HIERARCHIES AT WORK

NEW DIRECTIONS IN CRITICAL THEORY

NEW DIRECTIONS IN CRITICAL THEORY

Amy Allen, Founding Editor

New Directions in Critical Theory presents outstanding classic and contemporary texts in the tradition of critical social theory, broadly construed. The series aims to renew and advance the program of critical social theory, with a particular focus on theorizing contemporary struggles around gender, race, sexuality, class, and globalization and their complex interconnections.

Critical Theories of Anti-Semitism, Jonathan Judaken

Subaltern Silence: A Postcolonial Genealogy, Kevin Olson

Contesting the Far Right: A Psychoanalytic Critical Theory Approach, Claudia Leeb

Another Universalism: Seyla Benhabib and the Future of Critical Theory, edited by Stefan Eich, Anna Jurkevics, Nishin Nathwani, and Nica Siegel

Fascist Mythologies: The History and Politics of Unreason in Borges, Freud, and Schmitt, Federico Finchelstein

Selected Writings on Media, Propaganda, and Political Communication, Siegfried Kracauer, edited by Jaeho Kang, Graeme Gilloch, and John Abromeit

Crisis Under Critique: How People Assess, Transform, and Respond to Critical Situations, edited by Didier Fassin and Axel Honneth

Praxis and Revolution: A Theory of Social Transformation, Eva von Redecker

Recognition and Ambivalence, edited by Heikki Ikäheimo, Kristina Lepold, and Titus Stahl

Hermeneutics as Critique: Science, Politics, Race and Culture, Lorenzo C. Simpson

Critique on the Couch: Why Critical Theory Needs Psychoanalysis, Amy Allen

Capitalism on Edge: How Fighting Precarity Can Achieve Radical Change Without Crisis or Utopia, Albena Azmanova

A Time for Critique, edited by Didier Fassin and Bernard E. Harcourt

Transitional Subjects: Critical Theory and Object Relations, edited by Amy Allen and Brian O'Connor

For a complete list of books in the series, please see the Columbia University Press website.

HIERARCHIES AT WORK

Race, World-Systems,
and Legal Distribution

EDITED BY KAREN ENGLE
AND NEVILLE HOAD

Columbia University Press

New York

Columbia University Press
Publishers Since 1893
New York   Chichester, West Sussex

Copyright © 2025 Columbia University Press
All rights reserved

Library of Congress Cataloging-in-Publication Data
Names: Engle, Karen, editor. | Hoad, Neville Wallace, 1966– editor.
Title: Hierarchies at work : race, world-systems, and legal distribution / edited by Karen Engle and Neville Hoad.
Description: New York : Columbia University Press, [2025] | Series: New directions in critical theory | Includes bibliographical references and index.
Identifiers: LCCN 2024048165 | ISBN 9780231212250 (trade paperback) | ISBN 9780231212243 (hardback) | ISBN 9780231559287 (ebook)
Subjects: LCSH: Race relations—Economic aspects. | Racism—Economic aspects. | Capitalism—Social aspects. | Labor market—Social aspects. | Income distribution. | Minorities—Legal status, laws, etc.
Classification: LCC HT1531 .H54 2025 | DDC 305.8—dc23/eng/20250221

Cover design: Milenda Nan Ok Lee
Cover art: Meghan Nguyen

GPSR Authorized Representative: Easy Access System Europe, Mustamäe tee 50, 10621 Tallinn, Estonia, gpsr.requests@easproject.com

In memory of Barbara Harlow

CONTENTS

Acknowledgments xi

Introduction 1
KAREN ENGLE AND NEVILLE HOAD

PART I. GLOBAL HIERARCHIES: RACIAL CAPITALISM, WORLD-SYSTEMS, AND LEGAL DISTRIBUTIONAL ANALYSES

1. Neville Alexander: Racial Capitalism South African Style 31
DENNIS DAVIS

2. Walter Rodney, World-Systems Theory, and Racial Capitalism 45
NICOLE BURROWES

3. Critical System Analysis and the Great Disparities 65
DAVID KENNEDY

4. Law Distributes: Ricardo, Marx, CLS   85
DUNCAN KENNEDY

5. Distributional Analytics and the TWAIL Tradition   122
VASUKI NESIAH

PART II. THE FUTURE OF WORK: CHALLENGES TO DOMINANT FRAMINGS

6. The Future of Work from a Victorian Past   145
NEVILLE HOAD

7. Recovering the Past and the Outside: Sites for New Imaginaries of the Future of Work   167
KERRY RITTICH

8. Financialization, Fissuring, and Global Futures of Work   196
JENNIFER BAIR

PART III. GLOBAL HIERARCHIES AT WORK: GROUNDED ACCOUNTS

9. Labors in Time and Subjectivity: Gender Nonconformity and Racial Capitalism in the Making of Eighteenth-Century New Orleans   213
VANJA HAMZIĆ

10. Garment Work, Refugees, and Resistance: The Jordan Compact   236
JENNIFER GORDON

11. Distributional Analysis and Supply Chain Interventions: Migrant Worker Organization in Vermont's Dairy Industry   260
JENNIFER BAIR

12. Beyond Essential: Growth, a Pandemic, and the Future of Expendable Workers in a "Progressive" Texas Boomtown   281
KAREN ENGLE AND SAMUEL TABORY

13. Land and Labor in the Colombian Palm Oil Industry   312
HELENA ALVIAR GARCÍA AND JORGE GONZÁLEZ JÁCOME

14. Dead Ends and Blind Alleys in the Future of Work: Notes from Italy   338
JORGE L. ESQUIROL

....

List of Contributors   369

Index   375

ACKNOWLEDGMENTS

This collection grew out of two workshops organized by the Bernard and Audre Rapoport Center for Human Rights and Justice at the University of Texas at Austin and the Harvard Institute for Global Law and Policy (IGLP) at Harvard Law School. We thank David Kennedy for his support and intellectual leadership through IGLP and all the participants at both workshops, especially those who authored chapters for this collection, continued to workshop and present their drafts at subsequent events, and worked closely with us on their chapters. We are also enormously grateful to Rapoport Center postgraduate fellow Cooper Christiancy for the tremendous thought and care that he put into the final preparation of the manuscript.

Many people who did not author chapters have participated in our collective conversations. Some who were particularly influential include Tendayi Achiume, Bedour Alaagra, Daniel Brinks, Dan Danielsen, Janet Halley, Walter Johnson, Pavithra Vasudevan, and Lucie White, in addition to Rapoport Center postdoctoral fellows Nina Ebner, Edward Shore, and Mishal Khan. We are grateful for their many contributions.

We very much appreciate those who provided logistical support for our workshops, particularly Kristen Verdeaux (IGLP) and Sarah Eliason (Rapoport Center), and the IGLP and Rapoport Center fellows, scholars, and interns who provided organizational, notetaking, and editorial assistance. These include Nadia Lambek, Giulia Oprea, Gowthaman Ranganathan, Eve Wang, and Danny Woodward.

We thank the Ford Foundation for supporting the Rapoport Center's broader research and advocacy projects on combating inequality, especially in the contexts of natural resource governance and labor. The University of Texas vice president for research provided funds for a month-long international virtual conference titled "Beyond the Future of Work: New Paradigms for Addressing Global Inequality," which provided the opportunity to expand our group of interlocutors and further develop some key ideas in this anthology. Texas Global facilitated a collaboration with the University of Cape Town Faculty of Law, which led to a South African conference on "Labor, Land, and Livelihoods in Crisis: New Conversations on the Future of Work."

HIERARCHIES AT WORK

INTRODUCTION

KAREN ENGLE AND NEVILLE HOAD

This book intervenes in two of the most significant scholarly and political discussions around economic injustice today: "inequality" and the "future of work." Those engaged in the former discussion point to rising rates of inequality of wealth and income since the 1970s, and many are preoccupied with the fact that an increasingly few individuals possess more income or wealth than an increasingly large percentage of the population. Those who focus on the future of work often either enthuse or panic about the extent to which advanced automation, artificial intelligence, and other forms of technological innovation are dramatically changing the nature of work.

The two discussions are related. Critics of economic inequality, for instance, might take aim at the substantial increase in gaps between the salaries of CEOs and most workers. At the same time, those who prognosticate about the impact of new or nascent technologies might consider whether they are likely to increase or decrease levels of inequality in income and wealth. Of course, there are many internal nuances and disagreements among the scholars, advocates, and commentators who engage in these conversations. Yet we contend that the dominant discourses in which they operate too often misunderstand or misidentify the "crises" they address. Specifically, their analyses elide many of the entrenched racialized and geographic hierarchies—facilitated by law—that have long created and maintained the very dynamics that they consider to be new.

This book aims to reframe inequality, the future of work, and their intersection by (re)turning to three methods for analyzing global hierarchies that emerged in the 1970s and early 1980s (ironically perhaps, a time of relative *equality* according to economic inequality theorists[1]). The first two, by theorizing racial capitalism and world-systems, seek to understand the organization of global capitalism around class, race, colonialism, and (under)development. The third, critical legal distributional analysis, calls attention to law's role in the unequal distribution of wealth and resources. Especially when thought together, these three approaches unmask elisions and enable more complete analyses of the complex legal, historical, productive, extractive, and distributive processes that enable the world's great disparities in power, wealth, and work.

This book works toward reframing the inequality and future-of-work discourses in three parts. Part 1 challenges dominant discourses around inequality by providing critical theories and analyses of racial capitalism, world-systems, and the role of law in distribution, while also connecting them with each other. Part 2 contests dominant discourses on the future of work, specifically their prevailing preoccupation with technology, by attending to the ways technology operates through or alongside—even while often obscuring—other racialized and gendered dynamics in the global hierarchies of work, including fissuring and financialization. Part 3 provides a series of powerful, grounded studies that interrogate some of these dynamics of work and livelihood, using the methods elaborated in part 1. Through a diverse set of historical, geographic, and political contexts ranging from the garment factories of Jordan and the palm oil fields of Colombia to United States dairy farms, these examinations push past both technological determinism and dominant inequality approaches that limit inquiry into the historic systemic production and reproduction of domination and subordination.

Our ultimate aim for this collection is to spur alternative legal, economic, and political imaginaries toward a more just future of work and livelihoods at levels both local and global. This introduction sets us on that path by following the trajectory of the book and then highlighting some alternative imaginaries that emerge in several chapters. Before turning to discussion of the three parts, however, a few more words about the dominant framings of inequality are in order.

Particularly after the global financial crisis of 2008, scholars, policy makers, advocates, and activists from a variety of disciplines and perspectives began to focus on economic inequality as particularly pernicious. Whether they concentrated on wealth or income inequality within countries, between countries, or among individuals around the world, critics generally agreed that at least extreme or toxic levels of inequality are harmful to the political economy, social contract, and moral good.

Even political leaders across the spectrum once concurred. In 2013, then U.S. president Barack Obama called economic inequality "the defining challenge of our time."[2] The Russian president Vladimir Putin had written only a year earlier that "the differentiation of incomes is unacceptable" and that the "most important task is to reduce material inequality."[3] In 2014, Pope Francis condemned economic inequality as "the root of all social evil."[4]

Efforts to expose, understand, and respond to inequality have swept through several disciplines—from economics and law to literature—as well as a variety of think tanks and advocacy groups. The runaway success of Richard Wilkinson and Kate Pickett's *The Spirit Level: Why More Equal Societies Almost Always Do Better* (2009), subsequently dwarfed by Thomas Piketty's best-selling *Capital in the 21st Century* (2014), signaled and precipitated this growing scholarly and public interest in economic inequality.

Especially in public discourse, critics have often provided shocking numbers or images to bring attention to economic inequality. In 2016, for instance, Oxfam reported that sixty-two people in the world owned as much wealth as the poorest half of the world's population.[5] Only a year later, it reported that a mere eight men own as much wealth as the poorest 3.6 billion people, leading Oxfam's chief executive officer to explain: "Last year we said we would have needed a double-decker bus to transport the 62 people we thought owned the same as the poorest 3.6 billion on the planet. In 2017, thanks to more accurate data, we find that in fact this group would fit in a single golf buggy."[6] For Oxfam, these pithy data points support a clear call to action. The subtitle of its 2023 report with similar data, for instance, reads "How we must tax the super-rich now to fight inequality."[7]

Whether they track trends and provide statistical accounts of wealth or income inequality[8] or engage in detailed explanations of the workings of capitalism that they argue lead to inequality,[9] the policy proposals of critics—if stated—generally focus on increased regulation and after-the-fact redistribution. As Albena Azmanova observes, "remonstrations against inequality present the matter of capitalism's numerous and grave failures as issues that can be easily tackled with a dose of redistributive policies and strengthened oversight."[10] And as David Kennedy puts it in chapter 3 of this book, "too often the inquiry [into "great disparities"] pulls back from inquiry into systemic foundations, returning to a familiar catalogue of diagnoses and reform suggestions that can be pursued within the system as it is." Such an approach, he contends, makes it difficult "to imagine the system itself as being organized around the reproduction of inequality."

Following Kennedy's impulse to see great economic disparities not as aberrational but as the very distributional point of larger structures at play, this book focuses on possibilities not so much for redistribution (although, under the current political economy, that is certainly needed) but for a radically different distribution to begin with. To gain a better understanding of global hierarchies and to move beyond contemporary inequality discourse, it brings together fundamental ideas from the three critical literatures.

GLOBAL HIERARCHIES: RACIAL CAPITALISM, WORLD-SYSTEMS, AND LEGAL DISTRIBUTIONAL ANALYSES

Particularly when thought together, racial capitalism, world-systems, and legal distributional analyses provide thicker accounts of distribution than we find in dominant accounts of inequality, including by attending to law's role in distribution in a global racialized capitalist political economy. Part 1 of the collection considers the three methods and their sometimes overlapping and contested genealogies. It allows for a deeper dive into and sometimes a heterodox take on the approaches as well as on many of the thinkers identified with them. We hope that readers who want to better understand and contest what is often shorthanded as "inequality" will find the chapters useful, perhaps even paradigm-shifting.

At the risk of gross oversimplification, we begin this section of the introduction with a brief statement about the three approaches and our methodological uses of them in this book. Because legal distributional analysis is less known to a multidisciplinary audience than are the lenses of racial capitalism and world-systems, we introduce it in a bit more detail than the others.

Racial capitalism, which argues that capitalism is always and already racial capitalism, provides us with an analytical framework for understanding the historical and ongoing ways in which racialization and racial stratification are fundamental to the emergence and operation of global capitalism. The term "racial capitalism" was first popularized in the 1970s by the South African intellectual and anti-apartheid activist Neville Alexander, who used the term to describe the political economy of South Africa, naming racial capitalism as the target of the national liberation movement's struggle against apartheid.[11] Alexander, who is the subject of Dennis Davis's chapter 1 in this book, theorized racial capitalism to argue against liberal claims that apartheid could be ended without ending capitalism, on the one hand, and Marxist claims that dismantling capitalism would necessarily lead to racial equality, on the other.

In a parallel move in the United States, Cedric Robinson's *Black Marxism: The Making of the Black Radical Tradition* (1983) is well known for developing the analytic and historiography of racial capitalism as a challenge to mainstream understandings of capitalism as well as to the race-blind Marxist critique of capitalism.

In addition, Robinson elaborated a Black radical tradition that has long opposed racial capitalism, pointing to earlier African diaspora thinkers such as W. E. B. Du Bois, C. L. R. James, and Richard Wright. This tradition, as Bedour Alagraa explains, is "a project of dislocating Marxism and Europe . . . from the center of contemporary theorizations about radicalism and liberation."[12]

Notwithstanding these early articulations of racial capitalism, use of the term began to skyrocket in the 2010s. A resurgence of interest in critiques of the contemporary global economy through the lens of racial capitalism is indicated in part by the publication of the third edition of *Black Marxism* (2020) with an updated foreword by Robin D. G. Kelley.[13] The 2023 publication of a collection of Alexander's essays, along with recent critical and comparative commentary that centers his work, also speak to the continuing importance of theories of racial capitalism for a number of countries, including contemporary South Africa— often held up as enduring the highest level of inequality in the world.[14]

World-systems analysis provides us with a framework for identifying the deeply uneven core-periphery political economic relations among and within national and regional economies undergirding global capitalism. It, too, has its roots in the 1970s. It was most prominently elaborated by Immanuel Wallerstein beginning in 1974, with the publication of the first of a four-volume series titled *The Modern World-System*. Wallerstein set forth the historical underpinnings, dating to the sixteenth century, of what he called a world-system. This global capitalist system is composed of core, peripheral, and semiperipheral economic activities, spaces, and polities that produce, sustain, and exacerbate massively unequal capital accumulation.

World-systems analysis built in part on dependency theory, which had originally emerged in Latin America in the 1950s to explain a cycle of underdevelopment between poor (peripheral) and rich (core) countries. Wallerstein identifies as key to his own world-systems analysis the then more recent dependency theory of the Guyanese activist and scholar Walter Rodney, whose argument is articulated most forcefully in his groundbreaking book *How Europe Underdeveloped Africa* (1972). As Nicole Burrowes details in chapter 2 of our book, among Rodney's broader intellectual contributions that Wallerstein identified were his consistent description of capitalism as a world-system and the commitment to think race and class together.

Theories of racial capitalism and world-systems share a number of key elements, influences, and even thinkers. Cedric Robinson, for instance, was also associated with Wallerstein and others who identified with world-systems analysis. At the same time, Robinson expressed concern about what he considered "the unifying language of world-systems theory," which he believed missed the significance of culture to both capitalism and the means to resist it. For Robinson, "capitalism has a specific culture" and "race, ethnicity, and gender were powerful procedures for the conduct of accumulation and value appropriation."[15]

Unlike the term "racial capitalism," the term "world-systems" has been used relatively widely (if with different meanings) since its early theorizing. Dependency theory, however, has experienced a recent resurgence perhaps not coincidentally at the same time as has attention to racial capitalism. Several books, for instance, claim to revisit and revise dependency theory for today.[16] Walter Rodney's work has received particular attention, with much of his writing having been republished (or published for the first time) since 2018.[17]

In her foreword to the 2018 reprint of *How Europe Underdeveloped Africa*, Angela Davis implicitly draws a connection between world-systems analysis and critiques of racial capitalism, as she calls for scholar-activists to "expand upon, and deepen" Rodney's underdevelopment theory. Reminiscent of Alexander and Robinson, she writes: "Those of us who refuse to concede that global capitalism represents the planet's best future and that Africa and the former third world are destined to remain forever ensconced in the poverty of 'underdevelopment' are confronted with this crucial question: how can we encourage radical critiques of capitalism as integral to struggles against racism as we also advance the recognition that we cannot envision the dismantling of capitalism as long as the structures of racism remain intact?"[18] Burrowes makes the connection even more explicit in chapter 2, pointing to the role that Rodney's Pan-Africanism played not only in his racial capitalist critique but in world-systems theory more generally.

Finally, critical *legal distributional analysis* allows us to map the often-backgrounded legal arrangements that make, maintain, and worsen massive unequal distribution. It shifts our attention to the distributive effects of (rather than the norms behind) even well-meaning law reform efforts, insisting that there are always winners and losers. Distributional analysis emerged in the late 1970s and early 1980s as a part of critical legal studies (CLS). The critique built on earlier insights from some legal realists in the 1920s and 1930s about the important role of private law (especially contracts and property) in conditioning social bargaining.

Largely attributable to Duncan Kennedy, who authors his own genealogy of the method in chapter 4 of this collection, CLS deployment of distributional analysis was meant to move beyond the two approaches that dominated private law theory in the 1970s and 1980s: mainstream law and economics and advocacy of protection for weak parties by statutory regulation.[19] Law and economics adherents aimed to use both public and private law to facilitate an "efficient" "free" market by decreasing regulation, lowering transaction costs, and protecting private property. Once efficiency was achieved, the proponents of law and economics believed (to varying degrees, depending on where they fell on the conservative-liberal scale) that the state could then redistribute, largely through tax and transfer. Their liberal opponents defended the existing post–New Deal regulatory structure and argued for its modest expansion on the ground that unequal bargaining power vitiated consent.

Both approaches, according to legal distributional analysis, miss the important role of supposedly neutral private legal rules in structuring maldistribution, on the one hand, and distribution that is retroactively made to seem efficient, on the other. As the legal realist Robert Hale recognized in the 1920s, the interpretation and enforcement of these backgrounded and naturalized legal rules determine and are in turn determined by the relative coercive power of various actors.[20] That is, the rules of property, contract, and tort law (along with the criminal law rules that reinforce them in some cases) are the "rules of the game of economic struggle."[21] Changing the background rules might therefore have a greater distributive effect than changing the foreground rules—distribution is more important than redistribution.

In the 2010s, "distributional analysis" as a method for critiquing existing legal regimes and normative proposals began to be articulated by critical legal theorists in fields ranging from law and development to comparative family law.[22] Scholars emphasized the need to attend to the distributive outcomes of law, in part by seeing what areas of law were obscured by the dominant fields' framings. In 2014, Janet Halley put together an informal document on "how to do a distributional analysis," primarily for her doctoral students at Harvard Law School, many of whom she shared with Duncan Kennedy and David Kennedy. She usefully published a version of it in 2018 in the concluding chapter to her coauthored book on governance feminism. Building in part on some of Duncan Kennedy's work and a chapter titled "Law and the Global Dynamics of Distribution" in David Kennedy's *World of Struggle* (2016), Halley describes the key steps for doing a distributional analysis: put aside one's own moral or normative lens to focus on distributive outcome; identify the struggle and players; identify the surplus at stake for the players in the struggles; identify the background legal rules in whose shadow the struggle is taking place; and, pulling it all together, reintroduce normative assessment by "imagin[ing] it otherwise."[23]

To generate a critical conversation among the three methods and their key thinkers, we invited the authors for part 1 of this collection to focus on one or more of the methods, principally through close analysis of the work of thinkers who they identify with the theories. The resulting chapters are authored by Dennis Davis (on Neville Alexander—racial capitalism), Nicole Burrowes (on Walter Rodney—racial capitalism and world-systems), David Kennedy (on Immanuel Wallerstein and Gunnar Myrdal—world-systems), Duncan Kennedy (on David Ricardo and Karl Marx—legal distributional analysis), and Vasuki Nesiah (on a variety of authors she identifies with Third World approaches to international law (TWAIL)—legal distributional analysis alongside racial capitalism and world-systems). Many more thinkers are discussed in these chapters, perhaps most notably Cedric Robinson and Eric Williams.

The first two chapters, by Dennis Davis and Nicole Burrowes, engage extensively with racial capitalism, each bringing in a figure who is (or they argue should be) key to the understanding of the Black radical tradition that is central to Robinson's critique of racial capitalism. These discussions of Alexander and Rodney provide important expositions of racial capitalism from the perspective of the Global South, namely, South Africa and the Caribbean. (In chapter 5, Vasuki Nesiah considers the work of Eric Williams as an important early contribution to racial capitalism as well.)

In chapter 1, Davis reads the life and work of Alexander to elucidate the South African genealogy of racial capitalism. Davis shows that Alexander effectively rewrote South African history to reveal the mutually determining intersections of prevailing forms of capital accumulation and racialization from the colonial era through post-apartheid policies that continue to disadvantage the poor and working classes. He usefully situates Alexander in debates beginning in the 1970s over whether racial subordination under apartheid could be overcome through a more rational or efficient system of capitalism, bringing into stark relief the question of whether racial subordination is necessary to capitalism.

Looking both backward and forward, Davis explains, "Alexander's application of racial capitalism to apartheid South Africa became the foundation for his pathbreaking work on how a democratic South Africa could redress the consequences of more than three hundred years of racist authoritarian rule." Contending that the leadership of the Black working class would be essential to a post-apartheid nation, Alexander insisted with uncanny prescience that Black liberation would be impossible under capitalism.

In chapter 2, Burrowes considers Rodney's thinking about race in relation to that of Alexander and Robinson, noting that Rodney saw race as a constituent part of the rise and persistence of capitalism and arguing that he embodied the Black radical tradition. Specifically, Burrowes demonstrates that Rodney's academic and political work—in and from a variety of geographic locations—provide compelling instances of the power of decentering Europe while using

Marxism both to enrich understandings of national liberation and anticolonialism and to provide a thicker conception of inequality.

Burrowes's chapter on Rodney is also one of the two chapters on world-systems theory and notes Wallerstein's acknowledgment of Rodney as a significant influence on his work. Tracing Rodney's world-systems thought in part to Latin American dependency theorists, she notes that he was among the first to apply their identification of core-peripheral global relations to Africa. For Rodney, "African economies are integrated into the structure of the developed capitalist economies . . . in a manner that is unfavorable to Africa and ensures that Africa is dependent on the big capitalist countries."[24] Burrowes contextualizes Rodney's dependency theory in the revolutionary milieu of the 1960s and 1970s, with attention to his movement-building work and political activism more generally—in Tanzania, the United States, and Guyana. Rodney's synthesis of racial capitalism and world-systems theory, she argues, emerged from this praxis.

In line with Wallerstein's recognition of Rodney's significant contributions to world-systems analysis, we note that Wallerstein saw important connections between race and underdevelopment in the work of Swedish economist Gunnar Myrdal. Reading *The American Dilemma* (1944), Myrdal's early formative work on racial oppression in the United States, alongside Mrydal's later work in the 1970s on unequal development within a social system, Wallerstein attributed to Myrdal's legacy the tenet that "racism and underdevelopment are constitutive of the capitalist world-economy as an historical system and are not curable maladies within the system."[25]

It is perhaps fitting, then, that David Kennedy's chapter on world-systems theory uses both Wallerstein and Myrdal in Kennedy's own identification and pursuit of a "critical system analysis" to argue that great disparities are features, not bugs, of the normal operations of the "system" of the political economy. Yet, Kennedy contrasts key elements of Wallerstein's approach to world-systems with Myrdal's conception of unequal development within a social system. Although Myrdal is not normally identified with world-systems theory (notwithstanding Wallerstein's nod to him), Kennedy uses this work, particularly its naming of a number of interrelated causal conditions, to challenge what he considers to be a *too* systemic or determinative account by Wallerstein. Kennedy explains, "In contrast to economic models that foreground a propensity to equilibrium, or even the recurring and predictable patterns Wallerstein saw as historically validating his theory, Myrdal proposes that the ubiquity of circular causation conduces rather to patterns of disequilibrium and instability—and . . . inequality."

Kennedy's purchase from bringing Wallerstein and Myrdal together is a robust system diagnostic that foregrounds the variety of ways, both predictable and unpredictable, that inequalities are reproduced and consolidated by the institutions of political economic life. Importantly, Kennedy brings his own critical distributional insights to bear by calling for foregrounding the *legal* arrangements that underlie these distributional outcomes, making his chapter an important overlap with and segue to the subsequent chapters focused on critical legal distributional analysis.

Although the genealogy of critical distributional analysis in law often begins with legal realism, as in our earlier account, Duncan Kennedy's chapter traces the method farther back—to Karl Marx read side-by-side with the classical economist David Ricardo. While these thinkers are generally seen as sharing little but a labor theory of value—which he intentionally sets aside—Kennedy argues that they are the progenitors of contemporary critical legal approaches to law and political economy. Notwithstanding their limited, even misguided, engagement with law, Kennedy insists that they nevertheless facilitate a critical analysis of the role of legal regimes in distribution and bargaining power, particularly in the distribution of surplus value. Using Ricardo's focus on rent-seeking by landowners and Marx's attention to capital accumulation in manufacturing, Kennedy demonstrates, in neoclassical economic terms and with models, how a variety of legal arrangements structure bargaining power and facilitate exploitative relationships— between landlord and farmer, for Ricardo, and capitalist and worker, for Marx. Put simply, law distributes.

Kennedy mines this analysis for possible contemporary legal interventions that might lead to "rent-seeking on behalf of the poor," proposing the identification of surpluses in any given regime and then finding the best legal distributive mechanisms to ensure that the surplus is distributed to benefit the poor. Kennedy focuses on low-income housing as his principal example but also makes clear the reach of his approach, noting the many places in which parties with grossly unequal bargaining power permit the unjust extraction of surplus: "The profits of individual slum landlords are a small subset of the mass of profit that enterprises of all kinds derive from dealings with the poor, from banks to auto and home insurance companies to supermarkets to holders of mortgage backed securities to pay day lenders to local appliance store owners."

In the final chapter of part 1, Nesiah uses distributional analysis to chart the writings of a variety of contemporary international legal scholars who began in the 1990s to work under the moniker TWAIL, or Third World approaches to international law. One of the founders of TWAIL, Nesiah identifies it as "an intellectual and political project that foregrounds the history of colonialism and neocolonialism in understanding international legal history and interpreting international laws and norms." Referencing Duncan Kennedy's chapter, she argues that "the constitutive role of property ownership in the Ricardo-cum-Marx story can be affirmed, extended, and analogized to the role that the afterlives of colonialism and slavery play in TWAIL analytics of surplus and the structuring of its distribution."

Nesiah uses Halley's elaboration of legal distributional analysis to mine TWAIL scholarship for examples of the method's use, including in arguments about the imbrication of debt and sovereignty and in the reading of migration as decolonization. She derives from these examples a repertoire of strategies for diagnosing and contesting the international legal arrangements underlying unequal distribution.

Nesiah explicitly writes Eric Williams, author of *Capitalism and Slavery* (1944), into the genealogy of TWAIL's distributional analysis, noting that he tracked "the surplus value generated by the triangular trade of enslaved peoples from Africa to cotton plantations in the Americas to the factories of Manchester in producing European wealth." Importantly, for Nesiah and many of the other TWAIL scholars she mentions, surplus does not accrue only in financial capital but in ethical and epistemic capital as well.

Claiming that "surplus appropriation from the Global North–based proletariat was subsidized, supplemented, and fueled by the dispossession and expropriation built into slave and colonial economies," Nesiah yokes together distributional analysis with world-systems and racial capitalist critiques. In tandem with our other chapters on method, and important for the remainder of the book, she suggests the ongoing explanatory power of the history of geographically and racially stratified forms of work, and the law that made it possible, for analyzing the future of work.

In sum, these methods demonstrate the need to address the complex, historical, productive, extractive, and distributive processes—undergirded by law—that enable the world's great disparities in power, wealth, and status. They make clear that responses to income and wealth inequality that aim to tame the excesses of capitalism or even to redistribute surpluses through tax and transfer, so long as they maintain the underlying historical processes of global racial capitalism, will do little to address systemically the gross disparities that we often label as inequality. That is, these methods move us well beyond a focus on income or wealth inequality by providing a complex analysis of the ways that many key forms of racial and geographic differentiation are inextricably tied to global capitalism. As we move to critiques of the dominant future-of-work discourses, these three methods help us further challenge many of the contemporary understandings of the dilemmas posed by the future of work.

THE FUTURE OF WORK: CHALLENGES TO DOMINANT FRAMINGS

Issues of technology pervade dominant discourses about the future of work. Many scholars, policy makers, and even labor rights advocates are highly optimistic about a future in which technological innovation, whether through the "free market" or state regulation, will eliminate the need for "unfulfilling" labor. Such innovations might also respond to perceived inefficiencies, or perhaps injustices, in the manufacturing, service, and knowledge economies. Even those who tend to be "techno-optimists," however, often express at least some concern about mass job displacement or limited social protection for workers caused by rapid advancements in artificial intelligence, automation, and robotics. Some seek to ameliorate these harms through greater or improved formalization of platform work or regulation of artificial intelligence. Others propose "skilling up" workers to be able to operate in a technologically focused economy. All these approaches—whether optimistic or pessimistic, diagnostic or prescriptive—are characterized by the centrality of technological change to their analysis.[26]

Here, along with our authors in part 2, we question both the novelty of these dominant preoccupations and their proposed solutions. In terms of novelty, both the excitement and despair expressed in contemporary discourses sometimes repeat almost compulsively the fantasies about industrial capitalism and development found during the height of territorial empire and later during early decolonization.

At least since the late nineteenth century, artists, academics, theorists, and policy makers have produced accounts of both dystopian and utopian images of worlds dominated by technological change. As Neville Hoad shows in chapter 6, in the Victorian period, anxieties about the place of technology in capitalism—including in its racialized, colonial, and gendered determinants and production—were often overt in imaginings of the future. Perhaps most famously, in *The Time Machine* (1895), H. G. Wells warned of a terrifying future in which class divisions, resulting from excessive levels of capitalist accumulation, harden into racial or even species divisions, with the former working class gaining the upper hand due to the closer contact it already had with technology. In that future world, the former overlords have devolved into feminized, pretty creatures who serve simply as food for the descendants of the former workers. Technology may have allowed for the descendants of the laboring classes to prevail, but a world in which livelihood and subsistence become cannibalism is clearly dystopian. Hoad contrasts *The Time Machine* with Oscar Wilde's utopian imaginary of technological innovation in "The Soul of Man Under Socialism" (1891). Wilde looked forward to a world where technological machinery would perform all "essential" or alienated labor, what he called "the slavery of machines." For him, a world without division of labor would become a world of human self-realization and flourishing.

Elsewhere, Miriam Cherry has also contested the novelty of today's preoccupations by showing a similar articulation of these anxieties and hopes about technological change by international labor policy makers in the 1960s. Revisiting International Labor Organization (ILO) debates around automation and its impact on labor during that period, she writes that "[w]hile the technological landscape has changed, both the optimism and fears for the future that were expressed in the 1960s seem incredibly familiar and current."[27]

In terms of proposed solutions, we suggest that those who privilege prognoses centered on the effects of changing technologies often miss other significant causes of contemporary worker precarity, not all of which are novel. These include a decline in labor union power and an increase in fissuring and financialization of the workplace.[28] In chapter 7 in this collection, Kerry Rittich refutes the focus on technology for failing to recognize that technology does not exist in a vacuum: "technology neither exists nor operates on its own; instead, it is a classic example of a hybrid actor." Elsewhere, Juan De Lara has provided a chilling illustration of technology as a hybrid actor in his critique of just-in-time manufacturing. Reprinting a 1993 patent drawing of wrist-worn barcode scanners that "turn warehouse workers into cyborg logistics laborers," De Lara uses the drawing to illustrate "how people and machines, data and flesh, combine to propel the [just-in-time] circulation of commodities."[29] Less literally, Rittich contends that what we might "experience as technology, at work and elsewhere, is technology intermixed with human action, modes of organization and classification, physical geography, etc." Those include the rise not only of just-in-time manufacturing but of an increase in "gig," or contract, work.

In that organizational vein, Jennifer Bair, in chapter 8, builds on David Weil's conception of the fissured workplace, which describes the replacement of the standard employment relationship. That is, corporations that once hired full-time employees increasingly distribute activities through networks of independent contractors and outsourcing arrangements.[30] Although most of Weil's work focuses on the United States, Bair considers the distributional changes wrought by the organization of global value chains, deploying a critique that she has elsewhere insisted be rooted in world-systems analysis.[31]

In chapter 8, Bair explains that global value chains facilitate fissuring at a more expansive scale. As companies draw "their organizational boundaries around those activities that deliver... the highest or most secure returns," the most profitable activities in the value chain (generally conducted in the Global North) are distanced from the least profitable activities (frequently located in the Global South). Fissuring is an organizational strategy with implications for inequality among countries as well as within them, though its influence is often underappreciated in dominant discourses that privilege advanced automation, AI, and other forms of technological developments as key drivers of change. Of course, even this fissured organization of work, Rittich argues, has long been embedded in capitalist production. She cites both Wallerstein and Max Weber to contend that "there is nothing new about the outsourcing of work; far from a transitional stage of capitalism, moreover, the 'putting out' of work to the home or countryside has long traveled in tandem with the growth of industrial employment."[32]

If the outsourcing of work is not new, neither is the informal work that accompanies it; the "standard" employment relationship was never the norm in most of the world. Partly for this reason, Rittich critiques the ILO's call for a "transition" from the informal to formal economy in response to what it identifies as a "transformative change in the world of work, driven by technological innovations, demographic shifts, environmental and climate change, and globalization, as well as at a time of persistent inequalities."[33] She contends that this approach to formalization—through the rule of law—is misplaced, largely because it treats (and defines) informal work as exceptional rather than as seeing it as the global norm. "Rather than imagine the periphery as the zone that needs to be 'brought in'... in order for work to become 'good,'" Rittich argues, "we might instead take work and the many ways it is organized in the Global South as the referent from which to ask new questions... about the legal infrastructure of work."[34]

Bair's Chapter 8 attributes rising precarity not only to increased fissuring but also to financialization. Companies on the high profitability end of supply chains, whose returns often reflect "the greater valorization of intangible activities over tangible ones," are investing their gains into financial—rather than fixed—assets, "a dynamic that may depress productivity growth and employment generation while rewarding the ownership class." Together fissuring and financialization, Bair contends, shift economic surplus toward intangible activities at the expense of tangible production, capital at the expense of labor, and the Global North at the expense of the Global South.

Even more significant than fissuring and financialization, for Rittich, are the gendered and racialized distinctions and hierarchies among workers that are central to the structuring of capitalism as well as to the distinction between paid work and unpaid social reproduction. As to the latter, she argues—invoking Silvia Federici and others—"we might think of the nonrecognition of unpaid care work as one of the keys to global inequality, a central part of how massive disparities in the returns to work are now produced."

If, as Hoad argues, speculative Victorian-era literature on the future of work refused to disarticulate imaginings of technology and capitalism from questions of gender, sexuality, and racial identities and relations, the same cannot be said of dominant future-of-work discourses today. In their attempts to constrain and channel new technologies or to remake workers to fit a technologically transformed world of work, these dominant discourses obscure the political-economic and legal structures at the heart not only of the future of work but its past and present.

Together the lenses of racial capitalism, world-systems, and critical legal distribution require attention to how these deep structures have defined and affected work, workers, and livelihoods. The final part of the collection facilitates that attention through a series of grounded systemic explorations.

GLOBAL HIERARCHIES AT WORK: GROUNDED ACCOUNTS

Understanding the distributive effects of law in producing and maintaining a world-system of globalized racial capitalism requires, as Jane Collins puts it, recovering "some of what neoclassical economics makes us forget: living, breathing, gendered, and raced bodies working under social relations that exploit them."[35] Such a move is analytic as much as recuperative, and requires taking account of the past and present in imagining a more just future of work and livelihood. In chapter 7, Kerry Rittich explains: "If one of the insights of racial capitalism is the foundational role played by race and racial categories in the organization of capitalist production in transnational enterprises in particular, then one challenge going forward seems clear: how to make the racially and ethnically marked worker more central to the analysis of work."

For part 3 of the collection, we invited scholars to analyze specific groups of workers, industries, development policies, or labor regimes through deployment of one or more of the three methods. The resulting chapters complicate and contest diagnoses of and prognoses for the future of work that overemphasize technological innovation as either threat or promise by calling attention to the many entrenched racialized and geographic hierarchies at work that create and maintain maldistribution, often through law.

The chapters span multiple temporalities and geographies: the racialized and gendered impact of multiple labor regimes on African and Indigenous peoples in eighteenth- and nineteenth-century New Orleans (Vanja Hamzić); the European Union's failed attempt to place Syrian refugees in the Jordanian garment manufacturing industry (Jennifer Gordon); the worker-driven social responsibility model of organizing undocumented migrant workers in the dairy industry in Vermont (Jennifer Bair); the impact of the "essential" work designation during COVID-19 on low-wage, largely undocumented construction workers in the "progressive" boomtown of Austin, Texas (Karen Engle and Sam Tabory); development-driven changes in the distribution of production in the oil palm industry in Colombia (Helena Alviar and Jorge González); and legal struggles over the past few decades around the treatment of workers in a southern Italian steel plant bought by foreign investors, considered alongside the state's detention of African (potential) workers (Jorge Esquirol).

Hamzić goes furthest back in time, exploring the intersection of racial capitalism and gender nonconformity through consideration of the work and lives of Senegambians, both enslaved and "free," in eighteenth-century New Orleans. Tracing their histories to the artisan class in Greater Senegambia, Hamzić describes fragments of their lives in Louisiana as they resisted the political economy of the plantation, often engaging with a number of other communities, including other Africans and Indigenous peoples. He argues that transatlantic slavery not only racialized but imposed a gender binary to facilitate racial capitalism's labor regimes through the category-making power of the law. Hamzić uses this history to imagine a decolonial future of work and livelihoods. He looks both to Greater Senegambian lifeworlds before slavery and to the interstices of the violent economic production of plantation slavery. In the latter, he locates and elucidates the often hidden livelihood strategies and resistances—including through social reproduction, sex work, and waged work—that he suggests could give rise to new imaginaries of work and livelihood today.

The remaining chapters revolve around the contemporary fissuring of production. As with Hamzić's chapter, they involve at some level the migration of workers, some as part of what Gordon has elsewhere termed "human supply chains."[36] Although Gordon uses the term to understand the regulation of migrant labor in the United States, we use it here more broadly to describe a variety of ways in which capitalism is and has long been organized, racialized, and gendered through the movement of workers within and across national and imperial lines.

Both Jorge Esquirol and Jennifer Gordon examine contemporary efforts to prevent increased migration of workers to Europe from the Global South. As one of two case studies he offers in chapter 14, Esquirol considers the politics around and the plight of mostly Eritrean migrants detained in 2018 on the

Diciotti, an Italian Coast Guard ship, for ten days off the coast of Italy. Using ideas that can be found in racial capitalism and world-systems analyses, he critiques the Italian state's racialization of, and denial of social protection (and sometimes even entry or rescue) to, those migrants arriving on its shores, often from former colonies. Once in the country, migrants experience the enormous precarity and exploitation that low-wage migrant workers face in most parts of the world. Although immigration and labor law both participate in this precarity, Esquirol deploys distributional analysis to highlight a variety of Italian and European Union laws that allocate power to "produce a situation in which democratic demands—such as worker interests—cannot permeate the protected encasement of neoliberal policies."

Gordon's chapter 10 takes us to the European Union's attempts to keep unwanted migrants far away from the shores of Europe by offering Jordan financial incentives to encourage Syrian refugees already living in Jordan to stay there. "Facing conflicting political pressures" around the increase in Syrian refugees, she explains, "the EU urgently sought a way to keep the Syrians out without appearing heartless in the face of their suffering." Gordon explores the unintended consequences and distributional effects of the resulting 2015 EU-Jordan Compact in which Jordan agreed to provide work permits to Syrians, mostly in free trade zones, in exchange for decreased tariffs for exports from Jordan to European factories as well as loans and other financial aid. The compact's architects assumed that most of the permits would go to Syrian women to allow them to work in the garment industry, displacing much of the South Asian migrant workforce. They were wrong.

Gordon follows Michel-Rolph Trouillot's notion of "motion in the system" for some of the reasons that David Kennedy turns to Myrdal—for a less determinist account of the global world-system than some theorists offer. She brings together Trouillot's insights with Robinson's critique of racial capitalism to explain how the EU architects miscalculated the global world-system and underestimated the agency of workers in the periphery to challenge the core. If capitalism imagines all workers as fungible, Gordon's case study demonstrates that even if capitalism has always racialized workers it does not do so in a consistent way. Specifically, in this instance, the EU architects' racialization of Syrian refugee women as fungible with South Asian migrant garment workers failed to account for other important factors, such as the disruptions to social reproduction that moving to export zones would cause Syrian refugees. In the end, Syrian men primarily used the work permits to formalize their status as they continued to engage in the same type of work they had done before—in the largely informal agricultural and construction sectors. Gordon insists that "this process formalized the workers but not the work," given that "improvements in pay and conditions have been slow to follow."

Two chapters, one by Jennifer Bair and another by Karen Engle and Samuel Tabory, consider undocumented workers in the United States whose work is central to two different industries and locales—dairy farming in Vermont and construction work in Austin, Texas. Both chapters mobilize ideas found in racial capitalism and world-systems theories in their distributional analyses of the laws that create and maintain low-wage and highly dangerous jobs that are structured to be filled by racialized migrant workers, who in turn become essential to the regional economy. The chapters consider not only the impact of immigration and labor law on creating these conditions but the myriad often backgrounded laws that, intentionally or not, make worker precarity highly profitable for businesses.

In chapter 11, Bair discusses the Vermont dairy industry, which generates 70 percent of the state's agricultural sales. Against a background of regional recognition of the dependence of dairy farms on undocumented migrant labor alongside heightened precarity for those who perform the work, Bair describes Milk with Dignity, a program developed by the rights group Migrant Justice. She focuses on the group's successful pressuring of Ben & Jerry's, the Vermont-based ice cream producer that espouses a progressive social justice mission, to sign an agreement to become a part of the program. Bair considers some of the promises and pitfalls of the agreement and confronts the enmeshment of immigration law, labor law, and racial capitalism that, resonant with Gordon's study, "draw[s] distinctions between laboring bodies and then use[s] these distinctions to naturalize the kinds of work bodies are assigned to do and the conditions under which they do it."

Through distributional analysis that she attributes directly to Duncan Kennedy's chapter in this book (see chapter 4), Bair analyzes the agreement, which is based on a worker-driven social responsibility model. It requires Ben & Jerry's to distribute some of its surplus further along the supply chain, principally by paying a premium to participating dairy farms to provide their workers with a direct monthly payment as well as to improve working conditions, including around health and safety.[37] Contending that whether the agreement will successfully shift the distribution of economic gains depends on other backgrounded legal rules, Bair calls special attention to the role of antitrust law in the agreement. She argues that the surplus at stake is derived not only from the exploitation of devalued migrant labor but also from antitrust law's exclusion of cooperatives which has undermined the security of small- and medium-sized dairy farmers. This result potentially weakens the power of Ben & Jerry's to effect change for farmworkers by complicating the very power imbalance upon which the agreement depends and activists often rely.

In chapter 12, Engle and Tabory similarly call attention to backgrounded legal rules—as well as backgrounded subsidies for corporations, including social reproduction—in their analysis of an early COVID-19 hotspot experienced by low-wage, largely undocumented, Latino construction workers in the "progressive" boomtown of Austin, Texas. Comparable to the dairy industry in Vermont, construction is key to the development of the Austin regional economy—so much so that shortly after the local government closed down construction sites due to COVID-19, the State of Texas ordered them reopened on the ground that construction work is "essential." That reopening coincided with a high rate of hospitalization for COVID-19 among the workers. The chapter uses ideas found in critiques of racial capitalism and world-systems theory in its distributional analysis of the connections between growth politics in Austin and the conditions of precarity experienced by these racialized—and expendable—workers from the Global South whose labor is fundamental to the material processes of that growth.

As with Bair's study, immigration, employment, and labor law are all central to Engle and Tabory's analysis. They also point to many other, often backgrounded, laws and policies that benefit large corporations while weakening the bargaining power of those working in low-wage jobs throughout the region. These include Texas state restrictions on local control, tax law and policy, and direct and indirect economic development subsidies that government actors insist (generally with little proof) are necessary to woo companies to the region. Engle and Tabory argue that these legal rules and policies work together not only to devalue the migrant labor that literally builds the city but to sustain the deeply racialized growth politics that have long shaped the region, first through legal segregation and later through gentrification. Engle and Tabory use the Austin example to call for imagining alternatives for the futures of work and livelihood in an urban-regional political economy—alternatives that embrace a radically different configuration of value not centered around growth.

In chapter 13, Alviar and González, although not addressing international migration, follow the changing organization of the palm oil industry in Colombia from the 1950s to the present, which is deeply intertwined with large-scale land dispossession and attendant internal migration. Along with Gordon, Bair, and Engle and Tabory, they consider the relationship between development and work. Through distributional analysis, they demonstrate many ways that capitalist elites in the industry have benefited over decades—at the cost of industrial workers, peasants, and Afro-descendant collective communities—whether through national development policies that promoted palm as a key import substitute, later international development priorities that used subsidies to encourage palm production as comparative advantage in export-led growth, or armed conflict. Arguing that comparative advantage does not come naturally, they identify multiple backgrounded private legal rules and subsidies that have facilitated the dispossession of peasant and communal Afro-descendant property as well as other rent-seeking activities of large palm growers and palm oil producers.

Since the 1990s, Alviar and González show, fissuring and financialization have facilitated the accumulation of wealth for shareholders and executives of large producers while decreasing the power and income of workers, including through outsourcing or other forms of subcontracting. Alviar and González begin their chapter by relating that in 2019, Indupalma, one of the largest palm producers in the country, declared bankruptcy and liquidated its assets, claiming that worker costs and demands were simply too high. The combination of fissuring and financialization, it seems, meant that ceasing to be an employer altogether had become a profitable option for the company.

Both racial capitalism and world-systems also play an important role in Alviar and González's chapter. The authors explicitly analyze Afro-descendant land expropriation through a racial capitalist critique. Their world-systems analysis is more implicit, but clear: Colombia's peripheral status in the global economy affected the many development policies, from import substitution and comparative advantage to foreign investment.

Esquirol' finds similar dynamics in southern Italy, juxtaposing his chapter 14 study of the detention of migrants on the *Diciotti* (discussed previously) with the long saga of what was once the largest steel mill plant in Europe, located in Taranto in one of the least developed regions of the country. Publicly owned for decades, the state privatized the plant after the 1980s economic crisis. New owners who purchased it in 1995 committed serious environmental violations, leading an Italian court to order the seizure of the plant in 2012, only for the state to sell it again in 2017—this time to ArcelorMittal, the world's largest steel multinational. The sale agreement explicitly required that the company maintain a certain number of jobs or suffer a financial penalty. In dynamics similar to Indupalma's declaration of bankruptcy in Alviar and González's telling, ArcelorMittal threatened to shut down the plant if it was not permitted to dramatically reduce the workforce, which would also shield it from paying for years of environmental harm. Ultimately, the government increased its budget deficit (for which it needs European Union approval) to intervene financially to keep the plant open.

Esquirol uses this tangled tale of public, private, and multinational ownership alongside the imposition and removal of national and international regulation to demonstrate the weakness of the dominant legal and political strategy for worker empowerment in Italy. That strategy, which demands inclusion in "the social" through the legal protection of *tutela*, he argues, is inherited from both Italian fascism and the 1970s welfare state. Esquirol asserts that the invocation of the social today erroneously assumes the same pressure points for labor, capital, and governments that were present in earlier eras. In a distributive analytical move that he applies to waged Italian workers as well as to the potential migrant workers that Italy attempts to keep at bay, Esquirol contends that, rather than attempting to claim inclusion in "the social," workers and their advocates should (re)engage with the background rules of private, commercial, and corporate law: "the interests of workers should be integrated in the background rules of the market, not merely segregated to offer protections from it."

We have provided here only a glimpse of the many insights found in the grounded accounts elucidated in the chapters in part 3, calling attention to their use of the methods of legal distribution, world-systems, and racial capitalism. Together, the chapters compellingly demonstrate how these methodological approaches offer a richer account of the hierarchies at work than those generally provided by the dominant inequality and future of work discourses. Along with the chapters in parts 1 and 2 of the collection, these chapters call for imaginaries well beyond the promise or critique of technological innovation.

ALTERNATIVE IMAGINARIES

As we have seen, dominant discourses about the future of work necessarily contain imaginaries, both descriptive and normative. Diagnoses proffered by scholars, pundits, and national and international institutions conjure significant transformations they believe are or will be produced by technological innovation. Some of their solutions, often responding to concerns about an increase in informal work, evoke an ahistorical and racialized nostalgia for "full" and "standard" employment as it was imagined to be at the height of worker power in the Global North during a fleeting moment of the twentieth century. In chapter 7, Rittich problematizes this "prevailing idea of 'normal' work, the path it projects for workers, and the limits it imposes on imagining work's possible futures."

Once we understand the world of work through the intersecting lenses of racial capitalism, world-systems theory, and legal distributional analysis, we can begin to rethink the distinctions often drawn among productive, reproductive, nonproductive, and waged and unwaged labor as well as among work, workers, land, and livelihoods. The chapters in this collection show that this rethinking would mount a serious, distributive challenge to the racialized, gendered, and geographic legal and normative orders of global capitalism—a challenge lacking in many of the critiques of inequality and of a technology-focused future of work. The challenge might begin with what Nesiah identifies in TWAIL literature as "reparative interventions," which she contends are about "working toward different futures." In particular, she argues that tracking the distribution of surplus can reveal the hidden rules of the game and, along with the mining of "dissident intellectual traditions," might "reconnoiter new terrain" in law.

To think alternative futures that are more rupture than repetition requires expanding the archives we consult. The speculative chapters by Hoad and Hamzić usefully turn to literary genres and historical sources often (dis)missed in dominant accounts of work, to (re)imagine both the past and future of work and livelihoods.

Given the explicitly racialized and gendered fury that animated Victorian debates about the future of work, the authors that Hoad discusses from that period could only conjure the alterity of future work by transfiguring race, gender, sexuality, and the state itself. In addition to the techno-optimism of Wilde and the uneven techno-pessimism of Wells (discussed previously) Hoad reads Edward Bulwer-Lytton's *The Coming Race* (1870) for its imagination of a world without productive labor and with reversed sexual agency and a withering away of the state. For each of these three authors' fantasies, then, a change in the future of work means some upheaval in dominant forms of governance, social reproduction, sexual desire, and gender identity.

Hamzić shows that we don't need to go to science fiction to reimagine the web of connections that informed work in the emergent world-system of racial capitalism. He animates archival fragments to tell stories of life, livelihoods, and loss in the double crossings between Senegambia and Louisiana over the course of the long eighteenth century. Through these fragments, he glimpses modes of living and practices of freedom in the historical alterity of the experiences of those who resisted, escaped, or refused—even if just for a moment—the imposition of a gender binary, the commodification of human flesh, land expropriation, and other manifestations of racial capitalism. These experiences suggest that, even in a long period of quotidian and unspeakable violence, there were and are other distributive possibilities to be seized.

In our delineation of these past futurities and resistances, we aim to spur additional imaginaries made possible by the critical methods expounded and deployed in the various chapters. One such imaginary that emerges, for instance, is a political economy not centered on growth. Local, national, or regional development policies—along with the legal infrastructure that sustains them—are at the heart of the chapters that address or deploy world-systems theory in each part of the book. A number of authors identify growth policies or aims as a significant source of precarious work and livelihoods. Alviar and González, for instance, connect land dispossession and worker precarity in Colombia largely through government policies related to economic development. Engle and Tabory link the precarity of low-wage migrant construction workers in the Austin, Texas region to the fast-paced growth promoted through numerous governmental subsidies and legal regimes.

Alviar and González remind us of the many alternatives to development models based principally on economic growth: those that "make the protection of national production the main goal; combine growth with redistribution; define growth in terms of sustainability; or more recently, center well-being, the environment, care, and a good living, *buen vivir*, for all." This eschewal of growth as the metric by which to gauge "progress" in the developing world could be seen in Myrdal's work too. As David Kennedy explains in chapter 3: "In analyzing postwar conditions of 'underdevelopment' in Asia, Myrdal forswore offering a specifically economic metric such as 'growth' or 'industrialization' for assessing progress in a developing nation. Only the people of a nation could assess their progress and only in the terms they chose to value."

If rejecting economic growth as the model of development might have been an option for some countries in the Global South, some argue that it is now (and maybe was then also) a necessity in the Global North. As Rittich puts it in chapter 7, "climate change and ecological crises and limits have now destabilized the ground—continuous economic growth—upon which improvements to work have traditionally been achieved."

Engle and Tabory take degrowth seriously, not as an outcome of economic crisis but as a deliberate policy. They push us to imagine what alternatives might exist for the future of work and livelihoods in an urban-regional political economy that is not centered on growth. Perhaps pursuing alternatives would not require as much upheaval as that undertaken by Hoad's Victorian writers, but it would require a radical (re)configuration of value—through both law and culture. That reconfiguration cannot be done without engagement with the very people—in Engle and Tabory's case, undocumented workers—whose ability to stay in the country and work depends on the very jobs that make their work and livelihoods precarious in multiple ways. Engle and Tabory cite the economic historian Stefania Barca's insistence that the degrowth movement must "take seriously workers' conditions and needs, as well as labour movements' concerns and dilemmas vis-à-vis ecology and the climate."[38]

Imagination is hard work. But it is of course not enough, and it cannot take place in an academic silo. We hope this book suggests and opens space for the emergence of new and revived modes of praxis that both provide a better understanding of the racialized, colonial, and gendered legal and political workings of global capitalism and prompt interventions that radically reconfigure the distribution of value, work, and livelihoods.

NOTES

1. See, for example, Thomas Piketty, *Capital in the Twenty-First Century* (Cambridge, MA: Belknap, 2014), 316–20.
2. President Barack Obama, "Remarks by the President on Economic Mobility," December 4, 2013, https://obamawhitehouse.archives.gov/the-press-office/2013/12/04/remarks-president-economic-mobility.
3. Quoted in Jason M. Breslow, "Inequality and the Putin Economy: Inside the Numbers," *PBS Frontline*, January 13, 2015, https://www.pbs.org/wgbh/frontline/article/inequality-and-the-putin-economy-inside-the-numbers/.
4. Andrew Brown, "Pope Francis Condemns Inequality, Thus Refusing to Play the Game," *The Guardian*, April 28, 2014, https://www.theguardian.com/commentisfree/2014/apr/28/pope-francis-condemns-inequality-john-paul.
5. Oxfam, *An Economy for the 1 Percent: How Privilege and Power in the Economy Drive Extreme Inequality and How This Can Be Stopped* (Oxford: Oxfam, 2016), 2, https://s3.amazonaws.com/oxfam-us/www/static/media/files/bp210-economy-one-percent-tax-havens-180116-en_0.pdf.
6. Mark Goldring, "Eight Men Own More Than 3.6 Billion People Do: Our Economic System Is Broken," *The Guardian*, January 16, 2017, https://www.theguardian.com/commentisfree/2017/jan/16/eight-people-earn-more-billion-economics-broken.
7. Martin-Brehm Christensen et al., *Survival of the Richest: How We Must Tax the Super-Rich Now to Fight Inequality* (Oxford: Oxfam International, 2023). In this report, Oxfam proclaims that the "81 billionaires hold more wealth than 50 percent of the world combined" and "10 billionaires own more than 200 million African women combined" (16).
8. For examples, see Christensen et al.; "Facts," Inequality.org, accessed July 6, 2023, https://inequality.org/facts/; Danny Dorling, *Inequality and the 1 percent* (New York: Verso, 2014); and Piketty, *Capital in the Twenty-First Century*.
9. For some examples, see James K. Galbraith, *Inequality: What Everyone Needs to Know* (Oxford: Oxford University Press, 2016); Thomas Piketty, *The Economics of Inequality* (Cambridge, MA: Belknap, 2015); Piketty, *Capital in the Twenty-First Century*; and Joseph E. Stiglitz, *The Price of Inequality: How Today's Divided Society Endangers Our Future* (New York: Norton, 2013).

10. Albena Asmanova, *Capitalism on Edge: How Fighting Precarity Can Achieve Radical Change Without Crisis or Utopia* (New York: Columbia University Press, 2020), 7.
11. See Neville Alexander, *Against Racial Capitalism: Selected Writings*, ed. Salim Vally and Enver Motala (London: Pluto, 2023).
12. Bedour Alagraa, "Cedric Robinson's *Black Marxism*: Thirty-Five Years Later," *C. L. R. James Journal* 24, nos. 1–2 (Fall 2018): 304. Robinson later noted, in an interview in 1999, that anticapitalism might also demand other radical traditions, "drawing their own power from alternative historical experiences." Cedric Robinson, "Capitalism, Marxism, and the Black Radical Tradition: An Interview with Cedric Robinson," interview by Chuck Morse, *Perspectives on Anarchist Theory* 3, no. 1 (Spring 1999): 7.
13. Cedric J. Robinson, *Black Marxism: The Making of a Black Radical Tradition*, 3rd ed. (1983; Chapel Hill: University of North Carolina Press, 2020). As of May 2024, Google Scholar shows the book has been cited nearly seven thousand times. See also Cedric J. Robinson, *Cedric J. Robinson on Racial Capitalism, Black Internationalism, and Cultures of Resistance*, ed. H. L. T. Quan (London: Pluto, 2019); Cedric J. Robinson, *An Anthropology of Marxism*, 2nd ed. (2001; Chapel Hill: University of North Carolina Press, 2019); and Joshua Myers, *Cedric Robinson: The Time of the Black Radical Tradition* (Cambridge: Polity, 2021).
14. See Alexander, *Against Racial Capitalism*. See also Zachary Levenson and Marcel Paret, "The Three Dialectics of Racial Capitalism: From South Africa to the U.S. and Back Again," *Du Bois Review: Social Science Research on Race* 20, no. 2 (2023): 333–51; Arun Kundnani, "What Is Racial Capitalism?," *Arun Kundnani on Race, Culture, and Empire*, October 15, 2020, https://www.kundnani.org/what-is-racial-capitalism/; and Peter James Hudson, "Racial Capitalism and the Dark Proletariat," *Boston Review*, February 20, 2018, https://www.bostonreview.net/forum_response/peter-james-hudson-racial-capitalism-and/.
15. Robinson, "Capitalism, Marxism, and the Black Radical Tradition," 7–8. See also Myers, *Cedric Robinson*, 127–39.
16. See, for example, Adrián Sotelo Valencia, *Sub-Imperialism Revisited: Dependency Theory in the Thought of Ruy Mauro Marini*, trans. Jacob Lagnado (Leiden: Brill, 2017); Barbara Stallings, *Dependency in the Twenty-First Century? The Political Economy of China-Latin America Relations* (Cambridge: Cambridge University Press, 2020); and Claudio Katz, *Dependency Theory After Fifty Years: The Continuing Relevance of Latin American Critical Thought*, trans. Stanley Malinowitz (Leiden: Brill, 2022).
17. See Walter Rodney, *How Europe Underdeveloped Africa* (1972; repr., New York: Verso, 2018); Walter Rodney, *The Russian Revolution: A View from the Third World*, ed. Robin D. G. Kelley and Jesse Benjamin (New York: Verso, 2018); Walter Rodney, *The Groundings with My Brothers* (1969; repr., London: Verso, 2019); and Walter Rodney, *Decolonial Marxism: Essays from the Pan-African Revolution*, ed. Asha Rodney, Patricia Rodney, Ben Mabie, and Jesse Benjamin (New York: Verso, 2022).
18. Angela Davis, foreword to Rodney, *How Europe Underdeveloped Africa*, 12–13.
19. See Duncan Kennedy, "Distributive and Paternalist Motives in Contract and Tort Law with Special Reference to Compulsory Terms and Unequal Bargaining Power,"

Maryland Law Review 41 (1982): 563–658. For his distributional critique of a liberal law and economics position, see Duncan Kennedy, "Cost-Benefit Analysis of Entitlement Problems: A Critique," *Stanford Law Review* 33, no. 3 (1981): 387–445, https://doi.org/10.2307/1228354.

20. Robert L. Hale, "Coercion and Distribution in a Supposedly Non-coercive State," *Political Science Quarterly* 38, no. 3 (1923): 470–94, https://doi.org/10.2307/2142367.
21. Duncan Kennedy, "The Stakes of Law, or Hale and Foucault," *Legal Studies Forum* 15 (1991): 327.
22. See, for example, David M. Trubek and Alvaro Santos, eds., *The New Law and Economic Development: A Critical Appraisal* (Cambridge: Cambridge University Press, 2006), 16–18; and Janet Halley and Kerry Rittich, "Critical Directions in Comparative Family Law: Genealogies and Contemporary Studies of Family Law Exceptionalism," *American Journal of Comparative Law* 58, no. 4 (2010): 753–75.
23. Janet Halley, "Distribution and Decision: Assessing Governance Feminism," in *Governance Feminism: An Introduction*, ed. Janet Halley, Prabha Kotiswaran, Rachel Rebouché, and Hila Shamir (Minneapolis: University of Minnesota Press, 2018), 253–67.
24. Rodney, *How Europe Underdeveloped Africa*, 30.
25. Immanuel Wallerstein, "The Myrdal Legacy: Racism and Underdevelopment as Dilemmas," *Cooperation and Conflict* 24, no. 1 (1989): 1, https://www.jstor.org/stable/45083690.
26. The literature on technological change and the future of work is massive. Some of that literature is engaged with by Kerry Rittich in chapter 7 of this collection. For a few examples of the positions described by international institutions, see "IMF Future of Work," *International Monetary Fund*, October 11, 2017, https://mediacenter.imf.org/news/imf-future-of-work/s/aad85c4c-9b5a-45c4-8dd2-2d8ab3398750; ILO Global Commission on the Future of Work, *Work for a Brighter Future* (Geneva: ILO 2019), 19, table 1; World Bank Group, *The Changing Nature of Work* (Washington, DC: World Bank Group, 2019), https://documents1.worldbank.org/curated/en/816281518818814423/pdf/2019-WDR-Report.pdf; World Economic Forum, *Preparing for the Future of Work*, https://www3.weforum.org/docs/WEF_System_Initiative_Future_Education_Gender_Work_Preparing_Future_Work_2-P. pdf; and "Future of Work," *Organization for Economic Cooperation and Development*, accessed July 11, 2023, https://www.oecd.org/future-of-work/.

    For a few legal scholarly interventions in this area, see Jeremias Prassl, *Humans as a Service: The Promise and Perils of Work in the Gig Economy* (Oxford: Oxford University Press, 2018); Veena B. Dubal, Ruth Berins Collier, and Christopher L. Carter, "Disrupting Regulation, Regulating Disruption: The Politics of Uber in the United States," *Perspectives on Politics* 16 (2018): 919–37, https://doi.org/10.1017/S1537592718001093; Frank Pasquale, *New Laws of Robotics: Defending Human Expertise in the Age of AI* (Cambridge, MA: Belknap Press of Harvard University Press, 2020); Cynthia Estlund, *Automation Anxiety: Why and How to Save Work* (Oxford: Oxford University Press, 2021); and Brishen Rogers, *Data and Democracy at Work: Advanced Information Technologies, Labor Law, and the New Working Class* (Cambridge, MA: MIT Press, 2023).

For examples of scholarship by economists grappling with technological disruption in work, see Richard Baldwin, *The Globotics Upheaval: Globalization, Robotics, and the Future of Work* (Oxford: Oxford University Press, 2019); Daron Acemoglu and Pascual Restrepo, "Automation and New Tasks: How Technology Displaces and Reinstates Labor," *Journal of Economic Perspectives* 33, no. 2 (2019): 3–30, https://doi.org/10.1257/jep.33.2.3; and Melline Somers, Angelos Theodorakopoulos, and Kerstin Hötte, "The Fear of Technology-Driven Unemployment and Its Empirical Base," *Center for Economic Policy Research*, June 10, 2022, https://cepr.org/voxeu/columns/fear-technology-driven-unemployment-and-its-empirical-base.

For some public commentary on the topic, see Clark Mindock, "Alexandria Ocasio-Cortez Says the Jobless in America Are 'Left to Die' but US Must 'Embrace Automation,'" *The Independent*, March 11, 2019, https://www.independent.co.uk/news/world/americas/us-politics/aoc-twitter-automation-jobless-die-sxsw-alexandria-ocasio-cortez-a8818191.html; Margaret O'Mara, "The Church of Techno-Optimism," *New York Times*, September 28, 2019, https://www.nytimes.com/2019/09/28/opinion/sunday/silicon-valley-techno-optimism.html; Kristen Broady, Anthony Barr, and Colleen Dougherty, "Workers Must Use Their Newfound Leverage to Protect Their Careers from Automation," *Brookings*, December 10, 2021, https://www.brookings.edu/articles/workers-must-use-their-newfound-leverage-to-protect-their-careers-from-automation/; and Dagny Dukach, "Research Roundup: How Technology Is Transforming Work," *Harvard Business Review*, November 7, 2022, https://hbr.org/2022/11/research-roundup-how-technology-is-transforming-work.

27. Miriam A. Cherry, "Back to the Future: A Continuity of Dialogue on Work and Technology at the ILO," *International Labour Review* 159, no. 1 (2020): 21, https://doi.org/10.1111/ilr.12156. See also Qingkun (Eric) Deng, "Technology's Impact on the Labor Market: Different This Time?," Futures of Work, November 29, 2022, https://futuresofwork.co.uk/2022/11/29/technologys-impact-on-the-labour-market-different-this-time/.

28. Cherry makes a similar point about the decline in union power and fissuring since 1960. See Cherry, "Back to the Future," 18.

29. Juan D. De Lara, *Inland Shift: Race, Space, and Capital in Southern California* (Oakland: University of California Press, 2018), 80 and Figure 13.

30. David Weil, *The Fissured Workplace: Why Work Became So Bad for So Many and What Can Be Done About It* (Cambridge, MA: Harvard University Press, 2014). Rittich's chapter 7 in this collection also references Weil in discussing the displacement of the standard employment relationship.

31. See Jennifer Bair, "Editor's Introduction: Commodity Chains in and of the World System," in "The Political Economy of Commodity Chains," ed. Jennifer Bair, special issue, *Journal of World-Systems Research* 20, no. 1 (Winter/Spring 2014): 1–10, https://doi.org/10.5195/jwsr.2014.574. Among other questions, Bair usefully asks "What is the relationship between commodity chains and the stratification of the world-system, and how, if at all, does this change over time?"; "Where does the surplus in commodity chains come from, and how are the returns to participation distributed among the actors in the chain?"; and "What kinds of structural and/or discursive openings do different commodity chains create for political organization

and/or resistance?" Bair, "Editor's Introduction," 3. Or, as David Kennedy explains, "When gains at the center are self-reinforcing and firms at the periphery find themselves increasingly unable to extract rents, the global value chain has unleashed a dualist dynamic of downgrading at the periphery and upgrading at the center." David Kennedy, *A World of Struggle: How Power, Law, and Expertise Shape Global Political Economy* (Princeton: Princeton University Press, 2016), 202.

32. Rittich, citing Immanuel Wallerstein, *The Modern World-System II: Mercantilism and the Consolidation of the European World-Economy 1600–1750* (Berkeley: University of California Press, 1980), 194; and Max Weber, *General Economic History* (New York: Transaction, 1992), 173.

33. International Labour Organization, *ILO Centenary Declaration for the Future of Work*, adopted June 21, 2019, I.A, http://www.ilo.org/global/about-the-ilo/mission-and-objectives/centenary-declaration/lang--en/index.htm. For calls for transition to formality, see International Labor Organization, *ILO Centenary Declaration*, II.A(xiv), III.B, and III.C(iv).

34. Some have even argued, in the context of temporary migrant labor schemes in the Global South, that workers sometimes find themselves in better bargaining positions in the informal rather than formal sector. Yiran Zhang, for instance, follows the work lives and relative bargaining power of undocumented Filipina domestic workers in China (over workers with temporary migrant visas) to challenge the orthodox account that formality invariably leads to better jobs for transnational migrant workers. Yiran Zhang, "Rethinking the Global Governance of Migrant Domestic Workers: The Heterodox Case of Informal Filipina Workers in China," *Georgetown Immigration Law Journal* 36, no. 3 (Spring 2022): 963–1015. Jennifer Gordon's chapter 10 in this volume provides examples of Syrian refugees in Jordan rejecting formal temporary migrant work programs in export zones, choosing instead to continue with informal and socially reproductive work.

35. Jane Collins, "A Feminist Approach to Overcoming the Closed Boxes of the Commodity Chain," in *Gendered Commodity Chains: Seeing Women's Work and Households in Global Production*, ed. Wilma Dunaway (Stanford: Stanford University Press: 2014), 27.

36. Jennifer Gordon, "Regulating the Human Supply Chain," *Iowa Law Review* 102 (2017): 445–504.

37. For discussion of other worker-driven social responsibility programs, see, generally, Daniel Brinks, Julia Dehm, Karen Engle, and Kate Taylor, eds., *Power, Participation, and Private Regulatory Initiatives* (Philadelphia: University of Pennsylvania Press, 2021), which includes chapters by Jessica Champagne on the Bangladesh Accord and Sean Sellers on the Fair Food Program.

38. See Stefania Barca, "An Alternative Worth Fighting For: Degrowth and the Liberation of Work," in *Towards a Political Economy of Degrowth*, ed. Ekaterina Chertovskaya et al. (New York: Rowman and Littlefield, 2019), 184.

PART I

Global Hierarchies

Racial Capitalism, World-Systems, and Legal Distributional Analyses

CHAPTER 1

NEVILLE ALEXANDER

Racial Capitalism South African Style

DENNIS DAVIS

To anyone familiar with the correct analysis of the Azanian liberation struggle, the contention that racialism is a creation of capitalism and can only be overthrown by a proletarian revolution is a load of shit. . . . The brutal processes of primitive accumulation and the establishment of a wealthy and powerful white ruling class over the African masses are overlooked in order to cater to the "historical" justification of the theory of "racial capitalism."
—Anonymous, "Neo Marxism and the Bogus Theory of Racial Capitalism"

The black working class has to act as a magnet that draws all the other oppressed layers of our society, organises them for the liberation struggle and imbues them with consistent democratic socialist ideas which alone spell death to the system of racial . . . capitalism as we know it today.
—Neville Alexander, "Nation and Ethnicity in South Africa" (1985)

The concept of racial capitalism emerged in South Africa in the 1970s as a reaction to liberal responses to the apartheid regime. These liberal responses, in essence, contended that the racial inequalities spawned by the apartheid system would be reformed through the development of a more rational system of capitalism. A number of Marxist scholars began to challenge this perspective, arguing that apartheid was not a deformation of capitalism and that capitalism was *always* racial capitalism.[1] Neville Alexander, a public intellectual and activist who spent a decade as a prisoner on Robben Island with Nelson Mandela, was the most prominent scholar among them. In Alexander's view, "the immediate goal of the national liberation struggle now being waged in South Africa is the destruction of the system of racial capitalism." He argued that the development of capitalism in South Africa was guided by the national bourgeoisie, a class of white capitalists who created a legal system that secured an unlimited supply of cheap Black labor through denial to the majority of political rights, restricted freedom of movement tied to the so-called native reserves, prohibition of the right to own property outside of the reserves, and a draconian system of influx control to ensure a supply of Black labor that could meet the demands of the mining sector.[2]

As the anonymous author quoted in this chapter's epigraph made clear, the turn to Marxism as a means of analyzing apartheid South Africa met with opposition not only from liberal scholars who contended that capitalist development would cause the termination of apartheid but also from those who argued that any attempt to explain apartheid through the prism of capitalism represented an attempt to obfuscate the *racism* at the core of the struggle—the construction of a new nation of Azania had to be built on victory over naked racism, which had characterized South Africa since the advent of Dutch colonialism in 1652.[3]

Although this chapter is devoted to the work of Alexander, it should be noted that by the early 1980s the theory of racial capitalism began to gain traction beyond the borders of South Africa. The implicit dialogue between theorists of racial capitalism in South Africa and those who employed the term to analyze other jurisdictions highlights important convergences and differences in the application thereof.

For American readers of the theory of racial capitalism, Cedric Robinson assumes the same importance that Neville Alexander does for South African audiences. In 1983, a few years after the first clutch of publications of analyses of racial capitalism in South Africa, Robinson published an important work titled *Black Marxism*. In it he expounded on the concept of racial capitalism, by which he meant that capitalism was inextricably linked, throughout its history, to the concept of race and racism. In Robinson's explanation, the system of capitalism had been built upon the transatlantic slave trade and the exploitation that was inherent in the colonial project. For Robinson, the concept of nonracial capitalism was nothing more than a figment.

Viewed within this context, Robinson's central argument was that Black radicalism required racially oppressed people, particularly those of African descent, who had been exploited by capitalism, to lead the liberation from this exploitative economic system. He wrote that racism was deeply imbricated in any capitalist system: "All capitalists believe the brutality of the slave system to be a practical necessity. Maroon settlements like those of Jamaica, Cuba, and North America had to be destroyed or failing that quarantined. They could not be allowed to contaminate a labor upon which so much depended." For similar reasons, Robinson argued that capitalism could never be uncoupled from a racist discourse with which it was inextricably linked: "The development, organization, and expansion of capitalist society pursued essentially racial directions, so too did social ideology. As a material force, then, it could be expected that racialism would inevitably permeate the social structures emergent from capitalism."[4]

That Robinson employed the term "racial capitalism" holds considerable significance for South Africa because it lent great weight to the challenge of the prevailing liberal orthodoxy, even within the African National Congress, that apartheid was antithetical to the capitalist system and that capitalism would therefore eventually cause the collapse of apartheid. In contrast, political theorists inspired by the Marxist tradition, in particular Alexander, argued that racism was vital to the development of South African capitalism. South African capitalism, powered as it was by the mining sector, created a reserve labor market based on the denial of basic rights to the majority of the population. Indeed, in this way, capitalism and apartheid were effectively conjoined twins.[5] For this reason, the apartheid state needed to be analyzed through its consistent responses to the changing demands of capital accumulation. These changes in the economic structure meant that the racist practices of South Africa had to be reconfigured to support the prevailing form of capital accumulation.

In this chapter, I explain Alexander's development of the concept of racial capitalism as it applied to South Africa, along with his unique perspective on the construction of a democratic South Africa. I contend that Alexander's application of racial capitalism to apartheid South Africa became the foundation for his pathbreaking work on how a democratic South Africa could redress the consequences of more than three hundred years of racist authoritarian rule.

WHO WAS NEVILLE ALEXANDER?

Neville Alexander was born on October 22, 1936, and died on August 27, 2012. His entire career was devoted to the construction of a country based on freedom and substantive equality for all. By the time of his death, he had contributed significantly to the defeat of the apartheid regime, and with the advent of democracy he became the foremost advocate of a language policy for a democratic country that was based on a clear idea of what might constitute a nonracial South Africa.[6]

His life was shaped by struggle. As a member of the National Liberation Front, which he cofounded, Alexander, along with most members of the front, was arrested in July 1963. After a lengthy criminal trial, he was convicted of conspiracy to commit sabotage and sentenced to ten years imprisonment on Robben Island. By this time he had a PhD, which was awarded to him in 1961 by the University of Tubingen for his dissertation, "Style Change in the Dramatic Work of Gerhart Hauptmann." The topic was developed from his study of German and particularly German drama at the University of Cape Town in the 1950s, which inspired an interest in language and linguistic diversity. He was rightly regarded as an intellectual revolutionary by the time he joined the Rivonia trialists, including Nelson Mandela, on the island.

Upon his release from prison in 1974, Alexander devoted much of his intellectual and political energy to the development of an appropriate language policy for a nonracial democratic South Africa by way of organizations such as the Project for the Study of Alternative Education in South Africa. Alexander recognized that English would be a dominant language in South Africa as a result of global political and economic development. But English, he argued, should not retain the hegemonic status that in turn disempowered indigenous languages and thus threatened the viability of nation building.

Throughout this period, he also wrote extensively on the relationship between the national struggle for liberation in South Africa and the potential future political vision for a democratic society. The relationships among racism, capitalism, the role of the working class, and the liberation struggles, as well as those among the process of nation building, the role of education, and social change, were crucial to his writings.[7] It is to these analyses of the South African political economy that I now turn.

ALEXANDER AND RACIAL CAPITALISM

In analyzing the economic aims of the apartheid regime in the 1970s, Alexander identified two main goals the regime sought to achieve. First, the state expanded the strategy of earlier governments that ruled the Union of South Africa by progressively emancipating indigenous capital from the metropolitan, thereby ensuring that the maximum amount of economic surplus generated by both mining and industry was reinvested in South African agriculture and secondary industries rather than being patriated to Europe in general and the United Kingdom in particular.

Fiscal and tariff policies, which were heavily weighted in favor of agriculture and secondary industries, became major policy tools used to promote the government's goals. At the same time, state-owned and parastatal corporations were developed to undertake and expand a program of import substitution with a view to strengthening the industrial base of indigenous capital and ensuring the highest possible price for agricultural products and base metals, thereby enhancing the interests of the mining and agricultural fractions of capital.

The second key goal of the apartheid regime when it came to power in 1948 was to develop methods to maintain a large supply of cheap Black labor once the so-called native reserve system had been eliminated as a viable reservoir of surplus labor needed to depress wages and promote capitalist profit. As a result, new systems of control over labor and subsidization of cheap labor throughout the rural areas had to be devised.

As Alexander writes, "With the discovery and exploitation of diamonds and later of gold, there was a giant leap in demand for labour which called for even more drastic measures. *The 'native', in the notorious words of Rhodes, had to be taught 'the dignity of labour'*, and it is at this point that the system of native reserves becomes a crucial component of the capitalist system as it has developed in the peculiar conditions of South Africa."[8]

To explain these developments, Alexander traced the history beginning with the discovery of precious gems and metals in South Africa in the 1860s. The reserves on which the vast majority of Black South Africans then lived bore the burden of supplying the bulk of the labor needed in the mines. This made possible the maintenance of a workforce that labored at sub-subsistence levels and hence at a minimum cost to the state and to capital because the rural homestead paid most of the reproductive labor costs in the system of short-term contract migrant work in the mines. In this way, the reserves were a source of subsidization of the low wages paid to miners and workers in the industrial sector of the economy. In support of his general argument, Alexander cited testimony from the Chamber of Mines to the Lansdowne Commission on Mine Wages of 1943: "The ability of the mines to maintain their native labour force by means of tribal natives from the Reserves at rates of pay which are adequate for this migratory class of native but inadequate for the detribalised native is a fundamental factor in the economy of the gold mining industry."[9]

By the 1940s, the reserves were no longer able to continue to sustain this subsidization of labor, in Alexander's words, because of "relative overpopulation, overstocking, backward methods of production, and the absence of most of the economically active population at any given time ... [which led to] the notorious poverty, malnutrition and mortality rates associated with the reserves."[10] The collapse of the reserve system meant that by 1948 the National Party was required to recreate a pool of cheap labor. Three decades of industrialization had resulted in a significant need for Black labor in the urban areas and a concomitant degradation of the rural reserves, which had subsidized the Black workforce and thus ensured a plentiful supply of cheap labor.

The National Party government responded by developing the "Bantustan policy" to prop up the reserves. Simultaneously, the government sought to develop a theory that, in Alexander's view, "appeared to jettison racism while actually building on its solid foundations."[11] The government created so-called independent homelands, one for each tribal group and governed by a coterie of pliable traditional chiefs. Its aim was to suppress labor power as much as possible while responding to foreign pressure exerted against the crude racism of existing government policy—hence the claim of "independence" in homelands for the majority of the population, conveniently divided by tribe and ethnic origin. In this way, the regime could argue that it recognized Black political aspirations while also ensuring that the homelands would continue to subsidize the supply of Black labor. The flow of Black labor from the homelands was further regulated by influx control measures in which only Black workers with a pass to enter the urban areas were allowed to do so.

For Alexander, this system of control—buttressed by an archipelago of legislation—reflected the racism that lay at the core of the development of capitalism in South Africa, in the same way that the doctrine of individual rights helped to develop the capitalism of England and France:

> The conventional bourgeois critique of racism, and many marxist variants thereof that are still current in the literature of the liberation movement, is based on a myth. This myth ... assumes that there is some optimum set of conditions under which capitalism—with a minimum of blood and tears—can flourish to infinity. One of these conditions is assumed to be equality of rights for individuals. Yet, historically, capital has been combined with all forms of labour, from slave labour to 'free' wage labour, in order to make possible the process of accumulation. In South Africa, racism with its concomitant forms of forced labour (i.e. labour recruited with coercive assistance of state organs rather than on the basis of some illusory contract between 'equal' buyer and seller of labour power meeting each other in the so-called free market as alleged in the textbooks on 'perfect competition') legitimated the accumulation of capital by a small class of local and foreign white capitalists.[12]

One of the significant implications of the apartheid system was the manner in which the vast majority of the population were educated during this period. Education policy was illustrative of the broader apartheid project and, for Alexander, a significant site where the articulation of race and capitalism in South African political economy becomes clear. "Because of its pivotal role in the reproduction of the relations of production, 'native education' was to be reconceived and restructured from the bottom up. It was to serve the purpose of perpetuating the capitalist system as it had developed in South Africa and not creating the illusion that black people would be permitted to graze in the green pastures of 'white civilisation'. In the notorious words of Dr Verwoerd, 'the Native' was to be taught that 'there was no place for him in "European society" above the level of certain forms of labour.'"[13]

Alexander accepted that the Bantustan strategy was designed in part to produce Black satellite capitalist systems operating within the Bantustans. This was essential to the reconstruction of a reserve army of labor needed to serve the needs of the capitalist economy. But "given the historical development of capitalism in South Africa and the white capitalists' almost complete monopoly of access to capital, there does not exist any mechanism whereby blacks could *independently* accumulate capital on any but a miniscule scale."[14] The basis of the Bantustan policy, in which nominal rights of governance would be granted to a cadre of "reliable" Black leaders, was a plan to develop an increasing reservoir of super-exploitable wage laborers who would never become peasants but neither would they ever be part of the bourgeois class.

Unlike Robinson, Alexander concentrated less on the global economy and more on the indigenous conditions of South Africa. Hence his conception of racial capitalism was employed as a key analytic tool to understand the nature of the apartheid state and its policies. Although his writings refer to the global workings of capitalism, they did not broaden to a detailed examination of the economics of the developed world. South Africa remained his exclusive concern, and the theories he developed were central to his major focus: the successful fight against apartheid. Thus he drew a distinction between the growth of capitalism in Europe, which in his view was a "relatively gradual and organic process," and capitalism in the conquered territories wherein "the process assumes the character of a cataclysm. Whole peoples disappear in the space of a few decades, cultural treasures and historical patterns are suddenly obliterated, and a painful process of adaptation to the new conditions begins. Imperialist rivalry changes the whole pre-existent territorial configuration."[15]

Significantly, Robinson eschewed the idea that South African capitalism had taken on an exceptional form. For him, it was inherent in the nature of capitalism that a division between wage and surplus labor would be created to reproduce the exploitation by capital of surplus value. In this way, differentiations between races, exploitation of the colonial by the colonizers, and the calibration of rights enjoyed by various forms of labor lay at the core of the capitalist enterprise. As Arun Kundnani has correctly observed, Robinson had turned the claim of South African capitalism on its head and developed a theory that placed race at the center of the capitalist system.[16]

TOWARD LIBERATION FROM RACIAL CAPITALISM

Alexander's concept of racial capitalism as analyzed in terms of the South African economic model was central to his conception of liberation from the nightmare of apartheid. It followed from his theory that the task for a country such as South Africa was to develop a cohesive conception of a nation if any liberation struggle was to throw off the shackles of racist rule. In the first place, the racial oppression of Black people was manifestly a function of the capitalist system. What was required, then, was the liquidation of those institutions and practices that had created and reinforced the racial structures of South African society that fueled the capitalist machine. In short, "this mean[t] nothing else than the abolition of capitalism." Viewed within this context, the South African nation had to consist "of all the people who are prepared to throw off the yoke of capitalist exploitation and racist oppression."[17] The struggle was a fight against any attempt to divide the South African population on the basis of language, religion, tribe, or caste, distinctions that were central to the reproduction of apartheid policy.

This new conception of democracy represented Alexander's solution to the "national question." Alexander argued that the nation at a political level does not belong to one or another class. In South Africa, the bourgeoise had promoted a capitalist project by dividing people who lived within the country and by making the nation exclusively a white nation—indeed, even an exclusively Afrikaner nation. In response, national liberation movements had to insist on uniting the people not only on a geographical and juridical level but also politically and culturally. Although the project of constructing the nation was a progressive one, Alexander noted that this was not necessarily an anticapitalist project—which is why, in his view, the development of a new South Africa had to be informed by a class perspective.

Employing the work of Antonio Gramsci, Alexander contended that the working class would need to become the leading, or hegemonic, class in order to set the terms upon which the new nation would be built.[18] Critically, because race and class overlapped in South Africa in the system of racial capitalism, unless a class revolution against capitalism took place, the dominant mode of production would continue to reproduce racial inequality.

Alexander's conception of nationalism built through the leadership of the working class was in sharp contrast to a liberal model of multiracialism as envisaged by the African National Congress (ANC). Alexander recalls his debates in prison on Robben Island with Nelson Mandela, who maintained that the South Africa nation was constituted by the Black population and all others were minorities.[19] For Alexander, only upon the idea of a nonracial society could a community of shared values and supportive solidarity be constructed. As he wrote: "I believe the only worthwhile non-racial project is the one that uses non-racial means. Just like democracy: you cannot bring about democracy by authoritarian means. For the very same reason I think one must accept that this struggle is going to continue. . . . The potential for chauvinist and black racist effects and spin-offs is very great, especially if those things can be linked to economic interest. That is why things like setting up companies where only blacks are allowed could become the thin edge of the wedge."[20]

Although he accepted that in the foreseeable future capitalism would not be destroyed, Alexander argued that the more radical the democratic project that could be constructed in South Africa, whereby the working class would gain hegemony in the struggle for democracy, the more the "very practices that come into being will eventually impact even on the policies of a capitalist state."[21] That Alexander made in this claim in 1993, a year before democracy dawned in South Africa, reflects the prescience of Alexander's concerns about the political project led by the ANC after it attained power in 1994.

Alexander acknowledged that nonracial capitalism was theoretically possible, but he insisted that it was historically impossible. Race and class had "overlapped with one another to such an extent that unless you have a class revolution against capitalism your mode of production reproduces racial inequality."[22] In this way, Alexander's argument about the nature of racial capitalism in South Africa was unanswerable. Throughout the apartheid period that formally ended in 1994, race and class were closely correlated. The displacement of Black South Africans from the land and unequal access to educational and employment opportunities shaped a racially skewed distribution of income.[23] Capitalism in South Africa was invariably racial.

RACIAL CAPITALISM NOW

Unless there was a radical distribution of resources within the lifetime of those who had finally seen apartheid replaced by a democratic rule, Alexander argued that visions of social transformation and of a national democratic revolution—and even of an African renaissance—could never be achieved. As he had argued with Mandela when both men were prisoners on Robben Island, it was not possible to build a united historical community if race continued to be essentialized. The centrality of race as a key analytic frame would make it all but impossible for racial thinking to disappear in a future democratic South Africa, and thus a South African nation united in the pursuit of a democratic project would not materialize.

For Alexander, the concept of racial capitalism explained the ways in which the South African state had derived economic and social value from the maintenance of racial identities. As such, the racial classifications employed by the apartheid state had to disappear for democracy to be born. If racial capitalism could be replaced by a society led by the working class, the maintenance of racial identity would begin to disappear and a truly nonracial, egalitarian society could emerge.

Alexander was not naïve in his outlook. He knew that his political vision would take time. He also understood that the notion of the rainbow nation, as proclaimed by Archbishop Desmond Tutu in 1994 at the time of the first democratic elections, was both hopelessly premature and, in any event, adopted the wrong approach. It was premature in that the fundamental material conditions that would permit a united nation to emerge from the racist past were simply not present. Without these material changes, it was impossible to envisage the social cohesion of a South African nation. It was also wrong because the image of the rainbow represented bands that were separated. For Alexander, the preferred metaphor was the Gariep River, where a multitude of streams from diverse origins flow together to form a mighty river.[24]

As Alexander predicted, race continues to be central to the existing South African capitalist model. More than two decades after the end of apartheid, the World Bank reported that race's contribution to income inequality in South Africa amounted to 41 percent, with education's contribution at 30 percent. Thus race, through its effect on both education and labor market outcomes, remains the key driver of South Africa's high levels of inequality.[25]

It is for these reasons that, in response to the ANC's focus on affirmative action based on race classification, Alexander argued that unless state institutions placed disadvantage rather than racial classification at the center of a transformative strategy, affirmative action would only benefit a narrow group of Black people. In his view, this constituency comprised rent seekers, hence the perpetuation of racial thinking at the expense of the working class and the perennially poor.

In a 2010 speech delivered just two years before his death, Alexander surveyed both the current policies of the trade union movement and the government led by the African National Congress and said that their policies "can at best lead to what I have already referred to as the consolidation of social democracy in the workers' movement. The entire strategy depends on a notion of the state as being essentially neutral. The final disillusionment will come, of course, when the oppressive apparatuses of the state, instead of supporting the exploited classes and other oppressed strata turn their weapons on the masses, to protect the interest of a capitalist class. The response of police personnel to many of the so-called service delivery protests prefigures what I am saying here."[26] If this depressing notion was not to find its way into reality, Alexander argued that what was needed was the creation of "the ideological and organisational means to build the counter-society that insulates the oppressed and exploited from the undermining and disempowering values and practices of bourgeois society. This goal [had to] once again become an integral part of the class struggle against exploitation and oppression."[27]

The importance of Neville Alexander's work cannot be overestimated within the context of the bleak political conditions of contemporary South Africa. To again emphasize racially based economic disparities, the monthly rent earnings of whites were more than three times higher than those of Black Africans. Between 2011 and 2015, the Gini coefficient reflected increases in the disparity between Black and white earners.[28]

The mountainous challenges posed by the history of apartheid have been greatly exacerbated during the past decade. Rent-seeking by the middle class, the capture of key state institutions in order to promote greater levels of plundering of state resources, a populist rhetoric that uses race for the purposes of personal gain, and a capitalist economy in which the vast majority of South Africans continue to enjoy precious little benefit represent the precise elements of the warning issued by Alexander. Contemporary South Africa affirms Alexander's contention that the failure to engage in material redistribution of resources in combination with the absence of construction of a nation led by the working class would reproduce a form of capitalism that would remain essentially racial, even if the Constitution of South Africa of 1996 claimed that it heralded the dawn of a nonracial, nonsexist democracy based on freedom, dignity, and equality for all.

In this sense, Alexander's work on the nature of racial capitalism in South Africa and the manner in which it developed and persists regrettably "alive and well" in contemporary South Africa remains vibrantly relevant. He was one of the few South African intellectuals who had the foresight, intellectual rigor, and courage to warn against the disastrous economic and political conditions that prevail in contemporary South Africa.

Given the socioeconomic conditions of contemporary South Africa, Alexander's warning should echo throughout the country: "We have seen that the national bourgeoisie have failed to complete the democratic revolution. The middle classes cannot be consistent since in their interest are generally speaking and their own consciousness, tied to the capitalist system. Hence only the black working class can take the task of completing the democratization of the country on its shoulders. It alone can unite all the oppressed and exploited classes."[29]

In his consistent insistence that race was not a valid biological entity but rather a social reality, Alexander hoped that a democratic post-apartheid South Africa that meaningfully addressed the consequences of the social reality born of more than three hundred years of colonial and apartheid racist rule could speak to transformative politics beyond the boundaries of South Africa. In summary, Alexander saw the development of a truly nonracial egalitarian South Africa as providing the way for the realization of the dream of a raceless and even a classless society.

NOTES

1. For an early exposition of the Marxist perspective, see Martin Legassick and David Hemson, *Foreign Investment and the Reproduction of Racial Capitalism in South Africa* (London: Anti-Apartheid Movement, 1976).
2. Neville Alexander, "Nation and Ethnicity in South Africa," in *Sow the Wind: Contemporary Speeches* (Johannesburg: Skotaville, 1985), 49, 51–52.
3. For opposition from liberal scholars, see Merle Lipton, *Capitalism and Apartheid: South Africa 1910–1984* (Aldershot, UK: Gower/M.T. Smith, 1985).
4. Cedric Robinson, *Black Marxism*, 2nd ed. (Chapel Hill: University of North Carolina Press, 2000), 40, 2.
5. Among these theorists were Martin Legassick, David Henson, Harold Wolpe, and Neville Alexander, all of whom were analyzed carefully in Alex Callinicos, ed., *South Africa Between Reform and Revolution: Conversations with South African Socialists* (London: Bookmarks, 1988), 84–88. See also Legassick and Henson, *Foreign Investment and the Reproduction of Racial Capitalism*.
6. Neville Alexander, *Language Educational Policy: National and Sub-national Identities in South Africa* (Strasbourg: Council of Europe, 2003).

7. See, particularly, Neville Alexander, *Sow the Wind: Contemporary Speeches* (Johannesburg: Skotaville, 1985); and Neville Alexander [No Sizwe, pseud.], *One Azania, One Nation: The National Question in South Africa*, digital edition (2013; London: Zed, 1979), https://www.marxists.org/archive/alexander/one-azania-one-nation.pdf.
8. Alexander, *One Azania, One Nation*, 59–60 (emphasis added).
9. Alexander, 61 (emphasis removed), quoting Oliver Walker, *Kaffirs Are Lively, Being Some Backstage Impressions of the South African Democracy* (London: V. Gollancz, 1948), 22.
10. Alexander, *One Azania, One Nation*, 67.
11. Alexander, *One Azania, One Nation*, 105.
12. Alexander, *One Azania, One Nation*, 105.
13. Alexander, *One Azania, One Nation*, 108, quoting A. N. Pelzer, ed., *Verwoerd aan die Woord—Toesprake 1948–1962* (Johannesburg: Afrikaanse Pers-Boekhandel, 1963), 77–78.
14. Alexander, *One Azania, One Nation*, 118–19.
15. Alexander, *One Azania, One Nation*, 276.
16. Arun Kundnani, "What Is Racial Capitalism?," *Arun Kundnani on Race, Culture, and Empire*, October 15, 2020, https://www.kundnani.org/what-is-racial-capitalism/.
17. Alexander, *One Azania, One Nation*, 289–90.
18. In particular, see Antonio Gramsci, *Selections from the Prison Notebooks*, ed. Geoffrey Nowell Smith, trans. Quintin Hoare (New York: International, 1971).
19. An interview with Alexander cited in Roland Czada, "Neville Alexander's Non-Racial, Inclusionary Vision of Nationhood," paper prepared for the Neville Alexander Commemorative Conference: *The Life and Times of Neville Alexander*, July 6–8, 2013, Nelson Mandela Metropolitan University, Port Elizabeth, South Africa.
20. Neville Alexander, "An Interview with Neville Alexander," interview by Hein Marais, *Work in Progress*, no. 93 (November 1993): 17, https://disa.ukzn.ac.za/sites/default/files/pdf_files/WpNov93.1608.2036.000.093.Nov1993.13.pdf.
21. Alexander, "An Interview with Neville Alexander," 17.
22. See Alexander, "An Interview with Neville Alexander," 16.
23. See Jeremy Seekings and Nicoli Nattrass, *Class, Race and Inequality in South Africa* (Scottsville: University of KwaZulu-Natal Press, 2006).
24. The Gariep River, otherwise known as the Orange River, is South Africa's largest river.
25. In this Alexander sadly was extremely prescient, according to Victor Sulla, Precious Zikhali, and Facundo Cuevas, *Inequality in Southern Africa: An Assessment of the Southern African Customs Union (English)* (Washington, DC: World Bank Group, 2022). The bank reported that South Africa is characterized by high wealth inequality and economic polarization across labor markets. Wealth inequality is higher than income inequality, with estimates showing that the top 10 percent of the population hold 71 percent of the country's wealth, whereas the bottom 60 percent hold only 7 percent. Wage inequality inflated by more than 10 percent between 1995 and 2015 when the Gini coefficient for wages rose from 58 to 69.
26. Neville Alexander, "South Africa—an Unfinished Revolution?," Strini Moodley Annual Memorial Lecture, University of KwaZulu-Natal, Durban, South Africa,

May 13, 2010, https://links.org.au/neville-alexander-south-africa-unfinished-revolution.
27. Alexander, "South Africa—an Unfinished Revolution?."
28. Statistics South Africa, *Inequality Trends in South Africa: A Multidimensional Diagnostic of Inequality* (Pretoria: Statistics South Africa, 2019), 151–53.
29. As quoted in Peter James Hudson, "Racial Capitalism and the Dark Proletariat," *Boston Review*, February 20, 2018, https://www.bostonreview.net/forum_response/peter-james-hudson-racial-capitalism-and/. According to Sulla, Zikhali, and Cuevas, *Inequality in Southern Africa*, South Africa is the most unequal country in the world with a consumption per capita Gini coefficient of 67 (as of 2018).

CHAPTER 2

WALTER RODNEY, WORLD-SYSTEMS THEORY, AND RACIAL CAPITALISM

NICOLE BURROWES

Writing about the aftermath of enslavement in British Guiana, the historian and activist Walter Rodney discussed how African people worked to reengineer their lives in ways that countered the oppressive nature of the plantation. He argued that they "began to put into practice, an alternative vision about the organization of work, about their culture, about their politics, and about what they expected in society. It was a vision they could not articulate under slavery, and this is where they came into conflict with the plantation system."[1] Throughout his life, Rodney consistently researched the histories of the "alternative visions" developed by racialized working people and the massive levels of inequality that shape our world.

In their 1981 introduction to Rodney's 1972 classic work, *How Europe Underdeveloped Africa*, three scholars who were leaders of the Institute of the Black World—Vincent Harding, Robert Hill, and William Strickland—posed a series of questions: "[H]ow shall we re-develop the world? Beginning with ourselves, beginning with where we are, what must we tear down, what must we build up, what foundations must we lay? Who shall we work with, what visions can we create, what hopes shall possess us? How shall we organize? How shall we be related to those who raise the same questions in South Africa, El Salvador, in Guyana? How shall we communicate with others the urgency of our time?" Written shortly after Walter Rodney's 1980 assassination, these inquiries drawn from Rodney's work continue to resonate. The scholars argued that a liberatory future depended on "these rigorous transformations."[2]

In this chapter, I consider Walter Rodney's life and scholarship to redraw the map of intellectuals who are considered central to world-systems theory and racial capitalism.[3] Rodney was one of the key people who influenced the development of both methods (and their intersection) for understanding the unequal North-South and racialized power relations under which capitalism thrives. Centering the frame around Rodney allows us to gesture toward a different genealogy of critical praxis that is relevant to current solutions; to engage his global, but locally grounded, interventions; and to return to the questions so provocatively laid out by Vincent Harding and his colleagues generations ago.

I pay particular attention to Rodney's movement-building work in multiple countries as well as various publications including his most popular work, *How Europe Underdeveloped Africa*; and his posthumously published book, *A History of Guyanese Working People, 1881–1905*. These texts demonstrate how Rodney influenced Immanuel Wallerstein, largely recognized as the leading thinker of the world-systems approach. They also help us unearth connections between Rodney's ideas and current notions of racial capitalism. Theorists of racial capitalism—including the South African thinker and revolutionary Neville Alexander, who Dennis Davis examines in this edited collection, and the African American scholar-activist Cedric Robinson—were animated by similar concerns and impulses about the axes of struggle, namely, a recognition of the importance of both race and class.[4] Rodney may have initially positioned himself differently about the origins of race, but he certainly thought about race in a flexible way and articulated that it was a constituent part of the rise of capitalism. Like Alexander, Rodney was concerned with the question of how to disrupt the "conditions of domination," and he was a part of the Black radical tradition that Robinson articulated as the antithesis to racial capitalism.[5]

Hailing from the Caribbean, Rodney was a Pan-Africanist and a Marxist.[6] Rodney applied and probed Marxist methodology to examine questions of race and colonialism, expanding its flexibility on the subject of the proletariat, extending historical analysis and centering on the societies that concerned him. Some contemporary scholars have ignored the Pan-Africanist aspect of his trajectory and cite him only as a Marxist. This problematic reading divorces him from a key tradition in world-systems and Black radical thought and ignores the reality that Rodney embodied: he bridged streams of analysis that were seemingly contradictory in some political and intellectual spaces. The political theorist Anthony Bogues points out that Rodney positioned himself as a Black Marxist: he was working to "Africanize" Marxism and was "preoccupied with creating a revolutionary ideology and theory that would emerge from the historical specific, the particular conditions of the black world."[7] Key tenets of Rodney's project included studying the multifaceted nature of exploitation, inequality, and the development of capitalism; exposing the myths of white supremacy and colonialism; exploring how the intersection of race and class functioned at various historical conjunctures; carefully documenting how working people (broadly defined) pursued new destinies; understanding and challenging neocolonial regimes; and building noncapitalist liberatory futures.

I explore some biographical detail to help readers understand the historical context and how Rodney's experience impacted his analysis and to explore key themes in this collection: world-systems theory, racial capitalism, and the future of work. Rodney was born and raised in British Guiana, South America, in 1942. He attended the University of the West Indies in Jamaica at a time that fundamentally transformed the intellectuals of his generation. By the age of twenty-four, he had completed his PhD in African history at the School of Oriental and African Studies (SOAS) in London. During his time in England, Rodney was a member of an influential Marxist study group led by the radicals C. L. R. James and Selma James.[8] C. L. R. James, a Trinidadian scholar and activist and a Black Marxist (specifically a Trotskyite), was the author of several formative works that would influence Rodney's approach to writing history, including *The Black Jacobins*, his groundbreaking text about the Haitian Revolution.[9] Selma James was a Jewish intellectual who worked on Caribbean movements for self-determination and later started the International Wages for Housework Campaign, cofounded the Global Women's Strike, and wrote several works with themes of gender, race, and labor. What did it mean to be a colonial subject trained by trailblazing scholars in the Caribbean, studying African history at SOAS, and participating in Marxist study groups led by anticolonial activists in London—all during a global moment of upheaval and revolution? By the time Rodney completed his doctorate, countries all over the world had thrown off the chains of colonialism. In fact, the year he completed his studies, 1966, was the same year that his home colony of British Guiana became the independent country of Guyana.

C. L. R. James later pointed out that Rodney was not a member of the independence generation in the anglophone Caribbean. Rather, he was part of the cohort that truly came of age during and in the aftermath of independence movements.[10] Rodney too saw himself in these terms: "I regard myself as a product of neo-colonial society as distinct from a colonial society."[11] James noted that Rodney benefited from those who had created the first Caribbean-centered histories in the anglophone Caribbean, and those who had already challenged imperialist scholarship. In addition to James himself, this group included Elsa Goveia, Eric Williams, W. E. B. Du Bois, George Padmore, Frantz Fanon, and others.[12] In other words, the ground on which Rodney walked was different from that of the generation that preceded him.

He was able to challenge the fundamental logic of colonialism, white supremacy, and capitalism. For example, Aimé Césaire—a poet, theorist, and politician from Martinique and a member of the anticolonial generation—challenged the very episteme of colonialism itself in the 1950s. He argued that colonization was never about "civilizing" the colonized, but in fact had the effect of decivilizing the colonizer instead. Césaire proposed that the Nazi regime was not an aberration but the culmination of practices that had been deemed acceptable in the colonies for generations.[13] In other words, Rodney matured under the postcolonial condition, engaging in an anti-neocolonial struggle versus an anticolonial struggle, and building on and expanding this tradition of exposing myths and logics—including serious critiques of neocolonialism and those nationalist leaders who did not govern their countries for the benefit of the majority of their peoples. As Bogues mentions, he was interested in "the relationships of rule inside the postcolony."[14]

After a brief stint in Tanzania in 1966, Rodney returned to Jamaica in 1967 as a lecturer teaching African history at the University of the West Indies. During the fervor of Black Power, Rodney also worked with some of the poorest and most marginalized populations in the country, including the religious and political group known as Rastafarians. While Rodney was attending the Congress of Black Writers in Canada in 1968, the Jamaican government led by Hugh Shearer used this as an opportunity to deem him a threat to the security of the state and ban him from returning to Jamaica. His banishment led to a series of uprisings in Jamaica, later dubbed "the Rodney riots," that challenged the Jamaican state around economic conditions, anti-Blackness, and neocolonialism. And in line with Rodney's teachings, as documented in the collection of his speeches, *The Groundings with My Brothers*, the uprising was also a call for Black Power—a break with imperialism, assumption of power by Black people at the grassroots, and a cultural remaking of society.[15]

The Groundings with My Brothers explored local conditions in Jamaica, global Black Power movements, and African history, and it served as a direct effort to build community with Black people around the dire conditions they faced. The activist-anthropologist Keisha-Khan Perry and others have expanded (and critiqued) the male-centered focus of *Groundings* while recognizing the importance of the call that it produced.[16] In *Groundings*, it is important to note that Rodney argued for a political understanding of Blackness and race. He argued that the structures of power were "white" and that nonwhite people were oppressed and "black." It is important to note that his definition of "black" included the South Asians of the Caribbean whose ancestors had come to the Americas as indentured labor in the wake of the end of enslavement. This flexible class-based definition of Blackness allowed him to build connections with Indo-Caribbean peoples, and this type of vision informed movements that would come later, including the Black Power Revolution that took place in Trinidad in 1970 and his multiracial work in Guyana during the 1970s.[17]

Central to this book was the Rastafarian concept of "grounding," which meant to *reason* with each other, to engage and build with people relationally, and to do so on equal footing. Patricia Rodney, Walter's partner in the movement and in life, discusses "grounding" as "a practice, a way of living." It was an approach "where academics and activism were integrated and inseparable in the pursuit of equality, justice and a common humanity."[18] As Rodney wrote in *Groundings*, "the Black intellectual, the Black academic, must attach himself to the activity of the Black masses."[19] He believed that he had to learn from those who were most vulnerable, those directly affected by the conditions of inequality, and that there needed to be a dialectical relationship, a relational experience, that could produce new understandings of the world. This way of being, Bogues points out, was a fundamental break with the behavior of traditional Caribbean intellectuals and elites.[20]

Walter and Patricia Rodney and their son Shaka met in London in the aftermath of the Rodney riots. Rodney ended up taking a solo trip to Cuba for a few months and returned to Dar es Salaam in June of 1969, remaining there until 1974. Patricia and Shaka had traveled ahead of him to Tanzania in early December of 1968. He would meet their daughter, Kanini, for the first time, as she had been born in March 1969. Their second daughter, Asha, was also born in Tanzania in 1971.[21]

The country was in the middle of a state-led African socialist experiment called "Ujamaa," which was crystallized by the independence president Julius Nyerere. Dar es Salaam served as a meeting ground for a host of African liberation movements and was a center for Pan-African debate and struggle. Rodney taught at the university during this flurry of activity. He created graduate programs in African history, developed a history teachers organization, and participated in heated discussions about the role of the university in the African revolution, all while rewriting African history, advocating for democratic governance, and reflecting on how to create a society that centered on the needs of everyday people. His early years in Guyana, his time at UWI in Jamaica and SOAS in London, his participation in the study group with Selma and C. L. R. James, his groundings with the Rastafarians, and his participation in building a new Tanzania were all part of what shaped how he thought about the project of colonial exploitation in Africa and the Caribbean. His life and educational experiences, inside and outside of the classroom, gave him a vision and an understanding of the relationship between the "core" and the "periphery"; the relationship among colonialism, capitalism, race, and class; the respect he had for the efforts of poor and working people; and his understandings of the world.

It was in Dar es Salaam that Rodney wrote *How Europe Underdeveloped Africa*, published in 1972 during this milieu of revolutionary activity and intense efforts to create new societies.[22] When the book emerged, a number of people were responding to modernization theory, the dominant paradigm for understanding inequality and underdevelopment at the time. Although tenets of modernization vary, it largely argues for a staged capitalist pathway from backwardness (both direct and implicit notions) to industrialization and growth. Rodney challenged the central tenets of modernization theory directly as newly independent societies were grappling with questions of development.

He was also invested in developing a particular corrective to the imperialist historiography of Africa. For example, he would argue that "the British colonialist school has a metropolitan and racial bias. It comes out most clearly in their references to pre-colonial Africa, but it is also present in their analysis of decolonization in a patronizing form." This type of analysis, he stated, came from "the British political ruling elite."[23] He reserved particular criticism for those who minimized the catastrophic impact of the trade in human captives and colonialism on Africa, as well as those who extolled the virtues of "development" brought to the continent through colonization or posed that colonization itself was a benevolent project.

Rodney wanted *How Europe Underdeveloped Africa* to be accessible. He published with independent presses—Tanzania Publishing House and Bogle L'Ouverture—and was most concerned that it be read by a wide cross section of people, particularly African youth, intellectuals, bureaucrats, and revolutionaries. His was a commentary on the postcolonial condition designed not only to impact the African present but also life in the Caribbean and the wider world. There were significant critiques of his work, but for those trying to understand inequality and affect change in Africa, the diaspora, and beyond, it was (is) invaluable.[24]

Rodney challenged the concepts of development and underdevelopment, explored questions about the core and periphery, exposed the logics of white supremacy and colonialism, and centered the importance of exploitation. Rodney considered questions of labor, environment, race, differentiation, culture, and a focus on the role of African elites. First, Rodney shifted the question of underdevelopment away from the discourse of modernization—rejecting the idea that developing societies needed to *train up*, *scale up*, and *industrialize up*— and away from implied and direct notions of African deficiency. He challenged those who imagined and understood inequality as preordained, fixed, and inevitable, arguing that the development and the accumulation of wealth in imperialist Europe was fundamentally the result of exploitation.

Rodney built on the work of Latin American dependency theorists who contended that the world consisted of a core and a periphery, and that it was integrated unevenly such that there were winners and losers.[25] Indeed, Rodney was among an early cohort of scholars who applied dependency theory to Africa.[26] Further, in *How Europe Underdeveloped Africa*, Rodney indicated that there was a world capitalist *system*, writing: "African economies are integrated into the structure of the developed capitalist economies; and they are integrated in a manner that is unfavorable to Africa and ensures that Africa is dependent on the big capitalist countries."[27] He argued that formerly colonized countries provided the raw materials and natural resources that allowed Western Europe to industrialize and build wealth. Furthermore, African societies suffered from the creation and development of extractive economies—which were not set up to benefit the people in those societies—and from a trade in human captives that drained the continent of its most precious resource. In this, he focused on the devasting impact of the trade in human beings on the continent. Indeed, for Rodney, development could not be understood outside of the context of the history of enslavement, colonialism, and capitalist extraction: "African development is possible only on the basis of a radical break with the international capitalist *system*, which has been the principal agency of underdevelopment of Africa over the last five centuries."[28]

Wallerstein himself later attributed a seminal role in world-systems theory to *How Europe Underdeveloped Africa*, noting—albeit in passing—that "we should recall that it was a relatively new theoretical standpoint only some 15 years ago, and Walter Rodney was one of the first to propagate it in his didactic book that was itself quite influential."[29] In the same article, Wallerstein examined three of Rodney's major works, *A History of the Upper Guinea Coast*, *How Europe Underdeveloped Africa*, and *A History of Guyanese Working People*. Wallerstein used all the books to elaborate upon Rodney's multiple contributions: "Rereading these three books successively makes it very clear how coherent an intellectual viewpoint Rodney held, and what in a sense was his long-term intellectual agenda. He seems to me to have tackled five main themes in his corpus: capitalism as a world-system, the so-called issue of agency, the nature of the class struggle and in particular the role of non-white 'middle class' elements, the structure of the working classes, and the interrelations of race and class."[30]

Rodney's critique was both external and internal. Beyond the role of European colonial extraction and slave trading, he reserved harsh criticism for African elites and accomplices who benefited from these international relations.

"None of these remarks are intended to remove the ultimate responsibility for development from the shoulders of Africans," he insisted. "Not only are there African accomplices within the imperialist system, but every African has a responsibility to understand the system and work for its overthrow."[31]

When one reads Walter Rodney's *How Europe Underdeveloped Africa* today, it is important to remember that (1) it was a corrective work—Rodney was responding to modernization theory, imperialist historiography, and the logics of white supremacy and capitalism; (2) it was a call to action—Rodney was interested in generating revolution on the continent and beyond; (3) Rodney's work was a progenitor in the development of world-systems analysis; and (4) the book continues to live, still relevant to many questions with which we continue to grapple, still eliciting responses and providing a model. For example, in one of his earlier works, the late African American historian Manning Marable used Rodney's framing to write his 1983 text, *How Capitalism Underdeveloped Black America*. More recently, in 2021, Hilary Beckles, a leading Barbadian scholar, published *How Britain Underdeveloped the Caribbean* to make the case for reparations for the region.[32]

By 1974, Rodney and his family decided to return to Guyana. He had been gone for fourteen years and yearned to return and be part of transformation at home. Patricia Rodney arrived first with the children in May, three months before Walter Rodney, setting up their living arrangements and landing a job. The children had to adjust to a new place, and even though their parents were born there, the transition was not easy—they identified as African, not Caribbean or Guyanese, and because Shaka's first language was KiSwahili, he had to transition to English.[33]

Rodney's work in the 1970s with various organizations, and his writings, demonstrate significant synergy with the concept we now refer to as racial capitalism. Rodney was part of a milieu of Caribbean thinkers who had been engaging these questions over time, including Claudia Jones, the Afro-Trinidadian communist, journalist, and organizer who wrote about race, class, gender, and imperialism and was deported from the United States for her activism; C. L. R. James (mentioned previously); and Oliver Cromwell Cox, the Trinidadian-born lawyer and sociologist who wrote extensively about the relationship between capitalism and race from the 1940s through the 1970s, his earliest work being *Caste, Class, and Race: A Study in Social Dynamics* (1948); and his trilogy: *Foundations of Capitalism* (1959), *Capitalism and American Leadership* (1962), and *Capitalism as a System* (1964).[34]

In June 1974, the Sixth Pan-African Congress was held in Tanzania, the first to occur in Africa. Rodney was ill and could not attend, but he had circulated a controversial document, "Towards the Sixth Pan-African Congress: Aspects of the International Class Struggle in Africa, the Caribbean and America," which was widely discussed.[35] The essay highlighted the contradictions between nationalism—which reinforced colonial boundaries—and Pan-Africanism. He argued for the importance of representing liberation movements and not simply heads of state. Furthermore, he issued a scathing critique of those who led newly independent states in ways that reproduced the divisions and economic exploitation of colonialism and modern capitalism. He highlighted the class contradictions that would plague the Congress if organizers were not vigilant in combating the overrepresentation of state governments and if liberation and popular movements were not there to represent themselves.

Before Rodney returned to Guyana, he traveled to Atlanta to support the work of the Institute of the Black World (IBW) as a lecturer and co-coordinator, along with William Strickland, of their Summer Research Symposium. Participants in the IBW described themselves as a "community of black scholars, artists, teachers and organizers" dedicated to "a new understanding of the past, present and future condition of the peoples of African descent."[36] The IBW 1974 symposium included public lectures, a six-week research component about "Social Structure and the Black Struggle," and a three-day conference to chart future directions for the Black Freedom Movement. The historian Derrick White, author of *The Challenge of Blackness: The Institute of the Black World and Political Activism in the 1970s*, demonstrates that the 1970s ideological debates in the Black Freedom Movement in the United States often centered on race versus class and socialism versus Black nationalism. For Rodney, class *and* race were critical categories of analysis. For the IBW, in their attempts to bring unity to the struggle in the United States and support for the Black struggle abroad, political economy was a necessary ingredient for their analyses. Rodney—who had been critical of Black neocolonial leadership and deeply understood the impact of white supremacy, colonialism, and capitalism on communities worldwide—supported them in their vision to chart a new analysis through their 1974 symposium. White argues that the discussions with and lectures by Rodney helped the IBW "expand their understanding of a racialized political economy."[37]

Rodney had been living abroad during the early 1960s when violence erupted between the two largest racialized groups in British Guiana—people of African descent and people of South Asian descent, called Africans and Indians in the Guyanese context.[38] Although this violence was certainly influenced by leadership, political differences, and racial tension within what was British Guiana at the time, it was fundamentally due to the British history of "divide and rule" in the colony, as well as British, and later CIA, machinations designed to split a multiracial movement and prevent Guyana from moving into the communist orbit during the Cold War.[39] Forbes Burnham, the prime minister turned president who would usher a racially divided British Guiana into an independent Guyana in 1966, devolved into a polarizing figure during his decades in power: he was an Afro-Guianese politician who fueled racial tensions to hold onto power fraudulently in a majority Indian-Black nation.

Rodney had been offered an academic position at the University of Guyana. However, the job was rescinded due to pressure from Burnham supporters on the Board of Governors of the university. Patricia Rodney would also have positions revoked as a result of her husband's political work.[40] Patricia and Walter would struggle to make a living during those years, 1974 to 1980, with Rodney obtaining brief temporary positions in North America and Europe to help support his family. Patricia's familial and intellectual labor and her emotional support were critical to his ability to participate in the movement in Guyana. Her story and contribution to these struggles is a critical area for further study.

Once Walter was back in the country with his family, he began to work with the left and multiracial coalition of different organizations and individuals founded in November 1974: the Working People's Alliance (WPA). The African Society for Cultural Relations with Independent Africa (ASCRIA); the Indian Political Revolutionary Associates (IPRA); the Working People's Vanguard Party (WPVP); and Ratoon, a leftist group of academics and teachers. They all came together to form the WPA, along with support from other groups such as the Movement Against Oppression (MAO).[41] Rodney became crucial to the political struggle in Guyana, as he drew large audiences from both racial groups and was able to speak to a broad spectrum of people, including bauxite miners, sugar workers, students, civil servants, teachers, and the urban poor. Burnham saw him as a troublemaker and as a threat to his administration. He was indeed a political threat—this Black citizen with a worldwide reputation who was a serious critic of the Burnham regime and had political sway across racial lines.

Rodney became a leading member of the WPA, which was committed to challenging racial polarization, fighting for economic justice and socialist government, and developing a popular political front to fight for democracy in lieu of what had become an authoritarian regime. Rodney was one of the WPA's key organizers, mobilizing across race and pointing out the hypocrisy of Forbes Burnham, whom he argued created a climate of fear and worked against the interests of all working people in the country. Despite the fact that many people suggested he leave the country for his and his family's safety, he felt that he needed to remain rooted there. He reasoned, how could he ask people to confront their fear if he chose to go into exile?[42] He was able to inspire those who were economically and politically disenfranchised, or simply fearful of the repercussions of taking a stand.

Leaders from the Institute of the Black World in Atlanta, Georgia, would work to support Rodney given the political backlash he faced from the Burnham regime. Supporters included the African American historian, theologian, and civil rights activist Vincent Harding, who also had personal ties to the Caribbean because his mother was Barbadian; Robert Hill, the Jamaican historian and activist most well-known for his work on Marcus Garvey; and William Strickland, the African American political scientist and civil rights and Black Power activist. These and other members of IBW approached several people to help organize activities that promoted Rodney's work in the United States.[43] The late James Turner, then the director of the Africana Studies and Research Center at Cornell, provided critical support. Immanuel Wallerstein was among those recruited to help. One of Rodney's positions abroad that helped to sustain his family was an academic appointment that he held at the State University of New York at Binghamton, where Wallerstein was the founding director of the Fernand Braudel Center.[44]

Rodney would return to his work in Guyana after his temporary stints in other places were completed. Often under duress due to his political work, Rodney also conducted the research for and wrote *A History of Guyanese Working People, 1885–1905*, published posthumously in 1981. In fact, he revised this book while in prison for his political activities, accused of arson.[45] A social history of British Guiana, the book explored the political economy of the country, the role and struggles of working people in national development, the constraints they faced, and how they challenged systems designed to control them. The nineteenth century marked the development of British Guiana's political economy and the ways in which planters and imperial capitalism made the Caribbean a center for plantations, raw materials, and cheap labor. According to Rodney, the capitalist class was fully fledged and well-defined in British Guiana, but "the differentiation of working class, peasantry, and middle class was incomplete."[46] He argued that ex-enslaved Africans became plantation workers immediately after slavery and then transitioned to become urban workers, peasantry, or some hybrid of the two.

In the British Caribbean, the end of enslavement led to the rise of indentured labor, but previous experiments informed this approach to control the plantation labor force. During the heat of the Haitian Revolution, from 1791 to 1804, when the enslaved people threw off the chains of slavery and imperial rule, Trinidad planters experimented with Asian indentured labor in 1803.[47] The rationale was to prevent the types of revolt that occurred in Haiti by bringing workers who could be kept distinct from African laborers, the assumption being that they would not band together against the plantocracy. Myriad indentured labor schemes emerged later after the 1834 abolition of enslavement in the British empire. The former owners of enslaved people were compensated to the tune of twenty million pounds in exchange for their "lost property." Worried that freed people would leave the plantation in droves and distressed about their new bargaining power, the imperial government and planters began importing workers from all over the world through indenture contracts, a phenomenon that Madhavi Kale refers to as an "imperial labor reallocation" strategy rather than simply a labor migration.[48] Some workers came from Madeira, Azores, China, Malta, the continent of Africa, and other West Indian countries, but the overwhelming majority came from India through the ports of Calcutta and Madras. The majority of Indian indentured laborers who went to the Caribbean landed in British Guiana. Rodney examined the policy surrounding Indian indentured labor and the conditions and stereotypes these laborers faced, as well as the ways in which race was used to divide a labor force in the interest of the sugar industry.

Rodney's *A History of Guyanese Working People* would become an important intervention in the development of Guyanese political economy, the struggles of working people, and the history of ethnic conflict born of colonial racial capitalism. He concluded that even though there was less conflict between Indians and Africans than one would expect given the economic competition, the development of a "plantation workers movement" was constrained and retarded due to the uses of "indentureship and racial competition." Yet it was during this same period, the late nineteenth century, that the groundwork was laid for the development of trade union organization, as he showed in his discussion of the riots that occurred in 1905.[49] Although these manifestations were more spontaneous than organized, the foundation had been established for later movements. In writing about the late nineteenth century, Rodney was making a deep intervention in the middle of the late twentieth century. He was arguing that the racial division that characterized the 1960s should not be read backward historically or projected deterministically into the future. In a context where those dispossessed of their labor were pitted against each other in the interests of the sugar industry and colonial proxy, the book pushed against history and understandings that portrayed ethnic conflict as inevitable and permanent and urged everyone to understand the true beneficiaries of these divisions—planters, the metropole, and their local elite accomplices. He also placed a spotlight on the daily struggles of the working people of British Guiana and their efforts to design their social worlds.

Rodney was imprisoned for his work in the WPA, and he was assassinated at the age of thirty-eight on June 13, 1980, before his book was completed, leaving behind a devastated family, community, and international comrades. The 2016 findings from a lengthy and controversial government inquiry into his death concluded the following: Gregory Smith, who gave Rodney a walkie talkie that was exploded remotely and killed him, "was acting as an agent of the State having been aided and abetted so to do, by individuals holding positions of leadership in State agencies and committed to carrying out the wishes of the PNC administration." Smith was given a new identity and spirited out of the country with support from high-ranking government officials. Furthermore, the report found that the Burnham regime was afraid of the large numbers of people who participated in WPA meetings, that Rodney had been infiltrating intelligence agencies by recruiting supporters, and that he was interfering with "the smooth operations" of the government—and indeed he was.[50]

In many ways, the concept of racial capitalism emerged from a desire to address both the racial and class dimensions of oppression in South Africa, to demonstrate the realities of racialism that was foundational to the development of capitalism. Rodney's work in the 1970s aligned in many ways with the ideas of Neville Alexander (South Africa) and Cedric Robinson (United States), which are often considered early articulations of an understanding of racial capitalism in the 1970s and early 1980s. Rodney extended Marxist analysis by centering Africa, Africans, enslaved people, and working people in the Caribbean in his work. Rodney cared deeply about issues of race and class and was nuanced in the ways in which he discussed how race and capitalist exploitation were intertwined with respect to varying local contexts. He certainly argued, as many proponents of racial capitalism do, that the historic development of capitalism was imbricated in histories of genocide, imperialism, and enslavement. Based on the concerns included in his body of work, I believe he would have included the system of indenture in this formulation. He also saw race and class as mutually constituted and demonstrated that struggles needed to be waged on both fronts. He was anticapitalist, anti-imperialist, and called for an end to Eurocentrism. Rodney also contended that racism was a mechanism used to divide working people.[51] Furthermore, similar to notions of race focused on differentiation and hierarchy, his understanding of Blackness was quite flexible, as it encompassed all those who were racially oppressed. Rodney promoted Blackness as a political category, as opposed to one based in phenotype or even culture.

Rodney argued that racism developed as a justification for enslavement and dispossession, stating that economics, rather than racism, led to the development of chattel slavery.[52] In this respect, he was more closely aligned with arguments advanced by the anticolonial Trinidadian scholar turned politician Eric Williams in his groundbreaking text *Capitalism and Slavery*, published in 1944.[53] However, Rodney also articulated positions that had resonance with Robinson's idea that racism developed in Europe as a mechanism of differentiation in feudal society:

> [T]he most striking feature is undoubtedly the rise of racism as a widespread and deeply rooted element in European thought.... It would be much too sweeping a statement to say that all racial and color prejudice in Europe derived from the enslavement of Africans and the exploitation of non-white peoples in the early centuries of international trade. There was also anti-Semitism at an even earlier date inside Europe and there is always an element of suspicion and incomprehension when peoples of different culture come together. However, it can be affirmed without reservation that the white racism which came to pervade the world was an integral part of the capitalist mode of production.[54]

In fact, Rodney concluded that chapter by arguing that "racism, violence, and brutality were the concomitants of the capitalist system when it extended itself abroad in the early centuries of international trade."[55] Furthermore, I suggest that some of Rodney's ideas anticipated the deep connections between colonialism and racial capitalism that scholars are making today.

As several scholars have pointed out, Robinson's seminal book *Black Marxism* was about more than racial capitalism.[56] It was centrally about those who fought against it and went about the business of challenging it: the Black radical tradition, or perhaps the "black heretical tradition" with respect to the gendered analysis that the historian Shauna Sweeney proffers.[57] As he had done in other places, Rodney continued the work of this tradition in Guyana, a phenomenon that Carol Boyce Davies refers to as the "Caribbean/black radical tradition," and Perry refers to as "the global black tradition."[58]

Rodney's work was instructive for suggesting new paradigms for considering the future of work, particularly in his approach to how working people sought self-determination over their work and lifeworlds in *A History of Guyanese Working People*, which remains relevant today. In the introduction written for its first publication, the Barbadian writer George Lamming offered a trenchant analysis of Rodney's contributions around some of the fundamental questions of work in his text: "Work makes possible a process of production, and the planters perceived this to be true. But work is also the essential base on which people struggle to create a design for social living. Planters could not perceive this to be true without contradicting their original reason for being there. The workers' achievement of humanizing the landscape and creating a design for social living had to be interpreted and dealt with as a threat to the foundations of the planter enterprise."[59]

How people over time have tried to socially engineer their lives, often counter to the plantation machine even as they were working within it, lays bare some of the contradictions of work. Central to this in my mind is the idea of social reproduction—the labor and caretaking that make it possible to live and to make life. *That* work, so often devalued, is so important for the functioning of human existence. Lamming articulated a central idea that emanated from Rodney that should be of deep interest to those thinking about these questions: "[Rodney] worked on the assumption that men deserved to be liberated from those hostile forms of ownership that are based exclusively on the principle of material self-interest that negate the fundamental purpose of work. At the deepest levels of a man's being it cannot make sense that he should voluntarily labor for those whose style of thinking declares them to be his enemies and whose triumph in the management of human affairs remains a persistent threat to the dignity of his person."[60]

Discussing the end of the nineteenth century, Rodney highlighted the hostility of these contradictions and the ways they circumscribed working peoples' lives. "On the contrary, capitalism slumps and market crises struck at the very fundamentals of working-class existence—namely the right to work and the right to earn a living wage." Yet, this right to work and the right to a living wage, subject to the volatility of capital, also translated into a lack of autonomy. In the post-emancipation period, Rodney argued that one who worked on the plantations should be called a "naked worker" rather than a "free worker," mainly "because the laborer has been divested of ownership of the means of survival."[61]

In conclusion, Rodney was a critical interlocutor for the development of world-systems theory; he articulated critical notions of colonial racial capitalism; he embodied the global Black radical tradition; and he provided important insights into the past, present, and future of work. In all these ways, he powerfully contributed on multiple fronts and continents. He advanced our understanding of how world-systems functioned historically. He undertook frontal assaults against Eurocentrism and white supremacy in scholarship, governance, elite orientation, and everyday interactions and cultural existence. He engaged in an activism predicated on building solidarity and confronting capitalism. And he organized against the continuities of the colonial politics of divide and rule that permeated postcolonial regimes. Finally, he illustrated that the mechanisms of plantocracy and colonialism were fundamentally about control and exploitation, so that any future we envision means that working people must have control over their lives and work.

As the historian Robin D. G. Kelley wrote in 2022 in the wake of the Movement for Black Lives, "it should be clear by now that Black radical imagination does not stand still; it lives, breathes, and moves with the people. The best we can do is catch a glimpse of how people in motion envisioned the future and what they did to try to enact that future. But every freedom dream shares a common desire to find better ways of being together without hierarchy and exclusion, without violence and domination, but with love, compassion, care, and friendship."[62] For Rodney, the "rigorous transformations" that Harding, Hill, and Strickland called for, and the freedom dreams that Kelley invoked, lay in the alternative counter-plantation visions that working people worked to build and create.

Rodney reminds us that groundings with those directly affected is central to any solution to global inequity—that capitalism will not save us, and it is not inevitable. He taught us that white supremacy and anti-Blackness murder our spirits, intellect, and bodies; that history is a critical tool for struggle and liberation; and finally, that the future of work would have to mean that those at the bottom of empire could socially engineer their own lives.

NOTES

1. Walter Rodney, "Plantation Society in Guyana," *Review (Fernand Braudel Center)* 4, no. 4 (Spring 1981): 647, https://www.jstor.org/stable/40240885.
2. Vincent Harding, Robert Hill, and William Strickland, introduction to *How Europe Underdeveloped Africa* by Walter Rodney (1972; repr., London: Verso, 2018), xxx, xxxi. All references in this chapter refer to this version published by Verso.
3. A special thanks to the Beyond Inequality working group, the editors of this volume, and Minkah Makalani for their generative commentary on drafts of this chapter.
4. Neville Alexander was part of a group of South African thinkers and activists who first used the term "racial capitalism" to explicate the relationship between the apartheid state and capitalism and to unite the struggles against white supremacy and capitalism in South Africa in the 1970s. This group included Martin Legassick, Harold Wolpe, and David Hemson. See also Cedric J. Robinson, *Black Marxism: The Making of the Black Radical Tradition* (1983; repr., Chapel Hill: University of North Carolina Press, 2000).
5. Crain Soudien, "What Would Neville Have Said?," in *Non-Racialism in South Africa: The Life and Times of Neville Alexander*, ed. Allan Zinn (Port Elizabeth: African Sun Media, 2016), 124.
6. Drawing on the analysis of C. L. R. James, historian Rupert Lewis describes Rodney as West Indian, Pan-African, and Marxist. See Rupert Lewis, *Walter Rodney's Intellectual and Political Thought* (Barbados: Press University of the West Indies, 1998), xi.
7. Anthony Bogues, *Black Heretics, Black Prophets: Radical Political Intellectuals* (2003; repr., London: Routledge, 2016), chap. 5, see pages 126, 136, and 138. In this chapter,

Bogues discusses Rodney's Marxism, including the tensions that existed in Rodney's distinction of Marxism's uses as a methodology versus an ideology and his recognition of the need for contextual specificity and creativity versus Marxism as a universal ideology.

8. Lewis, *Walter Rodney's Intellectual and Political Thought*, 37–38.
9. C. L. R. James, *The Black Jacobins: Toussaint L'Ouverture and the San Domingo Revolution* (1938; repr., New York: Vintage, 1963).
10. Lewis, *Walter Rodney's Intellectual and Political Thought*, 116.
11. Walter Rodney, *Walter Rodney Speaks: The Making of an African Intellectual* (Trenton, South Africa: Africa World, 1990), 33.
12. Lewis, *Walter Rodney's Intellectual and Political Thought*, 36–37.
13. Aimé Césaire and Robin D. G. Kelley, *Discourse on Colonialism* (New York: Monthly Review, 2000).
14. Bogues, *Black Heretics*, 142.
15. Walter Rodney, *The Groundings with My Brothers*, rev. ed. (1969; repr., Brooklyn, NY: Verso, 2019), 24. This book also helped to establish the independent Pan-African press, Bogle L'Ouverture publishers. Patricia Rodney, "Living the Groundings, A Personal Context," in Rodney, *The Groundings with My Brothers*, 82.
16. In the introduction to Rodney, *The Groundings with My Brothers*, xix–xx, Carol Boyce Davies argues that the focus of *Groundings* was decidedly male, and she highlights the role of Black women such as Claudia Jones, who worked for transformational politics; Davies also cites Perry, who argues for a central place for Black women in Latin America in the struggle for Black liberation, calling them "sister outsiders" of the Americas, and the need to recognize the complex experiences of Black women in the project of building diasporic and feminist solidarity. Keisha-Khan Y. Perry, "The Groundings with My Sisters: Toward a Black Diasporic Feminist Agenda in the Americas," *Rewriting Dispersal: Africana Gender Studies* 7, no. 2 (Spring 2009), https://sfonline.barnard.edu/africana/print_perry.htm. Monique Bedasse argues that we "must critique Rodney for having given the impression that he grounded only with Rastafari 'brothers' and not with sisters," in her commentary in Anakwa Dwamena, "Groundings with Walter Rodney: An Interview with Monique Bedasse, Erin MacLeod, Nijah Cunningham, Matthew J. Smith, and Jesse Benjamin," *Africa Is a Country*, August 18, 2019, https://africasacountry.com/2019/08/groundings-with-walter-rodney.
17. For important discussions, see Kate Quinn, ed., *Black Power in the Caribbean* (Gainesville: University Press of Florida, 2014); and Michael O. West, "Seeing Darkly: Guyana, Black Power, and Walter Rodney's Expulsion from Jamaica," *Small Axe: A Journal of Criticism* 12, no. 1 (2008): 93–104, https://doi.org/10.1215/-12-1-93.
18. Rodney, "Living the Groundings," 77, 85.
19. Rodney, *The Groundings with My Brothers*, 67.
20. Bogues, *Black Heretics*, 129.
21. Rodney, "Living the Groundings," 82–83.
22. Walter Rodney, *How Europe Underdeveloped Africa* (London: Bogle L'Ouverture, 1972).
23. Walter Rodney, *Decolonial Marxism: Essays from the Pan-African Revolution*, ed. Asha Rodney, Patricia Rodney, Ben Mabie, and Jesse Benjamin (London: Verso, 2022), 184.

24. Critics held that it was polemic; that the book oversimplified conditions across the continent; that it did not pay sufficient attention to internal African politics, sovereignty, and agency; and that it overstates the transfer of surplus and benefits to Europe. Unfortunately, some scholars have erroneously argued that Africans were rendered passive in Rodney's text. For a more recent example, see John Thornton, *Africa and Africans in the Making of the Atlantic World, 1400–1800*, 2nd ed. (Cambridge: Cambridge University Press, 1997), 4. Thornton also leveled this critique against André Gunder Frank, Immanuel Wallerstein, and Eric Wolf. He argued that all four scholars combined an Annalist school of history with a neo-Marxist framework that rendered Africans as passive victims in the development of the Atlantic, unwittingly reinforcing a Eurocentric perspective. Because Thornton challenged Rodney's conclusions several times in his book, historian Herman Bennett included a clear critique of Thornton's "mischaracterization" of Rodney's work in *African Kings and Black Slaves: Sovereignty and Dispossession in the Early Modern Atlantic*. Engaging Rodney's *A History of the Upper Guinea Coast*, Bennett argued that "Rodney questioned the idea of European dominance in the earliest engagement with Africans." Meanwhile, Thornton "flattened a layered political history, which Rodney had built around elites, power, political authority, and sovereignty." See Herman Bennett, *African Kings and Black Slaves: Sovereignty and Dispossession in the Early Modern Atlantic* (Philadelphia: University of Pennsylvania Press, 2019), 24–25.
25. These scholars included Raul Prebisch, Theotonio dos Santos, Fernando Henrique Cardoso, and André Gunder Frank.
26. For example, Samir Amin, Colin Leys, Claude Ake, and Timothy Shaw. See Rodney, *Walter Rodney Speaks*, 67n14. Wallerstein also noted that he was in conversation with dependency theorists Amin and Frank. See Immanuel Maurice Wallerstein, *The Modern World-System* (Berkeley: University of California Press, 2011), 1: xviii.
27. Rodney, *How Europe Underdeveloped Africa*, 30–31.
28. Rodney, *How Europe Underdeveloped Africa*, xiii (emphasis added).
29. Immanuel Wallerstein, "Review: Walter Rodney: The Historian as Spokesman for Historical Forces," *American Ethnologist* 13, no. 2 (May 1986): 330, https://www.jstor.org/stable/644136.
30. Wallerstein, "Review," 330.
31. Walter Rodney, *How Europe Underdeveloped Africa*, 34.
32. See, for example, Manning Marable, *How Capitalism Underdeveloped Black America: Problems in Race, Political Economy, and Society* (Boston: South End, 1983); and more recently, Hilary Beckles, *How Britain Underdeveloped the Caribbean: A Reparation Response to Europe's Legacy of Plunder and Poverty* (Kingston: University of the West Indies Press, 2021).
33. Lewis, *Walter Rodney's Intellectual and Political Thought*, 186, 182.
34. See Carole Boyce Davies, *Left of Karl Marx: The Political Life of Black Communist Claudia Jones* (Durham, NC: Duke University Press, 2007); Oliver C. Cox, *Caste, Class and Race: A Study in Social Dynamics* (New York: Monthly Review, 1948); Oliver C. Cox, *The Foundations of Capitalism* (London: Peter Owen, 1959); Oliver C. Cox, *Capitalism and American Leadership* (New York: Philosophical Library, 1962); and Oliver C. Cox, *Capitalism as a System* (New York: Monthly Review, 1964).

35. Walter Rodney, "Towards the Sixth Pan-African Congress: Aspects of the International Class Struggle in Africa, the Caribbean and America," in *Resolutions and Selected Speeches from the Sixth Pan African Congress*, ed. Pan-African Congress (Dar es Salaam: Tanzania, 1976).

36. Institute of the Black World, "The Institute of the Black World Martin Luther King, Jr. Memorial Center Atlanta, Georgia Statement of Purpose and Program Fall, 1969," *The Massachusetts Review* 10, no. 4 (Autumn 1969): 713, http://www.jstor.org/stable/25087919.

37. Derrick E. White, *The Challenge of Blackness: The Institute of the Black World and Political Activism in the 1970s* (Gainesville: University Press of Florida, 2011), 154.

38. Although different in context, South Africa also experienced African-Indian violence in 1949 in Durban. See Ravi K. Thiara, "The African-Indian Antithesis? The 1949 Durban 'Riots' in South Africa," in *Thinking Identities: Explorations in Sociology*, ed. Avtar Brah, Mary J. Hickman, and Máirtín Mac an Ghaill (London: Palgrave Macmillan, 1999), 161–84.

39. Colin Palmer, *Cheddi Jagan and the Politics of Power: British Guiana's Struggle for Independence* (Chapel Hill: University of North Carolina Press, 2010); and Andaiye and D. Alissa Trotz, "1964: The Rupture of Neighborliness and Its Legacy for Indian /African Relations [2008; 2018]," in Andaiye, *The Point Is to Change the World: Selected Writings of Andaiye*, ed. D. Alissa Trotz (London: Pluto, 2020), 58–76.

40. Patricia Rodney, "Living the Groundings," 184.

41. Nigel D. Westmaas, "Resisting Orthodoxy: Notes on the Origins and Ideology of the Working People's Alliance," *Small Axe: A Journal of Criticism* 8, no. 1 (2004): 70, https://doi.org/10.1353/smx.2004.0015.

42. Lewis, *Walter Rodney's Intellectual and Political Thought*, 186.

43. Harding, Hill, and Strickland, introduction to Rodney, *How Europe Underdeveloped Africa*, xxv–xxvi.

44. Fernand Braudel Center, "Statement on the Death of Walter Rodney," *Review* 4, no. 4 (Spring 1981): 641, https://www.jstor.org/stable/40240884.

45. Lewis, *Walter Rodney's Intellectual and Political Thought*, 189.

46. Walter Rodney, *A History of Guyanese Working People, 1885–1905* (Baltimore: Johns Hopkins University Press, 1981), 218.

47. Lisa Lowe, *The Intimacies of Four Continents* (Durham, NC: Duke University Press, 2015), 22–23, 25–26.

48. Madhavi Kale, *Fragments of Empire: Capital, Slavery, and Indian Indentured Labor Migration in the British Caribbean* (Philadelphia: University of Pennsylvania Press, 1998), 5.

49. Rodney, *A History of Guyanese Working People*, 219.

50. Richard L. Cheltenham, Seenath Jairam, and Jacqueline Samuels-Browne, *The Commission of Inquiry Appointed to Enquire and Report on the Circumstances Surrounding the Death in an Explosion of the Late Dr. Walter Rodney on Thirteenth Day of June, One Thousand Nine Hundred and Eighty at Georetown [sic] Volume 1: Report and Appendices* (Georgetown: Government of Guyana, February 2016), 102, 103. This report can be accessed from The Walter Rodney Foundation, https://www.walterrodneyfoundation.org/coi.

51. Rodney, *A History of Guyanese Working People, 1881–1905*, see chap. 7 especially.
52. Rodney, *How Europe Underdeveloped Africa*, 103; and Rodney, *The Groundings with My Brothers*, 74.
53. Eric Eustace Williams, *Capitalism & Slavery*, rev. ed. (1944; repr., Chapel Hill: University of North Carolina Press, 1994).
54. Rodney, *How Europe Underdeveloped Africa*, 103.
55. Rodney, *How Europe Underdeveloped Africa*, 103.
56. Bedour Alagraa, "Cedric Robinson's *Black Marxism*: Thirty-Five Years Later," *The C. L. R. James Journal* 24, nos. 1–2 (Fall 2018): 309, https://doi.org/10.5840/clrjames2018241/262.
57. Shauna J. Sweeney, "Gendering Racial Capitalism and the Black Heretical Tradition," in *Histories of Racial Capitalism*, ed. Justin Leroy and Destin Jenkins (New York: Columbia University Press, 2021), 53–84.
58. Davies, introduction to Walter Rodney, *The Groundings with My Brothers*, xxi; and Perry, "The Groundings with My Sisters."
59. Lamming, introduction to Rodney, *A History of Guyanese Working People*, xix.
60. Lamming, introduction to Rodney, *A History of Guyanese Working People*, xxv.
61. Rodney, *A History of Guyanese Working People*, 29, 32.
62. Robin D. G. Kelley, "Twenty Years of *Freedom Dreams*," *Boston Review*, August 1, 2022, https://bostonreview.net/articles/twenty-years-of-freedom-dreams/.

CHAPTER 3

CRITICAL SYSTEM ANALYSIS AND THE GREAT DISPARITIES

DAVID KENNEDY

In the years since the 2009 financial crisis, worry about inequality has preoccupied scholars and cultural commentators, just as security and the vagaries of distant wars dominated discussion in the decade after September 11, 2001. Great disparities in wealth, power, and cultural significance have taken center stage in part because they seem to threaten the sustainability of governance capacity, effective economic management, cultural understanding, and tolerance. Worry about system sustainability reflects a broader loss of confidence in the public interest orientation and governance capabilities of the political, economic, and social mechanisms within which one might do something about inequality. In particular, when sharp and visible differences animate polarization, populism, and mistrust of experts and government, they threaten the ability to tackle all the other pressing issues of the day—from climate change to poverty or pandemics.

In such an unsettled time, many scholars and policy makers have doubled down on familiar ideas and policy proposals. But there is also an appetite for rethinking and for revisiting heterodox literatures that had become dormant in the law reform and policy literature. In particular, worry about system sustainability has brought new attention to "the system"—its capabilities and inherent limitations. Words like "structural" or "systemic" have crept into the discussion, which might be thought to implicate the foundational arrangements of the society in its patterns of subordination, although these terms are often softened to mean something more like "serious" or "hard to change." In a similar way, the term "political economy" frequently appears in American legal and social science commentary as a mark of progressive and reformist aspirations. Floating free of its classical lineage, the term suggests that markets and governments are part of a larger whole whose structure and functioning can be studied and opened for revision. In legal circles, the "political economy" has become a flag for resistance to the complacent and technocratic specialization so common in the contemporary American legal academy, suggesting that law may be constitutive of political and economic disparities as much as it may also serve to remedy them.

Nevertheless, the persistence of widely shared default images of the society and governance system have made it difficult to think wholistically, structurally, or systemically about the great disparities in political and economic life. Instead, too often the inquiry pulls back from inquiry into systemic foundations, returning to a familiar catalogue of diagnoses and reform suggestions that can be pursued within the system as it is. In North American commentary, the idea that the American polity and its governance machinery are constructed on the basis of equality, that the government normally attends to the general public interest, or that the economy is a terrain for bargains and exchange when not distorted by discrimination or monopoly power make it more difficult to place the disparities in wealth and power among groups in society at the center of the analysis or to imagine the system itself as being organized around the reproduction of inequality.

We all carry around notions we learned early on about how our society's political and economic arrangements normally operate. The word "system" typically refers to these arrangements: the "American system" with the political or economic "systems" we have long known. Unfortunately, to examine the great disparities through the prism of this common sense is to look through a glass darkly. It is hard to place great disparities in power at the center of the analysis if you imagine that both constitutional democracy and a competitive market were designed precisely to prevent anyone—or any group—from dominating, an idea that throws a mist over patterns of subordination. The worrisome disparities seem exceptional, if enduring and frustratingly intractable, in a society ostensibly organized to prevent just that.

In this chapter, I explore two well-known heterodox intellectual traditions that aim to get behind these obscuring, if common, images: Immanuel Wallerstein's "world-systems theory" and Gunnar Myrdal's institutionalist analysis of unequal development within a "social system." In the critical traditions they exemplify, "the system" is not at all obvious or familiar: it needs to be discovered, analyzed, and illuminated by intellectual work. The work of analysis is to identify the underlying dynamics that give economic and political power its shape and direction. These underlying patterns have their own dynamics, lead actors, and plotlines.

Wallerstein and Myrdal approach the search for systematic patterns within or beneath political, economic, and social arrangements in different ways. I bring them together to identify elements in their analyses that open the door to thinking more critically about the relationship between routine arrangements—including legal arrangements—and patterns of subordination and inequality. Although law is not their focal point, their analytic styles are particularly suggestive for legal scholars working in critical traditions that focus attention on the distributive—and unequal—significance of legal arrangements.

The strength of these traditions is their focus on the unequal relationships among groups that cut across the society. Both offer pathways to see political, economic, and social hierarchies among groups—regions, sectors, communities, elites, and everyone else—as the central drivers in dynamics that generate and reproduce disparity. Starting there, they search for the recurring patterns and structuring arrangements that channel the dynamic interactions between those groups. It is then a short step to mapping the arrangements of public or private authority that reinforce or impede those patterns, offering an opening for legal scholars to bring the constitutive role of law in the great disparities into focus.

There is an unfortunate tendency to associate a critical system analysis with a mechanical or logical determinism. People often talk about systems like "capitalism," "imperialism," "colonialism," and "patriarchy" as if they were forged in steel, with actors, motivations, conflicts, and recurring patterns that simply cannot be broken by altering their forms: they are what they are. This kind of interpretation can be pretty bleak, even somewhat paranoid, if also thrilling in the sense of one key unlocks all doors. Without denying the rhetorical and political power that can be wielded in this way, that's not my approach.

I place Wallerstein and Myrdal together to illustrate a less determinative, more suggestive way to harness structural or systemic analyses—more recurring historical or sociological patterns it is hard to ignore once they've been identified or patterns that suggest hypotheses to explore than logics to sacralize. Harnessing critical system ideas in this spirit does open the door to legal analysis that may illuminate just how malleable apparently inevitable disparities may turn out to be. To illustrate how this might work, let me briefly describe some key elements in Wallerstein's approach to "world-systems" and Myrdal's analysis of unequal development within a "social system."

IMMANUEL WALLERSTEIN'S WORLD-SYSTEMS ANALYSIS

Immanuel Wallerstein was a leading American sociologist and prominent critic of "globalization" who wrote extensively about global economic and political history and the operations of capitalism. His now classic foundational account of "world-system" analysis illustrates many of the critical elements that recur in structural accounts of system dynamics.[1]

Wallerstein's broad concern is the historical tendency of wealth to accumulate in some parts of the world and not in others. He starts with an image of the world divided and unequal—that's what he believes needs explaining. Drawing terminology from economic dependency theories, he redescribes the world in broad groups of countries he labels the "center," "semiperiphery," and "periphery." He then sets out to explain how economic actors in the center accumulate a great deal while those elsewhere can work terribly hard and accumulate far less. How is this distribution reproduced and consolidated? The mainspring turns out to be a dynamic process of specialization in which countries find themselves specializing in productive activities offering wildly divergent opportunities to accumulate wealth. But how does that happen?

The explanation requires identification of the key—largely institutional, in the broadest sense—arrangements that structure economic and political life in ways conducive to the reproduction and entrenchment of this pattern of specialization. This leads Wallerstein to a broad historical assessment of the world situation. He claims that two features have remained constant since the sixteenth century: "It is and always has been a *world-economy*. It is and always has been a *capitalist* world-economy."[2] Not unusual observations. The key is the way he unpacks these terms, the institutional elements he identifies as both stable over time and significant in maintaining the division of productive activities that leads to such dramatic differences in wealth among his three groups.

First, he outlines an arrangement of political powers and cultural identities:

> A defining feature of a world-economy is that it is *not* bounded by a unitary political structure. Rather, there are many political units inside the world-economy, loosely tied together in our modern world system in an interstate system. And a world-economy contains many cultures and groups—practicing many religions, speaking many languages, differing in their everyday patterns.... What unifies the structure most is the division of labor which is constituted within it.[3]

Meanwhile, economic activity is global in the sense that economic actors are able to arrange production and commerce in a way that crosses boundaries between both political units and cultures. Economic activity on a global scale is neither culturally diversified nor geographically confined: it operates on an international and cross-cultural basis. The result, however, is anything but homogenous. Rather, a "division of labor" is "constituted within it" as areas of the world specialize in modes of production with sharply different returns.

How is a division of labor "constituted within it"? The key turns out to be the *animating driver* shared by the world's economic actors: endless accumulation. Once economic actors give priority to endless accumulation in a world economic space internally divided politically and culturally, a division of labor will arise. As Wallerstein states:

> Capitalism is not the mere existence of persons or firms producing for sale on the market with the intention of obtaining a profit. Such persons or firms have existed for thousands of years all across the world. Nor is the existence of persons working for wages sufficient as a definition. Wage-labor has also been known for thousands of years. We are in a capitalist system only when the system gives priority to the *endless* accumulation of capital. . . . Endless accumulation is a quite simple concept: it means that people and firms are accumulating capital in order to accumulate still more capital, a process that is continual and endless.[4]

Crucially, this drive is not some inherent or natural characteristic of firms and people: it is generated by foundational institutional, cultural—even psychological—arrangements. As Wallerstein sees it:

> If we say that a system "gives priority" to such endless accumulation, it means that there exist structural mechanisms by which those who act with other motivations are penalized in some way, and are eventually eliminated from the social scene, whereas those who act with the appropriate motivations are rewarded and, if successful, enriched.[5]

For Wallerstein, the dominant "structural mechanism" is rapacious competition among firms, each seeking to drive their competitors from the market by garnering one or another form of monopoly power. For legal scholars, of course, the significance of legal arrangements in structuring this "mechanism" is readily apparent.

The "world market" then provides the ambit for this animus. Economic actors comport themselves in relation to global opportunities and global competitive threats. As Wallerstein presents it, the existence of a freely competitive world market is more fantasy than reality. It is not that all economic actors actually do seek to accumulate capital globally; rather, they arrange their affairs as if this were both a possibility and, should they face competition from actors worldwide, a potential threat. For a global division of labor to arise, he argues, a world market need only exist "in principle" as a "virtual market" which acts "as a magnet for all producers and buyers, whose pull is a constant political factor in the decision-making of everyone."[6] Wallerstein says that

> this complete virtual world market is a reality in that it influences all decision making, but it never functions fully and freely (that is, without interference.) The totally free market functions as an ideology, a myth, and a constraining influence, but never as a day-to-day reality.[7]

A global division of labor arises as economic actors animated by the priority to accumulate capital with the allure—and fear—of a global market instrumentalize the political and cultural differences that pervade the interstate system in the search for monopoly advantage. The territorial divisions in political and cultural life are crucial. As long as capital accumulators have a world economy at their disposal—at least in their minds' eye—while political actors remain tied to their territory, there is no danger that political priorities will displace capital accumulation as the prime directive. Social or political action on a global scale that might likewise displace the priority of capital accumulation is foreclosed by the human challenges of coordinated action. States would need to join together—or give way to a determined global hegemon—to place other political objectives ahead of capital accumulation. Their diversity operates as a guardrail against global policy. The world-system will remain a capitalist system.

So now we have identified a great disparity among groups of states, the animating driver for the key (economic) actors, and the large scale political, cultural, and economic arrangements, both psychological and institutional, within which they operate. Although Wallerstein rarely foregrounds the *legal* architecture of this world-system, the constitutive significance of legal arrangements is easy to see. Legal norms and institutions establish economic actors oriented to capital accumulation, ratify the association of political sovereignty with territory, and enable global economic transactions by enforcing property and contract globally (absolutely in principle, if qualifiedly in practice). If you are a citizen here, you can't participate in politics there, but if you own something here, you will also own it when you step off the plane there. You and everyone else understand this to be the case.

Once the elements are on the table, to see how the world-system generates a division of labor with great disparities in wealth and opportunity, we need to turn it on. What historical patterns can we observe that may offer a window on the dynamics in play? Wallerstein analyzes long economic cycles of boom and bust to understand where and how opportunities for capital accumulation are concentrated. He observes that robust gains are repeatedly realized in "lead industries" that identify and exploit innovation to achieve, at least for a time, some monopoly power. These "leading" industries come to be concentrated in "the center," available only sporadically in "the semiperiphery," and rarely in "the periphery." Gains are less available in industries that have become more competitive, which are found more frequently in the periphery.

This distribution of monopoly power is sustained, he argues, as technological change shifts monopoly opportunities from one "lead industry" to its successors. In a dynamic world market, capital accumulation is only possible, Wallerstein argues, for actors whose exposure to competition is limited, enabling them to produce and sell into markets where they enjoy some monopoly power. Perfect competition would reduce sellers to "an absolutely minuscule level of profit," making "the capitalist game entirely uninteresting." Whether or not they admit it, what sellers prefer is an element of monopoly power. Initially, the potential for monopoly power arises in industries that identify and benefit from innovations—in process, product, strategy—which offer some measure of monopoly power. This monopoly power can be prolonged—and sometimes acquired—with "the support of the machinery of a relatively strong state, one which can enforce a quasi-monopoly."[8] Again, we can imagine the significance of legal arrangements: entitlements to exclude arranged and enforced by state power are central to monopoly power.

As a result, economic actors are constantly searching for opportunities to impede competitive pressures, both through innovations and by harnessing the authority and cultural distinctiveness of the nations in which they operate. In this, they benefit from a multiplicity of states that can be played off against one another in the search for competitive advantage. But not all states are equally able to assist. The capacity to facilitate monopoly power is itself unequally distributed among states: large "strong states" in the "center" are more able to do this than smaller, weaker states at the "periphery." For those in between, it is sometimes possible, and sometimes not. There are all kinds of historical reasons for these differences in relative power. They net out for these purposes as significant differences in what states have to offer economic actors—for example, preferential access to investment capital and protection of intellectual property versus regulatory forbearance equally available in every other peripheral nation. The key factor, then, in successful capital accumulation is the relationship between relative monopoly power and the support from a relatively "strong state."

In Wallerstein's account, the monopolistic potential in what he terms "lead" industries may begin high, protected by a "core" state, but will likely decline over time. As rivals gain access to the technology and to the monopoly enforcing capabilities of other sovereigns, "quasi-monopolies are self-liquidating."[9]

> But [quasi-monopolies] last long enough (say thirty years) to ensure considerable accumulation of capital by those who control the quasi-monopolies. When a

quasi-monopoly does cease to exist, the large accumulators of capital simply move their capital to new leading products or whole new leading industries. The result is a cycle of leading products. . . . As for the once-leading industries past their prime, they become more and more "competitive," that is, less and less profitable.[10]

As a once lead industry becomes just another competitive industry, prices decline, supplies rise, wages fall, and it will be easier for the industry to get a foothold outside the center—and for players outside the center to get a foothold in the industry. In each boom-and-bust cycle, the new leading industry strengthens the capabilities of actors in the center to invest in the next big thing while financing the movement of production in increasingly competitive industries elsewhere. Nations in the periphery end up specializing in the highly competitive industries they are able to attract.

It is the geographic distribution of lead industries and the quasi-monopoly power that generates what Wallerstein identifies as an "axial division of labor" between nations that specialize in "core-like products and peripheral products." The key to their relative position in the world-system is the inherent capital accumulation possibilities in core and peripheral industries. The result is a "constant flow of surplus-value from the producers of peripheral products to the producers of core-like products."[11] Successful capital accumulators in the first lead industry can shift their capital to new lead industries as they arise, peripheral nations must await the access that comes as lead monopoly power again erodes. Over time, the rise and fall of "leading products" reproduces a distribution of peripheral products to nations in the periphery.

It is a good story. One might raise—and people have raised—lots of questions about its historical accuracy and the significance of the particular dynamics Wallerstein identifies. Is this pattern as mechanically determined as his long historical narrative seems to suggest? Aren't there other forces at work? Countervailing forces? Is it really all just the rise and fall of relative monopoly in leading industries? What about the distribution of resources or demographics? What about wars? What about the global hegemony of leading states or the ongoing impact of imperialism and colonialism and racism?

These are all good questions that suggest other potentially valuable systemic interpretations. For my critical purposes, however, it doesn't matter so much if Wallerstein's historical observations are as decisive or as significant as Wallerstein suggests. He has identified elements, relationships and dynamics that are suggestive for diagnosing causes for persistent inequality. His story pierces beneath images of the international system that more conventional commentary nudges us toward: an international order of equal sovereigns or a trading system characterized by bargaining and (notionally equal) exchange in which competition is more universally salient, monopoly an unfortunate exception, and "gains from trade" more generally available than habitually concentrated.

Once he points it out, the difference in relative competitive exposure of firms in wealthy and poorer nations does seem rather pronounced. It seems commonsensical that this would influence the distribution of wealth. Let's investigate: what arrangements allow relative monopoly power to accumulate and to disperse geographically? Precisely this question ought to stimulate legal research: how do the legal arrangements that enable global economic activity while territorially concentrating politics and culture influence the distribution of innovation or relative monopoly power? What legal and institutional arrangements encourage profitable new industries to arise at the center and then drift to the periphery as they become more competitive?

Although I am confident that Wallerstein was ethically and politically committed to reducing global disparities, his analysis is descriptive rather than normative. He doesn't tell us how much inequality is "too much," and his analytic tone is very "just the facts, thought you'd like to know." You might think it grand that the system concentrates gains on leading innovative industries, and altogether appropriate, even salutary, that other economic possibilities are pushed to the periphery where they provide otherwise unavailable jobs. Only political or ethical conviction can tell you whether this is a good thing or a bad thing. The point of critical system diagnostics is to figure out *how* it happens. And where to look for the structures that generate the great disparities should they trouble you.

GUNNAR MYRDAL'S ECONOMIC INSTITUTIONALISM: CUMULATIVE CAUSATION IN A SOCIAL SYSTEM

Gunnar Myrdal was a Swedish economist and Nobel Prize laureate who focused on the international economics of development. Unlike Wallerstein, Myrdal is not usually considered a "systems theorist." He was known as an "institutionalist" economist who aimed to develop economic models to endogenize social, cultural, political, and institutional variables. For him, the complexity of a society's economic patterns could only be understood through a rigorous exploration of the contexts within which they occurred. The result would not be a mechanical picture of economic patterns but a richer understanding of the dynamic tendencies in society.

I place Myrdal in conversation with Wallerstein because the approach he takes to the dynamics of a social system characterized by inequality offers a contrasting way to model the reproduction of great disparities. Indeed, Myrdal's economic institutionalism is so capacious in its endogenization of social, cultural, and political factors as to seem anything but systematic. Nevertheless, it is equally suggestive for efforts to identify the legal arrangements that reproduce—or might reduce—those disparities.

Like Wallerstein, who acknowledged Myrdal's influence on his thought, Myrdal's analytic objective was descriptive rather than normative, however passionately he may have felt about the inequalities he analyzed.[12] In analyzing postwar conditions of "underdevelopment" in Asia, Myrdal forswore offering a specifically economic metric such as "growth" or "industrialization" for assessing progress in a developing nation. Only the people of a nation could assess their progress and only in the terms they chose to value. He describes his analytic approach to development this way:

> When conditions are characterized as in various respects undesirable for an underdeveloped country, this judgment is made not from the speculative and a priori point of view of some form of "welfare economics," nor is it made in terms of some postulated absolute ethical norms. The conditions are deemed unfavorable simply from the point of view of the concrete development goals of the people of that country or, more precisely, of those who in that country decide policy.[13]

In his studies of social dynamics, Myrdal takes what he calls "the social system" as the object of his analysis. In speaking of South Asian development, for example, he defines a "social system" this way:

> The system consists of a great number of conditions that are causally interrelated, in that a change in one will cause changes in others. We classify the conditions in six broad categories: (1) output and incomes; (2) conditions of production; (3) levels of living; (4) attitudes toward life and work; (5) institutions; (6) policies.[14]

Myrdal aims to model the operations of such a social system, although he acknowledges that "we regard the generalizations making up our 'theory' as highly tentative and often conjectural."[15] Unlike Wallerstein, he does not begin with a cartography of groups or actors and their animating drives. That comes later. He starts with an observation about causation in social systems that he terms "circular causation." He describes the "basic concept" of circular causation as the interdependence of the various conditions in a society so that they are "the cause of each other."[16] A change in any one condition will tend to generate change in other conditions. He proposes this pattern of interactive change as a prime dynamic universal across social systems:

> If initially the system was in balance, the circular interdependence of the conditions in the social system would thus give rise to a cumulative process of change of that entire system, proceeding in the same direction as the primary change and affecting most or all conditions in the system. If, as is more probable, the system is not in balance but already changing in one direction or another, and if there is not one primary change but a number of simultaneous changes, the causal interdependence within the system would also make this more complex process cumulative.[17]

Where Wallerstein began with a social structure—a cartography of national units in a global economy—Myrdal begins with a principle of change. The "social system" is simply the sum of conditions that influence one another in a society, among which he lists "policies, institutions, attitudes toward life and work, levels of living, conditions of production, and output and incomes" as elements that might be relevant in thinking about development.

> *The preceding enumeration and comments are in the broadest sense our "theory."* They are made to demonstrate in the abstract the mechanism of causal interdependence of all the undesirable conditions in an underdeveloped country.[18]

In contrast to economic models that foreground a propensity to equilibrium, or even the recurring and predictable patterns Wallerstein saw as historically validating his theory, Myrdal proposes that the ubiquity of circular causation conduces rather to patterns of disequilibrium and instability—and, as we shall see, inequality.

> *Prima facie* this causal interdependence would seem to indicate a highly unstable social system. It is, of course, conceivable that at a particular point in time the various conditions should have attained precisely such levels as to represent a balance between the forces. . . . But, first, there would seem to be no reason to expect that, except by rare chance, a social system would ever fulfill the requirements of such balance. Secondly, the balance, if established, would be broken as soon as some outside event or some policy intervention at home moved one or several of the conditions up or down. Any such change in some conditions

would tend to cause other conditions to move in the same direction and these secondary changes would, in their turn, result in tertiary changes all around the system, and so on in a circular fashion.[19]

We have come some way from Wallerstein to anticipate an immense complexity of interdependent changes unlikely to stabilize in any particular direction. Because a change pretty much anywhere could lead to a change elsewhere, the analysis necessary to relate all the possible conditions that might, when shifted, move things one way or the other would require an analysis of unmanageable complexity, resulting in an irreducible "indeterminacy" in the dynamic development of a society. That systemic indeterminacy would seem to rule out a priori identification of prime levers or leading indicators. As Myrdal states:

> Subject to this inescapable indeterminacy, the movement of the whole social system upwards is what all of us in fact mean by development. There is no escape from that if we want to be realistic.[20]

Nevertheless, Myrdal is also well-known for his effort to account for patterns of unequal development. Starting from the principle of circular causation, he elaborated a general theory of the persistence—even deepening—of underdevelopment in some regions while other regions advanced, precisely the kind of disparity Wallerstein also sought to explain. In his now famous essay on the development dynamics between more and less wealthy regions, Myrdal focused attention on the dynamic relationships between differently situated regions in a social system without framing them in a constituted "structure."[21] Once their dynamics have been understood, the role of institutional arrangements in impeding or speeding those dynamics could be identified.

The animating principle in Myrdal's story is not a prime directive such as "endless capital accumulation" but the social dynamics of cumulative causation: the tendency for changes to lead to follow-on changes that he divides loosely between those that reinforce the direction of the initial change, termed "spread effects," and those that undermine it, or "backwash effects." Myrdal puts it this way:

> I have suggested that the principle of interlocking, circular interdependence within a process of cumulative causation has validity over the entire field of social relations. It should be the main hypothesis when studying economic underdevelopment and development.[22]

With this hypothesis in mind, he aims to identify situations in which backwash effects may predominate over spread effects, contributing to the differences one often observes between the wealth of two regions in a society. Think northern and southern Italy, the American coasts and the rural Midwest, or the Global North and the Global South. In the normal course, he suggests, gains in one region are self-reinforcing:

> The system is by itself not moving toward any sort of balance between forces but is constantly on the move away from such a situation. In the normal case a change does not call forth countervailing changes but, instead, supporting changes, which move the system in the same direction as the first change but much further. Because of such circular causation a social process tends to become cumulative and often to gather speed at an accelerating rate.[23]

In a society with unequal regions, however, the process of cumulative change could impact the two regions quite differently: "It is easy to see how expansion in one locality has 'backwash effects' in other localities."[24]

This is a tendency, not an iron law. Growth in the North draws capital and skilled labor from the South, but it may also stimulate growth in the South by increasing demand for commodities or skills situated there or by generating remittances. Myrdal emphasizes that there is no reason to anticipate a priori that these forces will cancel one another out or that the spread—or backwash—effects will dominate. It depends, he says, on all kinds of social, institutional, and other conditions. This suggests a direction for research: to identify the arrangements that affect these dynamics. And then to decide how desirable changes might be advanced and undesirable changes impeded.

To get there, he identifies the "media" through which spread and backwash effects move from the region that is growing to the less developed region:

> The movements of labour, capital, goods and services do not by themselves counteract the natural tendency to regional inequality. By themselves, migration, capital movements and trade are rather the media through which the cumulative process evolves—upwards in the lucky regions and downwards in the unlucky ones.[25]

Altering the trajectory of these "media" will alter the relationship between spread and backwash effects. We can now imagine a diagnostic for identifying factors that may influence patterns of social change: what arrangements enable these "media" to generate spread or backwash effects. Find these and possible openings to blunt those effects will be visible.

Crucially, Myrdal does not imagine the state as an autonomous actor considering what to do about the impact of these effects on overall public interest. The state is part of the "social system" and will also be pushed and pulled by patterns of cumulative causation. For example, a positive change in one region may give that region more sway in government institutions leading to policy changes that further concentrate spread effects there and backwash effects elsewhere. The state—and the law—is at once cause, effect, and bystander.

Nor does Myrdal distinguish public regulatory mechanisms sharply from the many other institutional arrangements that may affect the "media" and animate the dynamics of spread and backwash. Instead, he defines "the state" as "all organized interferences with the market forces," embracing anything that would shift the patterns of cumulative causation, altering the patterns of spread and backwash effects. Any of these organized interferences may intensify or alleviate spread and backwash effects—or may be irrelevant to their operation.

This suggests a direction for legal diagnostics: what legal arrangements influence the media through which spread and backwash effects are transmitted? Some of these may be directly regulatory or redistributional: the state may prohibit backwash reinforcing patterns of migration or financial flows or may tax and redistribute to compensate for those effects. A legal sensibility attuned to the structuring work of private law would expand Myrdal's focus on "interferences with the market forces" to the conditions that constitute those forces. Law will be constitutive of the flows themselves: patterns of property ownership and contractual enforceability, the institutional structure of finance, the legal structure of firms—all will be relevant here as they were in Wallerstein's analysis.

Myrdal contrasts usefully with Wallerstein precisely because there is so little "structure" in his system. Like Wallerstein, he begins with an interest in the great disparities and imagines the "social system" as a relationship among regions that are both related to one another (in the same "social system") and unequal. He foregrounds a principle of social change in a situation of radical complexity and a series of hypotheses about the sorts of tendencies that may develop between differently situated regions. It is precisely the extreme generality of his analytic that makes it a useful starting point for figuring out how legal or institutional arrangements might generate inequality between rich and poor nations, leading and lagging sectors, suburbs and cities, or among differently situated groups, classes, races, or genders. What are the social patterns and institutional arrangements through which positive changes in one area intensify negative changes in another?

CRITICAL SYSTEM ANALYTICS AND LEGAL ANALYSIS

Wallerstein and Myrdal honed their approaches to system dynamics before the outpouring of social science commentary on national and international inequality of the last decade or so. Some of that literature does aim to link the inequalities that trouble with an underlying "system" or "structure." Although the contours of those systems are often left somewhat vague or unspecified, Wallerstein, in particular, has spawned a range of follow-up efforts to extend his analysis of the "world-system." Unfortunately, the bulk of recent commentary on inequality opts rather for a more conventional understanding of "the system" that identifies some inequalities as troubling departures from how things normally operate and offers the familiar national political institutions as the terrain in which they might be remedied. Thinking this way can constrain inquiry into the "causes" of inequality to those one can realistically imagine being remedied by those institutions in real political time. I bring Myrdal and Wallerstein together to suggest how what I would call "critical system analytics" might enrich the analysis, particularly for those seeking to understand law's role not only in remedying but in reproducing inequality.

The contrast between these critical system frameworks and a more commonsense image of, say, "the American system" is easy to sketch. A conventional picture of "the system" typically focuses on the national situation: the national economy, the national political order. That's where inequalities can most readily be seen and, more important, be addressed through the normal operations of the political process. The goal of social scientific inquiry undertaken within that frame is to illuminate the causes to orient those remedies. Thinking globally, the focus is usually inequality "between" nations, which may seem easy to measure; but absent a plausible "global governance" reference point, it is more difficult to imagine remedying through measures analogous to those that can be imagined in the conventional national political process. Global inequalities can be recognized and lamented, but the remedy—and therefore the causes worth establishing—will be found nationally.

The troubling inequalities within the nation are those that seem aberrational in a system understood to be oriented both toward equality and toward the economic reward of merit. In a world where wages are normally thought to reflect the marginal productivity of labor, inequalities become problematic, for example, when they arise from merit being disregarded through discrimination or legacy inheritance. Inequalities at the bottom are troubling when they amount to precarity—and exclusion from normal economic or political life—and at the top when they threaten to corrupt the normal operations of the political system. Once such troubling disparities have been identified, their cause can be sought in specific obstacles to the normal operations of political representation and economic opportunity such as ongoing bias, educational differences, the legacy burdens of debt, or advantages of family wealth.

Social scientific study may bring innumerable causes to light, but the causes most worth identifying are those for which there are remedies the known political system might realistically undertake. It is easy, in this spirit, to bring law to the table as a remedial tool, enforcing rules against discrimination and monopoly power, revising election law to disempower the super wealthy, or revisiting prior legal efforts along these lines that have been poorly implemented or insufficiently enforced. Legal arrangements in the system's foundations—or routinely constitutive of inequality—get less air time.

Many remedies identified in this way probably ought to be tried. But much is missed that would be visible were one to begin with what I am calling "critical system analytics" suggests: patterns of disparity between loosely defined groups—"regions" for Myrdal, and nations of the "periphery, semiperiphery, and center" for Wallerstein. Observed differences are the starting point, and the "system" is whatever keeps them going. The system here is a space of differentiation. Moreover, starting with unequal relationships among groups turns one's attention to power differences, to winners and losers, dominators and dominated. What arrangements have the winners instrumentalized to secure their gains? What dynamics reinforce their powers? The system now is also a hierarchy: inequality is its métier.

The "structure" of such a system lies not in a stable constitutional framework or governance process, but in patterns that can only be uncovered historically or sociologically. Rather than gravitating toward stability or equilibrium with acceptable levels of inequality, a system built for persistent disparity orients one's expectations to instability and hierarchy. Such a system is an achievement of winners: a historical consolidation of powers and entitlements that lasts as long as it is not overturned or rebuilt to generate other patterns of power or wealth.

Reframing "the system" in this way suggests a wider range of "causes" for ongoing disparities and a wider range of potential sites for remedial action. The arrangements that constitute or reproduce inequality probably will include the normal operation of political and economic arrangements: for Wallerstein whatever undergirds the cartography of a global economy amid national polities or contributes to the capability of some economic actors to reproduce monopoly power in one industry after another while others find themselves consigned to more competitive pursuits; and for Myrdal, all the influences that affect the "media" through which chains of cumulative causation encourage backwash rather than spread effects.

A further advantage of approaching disparities in the style of Myrdal or Wallerstein is liberation from the national frame as a boundary between local/national and international dynamics. If you are thinking of "the system" as "the American system," for example, it is obvious that things elsewhere have to be thought about differently: other nations have other constitutional arrangements. It is easy to fall into imagining the "system" of "global governance" as somehow analogous to national arrangements, if more primitive or ineffective.

By shifting the focus from sovereign jurisdictional units to "groups," the analytic modes introduced by Wallerstein or Myrdal move easily by analogy from local to global dynamics. Wallerstein's analysis of "lead industries" clustering in the center as competitive industries are dispersed to the periphery could as well describe the relations between Silicon Valley or Boston's biotech centers and the low wage service sectors—warehousing, logistics, distribution—arising in the old industrial Midwest after their manufacturing prowess moved off shore. Myrdal's conception of the "state" as the arrangements that speed or impede cumulative causation translates easily from an institutional analysis of relations within a city or between regions to relations between nations or regions of the world. At whatever scale, one simply identifies the arrangements, wherever located, that structure the movements in capital, labor, goods, or technology, the "media" through which spread and backwash effects occur. Global inequalities would be constituted—"governed"—by a wide range of legal and institutional arrangements, many of them quite local, rather than be imagined to arise between nations under the loose purview of explicitly "global governance" institutions.

Critical system stories—like Myrdal's or Wallerstein's—are often developed outside the legal field, and it is not surprising that they mention law only sporadically, often with a conventional outsider's view of law as primarily a regulatory overlay on economic activity. Legal scholars also often focus on law's regulatory potential as a remedy. Nevertheless, from within the legal field, it is easy to see law's broader significance to the dynamics Myrdal or Wallerstein identify, often by drawing on realist and critical traditions in law that foreground law's distributional impact as well as law's constitutive—and therefore alterable—role in the arrangements treated commonsensically as "the system."

In his contribution to this volume, Duncan Kennedy analyzes Marx and Ricardo as critical system theorists in much the way I have analyzed Myrdal and Wallerstein. His analysis of their narratives points directly to the constitutive and distributional significance of legal arrangements. Take Marx, dramatically simplified: where capitalists own the means of production, competition among workers allocates the gains from production to the capitalist, alienating the laborer from the product of their labor. Remedy: empower the proletariat to own the means of production. Expropriating the capitalists won't lead to a decline in production; their gain is all surplus resulting from their "ownership." From a legal perspective, "ownership of the means of production" placing workers in competition with one another turns out to be a complex legal regime constituted by a background regime of entitlements that could be put together in various ways. The relationship between capitalists and workers might not only be regulated differently, it might be *established* differently. In this way, the critical system/structural relationship Marx foregrounds opens the door to analysis of its legal foundations and their potential alteration.

Or take Ricardo: as the population grows, increasing demand for food brings ever more unproductive land into cultivation, raising the price of food and enriching landlords who hold the most productive land at the cost of consumers facing ever higher prices. Ricardo looks directly at law for a remedy: repeal the corn laws, reduce the price of food, and impoverish those landlords. As Kennedy explains, impoverishing the landlords won't lead to a decline in production because their gain is all surplus resulting from their ownership of the productive land. Again here the legal constructions—both ideological and institutional—that enable this pattern are complex: ownership of the land, the authority of tenant farmers, the market for grain, access to credit, patterns of trade, and on and on—all legally constructed. And all able to be organized in a variety of ways that may intensify or reduce the landlord's ability to extract "unearned" gains. Indeed, that's why Ricardo focuses on the tariff. But "owning" land, like the relationship among "owners" and "farmers" or "farm workers," can be legally arranged to strengthen or weaken the relative powers of each group.

Working in these traditions, the puzzle for legal analysis is to understand the underlying drivers and dynamics of political or economic activity rather than to mind the guardrails within which it rolls. The "laws" that matter are less the visible constitutional or regulatory norms than the legal and institutional arrangements that reinforce patterns of inequality in power, wealth, status, or opportunity. Following Wallerstein, these would be the laws that constitute a world of local sovereigns, enable the promise of a global economy, and that "give priority" to endless capital accumulation. Following Myrdal, one would look to the legal arrangements that speed or impede any of the "media" through which spread and backwash effects are brought to bear.

Bringing this "critical" and "realist" attention to law's constitutive significance in conversation with critical system analytics focuses attention on law's role in the construction of the groups, the production and distribution of stakes among them, and the consolidation of gains. That law distributes—rather, or alongside, constitutionally ordering or regulating or judging—is familiar to lobbyists and other participants in everyday struggles. People readily understand that legal arrangements distribute when they affect the bargaining power of people struggling with one another; when they mark the line where coercion will enforce an allocation, excluding others from political authority or economic gain; or when they privilege some actors to injure others without recourse. The pressures of economic competition arise from the legal permission to use what one owns as ruthlessly as one wishes to the detriment of other property and business owners. Law's distributional significance thus extends to the foundational entitlement regimes that constitute political and economic activity. Law also offers both an ideological picture of political and economic life that sinks deep into common sense and an ideological vocabulary of contestation, each of which influences the distribution of stakes and the imaginary and factual terrain on which struggle takes place.

The dynamic element is also readily grasped. Because struggle is an iterative affair, people fight for an improved starting position in the next round by locking in gains and defending their dominance as entitlements. In this sense, legal entitlements mark the fault lines between winners and losers in past struggles and affect the alliances and trajectories for the next round. Over time, gains and losses compound as legal entitlements and authority sparking dynamics of inequality between groups, sectors, regions, and nations. From colonial governance to modern trade and investment, for example, legal arrangements have consolidated the distribution of rents from global economic activity and the political authority of those committed to the stability of that outcome. That's how "centers" become and stay "centers," or how leading regions reproduce their ability to benefit from spread effects while subjecting others to repeated doses of backwash.

In short, replacing a commonsense image of "the system" where inequality is aberrational but remediable with a picture identifying the dynamic reproduction of inequality as a feature rather than a bug allows legal ideas, institutions, and entitlements to serve as a red thread to unravel the great disparities of inequality and domination.

NOTES

My thanks to Richard Clements, Nafay Choudhury, Trace Dodge, Karen Engle, Janet Halley, Neville Hoad, Duncan Kennedy, Nadia Lambek, Veronica Pecile, Love Ronnelid, Michele Tedeschini, and Lucie White.

1. See Immanuel Wallerstein, *World-Systems Analysis: An Introduction* (Durham, NC: Duke University Press, 2004), for a useful introduction to his general approach.
2. Wallerstein, *World-Systems Analysis*, 23.
3. Wallerstein, *World-Systems Analysis*, 23.
4. Wallerstein, *World-Systems Analysis*, 23–24.
5. Wallerstein, *World-Systems Analysis*, 24.
6. Wallerstein, *World-Systems Analysis*, 25.
7. Wallerstein, *World-Systems Analysis*, 25.
8. Wallerstein, *World-Systems Analysis*, 25–26.
9. Wallerstein, *World-Systems Analysis*, 26.
10. Wallerstein, *World-Systems Analysis*, 26.
11. Wallerstein, *World-Systems Analysis*, 27–28.
12. On Myrdal's influence, see Immanuel Wallerstein, "The Myrdal Legacy: Racism and Underdevelopment as Dilemmas," *Cooperation and Conflict* 24 (1989): 1–18.
13. Gunnar Myrdal, "The Mechanism of Underdevelopment and Development and a Sketch of an Elementary Theory of Planning for Development," in Gunnar Myrdal, *An Approach to the Asian Drama: Methodological and Theoretical. Selections from Asian Drama: An Inquiry Into the Poverty of Nations, A Twentieth Century Fund Study* (New York: Vintage, 1970), 1166.
14. Myrdal, "The Mechanism of Underdevelopment and Development," 1859–60.
15. Myrdal, "The Mechanism of Underdevelopment and Development," 1860.
16. Myrdal, "The Mechanism of Underdevelopment and Development," 1870.
17. Myrdal, "The Mechanism of Underdevelopment and Development," 1870.
18. Myrdal, "The Mechanism of Underdevelopment and Development," 1863.
19. Myrdal, "The Mechanism of Underdevelopment and Development," 1871.
20. Myrdal, "The Mechanism of Underdevelopment and Development," 1868.
21. Gunnar Myrdal, *Economic Theory and Underdeveloped Regions* (New York: Harper and Row, 1971).
22. Myrdal, *Economic Theory*, 23.
23. Myrdal, *Economic Theory*, 13.
24. Myrdal, *Economic Theory*, 27.
25. Myrdal, *Economic Theory*, 27.

CHAPTER 4

LAW DISTRIBUTES

Ricardo, Marx, CLS

DUNCAN KENNEDY

In this chapter, I tell the story of the origins and the birth of the practice of left politically motivated distributional analysis of legal rules associated with the American critical legal studies (CLS) movement. Its origins are in classical economics, in the theories of economic surplus and its distribution that David Ricardo and Karl Marx developed for their very different critical purposes. Distributional analysis largely responded to the utter inability of mainstream economic analysis to theorize the 1960s crisis of the Black poor in deteriorating urban neighborhoods.

The long first part of this chapter is a detailed account of both the static and dynamic surplus analysis of Ricardo and Marx through a presentist lens. That is, it ignores their allegiance to the labor theory of value and restates in neoclassical terms their importance for CLS. They developed a model in which a legal regime distributes surpluses, helping some at the expense of others, and sets in motion a chain of further distributional changes in particular directions, for example, stagnation or growth, accumulation and impoverishment.

Marx and Ricardo invented distributional analysis, but they did not conceptualize it as distributional analysis of *legal regimes*. In fact, law figures in their work in a very mechanical, unorganic way, as a kind of inert background against which an economic conflict plays out. This is not surprising seen in the context of the widely shared legal formalist ideas of their time.

Within their larger projects, Ricardo and Marx each worked out models of how a change in a particular legal rule could work a large transfer of surplus away from the strong party in a bargaining relationship without the strong party being able to shift the burden to the weak party. This striking accomplishment has been ignored both by mainstream law and economics and by the welcome revival of left-of-liberal work on law and political economy.

In the second part of the chapter, I restate their ideas in the "post-realist" language of mainstream contemporary American legal thought. The post-realist legal lens shows how highly variable legal rules erratically applied—rather than the abstract ideas of absolute property and freedom of contract—strongly influence the relative bargaining power of the parties to transactions between strong and weak parties. This is true *across the board* rather than only in the particular circumstances worked out by Ricardo and Marx.

The great question they help answer is how to decide when redistributive interventions will or will not, have or have not, "hurt the people they are trying to help." In the last part of the chapter, I introduce this ("neo-Ricardian") approach as it has developed in the United States since the late 1960s, contrasting it with familiar liberal approaches. I use the distributional analysis of pro-tenant rules in low-income urban housing markets as an example.

The normative orientation of distributional analysis is toward distribution in favor of subordinated groups ("rent-seeking on behalf of the poor") rather than toward efficiency, and toward work on transformable background rules of public and private law rather than toward politically unattainable reform by tax and spend, large scale reregulation, or decommodification.

My hope is that the exposition will be intelligible equally to lawyers with no economics and to economists with no law.

RICARDO AND MARX ON THE DISTRIBUTION OF SURPLUS

Ricardo on Rent: Statics

Ricardo (1772–1823), like Marx (1814–1883) and the other classical economists, believed in the labor theory of value. "Value" is determined by "labor equivalents" and then determines "in the long run" the prices of commodities through competition. In both Ricardo and Marx, the theory was an important determinant of the distribution of surpluses throughout the economy. Because I share the neoclassical conviction that the labor theory of value is not useful in the way the classics thought it was, I am going to translate their insights into the neoclassical language familiar in first year college microeconomics courses.[1] I mean no insult to the orthodox!

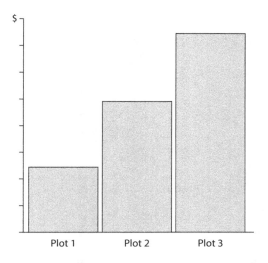

FIGURE 4.1 Cost of production

SOIL OF VARYING FERTILITY

Ricardo's highly abstract model of the rent of agricultural land is the starting point for the analytic. He posits something called the "original and indestructible power of the soil," meaning its fertility before it has been developed for commercial agriculture.[2] I am going to interpret this for our purposes as "a given acre is more fertile than another acre if it costs less than on the other to produce a bushel of wheat, assuming the same amount of labor, equipment, fertilizer, and tractors, or barns, or whatever." So the idea is that the most fertile land has the lowest cost of production.[3]

In figure 4.1 the vertical columns represent pieces of land arrayed from more to less fertile. The vertical axis is dollars. It gets progressively more expensive to produce a bushel of wheat as we go from left to right. Out of this very simple idea of different levels of fertility arrayed in a progression from more to less fertile, Ricardo is going to build an *enormous* apparatus. The whole history and future of the world is going to be summarized in that little idea.

THE DEMAND FOR FOOD

The second part of the model is demand for food (figure 4.2). The idea is that people have money, and they will offer money for food. How much food they

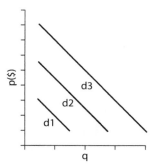

FIGURE 4.2 Demand curves

buy depends on how much it costs them and on how much money they have to spend. The more it costs, the less they want or demand.[4]

If the price of food is low, people want a lot of food. As the price of food rises, they want less and less. At a very high price for food, very little will be demanded. If circumstances change, for example, because there are a lot more people with a lot more money buying in the market, the demand curve shifts, moving to the right, as in Figure 4.2. At a given price, there is more demand. But it is still true in the new situation that the quantity demanded will go up and down as prices change. Just keep this in mind when I discuss the setup between the parties who are producing the food in response to this demand.

LANDLORDS AND FARMERS

Ricardo starts from a very stylized deliberately distorted (for the purposes of his argument) model of agriculture in England in his time. In his model the land is owned exclusively by people called landlords. He recognizes that in real life they're varied, but in his model they aren't. In his model the landlords just provide land. They live, say, in London. Their favorite author is Jane Austen, who is writing about them at that very moment. They have country houses on their estates, which are abandoned to employees and servants who look after the premises and others who are managing the business while they're going to balls "in town." Their business life in the model is strictly limited to choosing tenants, collecting the rent they've agreed to pay, and evicting them if they fail to pay or otherwise violate their lease terms. *Landlords don't do anything other than these three things.*[5]

These tenants are called "farmers," and they are not to be confused with the tenants of urban residential premises. These tenants are capitalists. The farmer in the advanced agriculture of the time rents a substantial piece of land and provides everything for the production of actual wheat. The farmer builds the buildings and buys the equipment needed, which is not very elaborate because it's no mechanized agriculture yet, but it will eventually be mechanized. And the farmer hires agricultural laborers. They don't figure in Ricardo's discussion at all—they're just subsumed in the general cost of production. In real life, the agricultural laborers were basically a destitute agricultural population that appears in every capitalist country in the beginning of capitalist agriculture. They have nothing, they live in barracks, and they are very deprived. They're paid a subsistence wage, which is barely enough to prevent starvation.[6]

THE IMPROVING LANDLORD

In Ricardo's model, all production is done by the farmers, who provide the capital, hire the laborers, raise the wheat, sell it in the local or national wheat market, and pay rent to the landlord. Contrary to Ricardo's model, many people think the single most important thing about the early economic development of England was not even manufacturing and the steam engine, it was the improving landlord.[7]

The improving landlord is a landlord who farms his land rather than renting it out. He is a capitalist as well as the owner. He kicks off his customary small holding tenants and builds an agribusiness. He drains the land, builds buildings and lays roads within the estate, all aimed at massively increasing the yield per acre of his land. And he collects all the proceeds of the sale of the wheat. He is, in Ricardo's analysis, both a landlord and a farmer.[8]

Ricardo's relentless focus on the *non*improving landlord has an obvious political as well as an analytic function. Rather than engaging in capitalist reinvestment, that landlord is pocketing his payment and going to the ball, so to speak. That's all he's doing. And his wife is buying her clothes in Paris not London. Ricardo is setting up the landlord class, mainly aristocrats and pseudo-aristocrats, in favor of, you might say, the bourgeoisie.

THE RENTAL MARKET FOR AGRICULTURAL LAND

The landlord collects rent. The question Ricardo addresses in the terms of his model is: How much rent? He defines rent as the return on the unimproved productive potential of the soil, which means in practice what you get if you do absolutely nothing but rent it out in the state in which you acquired it and then collect the payment owed. In other words, the rent is what you get, *just by owning the land*.[9] Well, why do you get *anything* for owning the land? The answer to that is that a farmer will pay for the right, the leasehold right, to raise crops on your land and to sell them. The farmer is going to pay you a part of the proceeds of sale. And that part is rent. If you're an improving landlord, you get a lot more than rent because you're also the owner of the farm animals and the machines, you hire the agricultural laborers, and you build the buildings. That's not rent, that's profit, meaning a return to capital.[10]

The next really basic idea is that the landlord rents the land to the farmer who offers the most rent. A background condition of the model, not mentioned because it's so obvious that Ricardo doesn't need to make it explicit, is that there are many more people who want to be farmers and have access to working capital so they could make a go of it than there are farms available for renting.[11]

THE FARMERS' OFFERS

The farmers make offers of rent for the land. They're saying, "I'll give you this much rent for this particular parcel." What they offer is a function of what they could get by investing their capital in a different parcel, or in a different activity. They want something that's better than their alternative inside or outside farming. They have various things they could do with their capital. They could go into small business, manufacturing, or trade, or they could invest the money in Bank of England bonds. Ricardo's idea is that there is an average rate of profit, adjusted for risk, in all these activities, which is equalized by competition. For entrepreneurs, a return to capital in farming that's better than the overall average will draw them to become farmers.[12]

This return isn't subsistence. It's not a category like the minimum necessary to survive, because these are capitalists. Depending on how much capital they have to invest, the average return on it in the form of profit might be a little or a great deal of money, and each of them can beat the average rate by skill in managing that particular farm. Farmers looking for land will calculate the probable profit on each parcel, and here the most important factor is fertility (but not the only factor, viz. location, etc.).[13] All the wheat produced by the three parcels in figure 4.1 with their different fertilities will be sold for the same price because buyers don't care which parcel it comes from, only about its quality, and quality is identical. Farmers have no reason to sell wheat that costs little to produce for less than the market price, so there's a single market price for wheat. Although the parcels have radically different fertilities, the farmers looking to rent will be willing to farm any of them for just a little more than the average rate of return to investment in other sectors.[14] The farmers don't care about the land, and they don't care about fertility. They only care about profit.

But if the wheat is all sold for the same price, why wouldn't the farmers who rent good land be making more than the farmers with bad land? It seems counterintuitive that all the farmers will get the same return on capital whether their cost per bushel is high or low. Remember that the fertility difference between good land and bad land exists for identical inputs of labor, equipment, and so forth. The farmer on good land gets his wheat for less cost than his neighbor and sells it for the same market price, so why doesn't he make more profit? Ricardo's answer is that he won't make more profit on each bushel of wheat because he will pay a sum equivalent to the difference in cost to the landlord as rent.[15] This is the hardest thing to grasp in the theory.

WHY THE LANDLORD GETS ALL THE SURPLUS

The first step to understanding the theory is to add the demand curve to our diagram of the three parcels (figure 4.3). The idea is that when there aren't many people and they aren't rich, their demand for wheat at any price is less than it will be with population growth and development. But even at this low starting point (demand curve d1), the farmer on the most fertile land, Plot 1, will be able to sell its product for a price that equals its cost of production, plus a little more than the overall average rate of profit.[16]

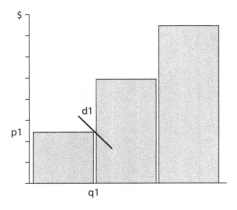

FIGURE 4.3 Bushels produced

The landlords who own Plots 2 and 3 won't be able to find farmers who want to rent from them even for a notional rent. Even paying zero rent, if the farmer puts in the cost of production on the land, he will have to sell at a loss. The market price for wheat is below the cost of production on all but the most fertile land. The landlord of Plot 1 is going to get a nominal rent payment, just enough to make it worth it for him to take the time to rent the land.[17] His land is just fertile enough so that it can produce wheat that will sell for enough to cover the cost of producing it, plus the necessary profit to the farmer.

Now suppose that population growth and income growth have increased demand for food. At any given price, more is demanded, so the demand curve has shifted to the right (d3). All the plots, at this new much higher market price (p3), are profitable, even Plot 3, the highest cost parcel. The landlord who owns Plot 3 can now find a farmer to rent at the standard average profit, just as was true for the landlord of Plot 1 in the old regime. That farmer will pay only nominal rent and receive, as all the other farmers do, the standard profit.

Now let's go back to the most fertile piece of land. On Plot 1, the farmer has produced the same amount of wheat as the farmer on Plot 3, but it's costing him much less than on Plot 3. Ricardo's idea is that when competing potential farmers approach the landlord who owns Plot 1, he will demand a rent equal to the whole difference between the cost of production (+average profit) and the expected market price for the produce of that plot.[18] Say the price of wheat is $60 (p3 in figure 4.4). The cost of production, which is $59 on Plot 3, is only $19 on Plot 1. The average profit, the farmer's alternative, is $1. The landlord will demand and get $40 in rent (r1), leaving the farmer with $20. The cost of

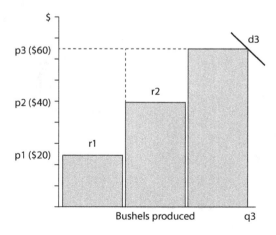

FIGURE 4.4 Rent (*r*)

production takes $19 of this, leaving the farmer with $1 profit, just the amount necessary to keep him from going elsewhere. The rent that goes to the landlord will be the whole difference between what it cost to produce a bushel on Plot 3 and the lower cost of production on Plot 1. If farmer 1 asks to pay less rent so he can make more than the absolute minimal standard profit that everybody gets, the landlord just says "bye-bye!" and puts up a little sign saying "farmer wanted." A line of a hundred people forms, and he waits for a person to say, "well, I'll do it for the standard profit."[19]

TAXING THE NONIMPROVING LANDLORD WOULD HAVE NO EFFICIENCY COST

Ricardo's great treatise is called "On the Principles of Political Economy and Taxation." One of the greatest issues of early nineteenth-century British politics was whether or not and by how much to tax landed wealth. At that time land was still the dominant kind of wealth, with manufacturing gaining fast but not there yet. Moreover, the owners of agricultural land were divided between large estate owners and smallholders, representing different social classes, and both distinct from the urban proletariat and varied bourgeoisie. The large landlords, improving and not improving, and the farmers, were locked in a struggle with the emerging capitalist bourgeoisie in manufacturing and finance. A major argument against taxing landlords, believed as gospel by a large part of conservative opinion, was that taxing landlords would "hurt the people you are trying to help," as it is commonly phrased today.

If his land was fertile, the landlord would raise the rent. If it wasn't fertile enough to be profitable after paying the tax, he would withdraw it from production. Passing the tax burden to farmers, all operating at mere standard profit, would require them to increase what they charged for the now smaller supply of wheat or go out of business. Bakers would increase the price of bread, the principal food stuff of the urban proletariat.

Ricardo's answer was that the tax, if it was on the unimproved value of the land, and not on capital investment of farmers or improving landlords, would have no effect on output, and so no effect on the price of bread.[20] The landlord on Plots 1 and 2 would have no takers for their land if they tried to raise the rent above what they were already charging. The farmers operate at normal profit, which means with no profit cushion that could absorb the rent increase. Landlords would have to leave rent where it was and "eat" the tax, that is, accept a reduction of their surplus (r1 and r2). As long as the tax left enough surplus to make it worth it for the landlords to keep it in production, it would stay in production.

Ricardo assumes (implicitly) that the market value of the land—the basis for taxing it—is simply a function of its productivity, in its "natural state" for commercial agriculture. For this reason, Plot 3 has little market value. Its infertility makes it barely productive enough to pay its costs. So a tax on the unimproved value of marginal land will be small or nominal, and neither the landlord nor the farmer will have any incentive to withdraw it from production. In sum, the tax will have no effect on the amount of land in production, and no effect on farmers' profit, and therefore no impact on the price of bread.[21]

In the language of neoclassical welfare economics, the tax has no efficiency cost. It is the equivalent of what is called "one shot after the fact redistribution." No actor who makes decisions will behave differently as a result of the tax as long as it doesn't drive the pure landlord to withdraw the land. Farmers, bakers, and consumers will confront the exact same price configuration as before the tax. The welfare loss to landlords is then measured in ethical/political terms against the benefits produced by the government's spending of the tax revenue.

This elegant piece of partisan political economic argument is the direct ancestor of an enormous amount of good, bad, and indifferent effort on behalf of the economically oppressed and the not oppressed alike. To my mind it was "epochal." For example, Henry George's single tax plan is a straightforward application.[22] But the idea is central to Marx as well. As you will see in Marx's dynamic analysis, the dynamic endpoint is the costless transfer of the ownership of the means of production to an as yet to be imagined organization of the social whole.

Marx's Theory of Profit: Statics

Now I'm going to do something that is somewhat underplayed in the Marxist and neo-Marxist literature but is clear to some generally liberal historians of economic thought. The idea is that there is a very close parallel between Ricardo's theory of rent and Marx's theory of profit in manufacturing under capitalism.[23]

THE PRODUCTION AND SALE OF COMMODITIES: LABOR AS "FERTILE"

Marx's capitalist is the owner of the means of production—a factory, machines in the factory, and raw materials. The owner pays workers (proletarians) who operate the whole thing and produce the goods that will be sold. In the pure form of the model, there are many more workers than capitalists: all the workers are identical and do identical work, and competition among workers drives them down to an identical subsistence wage, which in Marx's terms represents the labor value of labor, or the labor cost of reproducing the labor force. The capitalist will sell the commodity on the (free) market for a price set by competition, both with other producers of his product and with all other products, which represents its (long run) labor value. What is left over is profit.

The most important idea in Marx's theory of capitalist economics is that the commodity sells for more than it costs the capitalist to produce it and that all of the difference goes to him and none to the worker. A day's proletarian labor costs the capitalist the subsistence wage but only a part of the day is necessary to produce enough commodities to cover the wage bill. Production after that point is pure profit for the capitalist. By contrast, increasing materials input raises cost by as much as it raises price. The nonlabor inputs are "inert" but the labor input is, by analogy to land in Ricardo, "fertile." This "surplus value" thesis is a good illustration of the daunting complexities of the labor theory of value. The non-Marxist mass of the economics profession rejected the "exploitation theory of profit" from the very beginning, proposing many alternatives designed to remove the stigma from the capitalist role. None of them need concern us given the demise of the labor theory of value.[24]

A NEO-RICARDIAN ACCOUNT OF MARXIAN PROFIT

Marx's account of profit assumes a perfectly competitive product market which is the mechanism driving price down to labor equivalents. Of course a major source of profit in actual capitalism has always been massive deviations from perfect competition so that market power of one kind or another dominates distributional outcomes. For competitive markets, a neo-Ricardian alternative to the labor theory of value would begin with a stock of capital (the actual physical and intellectual means of production) fixed at a particular moment. Imagine that all firms in the market get the same price for the identical product but that their costs vary widely. Although their technology is identical, firms differ in terms of location (transport cost of both supply and distribution; more or less favorable weather). Some are older than others, which is sometimes a major advantage and sometimes a major disadvantage (accumulated goodwill vs. worn out equipment). Still assuming perfect competition in the product and factor markets, ownership of brand names and protectable trade secrets is a major source of surplus along with favorable contractual deals with suppliers and customers. Then there are the (Schumpeterian) competitive advantages, derived from having been the "first mover" in an industrial innovation, generating surpluses that can persist long after the industry has become competitive.

In other words, the firms are positioned along a cost curve that looks just like the sequence from Plots 1 to 2 to 3. The demand curves for the commodity the firms produce are like d1, d2, and d3 in figure 4.2. The surplus generated by Marxian Firm 1 is available for distribution between the capitalist and the workers, just like the surplus of Ricardian Plot 1 is to be distributed between the landlord and the farmer. If the capitalists get everything above the workers' subsistence, it will be because the number of factory jobs is momentarily fixed, a far larger number of potential factory workers are willing to work for subsistence, and there is greater feasibility for concerted action among capitalists than among workers (for many reasons).[25]

Firm 2 generates less surplus, but again it all goes to the capitalist. Firm 3 is just breaking even, with the workers receiving their subsistence wage and the capitalist making barely enough profit to keep him afloat.

Marx recognizes all of these differences in costs as things that happen, but for him they are incidents in the process by which competition drives the price of the product to correspond to labor time.[26] In this alternative neoclassical version, profit is even more closely analogous to Ricardian rent than in Marx's account because it is the differences between firms, operating like the differences between plots of land that accounts for it. The differences are what distributional analysis works with rather than deviations from the truth of the labor theory of value.

THE NEO-RICARDIAN NEOCLASSICAL CASE AGAINST CAPITALIST APPROPRIATION OF THE SURPLUS

In a neoclassical version of the argument that the workers should get more than subsistence even in a competitive economy, we begin with Ricardo's distinction between the pure landlord and the improving landlord. The pure capitalist in Marx's model is like the pure landlord in Ricardo's model. He owns the means of production but is not involved in the actual production process. Managers, who are the equivalent of Ricardian farmers, hire labor and purchase material inputs and direct their allocation. They perform the entrepreneurial function of adjusting prices and outputs to the demands of competition. Marxian profit is the return to "mere" ownership of the means of production, rather than of land, and it is distributed through dividend checks and bond coupons rather than through rent payments.

The reward for management, including entrepreneurship (bonuses to the CEO), even if it is a very large amount of money, is not profit but compensation for labor. Compare this with the Berle and Means theory of the separation of ownership and control in the most advanced capitalist enterprises emerging before and after World War I.[27] Managers, not owners, do all the things that generate surplus but not as an inevitable result of labor fertility. They make the choices that generate the highly differentiated costs between firms that translate into variable surpluses when the goods are sold at a single competitive price.

The owner-entrepreneur in capitalist markets is the exact equivalent of Ricardo's improving landlord. Unlike the dividend-check-casher coupon-clipper, he works hard at management. But we can in theory distinguish between the two parts of his return, even though it is difficult or impossible to do so in practice. The return to simple ownership of the means of production, to holding the shares or the bonds, is like the rent for unimproved farmland, simply unearned, not the product of any aspect of the situation that gives the capitalist as mere owner an ethical claim to the product.

There are many complexities and shortcomings to the ethical argument, but they don't concern us because we are looking at the uses of the Marxist model in order to understand how to do distributional analysis of changes in legal rules. The political motive for the analysis is to support distributive change in a radically egalitarian direction.

For Both Ricardo and Marx, "Mere Ownership" Permits Appropriation of All the Surplus

For Ricardo, mere ownership of agricultural land permits the landlord to appropriate the surplus from the sale of the wheat, meaning everything above the costs of production plus a minimal return to the capitalist farmer. For Marx, mere ownership of the means of production permits the capitalist to appropriate the surplus from the sale of the commodity, meaning everything above the costs of production, including the cost of reproducing the proletarian labor force, plus the return to the management function.

In the neoclassical version of surplus that I have been tortuously pursuing, as in Marx's classical version, distribution is determined through the complex legal *concept* of ownership as it plays out in the equally complex *social practice* of ownership. Both the theory of property as concept and its study as social practice are as different today from their version in Ricardo and Marx as the labor theory of value is from neoclassicism. In short, we need to critique and reconstruct both authors in light of the contemporary post-legal-realist version of what law "is" and how it works.

But first let's examine the dynamics of the models.

DYNAMICS OF THE MODELS

Ricardo's Dynamic: Higher and Higher Rent Strangles Investment

Ricardo's basic idea is that the size of the population determines the demand for food. If the economy is growing, the population will grow. The growth in demand will drive up the price of bread. At the new high prices, the less fertile land (Plot 3) will become profitable. The owners of that land will receive minimal rent because farmers making only the break-even price given the high cost of production will offer no more than it takes to get the landlord to bring the land into production. However, previously marginal land is now profitable, so there will be increased rent for landlords who previously received only a pittance (r2 on Plot 2), and the landlords of the most fertile land will make a lot more than ever before (r1 on Plot 1).[28]

At first glance it would seem that as long as there is land to bring into cultivation this can go on indefinitely as the economy develops and the population gets fed as it grows. The problem is that the price of bread determines the cost of production of manufactured goods.[29] Urban labor paid at subsistence has to consume its minimal daily ration, so capitalist manufacturers will have to increase wages as the price of bread goes up. Ricardo thinks the market price of manufactured goods is determined by labor inputs that haven't changed with higher wages (even though the capitalist has to pay more for that labor).[30] (In neoclassical terms, we would expect that the capitalist will be unable to pass along the full cost increase to consumers, depending on the elasticity of demand.) That means some capitalists will have to "eat" some of the cost, and those on the margin of profitability will go out of business. The profit on capital in general (the average return we saw in the case of the farmer) will fall.

As less and less fertile land is brought into cultivation, the price of bread continues to rise and standard profit keeps falling, shrinking the amount of manufacturing profit available for new investment and driving up the standard interest rate. Entrepreneurs in the manufacturing sector are caught in a classic profit squeeze between higher wages and higher credit costs.[31]

But what about the increased rent? Why wouldn't the landlords loan their increased rental income to the capitalists, keeping the machine going through a capital market rather than by retained earnings? Again, according to Ricardo, the problem with this is that the landlords are not going to invest their new income in building British industry either in person or by loaning to capitalist entrepreneurs. They're going to spend it on balls and on *imported* Paris fashions for their wives and daughters and mistresses. They're going to spend it on food, not for armies of proletarians but for armies of household servants, and on real estate, yes, but on unbelievably beautiful country houses, not factory buildings. Not "productive activity."[32] In this situation, rent increases shrink the supply of capital available to industry and choke development. Ricardo's end result is stagnation, or if the population continues to grow, a Malthusian descent into famine.[33]

THE SOLUTION: REPEAL THE "CORN LAWS"

In Ricardo's time and for twenty years after his death, Britain imposed a tariff on imported grain ("the corn laws"). In Ricardo's time, immediately following fifteen years of war against Napoleon, the rationale for the tariff was to maintain self-sufficiency in grain (=bread) for national security reasons. But everyone also understood that it was about preserving the system of aristocratic and nouveau agricultural wealth, which was sitting on top of a smallholder sector, a large mass of agricultural laborers, and another mass of household servants. Partly because of the obvious significance of the tariff, the landlord class reinvested a significant part of its rents in controlling politics. The system was far from anything like universal manhood suffrage; what voting occurred was almost comically rigged to maximize conservative votes and was paralyzed by large scale networks of corruption.[34]

Ricardo based his stagnation argument on little more than the insanely abstract model outlined earlier. But if you believed it even in a much more qualified and nuanced form, it argued powerfully for repealing the corn laws. The reason for this was that the cost of production of British wheat was already in 1821 far higher than the cost of production, plus shipping cost, of foreign wheat. Over the ensuing years, the difference would get larger and larger as the United States and Canada opened vast new wheat land from Ohio outward toward Montana and Saskatchewan and began to mechanize production. Meanwhile steam replaced sail for transport across the Atlantic.

Without the corn laws, according to the reformers of the period, only the most fertile British land (Plot 1) was competitive with foreign wheat. Without the tariff, the less fertile land (Plots 2 and 3) would go out of production. The owners would have zero rent, and their farmers would be bankrupted unless they figured it out fast enough in advance to bail before the crash. Cheap foreign wheat would drive down the price of bread, permitting stable wage rates far below what was coming under the old regime as population growth drove demand beyond the availability of fertile land. Cheap bread would mean high profits, permitting the capitalist class to keep growing the economy.

Like a tax on unimproved agricultural land, the large reduction of landlords' rent would increase total wealth. It would divert the surplus from unproductive (balls, servants, houses) to productive use in the short run and from stagnation to growth in the long run. To fully grasp this, we need but will not explore here Ricardo's second amazing invention, the theory of comparative advantage, in which, Britain specialized in manufactured goods and the United States specialized in farm products, would both be better off than they would be producing each of the goods for themselves.

So, for Ricardo, the choice is either stagnation or abolish the corn laws and expropriate a part of the property of the landlord class, by eliminating their legal device. Note that it's a *legal* device. The whole thing turns on a tariff: a legislatively enacted provision, valid under general law, and applied in such a way as to completely change the distribution of income without either a tax or a domestic regulation.

By the way, that's not critical legal studies. That's just the normal distributional analysis of legislation. CLS distributional analysis means doing the same thing not with having or not having a tariff, but with having or not having freedom of contract or, say, fault-based tort law or the free movement of capital between American states. The critical move is to take the distributive analytic developed by Ricardo for a tariff—a public law measure that was foregrounded as a highly salient political economic issue—and apply it to something completely different, such as a taken for granted background rule.

Marx's Dynamic: Socialism in the Womb of Capitalism

The premises of Marx's dynamic model is this: the manufacturing sector of the capitalist economy grows through the reinvestment of profits by manufacturing firms, a process known by the talismanic phrase *capital accumulation*.

THE LOGIC OF CAPITAL ACCUMULATION

Capital accumulation requires the pure owners to refrain from consuming in the unproductive mode of landlords. They gain through the mere fact of ownership the legal right to control the whole surplus of price over cost generated in their factories. But because the manufacturing sector is highly competitive, they have to reinvest at least a large part of their profits in the business. In Marx's phrase, whether he likes it or not, the capitalist has to behave as a miser, sacrificing his own consumption in order to maintain or increase his wealth.[35]

The need to reinvest to stave off competition is a function of two characteristics of the modern capitalist manufacturing sector as Marx understands it. First, the manufacturing sector undergoes a continuous process of technological innovation, reducing the cost of production. Technology includes steam to coal power, assembly line technology, and the like. Innovating requires capital beyond what is needed to maintain a steady state because it requires constant investment in new equipment.[36] The possibility of reducing costs and making Schumpeterian profits before rivals could catch up is the main driver of technological innovation.

Second, along with the technological dimension, there is an organizational dimension, the rationalization of production.[37] Tech innovation permitted more and more intense specialization in the production process (the division of labor). In the first phase, as the process of division intensifies, larger and larger numbers of specialized workers in each firm are required to produce each unit of output, and the contribution of each worker to a unit becomes smaller and smaller. Large agglomerations of workers, each making a tiny contribution per unit, can produce vastly more units together than a collection of individuals or small teams handling all aspects of production.

In the second phase, mechanization replaces the tools of classic Smithian pin making. The machines for individual pieces are combined into the assembly line, and the work of "tending" the assembly line is, so to speak, facilitative rather than in any way autonomous. As such, innovation makes it simpler and more repetitive and divides tasks not according to skill but according to whether they are more suited psycho-physically to men, women, or children.

The logic of specialization is progressive in the sense of developing through technological innovation in the single direction of larger and larger production units, but fewer and fewer of them. Every innovation that reduces costs allows the innovating firm to undercut its rivals and steal their market share. The larger firm can afford a more elaborate specialization incentivizing yet more tech innovation.[38]

THE CAPITALIST SOCIALIZATION OF PRODUCTION

The larger and larger units based on more and more elaborate divisions of labor are *managed*. The logic of the competitive market is wholly absent inside the modern factory. Its ethos is intricately planned cooperation of thousands of people, each with a role dependent on coordination with all the other roles in the production process. The goal is efficiency in the sense of producing a desired product at the least cost in the resources of land, labor, and capital.[39] In short, in Weber's phrasing of Marx's insight, capitalist development substitutes rationally goal-oriented bureaucracy for markets and competition.[40]

Capitalist development enormously increases society's productive capacity by socializing it. In liberal fantasy, economic life is based on the exercise of their contractual free choices by all kinds of owners and all kinds of workers. In fact, according to Marx, the workers have no say at all in any aspect of the production process—they sign away their property right in their own labor at the factory gate.[41] As owners delegate more and more to managers, a steel manufacturing company might employ several thousand workers and managers for the benefit of several hundred thousand completely passive stockholders. From the functional point of view, the capitalist is a sort of appendix to a giant bureaucratic organization.

THE SOCIAL ROLES OF LANDLORD AND CAPITALIST

Whereas Ricardo's landlord is a strictly socially negative being who we could, as revolutionaries, gladly do without, Marx's capitalist is the author of the modern world. The extreme poverty of the masses of his day is not just or mainly a function of the maldistribution of income between capitalists and workers. There just isn't enough output of goods and services for everyone to live a modestly good material life. Moreover, the utopian hope for freedom from want goes along with the utopian hope for freedom from the need to work long hours to produce that modestly good material life.

The capitalist's miserly behavior as a profit-obsessed accumulator and reinvestor is opening the way to a radically different future for all of humanity. This is very Hegelian; the cunning of history, aka the system logic of capitalism, obliges totally selfish actors who have not the *slightest* desire for anything except money to act in a way that will make it possible for everyone in the society to be rich when the accumulation process has taken its course.

On the way, there is the "ah-hah" moment when productive capacity is great enough so everyone could be modestly well off, and everyone is already organized in a socialist system, with owners cashing checks and coupon-clipping away. "The consciousness of the proletariat" then realizes this truth.[42] The true or pure capitalist class is holding *their* property titles, *their* stocks and bonds, on behalf of all of us, while inflicting the chaos of more and more concentrated capital and commodity markets. Since production is already socialized, all that will remain will be to flip the ownership from private to public as the first step on the road to communism. It can be done in seconds. And nothing has to change at the enterprise level because the owners aren't doing anything unless, of course, "we," the new owners, have new ideas about how "we" should deploy "our" labor power using "our" means of production. Revolution means not the violent destruction of a functioning economic order, as happened in the liberal revolution against feudalism, but the birth of the socialist baby from its capitalist womb.[43]

THE SYSTEM THREATENS TO DESTROY ITSELF

There is a flaw, a "contradiction" in this historical formation, typically Hegelian, which is precisely that economic activity along this path is driven by competition among present-oriented amoral individualist actors. Firms compete with each other for market share under the ground rules of property and contract, in a zero-sum game: cut costs further than your rival and expand or disappear. For this reason, the competitive free market is systemically prone to crises of over- and underproduction, booms and busts.[44]

Capitalists have no ethical commitment to the welfare or even the long run survival of the system in which they are the prime decision makers. They aim to survive as individuals by conquering through whatever means, legal or illegal, moral or immoral, may be current in the industry. The long run socially beneficial option is reinvestment in technological advance. The ever-present dark option is to reduce labor costs by sweating the workforce, particularly by demanding a longer working day for a constant wage.[45]

In Marx's model, the position of capital in relation to labor was strong enough so that firms could improve their positions vis-à-vis competitors by driving the actual wage to a version of subsistence that was abysmal by the standards that prevailed in the precapitalist labor market and under conditions of social disintegration and consequent degradation worse than the worst version of rural life. That went for men, women, and children alike, twelve hours a day, seven days a week. On the downside of the business cycle, the capitalist survival strategy was to reduce the wage below the reproduction rate to actual death by starvation levels.

Marx's brilliant portrayal of the transformation of the labor process in the factory adds a second dimension. The assembly line was organized to reduce the workers from cooperators in the division of labor to "appendages" of the machine. In his picture, the human consequences of mechanization are in some ways more chilling than those of starvation wages. Workers are not just deskilled, their humanity is brutally stunted by the repetitive work regime.

The combination of immiseration with dehumanization on the assembly line, according to Marx, had begun to threaten the reproduction of labor power and therefore the whole system.[46] The answer was a new synthesis, also very Hegelian, namely, social democracy in the form of formation of unions, factory legislation, and education.[47] These could stabilize the system so that its productive dynamic could continue to the moment when the working class could take power.[48] (Another contradiction another overcoming.)

FACTORY LEGISLATION REDISTRIBUTES TO WORKERS WITH MINIMAL EFFICIENCY COSTS

Here we come to another striking parallel between Ricardo and Marx on the distributive consequences of legal innovation. In Marx's model, workers are paid by the day for a number of hours fixed by the employer. The wage fluctuates around the reproduction cost of labor. The system-threatening capitalist strategy that Marx describes in meticulous detail is the lengthening of the working day in order to increase the amount of "unpaid" labor. A certain number of hours of work increase the value and hence the selling price of the product by an amount necessary to pay the daily wage. Further hours of labor further increase the price of the product, and that increase is pure profit on the means of production employed.

Legislation fixing the length of the working day at a number of hours shorter than the number prevailing in the unregulated market cannot affect the daily wage. A shorter day for the same wage is an unequivocal gain for workers and a loss for capitalists because beyond the very short run they can't reduce the wage in response to the regulation.[49] The workers at the edge of subsistence are like Ricardo's farmers who can't pay more rent because they are already operating for the minimum average profit necessary to keep them in business.

The industrialists argued that the limitation would cause a reduction in output and large efficiency costs from having to employ more workers in shorter shifts. But as long as the reduction in hours, for the constant wage, leaves some profit, and all firms are regulated in the same way, capitalists have no motive to cut production. They will "eat the loss" of surplus. Cutting production would just reduce profits further, beyond the loss caused by the regulation. As for the efficiency costs, Marx quotes the famous British factory inspectors' reports showing that the supposed massive inconveniences "vanished like snow in the sunlight" as firms quickly adjusted without loss of productive capacity.

Like Ricardo in his discussions of the taxation of landlord wealth and the abolition of the corn laws, Marx was here engaged in one of the premier activities of present-day lawyer/economist policy analysts, namely, assessing the distributive consequences of legal rule changes. Unlike Ricardo, he is doing it in the familiar mode of social democrats responding to self-styled benevolent free-marketeers who claim that all do-gooding on behalf of the poor is self-defeating ("hurts the people").

The rest of this chapter explores how the Ricardo/Marx analytic might be applied to the particular form of social democratic reform that tries to redistribute, more or less "structurally," by modifying the background rules of private law that Ricardo and Marx either unreflectively presuppose or misconceive.

CRITIQUE AND RECONSTRUCTION OF THE ROLE OF LAW IN RICARDO AND MARX

In Ricardo's model, the factors determining the distribution of surplus are the fertility of the land, the cost of production, the demand for wheat, and the ownership rights of landlords under a regime of freedom of contract. Under these assumptions, landlords receive the whole surplus. Ricardo makes no formal or explicit assumptions at all about the legal context.

For Marx, the factors determining the rate of profit are the cost of labor, the costs of nonlabor means of production, the demand for the commodity, and the resulting market price (once again, if we simply ignore the labor theory of value). Under these assumptions, the capitalist owners of the means of production receive the whole profit, that is, the whole surplus.

However, Marx treats the abstract legal concepts of property and contract as having necessary specific meanings when operationalized at the level of particular legal rules governing production and distribution. The meanings he derives are those of the extreme laissez-faire private law regime of mid-nineteenth-century Western Europe (philosophized by Hegel and abstracted by Savigny). The upshot is that the commodity form is contingent, the product of class conflict through history, but it determines, in its abstraction, the legal regime that determines the distribution of surplus under capitalism.

Contemporary Legal Thought vs. Marx's Legal Formalism

It is not possible to predict what a capitalist legal regime is or will be in the real world or to predict its effects by reasoning from the abstract concepts of absolute property and free contract. Here I aim to bring contemporary mainstream American legal theory into contact with neoclassical welfare economics as it applies to wage and rent bargains. The mainstream legal theoretical view is that the ideas of private property and freedom of contract are vague or contradictory or open to conflicting but equally legally plausible interpretations (depending on the genre of critique). The actual order of enforceable formal state law has never followed and could not follow from the "logic of the commodity form" or "property and contract" because of their (relative) indeterminacy. Actual regimes of positive law consist of highly contextual rules emerging from free-for-all political/economic conflict. Supposing that they care, the actors (including judges) with legislative or other law-making power have been and are only very loosely bound or constrained by ideas about what the abstractions require.

The play in the joints may be more or less, and it is differently theorized by different legal theory schools. It is nonetheless obviously large enough in practice so that very left-wing and very right-wing versions of capitalism can claim liberal or Liberal fidelity. While pursuing a "hermeneutic of suspicion" against their enemies, all ideological formations defend their radically different rule choices as consistent with the abstractions. It is the actual ground level positive regime of state law that emerges from their continuous conflicting law-making projects, rather than the abstractions, that determines distributive outcomes.[50]

Reconstructing the Legal Presuppositions of Ricardian Rent

Unlike Marx, Ricardo has nothing at all to say about the legal regime underlying his model. But his presupposition, as best as I can reconstruct it, is the same as Marx's explicit idea and is shared with modern day neoclassical welfare economists. It is that the property regime in force will clearly identify someone as the owner. He will enjoy very strong legal entitlements about what is going to be done on the land that he owns. Landlords will operate in a regime of virtually complete freedom of contract when it comes to their transactions with farmers and farmers likewise in transactions through intermediaries with the wheat market. In these bargaining relationships, neither party will have the right to "threaten" the other in any way, except for threatening not to transact at all.

The statement that the landlord appropriates "all the surplus" also seems to presuppose that the landlord can enforce the rent bargain that emerges from the exercise of these legal entitlements. He can get a state agency to adjudicate his claim and then order a judgment in his favor that will be carried out with official force if necessary. And enforcement is free as well as easy—landlords have nothing to fear from litigation.

Bargaining Power as the Determinant of the Distribution of Surplus

In both models, the key is that there is no meaningful bargaining either between landlords and farmers or between capitalists and workers. In each case, the labor theory of value seems to dictate the winner take all outcome, with the famer and worker each getting the "value" of what is offered. A neoclassical read, by contrast, might imagine that all the farmers/workers are identical, more numerous than employers, prevented from any kind of combination, and all willing to work for a common minimum if nothing better is offered. In contrast, the landlords and capitalists (not "farmers") are positioned to "hold out" until the others come down to the minimum rent/wage.

The picture of zero bargaining power makes sense given the assumptions of the model, but it is my reconstruction rather than what they wrote, again because the labor theory of value led them astray. As soon as we make the model a tiny bit more complex, bargaining power will reemerge as the best way to understand the outcomes. In the Ricardo case, differences among farmers will generate bargaining power for some farmers, allowing them to demand a share of surplus.

Some farmers will be "better at it" than others, in the sense that for any number of reasons they can produce at less cost and generate more surplus than the average. They will get a premium in the form of lower rent, that is, some share of the "surplus surplus" they generate. Even among equally productive farmers, some are better than others from the landlord's point of view. For example, a farmer who has been of standard quality for a particular landlord for a long period of time should have a higher than normal value to the landlord because reengaging him saves the "costs of search" and the risks of mistaken choice in replacing him.

This analytic is the same as that I proposed for a capitalist firm in the discussion of the Marx model, and it applies to landlords as firms as well. Some will be better than others at their single task of selecting and checking up on farmers, and so benefit from the surplus surplus, and so forth. The disposition of the surplus surplus, and symmetrically of losses, will occur through bargaining in which each side, not just the landlord, has some degree of power.

How much power? A multitude of factors affect the outcome, but we are interested in the legal regime. There are systemic advantages and disadvantages generated by the legal regime, in the sense that changes in the regime in a given direction will advantage some and disadvantage others, both between and within the classes. There are valuable rights on both sides rather than only on the stronger side. This is the important realist insight of the legal institutional economist Robert Hale.[51]

Legal Rules Powerfully Affect Bargaining Power

When we set out to analyze the impact of legal rules on party bargaining power, we can't start at the level of "property" or "contract," these are vague and indeterminate abstractions, not rules at all in the sense we are looking for. To repeat, the rules are contingent outcomes, each one the crystallization or result of a particular complex decision process in a particular political/economic conjuncture.[52] So we start with rules of positive law, of state law, which we identify in the normal lawyer way.

At every stage of capitalist development there have been multiple layered legal orders surviving within state law, with contradictory relationships to the rules of the presupposed models. We can trace historically and model analytically how the ability of parties to appeal from one normative order to another can influence outcomes. Moreover, even where the formal, official, supposedly state enforced order has been clear, there have always been areas where it was resisted or just not enforced or defied by "informal" counternorms enforced by nonstate actors. Once again, we can trace these historically and model them analytically.[53]

Ricardian Examples

Modeling distributional effects on the basis of the actual rules and institutional practices in force is a radically different enterprise than modeling them assuming absolute property rights, freedom of contract, no threats other than walking away, costless enforcement, and so on. First of all, not all the landlords are the same, as we've seen already. Let's imagine a Ricardo-era farmer on a five-year lease and who has done a significant amount of improvement of the property that belongs to the landlord if the lease is terminated. From the landlord's point of view, it is a good deal because he's above average as a producer and replacing him means search costs and uncertainty.

The lease comes up for renegotiation. The landlord offers to renew at the old rent, representing the standard rate of profit on capital. The sitting farmer says: "I am not going to do it. That's *much* more rent than I'm willing to pay." The landlord says: "Okay, I'll take a 10 percent rent reduction." The farmer responds, "You jest." Things go downhill from there. The landlord has on the tip of his tongue to respond, "Okay, out with the old! Bring in the new!" But what will happen, he thinks, if he refuses to renew and takes on a new farmer?

Begin with an imaginary extreme case (we are modeling not writing social history!). All these buildings have been built by the farmer, but the lease says that they all belong to the landlord. "Where is the nearest fire department?" is a question that might go through the minds of the parties. Let's imagine that in this English countryside there are volunteers and bubbling brooks and guys with pumps. They pump the water out, carry it around on horse drawn wagons, and pump it out on site. Why is this relevant? Because there's a possibility that if the farmer experiences extreme outrage at ethically condemned landlord behavior—or has a criminal bent—maybe he is going to try to burn the place down.

Even an explicit threat to burn the place down is not a crime without an overt "act" of some kind. The farmer has little to lose by threatening, but of course if the barn does burn the threat will play a big part in a criminal case against him. Perhaps he never says anything remotely threatening, but everyone knows that there is a possibility in this kind of situation and more specifically with these actors in this drama. The possibility, maybe conveyed nonverbally, can play a significant role in the negotiation. This is a gap in the legal system from the landlord's point of view but a beneficial concession to the difficulties of proof from the farmer's point of view. The consequence should be better bargains for farmers, maybe only for plausibly threatening ones, but if they are hard to tell from the nice guys, then for all farmers.

But you say the whole point of the Ricardian presupposition is that the legal order should respond if not to implicit threats then certainly to actual arson. That should drastically reduce the credibility of overt or implicit threats and partially restore landlord bargaining power (BP). But now let's imagine that rural criminal law is in the hands of the justices of the peace who are . . . the landlords. Up landlord BP. Now add that enforcement is by a posse of the local landlords, a voluntary activity with only the vaguest rules about what the posse can do, and landlord BP increases even more. The rules governing harms that can be inflicted either in the course of bargaining or in the event of rupture are major determinants of bargaining power. They are virtually never discussed in either the economics or law and economics literature.[54]

A more moderate and technical and lawyerlike example is the law of distraint. Distraint is the right of the landlord, when owed rent, to enter the premises and take personal property off the premises, as a security for the future payment of the rent. Distraint doesn't exist in modern American landlord-tenant law. A landlord who tried it would probably face criminal trespass charges and anyway has plenty of other brutal remedies available. But distraint in its day was an effective threat. It was a socioeconomic catastrophe to have a constable come into your house and "temporarily" take away everything of value.

But what if distraint in the countryside were a self-help remedy—no help from the state, such as it was. That would reduce landlord BP unless landlords had domestics with arms, and so on. The parties bargain with each other over the surplus "in the Shadow of the [actual] Law [in force]."[55] It's a free market system. Everybody is actively picking strategies and making moves. The outcome is the highly uncertain product of everyone going at each other. It looks as though agency is everywhere. It looks as though they're the masters and mistresses of their own fate because they bargained to closure. And each side respected the legal rights of the other, so neither has a ground for complaint.

But remember the basic CLS idea that neither the abstract concept of property nor that of contract (and certainly not the chaos of tort theory) gives a plausible description of what the rules are going to be in actual countrysides and urban neighborhoods. The efforts of Kant, Bentham, Rawls, Dworkin, and Posner to demonstrate what they ought to be (not even guessing at what they are in any particular place or time) are not convincing to any lawyer or law professor I know. Nonetheless these variable rules about what you can do to harm the other during bargaining or threaten to do after rupture very often determine outcomes. The point: the landlord isn't going to get the difference between an imagined pure cost of production and the market price. Different landlords confronting different farmers will get different outcomes.

How to Explain Gross Over-Reward of Landlords and Capitalists

One conclusion that follows from the discussion to this point is that if the actual real-life pattern of distribution seems to grossly over-reward capitalists and landlords, it is not because commodities have legal form and their necessary legal form is determined by the abstract ideas of property and contract. The gross over-reward is the consequence of bargaining based on entitlements to property and contract rules, but these are the product of contestation between social forces only marginally constrained by fidelity to the abstractions. The abstract commodity legal form is a historical artifact not an eternal truth, just as Marx demonstrated. But the same is true of its instantiation in positive law on the books and pluralist law in action.

Recognizing that the distribution of income and wealth emerges from bargaining structured by the contingent and incoherent ensemble of legal rules renders the distribution contingent as well. That doesn't make it any less grossly unjust. The CLS distributional analysis approach works to make it intelligible in all its nastiness through the (Marx inspired) analytics of law and political economy rather than through a conceptual definition of capitalism and the labor theory of value. In this version, political economy starts with groups led by elites, understood not just as collections of individuals but as collectives (usually, but not always, loose) with goals and strategies that are based on shared material and ideological, or "ideal," interests. They cooperate in social production and reproduction and are at the same time in conflict over the distribution of stakes that are both material and "ideal." Relations of domination and subordination are pervasive.

The stakes include the resources necessary for success in the next iteration of the conflict as it unfolds within the institutionally established rules of the game, including law and in our case prominently, but not exclusively the law of property and contract. The framework is given at any particular moment but is in constant modification because the rules of the game are among its objects.[56]

Reformers Address the Models' Alleged Outcomes in Various Ways

The gross over-reward of landlords and capitalists has motivated many different arguments for social reform. For Ricardo, tax rent and abolish the corn laws; for Marx, expropriate the expropriators. All the way to the contemporary moment, the model of surplus appropriation, recontextualized and without the technical apparatus of the labor theory of value, has served as one analytical basis for dozens of proposals and kinds of proposals as to "what is to be done."

If you believe gross inequality follows ineluctably from the operation of the commodity form, meaning property and contract law systems, we should promote these four ideas. First, *social democratic regulatory regimes*, including everything from factory laws, rent control, and minimum wage law, through farm subsidies and (compensated) land reform, and on to the legal protection of worker associations and through to labor law, public utility law, regulation of financial institutions, and consumer protection law. The public interest, social welfare, and social and economic rights should be used as guides. *Second, progressive taxation of income from land and capital and redistributive government spending* from compulsory public education to health care to straightforward income support. *Third, "public not private property,"* as in publicly owned railroads, public housing, state owned and run hospitals and nursing homes, state owned banks, and state ownership of key industries such as coal and steel (the British Labor Party's "commanding heights of the economy"). *Fourth, "abolishing the commodity form"* for land use and control of the means of production—the kolkhoz and the Soviet industrial "enterprise." The commons.

Like Ricardo and Marx themselves, each of these four modes either ignores private law altogether or presupposes it as having its own internal commodity logic. Law seen this way is a necessary but nonproblematic neutral institutional background condition for working out the autonomous logics of options 1 through 3 or the enemy to be done away with altogether in option 4.

THE CLS APPROPRIATION OF THE RICARDO/MARX MODEL OF THE DISTRIBUTION OF SURPLUSES AMONG SOCIOECONOMIC GROUPS

The "left institutionalist/legal realist/CLS strand" I pursue here is not inconsistent with any of the above, but it is sharply distinct and much less well known.

Antisubordination, Political Economy Analytics, Constructive/ Defensive Program, Both Structural and Palliative

This CLS distributive agenda is: Promote egalitarian distributional change and economic and social reconstruction in the interests of people who are oppressed and exploited more or less permanently, within the U.S. political economy.[57] Equally, and at times more important, defend distributive arrangements that favor the oppressed and exploited against roll back powered by the neoliberal claim that they everywhere and always "hurt the people they are trying to help." Apply conventional neoclassical welfare economics to legal distributional questions that arise when we take seriously the idea that the rules of private law, as distinct from tax and spend and regulation, powerfully influence distribution. They do this because they "constitute" the bargaining power of economic actors. They do this "before" taxation and regulation.

The argument is that pro-poor private law rules will in many circumstances force the strong party (landlord, bank, retail merchant, gentrifier, mortgage investor) to "eat" the benefit from surplus. The mechanisms of the Ricardian tax on landlords and the Marxian defense of factory legislation still work on contemporary private law transactional regimes. This is true whether the rule changes in question are merely palliative of oppression and exploitation (but still better than nothing) or "structural," meaning promising substantial and permanent shifts in surplus in an egalitarian direction. We abstract and redeploy this analytic for other legal contexts, as we have already done to one degree or another for public international law, local government law, family law, and the law of race.[58]

Birth of Contemporary Neo-Ricardian Distributional Analysis: Low-Income Housing Markets

Contemporary legal distributional analysis was born in the late 1960s and early 1970s out of the political/economic crisis centered on the racial transformation of American cities and its impact on housing: the continuous arrival in northern cities of large numbers of Black migrants from the Jim Crow South; government-supported white flight from the inner city and close-in suburbs; and the transition from white to all-Black and very poor neighborhoods. Poor Black neighborhoods underwent disinvestment by the housing and financial sectors and by the withdrawal of health and sanitation services by large city governments.[59]

After Nixon's victory in 1968 the federal government adopted a hands-off policy in the face of the downward spirals in poor Black neighborhoods, along with an ineffectual "Black capitalism" strategy. The post–Warren Supreme Court rejected attempts to force integration of suburban housing and schools under the Civil Rights Acts, as well as the argument that segregated inner city schools should have equal funding with rich white suburban ones. Around 1980 the return of the upper middle class to the inner city set off a second wave of massive neighborhood change via gentrification and displacement of poor by rich residents.

During the whole period since 1968, including downward spirals and gentrifying bubbles, the types of proposals discussed at the end of this book have had little traction. Reformers have been unable to adopt tax and spend or sweeping regulation in favor of poor neighborhoods. Government ownership has been so "out of fashion" in the neoliberal fever that tearing down public housing projects has been more common than building them. Decommodification has been a vital social practice—but only in communes and cults and housing and food co-ops.

In this situation, it made sense to apply distributional analysis to the more granular level of the existing common law and statutory legal regimes that obviously impacted poor Black neighborhoods in their relationship to rich white suburbs. The motive was to find distributive arguments favoring the poor under the existing political circumstances. This involved finding the economics literature that described the market in question and figuring out where there were surpluses in the existing regime to be defended against neoliberal attack or to be pursued for transfer to the poor—whether at the expense of landlords, banks, taxpayers, investors, insurance companies, rich tenants, or rich homeowners, to name some obvious targets. The next steps are closely parallel to Ricardo's analyses of taxes on the pure rent of land and the elimination of tariffs on wheat. The ways different kinds of legal rules, informal norms, and lacunae impact the rent bargain for poor ghetto tenants are similar to the way "distraint," or the landlords' justices of the peace with a posse to enforce the rules, influences rent in the revised Ricardo model.

Ricardo, Marx, and Ackerman

In 1971 Bruce Ackerman, then an assistant professor at the University of Pennsylvania Law School, published "Regulating Slum Housing Markets on Behalf of the Poor: Of Housing Codes, Housing Subsidies and Income Redistribution Policy," arguing for across the board enforcement of already existing housing codes in slum neighborhoods.[60] I think this is the first contemporary example of neo-Ricardian legal distributional analysis of the kind I've been discussing, and fifty years later it is still one of the most important. Ackerman argued that most landlords would absorb the increased costs of improving conditions, accepting reduced surplus without raising the rent.

Both conservatives and liberals believed that the reason for poor slum conditions was that the incomes of the poor were not large enough to pay for decent housing. The only feasible answers to slum conditions were public housing and subsidized new construction.[61] Ackerman's solution involved just a little public or a little subsidized housing but proposed to deliver a massive improvement of slum conditions at the expense of landlords and banks (!!). All at easily controlled efficiency costs (!!!).

Throughout the 1970s and 1980s, there was a combination of political mobilization of poor neighborhoods with committed legal representation through federally funded neighborhood legal services offices. The policy debates were consequently more than academic and represented a minority strand in both legal scholarship and activist practice. As the housing analytic developed over the years, other strands of CLS work abstracted, transposed, and reapplied it to understand other fields of conflict between strong and weak parties, as previously mentioned.

A Left of Liberal vs. Liberal Rationale for Rent-Seeking on Behalf of the Poor

Ackerman's 1971 article clearly formulated and addressed, I think for the first time in a liberal mode, the controversial ethics of instrumentalizing private law background rules to redistribute transactional surpluses from strong to weak parties. In his model, enforcing the housing code, which had been an unenforced dead letter, would, if it worked, deliberately impose a one-shot reduction in the market value of slum buildings. That would give rise to this question: "Why is it fair to impose a special obligation upon slum landlords to redistribute their wealth beyond that assumed by the rest of the population who simply pay their allotted share of the progressive income and estate tax?"[62] This question is no less germane to debates about regulation today, in the age of the Consumer Protection Bureau, the revival of the rent control debate, and the "eviction crisis," than it was in the age of summer ghetto riots and George Wallace's presidential campaigns.[63]

Ackerman's justification, in answer to his own question, relied on his criticism of the landlord for constant "disregard for human personality" and for "weaving the larger social injustice of the maldistribution of income into the fabric of [the landlord's] life."[64] But opportunistic rent-seeking on behalf of the poor, it seems to me, doesn't rest on the moralistic critique of the individual slum landlord. My own answer, which I think is reflective of what various other CLS inspired authors might say as well, is that the profits of individual slum landlords are a small subset of the mass of profit that enterprises of all kinds derive from dealings with the poor, from banks to auto and home insurance companies to supermarkets to holders of mortgage backed securities to pay day lenders to local appliance store owners. In the transactions in question, the superior bargaining power of the strong party extracts an arbitrary and unjust share of the available surplus.[65]

Targeted intervention through the legal regime governing the transaction can reallocate some or all of the surplus to, for example, neighborhood residents, just as Ackerman painstakingly and convincingly demonstrated. Activists, lawyers, and nonlawyers who have legal tools, ranging from local regulations (as in the housing code) to class actions to focused neighborhood litigation campaigns to individual representation, should use them opportunistically against any of the strong parties wherever they are likely to work.

The ethical justification for opportunism, that is, going after whichever exploiting transaction partner appears vulnerable to local expropriation, is first that the profit in question has no ethical claim to respect. Second, given the very limited power that the system makes available for the defense of the interests of the poor, whoever has a chance to use some of it has to use it situationally or not at all.

This does not preclude, indeed it seems to demand, that the opportunistic intervention take into account *to some extent* the varying degrees of reciprocal vulnerability of exploiters, for example, upwardly mobile Black owner-occupant landlords of slum buildings.[66] However, as an activist, I put myself (yes, of course, unsolicited) in the position of trying to represent, both politically and professionally, the interests of a class of people in a fight with another class or group. With that commitment and commitment to the particularity of "the situation," I think it is ethically unproblematic to deploy what legal resources we can muster to go after strong party rents wherever we can find them and to defend historic social democratic successes against neoliberal clawback.

In this current, we attempt rent-seeking on behalf of the poor as a tactic of expropriation in what we see as the macro-systemic group conflict over distribution between strong and weak parties. We hope we are on the right side, and that our commitment to act for that side won't turn out to have been a wrong choice. We also hope without guarantees that ethically uneasy self-selection into the advocate role deploying our elite status perks won't one day seem counterproductive for the cause, and arrogant to boot. It is reassuring that given our far marginality vis-à-vis power it is unlikely that we can do a lot of harm. What we say and do in the battle is, of course, subject to all kinds of restrictive moral imperatives. Although it is a battle and subject to the logic of conflict rather than cooperation or compromise, it is nothing like a Schmittian crisis in which the exception suspends the rule.[67] But neither is it Ackerman's question: "What are the obligations of a citizen of an unjust state that is capable of reformation?"

When trying to decide "how far to go," opportunistically, against the property rights of the other side, I think the most helpful reference may be to notions such as "don't target innocents," "when you can't avoid hurting them, observe an idea of proportionality in terms of the gains obtained at their expense," and "excessive force is wrong no matter the provocation." In short, in rent-seeking on behalf of the poor, the heavily reconstructed but still decisionist doctrines of the modern law of war may be more useful than the hopeful legalism of liberal political theory.[68]

NOTES

1. Joseph A. Schumpeter, *History of Economic Analysis* (Hove, East Sussex: Psychology, 1954); and Ben Seligman, *Main Currents in Modern Economic Thought* (New York: Free Press of Glencoe, 1962).
2. David Ricardo, *The Works and Correspondence of David Ricardo*, ed. Piero Sraffa in collaboration with M. H. Dobb, vol. 1, *Principles of Political Economy and Taxation* (1817) (Indianapolis: Liberty Fund, 2005), 65.
3. Ricardo, *The Works and Correspondence*, 1:69–70.
4. Ricardo, *The Works and Correspondence*, 1:79.
5. Ricardo, *The Works and Correspondence*, 1:67–69.
6. Edward Palmer Thompson, *The Making of the English Working Class* (New York: Vintage, 1966), 213–34; or what Marx calls "primitive accumulation." See Karl Marx, *Capital: A Critique of Political Economy*, vol. 1, *The Process of Production of Capital* (Moscow: Progress, 1887), 1:506–47.
7. Ricardo, *The Works and Correspondence*, 1:126.
8. Ricardo, *The Works and Correspondence*, 1:79–80.
9. Ricardo, *The Works and Correspondence*, 1:68–69, 1:79.
10. Ricardo, *The Works and Correspondence*, 1:67–68.
11. This is made explicit by Eric Roll in Eric Roll, *A History of Economic Thought*, 3rd ed. (Hoboken, NJ: Prentice Hall, 1953), 80–85.
12. Ricardo, *The Works and Correspondence*, 1:71–72.
13. Ricardo, *The Works and Correspondence*, 1:70.
14. Ricardo, *The Works and Correspondence*, 1:72.
15. Ricardo, *The Works and Correspondence*, 1:74.
16. Ricardo, *The Works and Correspondence*, 1:69.
17. Ricardo, *The Works and Correspondence*, 1:69–70.
18. Ricardo, *The Works and Correspondence*, 1:74.
19. Ricardo, *The Works and Correspondence*, 1:72.
20. Ricardo, *The Works and Correspondence*, 1:173–75.
21. Ricardo, *The Works and Correspondence*, 1:173.
22. Henry George, *Progress and Poverty: An Inquiry Into the Cause of Industrial Depressions and of Increase of Want with Increase of Wealth: The Remedy* (New York: D. Appleton, 1882).
23. William J. Barber, *A History of Economic Thought* (Middleton, CT: Wesleyan University Press, 2009), 124–53.
24. Marx, *Capital*, 1:150–61.

25. The reason that large numbers of factory workers are available to work for subsistence wages is that Ricardo's improving landlords in alliance with innovating capitalist farmers have driven the agricultural population off the land as they reduced the labor input to agriculture while enormously expanding productivity (the "enclosure movement"). Once they are in the city en masse, a capitalist who paid more than a subsistence wage would be put out of business by his more "rational" competitors. See Marx, *Capital*, 1:506–43.
26. Marx, *Capital*, 1:27–60.
27. Adolf Augustus Berle and Gardiner Coit Means, *The Modern Corporation and Private Property* (New York: Macmillan, 1933).
28. Ricardo, *The Works and Correspondence*, 1:78–79.
29. Ricardo, *The Works and Correspondence*, 1:93.
30. Ricardo, *The Works and Correspondence*, 1:111–12.
31. Emery Kay Hunt and Mark Lautzenheiser, *History of Economic Thought: A Critical Perspective* (London: Routledge, 2011), 96–98.
32. On the significance of the productive/unproductive distinction in classical economics, see Donald Harris, "The Classical Theory of Economic Growth," in *The New Palgrave Dictionary of Economics*, ed. Matias Vernengo, Esteban Perez Caldentey, and Barkley J. Rosser Jr, 2nd ed. (London: Macmillan, 2007).
33. Ricardo, *The Works and Correspondence*, 1:78–79.
34. Hunt and Lautzenheiser, *History of Economic Thought*, 70–71.
35. Marx, *Capital*, 1:434–505.
36. Marx, *Capital*, 1:261–328.
37. Marx, *Capital*, 1:261–328.
38. Marx, *Capital*, 1:438–42.
39. Marx, *Capital*, 1:261–328.
40. Max Weber, "Politics as a Vocation," in *From Max Weber: Essays in Sociology*, trans. and ed. H. H. Gerth and C. Wright Mills (London: Routledge, 2009), 77–128.
41. Marx, *Capital*, 1:284–87.
42. Compare with Georg Lukács, "Reification and the Consciousness of the Proletariat," in *History and Class Consciousness: Studies in Marxist Dialectics*, trans. Rodney Livingstone (London: Merlin, 1967), 83–222.
43. Compare with Karl Renner, *The Institutions of Private Law and Their Social Functions* (London: Routledge & K. Paul, 1949).
44. Marx, *Capital*, 1:261–328.
45. Marx, *Capital*, 1:261–328.
46. "Modern Industry, indeed, compels society, *under penalty of death*, to replace the detail-worker of to-day, grappled by life-long repetition of one and the same trivial operation, and thus reduced to the mere fragment of a man, by the fully developed individual, fit for a variety of labours, ready to face any change of production, and to whom the different social functions he performs, are but so many modes of giving free scope to his own natural and acquired powers." Marx, *Capital*, 1:19.
47. This is Hegelian not just because it is dialectical but because this particular dialectic is fully anticipated/predicted in Hegel's Philosophy of Right. See Aldo Schiavone, *Alle Origini Del Diritto Borghese Hegel Contro Savigny* (Roma-Bari, Italy: Laterza, 1984).

48. "In England the process of social disintegration is palpable. When it has reached a certain point, it must react on the Continent. There it will take a form more brutal or more humane, according to the degree of development of the working class itself. Apart from higher motives, therefore, their own most important interests dictate to the classes that are for the nonce the ruling ones, the removal of all legally removable hindrances to the free development of the working class." Marx, *Capital*, 1:7.
49. It is interesting that Marx supports this claim with the observation that workers tell inspectors that the reduction in hours is so valuable that they would want it even if it cost some wage reduction (not that it has caused one). Marx, *Capital*, 1:276–78.
50. Felix S. Cohen, "Transcendental Nonsense and the Functional Approach," *Columbia Law Review* 35, no. 6 (1935): 809–49, https://doi.org/10.2307/1116300. See also Duncan Kennedy, *A Critique of Adjudication [fin de siècle]* (Cambridge, MA: Harvard University Press, 2009).
51. Robert L. Hale, "Coercion and Distribution in a Supposedly Non-Coercive State," *Political Science Quarterly* 38, no. 3 (1923): 470–94, https://doi.org/10.2307/2142367; and Duncan Kennedy, "The Stakes of Law, or Hale and Foucault," *Legal Studies Forum* 15, no. 4 (1991): 327–66.
52. When rules fit together in a coherent way, they make sense not because they follow from an abstraction, even a modest level abstraction, but because they represent analogous resolutions of perennial conflicts, like, say, the conflict between landlords and farmers phrased in the common (indeterminate) legal *langue*.
53. Boaventura de Sousa Santos, "Law: A Map of Misreading. Toward a Postmodern Conception of Law," *Journal of Law and Society* 14, no. 3 (1987): 279–302, https://doi.org/10.2307/1410186.
54. But see Arthur Allen Leff, "Injury, Ignorance and Spite. The Dynamics of Coercive Collection," *Yale Law Journal* 80, no. 1 (1970):1–46, https://doi.org/10.2307/795095.
55. Robert H. Mnookin and Lewis Kornhauser, "Bargaining in the Shadow of the Law: The Case of Divorce," *Yale Law Journal* 80, no. 5 (1979): 950–98, https://doi.org/10.2307/795824.
56. Karl Marx, *The Eighteenth Brumaire of Louis Bonaparte*, trans. Daniel De Leon (New York: International, 1898). Among many examples of this notion of political economy that I find inspiring are W. E. B. Du Bois, *Black Reconstruction in America: An Essay Toward a History of the Part Which Black Folk Played in the Attempt to Reconstruct Democracy in America, 1860–1880* (New York: Oxford University Press, 2007); and Yves Dezalay and Bryant Garth, *The Internationalization of Palace Wars: Lawyers, Economists, and the Contest to Transform Latin American States* (Chicago, IL: University of Chicago Press, 2002). See also Catharine A. MacKinnon, "Feminism, Marxism, Method, and the State: An Agenda for Theory," *Signs: Journal of Women in Culture and Society* 7, no. 3 (1982): 515–44, https://www.jstor.org/stable/3173853; and Catharine MacKinnon, "Marxism, Feminism, Method, and the State: Toward Feminist Jurisprudence," *Signs: Journal of Women in Culture and Society* 8, no. 4 (April 1982): 635–58, https://www.jstor.org/stable/3173687. Another inspiration is Antonio Gramsci, *Selections from the Prison Notebooks*, ed. Quentin Hoare and Geoffrey N. Smith (New York: International, 1971). For a political economy inspired analysis of law, see Duncan Kennedy, "Legal Economics of U.S.

Low Income Housing Markets in Light of 'Informality' Analysis," *Journal of Law in Society* 4, no. 1 (2002): 71–98; Duncan Kennedy, "African Poverty," *Washington Law Review* 87, no. 1 (2012): 205–35; Duncan Kennedy, "Commentary on Anti-Eviction and Development in the Global South," in *Stones of Hope: How African Activists Reclaim Human Rights to Challenge Global Poverty*, ed. Lucie E. White and Jeremy Perelman (Stanford, CA: Stanford University Press, 2010), 41–50; and Duncan Kennedy, "A Political Economy of Contemporary Legality," in *The Law of Political Economy: Transformation in the Function of Law*, ed. Pool Kjaer (Cambridge: Cambridge University Press, 2020), 89–124.

57. Ruth Colker, "Anti-Subordination Above All: Sex, Race, and Equal Protection," *NYU Law Review* 61, no. 6 (1986): 1003–66, http://hdl.handle.net/1811/87218.

58. For public international law, see David Kennedy, *A World of Struggle* (Princeton, NJ: Princeton University Press, 2018). For local government law, see Gerald Frug, "The City as a Legal Concept," *Harvard Law Review* 93, no. 6 (1980): 1057, https://doi.org/10.2307/1340702; and Gerald E. Frug, *City Making* (Princeton, NJ: Princeton University Press, 2001). For family law, see Janet Halley, Prabha Kotiswaran, Rachel Rebouché, and Hila Shamir, eds., *Governance Feminism: An Introduction* (Minneapolis: University of Minnesota Press, 2018). For the law of race, see Alan Freeman, "Antidiscrimination Law from 1954 to 1989: Uncertainty, Contradiction, Rationalization, Denial," in *The Politics of Law: A Progressive Critique*, ed. David Kairys (New York: Pantheon, 1990), 121–50; Cheryl Harris, "Whiteness as Property," *Harvard Law Review* 106, no. 8 (1993): 1707, https://doi.org/10.2307/1341787; and Richard Ford, "The Boundaries of Race: Political Geography in Legal Analysis," *Harvard Law Review* 107, no. 8 (1994): 1841–921, https://doi.org/10.2307/1341760.

59. Daniel Roland Fusfeld and Timothy Mason Bates, *The Political Economy of the Urban Ghetto* (Carbondale, IL: SIU, 1984); William Julius Wilson, *The Truly Disadvantaged: The Inner City, the Underclass, and Public Policy* (Chicago: University of Chicago Press, 2012); and Isabel Wilkerson, *The Warmth of Other Suns: The Epic Story of America's Great Migration* (New York: Random House, 2010).

60. Bruce Ackerman, "Regulating Slum Housing Markets on Behalf of the Poor: Of Housing Codes, Housing Subsidies and Income Redistribution Policy," *Yale Law Journal* 80, no. 6 (May 1971): 1093–197, https://doi.org/10.2307/795276.

61. This was the despairing liberal as well as the gleeful neoliberal view. See Joseph L. Sax and Fred J. Hiestand, "Slumlordism as a Tort," *Michigan Law Review* 65, no. 5 (1966): 869–92, https://doi.org/10.2307/1287089; and Walter J. Blum and Allison Dunham, "Slumlordism as a Tort–A Dissenting View," *Michigan Law Review* 66, no. 3 (January 1968): 451–64, https://doi.org/10.2307/1287246. Also, seemingly still unclear on the existence of landlord profits well after Ackerman's article, see Mark H. Lazerson, "In the Halls of Justice, the Only Justice Is in the Halls," in *The Politics of Informal Justice*, ed. Richard Abel, 2 vols. (New York: Academic, 1982), 1:119–63.

62. Ackerman, "Regulating Slum Housing Markets," 1169.

63. It is also the subject of an intense long-running debate in the law and economics literature initiated by Louis Kaplow and Steven Shavell arguing that redistribution through private law rules was inferior to tax and spend because it was less efficient, a priori. Louis Kaplow and Steven Shavell, "Why the Legal System Is Less Efficient

Than the Income Tax in Redistributing Income," *Journal of Legal Studies* 23, no. 2 (1994): 667–82, https://doi.org/10.1086/467941. For a review of the debate, see Matthew Dimick, "The Law and Economics of Redistribution," *Annual Review of Law and Social Science* 15 (2019): 559–82, https://doi.org/10.1146/annurev-lawsocsci-101518-043037. For my critique of Kaplow and Shavell, see Duncan Kennedy, "Law-and-Economics from the Perspective of Critical Legal Studies," in *The New Palgrave Dictionary of Economics and the Law*, ed. Peter Newman, 3 vols. (New York: Macmillan Reference, 1998), 465–74.

64. Ackerman, "Regulating Slum Housing Markets, 1177.
65. Fusfeld and Bates, *Political Economy*.
66. Ackerman, "Regulating Slum Housing Markets," 1174–75. I think his take in 1971 is still convincing against the tendency of white liberals to defend Black economic exploitation in the Black community that would look outrageous if claimed for business in general.
67. No, dear reader, nothing Schmittian here. Compare with Duncan Kennedy, "A Semiotics of Critique," *Cardozo Law Review* 22, nos. 3–4 (2000): 1147–90.
68. David Kennedy, *Of War and Law* (Princeton, NJ: Princeton University Press, 2006). The legal realist antecedents of this frame are in the scholarly debate about unfair competition in the 1930s.

CHAPTER 5

DISTRIBUTIONAL ANALYTICS AND THE TWAIL TRADITION

VASUKI NESIAH

Third World approaches to international law (TWAIL) emerged in the 1990s as an intellectual and political project that foregrounds the history of colonialism and neocolonialism in understanding international legal history and interpreting international laws and norms.[1] This reference to the "third world" is not only about geography but also about the dynamics of political history and international law's imbrication with colonialism, slavery, and capitalism.[2] TWAIL has expanded over the years and constitutes a diverse network of critically oriented scholars (largely of international law) who attend in different ways to the imbrication of the histories and legacies of colonialism and slavery in the legal, economic, and institutional architecture that enables, legitimizes, and reproduces an unjust world order. There are at least three foci of TWAIL scholarship: the politics of resources, the politics of knowledge, and the politics of the discipline. These three themes often function as intertwined lenses in unpacking and investigating the relationship between international law and the political economy of world-systems, international legal epistemologies, and the professional and practice dimensions of international law.

At the heart of each of these foci is an analysis of the uneven distribution of wealth and resources that underlies international legal arrangements. That analysis is not surprising given that TWAIL can be situated in relation to several left critical approaches to law, including "distributional analysis." Those who use the term "distributional analysis" within legal academia often reference a genealogy drawing from Marxism, more proximately critical legal studies, and those identified with heterodox approaches in international law.[3] In chapter 4 in this book, Duncan Kennedy offered a specific genealogy of left legal distributional analysis that drew from David Ricardo and Karl Marx. Kennedy highlights the role of property ownership in the Ricardo- and Marx-derived analytical frame regarding economic surplus and its distribution. The constitutive role of property ownership in the Ricardo-cum-Marx story can be affirmed, extended, and analogized to the role that the afterlives of colonialism and slavery play in TWAIL analytics of surplus and the structuring of its distribution.[4]

Marxist traditions have an important presence in TWAIL scholarship. Some have drawn from canonical works in Marxist legal analysis (such as Pashukanis's analysis of capitalist legal form or E. P. Thompson's analysis of law and class), others have drawn on critical approaches that may not always identify as Marxist but do identify as a left critique of liberal legalism that bears strong Marxist influences (such as critical legal studies in the United States or the UK, or left legal movements elsewhere).[5] However, those are not the only paths to distributional analysis within TWAIL scholarship. Significantly, TWAIL analysis of distribution has been shaped by intellectual traditions (originally from the Global South) that were themselves responding to the racial capitalist conjuncture of the postcolonial period. This included projects with roots outside of the legal academy, such as political economy (for example, the Latin American scholars of dependency associated with CEPAL who studied the world economic system forged by colonialism and capitalism) and cultural studies (scholars such as Edward Said and Gayatri Spivak, who studied the co-constitutive dynamics of power and knowledge in the colonial and postcolonial experience).[6] As I will discuss further, this insight into the mutually constitutive relationship between material dispossession and epistemic injustice has been vitally important in TWAIL analysis of surplus appropriation and dispossession. Within law, Bandung-era jurists, such as Mohammed Bedjaoui and George Abi Saab, have been especially influential in TWAIL understandings of how Global South actors may navigate the international legal system in the postcolonial era; they are sometimes referred to as TWAIL I in acknowledgment of an intergenerational debt to an earlier generation of anti-imperialist legal thinkers.[7] The Black radical tradition has also been important—be it through theorists of earlier generations such as W. E. B. Du Bois and C. L. R. James, or more contemporary critical race theory scholars such as Cheryl Harris and Hope Lewis.[8] A signature feature of TWAIL from its founding has been intellectual diversity and eclectic methodological debts with no politburo defining its boundaries. Thus TWAIL has largely emerged organically in ways that might be situated in a dialectic between the self-definition and affiliations of individual scholars and the scholarship that is anchored in the core claim referenced earlier about the centrality of the history of colonialism and neocolonialism in understanding international legal history and interpreting international laws and norms.

In the following pages, I seek to convey this theoretical eclecticism, but it does not do justice to the diversity of TWAIL work, or offer a comprehensive reading of TWAIL scholarship.[9] Indeed, there are many TWAILers (including some of those whose work I reference later) for whom distributional analysis as I describe it may not be a methodological orientation with which they affiliate, just as there are many who use the language of distributional analysis who may not understand TWAIL work in those terms. This chapter is a small window into TWAIL scholarship that is shaped by my own interest in conveying the intellectual and political yield of a TWAIL orientation in performing distributional analysis. This is, in other words, both a literature review and an argument for TWAIL-inflected distributional analytics.

Within the terms of this chapter, distributional analysis is not a sharply defined method but a repertoire of strategies. In elaborating these strategies, I draw from Janet Halley's description of the three steps of distributional analysis in relation to governance feminism. The four strategies I identify here do not map precisely onto Halley's three steps, but they are indebted to her description and the way she illuminates the logic of assessing the consequences of a law, a norm, or a policy. What I offer here is a mapping of how TWAIL scholarship takes account of the afterlives of colonialism and slavery in conducting distributional analysis to assess a new legal/policy intervention or in a retrospective assessment of a past intervention. I identify four strategies of distributional analysis employed by various TWAIL projects. These are not sequential strategies, but there is some value in spotlighting each of them in turn, even though in any particular project they may be intertwined dimensions. In fact, even in my discussion of any one strategy, you can see the shadows of other strategies.

TRACKING CAPITAL ACCUMULATION: IDENTIFYING THE SURPLUS

For many TWAIL scholars, the starting point for their analysis is tracking the accumulation of capital to identify an area of international law or an approach to international law that produces systematic winners and losers. Janet Halley refers to this preliminary analytical move as "identifying the surplus at stake," referring to what might be the potential profit or, concomitantly, the potential losses.[10]

The notion of "surplus value" invoked by this articulation of distributional analysis draws on Marx's description of labor's contribution to capital accumulation as the difference between the price of a product and the cost of its manufacture and distribution; capitalist profits arise through appropriation of that surplus value.[11] In a Marxist critique of political economy, that appropriation is simultaneously enabled and hidden by how claims over the means of production are structured by the interplay of several background structural and ideological elements. These include property law, factors that shaped the supply and demand of wage labor, the sociocultural dynamics of commodity fetishism, conceptions of the right to private property and inheritance and factors that help legitimize them, and more. The identification of the surplus does the critical, one may even say subversive, work of exposing the fact of capital accumulation off the backs of others through these embedded dimensions of business as usual.

In the context of TWAIL analysis of world-systems, the interplay of background structural and ideological elements may include international law and institutions; the factors that range from national sovereignty to the legal and sociocultural dynamics of the mobility and immobility of capital, goods, and people; conceptions of world history; and frameworks of trade, human rights etc. that help legitimize the dominant world order and enable the production and reproduction of capital accumulation and dispossession. Identifying the surplus entails mapping this interplay of elements in the particular context of profit and loss that is being analyzed; the context can vary—it could be an international trade deal, an environmental policy initiative, a humanitarian intervention, etc. Notably, a focus on the profit/loss assessment of specific local transactions/ negotiations between the stronger and weaker party is not the same as structural capital accumulation, including the way that multiple technologies of accumulation intersect and accrete over a longer historical period.[12] One way in which the colonial power/knowledge nexus referenced earlier informs the understanding of capital accumulation and dispossession in my account of relevant TWAIL scholarship is that it calls for a more capacious vocabulary of capital to refer not only to material resources but also epistemic resources. Thus the following discussion describes TWAIL analysis that focuses on material distribution as well as on the distribution of other registers of capital, such as expertise capital or humanitarian capital.

A TWAIL-simpatico history of capitalism reads colonialism and slavery as central to the dynamics that Marx theorized. Surplus appropriation from the Global North–based proletariat was subsidized, supplemented, and fueled by the dispossession and expropriation built into slave and colonial economies. Scholars as diverse as Rosa Luxemburg and Eric Williams spoke to these racial capitalist histories of property ownership and labor relations.[13] In this way, one can see this version of the TWAIL story as part of the same analytical family as that referenced by Duncan Kennedy, but also distinct in important ways.

The TWAIL critique and elaboration of the classical Marxist story of surplus appropriation can be seen as parallel to the work of feminist social reproduction theorists (such as Silvia Federici and Nancy Fraser) in foregrounding the domestic sphere as an often-ignored realm of subsidy, supplement and fuel of capitalist production. This idea of surplus appropriation through a whole range of background rules and ideologies, from the family to the colony, has been central to theorizing racial-capitalist exploitation and the structural conditions that enable it. Identifying the surplus that has been appropriated is sometimes obvious (slavery, for instance), but even though obvious it is also "forgotten"/normalized/backgrounded into the status quo.[14]

Much TWAIL scholarship on development has focused on identifying postcolonial moments of surplus appropriation by reframing a trade contract or a development loan as a moment of capital accumulation by the Global North, or concomitantly, a moment of capital dispossession of the Global South. For instance, Sundhya Pahuja's *Decolonising International Law* shows how international trade transactions, legal protections of foreign investors, development loans, and other dimensions of the development apparatus are structured in ways that are premised on theories and projects of universality and the rule of law that facilitate surplus appropriation by international and local rent-seeking elites.[15] Specifically, Pahuja identifies a surplus at stake in the "ruling rationality" of developmentalism and traces how the theories and projects it entails (the default orientation toward privileging the protection of foreign capital, for instance) shapes the terrain of bargaining.

For some TWAIL scholars, tracking the surplus has meant understanding where the "action" takes place. For James Gathii, this has meant going to the World Trade Organization (WTO) as a forum through which the ideologies, laws, and institutions that shape the international trade regime are negotiated.[16] In addition, Gathii argues that really following the surplus requires working out the complex interplay between the WTO's behind-the-scenes maneuvering and its front stage deals—i.e. there are background rules to the background rules. Thus a process of nested surplus accumulation must be taken into account in mapping the landscape and developing bargaining strategy to ensure one is playing with all eyes open about where and when surplus appropriation is taking place in the process of trade negotiations.[17]

Although he might not use the language of "surplus," Balakrishnan Rajagopal's *International Law from Below* identifies a surplus at stake in approaching international law from the perspective and agendas of international institutions as opposed to the perspective and agendas of transnational social movements.[18] These competing perspectives shadow and shape the relative bargaining power of different actors and, concomitantly, how that surplus is distributed. Thus, for instance, Rajagopal demonstrates how the perspective of international institutions empowers the relative bargaining position of the Global North, and that, in turn can further embed Global North interests in the functioning of international institutions so that the weight of the distributive consequences is exacerbated.

As noted earlier, within TWAIL scholarship as with distributional analysis more generally, identifying the surplus is not just a project of following the money. For instance, among other interventions, John Reynolds's *Emergency, Empire and International Law* is an analysis of what we might term "security capital."[19] Powerful states accumulate and deploy "security capital" by normalizing emergency rule while maintain the mythos of exceptionality. Often the argument is that powerful states need to take exceptional measures to ensure greater security for all. Reynolds's analysis helps show that what should concern us is not security per se but the distribution of security (how powerful actors accumulate it by rendering vulnerable actors even more insecure) and the mechanics of accumulating that surplus security. Ntina Tzouvala's recent book, *Capitalism as Civilisation*, tracks the surplus at stake in the discourse of civilization; she attends to the appropriation work done by the exclusions and hierarchies sutured together by the racial-capitalist and imperial logics of civilization talk in fashioning international law as a complement to the demands of global capital.[20] In a similar vein, I have analyzed how the abolition of the slave trade in the British Empire was framed as a mark of civilization. With humanitarian virtue as the currency of civilization, the British were keen to accrue "civilization capital" when an imperial system of slave labor was transitioned into an imperial system of indentured labor. The surplus appropriated from these imperial labor systems at the moment of transition was not only economic capital but also a civilizational capital that helped fuel, legitimize, and consolidate a new era of humanitarian imperialism.[21]

Much TWAIL work has focused on an accumulation of "humanitarian capital" through institutions such as the International Criminal Court or through international humanitarian and human rights law and policy. For instance, Ratna Kapur's *Gender, Alterity, and Human Rights* identifies the surplus in the ethical hierarchies that are invoked and cemented in the international human rights framework and the way this humanitarian capital accrues to empire and further dispossesses the colonized of their ethical voice.[22] This kind of work is central in showing that, as with all moments of surplus appropriation, in human rights too there are winners and losers—some people are accumulating ethical voice in the circuits of humanitarian talk and action, whereas others are being dispossessed of ethical voice in these same circuits.[23] In other words, there is profit in accumulating and wielding humanitarian capital—as is true of appropriating the surplus/capital accumulation more generally.

Kapur's approach to identifying injustices in the distribution of ethical voice jibes with Boaventura de Sousa Santos's tracking of epistemic voice in his discussion of "cognitive injustice." Cognitive injustice speaks to systematic winners and losers in the circulation of epistemic claims that profit from meaning-making; I read de Sousa Santos's attention to "ecologies of knowledge" as identifying an epistemic surplus.[24] For instance, in the arena of agriculture and development, monocultures have created maldistribution by reducing biodiversity and empowering powerful agricultural actors. In parallel ways an "epistemological monoculture" creates an epistemic ecosystem that delegitimizes and marginalizes some knowledge in ways that allows powerful actors to accumulate epistemic surplus.[25] The cognitive injustice that de Sousa Santos analyzes as the result of epistemic surplus appropriation is another way of referencing what Gayatri Chakravorty Spivak, following Foucault, refers to as "subjugated knowledge."[26]

Whatever the register—be it financial capital, ethical capital, or epistemic capital—identifying the surplus that has been appropriated is central to TWAIL analyses because the injustice of this appropriation is often the political imperative driving TWAIL critique.

MAKING A DOUBLE MOVE REGARDING NORMATIVE QUESTIONS

The injustice of surplus appropriation segues into a second register of how various TWAIL projects employ distributional analysis by invoking, but also interrogating, normative questions. TWAIL's prime directive is an avowedly normative project of anti-imperialism aimed at challenging the injustices of surplus appropriation that I just discussed. However, TWAIL scholars also interrogate how anti-imperialism has been defined and the laws and policies with which it has been identified. For instance, the 1955 Bandung Conference was invested in statehood and sovereignty as the necessary platform for anti-imperialism, but contemporary TWAIL scholars have interrogated statehood as sometimes reproducing colonial governance technologies and as an extension of imperialism rather than its counter.[27]

For Janet Halley, distributional analysis may begin by "separating is from ought." That is, it focuses on the work that law does instead of being blinded by law's constitutive justifications.[28] Peeling off normative blinders may help us see dimensions of the legal order that we otherwise wouldn't.

Helena Alviar García's work on the paradox of continued substantial inequality in an era of progressive law reform in Colombia is exemplary here. Her inquiry is prompted precisely by the fact that she is troubled by persistent inequality, but she then brackets how that normative agenda motivates a variety of left and liberal law reform initiatives in order to better analyze these reforms, and probe the unexpected consequences of a "culture of legality." This "double move" of normative investments alongside the bracketing of the intended normative agenda of these reforms, helps her understand how legalism contributed to reproducing social inequality despite the fact that progressive energies were directed at addressing inequalities in the text of the law.[29]

While normative agendas may motivate the inquiry in the first place the double move is a way to describe an analytical ground clearing operation to better understand how things work. It is, of course, impossible to suspend the normative—it saturates every question. How we identify the surplus—which actors are seen as relevant, what counts as maldistribution, what determines decision points, etc.—are all normative issues. However, rather than have our analysis boxed within normative framings of law and policy, distributional analysis helps unpack how received normative vocabularies might function as decoys, distracting from critical analysis or obscuring how things work.[30]

A commitment to sovereign equality might be another way to understand the normative commitments of TWAIL. Yet here too the double move in relation to the normative has been central to canonical TWAIL interventions, such as in Antony Anghie's book, *Imperialism, Sovereignty and the Making of International Law*.[31] At one level, his work seems motivated by the injustices of sovereign inequality as manifest, for instance, in the League of Nations mandate system and the trusteeship system in the UN era, including in how these inequalities played out in cases such as Australia's phosphate mining in the Republic of Nauru. However, in the book, he temporarily brackets normative questions about sovereign equality and focuses instead on *how* sovereignty actually works: with this focus, he shows that the dynamic of difference produces hierarchy even within—especially within—an apparently universal standard of sovereignty. Specifically, Anghie demonstrates that this universal standard, rather than being the path to equality, has become the scaffolding for hierarchy. For the colonized aspiring to be independent sovereign nation-states, their relationship to the universal standard was defined through lack, a need for tutelage; whereas others are recognized as always already sovereign so that the universal standard of sovereignty becomes precisely the route to the accumulation of what we might term "sovereignty capital."[32]

Anghie gets to these analytical insights not by reiterating the injustice of sovereign inequality but by focusing on the mechanics of accumulation, including how notions of race and cultural difference come to be constitutive of the universal standard. Although a normative commitment to sovereign equality remains a reference point for Anghie's work, his project is directed at interrogating the terms of equality. Sovereign equality is both a norm he is invested in and one that he temporarily brackets to analyze *how* the notion of sovereign equality can be precisely the vehicle for the appropriation of "surplus sovereignty" in the colonial encounter.

One dimension of the double move regarding normative questions is that it also calls for paying attention to outcome rather than motive. In my own work on the history of international criminal law (ICL) and the history of international conflict feminism (ICF), I have bracketed the humanitarian motives that are heralded in a range of ICL projects (such as the abolition of slavery in relation to the mid-nineteenth century tribunals), or the feminist motives that are heralded in a range of ICF projects (such as the inclusion of women through the "women, peace and security" agenda) to argue that these projects are about powerful actors (imperial Britain and the Security Council, respectively) arrogating authority to speak in the voice of the universal (or, in today's vernacular, "all lives matter").[33] Similarly, Usha Natarajan, in her work on the environment, analyzes legal and policy interventions not in terms of whether those interventions are in fact motivated by an environmentalist ethos but by focusing instead on *how* particular interventions are advanced and what some of the distributive consequences (intended or not) are of those interventions.[34]

The questions of motive—Are they environmentalist? Did they intend to exploit? Are they sexist? Are they racist?, etc.—are not always irrelevant questions. However, they can function as distractions from distributional analysis of how certain laws and policies are structurally sexist, racist, and exploitative. Laws advanced in the name of principles such as antiracism, for instance, might still have structurally racist consequences. In this vein, the double move often entails identifying and throwing a spotlight on commonsense normative vocabularies (such as antiracism or nondiscrimination) while at the same time normalizing the vocabularies that are not usually invoked with such a normative charge (such as considering racial privilege as a kind of property). In this regard, TWAIL scholars have been enormously influenced by critical race theory scholar Cheryl Harris's article, "Whiteness as Property," which speaks of racialization as not only about identity and affiliation but also, fundamentally, a project of stealth material distribution.[35] Rather than claim identities that are themselves "wounded attachments," we may be better positioned to see *how* identities do different kinds of distributional work even when they travel unmarked.[36]

Relatedly, bracketing the normative can surface other historical processes. For instance, by bracketing the antislavery motives of abolitionists, the historian Eric Williams was better positioned to unpack the other drivers of abolition and its consequences. Williams offers a cleareyed analysis of how the shift from mercantile capitalism to industrial capitalism changed the profitability equation for those who profited from both slavery and wage labor.[37] Although normative issues undergird all of Williams's questions, his normative commitments are present only as background for much of *Capitalism and Slavery* because the normative cause of abolition can also be a blinder defining what a historian of that period sees and doesn't see. By focusing on the "how"—the mechanics of trade, industrialization, and capital accumulation—he is able to track the surplus value generated by the triangular trade of enslaved peoples from Africa to cotton plantations in the Americas to the factories of Manchester in producing European wealth and thereby offer a deeper analysis of the costs and benefits of abolition.[38]

In that spirit, let me now delve more deeply into the third element in the distributive analysis repertoire, which is precisely the "how" question that the bracketing of the normative often allows.

DESCRIBING HOW THINGS WORK: THE MECHANICS OF SURPLUS APPROPRIATION

The core analytical work of TWAIL's distributional analysis is the third register, which we turn to now: tracking *how* surplus is accumulated. In much TWAIL work, including the scholarship referenced previously, the double move on normative questions is a ground-clearing operation that enables scholars to be better positioned to track capital accumulation (financial and otherwise) by understanding the *mechanics* of appropriation. The work I have referenced in relation to the first two registers of identifying the surplus or making the double move on the normative questions also focuses on the "how" question—sometimes this has entailed investigation of how different legal rules work (such as Anghie's work on how the dynamic of difference gets deployed in defining rules of sovereignty), or it may be about how institutions work (such as Gathii's work on the front stage/back stage dynamic of the WTO), or how particular individuals and traditions pursue their projects (such as Natarajan's work on green washing), or how the psychological imperatives of domination and subjugation work (such as is implicit in Kapur's work on who gets to claim humanitarian judgment), or how different invocations of and interventions in the domain of what we may call the culture of economics and the economics of culture work (such as Alviar's work on the culture of legality in Colombian jurisprudence). The "how" question flips a thematic focus (such as development as an arena of surplus appropriation) into a question (if there is dispossession through development, how does it take place?).

The work of TWAIL scholars on surplus generated through land and natural resource expropriation is especially illuminating in showing that even if the answer to the "how" question includes guns and theft at the moment of colonial encounter, it also includes law and the legal imagination. Because background laws and norms continue to be key to ongoing technologies of colonial governance, asking the "how" questions entails focusing analytical energies on describing the legal and ideological technologies of dispossession. This internal critique of law has a long tradition in legal scholarship (often identified with the legal realists), but it also has a resonance in other disciplines. For instance, the cultural studies scholar La Paperson tells a similar story about how "technologies to make land into property also remade Indigenous African bodies" and paved the way for capital accumulation. In his case, the technologies extend from prioritizing the written word and title (over oral traditions and occupancy) to legal rules creating a new private property market.[39]

In a series of articles on international environmental law, Karin Mickelson has traced how legal frameworks for property and territory, such as *terra nullius*, *res communis*, and the common heritage of mankind, helped enable settler colonial surplus appropriation.[40] She shows how instrumental notions of economically productive and efficient uses of the natural environment have empowered and legitimized the reach of these legal frameworks into the contemporary moment so that narrowly economistic notions of productivity and efficiency can function like a new version of *terra nullius* that dispossesses Indigenous communities and other vulnerable groups whose relationship to land or property might be sustainable and valuable on many fronts but not commodifiable. Hernando de Soto's notion of dead capital may be analogous to this "neo-*terra nullius*" discourse to which Mickelson points.[41] Julia Dehm's analysis shows how carbon offset schemes and the tenure reform policies that accompany them have pulled forest-dwelling Indigenous people into the market economy and resulted in further dispossession.[42] Sylvia Kang'ara looks beyond property law, tracking how land expropriation gets absorbed into notions of modernity, international market logics, and human rights discourse to connect the dots between family law in Kenya and transnational governance.[43]

Mickelson, Dehm, and Kang'ara may be motivated by the injustices and violence of land dispossession, but the analytical focus of their project is to probe the ideological/cultural/legal mechanics of *how* land gets reframed as efficient property, how Indigenous land gets framed as *terra nullius*, or how the legal architecture of individual property rights plays out in conception of the modern family and so on.

Luis Eslava critiques the international/local binary, using the "how" question to demonstrate how the binary functions to produce and reproduce various maldistributions by invisibilizing international law's presence in the quotidian dimensions of the local.[44] A related strategy, undertaken in describing the "how" of capital accumulation and dispossession, is to describe how there has come to be a naturalizing of the public/private dichotomy in international law, and the yield of that dichotomy for an empowered private sphere. For instance, Martii Koskenniemi makes the argument that the public/private distinction in international law has made us focus on public international law while so much of the action of ongoing colonial appropriation takes place through private law rules on property and trade.[45] Thus he takes pains to describe *how* international law was made to naturalize notions of private property and free trade and how that naturalization works alongside that of the public/private boundary itself to produce the world that capitalism and empire have birthed.

Directing the "how" question to surplus appropriation in international trade, Bhupinder Chimni describes the background laws and institutions that shadow bargaining to produce a maldistributive tilt to trade negotiations.[46] These background rules, he argues, naturalize the history of wealth and trade advantages accumulated and dispossessed through colonialism or postcolonial institutions such as the World Bank and the International Monetary Fund, but they are relegated to the background, invisible to the formal terms of the bargaining process.[47] This kind of work to make visible something that is obscured in received framings of an issue goes to the core of TWAIL analytics. Describing the mechanics of distribution and unmasking how appropriation happens is important, but that in itself is not enough. We may need to change the ground on which people act.

REPARATIVE INTERVENTIONS

The fourth register of TWAIL distributional analytics takes on the challenge of thinking about the future. Doing distributional analysis can open up the rules of the game to help us understand how it works, but how do we move from that understanding to resistance and alternative futures? The reparative in my usage here is not about analyzing the future of work but about working toward different futures. How can distributive analysis contribute to interventions that challenge existing distribution and work toward alternative distributive outcomes? In much TWAIL work, the description of the technologies of maldistribution can themselves be the resistance—thus, if Kapur's work makes us less wedded to the discourse of rights when we see how it can be a trap not salvation, or if Dehm's work makes us more alert to popular environmentally sustainable development policies when we see that carbon trading is weaponized to profit some and dispossess others—these analytic descriptions of how things "really" work may themselves change the ground on which we act. Mapping the technologies of governance and reproduction in surplus appropriation, distributional analysis can help us identify false dawns and imagine alternatives. This may be especially true when distributional analysis challenges the dominant normative assumptions (the work of human rights) or the dominant expertise (the development paradigm promulgated from the International Financial Institutions). In this way, the cumulative weight of this unmasking may prod us to widen our political imagination, experiment with alternative approaches, and explore new paths to transform the distributive tilt of the received law and policy landscape. Fusing the very different conceptions of the reparative advanced by Eve Sedgwick and Priyamvada Gopal, these paths are what I refer to as reparative interventions.[48]

Eve Sedgwick speaks of reparative reading practices that attend to "the many ways selves and communities succeed in extracting sustenance from the object of a culture—even of a culture whose avowed desire has often been not to sustain them." She speaks of the importance of such practices given the overwhelming critical focus on unmasking the way things really work. She argues that "the hermeneutics of suspicion," this "paranoid reading" of the way things are, can be valuable, but if it monopolizes critical energies, it can be disabling of radical change.[49] Priyamvada Gopal speaks of reparative history as one that foregrounds past struggles of resistance. It challenges historical amnesia about lessons learned from expressions of dissent among oppressed peoples of the Global South and elsewhere.[50] TWAIL approaches to resistance include both these senses of the reparative—future oriented and experimental in pursuing alternative distributive ends, but also mining past struggles that spoke to other ways of being in the world in which the distributions of meanings and resources could have been otherwise.

Let me close then with a number of interventions that we can frame in this dual register that mine international law to develop immanent critique as if different dimensions of the international legal tradition could be interpreted and reconstituted differently.[51] From the New International Economic Order to the UN Conference on Trade and Development, and the Chagos Islands Case to the Case on the Wall in Palestine, a long history of TWAIL interventions have tried to change the distributive landscape by identifying and exploiting "gaps, conflicts, and ambiguities."[52] My own work has sought to do this by challenging the sovereign debt problem through the legal principle of "odious debt" as a concept that renders visible different dimensions of the background economic order that have been constitutive of postcolonial sovereignty and the histories of trade and aid that have engendered debt. At the same time, it is also a forward-looking experiment that seeks to interrupt settled distributions of debt obligations and advance new ways of stitching together doctrine and precedent, authorized interpretations, and persuasive reinterpretations to make insurgent legal claims.[53] Tendayi Achiume's work on migration as a form of decolonization offers a terrific example of an intervention that radically challenges settled legal interpretation of migration and borders to fundamentally reframe how a problem is defined.[54] It is a reframing that seeks to redistribute how the international legal framework settles the rights and responsibilities of migrants and the countries into which they are migrating.

For many TWAIL scholars, resistance involves challenging the distribution of political and legal space for resistance. It is about both describing the limits of international law and identifying spaces for new directions that are not overdetermined by the histories of colonialism, capitalism, and slavery. Liliana Obregón's exploration of peripheral histories of international law to challenge Eurocentric international legal history offers an example of such an effort.[55] Nahed Samour's work on Islamic law makes a parallel intervention by reinventing and renewing a tradition.[56] We see an ambitious effort to open up spaces for resistance within international law in Bhupinder Chimni's work to redistribute the sources of customary international law by paying attention to interventions in international law and policy that have "roots in a decolonized, self-determined, and plural cultural and political international order."[57] We can see a similar ambition in James Gathii's "The Promise of International Law," in which he advocates for going "outside the beltway of our discipline to places often unfamiliar in our textbooks and the locations where we practice and teach international law." For instance, he urges that we attend to rural social movements in the Global South that challenge the WTO rules about commodity flows and agricultural products "not only in resisting rules made from above, but in forging new ones that reflect their concerns."[58] We can see these as efforts that seek to challenge the distribution of spaces of resistance—i.e., what interventions are considered legitimate and are audible in international law—by redefining what are considered legitimate sources of law.

This process of reinterpretation recalls the toy box (vs. tool box) metaphor that Fred Moten and Stefano Harney use to describe the analytical play that opens up different ways of understanding or acting, by deploying a strategy differently from whatever end use was originally intended.[59] New forms of play are informed and inflected by recalling previous histories of resistance. Noura Erakat's book, *Justice for Some*, provides a powerful history of this approach to interpreting and reinterpreting international law and institutions through her analysis of public interest lawyering on the question of Palestine in the international plane.[60] It conveys the seriousness and high stakes of that interpretive play, but also how this orientation can open up even the most intractable circumstances to forward oriented engagement. In a similar spirit, Adil Khan's work on Upendra Baxi offers an imaginative reading of Baxi's work as presenting a particular style of international legal engagement that augments the reach of dissident lawyering in times of crisis.[61] Khan speaks of this as "an orientation towards authorization that puts forth demands for alternative future worlds without positing these just futures as regulative foundations that speak a single international law to the present."[62] Baxi's adroit navigation of international law through this orientation creates spaces for alternative distributive outcomes without fixing theses as regulatory foundations. Hani Sayed's analysis of an earlier generation of third world lawyers, Amar Bhatia's work on Indigenous law, Michael Fakhri's work on food sovereignty, and Ratna Kapur's work on freedom are all incisive and imaginative projects in this spirit.[63] Pooja Parmar captures the resistance work of these reorientations by speaking to it as the accumulation of third worldist epistemic resources.[64] Circling back to where we started, we can understand these interventions as accumulating surplus lost to colonialism, slavery, and their afterlives—a reparative "tactic of expropriation" as Duncan Kennedy describes it in chapter 4 of this book.

From Palestine to the NIEO, the history of TWAIL engagements with international law also present a caution. Everyone, including powerful actors who benefit from the system, are making calculations, developing strategies, and plotting alternatives that might even be worse than what we have seen so far. That risk may be a cotraveler of TWAIL interventions but also a risk we cannot not take if we want to imagine transformations of a maldistributive world-system. With risk and promise, TWAIL interventions have sought to deploy distributional analysis to reconnoiter new terrain in international law, mine dissident intellectual traditions, and work toward alternative futures.[65]

NOTES

Many thanks to Mishal Khan and Orlando Ochoa for their comments, help with citations, and much more.

1. For more on TWAIL, see James T. Gathii, "TWAIL: A Brief History of Its Origins, Its Decentralized Network, and a Tentative Bibliography," *Trade Law and Development* 3, no. 1 (2011): 26–64; Luis Eslava, "TWAIL Coordinates," *Critical Legal Thinking*, April 2, 2019, https://criticallegalthinking.com/2019/04/02/twail-coordinates/; Usha Natarajan, John Reynolds, Amar Bhatia, and Sujith Xavier, "TWAIL: On Praxis and the Intellectual," *Third World Quarterly* 37, no. 11 (2016): 1946–56, https://doi.org/10.1080/01436597.2016.1209971; and Antony Anghie, "Rethinking International Law: A TWAIL Retrospective," *European Journal of International Law* 34, no. 1 (2023): 7–112, https://doi.org/10.1093/ejil/chad005.

2. As such, for many TWAILers, "third world" refers not only to countries in the Global South but also the "third world in the first world"—so Baltimore and Flint, not just Bandung and Freetown.

3. My own framing of distributional analysis in this chapter is indebted to Janet Halley, "Distribution and Decision: Assessing Governance Feminism," in *Governance Feminism: An Introduction*, ed. Janet Halley, Prabha Kotiswaran, Rachel Rebouché, and Hila Shamir (Minneapolis: University of Minnesota Press, 2018), 253–67.

4. In addition, or alternatively, as I will elaborate further, TWAILers could also offer an internal critique of Marx's story of industrial capitalism as not accounting adequately for the role of surplus appropriation from colonial and slave economies.

5. B. S. Chimni's magisterial *International Law and World Order: A Critique of Contemporary Approaches* (New York: Columbia University Press, 2017) is critical here, but he is part of a rich lineage of Marxist legal analysis that includes several contemporary scholars such as Robert Knox, China Miéville, and Umut Özsu—each with their own distinct relationship to TWAIL.

6. CEPAL is the United Nations Commission for Latin America and the Caribbean, which played a pivotal role in conceptualizing the New International Economic Order (NIEO) under the leadership of Raul Prebisch. For more on the work of these scholars and their impact on economic policy, see María Margarita Fajardo Hernández, *The World That Latin America Created: The United Nations Economic Commission for Latin America in the Development Era* (Cambridge, MA: Harvard University Press, 2022).

7. Hani Sayed, "On the Political Limits of Pragmatism: Third Worldist International Lawyers and International Institutions" (unpublished manuscript, May 30, 2016), Adobe PDF file; and Adil Hasan Khan, "International Lawyers in the Aftermath of Disasters: Inheriting from Radhabinod Pal and Upendra Baxi," *Third World Quarterly* 37, no. 11 (2016): 2061–79, https://doi.org/10.1080/01436597.2016.1191940.

8. James Thuo Gathii, "The Promise of International Law: A Third World View," *American University International Law Review* 36, no. 3 (2021): 377–477, https://doi.org/10.1017/amp.2021.87.

9. In addition, I refer not only to projects and interventions by scholars who describe themselves as TWAILers but also others, such as the Spanish contribution to international law by Martii Koskenniemi "Empire and International Law: The Real Spanish Contribution," *University of Toronto Law Journal* 61, no. 1 (Winter 2011): 1–36, https://www.jstor.org/stable/23018686; and the influential book by the late Eric Williams, *Capitalism and Slavery* (Chapel Hill: University of North Carolina Press, 1994), which I situate within a TWAIL tradition even if the authors themselves may not have described these interventions as TWAIL projects.
10. Halley, "Distribution and Decision," 256.
11. Karl Marx, *Capital: A Critique of Political Economy* (1867; repr., Moscow: Progress, 1977).
12. This clarification was prompted by Duncan Kennedy's observation that there is often a slippage between the profit/loss assessment of specific transactions between stronger and weaker parties and capital accumulation in the structural sense to which Marx spoke. In some TWAIL work, the focus on transactions between stronger and weaker parties can be helpful as windows into capital accumulation in that more structural sense. Rather than a conflation of that profit/loss assessment with capital accumulation, it can be the entry point for probing specific instances of profit/loss transaction as symptomatic of a dimension of capital accumulation. In fact, one of the most interesting aspects of TWAIL work is when the distributive analysis shows that there is capital accumulation despite localized loss by the stronger party. This kind of work can enable a better mapping of the relationship between local transactions and capital accumulation.
13. Marx saw capitalism's drive to profit as fueling imperial expansion and a relentless search for new arenas of expropriation. At the same time, there have been historic debates about how the role of the imperial and slave economies were underappreciated in different ways in traditional Marxist analysis of surplus appropriation in the Global North. One area where there has been much recent work speaks to how "primitive accumulation" (that Marx understood as a precapitalist system) is in fact simultaneous with capitalism in many contexts and may have a complex symbiotic relationship with industrial capitalism and the classical model of surplus appropriation from the proletariat—those who own the means of production. For an account of the intellectual history of racial capitalism that tells this story in relation to the political economy of apartheid South Africa, see Arun Kundnani, "What Is Racial Capitalism?," *Arun Kundnani on Race, Culture, and Empire*, October 15, 2020, https://www.kundnani.org/what-is-racial-capitalism/.
14. In chapter after chapter, these arguments about the profitable political economy of the slave trade are made by Eric Williams in *Capitalism and Slavery*. As noted by Nicole Burrowes, scholars such as Walter Rodney foregrounded the long reach of colonial world-making that enabled postcolonial surplus appropriation. In this book, see chapter 2 by Nicole Burrowes, "Walter Rodney, World-Systems Theory, and Racial Capitalism." Also see, Walter Rodney, *How Europe Underdeveloped Africa* (London: Verso Books, 2018). In a similar spirit, see the dependency theorist Andre Gunder Frank, "The Development of Underdevelopment," *Monthly Review* 18,

no. 4 (September 1966): 17–31, https://doi.org/10.14452/MR-018-04-1966-08_3. The tracing of American slavery's surplus and the historical dynamic of surplus appropriation that it begets from "Two hundred fifty years of slavery. Ninety years of Jim Crow. Sixty years of separate but equal. Thirty-five years of racist housing policy" is at the core of Ta-Nehisi Coates, "The Case for Reparations," *The Atlantic*, June 2014, https://www.theatlantic.com/magazine/archive/2014/06/the-case-for-reparations/361631/.

15. Sundhya Pahuja, *Decolonising International Law: Development, Economic Growth, and the Politics of Universality* (Cambridge: Cambridge University Press, 2011).
16. James Thuo Gathii, "Process and Substance in WTO Reform," *Rutgers Law Review* 56, no. 4 (2004): 885–925.
17. James Thuo Gathii, "The High Stakes of WTO Reform," as reviewed by Fatoumata Jawara and Aileen Kwa, "Behind the Scenes at the WTO: The Real World of Trade Negotiations/The Lessons of Cancun," *Michigan Law Review* 104, no. 6 (May 2006): 1361–86, https://www.jstor.org/stable/40041439.
18. Balakrishnan Rajagopal, *International Law from Below* (Cambridge: Cambridge University Press, 2003).
19. John Reynolds, *Emergency, Empire and International Law* (Cambridge: Cambridge University Press, 2017).
20. Ntina Tzouvala, *Capitalism as Civilisation: A History of International Law* (Cambridge: Cambridge University Press, 2020). These intertwined genealogies resonate with the processes that scholars of racial capitalism such as Eric Williams and Cedric Robinson (among others) have spoken to. Williams, *Capitalism and Slavery*; Cedric J. Robinson, *Black Marxism: The Making of the Black Radical Tradition*, 2nd ed. (1983; repr., Chapel Hill: University of North Carolina Press, 2000); and Walter Johnson, *River of Dark Dreams: Slavery and Empire in the Cotton Kingdom* (Cambridge, MA: Belknap, 2017).
21. Vasuki Nesiah, "Slavery's Afterlives: Humanitarian Imperialism and Free Contract," *AJIL Unbound* 117 (2023): 66–70, https://doi.org/10.1017/aju.2023.7.
22. Ratna Kapur, *Gender, Alterity, and Human Rights: Freedom in a Fishbowl* (Cheltenham, UK: Edward Elgar, 2018).
23. This does not mean that the structural "losers" do not resist in ways that may make them "winners" in a different register. In some ways, the performance of loss (through mimicry, for instance) may offer productive ground to destabilize "the winnings." See Homi Bhabha, "Of Mimicry and Man: The Ambivalence of Colonial Discourse," *Discipleship: A Special Issue on Psychoanalysis* 28 (Spring 1984): 125–33, https://doi.org/10.2307/778467.
24. Boaventura de Sousa Santos, *Epistemologies of the South: Justice Against Epistemicide* (London: Routledge, 2014), 6; see also Miranda Fricker, *Epistemic Injustice: Power and the Ethics of Knowing* (Oxford: Oxford University Press, 2009).
25. Lorraine Code, *Ecological Thinking: The Politics of Epistemic Location* (Oxford: Oxford University Press, 2006), 8.
26. Gayatri Chakravorty Spivak, "Can the Subaltern Speak?," in *Marxism and the Interpretation of Culture*, ed. Cary Nelson and Lawrence Grossberg (Champaign: University of Illinois Press, 1988), 271.

27. Cyra Akila Choudhury, "From Bandung 1955 to Bangladesh 1971: Postcolonial Self-Determination and Third-World Failures in South Asia," in *Bandung, Global History and International Law: Critical Pasts and Pending Futures*, ed. Luis Eslava, Vasuki Nesiah, and Michael Fakhri (Cambridge: Cambridge University Press, 2017), 322–36; and Luwam Dirar, "Rethinking the Concept of Colonialism in Bandung and Its African Union Aftermath," in *Global History and International Law: Critical Pasts and Pending Futures*, ed. Luis Eslava, Vasuki Nesiah, and Michael Fakhri (Cambridge: Cambridge University Press, 2017), 355–66.
28. Halley, "Distribution and Decision." Halley's discussion builds on the work of legal realists Oliver Wendell Holmes and Karl Llewellyn.
29. Helena Alviar García, "Legal Reform, Social Policy, and Gendered Redistribution in Colombia: The Role of the Family," *American University Journal of Gender, Social Policy and the Law* 19, no. 2 (2011): 577–99.
30. David Kennedy, *The Dark Side of Virtue: International Humanitarianism Reassessed* (Princeton, NJ: Princeton University Press, 2004).
31. Antony Anghie, *Imperialism, Sovereignty and the Making of International Law* (Cambridge: Cambridge University Press, 2005).
32. Antony Anghie, "'The Heart of My Home': Colonialism, Environmental Damage, and the Nauru Case," *Harvard International Law Journal* 34, no. 2 (1993): 452–53; Memorial of the Republic of Nauru, "Certain Phosphate Lands in Nauru (Nauru v Australia)," March 20, 1990, 58–59, https://www.icj-cij.org/sites/default/files/case-related/80/6655.pdf; and Anghie, *Imperialism*.
33. Vasuki Nesiah, "'A Mad and Melancholy Record': The Crisis of International Law Histories," *Notre Dame Journal of International & Comparative Law* 11, no. 2 (2021): 232–55; and Vasuki Nesiah, *International Conflict Feminism* (Philadelphia: University of Pennsylvania Press, 2024).
34. Usha Natarajan, "TWAIL and the Environment: The State of Nature, the Nature of the State, and the Arab Spring," *Oregon Review of International Law* 14, no. 1 (2012): 177–202.
35. Cheryl Harris, "Whiteness as Property," *Harvard Law Review* 106, no. 8 (June 1993): 1707–91, https://doi.org/10.2307/1341787.
36. For more on wounded attachments, see Wendy Brown, *States of Injury: Power and Freedom in Late Modernity* (Princeton, NJ: Princeton University Press, 1995).
37. Williams, *Capitalism and Slavery*.
38. Williams's project illuminates the economic dynamics that enabled the cotton gin and its parallels in other areas of industry—from shipbuilding in Liverpool, to sugar refineries, to metallurgy and weapons manufacture, to British industrialization more generally.
39. La Paperson, *A Third University Is Possible* (Minneapolis: University of Minnesota Press, 2017); La Paperson, "A Ghetto Land Pedagogy: An Antidote for Environmentalism," *Environmental Education Research* 20, no. 1 (2014): 115–30, https://doi.org/10.1080/13504622.2013.865115; and John Reynolds, "Disrupting Civility: Amateur Intellectuals, International Lawyers and TWAIL as Praxis," *Third World Quarterly* 37, no. 11 (2016): 2098–118, https://doi.org/10.1080/01436597.2016.1197038.

40. Karin Mickelson, "Common Heritage of Mankind as a Limit to Exploitation of the Global Commons," *European Journal of International Law* 30, no. 2 (May 2019): 635–63, https://doi.org/10.1093/ejil/chz023; and Karin Mickelson, "The Maps of International Law: Perceptions of Nature in the Classification of Territory," *Leiden Journal of International Law* 27, no. 3 (September 2014): 621–39, https://doi.org/10.1017/S0922156514000235.
41. Hernando de Soto, *The Mystery of Capital: Why Capitalism Triumphs in the West and Fails Everywhere Else* (New York: Basic Books, 2000).
42. Julia Dehm, "Indigenous Peoples and REDD+ Safeguards: Rights as Resistance or as Disciplinary Inclusion in the Green Economy?," *Journal of Human Rights & the Environment* 7, no. 2 (September 2016): 170–217, https://doi.org/10.4337/jhre.2016.02.01.
43. Sylvia Wairimu Kang'ara, "Beyond Bed and Bread: Making the African State Through Marriage Law Reform—Constitutive and Transformative Influences of Anglo-American Legal Thought," *Hastings Race and Poverty Law Journal* 9, no. 2 (2012): 353–96.
44. Luis Eslava, *Local Space, Global Life: The Everyday Operation of International Law and Development* (Cambridge: Cambridge University Press, 2015).
45. Koskenniemi, "Empire and International Law." See also Duncan Kennedy, "Three Globalizations of Law and Legal Thought: 1850–2000," in *The New Law and Economic Development: A Critical Perspective*, ed. David M. Trubek and Alvaro Santos (Cambridge: Cambridge University Press, 2006), 19–73.
46. Bhupinder S. Chimni, "International Institutions Today: An Imperial Global State in the Making," *European Journal of International Law* 15, no. 1 (February 2004): 1–37, https://doi.org/10.1093/ejil/15.1.1.
47. For instance, the conditionalities imposed by the International Financial Institutions (IFIs) through their aid agreements target protectionism in the Global South and push for trade liberalization as if the WTO-monitored trade landscape were "free and fair." This is an adverse environment for countries bearing the legacies of colonial and postcolonial economic exploitation and vulnerability, and the exercise of quasi-sovereign powers by institutions like the IFIs and the WTO further undermines Global South sovereignty and exacerbates their vulnerability to global markets. In this way, Chimni's focus on the "how" of capital accumulation leads him to study and describe how these countries forge trade deals and economic paths in the shadow of international institutions, international economic law, and the interests of a transnational capitalist class.
48. Eve Sedgwick, *Touching Feeling: Affect, Pedagogy, Performativity* (Durham, NC: Duke University Press, 2002); and Priyamvada Gopal, *Insurgent Empire* (London: Verso, 2019).
49. Eve Kosofsky Sedgwick, "Paranoid Reading and Reparative Reading, or, You're So Paranoid, You Probably Think This Essay Is About You," in Eve Sedgwick, *Touching Feeling: Affect, Pedagogy, Performativity* (Durham, NC: Duke University Press, 2002), 150–51.
50. Gopal, *Insurgent Empire*.

51. In effect this treats the future of international law as if it were a "weird cocktail" created from the ingredients of international law as we know it but mixed differently. Dan Danielson invoked the metaphor of a "weird cocktail" in his intervention at a *Future of Work* workshop in Austin in 2018. The metaphor became a repeated reference point during that meeting. As I invoke it here, traveling the "weird cocktail" path entails identifying the opportunities for new experiments to push and pull, sip and spit, the received apparatus to test its yield.

52. Duncan Kennedy, "The Critique of Rights in Critical Legal Studies," in *Left Legalism/Left Critique*, ed. Wendy Brown and Janet Halley (Durham, NC: Duke University Press, 2002), 178–228.

53. Vasuki Nesiah, "A Double Take on Debt: Reparations Claims and Regimes of Visibility in a Politics of Refusal," *Osgoode Hall Law Journal* 59, no. 1 (Winter 2022): 153–87.

54. E. Tendayi Achiume, "Migration as Decolonization," *Stanford Law Review* 71, no. 6 (2019): 1565.

55. Liliana Obregón, "Peripheral Histories of International Law," *Annual Review of Law and Social Science* 15 (October 2019): 437–51, https://doi.org/10.1146/annurev-lawsocsci-110316-113348.

56. Nahed Samour, "Modernized Islamic International Law Concepts as a Third World Approach to International Law," *Heidelberg Journal of International Law* 72 (2012): 543–77.

57. Bhupinder S. Chimni, "Customary International Law: A Third World Perspective," *American Journal of International Law* 112, no. 1 (2018): 1–46, https://doi.org/10.1017/ajil.2018.12.

58. Gathii, "The Promise of International Law," 413.

59. Stefano Harney and Fred Moten, *The Undercommons: Fugitive Planning & Black Study* (Wivenhoe, UK: Minor Compositions, 2013).

60. Noura Erakat, *Justice for Some: Law and the Question of Palestine* (Stanford, CA: Stanford University Press, 2019).

61. Khan, "International Lawyers in the Aftermath of Disasters," 2061–79.

62. Adil Hasan Khan, "'... Those who ... Lost their Utopias ... but ... still Rebel ...': Taking up Upendra Baxi's Bequixotements in Times of Crisis," *Jindal Global Law Review* 9 (2018): 179, https://doi.org/10.1007/s41020-018-0075-1.

63. Sayed, "Political Limits of Pragmatism"; Amar Bhatia, "The South of the North: Building on Critical Approaches to International Law with Lessons from the Fourth World," *Oregon Review of International Law* 14, no. 1 (2012): 131–76; Michael Fakhri, "Third World Sovereignty, Indigenous Sovereignty, and Food Sovereignty: Living with Sovereignty Despite the Map," *Transnational Legal Theory* 9, nos. 3–4 (2018): 218–53, https://doi.org/10.1080/20414005.2018.1563748; and Kapur, *Gender, Alterity*.

64. Pooja Parmar, "TWAIL: An Epistemological Inquiry," *International Community Law Review* 10, no. 4 (2008): 363–70, https://doi.org/10.1163/157181208X361421.

65. Bhatia, "The South of the North;" Fakhri, "Third World Sovereignty;" and Kapur, *Gender, Alterity*.

PART II

The Future of Work

Challenges to Dominant Framings

CHAPTER 6

THE FUTURE OF WORK FROM A VICTORIAN PAST

NEVILLE HOAD

By the sweat of your brow, you will eat your food.
—Genesis 3:19

Free beer tomorrow
—bar sign

In the thirty years or so before Max Weber famously yoked the rise of capitalism to the Protestant work ethic, a range of writers in the English-speaking world fretted and fantasized about work, its definition, its value, and its future—especially in relation to the political economy.[1] The Victorians experienced the question of the future of work as something like a crisis.[2] In this chapter, I explore three imaginative responses to that perception of crisis: Oscar Wilde's 1891 essay "The Soul of Man Under Socialism," and two novels—H. G. Wells's *The Time Machine* (1895), and an understudied precursor to the above-mentioned texts, Edward Bulwer-Lytton's *The Coming Race* (1871). Wilde offers an optimistic vision of a society in which machines would do the work that he deems unfit for humans and thus all *human* labor becomes a form of self-expression. *The Time Machine* reveals a distant future in which the class divisions of late-nineteenth-century Britain have developed into species differences, and the former working classes, now the Morlocks, ranch and eat the Eloi, the former middle and upper classes. Contact with machinery and engagement with work is seen as what gave the Morlocks the evolutionary advantage. Bulwer-Lytton imagines an underground world where the magical substance of

Vril (not unrelated to electricity, which is emerging as a powerful force in this late-nineteenth-century moment) is a vitalist technology that removes any need for productive labor.

All three texts demonstrate the necessity of not thinking about work in a vacuum, siloed off from questions of race, gender, and the role of the state. Our current framings of the future of work, both techno-optimist and techno-pessimist—the machines, the robots, or even the Vril are coming to save us or destroy us—have much to learn from both their hopeful fantasies and their deepest fears about what happens when we try to remove formal employment and waged labor from our imaginative horizons about the future of work.

These three texts were part of a much wider set of Victorian imaginings about the future of work. Some key examples here might include Samuel Butler's 1872 novel *Erewhon*, which may have been the first novel to use Darwinian theories of evolution to suggest that machines could develop consciousness—the Erewhonians therefore ban all machines.[3] The American, Edward Bellamy, in his 1888 best-seller *Looking Backward*, has a Rip Van Winkle–like protagonist wake up in Boston in the year 2000 to find a world in which all industry has been nationalized.[4] There is equal distribution of resources and something that looks like universal basic income (UBI) and, as in *Erewhon*, "criminality" has become a medical concern, not a criminal one. William Morris's 1890 *News from Nowhere* employs a similar time-traveler conceit and responds fairly directly to Bellamy's novel.[5] Morris imagines a communist utopia in which work and leisure have entirely blurred—the cash economy has disappeared—and the world has returned to a well-fed, beautifully crafted, distinctly white, and English medievalism where "from each according to his abilities, to each according to his needs" has been tweaked into "make what gives you pleasure to make, take what you need."[6] One could also add Richard Jefferies's *After London; Or, Wild England* (1885) as arguably the first climate disaster novel in which environmental changes force a radical restructuring of both social relations and human interactions with the natural world.[7] In Jefferies's story, the mouth of the Thames and other major rivers on the island of Great Britain have silted over due to human commercial activity, and London ends up under a poisonous lake and surrounded by swampland. Domestic animals turn feral, nature returns in full force, and political economy relapses into barbarism—taking shape in the form of a state (such as it is) based on raiding and brigrandry in the fantasy of a debased and dystopian medievalism.

Thus a wealth of literary texts can constitute significant bibliographic resources for Victorian debates about the future of work, although there are no doubt many other possible archives, such as the huge literature around social and political reform, perhaps inaugurated by Henry Mayhew's mid-nineteenth-century epic *London Labour and the London Poor* (1864).[8] These other texts, however, are more focused on the realist description and critique of labor, livelihoods, and governance in their present moment of writing—although they inevitably gesture toward the future.

Because I am interested in futurity, which is definitionally speculative, and in collating intellectual and political resources for the generation of new imaginaries for work in its full panoply of meanings, I focus on speculative fiction with the exception of "The Soul of Man Under Socialism," which is a highly speculative text, but in the genre of the essay.[9] I have chosen to discuss these particular three texts because they are in dialogue with the many mentioned previously and because they push particularly hard at the question of work and its antonyms and cognates—art, leisure, pleasure, livelihood, and so on—refusing to disarticulate imaginings of the future of work from questions of gender, sexuality, racial identities and relationships, and the role of the state.

As my brief summary of these texts suggests, late-twentieth- and early-twenty-first-century framings of the future of work share many similarities with those of the turn of the twentieth century. Wilde can be seen as a precursor of the kind of techno-optimist that prefigures many of the fourth industrial revolution boosters, albeit with an aesthetic twist. Similarly, Bulwer-Lytton gives us technology as transforming magic.[10] In the mode of satire, Butler offers depictions of dire techno-pessimism. Jefferies imagines environmental disaster as the end of work as we knew it. And if Bulwer-Lytton does not quite describe a world of racial capitalism, he certainly provides a world of racialized primitive accumulation in the mode of threat, and Wells writes a future in which divisions of labor are racialized into species difference in a frightening allegory of the future of capitalism.

Morris's nostalgic medievalism further parallels the "ahistorical and racialized nostalgia for 'full' and 'standard' employment"—the nostalgic Keynesianism—of this moment of writing as outlined in the introduction to this book.

In *The Coming Race, The Time Machine*, and "The Soul of Man Under Socialism," worlds free of alienated labor are further imagined through rather complicated gendered and racialized terms. These imaginings can be read in the overdetermined terms of the uneven uptake of Darwinian theories of evolution, galloping proletarianization at home and forced labor abroad, simmering anxieties about the gendered division of labor and white women's political and economic enfranchisement, panics about nonreproductive/procreative sexual desires, and the context (and metaphors) of expanding British colonialism and capitalism. Although produced under very different historical circumstances than our own, many of the questions they raise about labor, gender, sexuality, governance, and race—morphed under changing conditions of production and reproduction—have not disappeared, and I return to past speculations about work and its futures to see how difficult it is to shift the imaginings of the future of work today.

UTOPIAN EMPIRE

Let us begin with Oscar Wilde's 1891 essay, "The Soul of Man Under Socialism," which after publication was arguably the most influential of all the previously mentioned works, at least in its translation and reception history, on socialism as it came to be in the long course of the twentieth century.[11] Wilde argues for art as the praxis for healing the wounds inflicted by the subjective experience of capitalism's division of labor. Like Karl Marx and William Morris before him, Wilde hated the "wretched lop-sided creatures we are being made by the excess of the division of labour in the modern occupations of life."[12] Unlike Morris's backward glance via Ruskin's romanticization of medieval economic and artistic production, Wilde shifts his utopic horizon both forward and backward: "Socialism, Communism, or whatever one chooses to call it, by converting private property into public wealth, and substituting cooperation for competition, will restore society to its proper condition of a thoroughly healthy organism, and ensure the material well-being of each member of the community."[13] Wilde, like his predecessors Morris and Ruskin, envisages a world in which some kinds of labor can be experienced as an intrinsic rather than extracted or extrinsic part of one's being, but he would agree with Marx on the question of alienated labor. Marx, in the *Economic and Philosophical Manuscripts* of 1844, offers the following description of alienated labor: "The fact simply applies that the object produced by labour, its product, now stands opposed to it as an alien being, as a power independent of the producer. . . . The performance of the work appears in the sphere of political economy as a vitiation of the worker, objectification as a loss and as servitude to the object, and appropriation as alienation."[14] Even as Wilde reads alienated labor more subjectively than Marx, he tries to imagine a world without alienated labor at all. He writes: "The fact is, that civilization requires slaves. The Greeks were quite right there. Unless there are slaves to do the ugly, horrible, uninteresting work, culture and contemplation become almost impossible. Human slavery is wrong, insecure and demoralising. On mechanical slavery, the slavery of the machine, the future of the world depends."[15]

For Wilde, the loss or delegation to machines of what in our current moment could be called "essential work" is an unequivocal moral and political good.[16] We are in the Wildean paradox of an aristocracy for everyone—no one should be economically compelled to do any work they don't want to do. Despite Wilde's avowal of revolutionary socialism, the essay reveals a deep affinity with Christian notions of redemption, which will later be expanded upon in *De Profundis*.[17] The notion that a future socialism will "restore" society to a prelapsarian state of organic wholeness and health rather than undergo a transformation gives the lie to the forward-looking impetus of Wilde's utopianism. Moreover, Wilde's invocation of "Greek slavery" might be somewhat disingenuous, when the model of transatlantic slavery that he does not invoke is in living memory, and the division of labor under the longue durée of European colonialism is always and already (to borrow a phrase) racialized.

In certain ways, Wilde attempts the impossible task of owning his own labor under capitalist relations of production, usually by denying or disavowing such labor. Two Wilde jokes encapsulate that impossibility nicely. Once, when asked about what he had done in a day, he responded: "I have spent most of the day putting in a comma and the rest of the day taking it out." And in a typical reversal of a temperance slogan, "drink is the curse of the working classes," Wilde asserts that "work is the curse of the drinking classes."[18] Not to my knowledge having read Marx, Wilde can only read the effects of capital subjectively, usually through a disavowed projective identification with the abjection of the worker, evident in the reversal of the aforementioned slogans about work and drinking in the subjective register of alienation. The appropriation of workers' labor by the capitalist class worries him less on moral and political grounds, except in terms of the bad feeling it produces, and Wilde does not attempt to imagine how his aesthetic Utopia could be instituted or governed.

More significant for my argument, Wilde employs a set of colonizing metaphors in the articulation of his utopian aspirations. The future of Humanity is imperial. "England will never be civilized until she has added Utopia to her dominions."[19] "A map of the world that does not include Utopia is not worth even glancing at, for it leaves out the one country at which Humanity is always landing. And when Humanity lands there, it looks out, and, seeing, a better country, sets sail. Progress is the realisation of Utopias."[20] In the time following the Sepoy Rebellion (1857) and the Congress of Berlin (1885), these imperial metaphors cannot be read innocently. In these distinctly Wildean pronouncements, it is possible to perceive both echoes of, and an ironic rejoinder to, Ruskin's famous inaugural lecture at Oxford in 1870:

> There is a destiny now possible to us, the highest ever set before a nation to be accepted or refused. Will you youths of England make your country again a royal throne of kings, a sceptered isle, for all the world a source of light, a centre of peace and mistress of learning and of the Arts, faithful guardian of time-tried principles? ... This is what England must do or perish: she must found colonies as fast and as far as she is able, formed of her most energetic and worthiest men; seizing every piece of fruitful wasteground she can set her feet on, and there teaching these colonists that their chief virtue is to be fidelity to their country, and their first aim is to advance the power of England by land and sea.[21]

Cecil Rhodes, empire-builder extraordinaire, overlapped with Wilde at Oxford, and although I cannot establish whether they ever met, both men were deeply impressed by Ruskin, taking from him diverging though not unrelated faiths in the sacred mission of civilization. But Wilde, as befitting a disciple of Pater, will not traffic in fruitfulness and abhors the energetic. If for Rhodes the future of work was materially colonial, for Wilde it was only metaphorically so. We are potentially in a huge historiographic debate about the history of capitalism and colonialism here. In *Imperialism: The Highest Stage of Capitalism* (1917), Lenin argues that European capitalism, once it has fully proletarianized its labor force, goes elsewhere in search of cheaper labor and new markets.[22] A world-systems theorist/historian like Giovanni Arrighi argues that the wealth created by the plundering of New World silver is what finances the beginning of the industrial revolution in Europe, so colonial pillage becomes a necessary condition for capitalist development rather than its consequence.[23] Another big question arises here: Where and how might we find imaginaries of progress, development, and advancement that are not materially or metaphorically imperial?

Theories of racial capitalism and their relation to world-systems theory discussed extensively elsewhere in this book are central to any discussion of the past, present, and future of work as we have come to know it. Wilde's slave-machines are intended to free the world of "unpleasant" or "undignified" labor, which might not be optimal for workers in a world where labor and livelihood remain linked, highlighting a tension between a focus on work and a focus on workers. Dustin Abnet, writing in the context of the United States, is also germane here: "Robots have remained potent fantasies for such men because they promise to resolve the fundamental tensions between American myths and American realties that have dominated the country's culture since the very beginning."[24] The appeal of such fantasies lies in how robots "offer a 'techno-fix' that promises to quickly and permanently settle social issues without much difficulty" and allows these men to maintain "the benefits of power and privilege without having to deal seriously with the demands of other people and any accompanying moral guilt."[25]

Wilde finds imperial metaphors irresistible and remains attached to the robot solution, but he firmly refuses a key premise of the colonial "civilizing mission." Throughout his life, he evinces a deep distrust of discourses of benevolence, which in the era of high British imperialism are frequently racialized and gendered. As a schoolboy, Wilde joked with his mother about forming a "Society for the Suppression of Virtue."[26] In "The Soul of Man Under Socialism," he asserts: "Accordingly, with admirable, though misdirected notions, they very seriously and very sentimentally set themselves to the task of remedying the evils that they see. But their remedies do not cure the disease: they merely prolong it. Indeed, their remedies are part of the disease. . . . Charity creates a multitude of sins."[27]

This distrust of benevolence is a multifaceted phenomenon in Victorian literature, useful for a range of political projects. Prior to Wilde, Dickens had already satirized white benevolence in relation to the colonies in the figure of Mrs. Jellyby in *Bleak House* (1853), who is so busy raising money for the missionaries in the upper Niger that she has no time to look after her own disorderly house.[28] She functions as a compound figure satirizing British colonialism. As a national/imperial emblem, she should literally get her own house in order first. She may also represent an antifeminist jab at women's greater involvement in the public sphere. Wilde's sustained distrust of those who take it on themselves to speak for others and to claim to "help" them is a recurring theme in his corpus and may mark a refusal of much of "the white man's burden," even as his utopian imaginings rely on imperial concept-metaphors.[29]

Through this distrust of white benevolence, Wilde anticipates some of the critiques shorthanded by the current maxim "the White Savior Industrial Complex," itself not unrelated to the emergence of a set of North Atlantic–funded NGOs and charitable foundations that seek to improve working and living conditions of people in the Global South, bypassing postcolonial states and generally not taking into account the large structural determinants of the global economy, such as sustained underdevelopment and debt service. (Africa is a net exporter of capital, largely through debt service.)[30] Teju Cole's famous series of tweets on the

White Savior Industrial Complex is a contemporary reworking of the Wildean critique of what has come to be called philanthrocapitalism:[31]

1. From Sachs to Kristof to Invisible Children to TED, the fastest growth industry in the U.S. is the White Savior Industrial Complex.
2. The white savior supports brutal policies in the morning, founds charities in the afternoon, and receives awards in the evening.
3. The banality of evil transmutes into the banality of sentimentality. The world is nothing but a problem to be solved by enthusiasm.
4. This world exists simply to satisfy the needs—including, importantly, the sentimental needs—of white people and Oprah.
5. The White Savior Industrial Complex is not about justice. It is about having a big emotional experience that validates privilege.
6. Feverish worry over that awful African warlord. But close to 1.5 million Iraqis died from an American war of choice. Worry about that.
7. I deeply respect American sentimentality, the way one respects a wounded hippo. You must keep an eye on it, for you know it is deadly.[32]

There are strong stylistic echoes of Wilde's preface to *The Picture of Dorian Gray* (1891) in the numbered list of aphorisms and the deceptively simple declarative sentences that shimmer into paradox. There is equally a strong distrust of benevolent sentimentality that we can also find in a range of Wildean aphorisms: "A little sincerity is a dangerous thing, and a great deal of it is absolutely fatal."[33] "Indeed, sentimentality is merely the back holiday of cynicism."[34] And "A sentimentalist is simply one who wants to have the luxury of an emotion without paying for it."[35]

The continuities between the earlier "civilizing mission" and the current "white savior industrial complex" are obvious, and the ideology of productivity is an important alibi for both of them. I write "alibi" because "theft" is one of work's antonyms. Joseph Conrad in *Heart of Darkness* (1899), arguably the novel that pushes hardest at the contradictions in the ideological justification of colonialism, acknowledges: "It was just robbery with violence, aggravated murder on a great scale, and men going at it blind which is very proper for those who tackle a darkness. The conquest of the earth, which mostly means taking it away from those who have a different complexion or slightly flatter noses than ourselves, is not a pretty thing when you look into it too much. What redeems it is the idea only."[36] Of course, Conrad is too smart to tell us what exactly this idea was/is, but Ruskin in that inaugural lecture might: that it is the task of English imperialism to make more of the world available for the extractive economies of what, a century after Ruskin's lecture, Cedric Robinson will term "racial capitalism." A certain version of Marx also calls this process "primitive accumulation," although I do not want to over-read the word "primitive" here.

One could argue that this productivity alibi of both the civilizing mission and the subsequent white savior industrial complex, which must necessarily obfuscate the terrible destruction that colonialism entailed, is supplemented ideologically by the slow popularizing and vulgarizing of Darwin's theory of evolution, which renders historical processes a kind of biological inevitability a la Engels. Engels is particularly trenchant in reading evolutionary theory as straight-up capitalist ideology: "The whole Darwinian theory of the struggle for existence is simply the transference from society to animate nature of Hobbes' theory of the war of every man against every man and the bourgeois economic theory of competition, along with the Malthusian theory of population. This feat having been accomplished . . . the same theories are next transferred back again from organic nature to history and their validity as eternal laws of human society declared to have been proved."[37]

However, the different domains of evolutionary theory and political economy at minimum complicate Engels's correlation. Although never a Social Darwinist in the strict sense of the term—Wilde is too resistant to biologically essentialist explanations and consistently privileges culture over nature epistemologically— it is possible to characterize moments of "The Soul of Man Under Socialism" as Social Darwinist: "Man will develop Individualism out of himself. Man is now so developing Individualism. To ask whether Individualism is practical is like asking whether Evolution is practical. Evolution is the law of Life, and there is no evolution except towards Individualism."[38]

For Wilde, individualism is a doctrine of self-expression predicated on ideas of self-completing, unalienated labor, and the pleasure that inheres in this labor that is not labor. We are to evolve from creatures of labor to creatures of leisure, from work to art. This is a fairly common fin-de-siècle fantasy/nightmare. Because of his constitutive Eurocentrism and his linkage of the project of civilization with the project of colonialism, Wilde's fantasy of a world free of unalienated labor remains oddly white or more generously racially homogenous, but still "wage labor bad" for everyone. And in the incoherent Social Darwinist rhetorics that Wilde deploys, for humanity to advance, wage labor must end and the state must no longer govern: "Now as the State is not to govern, it may be asked what the State is to do. The State is to be a voluntary association that will organise labour, and be the manufacturer and distributor of necessary commodities. The State is to make what is useful. The individual is to make what is beautiful."[39] Wilde thus wants to remove basic provisioning from the so-called free market and hand it over to the state, so the individual is liberated for aesthetic pursuits.

SEXUALITY, GENDER, RACE, AND LABOR: IMPOSSIBLE IMBRICATIONS

Two roughly contemporaneous dystopic novels by H. G. Wells and Edward Bulwer-Lytton share the same imaginative horizon of Wilde—worlds free of unalienated labor—but provide interesting counterpoints to his thought in that they return to the necessity, even desirability, of racialized alienated labor fairly explicitly. H. G. Wells's *The Time Machine* (1888 to 1895) explores the Wildean premise that evolution must be connected with the abolition of alienated labor, but in the mode of catastrophe rather than celebration. Narratologically, *The Time Machine* is framed as carefully as Conrad's *Heart of Darkness*. The double narrative removal of the frame-tales in both *Heart of Darkness* and *The Time Machine* suggests affinities between the suspect reliability of stories of colonial journeys and journeys into the future. Both spatial and temporal alterity need to be handled with the circumspection accorded to hearsay. It is not merely coincidental that the birth of science fiction writing is coincidental with the golden age of imperial travel fiction.[40]

In terms of genre, science fiction is frequently the heir to colonial travel yarns. Not for nothing does the subtitle of the television series *Star Trek* read "Space: The Final Frontier." The attempt to imagine the alterity of futurity—across a staggering array of genres and thinkers, including current prognoses on the future of work—remains seriously indebted to the narrative strategies and tropes of colonial encounters. Elon Musk is far from the first person to dream of colonizing Mars. Edgar Rice Burroughs of *Tarzan* fame wrote a deliciously bad series of novels on this topic starting in 1912, known as the *Barsoom* series (so named because Barsoom is the native Martian word for Mars).[41] *Total Recall* (1990) is an extraordinarily prescient Arnold Schwarzenegger film (loosely based on a Philip K. Dick story) partially set on Mars about the commodification of both air and memory.[42] Current talk about the fourth industrial revolution and the promise that technology will reduce our labor and improve our lives continues the techno-optimism around machines found in Wilde's essays, but the power of Vril in *The Coming Race* to destroy equally anticipates the long-held fears about the dangers of technology for the future of work, global political economy, and the very Earth itself.

Technology, however, has lost its determinative force in Wells's fantasy of the future of work, and it is instead on the terrain of basic provisioning that the real horror resides. Like Wilde, Wells imagines the future, or at least the surface part of it, as free from labor: The Eloi have evolved into creatures of perfect leisure. They live off the fruit of the land and seem unencumbered by the need to work:

"They spent all their time in playing gently, in bathing in the river, in making love in a half playful fashion, in eating fruit and sleeping. I could not see how things were kept going."[43]

Yet what becomes chillingly clear throughout the narrative is that they are simply fatted cattle for the carnivorous Morlocks who live and labor underground. Wells's use of Darwinian evolutionary principles is striking. Over the centuries, humanity has evolved into two distinct species along class lines. The erstwhile social division of class has become an imagined biological one of race tending to species:

> So as I see it, the Upper-world man had drifted towards his feeble prettiness, and the Underworld to mere mechanical industry.... Apparently, as time went on, the feeding of the Underworld, however it was effected, had become disjointed. Mother Necessity, who had been staved off for a few thousand years, came back again, and she began below. The Underworld, being in contact with machinery, which, however perfect, still needs some little thought outside habit, had probably retained perforce rather more initiative, if less of every other human character, than the upper. And when other meat failed them, they turned to what old habit had hitherto forbidden.[44]

Unlike Wilde's progressivism, which sees evolution moving inexorably toward "Individualism" and the end of alienated labor and attendant class divisions, Wells here deploys the rhetoric of another all-purpose late-nineteenth-century euphemism for the temporal production of human differences—degeneration.[45] Both Eloi and Morlocks have degenerated, the former into a helpless effeteness, the latter into cannibalistic barbarism. The future of gender or the gendering of the future is key in this warning about class, labor, and the implied dignity of work. Lack of clear gender dimorphism is clearly degenerate for Wells. A masculine work ethic is implicitly validated in the sense that, for the ruling classes to avert Wells's imagined scenario, they must remain productive and not give themselves over to the pleasures of the senses. The novella, like the utopian thought of Wilde and Morris, contains an implicit critique of capitalist divisions of labor, pushed through Darwinian evolution to an extreme. Despite Wells's commitments to socialism, some eradication of the class-split only seems necessary to avoid the dehumanizing triumph of the lower orders.

Wells's novel is often read as a critique of late-nineteenth-century industrial capitalism either through the implication that if the capitalist/working class split is not ameliorated, the moral horror of cannibalism will result; or through directly analogizing capitalism with cannibalism, even if the class hierarchy is reversed. Despite these readings, the moral horror of cannibalism can at a second remove be read also as the result of the collapse of both wage labor and the institutions of private property. In Wilde, if private property can be read as the enemy of individualism, in Wells's novella, private property may be something like a condition for individualism. It appears that in the future world of *The Time Machine*, there has been a return to the commons as much as there has been a degeneration back to fantasies of natural man, and a world prior to easily visible gender differentiation. Our time-traveler struggles to tell the Eloi apart and does not even bother attempting to individuate the Morlocks. Only heterosexual romance seems able to produce individuation when the narrator names an Eloi he likes "Weena." Our time-traveler is further an inadequate anthropologist of the future. Readers learn nothing of kinship or reproduction in this future world. More important for our purposes, neither Eloi nor Morlock *work*. The Eloi initially appear to live in a kind of prelapsarian Edenic bliss, subsisting on the freely given bounty of the earth. The Morlocks live by eating the Eloi. There does not seem to be any gendered division of labor in either group. There is no evidence that the Morlocks own the Eloi or trade them. The relation is one of pure predation. The novella finds a world without productive wage labor terrifying and legitimates by reversal the sanctity of private property. For Wells, the idea of the commons provides no redemptive fantasy or utopian horizon. However, this predation appears gendered—the Morlocks embody rapacious masculinity and the Eloi are effeminate with their "Dresden-china type of prettiness."[46]

Fascinatingly, even in this relation of pure predation, partially metaphorized through gender and a racial reversal of sorts, what the two new human species share is a radical gender indeterminacy and relatedly a possibly sexual polymorphous perversity. The terror of the far future is produced not just by the loss of productive labor, and cannibalism is not the only figuration of reproductive crisis. The initial encounter with the Eloi is described in these terms:

> And then looking more nearly into their features, I saw some further peculiarities in their Dresden-china type of prettiness. Their hair which was uniformly curly came to a sharp end at the neck and cheek; there was not the faintest suggestion of it on the face; and their ears were singularly minute. Their mouths were small with bright red rather thin lips and their little chins ran to a point.[47]
>
> . . .
>
> I perceived that they all had the same form of costume, the same soft hairless visage, and the same girlish rotundity of limb. . . . In costume, and in all the differences of texture and bearing that now mark the sexes from each other, these people of the future were alike. And the children seemed to my eyes but the miniatures of their parent.[48]

Clearly, the dominant trope for figuring these more advanced (in that they inhabit futurity) people is that of the lack of developmental differentiation, both along the lines of age and gender. Men cannot easily be distinguished from women. Moreover, they have the attributes of nineteenth-century children and to bring that point home more forcefully, cannot satisfactorily be distinguished from their own children. Again, the collapse between space and time that Social Darwinism encourages is visible in the rendering of alterity. The developmental difference (in this case, degeneration) of the Eloi is figured precisely in the same terms as the spatial difference of colonized peoples in Wells's own time.[49] The Eloi are white and so are the Morlocks, which prompts one to wonder whether for Wells that blackness is so evolutionarily backward that in the future even the most retrograde elements will have to be white. Even so, the Eloi are understood as children, a classic trope justifying the European conquest of other spaces. Even as he criticizes the excesses of capitalist divisions of labor, Wells is forced to argue the paradox that in the future there will be arrested development. While the Eloi are, over the course of the narrative, allowed gender differentiation, and in the character of the unfortunate Weena, individuation, the cannibalistic Morlocks can be granted neither: Ape-like and silent, male cannot easily be distinguished from female. Interestingly, the gender indeterminacy seems to go in the opposite direction for the Eloi and Morlocks. Morlocks's gender cannot be distinguished because female Morlocks appear masculine, whereas Eloi gender cannot be distinguished because male Eloi have feminine traits.

The Morlocks are a frightening composite of nineteenth-century stereotypes of the industrial working class from whom they have descended and the phantasmatic figure of the cannibalistic savage in desperate need of the light of European civilization. (What saves the narrator from destruction at their hands are four safety matches—ironically termed "Lucifers.")

In this dual world of shared gender indeterminacy and divided effete, meaningless pleasure and voracious cannibalistic appetite, physical contact—touch—is epistemologically and affectively complicated for our time-traveler. First contact with both human species of the future provokes a strange mix of anxiety and pleasure. With regard to the Eloi: "He came a step forward and then touched my hand. Then I felt other soft tentacles on my back and shoulders."[50] Since we are in daylight and our narrator can see that the Eloi are pretty and unthreatening, he feels no need to panic.

Initially, it would seem that the first encounter with the Morlocks could be similar: "I was roused by a soft hand touching my face . . . and while I stood in the dark a hand touched mine, lank fingers came feeling over my face, and I was sensible of a peculiar unpleasant odor. I fancied I heard the breathing of a crowd of those dreadful little beings about me. I felt the box of matches in my hand being gently disengaged, and other hands behind me plucking at my clothing."[51]

In both instances, the movement from one hand to many hands is speedy and invokes a kind of orgiastic thrill. The first Eloi goes for the hand, the Morlock, the face; individual contact is from the front, group touch from behind. The undifferentiated touch is initially pleasurable. Even the touch of the Morlocks is soft and gentle, at first. The touch of the Eloi is understood as epistemological, as an unthreatening childish curiosity: "They wanted to make sure that I was real." The touch of the Morlocks is much more foreboding and compounded by smell. Yet at this point in the narrative, the narrator is unaware of their cannibalistic practices. The time-traveler experiences a moment of panic: "The sudden realization of my ignorance of their ways of thinking and doing came home to me very vividly in the darkness."[52]

There is momentary confusion as to what appetite of the Morlocks the time-traveler will be used to satisfy. It is not as if the Morlocks fall on him like beasts of prey devouring him limb from limb. Elements of mass seduction are present: the touch is gentle and exploratory; clothing is coyly plucked at. Arguably, both initial tactile encounters with the Eloi and the Morlocks can be seen to prefigure what comes to be known in twentieth-century jurisprudence as the homosexual panic defense.[53] The time-traveler is in both instances groped from behind by part-objects attached to uncertainly gendered and sexualized bodies. The imputed lust the amorphously gendered Morlocks have for his body is ultimately driven by hunger, not sexual desire, but the two appetites are dangerously converging in this scene, and the relay between knowing and feeling can only induce violence in our protagonist that must then be understood as self-defense. In a world of gender confusion, the time-traveler experiences the desire for his male flesh as childish curiosity, cannibalistic hunger, and nascent homosexual panic. Wells is a deeply proto-Freudian thinker here, anticipating the narration of human origins in *Totem and Taboo* granted in the displaced mode of degeneration. The time-traveler must avoid becoming the totemic meal and avoid joining the expelled band of brothers who became strong enough, perhaps through homosexual feelings and acts, to kill the father to institute human sociality in the phylogeny of the very idea of culture.[54] The people of the future seem to be sliding back across the border between culture and nature. They don't work—they just touch and eat—their labor appears purely reproductive, if that.

The future—which for Wells must also be the past, if one takes seriously the idea of degeneration as an epistemology of sorts—like the colonies represents both a space of alterity in both gender and sexual norms for the white, male, about-to-be heterosexual exploring Victorian subject, but also a destabilizing fantasy of his past, a desublimating repetition that blurs all differences.

How does one read cannibalism in the novel? As a barely conscious recognition of the violence and destruction of the incorporation of racialized other humans into the global imperial economy in the mode of allegory? As a terror of what basic provisioning may be reduced to in a world without work? As a metaphor for the reification, the blurred line between people and things in the world as structured by the fetish character of the commodity? The terror of a world where there is only reproductive labor? As a moral warning—if you relinquish work like the Eloi, you deserve to be eaten? All of the above?

Bulwer-Lytton's *The Coming Race* presents a similar set of questions even though it is set at the same time of his narrator but in another place, the depths of the earth.[55] However, as the title and the last lines of the novel suggest, the underworld is a harbinger of the future: "I have thought it my duty to my fellow-men to place on record these forewarnings of The Coming Race."[56] The novel plays with versions of different gender and labor norms in a similar popular evolutionary paradigm to the Wells text, but reflects more explicit engagement with the colonial context. The continued well-being of the community of the racially superior Vril-ya is dependent on continuing imperial expansion. As the child Vril-ya Tae explains to Tish, our human narrator, in the world beneath the surface of the earth: "Of course, we cannot settle in lands already occupied by the Vril-ya, and if we take the cultivated lands of other races of Ann [humanity], we must utterly destroy the previous inhabitants. Sometimes, as it is, we take wastespots, and find that a troublesome, quarrelsome race of Ann [humanity]... resents our vicinity and picks a quarrel with us, thus, of course, as menacing our welfare, we destroy it."[57]

The link between colonialism and Utopia/futurity that Wilde will subsequently express metaphorically is by Bulwer-Lytton enacted in a narrative. The Vril-ya are continually in search of new lands, sometimes termed "wastespots," in order to make them productive, but they will also take via conquest the cultivated land of other races of Ann—the novel's term for humans. (The children of the Vril-ya compose the military on account of children's "natural" viciousness.) The Vril-ya understanding of the need to "utterly destroy the previous inhabitants" of their imperial possessions prefigures much later analyses of "disaster capitalism" and the booster phrase "creative destruction" or "creative disruption," allowing us to see that willy-nilly they are ideological echoes of the political economy of colonialism.[58] Bulwer-Lytton's biographical colonial connections are clearer than Wells's or Wilde's. Bulwer-Lytton, when he was the British Colonial Secretary in 1858, exhorted MPs "to fulfill the mission of the Anglo-Saxon race, in spreading intelligence, freedom and Christian faith, wherever Providence gives us the dominion of the earth."[59] The colonial exploits of the Vril-ya follow precisely such instructions—if one substitutes Vril-ya for Anglo-Saxon and Vril for intelligence, freedom, and Christian faith—yet Lytton sets his novel underground somewhere in the United States. Glancingly, one could read *The Coming Race* as something like an intraracial allegory that anticipates the passing of the imperial torch from Britain to the United States some thirty years before Rudyard Kipling writes the lines that ironically are often taken to define the British Empire, but actually mark its imagined transference of authority to the Americans, who in the famous poem are urged:

> Take up the white man's burden,
>   Send forth the best ye breed.
> Go bind your sons to exile
>   To serve your captives' need;
> To wait in heavy harness
>   On fluttered folk and wild—
> Your new-caught, sullen peoples,
>   Half devil and half child.[60]

The American Vril-ya are phenotypically represented as recognizable fantasies of Native Americans: tall, reddish-bronze in color, feathered headdresses have slipped down to shoulders to become wings, but most alarmingly, rather than enacting a world of gender indeterminacy, the world of the Vril-ya is a world of gender inversion, and the magical substance of Vril ensures that no labor is required at all for basic provisioning. Women are stronger, more intelligent, and only just contained by a patriarchal order. The demise of the figure of the productive worker is coterminous with the disappearance of the male provider—both staple figurations in the long imaginaries of the past, present, and future of work. Although women occupy most positions of intellectual leadership, the ultimate authority of the Vril-ya is still a man. Most important, in matters of sexual desire, women take the initiative. Tellingly, Darwin's *The Descent of Man* is published in the same year as *The Coming Race*. In Bulwer-Lytton's Darwinian schema, the Vril-ya women have agency in sexual selection. The narrator is acutely uncomfortable being the object of Zee's affections, experiencing being actively wooed by a woman as emasculating in both gender and racial terms: "Is it that, among the race I belong to, man's pride so far influences his passions that woman loses to him her special charm of woman if he feels her to be in all things eminently superior to himself? But by what strange infatuation could this peerless daughter of a race which, in the supremacy of its powers and the felicity of its conditions, ranked all other races in the category of barbarians, have deigned to honour me with her preference?"[61]

While the Vril-ya deploy Vril to ensure that no one in their society lacks the essentials for living, the narrator is distressed not just by their reversal of gender roles in courtship and his recognition of their racial superiority, but also by what he perceives as their artistic mediocrity. Unlike Wilde, who argues that freedom from want is what enables human creativity, Bulwer-Lytton (like Wells) suggests the necessity of striving—that greatness requires hardship and the working to overcome it.

In *The Coming Race*, *The Time Machine*, and "The Soul of Man Under Socialism," imaginings of worlds free of alienated labor are thought through in the complicated gendered and racialized terms of the uneven uptake of Darwinian evolution and informed by the context (and metaphors) of British colonialism. Tellingly, only Wilde, perhaps because it is too close to home, fails to pose the question of how a world without economic divisions of productive and reproductive labor can sustain gender differentiation and the attendant normativity of what anachronistically can be called heterosexual desire.

What import, if any, may my opening version of Wilde's understanding of art and labor have upon questions of the future of race, gender, sexuality, and work? Or will we have to change race, gender, and sexuality to shift the future of work? If the capacity for pleasure rather than the necessity of labor—productive and reproductive—is posited as the defining essence of humanity, sexuality is easily and dangerously severed from reproduction. If Walter Pater's dictum that value resides in the experience itself rather than the fruit of experience is applied to questions of sexual desire, reproductive heterosexuality loses its social usefulness.

Both Wells and Bulwer-Lytton reassert the imperative of work/labor for civilization in ways that run counter to Wilde, although all three ultimately measure civilization in aesthetic terms. In *The Time Machine*, the Eloi make nothing, let alone art. They cannot produce anything of aesthetic value, although they may be themselves of aesthetic value—they look good enough to eat. But being too enfeebled by centuries of ease, they cannot even defend themselves against the ravenous Morlocks. Similarly, the invincibility and material comfort the Vril-ya possess by virtue of their technological advancement and their possession of the magical power of the Vril renders the idea of alienated labor redundant. Therefore, they have produced no great literature, painting, or music for centuries. Darwinian in a different way from Wilde, Wells and Bulwer-Lytton both assert the importance of struggle aesthetically. Here is Tish speaking to Aph-Lin in *The Coming Race:* "I could not help expressing to Aph-Lin my surprise that a community in which mechanical science had made so marvelous a progress and in which intellectual civilisation had exhibited itself in realising those objects for the happiness of the people . . . should nevertheless, be so wholly without a contemporaneous literature." Aph-Lin replies in no uncertain terms that without passion, want, and struggle, literature cannot survive. The Vril-ya through the magical power of Vril have precisely the slavery of machines that Wilde calls for in "The Soul of Man Under Socialism"—"[where] mechanical science had made so marvelous a progress."[62]

All three texts valorize (with a few qualifications) the imagined evolutionary advantages of technology in radically different ways. *The Time Machine* can be read as representing deep terror as to what may happen if the leisured classes lose control of the means of production, by losing control of technology, to the working classes over the evolutionary long-term. Familiarity with machinery is ultimately what gives the Morlocks the edge in the struggle for life, and the novel thus obliquely, yet deeply, insists on the dignity of manual labor. In *The Coming Race*, Bulwer-Lytton's vision of a world without alienated labor is a world civilizationally impoverished, a world without poverty, but dependent on brutal force and colonial expansion and frighteningly emasculating. Both Wells and Bulwer-Lytton can only imagine a world without work as degeneration, and the future and underground races are civilizationally inferior to their own, although that inferiority is most felt by Bulwer-Lytton in the inability of the Vril-ya, for all their technological greatness, to make great art.

My three selected texts have radically different conceptions on the role of the state and questions of governance in their generation of new imaginaries of work. For Wilde in "The Soul of Man Under Socialism," the state is to make all that is useful or necessary for social reproduction, and the individuals will make what pleases them. For Wells, the state has withered away altogether and the results are disastrous. In *The Coming Race*, the state is barely vestigial, its leadership is largely ceremonial, and it does not need to have anything to do with provisioning.

For Wilde, a future without alienated labor or a future without labor at all is hoped for without reservation. His notions of what constitutes civilization are dependent, like Bulwer-Lytton and Wells, on European aesthetic canons and standards and remain in most instances normatively white and male. Nevertheless, his vision of a future aristocracy for all is unencumbered by warnings of the dire consequences of transforming nineteenth-century class, racial, and gender divisions. All three texts reveal that questions of transformed labor and work relations cannot be thought separately from imaginings of race, gender, sexuality, and governance. Current framings of the future of work—diagnostic and prescriptive, techno-optimist and techno-pessimist—would do well to remember these earlier optimistic fantasies and wild terrors that still shape our imaginaries of the future of work.

NOTES

This chapter greatly benefited from being workshopped by the members of the Beyond Inequality seminar on Zoom in the summer of 2021. Giulia Adelina Oprea gave most helpful feedback on an earlier draft, and Cooper Christiancy's comments smoothed out inconsistencies and generally improved the piece. Thanks also to my coeditor Karen Engle, for, inter alia, seeing how a disciplinary outlier chapter like this one could work.

1. Max Weber, *The Protestant Ethic and the "Spirit" of Capitalism and Other Writings*, trans. Peter Baehr and Gordon C. Wells (New York: Penguin, 2002).
2. For another account that also contextualizes modern worries about newly automated work via reference to the 1800s, see Qingkun (Eric) Deng, "Technology's Impact on the Labor Market: Different This Time?," *Futures of Work*, November 29, 2022, https://futuresofwork.co.uk/2022/11/29/technologys-impact-on-the-labour-market-different-this-time/.
3. Samuel Butler, *Erewhon* (Harmondsworth, UK: Penguin, 1970).
4. Edward Bellamy, *Looking Backward: From 2000 to 1887* (Bedford, MA: Applewood, 2000).
5. William Morris, *News from Nowhere: An Epoch of Rest, Being Some Chapters from a Utopian Romance* (New York: Vanguard, 1926).
6. For a transatlantic working through of cognate issues, see Charlotte Perkins Gilman's *Herland* (1915) which describes a world free of both men and private property, but the work of the Herlanders is a secondary concern to the inability of the three male travelers to comprehend an egalitarian society comprised entirely of women. Charlotte Perkins Gilman, *Herland* (New York: Pantheon, 1979). This story was first published in 1915 as a serial in Gilman's own magazine, *The Forerunner*.
7. Richard Jefferies, *After London; Or, Wild England* (London: Cassell, 1886).
8. Henry Mayhew, *London Labour and the London Poor* (London: C. Griffin, 1864). Henry Mayhew would provide a much more realist context for thinking through Victorian worries about the future of work.
9. Oscar Wilde, "The Soul of Man Under Socialism," in *The Complete Works of Oscar Wilde: Stories, Plays, Poems, & Essays* (London: HarperPerennial, 2008), 1079–1104.
10. Oscar Wilde's techno-optimism finds a modern analog in the utopian platform of "fully automated luxury communism" (which is characterized by echoes of Wildean irony): "After the realm of speculation, we draw upon the world as it is, or rather as it is becoming. Here we examine seemingly disparate technologies—in automation, energy, resources, health and food—before concluding that the foundations are cohering for a society beyond both scarcity and work." Aaron Bastani, *Fully Automated Luxury Communism: A Manifesto* (London: Verso, 2019), 12; Daphne Luchtenberg, "The Fourth Industrial Revolution Will Be People-Powered," *McKinsey & Company*, January 17, 2022, https://www.mckinsey.com/capabilities/operations/our-insights/the-fourth-industrial-revolution-will-be-people-powered; Edward Bulwer-Lytton, *The Coming Race* (New York: Francis B. Felt, 1871).
11. Betsy F. Moeller-Sally, "Oscar Wilde and the Culture of Russian Modernism," *The Slavic and East European Journal* 34, no. 4 (Winter 1990): 459–72.

12. William Morris, *The Collected Works of William Morris* (New York: Cambridge University Press, 2012), 22: 338.
13. Wilde, *The Soul of Man*, 1080.
14. Karl Marx, *Economic and Philosophic Manuscripts of 1844* (New York: International, 1964), 122.
15. Wilde, *The Soul of Man*, 1089.
16. In this fantasy of the slavery of the machine, Wilde could be a case study in Dustin Abnet's reading of robots in American history: "Robots have been primarily imagined and built by men whose gender, whiteness, training, or wealth has taught them that they were entitled to privilege." Dustin A. Abnet, *The American Robot: A Cultural History* (Chicago: University of Chicago Press, 2020), 8, ProQuest Ebook Central.
17. Oscar Wilde, *De Profundis* (London: Methuen, 1912).
18. Joseph R. Gusfield, "Social Structure and Moral Reform: A Study of the Woman's Christian Temperance Union," *American Journal of Sociology* 61, no. 3 (1955): 225; and Frank Harris, *Oscar Wilde: His Life and Confessions* (New York: printed by author, 1916), 1:166.
19. Oscar Wilde, *The Wit and Humor of Oscar Wilde*, ed. Alvin Redman (New York: Dover, 2012), 118.
20. Wilde, *The Soul of Man*, 1089.
21. John Ruskin, "Imperial Duty" (speech, Oxford, February 8, 1870), https://www.sahistory.org.za/archive/imperial-duty-john-ruskin-oxford-8-february-1870-0.
22. Vladimir Il'ich Lenin, *Imperialism: The Highest Stage of Capitalism* (London: Pluto, 1996).
23. Giovanni Arrighi, "The Global Market," *Journal of World-Systems Research* 5, no. 2 (August 26, 1999): 216–51.
24. Abnet, *The American Robot*, 9.
25. Abnet, *The American Robot*, 9–10. See also Gregory Jerome Hampton, *Imagining Slaves and Robots in Literature, Film, and Popular Culture: Reinventing Yesterday's Slave with Tomorrow's Robot* (Lanham, MD: Lexington, 2015); and Neda Atanasoski and Kalindi Vora, *Surrogate Humanity: Race, Robots, and the Politics of Technological Futures* (Durham, NC: Duke University Press, 2019).
26. Richard Ellmann, *Oscar Wilde* (London: Hamish Hamilton, 1987).
27. Wilde, *The Soul of Man*, 1079.
28. Charles Dickens, *Bleak House* (London: Bradbury & Evans, 1853).
29. The gendering of discourses of imperial benevolence is too large a topic to engage here, but a key contradiction can be noted between the feminization of imperial benevolence in a figure such as Mrs. Jellyby and the muscular Christianity of the book *Tom Brown's Schooldays* (1857). Thomas Hughes, *Tom Brown's Schooldays* (Oxford: Oxford World Classics, 2008).
30. J. K. Thisen, "The Design of Structural Adjustment Programs: The African Alternative Framework," *Africa Development / Afrique et Développement* 16, no. 1 (1991): 115–64, http://www.jstor.org/stable/43657880.
31. Matthew Bishop and Michael Green, *Philanthrocapitalism: How the Rich Can Save the World* (London: Bloomsbury, 2008).

32. Teju Cole, "The White-Savior Industrial Complex," *The Atlantic*, March 21, 2012, https://www.theatlantic.com/international/archive/2012/03/the-white-savior-industrial-complex/254843/.
33. Wilde, *The Wit and Humor of Oscar Wilde*, 113.
34. Oscar Wilde, *The Picture of Dorian Grey and Other Writings* (New York: Simon & Schuster, 2005), 353.
35. Wilde, *The Picture of Dorian Grey*, 348.
36. Joseph Conrad, *Heart of Darkness: An Authoritative Text, Backgrounds and Sources, Essays in Criticism* (New York: Norton, 1963), 69.
37. Friedrich Engels, "Engels and Darwin—Letter to Lavrov," ed. Dona Torr, *Labor Monthly* 18, no. 7 (1936): 437–42.
38. Wilde, *The Soul of Man*, 1100–1101.
39. Wilde, *The Soul of Man*, 1088.
40. See John Rieder, *Colonialism and the Emergence of Science Fiction* (Middletown, CT: Wesleyan University Press: 2008), and Patricia Kerslake, *Science Fiction and Empire* (Liverpool: Liverpool University Press, 2007), for the lineaments of the ideological and material connections between the emergence of science fiction as a recognizable genre and nineteenth-century European Empire.
41. Edgar Rice Burroughs, *Barsoom Series*, 3 vols. (New York: Penguin Random House, 1985).
42. *Total Recall*, directed by Paul Verhoeven (Culver City, CA: Tri-Star Pictures, 1990).
43. H. G. Wells, *The Definitive Time Machine: A Critical Edition of H.G. Wells's Scientific Romance*, ed. Harry M Geduld (Bloomington: Indiana University Press, 1987), 57.
44. Wells, *The Definitive Time Machine*, 82.
45. Max Simon Nordau, *Degeneration* (New York: D. Appleton, 1985). See also Alexander Scherr, "The Morlock-Eloi Illusion: Shifting Monstrosities in H.G. Wells' The Time Machine in the Context of the Degeneration Discourse," *Anglistik: International Journal of English Studies* 30, no. 3 (Winter 2019): 121–33.
46. Wells, *The Definitive Time Machine*, 45.
47. Wells, *The Definitive Time Machine*, 45.
48. Wells, *The Definitive Time Machine*, 49.
49. Johannes Fabian, *Time and the Other: How Anthropology Makes Its Object* (New York: Columbia University Press, 1983). Johannes Fabian offers the most rigorous account of how the spatialization of time produces racial difference.
50. Wells, *The Definitive Time Machine*, 45.
51. Wells, *The Definitive Time Machine*, 67.
52. Wells, *The Definitive Time Machine*, 67
53. Describing the homosexual panic defense, law professor Cynthia Lee writes that "borrowing from Kempf's Homosexual Panic Disorder theory, male defendants charged with murdering gay men have sought mitigation or exoneration by claiming gay panic, either as a manifestation of mental disease or defect or as support for a claim of provocation or self-defense." Cynthia Lee, "The Gay Panic Defense," *University of California-Davis Law Review* 42 (2008): 489. As Lee alludes, the homosexual panic defense was derived from the purported Homosexual Panic Disorder, proposed by psychiatrist Edward J. Kempf in 1920 as "panic due to the pressure of

uncontrollable perverse sexual cravings." Edward J. Kempf, "The Psychology of the Acute Homosexual Panic," in *Psychopathology* (St. Louis: C.V. Mosby, 1921), 477. See also Robert G. Bagnall, Patrick C. Gallagher, and Joni L. Goldstein, "Burdens on Gay Litigants and Bias in the Court System: Homosexual Panic, Child Custody, and Anonymous Parties," *Harvard Civil Rights-Civil Liberties Law Review* 19, no. 2 (Summer 1984): 499. The doctrinal basis for the gay panic defense can usually be conceptualized through distinct yet interconnected legal theories that suggest lack of guilt or diminished guilt (and therefore diminished punishment) due to insanity or diminished capacity prompted by hysteria triggered by latent homosexuality, heat of passion or provocation brought on by unwanted homosexual overtures, and self-defense due to perceptions of threat caused by homosexual advances. See Lee, "Gay Panic Defense," 489–509. The defense is often enabled by the leeway given to (presumably heterosexual) men to violently protect their heterosexuality and masculinity from the "threat" of non-normative sexuality. Lee, "Gay Panic Defense," 507–8. In this regard, it is important to note that the concept has not been limited only to violence against homosexual men. For example, the murder trial following the killing of seventeen-year-old Gwen Araujo in 2002 by four men featured a "trans panic defense." See Moya Lloyd, "Heteronormativity and/as Violence: The 'Sexing' of Gwen Araujo," *Hypatia* 28, no. 4 (Fall 2013): 818–34.

54. Sigmund Freud, *Totem and Taboo: Some Points of Agreement Between the Mental Lives of Savages and Neurotics* (London: Routledge, 2014).
55. Jules Verne's *Journey to the Center of the Earth* (1864) is something of a precursor to Bulwer-Lytton's novel. *The Coming Race* had an interesting future ahead. See Boris Kachka, "The Nazis Came from Middle Earth (and Possibly Still Live There)," *New York Magazine*, November 15, 2013, https://nymag.com/news/features/conspiracy-theories/nazi-vril-society/. According to myth, it will become one of Adolf Hitler's favorite novels.
56. Bulwer-Lytton, *The Coming Race*, 126.
57. Bulwer-Lytton, *The Coming Race*, 209.
58. Mike Davis, *Late Victorian Holocausts: El Niño Famines and the Making of the Third World* (London: Verso, 2017).
59. Peter Fryer, *Staying Power: Black People in Britain Since 1504* (Atlantic Highlands, NJ: Humanities, 1984), 182.
60. Rudyard Kipling, "The White Man's Burden," *The Times* (London), February 4, 1899. This poem was also sent to Teddy Roosevelt to encourage American imperial ambitions. Anjuli Fatima Raza Kolb, *Epidemic Empire: Colonialism, Contagion, Terror, 1817–2020* (Chicago: University of Chicago Press, 2021), 1.
61. Bulwer-Lytton, *The Coming Race*, 142–43.
62. Bulwer-Lytton, *The Coming Race*, 112.

CHAPTER 7

RECOVERING THE PAST AND THE OUTSIDE

Sites for New Imaginaries of the Future of Work

KERRY RITTICH

The "future of work" lies at the center of a panoply of social and political disturbances and challenges. Both in the Global South and in the Global North, it is now recognized that for a rising number of workers, work has become insecure, fragmented, and unstable, while for others it remains an enduring source of struggle and disadvantage. At the same time, work's significance to social, economic, and political crises has (re)surfaced with a vengeance, if in immensely varied ways. Now, as in the past, the experience of insecurity, struggle, and disadvantage at work spills over in myriad directions, destabilizing households, transforming communities, and upending political settlements. Almost everywhere, far from a defined and purely private concern, the conditions under which work is performed turn out to be connected, even central, to major social and political challenges—economic inequality, social inclusion, racial fracturing, gender equality, and democratic legitimacy and participation among them.

Addressing these challenges going forward is no easy matter, at least via the strategies of the past: for one, climate change and ecological crises and limits have now destabilized the ground—continuous economic growth—upon which improvements to work have traditionally been achieved; for another, existing legal and political institutions often seem inadequate to address events and phenomena that traverse borders in a transnationalized world of production. It is also becoming clear that aspirations for democracy and greater economic, social, and racial justice can *themselves* be approached as questions of work: it seems unlikely that such aspirations can be realized without attention to how they are advanced—or undermined—by developments at work. This puts work at the center of important social and political issues, making the future of work part of the solution as well as part of the problem.

Amid these tectonic changes and challenges, myriad visions of the future of work, along with projects to realize those visions, are now in circulation, many of which come from international institutions. Charting the promise and perils of the road ahead, these future-of-work projects come saturated with the goals of "decent" or "better" work and efficient labor markets, fueled by technological innovation and an ever more skilled, productive, and responsive labor force. These goals, along with the means to reach them, are presented as complementary, at least if pursued in their ideal forms. They are now also understood as universalizable, that is, relevant and applicable to workers whatever their personal or national circumstances.

Taking these projects as a starting point, in this chapter I challenge such claims, examining the enduring connections between work and distributive injustice, those that track the fault lines of race and gender as well as those that reflect the traditional concerns of labor in its conflicts with capital. Throughout I suggest that the future of work be read, and told, as a story of the present and the past of work. Reading that past, while refusing or reversing some conventional assumptions—about what constitutes the past of work rather than its present and about the work that is normal rather than exceptional—this discussion draws on histories of racial capitalism and analyses of social reproduction to capture a more complex picture of the position of workers and thereby set the ground for a broader conception of distributive justice and the "law of work" that underpins it. My aim, sketched in broad overview with illustrative examples, is to recover elements of that past that are imagined as marginal or outside the story of work and to use those elements to assess the projected future of work. As we think about what makes work "better" or "worse," part of the task is looking at work's boundaries and territory: what we see *as* work, and what we see as being beyond its borders.

I begin by surveying the current landscape of work, considering transformations now underway and identifying some foundational assumptions that underpin current projects on the future of work by international institutions. Using the example of technology at work, I consider where those assumptions—and hence different pathways to the future of work—might be uncertain or contingent on decisions about the legal infrastructure *of* work. I then describe three strategies or "moves" to both reveal and better assess the possibilities of distributive justice at work going forward. The first move is to consider past efforts to improve work, exploring the consequences of labor commodification and market engagement for workers at earlier moments in time. The second is to look at labor's "outside," to forms of work, such as informal work, that are not imagined as central to the future of work. The third involves expanding the scope of distributional analysis at work, taking up the racial stratification of work and the neglected domain of unpaid labor.

SURVEYING THE LANDSCAPE OF WORK

A convergence of developments has transformed the landscape of work, at the same time upending the foundations of economic and social life across the industrialized world. At the center of this upheaval is a significant erosion, now quite advanced, of the work relationship that both anchored the organization of work in the industrialized world and, during the twentieth century, provided the normative foundation for labor law and much of social policy: the standard employment relationship (SER). As its presence has faded, a profusion of alternative work forms and relations has emerged in its stead, many of which are proving to be both precarious and insecure for workers—even as they generate significant benefits for those who control the terms of work and those who consume the services and products that workers create.[1] In tandem with the erosion of the SER—indeed, fueling that erosion—is a parallel undermining of the institutions of worker representation, namely, trade unions. The result of this loss of collective voice is declining influence of workers, both over the terms and conditions under which they labor and within the political arenas in which the regulatory stakes of work are negotiated and settled.

These transformations are but the surface phenomena of more fundamental shifts in the ground of work, the contributing factors of which are, at this point, multiple and deeply intertwined. They include the decline of manufacturing and the rise of the service economy; the increasing utilization of "just in time," often task oriented, labor; the displacement of employment by "gig" or contract work; and the related fragmentation or "fissuring" of workplace relations.[2] These developments, in turn, are connected to technological and digital innovations that, along with the rise of value chains and processes of financialization, have transformed the economy writ large.

Yet most workers in the Global South have never worked in waged employment, let alone that of the "standard" kind. Although modernization narratives have long posited a future tracking that of the Global North as countries developed, when it comes to work, any such assumption is now manifestly unsafe. Whatever the future holds, in the Global South some—and perhaps much— work is certain to take different forms, engage new problems, and require responses unlike those familiar in the Global North. Indeed, the future of work in the North is itself uncharted territory, as the entry of low-cost labor into the circuits of global production has traveled in tandem with the proliferation of atypical and "informal" types of work within postindustrial economies too. Arguably, one problem lies with the prevailing idea of "normal" work, the path it projects forward for workers, and the limits it imposes on imagining work's possible futures.[3] As a guide to the future of work, traditional benchmarks are losing their power and, in some cases, their relevance as well.

THE FUTURE OF WORK: OVERLAPPING AND CONVERGING INSTITUTIONAL VISIONS

Emanating from international institutions devoted to matters of finance, development, and human rights, as well as labor, is a series of narratives and projects reflecting contending imaginaries around the future of work. Each institution sees the landscape of work through the prism of its principal mandate and concerns, each evaluates the challenges on the horizon accordingly, each proposes strategies by which to move forward, and each competes for allegiance, especially when it comes to the pressing issue of "what is to be done."

For some, workers have nothing to fear: the future looks bright, as long as they successfully adapt to the demands of the emerging world of work by "upping their game."[4] For others, the future is one of increased precarity in which workers face threats that, if not successfully addressed through law and policy, stand to seriously trouble both the path forward and the end results.

The World Bank and, as might be expected, the International Labor Organization (ILO) have been especially engaged in these narratives and projects. The World Bank charts an optimistic future of work, one in which, as long as the right policies are pursued and the appropriate rules and institutions are in place, workers can expect to see benefits commensurate with the skill or human capital they accumulate and successfully deploy. Along with jobs themselves, these benefits include greater flexibility and autonomy generated by technological and digital innovations; upward social as well as economic mobility through the adoption of entrepreneurial attitudes and practices at work; and income gains and improved working conditions through increased productivity realized through the formalization of work.[5]

The ILO, for its part, has long sought a brighter future by strengthening the recognition of fundamental principles and rights at work.[6] Along with the extension of labor and social protections to excluded workers, measures to ease transitions between jobs in an increasingly unstable labor market, and initiatives to promote the participation of groups such as women and youth, the practical realization of an extended range of rights at work—now threatened by developments such as platform and supply chain work—in the eyes of the ILO remains crucial to a future at work that ensures inclusive and sustainable economic growth.[7]

Each vision contains both utopian and dystopian elements, all of which are firmly rooted in present dilemmas of work. Although they diverge and even conflict in some respects, there is a zone of convergence or overlap in these visions. Despite differences in the weight they are accorded as well their implications in the policy calculus, almost all institutions subscribe to the following propositions concerning the future of work.[8] We might think of these propositions as interlinked articles of faith and fact that form the knowledge base and influence the consciousness of experts as they consider the future of work.

The first, and most basic, proposition is *the inevitability of constant upheaval and change at work*. Imagine a dynamic world of changing products and services, catalyzing continual modifications to the processes by which they are created and delivered, all accompanied by increasingly unstable work patterns, routines, and demands. Whether this scenario is styled as a source of opportunity through processes of "creative destruction," one of growing precarity and insecurity for workers, or some mixture of each, the need for responsive and continuous adaptation on the part of workers is a given.[9]

The second proposition is the fact—and intensity—of *global competition for work*. Whatever the challenges posed by globalized markets, and despite calls to "reshore" production in the wake of supply chain disruptions provoked by geopolitical rivalries, military conflict, and pandemics, no one imagines a future in which workers are insulated within national markets from global trends at work.

The third proposition is *the centrality of technology and innovation to the organization, and reorganization, of work and production*. For most institutional actors, this centrality is simply axiomatic. The ILO is alert to technology's emerging risks to workers, but others, claiming that such fears are overdrawn if not simply wrong, emphasize technology's benefits. In the words of the World Bank, "the pace of innovation will determine whether new sectors or tasks emerge to counterbalance the decline of old sectors and routine jobs as technology costs decline."[10]

Because of the conjoined claims that higher productivity drives economic growth while better work tracks gains in worker productivity, the fourth proposition concerns *the need for greater skill and capacity to adapt to technological change*. For the ILO, the preferred language is "increasing investment in peoples' capabilities."[11] For the World Bank, the challenge is fixing the "human capital gap," with "human capital" encompassing the cognitive, behavioral, and dispositional traits—including "perseverance, collaboration, and empathy"—that conduce to success within dynamic, innovative labor markets.[12]

Fifth is *the importance of formalizing labor markets*. Whether informality is perceived as a problem because of its association with poor work or whether the concern is low levels of productivity, immense confidence is reposed in the rule of law to solve labor market problems.

Finally, all mainstream international institutions now subscribe to the premise that *the private sector is the principal source of economic growth and job creation.* Whatever the appropriate role of the state in the production of jobs and the regulation of labor markets—a matter on which historic differences among labor and finance institutions remain—everyone is of the view that workers' fates will largely be disposed by the decisions taken by private actors in the market for labor.[13]

Yet each one of these assumptions deserves deeper scrutiny. Rather than constituting a clear guide to action, on reflection they open further lines of inquiry, revealing possible complications or contextual differences that might vary or even upend the path to the future of work. Consider the following: although upheaval in labor and production both destroys and creates work opportunities, many people, and in some regions the majority, still work in traditional economic activities such as agriculture, fishing, or forestry, trading in local rather than "global" markets. When upheaval *does* move such people into new forms of work, their relative position—at the bottom of the labor market—often remains unchanged.

Relentless competition among workers *does* seem hard-wired into globalized markets, especially within production and service-delivery organized via supply chains. However, the degree and intensity of that competition varies significantly, as do the consequences for workers. Territories and borders still matter, as do the rules, policies, and programs implemented to manage the processes of investment and exchange in which work takes place.[14] "Competition" seems an inadequate description of the way that workers are sorted within jobs or markets for labor in any event. Although the benefits of greater skill and adaptability may seem obvious, it can be difficult to attribute workers' status either to skill and entrepreneurial spirit or their lack. Historical distinctions among workers, including along lines of race and gender, provide compelling counternarratives in many cases. And where in this narrative should we locate the (re)structuring of work, an important driver of precarious work, or corporate mergers that concentrate market power and reduce labor market competition in general?

Technological innovation certainly drives labor market change. Yet its relation to productivity and income gains for workers is highly contingent. Freedom and flexibility are the watchwords of technology's upsides for workers, but technology's downsides are already well-established in contexts such as platform work.[15] It may be unhelpful to imagine technology, at least on its own, as either the engine of progress or an ineluctable source of disadvantage for workers. For related reasons, at least some of technology's benefits—and risks—remain up for grabs. *Do labor markets operating under the "rule of law" reliably deliver improved labor* market outcomes?[16] Although the benefits of formalizing legal entitlements at work are among the most sacred of beliefs, whether, how, and for whom those benefits materialize are puzzles that remain to be fully explored.

Finally, although the private sector's significance to work seems indisputable, in the end its role cannot be separated from a raft of public institutions, decisions, and actions. Indeed, invocation of "the private" may obscure the many conflicts *within* economic relations, veiling the pivotal role played by states in empowering private actors and constructing the terrain on which conflicts among them play out.

These questions do no more than suggest the complexities to be traversed. One way to illustrate their significance to the future of work, however, is through a brief review of the possibilities of technology for workers.

TECHNOLOGY AT WORK

Innovation driven by technological change is now imagined as the elixir of growth. But technology-based growth models may be ill-conceived or at least limited as modes of catalyzing greater economic productivity and efficiency. Rather than spectacular innovations such as the digital revolution of Silicon Valley, the most productive forms of innovation may involve piecemeal change achieved through more prosaic investments in people, processes, and preexisting local advantages.[17] There are, in addition, reasons to think that innovation agendas centered on robotics and artificial intelligence primarily reflect the concerns of industrialized states rather than those in the Global South.[18] Nonetheless, there can be little doubt that technology as a transformative force occupies center stage when it comes to the future of work.

Whatever its immanent possibilities for advancing equality and inclusion, so far technology has proved to be, at best, a mixed blessing for workers, serving firm objectives in ways that go beyond mere "efficiency" enhancement as classically understood.[19] Technology's downside for workers is not limited to the displacement of labor by machines—an old, and enduring, phenomenon, especially in the manufacturing sector where automation is a major factor in the decline of jobs. Technology has provided new modes of exercising control over workers, enabling more intense surveillance of workers and facilitating micro-adjustments to the pace and intensity of work. In so doing, it has also conferred unusual powers on the employer to change the terms, conditions, and rewards received by workers.

Algorithms under the exclusive, proprietary control of the employer enable the allocation and monitoring of labor with unprecedented precision, permitting firms to speed up task completion rates and rank performance levels, often without any communication with the workers involved.[20] They also allow firms to calculate exactly how much—and how little—workers can be expected to tolerate, and to calibrate the terms and conditions of work accordingly.[21] When applied to rapidly accumulating human resource and social network data, algorithms provide opportunities for expanded wage discrimination as well.[22]

To the extent that they intensify the subordination and control against which workers have always sought to exercise countervailing power, such practices look like the latest iteration of a familiar problem. Yet whether the workplace problems generated by technology are old or new, there are good reasons for fundamentally reformulating the questions around technology. One reason is that technology neither exists nor operates on its own; instead, it is a classic example of a hybrid actor.[23] What we experience as technology, at work and elsewhere, is technology intermixed with human action, modes of organization and classification, physical geography, etc. Rather than an independent force or entity, we may be better off approaching technology as part of a complex or amalgam of mechanisms, institutions, practices, spatial arrangements, and forms of knowledge—whose effects or consequences vary dynamically with the combination and arrangement of elements involved.

Technology at work is situated within productive relations and organizational networks; those relations and networks, in turn, operate through norms, rules, and institutions, social and cultural as well as legal.[24] The manner in which technology becomes conjoined with social practices and legal institutions influences its character, scope, and use. As is the case with other productive resources, technology is governed by legal rules and institutions conferring powers and immunities and also imposing limits and constraints on its users and "stakeholders."[25] Decisions about these entitlements, those operating directly on technology as well as those operating in the background—from the private law regimes of property and contract to corporate, tax, and antitrust law—stand to affect whether workers (and others) derive technology's benefits or suffer its burdens, in what ways, and by how much.[26] At the same time, technology may itself act on workers' rights—making it more difficult to exercise associational freedoms at work or, by contrast, enabling new modes of organizing geographically dispersed workers.[27]

To mention one obvious point of interest, it matters who controls the technology behind digital and platform work. Although it could conceivably be otherwise, this control almost invariably rests with firms, who use their property rights to ensure that it is their interests and commercial aims, rather than those of workers, consumers, and others, that prevail in technology's use.[28] Competition or antitrust law then reinforces this control, enabling platform-based firms to use the corporate form to determine unilaterally the price of their services—even as they claim that those who actually deliver those services form no part of their enterprises. Those same rules then preclude those "independent contractors" from coordinating their actions to respond in like manner, for example, by raising the price of their labor or withdrawing it entirely.[29]

The issues surrounding technology illustrate a more general issue for the future of work: whether, and how much, workers stand to lose or benefit in the new economy is contingent on the legal infrastructure *of* work, parts of which remain up for grabs; others of which although long settled are newly contested; and still others, like the employer's entitlement to govern the workplace and control the products of labor, are taken simply as naturalized elements of the ecosystem in which market economies operate.

As we have seen, institutional narratives concerning the future of work typically place workers on a path toward greater engagement with the market, promising gains through investments in human capital and entrepreneurial initiative, as long as their labor is organized under the rule of law and freedom of contract. If this path now appears to be perilous, these perils are not new. Both in the center and in the periphery, such promises have often failed to deliver, at least for workers.

To begin with a frank admission: we don't *know* what the future of work will look like. However, there seems little reason to assume *either* that it will unfold in accordance with modernist imaginaries *or* that it will be entirely discontinuous from what came before.[30] As with the present, it will carry elements of the past along with it. Without suggesting that this exhausts the possibilities, here I describe three moves that might help us think—and move forward—on this uncertain terrain.

The Past in the Present

The first move is to suspend or bracket the normative goals and advertised objectives around work to inquire what has traveled with projects to civilize or "improve" work in the past and to further ask who and what such projects have left behind or to the side. The aim here is to better see the future by reflecting on the past, indeed, to recover pasts of work that may be still with us. What we need, in the realm of work as elsewhere, is a genealogy of the present.[31] If part of the point is to render the present contingent by disrupting the idea that things had to become as they are, genealogical inquiry may equally serve to uncover disavowed connections and continuities with practices we think we have left behind.[32] We might ask, then, about work's histories and practices within global capitalism, inquiring how they connect to the forms of work and the predicaments workers face today. For example, what do (subaltern) histories of work suggest about the work relations sustained within transnationalized markets or the norms under which different workers labor? What counternarratives do they put in circulation, what problems do they help illuminate, and what paths forward do they suggest?

To begin, such histories remind us, ideologies of free trade and commerce notwithstanding, that unfree labor has long coexisted with free labor within globalized capitalist production.[33] For example, after abolition and a period of compulsory apprenticeships, enslaved plantation labor was replaced by indentured labor, a practice not ended until well into the twentieth century.[34] It is unclear that trafficking, indenture, and forced labor can always be distinguished from coercive forms of work within supply chains now; to the contrary, there are numerous points of connection between them.[35]

How much *can* workers expect from markets for labor organized under conditions of competitive contracting? It is worth recalling that the markets in "free" labor produced through legally sanctioned dispossession and the commodification of common resources were initially disastrous for workers, and not only in the colonial periphery.[36] Reading Oliver Goldsmith's celebrated meditation on the transformation of the English countryside amidst the industrial revolution, "Ill fares the land," David Bromwich notes that, whatever the promise of free contracting for work, many found themselves in a condition of "masterless servitude," leading lives of permanent displacement and destitution.[37] Far from an exceptional phenomenon, the creation of markets in wage labor and land routinely produced, along with desperate conditions of work, acute economic insecurity arising from the subjection of workers to the vagaries of market cycles and the rigors of competition as well as the arbitrary power of their employers. Out of those cataclysmic effects came the storied rise and backlash of the "social" against market forces described by Karl Polanyi, as well as the beginnings of labor law and the creation of the working class itself.[38]

Yet bad work and economic insecurity are hardly problems that have been conclusively "solved"; as the present moment confirms, they have a wicked tendency to recur. Amid today's relentless promotion of market engagement, it seems important to recall this history and to weigh the displacements and upheaval in social life that the commodification of labor and consumption may still provoke. Here, Furnivall's account of the consequences of the introduction of the rule of law and labor contracting in Burma (now Myanmar) stands as a cautionary tale. The "evils" that followed—from dysfunctional political institutions to increased crime and corruption and the routine immiseration of the agrarian populace—were all, in Furnivall's view, attributable to "the disintegration of social life through the inadequacy of law to control the working of anti-social economic forces."[39] For most, the introduction of law-governed markets constrained economic options, undercutting rather than enhancing economic security for the population as a whole. Polanyi famously made similar observations, linking the catastrophes that routinely befell those in the colonies as well as those at home to the liquidating force exerted by markets for labor, land, and money on the basic institutions of social and community life.[40]

But might market labor nonetheless promise greater freedom today? To what extent can workers expect to benefit from participating in law-governed markets, should they choose, or be compelled, to take this route? As described previously, dreams of the future of work are shot through with the promise of formalization.[41] Informal labor markets may indeed incubate dismal working conditions or perpetuate low levels of productivity—although, it seems only fair to note that reforms instituted in the Global South to spur investment and economic growth may themselves contribute to the expansion of informality.[42] Like informal housing, informal work routinely grows in the course of urbanization and development.[43] But along with other forms of precarious work, informal work now thrives within developed economies as well.[44] Put otherwise, the benefits of the rule of law for workers remain contingent; depending on the entitlements that are formalized and how they affect local practices, the possibilities, in both directions, are legion.[45] In some cases, formalization has left workers subject to new financial obligations without access to the social benefits that their tax contributions help fund.[46] And by displacing people from resources to which they previously had access, the titling and formalization of land may actually increase levels of informal labor—witness the many people who now migrate to urban centers in search of work even as the countryside "develops," a phenomenon visible all over the world, and the proliferation of informal markets in the rapidly expanding cities that inevitably follows. Yet in the North as well as the South, informal working arrangements may also provide workers with benefits or income greater than those available in formal work—think of the attractions of sex work or "under the table" arrangements that workers themselves adopt instead of—or on top of—formal employment and other licit work.

As we have seen, enhanced productivity through the cultivation of skills now dominates narratives about the future of work. But who gains? Workers now see diminishing returns from their market labor, as wages have remained flat despite rising levels of labor productivity.[47] This is a symptom of a general shift in the global balance of power: amid cross-cutting gains and losses at the local, national, and sectoral levels, workers' incomes have been sharply reduced relative to those of capital holders.[48] Given the direction in which the benefits of productivity now systematically flow, workers might well ask: for whom are they investing in their human capital?

Even in the absence of overt force and violence, contemporary markets remain sites of coercion. One source of coercion proves to be the obligation to labor due to financial pressures generated by debt. As was the case with earlier modernizing reforms,[49] the traps of indebtedness surface routinely for those now targeted for "financial inclusion,"[50] whether in aid of entrepreneurial development,[51] the "empowerment" of women,[52] reconstruction in the wake of armed conflict,[53] or all of the above. Indeed, debt follows so frequently from such initiatives that there may be reasons to see them as indelibly linked.

Debt-driven labor is now a constant companion of those in the postindustrial middle class too, as stagnant incomes fail to match rising household expenses and reliance on debt becomes simply a strategy of economic management, even survival. In the present as in the past, the problem is not merely that the promised rewards of market engagement do not always materialize. It is that so many find themselves working to service financial obligations whose burdens exceed any possible gain, bearing increased economic risks arising from events over which they have no control, and often doing so at the cost of the resources and relationships that formerly sustained both individual and collective life. Nor are these the only adverse effects; it is now clear that household debt plays a key role in economic recessions and financial crises as well.[54]

How innovative is gig work, and what might workers expect to gain from it? As both Max Weber and Immanuel Wallerstein observed, there is nothing new about the outsourcing of work; far from a transitional stage of capitalism, moreover, the "putting out" of work to the home or countryside has long traveled in tandem with the growth of industrial employment.[55] The logics behind such organizational tactics provide ongoing indications as to the results workers might expect now: to lower the costs of production; to externalize commercial risks; to circumvent worker associations such as guilds and the labor standards they seek to uphold; and to exploit the position of those with limited options in the market for labor.

In short, indebtedness is a routine companion of the contractualization of labor, while informality has endured, and in some cases expanded, with processes of industrialization and development. Given their role in the past of work, exploring these entanglements and their enabling conditions should be on the agenda for any "future of work" initiative invested in the promise of markets for workers.

Labor's Outside

In addition to recovering insights from subordinated or forgotten histories of work, inconvenient results of prior colonial interventions included, the second move is to look at labor's outside, to forms of work that are not imagined as part of the future, or even part of the world, of work at all. The strategy here is to perform a series of reversals on the assumptions underpinning "normal" work: its character and location; the identity of those who labor and the nature of their demands; the law and governance that both shapes work and to which it is a response; the trajectory of its evolution, etc. Such reversals not only bring a raft of new workers into the picture, repositioning them from "margin to center," they also reveal the limits of the conceptual structures that now govern work, channeling its future possibilities as well as its present forms.[56]

Here we might decenter formal, waged work and de-exceptionalize the many forms of work that now fall at the margins or outside the gaze of labor law and policy, seeing waged work as a subset of the larger field of productive labor and its normative centrality a contingent rather than a necessary feature of the future of work. The collateral move or "flip" is to take work relations in the Global South seriously, not as a "past" of work that must be overcome through processes of modernization and economic development but rather as an important ground out of which the future of work will itself emerge. Rather than imagine the periphery as the zone that needs to be "brought in"—whether from the (traditional, static) past of subsistence to the technological, market-oriented, innovative present; from lawless informal markets to those governed by rules and rights; or from the local to the global—in order for work to become "good," we might instead take work and the many ways it is organized in the Global South as the referent from which to ask new questions: for example, about the legal infrastructure of work; its economic, social, and familial context; the macroeconomic conditions of its (im)possibility, etc. Still more, we might take these work relations as sources of normative authority and sites of institutional intelligence themselves.[57]

Such a reversal might, for example, involve taking informality, rather than formality, as a "normal" condition of work.[58] Rather than imagine informal workers as in need of the classic protections afforded to employees, we could take the full ambit of their demands on their own terms, as part of the political, legal, and institutional agenda for building the future of work. Put differently, rather than universalize the reach of the law of work as we know it, we could pay more attention to the place of law in the worlds in which such workers live and in the predicaments that they now face. Consider, for example, the complex labor, social, and legal arrangements that organize the lives of sex workers in Sonagachi, Kolkata;[59] the delivery drivers in the large cities of Africa such as Lagos;[60] or those in the Landless Workers Movement in Brazil.[61] Tracking how workers navigate such arrangements, the barriers they encounter in their working lives, the opportunities they exploit and the practices they seek to change, how they organize to do so, and the varied laws, institutions, and actors that they engage in the process, it is already clear that we would emerge with a transformative agenda that far exceeds the ambitions of labor law as it now stands.[62] In some contexts, we might revisit conventional narratives of informality altogether, no longer seeing informal work simply as a state of lack or failure but rather as part of a complex, unstable world of activities and social relations through which individuals and collectives sustain life in a precariously urbanized world.[63]

Embracing the insights of racial capitalism, we might continue the task of recuperating histories of enslavement, indenture, and forced labor.[64] Rather than treat these legacies of the past as tangential to work today, we could investigate them as sources of practices and patterns at work with which we must still contend, illuminating questions such as how populations of workers are distributed within and across labor markets and how hierarchical relations have become normalized and accepted at work.

Finally, we could consider the many workers who labor outside the market, doing various forms of subsistence and unpaid work either in addition to or instead of market work. Reversing or refusing outright the public/private polarity, this endeavor would take unpaid domestic work as worthy of attention in its own right as well as work that is unavoidably entangled in questions of distributive justice in the labor market.[65] As the following discussion suggests, this involves questioning the received idea of work, along with the subjectivity of the worker, in fundamental ways.

Distributional Analysis Revisited

Bearing in mind the ongoing presence and weight of history and having brought informal and other marginalized forms of work inside the future of work, the third move is to inquire into the mechanics that sustain this world: the ways in which it is constructed, how it is connected—or distinguished—from other social and economic spaces and, once (re)configured, how resources, bodies, labor, income, and status are allocated, and move, within it. We might think of the task as *distributional analysis* that includes all of the rules and norms that structure the struggle over the surplus as it now exists and extend to consider how valuable work itself is made and unmade in the course of legal, economic, and political transformation; how determinations about value are affected by disciplinary practices; and to which bodies and activities value ultimately becomes attached.[66] We might, for example, investigate how productive activities are classified (and reclassified) and how people are positioned as workers as a result, both within settled arrangements and when those arrangements are subject to change. For it turns out that the constitution of new markets, the (re)assignment of tasks and responsibilities to individuals and households, enterprises or the state, or simply the decision that concerns such as child care form part of the world of production or in contrast fall within the private domain can all be consequential ways to reallocate resources and power at home and at work, thereby affecting the ultimate distribution of goods, income, labor, and leisure among social groups.[67]

The underlying normative or political project is to explain persistent phenomena such as systemic gender and racial segmentation of workplaces and labor forces and their interconnections with economic inequality, phenomena that stand to trouble the future as much as they afflict the past and present of work. The theoretical ambition is to point to ways in which we might do so by better connecting distributional analysis within law to insights within social theory, history, racial capitalism, and beyond.

Determining what such a research agenda might involve and pursuing it down different pathways is *itself* the work of the future of work. Put another way, the future of work is an analytic and an epistemological project as well as a social and a political one: the manner in which we (re)imagine the world of work and how it is populated, how we study its organizational forms and characteristic dilemmas, and how we identity the authoritative forms of knowledge *about* work are, to some degree, how we will *make* the future of work. There are various levels and modes in which such inquiries can be conducted, but one strategy is simply to look at the way work is seen, and at a granular level made, through decisions about legal rules, forms, and institutions. Drawing on historical knowledge, what follows illustrates some of the possibilities of such a flipped or reversed optic on the future of work, possibilities that might permit us to extend the forms of distributive analysis already available within the critical legal arsenal while simultaneously drawing on analyses of social reproduction and incorporating insights from studies of racial capitalism.

DISTRIBUTIONAL ANALYSIS AT WORK: BEYOND LABOR AND CAPITAL

The systematically unequal benefits derived by workers and capital from labor contracting is a phenomenon noted as far back as Adam Smith. Smith traced those disparate rewards to unequal access to the resources needed for survival (in general, employers have such resources; waged workers, by definition, do not), a state of affairs ensuring that employers can "hold out" and effectively set the terms and conditions of work.[68] Progressive and Realist legal scholars located the source of that bargaining asymmetry in property law, observing that control over resources flowed from the delegated sovereignty and coercive power, including over labor contracting, that owners are able to exercise through law.[69] The foundations of work relations in private law revealed, the project of labor law within liberal capitalist societies has been understood as the legal construction of workers' countervailing power.[70]

Work relations have already played a pivotal role in the development of distributional analysis within law.[71] But there are lines of power and forms of capital in circulation at work—cultural, social, and human as well as material—that remain to be fully tracked, and spaces of labor and production into which it can be extended further.

Racialization at Work

"Workers" are often invoked in discussions about the future of work as if, apart from differences in their capacities, effort, and experience, they are largely interchangeable. Modernist analyses of work, whether rooted in liberalism, Marxism, or neoclassical and institutional economics, all pivot around the relationship between labor and capital. Yet histories of racial capitalism upend any presumption that workers all share a common position or identity at work, as well as the related idea that the racial stratification of labor is in any way exceptional.

Intellectuals in the Black radical tradition have long confirmed the intimate connection between racialization and the procurement of labor within capitalist enterprise.[72] If one of the insights of racial capitalism is the foundational role played by race and racial categories in the organization of capitalist production in transnational enterprises in particular, then one challenge going forward seems clear: how to make the racially and ethnically marked worker more central to the analysis of work. Although work itself is routinely organized along racial as well as gender lines, this phenomenon is treated as if it were a peripheral, even exceptional, feature of work rather than part of the very structure of work relations themselves. Exploring this critical, if neglected, register in which labor-capital relations operate thus stands to deepen the understanding of capitalism's fundamental dynamics.

A focus on racialization may also disrupt the distinction between labor and capital itself. For example, enslaved women's bodies served a dual function within cotton production, the commodity around which nineteenth-century global capitalism turned: they were both the foundation of further capital accumulation, backstopping the credit plantation owners used to expand their operations and keep them afloat, as well as a direct source of labor on which those operations depended.[73] As suggested in the following text, there are still sources of labor and capital that require an accounting, many of which track lines of race and gender.

The foundational shift here is to question the idea that the conflict between labor and capital is always the primary axis of distributional struggle, even as it remains of central interest; the project then becomes to rethink the legal interventions that might follow when differences among workers surface as sites of conflict at work. Within liberal legal orders, ascriptive differences among workers, those made on the basis of race, religion, gender, sexuality, and other quasi-immutable traits, are typically treated as deviations from otherwise neutral hiring and management practices arising from discrimination on the part of those suffering (or benefiting!) from bias, bad values, or outright prejudice, to be remedied by the recognition and enforcement of human and constitutional rights stipulating equal treatment at work. The limits of such legal strategies have been well-mapped in feminist and critical race scholarship: for example, at work as elsewhere, in the face of antecedent inequality, equality of contract may have the perverse effect of entrenching rather than alleviating gender and racial disparities.[74]

We could, however, imagine—and adopt—another strategy, one directed at exposing how such differentiated workplaces are legally enabled and institutionally organized in the first place. Here, the idea is to see law's norms and rules as instruments for the construction of difference, as well as vectors along which material rewards and symbolic distinctions among workers (still) travel.

If whiteness itself is a form of capital, and if there are material as well as psychological wages of whiteness, then unpacking racialization at work involves taking the workplace and work relations as central sites for the deployment of racial categories and the creation of racial differences.[75]

Here, too, the past is instructive, and in the metropole as well as the periphery. Because the origins of such practices lie in colonial labor practices and the transatlantic slave trade, one track involves following where racialization manifests directly, as in the transmutation of slavery into "civilizing" forced labor underwritten by international legal instruments such as the interwar Native Labour Code or in the ongoing uses of convict labor, protected in the United States by the Thirteenth Amendment.[76] But it is also worth tracing how racialization at work manifests indirectly, through modern legal and policy instruments. For example, it has long been established that employer resistance to labor organizing by Black workers took legal form in the exclusion of agricultural and domestic workers from the National Labor Relations Act.[77] That exclusion continues today, in tandem with "right to work" laws that operate across the same region and effectively preclude labor organizing entirely.[78] Thus facially neutral rules may form part of the mechanisms by which racialization, and racial disadvantage, are created or sustained at work, and past histories may be relevant to how those rules work, and are used, in practice. In some places the fabric of union organizing today may still be inseparable from histories of Black resistance at work: consider the pertinence of the organizing efforts of Black industrial workers, many of whom were communists, in the steel mills of Alabama in the 1930s to the central role of Black warehouse workers in current labor struggles with postindustrial giant Amazon, underway in the very locale where that organizing previously had its epicenter—Bessemer, Alabama.[79]

A capacious approach to distributive justice at work also engages the status of unpaid labor, labor that in many contexts intersects with racialization at work. An important domain of interest here is care work, which remains a profoundly gendered form of work. In the context of feminized, precarious labor markets, the demands of household care work, along with the undercompensation of care work in the market, have resurfaced as central sites of injustice for women. The results of these competing demands, especially crushing for racialized women, were identified by Claudia Jones, who noted that the "super-exploitation" of Black women in the United States was rooted not only in the racialization of care work but in their labor market position as vastly underpaid domestic workers overwhelmingly responsible for providing their own household income and care labor as well.[80] This takes us to the place of unpaid work in the future of work.

UNPAID WORK AS WORK

Notwithstanding the massive amount of productive labor that is performed outside of the market, future-of-work discussions presuppose that in the future, as in the past, the work that is the proper object of our attention, that should be made "better," remains paid work. Subsistence work is largely imagined as a relic of premodern life, to be displaced as economies modernize and the production of goods and services is directed toward trade rather than consumption. Unpaid domestic care work, if it is recognized at all, typically comes into the picture when it threatens to impede women's participation in the market. Here, the standard responses are that men should do more of it so that its burdens are more equally shared, or that employers need to become more "flexible" so that women can better accommodate the demands of family to paid work.[81] Indeed, influential institutions such as the World Bank have proposed that market engagement itself will catalyze a redistribution of the burdens of unpaid work.[82]

Notice in these responses that unpaid work is a subject of interest *not* because it matters as work in its own right but because of its potential conflict with work that *does* count: market labor. Notice also that those who perform domestic work do not materialize as workers—unless and until they work for pay. Underpinning these assumptions are growth models that fail to recognize unpaid work as productive, despite its now well-documented contribution to the economy.[83] These have been described as artifacts of a "social system of production that does not recognize the production and reproduction of the worker as a social-economic activity, and a source of capital accumulation, but mystifies it instead as a natural resource or a personal service, while profiting from the wageless condition of the labor involved."[84]

The work of unpaid care, or social reproduction, is a long-standing subject of feminist activism and scholarship.[85] Recognizing such work as work remains a pressing distributional concern, especially in the context of growing labor market demands accompanied by inadequate public support for the care services that are indispensable to human life. Indeed, we might think of the nonrecognition of unpaid care work as one of the keys to global inequality, a central part of how massive disparities in the returns to work are now produced.[86] Unpaid work constitutes an effective "tax" on women's labor market participation, that is, it is work that (mostly) women must do on top of their work in the labor market.[87] But unpaid work also underwrites the performance of waged labor; it is thus an unacknowledged subsidy, part of how production in the market is itself produced.[88] Imagine a worker situated at the intersection of market and nonmarket economies, engaged in the work of both, faced with the now routine suggestion that she should engage in more "productive" market work, perhaps even in the name of gender equality or "empowerment." As long as nonmarket work does not count as work, or is only notionally counted, one response might well be, in the words of Mariarosa Dalla Costa and Selma James, "we have worked enough."[89]

The key to an expanded distributional analysis here is destabilizing these nested assumptions about the forms of work that "matter" and denaturalizing the market-centered frame in which discussions about labor in the future of work are conducted. Extending the reach of distributional analysis into the household, and into the community as well, both generates a more complete picture of the labor that is actually performed and places in view more of the resources on which the functioning of market-based enterprise draws and depends.

Multiple resources and activities pertinent to the distributive justice questions surrounding work traverse this line. For example, social networks—in the form of kinship and other forms of support—might be important both to the capacity to generate income and the ability to survive its absence; access to leisure will be similarly affected.[90] Valuable resources might come from the state—think of the array of possible benefits and subsidies, from welfare, health, and education to transportation, credit, and housing—but also from NGOs and other private actors. Access to private property remains important, but the allocation of communal and public assets matters just as much.[91] Evaluating the advantages and disadvantages of these arrangements requires recognizing the proliferation of norms, rules, and institutions that operate on work relations in particular social and economic contexts, as well as the interactions among them.[92]

Redrawing—and opening up—the frame of work suggests multiple possibilities when it comes to legal and policy interventions. A key move, however, is reversing the normative subject underpinning the law of work. Although workers now are as likely to be female as male, this subject remains the "unencumbered" worker, free to devote attention to (paid) work and able to respond to market demands unfettered by family and other "nonwork" obligations.[93] As has long been proposed, the replacement would be the encumbered worker: that is, to presume as the norm rather than the exception that workers carry obligations of unpaid labor, and to consider how these obligations transform how we imagine the future of work.[94]

In the course of the COVID-19 pandemic, such possibilities moved from the speculative into the domain of the real, as distinctions between working and nonworking time and space eroded and the demands of caring for children, the ill, and the elderly palpably conflicted with those of labor market work.[95] But the encumbered worker may be a better descriptor of the situation of workers globally in any event. In economies without the historical division of home from work, where land, labor, and money are not fully commodified and people engage in significant amounts of subsistence labor, there may be no reason to distinguish "reproductive" from "productive" labor, and there may be no uncontroversial, nonideological basis on which to do so.[96] Indeed, this may be true in general: in the many precariously situated low-income households within economies in which waged labor is fully entrenched, where income is inadequate to support the requirements of life, people must—and do—engage in subsistence activities as well as paid work to survive.[97]

To recap, as the histories and problematics of racialization at work and the burdens of care work reveal, a more complete accounting of distributive justice in any future of work will necessarily involve a significant transformation in the imagination of that future: around how workers are distinguished as well as the concerns and conditions they share; about the relevant spaces of work and their relation to labor and production in the market; and indeed, about how we conceive of work itself.

REVISITING THE FUTURE OF WORK

At this point, we emerge with a better sense of the terrain on which the future of work will unfold along with some strategies to approach the questions of justice placed before us. One salient feature of this terrain is the presence of the past. Far from a brave new world, the future of work now engages questions that have surfaced before, at earlier moments of social and economic transformation. They include what workers can expect, and what they must endure, in the course of economic modernization and development; what the commodification of labor portends in terms of gains—and losses—in welfare and economic security, and for whom; how the risks and opportunities of technological innovation are distributed; who holds power and who is subordinated at work, and by what means; and even what materializes as labor as opposed to what is marginal or falls outside its ambit altogether.

Helping to steer those myriad possible futures, as before, are decisions and choices about the social and legal organization of work. For example, it is already evident that institutional arrangements around technology are important sources of social and economic advantage and disadvantage at work. At this point, we can see that their significance extends still further: those arrangements help "make" the landscape of work, giving shape to the entities that populate it. Thus we might identify decisions *about* these norms and institutions as mechanisms by which different futures of work will be enabled, impeded or foreclosed entirely.

A more granular focus on this legal and institutional terrain, both at moments of transition and over the longue durée, may help explicate the vast, and enduring, differences among workers too: the nature and forms of work they undertake; the conditions under which they do it; the rewards they enjoy from their efforts; and whether they are seen as "workers" at all. Now, as before, differences often fall along lines of race, color, sex, and gender; indeed, such differences may be expressly mobilized through the organization of work.

In light of these pervasive differences, one question is whether it makes sense to speak of the future of work in the singular rather than the plural. Whatever the answer to that question, this much seems clear: the "worker" *simpliciter* is an inadequate subject of analysis. Rather, differences *among* workers warrant much more attention going forward than they have received in the past, as structural rather than epiphenomenal features of the world of work. Comprehending such differences—and moving to disrupt them, especially where they are attached to material and symbolic disadvantage—in turn requires a more complete appraisal of the practices and institutions that organize work relations and, along with a wider aperture on the spaces of work itself, a closer tracking of the vectors along which labor and other resources move.

Some of this work, of course, can be done with the tools of distributional analysis that are already in hand. But if distributional analysis is to fully reveal the stakes of legal and social arrangements at work, it must trace the flows of labor along more, and different, trajectories than it has in the past, moving beyond employment and labor markets, crossing into the household, traversing the field, farm, and forests, and probing informal urban spaces where work, habitation, and consumption may all be intermingled. Still more, it must look at the norms, practices, and institutions by which these spaces and relations of work are constructed; how patterns at work shift with changing access to resources and technology; how ideologies and networks of power channel people through the maze of work relations; and how race, gender, and other social differences themselves may be (re)produced as a result. These events, processes, and decisions all hold immense significance, both for particular groups of workers and for workers in general. Put simply, they lie at the heart of conundrums of distributive justice at work.

Finally, we should expect to see new conjunctions of interests and identities and even new forms of consciousness emerge as questions around work become entangled with transformed visions of economic development and heightened attention to ecology; such shifting alignments and new understandings may, in turn, provoke reconfigured relations—personal as well as social, economic, and political—within and across borders. Fortunately, there are myriad resources available to assist in unpacking these phenomena and their implications for work: in the literatures that examine the connections of race and colonialism with capitalism; in feminist analyses of social reproduction; and beyond.

NOTES

1. Guy Standing, *The Precariat: The New Dangerous Class* (London: Bloomsbury Academic, 2011); and Robert Reich, *Supercapitalism: The Transformation of Business, Democracy, and Everyday Life* (New York: Knopf, 2007).
2. For task oriented labor, see Jeremias Prassl, *Humans as a Service: The Promise and Perils of Work in the Gig Economy* (Oxford: Oxford University Press, 2018). For the fragmentation of workplace relations, see David Weil, *The Fissured Workplace: Why Work Became So Bad for So Many and What Can Be Done to Improve It* (Cambridge, MA: Harvard University Press, 2014).
3. International Labour Organization, *Decent Work in the Informal Economy* (Geneva: International Labour Office, 2002).
4. World Bank Group, *World Development Report 2019: The Changing Nature of Work* (Washington, DC: World Bank, 2019).
5. World Bank Group, *World Development Report 2019*; World Bank Group, *Doing Business 2019: Training for Reform* (Washington, DC: World Bank, 2019).
6. International Labour Organization, "Declaration on Fundamental Principles and Rights at Work," adopted June 18, 1998, https://www.ilo.org/declaration/lang--en/index.htm.
7. International Labour Organization, *ILO Centenary Declaration for the Future of Work*, adopted June 21, 2019, http://www.ilo.org/global/about-the-ilo/mission-and-objectives/centenary-declaration/lang--en/index.htm.
8. Vicente Silva, "The ILO and the Future of Work: The Politics of Global Labour Policy," *Global Social Policy* 22, no. 2 (2022): 341–58, https://doi.org/10.1177/14680181211004853.
9. World Bank Group, *World Development Report 2019*; Standing, *Precariat*; and Global Commission on the Future of Work, *Work for a Brighter Future* (Geneva: International Labour Office, 2019).
10. World Bank Group, *World Development Report 2019*, 12.
11. Global Commission on the Future of Work, *Work for a Brighter Future*.
12. Jim Yong Kim, foreword to *World Development Report 2019* by the World Bank Group, vii–viii.
13. Kerry Rittich, "Two Institutional Paths Toward the Future of Work—And a View from the Edge of the Field," in *Social Justice and the World of Work: Possible Global Futures*, ed. Brian Langille and Anne Trebilcock (Oxford: Hart, 2023), 43.

14. Dan Danielsen, "How Corporations Govern: Taking Corporate Power Seriously in Transnational Regulation and Governance," *Harvard Journal of International Law* 46 (2005): 411.
15. See World Bank, *World Development Report 2019*; World Bank, *World Development Report 2021: Data for Better Lives* (Washington, DC: World Bank, 2021); and Global Commission on the Future of Work, *Work for a Brighter Future*, 43.
16. Commission on Legal Empowerment of the Poor, *Making the Law Work for Everyone* (New York: United Nations Development Programme 2008).
17. Dan Breznitz, *Innovation in Real Places: Strategies for Prosperity in an Unforgiving World* (Oxford: Oxford University Press, 2021).
18. Vicente Silva, "The ILO and the Future of Work."
19. Orly Lobel, *The Equality Machine: Harnessing Digital Technology for a Bright, More Inclusive Future* (New York: Public Affairs, 2022); Valerio De Stefano, ed., "Crowdsourcing, the Gig-Economy, and the Law," special issue, *Comparative Labor Law and Policy Journal* 37, no. 3 (2016); and Prassl, *Humans as a Service*.
20. Brishen Rogers, *Data and Democracy at Work: Advanced Informational Technologies, Labor Law, and the New Working Class* (Cambridge, MA: MIT Press, 2023).
21. Brishen Rogers, "Workplace Privacy and Associational Power," in *Data and Democracy at Work: Advanced Informational Technologies, Labor Law, and the New Working Class* (Cambridge, MA: MIT Press, 2023), 81–103.
22. Suresh Naidu, Eric Posner, and Glenn Weyl, "Antitrust Remedies for Labor Market Power," *Harvard Law Review* 132 (2018): 536, 558.
23. Michel Callon and Bruno Latour, "Unscrewing the Big Leviathan: How Actors Macro-Structure Reality and How Sociologists Help Them to Do So," in *Advances in Social Theory and Methodology: Toward an Integration of Micro- and Macro-Sociologies*, ed. Aaron Victor Cicourel and K. Knorr-Cetina (Boston: Routledge & Kegan Paul, 1981), 277–303.
24. Julie Cohen, *Between Truth and Power: The Legal Constructions of Informational Capitalism* (New York: Oxford University Press, 2019).
25. Cohen, *Between Truth and Power*. For the general argument, see Wesley Newcomb Hohfeld, "Some Fundamental Legal Conceptions as Applied in Legal Reasoning," *Yale Law Journal* 23 (1913): 16, https://doi.org/10.2307/785533.
26. Cohen, *Between Truth and Power*, 50.
27. Rogers, *Data and Democracy at Work*.
28. See, for example, Heller v. Uber Technologies Inc., 2019 CanLII ONCA 1 (Can. ON CA); Canadian Union of Postal Workers v. Foodora Inc. d.b.a. Foodora, 2020 CanLII 16750 (Can. ON LRB).
29. Sanjukta Paul, "Fissuring and the Firm Exception," *Law and Contemporary Problems* 82 (2019): 65.
30. Christopher Chitty, *Sexual Hegemony: Statecraft, Sodomy, and Capital in the Rise of the World System* (Durham, NC: Duke University Press, 2020), 185.
31. Anne Orford, *International Law and the Politics of History* (Cambridge: Cambridge University Press, 2021).
32. Michel Foucault, "Nietzsche, Genealogy, History," in *Language, Counter-memory, Practice: Selected Essays and Interviews* (Ithaca, NY: Cornell University Press, 1977), 139–64; and Ben Golder, "Contemporary Legal Genealogies," in *Searching for*

Contemporary Legal Thought, ed. Justin Desautels-Stein and Christopher Tomlins (Cambridge: Cambridge University Press, 2017), 80.
33. Christopher Tomlins, *Freedom Bound: Law, Labor, and Civic Identity in Colonizing English America, 1580–1865* (Cambridge: Cambridge University Press, 2010).
34. For one account regarding indentured labor, see Walter Rodney, *A History of the Guyanese Working Peoples, 1881–1905* (Baltimore: Johns Hopkins, 1981). Also see, Tayyab Mahmud, "Cheaper Than a Slave: Indentured Labor, Colonialism, and Capitalism," *Whittier Law Review* 34, no. 2 (2013): 215.
35. Janet Halley, "Trafficking and the Modern Indenture," in *Revisiting the Law and Governance of Trafficking, Forced Labor and Modern Trafficking*, ed. Prabha Kotiswaran (Cambridge: Cambridge University Press, 2017), 179; and Kerry Rittich, "Representing, Counting, Valuing: Managing Definitional Uncertainty in the Law of Trafficking," in *Revisiting the Law and Governance of Trafficking, Forced Labor and Modern Trafficking*, ed. Prabha Kotiswaran (Cambridge: Cambridge University Press, 2017), 238.
36. Edward Palmer Thompson, *The Making of the English Working Class* (London: Vintage, 1966).
37. David Bromwich, "Market Rationalization," in *Private Government: How Employers Rule Our Lives (and Why We Don't Talk, about It)*, ed. Elizabeth Anderson (Princeton, NJ: Princeton University Press, 2017), 95.
38. Karl Polanyi, *The Great Transformation: The Political and Economic Origins of Our Time* (1944; repr., Boston: Beacon, 1957); and Thompson, *The Making of the English Working Class*.
39. John Sydenham Furnivall, *Colonial Policy and Practice: A Comparative Study of Burma and Netherlands India* (Cambridge: Cambridge University Press, 1948), ix.
40. Polanyi, *The Great Transformation*, 159–60.
41. Kerry Rittich, "Historicizing Labour and Development: Labour Market Formalization Through the Lens of British Colonial Administration," in *Re-Imagining Labour Law for Development*, ed. Diamond Ashiagbor (Oxford: Hart, 2019), 21; and Donatella Allessandrini et al., "The Dream of Formality: Racialization Otherwise and International Economic Law," *Journal of International Economic Law* 25 (2022): 207, https://doi.org/10.1093/jiel/jgac016.
42. International Labour Organization, *Decent Work in the Informal Economy*; and World Bank, *World Development Report 2019*.
43. See, for example, Jorge Esquirol, "Titling and Untitled Housing in Panama City," *Tennessee Journal of Law and Policy* 4 (2008): 1.
44. Standing, *Precariat*.
45. Kerry Rittich, "Formality and Informality in the Law of Work," in *The Daunting Enterprise of the Law: Essays in Honour of Harry W. Arthurs*, ed. Simon Archer, Daniel Drache, and Peer Zumbansen (Montreal and Kingston: McGill-Queen's University Press, 2017), 109.
46. Guy Fiti Sinclair, *To Reform the World: International Organizations and the Making of Modern States* (Oxford: Oxford University Press, 2017), 90.
47. Lawrence Mishel, *The Wedges Between Productivity and Median Compensation Growth* (Washington, DC: Economic Policy Institute, 2012), https://www.epi.org/publication/ib330-productivity-vs-compensation/.

48. Branko Milanovic, *Capitalism Alone: The Future of the System That Rules the World* (Cambridge, MA: Harvard Belknap, 2019), 15.
49. Furnivall, *Colonial Policy and Practice*.
50. David Roodman, *Due Diligence: An Impertinent Inquiry Into Microfinance* (Washington, DC: Center for Global Development, 2012); and Veronica Gago, "A Feminist Economics of Exploitation and Extraction," in *Feminist International: How to Change Everything*, trans. Liz Mason-Deese (London: Verso, 2020), 115–54.
51. See Abhijit V. Bannerjee and Esther Duflo, "Barefoot Hedge-Fund Managers," in *Poor Economics: A Radical Rethinking of the Way to Fight Global Poverty* (New York: Public Affairs, 2011), 133–56.
52. Tara Cookson, *Unjust Conditions: Women's Work and the Hidden Costs of Cash Transfer Programs* (Oakland: University of California Press, 2018).
53. Vasuki Nesiah, "Indebted: The Cruel Optimism of Leaning in to Empowerment," in *Governance Feminism: Notes From the Field*, ed. Janet Halley et al. (Minneapolis: University of Minnesota Press, 2019), 505.
54. Atif Mian and Amir Sufi, *House of Debt: How They (and You) Caused the Great Recession, and How We Can Prevent It from Happening Again* (Chicago: University of Chicago Press, 2014).
55. Immanuel Wallerstein, *The Modern World-System II: Mercantilism and the Consolidation of the European World-Economy 1600–1750* (Berkeley: University of California Press, 1980), 194; and Max Weber, *General Economic History* (New York: Transaction, 1992), 173, discussed in Matthew Finkin, "Beclouded Work, Beclouded Workers in Historical Perspective," *Comparative Labor Law and Policy Journal* 37 (2016): 603.
56. Diamond Ashiagbor and Kerry Rittich, "Labour and Labour Law in the Project of International Development," in *Oxford Handbook of International Law and Development*, ed. Ruth Buchanan, Luis Eslava, and Sundhya Pahuja (Oxford: Oxford University Press, 2024), 457–76.
57. Boaventura de Sousa Santos, *The End of Cognitive Empire: The Coming of Age of Epistemologies of the South* (Durham, NC: Duke University Press, 2018).
58. Rittich, "Formality and Informality in the Law of Work"; and Rittich, "Historicizing Labour and Development."
59. Prabha Kotiswaran, "Born Unto Brothels: Sex Work in a Kolkata Red-Light Area," in *Dangerous Sex, Invisible Labor: Sex Work and the Law in India* (Princeton, NJ: Princeton University Press, 2011), 137–82.
60. Daniel E. Agbiboa, *They Eat Our Sweat: Transport Labor, Corruption, and Everyday Survival in Urban Nigeria* (Oxford: Oxford University Press, 2022).
61. George Meszaros, *Social Movements, Law, and the Politics of Land Reform: Lessons from Brazil* (Oxford: Routledge, 2013).
62. Balakrishnan Rajagopal, "Markets, Gender and Identity: A Case Study of the Working Women's Forum as a Social Movement," in *International Law from Below: Development, Social Movements and Third World Resistance* (Cambridge: Cambridge University Press, 2003), 277–88.
63. AbdouMalik Simone, *Improvised Lives: Rhythms of Endurance in an Urban South* (Cambridge, UK: Polity, 2018).

64. Mahmud, "Cheaper Than a Slave."
65. Silvia Federici, *Caliban and the Witch: Women, the Body and Primitive Accumulation* (Brooklyn, NY: Autonomedia, 2006).
66. See Janet Halley, "Distribution and Decision: Assessing Governance Feminism," in *Governance Feminism: Notes From the Field*, ed. Janet Halley et al. (Minneapolis: University of Minnesota Press, 2019), 253; Mariana Mazzucato, *The Value of Everything: Making and Taking in the Global Economy* (London: Allen Lane, 2018); and Caitlin Rosenthal, *Accounting for Slavery: Masters and Management* (Cambridge, MA: Harvard University Press, 2018).
67. For a discussion of this process in the context of the "transition" from plan to market economies, see Kerry Rittich, *Recharacterizing Restructuring: Gender, Law and Distribution in Market Reform* (The Hague: Kluwer Law, 2002).
68. Adam Smith, *An Inquiry Into the Nature and Causes of the Wealth of Nations* (London: W. Strahan and T. Cadell, 1776).
69. Morris Cohen, "Property and Sovereignty," *Cornell Law Quarterly* 13 (1927): 8; and Robert Hale, "Freedom and Coercion in a Supposedly Non-Coercive State," *Political Science Quarterly* 38 (1923): 470, https://doi.org/10.2307/2142367.
70. Paul Davies and Mark Freedland, *Kahn-Freund's Labour and the Law*, 3rd. ed. (London: Stevens and Sons, 1983), 81; and Karl Klare, "Countervailing Workers' Power as a Regulatory Strategy," in *Legal Regulation of the Employment Relation*, ed. Hugh Collins, Paul Davies, and Roger Rideout (The Hague: Kluwer Law International, 2000).
71. See, for example, the case excerpts in William Fisher III, Morton J. Horwitz, and Thomas A. Reed, eds., *American Legal Realism* (New York: Oxford University Press, 1993).
72. See, for example, Walter Johnson, "Forum: To Remake the World: Slavery, Racial Capitalism and Justice," *Boston Review*, February 2017, https://bostonreview.net/forum/walter-johnson-to-remake-the-world (discussing W. E. B. Du Bois, "The Souls of White Folk" (1920), W. E. B. Du Bois, *Black Reconstruction*, and Cedric Robinson, *Black Marxism*); Cedric Robinson, *Black Marxism: The Making of the Black Radical Tradition*, 3rd. ed. (Chapel Hill: University of North Carolina Press, 2021); and Eric Williams, *Capitalism and Slavery*, 3rd ed. (Chapel Hill: University of North Carolina Press, 2021).
73. Walter Johnson, *River of Dark Dreams: Slavery and Empire in the Cotton Kingdom* (Cambridge, MA: Harvard Belknap, 2013); and Johnson, "To Remake the World."
74. Kimberlé Crenshaw et al., introduction to *Critical Race Theory: The Key Writings That Formed the Movement* (New York: New Press, 1995), xiii–xxxii.
75. Cheryl Harris, "Whiteness as Property," *Harvard Law Review* 106 (1993): 1710, https://doi.org/10.2307/1341787; and W. E. B. Du Bois, *Black Reconstruction in America* (New York: Russell and Russell, 1935), 700–1.
76. Daniel Maul, *The International Labour Organization: 100 Years of Global Social Policy* (Geneva: ILO, 2019); Chris Gevers, "Refiguring Slavery Through International Law: The 1926 Slavery Convention, the 'Native Labor Code' and Racial Capitalism," *Journal of International Economic Law* 25, no. 2 (June 2022): 312–33; and Douglas A. Blackmon, *Slavery by Another Name: The Re-Enslavement of Black Americans from the Civil War to World War Two* (New York: Anchor, 2009).

77. United States Code: National Labor Relations, 29 U.S.C. §§ 151–166 (Suppl. 2 1934).
78. Archibald Cox et al., *Labor Law: Cases and Materials*, 11th ed. (Westbury, NY: Foundation, 1991), 1117–20.
79. Robin D. G. Kelley, *Hammer and Hoe* (Chapel Hill: University of North Carolina Press, 1990); and Robin D. G. Kelley, "Amazon Union Drives Builds on Decades of Black Labor Activism in Alabama," *Democracy Now*, March 29, 2021, https://www.democracynow.org/2021/3/29/robin_dg_kelley_amazon_union_drive.
80. Carol Boyce Davies, *Left of Karl Marx: The Political Life of Black Communist Claudia Jones* (Durham, NC: Duke University Press, 2007).
81. See, for example, Global Commission on the Future of Work, *Work for a Brighter Future*.
82. Kerry Rittich, "Engendering Development/Marketing Equality," *Albany Law Review* 67 (2003): 575.
83. Marilyn Waring, *If Women Counted: A New Feminist Economics* (New York: Harper Collins, 1988); and Duncan Ironmonger, "Counting Outputs, Capital Inputs, and Caring Labor: Estimating Gross Household Product," *Feminist Economics* 2, no. 1 (1996): 37.
84. Federici, *Caliban and the Witch*, 8.
85. Margaret E. Reid, *Economics of Household Production* (New York: Wiley, 1934); and Mariarosa Dalla Costa and Selma James, "The Power of Women and the Subversion of the Community," in *Sex, Race and Class*, ed. Selma James (London: PM Press, 2012), 43–59.
86. Oxfam International, *Time to Care: Unpaid and Underpaid Care Work and the Global Inequality Crisis* (Oxford: Oxfam International, 2020), https://www.oxfam.ca/wp-content/uploads/2020/01/Time-to-Care-Report-January-20-2020-EN-Final.pdf.
87. Ingrid Palmer, "Public Finance from a Gender Perspective," *World Development* 23 (1995): 1981, https://doi.org/10.1016/0305-750X(95)00084-P.
88. Veronica Gago, *Feminist International: How to Change Everything*, trans. Liz Mason-Deese (London: Verso, 2020).
89. Global Commission on the Future of Work, *Work for a Brighter Future*; and Dalla Costa and James, "The Power of Women and the Subversion of the Community," 59.
90. Bina Agarwal, "'Bargaining' and Gender Relations: Within and Beyond the Household," *Feminist Economics* 3, no. 1 (1996): 1, https://doi.org/10.1080/135457097338799; and Gago, *Feminist International*.
91. Agarwal, "'Bargaining' and Gender Relations."
92. For a parallel analysis with respect to the family, including the economic household, and a model of how such rules might be taxonomized, see Janet Halley and Kerry Rittich, "Critical Directions in Comparative Family Law: Genealogies and Contemporary Studies of Family Law Exceptionalism," *American Journal of Comparative Law* 58 (2010): 753–75, https://doi.org/10.5131/ajcl.2010.0001.
93. For a collection of studies exploring this norm and its effects, see Joanne Conaghan and Kerry Rittich, eds., *Labour Law, Work and Family: Critical and Comparative Perspectives* (Oxford: Oxford University Press, 2005).

94. Nancy Fraser, "After the Family Wage: A Postindustrial Thought Experiment," in *Justice Interruptus: Critical Reflections on the "Postsocialist" Condition* (New York: Routledge, 1997), 41; and Gosta Esping-Anderson, "Towards a Post-Industrial Gender Contract," in *The Future of Work, Employment and Social Protection*, ed. Peter Auer and Bernard Gazier (Geneva: International Labour Organization, 2002), 109.

95. Jim Stanford, *10 Ways the COVID-19 Pandemic Must Change Work for Good* (Vancouver: Centre For Future Work, June 2020), https://centreforfuturework.ca/wp-content/uploads/2020/06/10Ways_work_must_change.pdf.

96. Polanyi, *The Great Transformation*; and Lourdes Beneria, "Paid and Unpaid Labor: Meanings and Debates," in *Gender, Development and Economics: Economics as if All People Mattered*, ed. Lourdes Beneria, Gunseli Berik, and Maria Floro, 2nd ed. (New York: Routledge, 2015), 178–226.

97. Lucy Williams, "Poor Women's Work Experiences: Gaps in the 'Work/Family' Discussion," in *Labour Law, Work and Family: Critical and Comparative Perspectives*, ed. Joanne Conaghan and Kerry Rittich (Oxford: Oxford University Press, 2005), 195.

CHAPTER 8

FINANCIALIZATION, FISSURING, AND GLOBAL FUTURES OF WORK

JENNIFER BAIR

Amid the cacophony of contemporary discussions around the future of work, robots have loomed particularly large in our collective imagination. Ever greater advances in automation and artificial intelligence (AI) are expected to drive profound changes in how, by whom, and where work is done. Some commentators are optimistic, envisioning a future in which human workers will be liberated from repetitive and boring tasks, but others worry about the labor-displacing effects of automation. In the United States and other high-wage economies, concerns focus on the anxiety that disruptive technologies create for individuals who are exhorted to stay ahead of a changing labor market by engaging in successive rounds of reskilling. In this scenario, the insecurity and precarity long experienced by manufacturing workers will extend to a broader swathe of the labor force, including white collar professionals, as largely deindustrialized societies grapple with what comes after a postindustrial economy.

The problem with anticipatory narratives of this sort is that they highlight the possibility and peril of future disruption in ways that can distract our attention from larger structural transformations that are underway. This chapter focuses on two such interrelated transformations that are already shaping the world of work in profound ways: fissuring and financialization. While there is a temptation to treat technology as an autonomous or disembedded force driving the pace and direction of change, we should instead ask how fissuring and financialization will *intersect* with AI and automation to create the future of work. Take, for example, concerns about the effects of advanced automation in developing economies, where the risks of dislocation are thought to include not just the displacement of workers but the disruption of the development process itself. This is because one of the sectors that some experts predict will be strongly affected by robotization is the type of labor-intensive manufacturing found primarily in parts of Asia, Latin America, and, to a lesser extent, Africa.

Until recently, activities such as soft goods production have proven stubbornly resistant to automation, which is why so much of this work left high-wage economies beginning in the 1960s. Over the past half century, shifting geographies of production created a global assembly line in which new industrial jobs and new working classes were generated in Taiwan, the Philippines, and Mexico. The epicenter of textile, apparel, and footwear manufacturing today is China, where garment factories alone employ some fifteen million workers. Employment in the industry there has begun to fall, but what is driving the decline is not automation but competition from lower-wage countries such as Cambodia, Bangladesh, and, most recently, Ethiopia.

One worry about the future of work is that technology will arrest the expansion of new frontiers on the global assembly line. If traditionally labor-intensive work can be automated, it "could eliminate lots of jobs very quickly, and block access to the global economy for further low-wage countries, in Africa for example."[1] In such a future, automated machines such as "sewbots" would eradicate the jobs that today connect poorer countries to global markets, kicking away the development ladder before the lowest-wage economies could begin to climb it.

For decades, such countries have been told that climbing the development ladder requires participating in global value chains (GVCs). A "value chain" refers to the sequential steps involved in the production of a good or service, from research, design, and product development to manufacturing, distribution, and marketing. In today's global economy, most value chains for even a simple manufactured good such as a T-shirt involve multiple producers stretched across multiple countries—thus the term *global* value chains. The most labor-intensive link in the chain is typically done in a country with low-cost labor. The conventional development paradigm has held that by participating in global value chains poorer countries can leverage their comparative advantage in cheap labor to generate employment and export revenue while also developing the physical and human capital needed to "move up" the value chain over time.

The process of moving up, or upgrading, along the value chain is captured in figure 8.1 by the so-called smile curve, which plots value-added against the sequential stages in the production process. Stan Shih, the founder of the Taiwanese electronics company Acer, developed the graphic in the 1990s to capture the dynamics of the personal computer industry.[2] Shih's insight was that companies like his were stuck at the bottom of the curve, manufacturing hardware for the mostly U.S.-based information technology firms that designed and sold computers. The challenge was to expand out from manufacturing tangible products

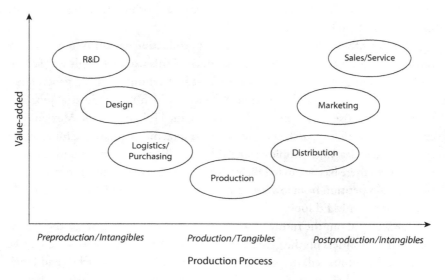

FIGURE 8.1 GVC smile curve: value-added

Source: Javier Lopez Gonzalez, "Using Foreign Factors to Enhance Domestic Export Performance: A Focus on Southeast Asia" (OECD Trade Policy Papers No. 191, Paris, 2016), https://doi.org/10.1787/5jlpq82v1jxw-en.

to include the "intangible" activities found at either end of the chain, including research and development, product design, branding, and marketing. Shih's analysis aptly captured the dynamics of the many industries that were beginning to be analyzed in a burgeoning academic and policy literature on global value chains. Although value chains vary in terms of length and complexity, there is significant consistency in the shape of the GVC smile curve. In other words, the relative distribution of value across the chain is strikingly similar for products as diverse as iPhones, blue jeans, or prepackaged bags of green beans.

At one level, the smile curve is a managerial tool—a way to diagnose opportunities for firms to capture value in an industry. Yet most references to the smile curve invoke it not as a guide to organizational strategy but as a representation of upgrading trajectories in the global economy. This toggling between the meso (firm) and the macro (country) levels of analysis is enabled by the correlation between an activity's location along the smile curve and the geographic location where the activity is carried out. The links at the bottom of the smile curve are where lower-wage countries tend to access the value chain. In terms of value added, returns to participation are relatively low at these links, but the employment impacts are substantial, as is clear when employment share instead of value-added is graphed on the y-axis (figure 8.2). But the impact of GVC

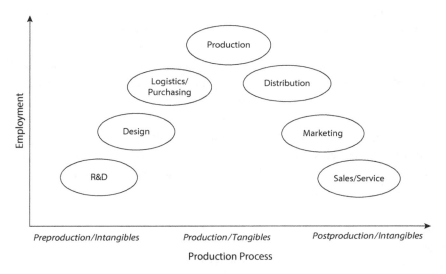

FIGURE 8.2 Reverse smile curve: employment share

Source: Javier Lopez Gonzalez, "Using Foreign Factors to Enhance Domestic Export Performance: A Focus on Southeast Asia" (OECD Trade Policy Papers No. 191, Paris, 2016), https://doi.org/10.1787/5jlpq82v1jxw-en.

participation goes beyond the employment effects in the present. According to the traditional development paradigm, incorporation into GVCs is supposed to put economies (or the firms comprising economies) on learning curves that they can use to move to higher value-added activities over time, either in the same chain—moving from apparel manufacturing to garment design—or, eventually, to chains in other industries or even sectors—moving from apparel manufacturing to the production of iPhones. Upgrading via value chain participation is the model of development widely shared by those concerned about a future of work in which the bottom of the smile curve falls out, closing off the opportunities that other countries have leveraged in the past.

Like all predictions and projections about the effects of technological change, to ask what the future of work will look like in East Africa, Central America, or South Asia is to invite a comparison between two unknowns: how these countries will be impacted by technological change, and the counterfactual—that is, where they will be if their current trajectories are unchanged by such developments. In this sense, grappling with the future of work demands an accounting of the recent past as well as the present, a reckoning with the course on which we are currently set.

Our present course is charted in important ways by the two interrelated processes I explore in this chapter. The first is fissuring—that is, the purposeful creation of a break or "fissure" in the production process in ways that allow a focal company to internalize more profitable activities and off-load less profitable ones on to independent contractors and the workers they employ. The second is financialization—that is, the greater valorization of intangible activities over tangible ones and the concomitant investment in financial rather than productive assets. Together, these trends are creating a world of work in which labor's share of income has fallen, and the smile curve is deepening in ways that are already making it difficult for low-wage countries to leverage value chains for development. These trends are critical for assessing the likely impacts of AI, automation, and other technical advances in shaping global futures of work.

FISSURING AND THE OFF-LOADING OF THE EMPLOYMENT RELATIONSHIP

Many debates about the future of work start from the premise that technology is the prime driver of change. What kind of work people will do in the future is presumed to depend, in large measure, on advances in technological capabilities such as AI and automation. Yet an equally important if sometimes overlooked force transforming the world of work is organizational change, which is reshaping how and where people work, what kind of returns they receive for their labor, and the degree to which they are protected by regulatory frameworks such as labor law. Within the United States, the growth in outsourcing and the increased use of temporary staffing agencies and other kinds of contingent labor has been cited as a factor contributing to relatively lackluster productivity growth and a prolonged period of wage stagnation. The economist David Weil has described these changes with the metaphor of the "fissured workplace."[3]

Fissuring can take multiple forms. The classic case is when a firm contracts out to an external entity work that was previously done in-house, but fissuring can also occur via a kind of internal subcontracting, as when workers employed by a temporary agency labor alongside those employed by the temp agency's client firm. What drives fissuring is not an advancing technology frontier or technical changes in the production process; rather, the fissured workplace is an organizational innovation on the part of firms seeking to shed less profitable activities that nevertheless remain necessary to deliver a good or service to the consumer. Fissuring is an outgrowth of the doctrine of shareholder value, which exhorts firms to dedicate their assets to core competencies—that is, those activities that generate returns to investors.⁴ However, as the definition of core competencies becomes ever narrower, the set of activities performed in-house shrinks and the remainder externalized to independent firms grows.

The fissured workplace, then, is the product of companies drawing their organizational boundaries around those activities that deliver (or are thought to deliver) the highest or most secure returns. This profitable core may be linked to, and indeed depend on, upstream or downstream activities, but whatever tasks or operations fall outside the boundaries of the focal firm can be managed via markets (i.e., spot transactions) or networks (i.e., longer-term contracting relationships). The logic of fissuring can be applied to a broad range of activities across sectors: from stocking warehouses to manufacturing garments, from digital editing to reading X-rays and other diagnostic technologies, from harvesting tomatoes to cleaning offices. In each case, fissuring is a mechanism that allows a company to shed the liabilities implied by the standard employment relationship. Fissuring transforms the potential employer into a client that purchases services from an independent supplier; the supplier, in turn, hires the workers necessary to deliver the contracted services. Moreover, as a client, the focal firm benefits from competition among service providers in the supplier market stimulated by the demand that fissuring generates.

Drawing the firm's boundaries around core competencies narrows the type of work, and thus the type of worker, that remains inside the organization. When janitors and security workers are employed by large firms that also hire software engineers and programmers, their wages are likely to be higher and their benefits better than their counterparts employed by cleaning companies or security contractors. In extreme cases, fissuring may even move workers from inside the firm to outside it, in which case they may find that, as employees of a contractor, they receive lower pay and fewer benefits for the same work they did when employed directly by the client firm. By externalizing work that was previously performed in-house, the client firm "transforms wage setting [within the firm] into a pricing problem [on the supplier market]."⁵ Fissuring, then, is a mechanism of market creation. It stimulates "a competitive market . . . in the form of a network of service providers" and substitutes this market for work that "in the past [would have been] handled internally through direct employment" by the client firm.⁶ Because the supplier firms that directly employ the bulk of the workforce operate in more competitive markets that are "separated from the locus of value creation," the result is often deteriorating conditions of employment.⁷

David Weil's magisterial analysis of fissuring focuses on the United States, where the fissured workplace is achieved via strategies such as domestic outsourcing, franchising, and the use of temporary workers. But the scope of the market created by fissuring can and does vary over time and across industries. In some industries, the market for suppliers is delimited spatially—either because the externalized activities are services that have to be performed in situ, such as cable installation, or because they involve physical resources or infrastructure that are fixed in place, such as coal deposits or cell towers. But for many other activities there are no such geographical restrictions on the scope of the market, and when firms contract with service providers in other countries or regions of the world, fissuring results in *global* value chains.

Global value chains do not arise spontaneously; they are brought into being through the decisions of particular actors—typically, but not always, multinational corporations. The actors that play the pivotal role in creating and managing value chains are referred to as lead firms. In this global version of fissuring, lead firms use their bargaining power over (potential) suppliers to reduce the cost of the goods and services they purchase. As Cédric Durand and Will Milberg have observed, induced "competition among suppliers acts also as competition among labor. . . . The decline in the wage share in numerous countries that accompanied the expansion of GVC trade after 1995 is consistent with this weakening position of labor."[8] Analyzing global value chains as a product of international fissuring provides a different perspective on the developmental opportunities posed by globalization. Although the smile curve posits value chains as developmental opportunity structures, Durand and Milberg's analysis leads to a less sanguine conclusion: that competition in the global supplier market weakens the bargaining power of developing-country suppliers, as well as that of the workers they employ.[9]

A particularly stark example is provided by Mark Anner's analysis of unit prices for cotton trousers (e.g., jeans and khaki pants) imported to the United States from leading suppliers.[10] Although there is some volatility in unit prices among countries and over time, the two countries whose unit values either stayed the same or declined—China and Bangladesh—have seen the largest increases in exports (figure 8.3). With the exception of Mexico, the prices among the major exporters have converged over the relevant period, suggesting increased benchmarking of suppliers by lead firms, most of which source from several of these countries.

If lead firms are paying less for the jeans they import from China and Bangladesh, what happens to the savings generated along this value chain? Some of it is passed on to consumers in the form of lower prices at retail, but much of the differential between the lead firm's cost and the consumer's price is captured by the lead firm. Using global value chains to procure the goods and services they sell has been an effective strategy for lead firms looking to boost profits. Drawing from research attempting to quantify the extent of the corporate profitability boost associated with globalization, the World Bank concludes that "the average

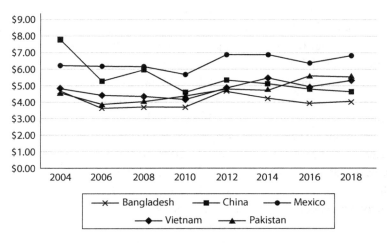

FIGURE 8.3 Unit prices for U.S. trouser imports.

Source: Author's calculations using OTEXA data for men's and boys' cotton trouser imports (category 347). Adapted from Mark Anner, "Squeezing Workers' Rights in Global Supply Chains: Purchasing Practices in the Bangladesh Garment Export Sector in Comparative Perspective," *Review of International Political Economy* 27, no. 2 (2020): 320–47, https://doi.org/10.1080/09692290.2019.1625426.

global markup increased by 46 percent between 1980 and 2016, with the largest increases accruing to the largest firms in Europe and North America and across a broad range of economic sectors."[11] The same World Bank publication is explicit in linking market concentration among lead firms, the bargaining power that they exercise over suppliers, and the distribution of returns between capital and labor: "The share of income accruing to workers—or how much of a country's GDP accrues to labor through wages as opposed to physical capital and profits—is the other side of the markup phenomenon: profits are rising, but labor's share of income is falling."[12] As the World Bank's observation suggests, when the market created by fissuring encompasses a vast global supply base, the resulting downward pressure on costs may manifest as a fall in labor's income share—a theme to which I return in the concluding section of this chapter.

FINANCIALIZATION AND THE VALORIZATION OF INTANGIBLE ASSETS

Fissuring is an organizational fix to the challenge of navigating the smile curve. Companies want to shed the activities located at the bottom of the curve by outsourcing to suppliers, but they also want to procure the goods and services produced outside the boundaries of the firm at a low cost. By becoming lead firms in value chains, they can leverage competition in the supply base, thereby reducing the amount of value that can be captured by suppliers and the workers they employ.

Yet squeezing suppliers in the middle of the chain—dropping the bottom—is only one route to a deeper smile curve. Increasing returns to the activities at the beginning and end of the chain—raising the sides—is another. What is critical about these links is that they entail intangible assets including "computerized information (such as databases and software), innovative property (such as patents, trademarks, and copyrights), and economic competencies (such as brand equity and organizational capital)."[13] Design, product development, and marketing activities generate higher returns not simply because they are more technology- or capital-intensive. These returns are, at least in part, rents created by legal regimes. Brands and copyrights are protected by intellectual property rights that generate monopoly rents for their owners.[14] They also serve as barriers to entry that make the sides of the smile curve steeper, and thereby make it more difficult for other firms to upgrade into these links in the chain.[15]

The proliferation of global value chains in the 1990s and 2000s has coincided with a strengthening of intellectual property rights, often via the negotiation and ratification of preferential trade agreements. Such agreements generally include stronger protections than those provided under the World Trade Organization's Trade-Related Aspects of Intellectual Property Rights (TRIPS) regime. These parallel trends—the expansion of global value chains and the strengthening of intellectual property rights—have been complementary; lead firms may be reluctant to externalize and outsource production to international suppliers in the absence of such protections, so they lobby for such rights to be strengthened. Stronger protections, once codified in new agreements, further contribute to the expansion of global value chains.

The use of legal affordances to valorize intangible assets is one factor driving the shape of the smile curve, but as Seabrooke and Wigan have argued, understanding the implications of global value chains requires analyzing not just where value is generated or captured but how the surplus generated by intangible assets is managed in ways that minimize tax liability, preserve the power of lead firms over other actors, and shield accumulated wealth from workers and governments.[16] In other words, we need to study *how* GVCs are generating surplus but also *where* and *to whom* the accrued profits are going. Many companies appear to be funneling these gains into financial assets rather than fixed investments, a dynamic that may depress productivity growth and employment generation while rewarding the ownership class.[17] Céline Baud and Cédric Durand, for example, demonstrate that global retailers based in the United States and Europe made aggressive use of global value chains in the 1990s to boost their profits. The profits enabled by international outsourcing were then distributed to shareholders or invested in financial assets.[18] Will Milberg and Deborah Winkler refer to this as the "offshoring-financialization" linkage.[19] From this perspective, the deepening of the smile curve reflects a broader transformation of capitalism, namely, the shift from an industrial-centered to a finance-centered regime of accumulation.[20]

The idea of an offshoring-financialization linkage connects financialization as a macro phenomenon to the organizational (and geographic) changes in production that fissuring enables. David Weil identifies the changing landscape of corporate governance and, more specifically, the rise of shareholder value, as the root cause of fissuring. The doctrine of shareholder value holds that the ultimate measure of a company's success is the value it delivers to the equity owners of the corporation—that is, the extent to which it enriches shareholders. Capital markets are understood to reward companies that pursue the shareholder model. Fissuring is a key way that companies demonstrate their commitment to this model, making decisions about which assets to own and which workers to employ, with an eye toward generating returns for investors.

CONCLUSION: THE FUTURE IS NOW

After the so-called third world debt crisis and the "lost decade" of the 1980s, the mainstream development consensus was that integration into, and upgrading along, global value chains presented the best, and possibly the only viable, path for countries across the radically heterogeneous (and constructed) space called the Global South. Yet as the *World Development Report* cited previously suggests, the GVC prescription for the developmental cure has come under strain. One factor is excess manufacturing capacity, which manifests in a vast global market of suppliers, as more and more countries angle for a spot on the global assembly line. This is consistent with the trade data I discussed in the prior section, which suggests that competition among garment manufacturers in Latin America, East Asia, and Southeast Asia—all vying for the orders of a smaller set of lead firms—drives a decline in unit values for U.S. clothing imports.

Similar dynamics can be found in other industries and geographies as well. Consider agricultural producers in Florida, Mexico, or Spain that want to sell fresh tomatoes to fast food restaurants; manufacturers of wire harnesses in

Vietnam, Indonesia, or Bulgaria wanting to supply auto assemblers; or software developers in India, Pakistan, or Russia offering their services via digital labor platforms such as Upwork. Service providers or suppliers like these compete at the bottom of the supply chain, operating in more competitive markets than those faced by client firms. The prices the client firm pays, and thus the wages the supplier's employees (or the independent contractor, in the case of labor platforms) receive, will reflect the greater intensity of this competition.

Fissuring negatively affects many individual workers, resulting, as Weil documents for the U.S. context, in stagnant wages and increased rates of labor violations.[21] It also has distributional consequences at the macro level, as reflected in labor's declining share of income. The magnitude of this decline varies across countries and world regions, but the trend itself is well-documented. In the case of the United States, labor's share of national income is estimated to have fallen somewhere between five and eight percentage points since the 1970s.[22] Although data from the Bureau of Labor Statistics suggest that labor's share started to fall as early as the 1960s, the trend was uneven and the pace of the decline was modest through the 1980s and early 1990s.[23] Following a brief reversal of this trend in the mid-1990s, the pace of the decline accelerated sharply. An analysis by McKinsey's Global Institute found that a full three-fourths of the fall in labor's share from 65.4 percent in 1947 to 56.7 percent in 2016 occurred after the year 2000.[24]

The decline has been particularly notable in the United States, but the same general trend is found throughout the higher-wage economies of the OECD. According to a survey by the IMF, thirty-five advanced economies saw labor's income share fall from around 54 percent in 1980 to 50.5 percent in 2014. The picture is more uneven in non-OECD countries, but here, too, labor's share has trended downward. In fifty-four developing economies, it fell from 39 percent in 1993 to 37.4 percent in 2014.[25] This decline has occurred even in countries considered to be among the most significant beneficiaries of globalization. China, which experienced both rapid growth and a substantial reduction in poverty over the last three decades, has nevertheless seen labor's share of income decline by just under three percentage points since 1990. These trends produce an increasingly complex landscape for understanding global inequality. Even as the inter-country inequality component of global inequality declines, intra-country inequality is growing in places as diverse as China, Indonesia, Sweden, Bolivia, Romania, and South Africa.[26]

The factors driving labor's declining income share are the subject of vigorous debate. Part of the difficulty lies in the messy reality that the causes are multiple and difficult to disentangle. What is less disputed is the scope of the transformation in the world of work that has occurred over this period in higher- and lower-wage economies alike. In the former, this transformation includes growth in short-term and temporary work, the erosion of internal labor markets, and a decline in the collective power of workers vis-à-vis employers—changes that, collectively, are sometimes referred to as "the decline of the standard employment relationship."

The standard employment relationship is the model of full-time employment associated with the Fordist period. Defined as a "stable, open-ended and direct arrangement between a dependent, full-time employee and their unitary employer," such a relationship is "standard" both because it refers to a "regulatory model" and because such a "model is expected to be the norm (with, in turn, non-standard forms of work being expected to be atypical)."[27] Temporary or part-time work (fixed-term or zero hour contracts) are departures from this standard, as are temporary agency work or other forms of labor contracting in which the worker does not have a "direct, subordinate relationship with [the] end user" of their labor.[28]

There are a few places in the world, such as the European Union, where many jobs continue to meet the "standard employment" definition, even if they account for a declining share of the total. From a global perspective, however, what is striking about the standard employment relationship is how decisively nonstandard it is. While there are few estimates of the prevalence of standard versus nonstandard employment globally, the ILO recently provided an estimate of total informal employment (a category that is inclusive of but not coterminous with nonstandard employment). It estimates that two billion people aged fifteen and over are engaged in informal employment, a number that represents 61.2 percent of the world's employed population.[29]

Because levels of social protection vary dramatically across countries and regions of the world, the consequences of working in the formal versus informal sector or being in a standard versus nonstandard employment relationship vary too. Yet what the available data suggest is that nonstandard employment, already high outside the developed country enclave of the OECD, is also increasing within it. Without conflating the meaning or experience of informal work in these different parts of the world, it is nevertheless possible to identify a kind of convergence of the Global North toward the Global South; more people in developed countries are today experiencing forms of work that diverge from the increasingly elusive "standard" of full-time, formal, and open-ended employment.

In this chapter, I have discussed fissuring and financialization as mutually reinforcing processes that, together, are deepening the smile curve and creating a world of work in which opportunities for secure and stable employment appear, like labor's share of income, to be on the decline. Importantly, these processes have been underway for some time. Although the technological developments we so often emphasize when we speculate on the future of work may well accelerate these trends, the causes of fissuring and financialization are political-economic, not scientific-technical. Discussions about the future of work must begin with a clear-eyed understanding of where we are and what it will take to shift course by intervening in the forces that are already at work making work's future.

NOTES

1. Aaron Benanav, "Automation and the Future of Work—2," *New Left Review* 120 (November/December 2019): 120.
2. Organization for Economic Cooperation and Development, *OECD Skills Outlook 2017: Skills and Global Value Chains* (2017), https://doi.org/10.1787/9789264273351-en.
3. David Weil, *The Fissured Workplace: Why Work Became So Bad for So Many and What Can Be Done About It* (Cambridge, MA: Harvard University Press, 2014).
4. William Lazonick and Mary O'Sullivan, "Maximising Shareholder Value: A New Ideology for Corporate Governance," *Economy and Society* 29, no. 1 (2000): 13–35, https://doi.org/10.1080/030851400360541.
5. Weil, *The Fissured Workplace*, 20.
6. Weil, *The Fissured Workplace*, 88.
7. Weil, *The Fissured Workplace*, 14.
8. Cédric Durand and William Milberg, "Intellectual Monopoly in Global Value Chains," *Review of International Political Economy* 27, no. 2 (2020): 409, https://doi.org/10.1080/09692290.2019.1660703.
9. Marion Werner, Jennifer Bair, and Victor Ramiro Fernández, "Linking Up to Development? Global Value Chains and the Making of a Post-Washington Consensus," *Development and Change* 45, no. 6 (2014): 1219–47, https://doi.org/10.1111/dech.12132.
10. Mark Anner, "Squeezing Workers' Rights in Global Supply Chains: Purchasing Practices in the Bangladesh Garment Export Sector in Comparative Perspective," *Review of International Political Economy* 27, no. 2 (2020): 320–47, https://doi.org/10.1080/09692290.2019.1625426. The Office of Textiles and Apparel at the U.S. Department of Commerce records apparel imports by volume and by dollar values. The unit value is calculated by dividing the value of imports by import volume (measured in square meters) and can be treated as a proxy for the price paid to suppliers by importers. See Mark Anner, Jennifer Bair, and Jeremy Blasi, "Towards Joint Liability in Global Supply Chains: Addressing the Root Causes of Labor Violations in International Subcontracting Networks," *Comparative Labor Law and Policy Journal* 35, no. 1 (2013): 1–43.
11. World Bank, *Trading for Development in the Age of Global Value Chains* (Washington, DC: World Bank, 2020), 83.
12. World Bank, *Trading for Development*, 86. Concerns about the degree to which global value chain dynamics are fueling market concentration and the rise of "superstar firms" (or oligopolistic market structures) are increasingly raised by mainstream

economists. See, for example, Mai Dao, Mitali Das, Zsoka Koczan, and Weicheng Lia, "Why Is Labor Receiving a Smaller Share of Global Income? Theory and Empirical Evidence," IMF Working Paper No. 17/169 (New York: International Monetary Fund, July 2017), https://www.imf.org/en/Publications/WP/Issues/2017/07/24/Why-Is-Labor-Receiving-a-Smaller-Share-of-Global-Income-Theory-and-Empirical-Evidence-45102; and Jan De Loecker, Jan Eeckhout, and Gabriel Unger, "The Rise of Market Power and the Macroeconomic Implications," *Quarterly Journal of Economics* 135, no. 2 (2020): 561–644, https://doi.org/10.1093/qje/qjz041.

13. Peter J. Buckley, Roger Strange, Marcel P. Timmer, and Gaaitzen de Vries, "Rent Appropriation in Global Value Chains: The Past, Present, and Future of Intangible Assets," *Global Strategy Journal* 12, no. 4 (2022): 679, https://doi.org/10.1002/gsj.1438.

14. Carlos Aguiar de Medeiros and Nicolas Trebat, "Inequality and Income Distribution in Global Value Chains," *Journal of Economic Issues* 51, no. 2 (2017): 401–8, https://doi.org/10.1080/00213624.2017.1320916; and Raphael Kaplinsky, "Rents and Inequality in Global Value Chains," in *Handbook of Global Value Chains*, ed. Stefano Ponte, Gary Rereffi, and Gale Raj-Reichert (Cheltenham, UK: Edward Elgar, 2019): 153–68.

15. Özgür Orhangazi, "The Role of Intangible Assets in Explaining the Investment–Profit Puzzle," *Cambridge Journal of Economics* 43, no. 5 (2019): 1251–85, https://doi.org/10.1093/cje/bey046.

16. Leonard Seabrooke and Duncan Wigan, "The Governance of Global Wealth Chains," *Review of International Political Economy* 24, no. 1 (2017): 1–29, https://doi.org/10.1080/09692290.2016.1268189; and Leonard Seabrooke and Duncan Wigan, "Asset Strategies in Global Wealth Chains," in *Global Wealth Chains*, ed. Leonard Seabrooke and Duncan Wigan (Oxford: Oxford University Press, 2022), 1–29.

17. William Milberg, "Shifting Sources and Uses of Profits: Sustaining US Financialization with Global Value Chains," *Economy and Society* 37, no. 3 (2008): 420–51, https://doi.org/10.1080/03085140802172706; and Herman Mark Schwartz, "Global Secular Stagnation and the Rise of Intellectual Property Monopoly," *Review of International Political Economy* 29, no. 5 (2022): 1448–76, https://doi.org/10.1080/09692290.2021.1918745.

18. Céline Baud and Cédric Durand, "Financialization, Globalization and the Making of Profits by Leading Retailers," *Socio-Economic Review* 10, no. 2 (2012): 241–66, https://doi.org/10.1093/ser/mwr016.

19. William Milberg and Deborah Winkler, *Outsourcing Economics: Global Value Chains in Capitalist Development* (New York: Cambridge University Press, 2013).

20. Robert Boyer, "Is a Finance-Led Growth Regime a Viable Alternative to Fordism? A Preliminary Analysis," *Economy and Society* 29, no. 1 (2000): 111–45, https://doi.org/10.1080/030851400360587. The term financialization is used to refer to multiple dynamics. See Natascha van der Zwan, "Making Sense of Financialization," *Socio-Economic Review* 12, no. 1 (2014): 99–129, https://doi.org/10.1093/ser/mwt020. Sociologist Greta Krippner defines it as "a pattern of accumulation in which profits accrue primarily through financial channels rather than through

trade and commodity production." Greta Krippner, "The Financialization of the American Economy," *Socio-Economic Review* 3, no. 2 (2005): 174–75, https://doi.org/10.1093/SER/mwi008. See also Giovanni Arrighi, *The Long Twentieth Century: Money, Power and the Origins of Our Times* (London: Verso, 1994).

21. Weil, *The Fissured Workplace*.
22. Gene M. Grossman and Ezra Oberfield, "The Elusive Explanation for the Declining Labor Share," *Annual Review of Economics* 14 (2022): 93–124, https://doi.org/10.1146/annurev-economics-080921-103046.
23. Michael D. Giandrea and Shawn Sprague, "Estimating the U.S. Labor Share," *Monthly Labor Review, U.S. Bureau of Labor Statistics* (February 2017), https://doi.org/10.21916/mlr.2017.7.
24. James Manyika et al., *A New Look at the Declining Labor Share of Income in the United States* (McKinsey Global Institute, 2019), 5–6, https://www.mckinsey.com/featured-insights/employment-and-growth/a-new-look-at-the-declining-labor-share-of-income-in-the-united-states.
25. International Monetary Fund, "Understanding the Downward Trend in Labor Income Shares," in *World Economic Outlook* (Washington, DC: April 2017), https://www.imf.org/en/Publications/WEO/Issues/2017/04/04/world-economic-outlook-april-2017.
26. Arthur S. Alderson and Roshan K. Pandian, "What Is Really Happening with Global Inequality?," *Sociology of Development* 4, no. 3 (2018): 261–81, https://doi.org/10.1525/sod.2018.4.3.261. Analyses of global inequality are highly sensitive to methodological choices, including income measures—currency exchange rate or purchasing power parity—and population-weighting. Much of the decline in poverty and between-country inequality after 2000 was thought to be driven by China, and to a lesser extent, India. However, more recent analyses show that population-weighted income inequality has declined since 2000, even when these populous countries are excluded. See Robert Wade, "Is Globalization Reducing Poverty and Inequality?," *World Development* 32, no. 4 (2004): 567–89, https://doi.org/10.1016/j.worlddev.2003.10.007; Christoph Lakner and Branko Milanovic, "Global Income Distribution: From the Fall of the Berlin Wall to the Great Recession," *World Bank Economic Review* 30, no. 2 (2016): 203–32, https://doi.org/10.1093/wber/lhv039; and Aldersen and Pandian, "What Is Really Happening."
27. Paul Schoukens and Alberto Barrio, "The Changing Concept of Work: When Does Typical Work Become Atypical?," *European Labour Law Journal* 8, no. 4 (2017): 308, https://doi.org/10.1177/2031952517743871.
28. International Labour Organization, *Non-Standard Employment Around the World: Understanding Challenges, Shaping Prospects* (Geneva: International Labour Organization, 2016), xxii; https://www.ilo.org/wcmsp5/groups/public/---dgreports/---dcomm/---publ/documents/publication/wcms_534326.pdf.
29. International Labour Organization, *Women and Men in the Informal Economy: A Statistical Picture* (Geneva: International Labour Organization, 2018), https://www.ilo.org/sites/default/files/2024-04/Women_men_informal_economy_statistical_picture.pdf.

PART III
Global Hierarchies at Work

Grounded Accounts

CHAPTER 9

LABORS IN TIME AND SUBJECTIVITY

Gender Nonconformity and Racial Capitalism in the Making of Eighteenth-Century New Orleans

VANJA HAMZIĆ

"I demand, on King's behalf," declared ceremoniously François Fleuriau, the *procureur general*, "that . . . Etienne La Rue, *mulâtre* prisoner accused, be declared duly charged and convicted of illicit carrying of arms." Fleuriau was speaking before the Superior Council of Louisiana in New Orleans, on the afternoon of May 18, 1747, wrapping up the prosecution's case against a twenty-two-year-old free person of color, who had arrived in this French colony as a pilot of *L'Unique*, a Compagnie des Indes' ship, from Senegambia. The trial documents describe La Rue as "a native of Senegal," Catholic, and a child of one "*seigneur* La Rue, a *nègre libre*," who on May 3 that year got into an altercation with three wounded French soldiers, also in their twenties, on the streets of New Orleans. As the record shows, the incident started when the soldier Jean Gaillard, "having met one La Rue, a *mulâtre*, . . . said jokingly [to La Rue]: '*Bonsoir, Seigneur Négritte*,' to which La Rue answered: '*Bonsoir, Seigneur Jean Foutre*'"—this swift exchange leading to another solider punching La Rue on the chin, having told La Rue: "Do you consider yourself insulted by being called *Seigneur Négritte*? You answer by abuse and he [Gaillard] tells you nothing to insult you."[1]

The council, as expected, decided for the prosecution and the trial documents were left to languish in the Cabildo, New Orleans' colonial-Spanish-era (1762–1801) city hall, as yet another remnant of the heavily classed and racialized "justice" at work in French Louisiana, of which New Orleans became capital in 1722, four years after the city's founding. Despite being free and a professional seafarer, La Rue was found guilty of possessing two pistols, which was forbidden under city ordinances due to La Rue's perceived racial designation (*mulâtre*, meaning "mulatto"). The soldiers' charges and La Rue's own evidence had been considered, but no soldier suffered legal consequences of any kind for clearly provoking the brawl. Centuries went by and, with them, a series of mistranslations, until an anthropologist finally recognized "the feminine form, diminutive" in *Négritte*, as well as that "*Foutre* is a very strong term, equivalent to 'fuck/fucking' in English."[2] She duly acknowledged the racialized nature and even "a heavy dose of sexual innuendo" in the soldiers' and La Rue's exchange, implying that La Rue essentially called Gaillard a "sodomite."[3] But no one could quite explain why the other soldier thought that Gaillard's gender-transgressive usage of *négritte* (lit. Black girl)—by then widely used across the French colonial world to police an emergent colonial gender binary as well as the attendant racialized hierarchies of personhood—should not have offended La Rue.[4]

The trial documents laconically fix La Rue's gender, age, occupation, and ethno-racial belonging in an *ordinary* way—a manner that appears consistent with the French recordkeeping legal, economic, and administrative enterprise of the time. But, in the mid-eighteenth century, this colonial ordinary was still very much in the making, and its archive nonetheless reveals a great deal of discordant, even jarring, details. La Rue's story is, however, typical in the history of early New Orleans in that its insurrectionary potential, its ways of telling a past that does not quite square with the colonial ordinary, is speculative and contingent on a critical analysis of the very way that extractive, dispossessive colonial ordinary came into being. Could La Rue's own senses of the self and the other *in time* have been incongruent to an extent, or altogether, with the surviving categories of colonial difference, such as race and gender? After all, the record suggests that, while proudly speaking of a Black father, La Rue did not necessarily self-identify as *mulâtre*, or endeavor to answer Gaillard's peculiar phrasing that caused the brawl with anything other than "I have pity on you; if you weren't sick, all three of you would pay for it!"[5] Besides, what could La Rue's designation as a free person of color from Senegambia, having a *job* deemed "respectable" by the colonial enterprise, mean vis-à-vis La Rue's position in New Orleans' French colonial society?

To probe these queries in a larger colonial context, in this chapter I engage the temporality of work and selfhood in its violent, dispossessive modes, which figure as an abiding feature of racial capitalism. Focusing on eighteenth-century New Orleans and its surroundings, I argue that gender nonconforming individuals and communities of color were systemically dispossessed, not only due to their perceived race and class, or social status, but also due to their gender difference. Bringing forth a range of resistive remnants of circum-Atlantic Black and Indigenous gender nonconformity, I focus on the distinct socio-temporal contexts of eighteenth-century New Orleans, which reveal a changing landscape of racial capitalist regulation of the gender binary and the sites of labor. I attempt to show how and why the commingling practices of work, gendering, and racialization mattered then, when they were imposed but also subverted and resisted as violent and dispossessive, especially with respect to the laborer's perceived forms of embodiment. But I also contend that their lingering presence matters still, proving an important corrective to the linear futurity of both work and subjectivity-making.

I start with a sketch of gender nonconformity in eighteenth-century Senegambia, from which not only La Rue and a small number of free persons of color came to French Louisiana but also some 3,909 enslaved people, who were brought there between 1720 and 1743.[6] Their incongruence relative to the colonial gender binary can be gauged from a series of scattered archival traces, starting with an open rebellion aboard a ship sailing toward Louisiana and the early labor patterns correspondent to their Senegambian occupational castes. What's more, enslaved Africans, forcefully mis-gendered though they may have been in Louisiana, encountered and formed alliances with Indigenous and even some European lower-class communities and labor force, some of whom were in their own ways resistant to the colonial gender binary and the class and racial divisions fundamental to early manifestations of racial capitalism.

Work mattered there in multiple intersecting ways. It mattered, for example, that some gender nonconforming enslaved Africans came from an *artisanal* status group, where their traditional occupations had set them apart socially and cosmologically, anchoring them in an alterity that could challenge and inspire rebellion against the new colonial ordinary, while their work skills also made them essential, in colonizers' eyes, for building and sustaining the ever-fragile settler-colonial sites of labor and life. Conversely, it is peculiar that spaces where "proper" work was deemed absent, such as illegal taverns, teemed with insurrectionary activity of "idlers" from across the racial and class divide.

Law mattered, too, as a chief device and repository of *categorical* ordering, evident in La Rue's case, but also as a means to regulate both work and "idleness" according to an overarching economic rationale of early capitalist racialized plantation society. Violent and unjust by design, colonial law was deployed (often unsuccessfully) mainly to "remind" lower classes, particularly those deemed legally enslaved, of their supposed place in the extractive, hierarchical lifeworlds of French and Spanish Louisiana, with the latter (as we shall see) more so than the former insisting on policing dress codes and sexual and gender propriety.

New Orleans, this uneasy city—which had been, from its very founding, designated as the devil's own domain for its ostensible sexual, gender, class, and racial transgressions—offers a unique insight into the centrality of socioeconomic alienation of certain forms of gender and bodily labor for the enduring project of racial capitalism.[7] But, in this chapter, I also ask what practices of temporal alienation, or *distemporalization*, such forms of labor would have to contend with, and just how, in turn, gender nonconforming subjectivities—whether enslaved or free—among New Orleanian communities of color organized and sustained their resistance to such systemic violence.[8] This is not only to query how the dominant knowledge-making patterns were interrupted in early New Orleans, but also to unsettle what still appears to be an abiding linear temporality of work and subjectivity. To understand the past or future of work and livelihood—or, indeed, time as a governing device—we must search for and engage resistive forms of embodiment, such as those in colonial Louisiana. And, with it, we should take seriously *temporal refuges* those embodiments conceived and relied on to work, rest, and live, however fleetingly, outside the colonial ordinary.

A LEAP IN SPACE AND TIME: FROM GREATER SENEGAMBIA TO FRENCH LOUISIANA

Eighteenth-century Louisianan Senegambians hailed from an exceptionally diverse region in West Africa, comprising not only the three crucial waterscapes—that of the Senegal and Gambia Rivers, and their tributaries, as well as of Senegal's Petite Côte in the Atlantic Ocean—but also the traditional Fulɓe heartlands of Bundu, Futa Jallon, and Futa Toro, as well as the Mande cultural zone, extending as far east as Bamako and Timbuktu and as far south as the Southern Rivers region, framed to the north by the Arabo-Berber Trarza and Brakna communities in present-day Mauritania. This vast territory was, in a sense, both postimperial and precolonial. The empires of Mali and Songhay, which for a long time had dominated Senegambian hinterlands and much of western Sudan, were succeeded by a welter of larger and smaller states, while the last truly imperial state, that of Great Fula, would see a steep decline, only to be fully eliminated in 1776 by the Imamate of Futa Toro.

European states and chartered companies, for their part, were still unable to engage in full-scale colonial experiments, not least due to constant power struggles between themselves, although the violence of the Atlantic trade in enslaved Africans led to an era of great social and political instability across Senegambia. During the seventeenth century, the Senegambian coast had been divided into French, Dutch, Portuguese, and English spheres of influence. A century later, the French and the English largely outpowered the rest, primarily because the forts at Saint-Louis (French) and James Island (English), built on small islands in the estuaries of the Senegal and the Gambia, gave their inhabitants effective control over much of riverine traffic taking place. Upstream trading posts, such as Saint-Joseph de Galam in Gajaaga on the upper Senegal River, ensured that the flow of enslaved Africans and goods from the interior toward the river's mouth would be as secure as possible. Another small but strategically important *entrepôt* was located on Île de Gorée, which operated its own network of trading villages along the Petite Côte.

Gender variance in eighteenth-century Greater Senegambian lifeworlds was a complex phenomenon, not least because it was related to a range of other expressions of belonging and personhood. Mande oral traditions, for example, attested to the existence of a gender-variant water spirit, called Faro, who was central to what has been termed as the Bamana (or *bambara*) religion.[9] Bamana societies also recognized the existence of the gender and socio-spiritual positionality of "[t]he hermaphrodite, [who,] being both male and female, is themself, materially, their own twin,"[10] in that their being-in-the-world did not necessarily require balancing the gendered forces within and without oneself, usually performed through a series of rituals, including scarification and marriage. Among Fulɓe, a well-known pre-Muslim genesis story suggested that the Supreme Being, called Geno, created the world from a single drop of milk, populating it at first with an array of gender nonspecific lesser deities (*laareeji*) and then with Kiikala, the first man, Naagara, the first woman, and Ndurbeele, the first bovine, a hermaphrodite who gave birth to the first twenty-two zebu cattle.[11] Various Senegambian communities also included "a gender role that is neither fully male nor female," denoted in Fulfulde as *samarooka* and in Wolof as *góor-jigéen*.[12]

But perhaps the most peculiar manifestation of Senegambian gender, sexual, societal, and cosmological diversity occurred among members of the endogamous *artisanal* status group, or caste, which is usually thought to have originated among the Mande, Wolof, and Soninke, only to be gradually adopted by a variety of Fulɓe, Arabo-Berber, and other populations of Greater Senegambia. As their collective name in Mande languages (*ɲamakalaw*) suggests, members of artisanal groups were thought to possess extraordinary access to the foundational life force, *ɲama*, and be persons with their own special temporality, access to history, and bodily and gender-variant properties. The *ɲamakalaw* (Wolof: ñeeño, Fulfulde: *nyeenyɓe*) occupied a deeply ambiguous position in society and were contradictorily described as feared, loathed, desired, necessary, and respected—all at the same time. They ordinarily made their living through specialized services they provided to the rest of the population. Numerous subdivisions existed. For example, among the Mande *ɲamakalaw*, *numuw* typically worked in metal, wood, and earth, and the *garankew* in leather. But the most famous and idiosyncratic of all were *jeliw*, known as griots, whose specific artistry (*jeliya*) extended wide and deep—from music, dance, companionship to warriors, and advice to nobles and local leaders to the art of oral history with its many mystical properties.

Griots' social segregation and behavioral difference did not go unnoticed in European travelogues and commercial literature of the time. John (Jean) Barbot, an employee of the Compagnie du Sénégal, called them "a sort of sycophants," who, being considered "infamous," were "much despis'd by all the other Blacks."[13] Dominique Harcourt Lamiral, a commercial agent in the French outpost of Saint-Louis, described with suspicion, in 1789, a griot always accompanying the local ruler, for whom "the King cares very much."[14] René-Claude Geoffroy de Villeneuve, who spent a total of four years in the region in the 1780s as aide de camp to a French governor and penned a four-tome bestseller on Senegal, similarly depicted the griots in constant presence of the *damel* of Kayor as "a species of histrions," and remarked of another aristocrat's "incapacity" as being related to his "passing his days surrounded with *guiriots* and *guiriottes*."[15] References to sexual intimacy, regardless of a griot's perceived gender, were either covert or overt. Villeneuve suggested, for example, contrary to popular travelogues, that women of Senegambia could not be easily seduced, "*si l'on en excepte les Guiriotes*," whom he readily accused of "almost always being courtesans by profession."[16] Others wondered exactly what went on between aristocrats and their griot advisors and entertainers. For instance, Armand Corre alarmingly wrote that "[i]n Boké, I saw a griot in the company of a Fulɓe prince, whose lascivious dances reflected the more intimate role he had to fulfil in the house of His Highness."[17]

Although members of the artisanal caste could sometimes be easier to notice in "New World" archives, due to their specific professions and sheer "otherness," Senegambians from diverse social strata and polities could become "captives" (*captifs*)—a term the French ordinarily used when they referred to the enslaved bound for the trans-oceanic commerce.[18] "Captivity" thus became an identity marker no matter the nature of an African *captif*'s "capture." Michel Jajolet de la Courbe, a French aristocrat who lived and worked in Senegambia in the last decades of the seventeenth and first decades of the eighteenth centuries, provided a simple definition for this term of art that emphasized the alleged "criminality" and "otherness" of the enslaved, while also alluding to the potential preference for griots: "The *captifs* are either people taken in war, or others who have committed some crime, or who are accused of sorcery, or who are of captive race."[19] Once so categorized, the *captifs* were ordered into "men," "women," and, occasionally, "children," or "boys" and "girls"—sometimes even before they would reach a European trading post.

But it was primarily a European *entrepôt* in West Africa, such as the French Saint-Louis and Île de Gorée, and then, a slaver's ship, that would serve as the spaces of heightened and forceful gendering and racialization of the *captifs*. As for racialized descriptions, the designation *nègre*, along with its age-stratified and gender-binary variants, was ubiquitous. The enslaved would be ordinarily denied the bodily markers of their cosmological, social, or gender difference and assigned a place on the ship, with "men" given the most and "girls" the least space, before they were sent onto the perilous voyage through the Middle Passage.[20] Thus the financial and symbolical disparity in "worth" ascribed to a *nègre* (Black man) as opposed to that of a *négrite*, *négritte*, or *négrillonne* (Black girl) undergirded the racial capitalist gender binary. And it is in this light that one might want to recall and reread my opening story, in which the French soldier in New Orleans calls the Senegambian La Rue *Seigneur Négritte*.

Open rebellions and conspiracies of the *captifs* aboard the slavers' ships were commonplace. On one such a vessel, *Le Courrier de Bourbon*, sailing in 1723 from Senegambia to Louisiana, a forty-five-year-old enslaved was identified as "the sorcerer (*sorcier*) who raised [the other *captifs*'] vain hopes" of liberation, for which, according to the ship's pilot, this likely griot was hoisted "to the top of the main mast and fire[d] on with rifles, until death ensued."[21] Enslavers' violence, cramming, chaining, malnutrition, and diseases account for high mortality of the enslaved aboard these ships, as with *La Venus*, which in 1729 embarked 400 *captifs* at Île de Gorée and landed 363 at the French fort in La Balize, Louisiana, of whom only 320 reached New Orleans.[22] This was in sharp contrast with the way the Compagnie des Indes' more privileged employees arrived to French Louisiana. One of those, the minor aristocrat Marc-Antoine Caillot, who arrived aboard *La Durance* to La Balize at roughly the same time as *La Venus*, spent his journey courting "a young lady" out of boredom, even though "she was not pretty at all," and enjoyed the sight of the ship's "officers, [who,] in order to amuse themselves," would trick the youngest members of the crew, aged thirteen to sixteen, into "pull[ing] their breeches down," only to be tied and whipped until "these poor creatures end[ed] up with bloody buttocks."[23] Such was the "New World" into which enslaved West Africans were sailing to become its principal forced laborers—an unstable, impoverished colony, more valued for its strategic position than for its early experimentations in plantation economy, a frontier society whose many nascent hierarchies (of gender, sexuality, labor) would be, at all times, deeply saturated with violence.[24]

When a slavers' ship arrived in French Louisiana, according to a contemporary report, "it was visited by surgeons, who separated the healthy from the sick, and put the latter under treatment," and there was a lottery held for the healthy, in which settlers who were entitled to purchase the enslaved each "drew from a bag a ticket whose number denoted the *Nègre* or *Négresse* who fell to them." The sick would be sold at auction, often for "as much as the others," given the frenzied bidding of settlers.[25] Insider connections often dictated who would be able to purchase *captifs*; the Company retained some "for its own use," with the colony's *commandant-général*, the *commissaire-ordonnateur*, and their protégés obtaining a large number between them. To New Orleans—where, as of 1721, more than two-thirds of the free households contained enslaved people—the *captifs* from West Africa "brought skill as well as brawn," having quickly "monolopolize[d] the colony's artisanal sector."[26] Cabinetmaker, blacksmith, metalworker, carpenter, and cooper were just some of the highly sought-after professions, which members of the Senegambian artisanal caste could easily excel in. Thus, in 1720, the Company exchanged three enslaved Africans for the *commandant-général's* "*Nègre* named Laurent, who is a good blacksmith," while the wages of the free skilled labor force began to fall dramatically, until some professions were nearly devoid of any such workers.[27] Senegambian blacksmiths (Mande: *numuw*; French: *forgerons*) in particular seem to have managed to forge a distinct identity and could be traced in the colonial archive for decades to come.[28]

Whether or not their labor was gendered, the enslaved Senegambians were traded in accordance with a common, racialized gender-binary matrix of human fungibility.[29] For instance, in 1722, the Compagnie des Indes in Louisiana "charged an average of 1,000 livres for a pièce d'Inde, ... the same price it charged the much wealthier planters in the French Caribbean."[30] *Pièce d'Inde* (Portuguese: *peça da Índia*; Spanish: *pieza de India*) was a unit of value adopted by the French from the enslavers undergirding the Iberian circum-Atlantic colonial project, who used it throughout the sixteenth to eighteenth centuries. It connoted the exchange value of a bolt of printed cloth from India (hence "piece of India"), the cost of an African *captif* deemed healthy, male, and between the ages of fourteen and thirty-five. This was a racial capitalist invention par excellence, not least because, as Sylvia Wynter has warned, "[t]he pieza framework required a repositioning of the mode of production in relation to the mode of domination. The former becomes a subset of the latter."[31] Used to establish quotas and tariffs, the *pièce d'Inde* enabled an early capitalist type of domination and enslavement that ushered in the mode of production based on a highly reductive and forceful concept of personhood of the enslaved. In Louisiana, those ordered into "women" generally sold for less than those deemed "men," although there were some exceptions, and the value of the Indigenous enslaved was several times less than *pièce d'Inde*.[32] These gendered and racialized variations notwithstanding, the Company's project in Louisiana was in constant peril; because it felt obliged to keep the charges for the enslaved's labor so high, most Louisianan colonists had to make use of its liberal credit schemes that, over time, swelled into a massive, multimillion livre debt.[33] And because those schemes allowed for a sudden large influx of West African *captifs* (according to an estimate, by 1726, the presumed racial composition of rural laborers in lower Louisiana was 85 percent Black), such a workforce was difficult to control, and it quickly immersed itself into the strong undercurrents of Indigenous and lower-class resistance.[34]

DISORDERLY LIAISONS: TRAJECTORIES OF LABOR, RESISTANCE, AND NONCONFORMITY

"I finally arrived in this famous city, which has been named *la Nouvelle Orléans*," noted, on January 10, 1722, a Jesuit priest, after an eventful journey down the Mississippi River to a town that had just been made the capital of French Louisiana. "Those, who have given it this name," he added, "have thought that *l'Orléans* is of feminine gender; but—who cares—custom has established it, and that is above the rules of grammar."[35] Thus the remark on New Orleans' misgendering joined the chorus of derisive descriptions of the city as a devilish, strange, and disorderly place. In 1717—after a series of unsuccessful economic experiments, which saw a royal charter for Louisiana awarded to a French financier, only for it to be returned to the crown—the colony, which at all times operated at a loss, was chartered to the Compagnie d'Occident, soon to be renamed the Compagnie des Indes. That same year, the Regent, Philippe, the Duc d'Orléans, after whom New Orleans was named, authorized mass deportations of *forçats* (forced immigrants) and *engagés* (indentured servants) to Louisiana. Those included convicts, *galériens* (French people enslaved on galleys), "licentious offspring" of the bourgeoisie, sex workers, minor felons, and *épouseuses* (women sent to be married to settlers), as well as poor people without occupation, described as "cheats" or "vagabonds."[36] They joined French-Canadian *coureurs des bois* (fur traders) and impoverished Euro-Louisianan peasantry and workers as the *petits*, a colonial version of the ancien régime's underclass, which would continue to be described as "wild," "debauched," and "lawless" by the *grands* (Company and state bureaucrats, ennobled officers, large landowners, rich merchants, and the clergy).

By that time, the *petits*, particularly the Canadian traders, had established lasting relations with Louisiana's Indigenous population, including "conversion, intermarriage, and *métissage*" (having offspring deemed interracial), whose lifestyles *à la façon du pays* involved trading with and often living in Indigenous villages and communities.[37] Although these relations were rarely equal (*coureurs des bois* were largely seen as male, and their partners or even enslaved as Indigenous women), they provided for a complex terrain of alliances and enmities that could be based on social status, labor, and cross-communal intimacies, rather than on the larger colonial, racialized hierarchies of belonging. They enabled, for example, a European observer who lived among the Natchez to note how this Indigenous nation used gender to "ridicule as an effeminacy" the way *coureurs des bois* and others connoted as "French, by chiefly frequenting the [Natchez] women, contracted their manner of speaking" the local language.[38]

The Natchez, who were sometimes seen as more like the French than the other Louisianan Indigenous nations, due to the ostensible "pre-eminence of the men" in their society (despite it being matrilineal and having many influential female leaders), and the Choctaw, the regular allies of the French, were also in a sufficiently long and close contact with settlers to leave an indelible trace of their sexual and gender nonconformity in the colonial archive.[39] For example, Jean-François-Benjamin Dumont de Montigny, a French colonial officer turned farmer and historian, in his *Mémoires historiques sur la Louisiane*, published in 1753, lamented the fact that "almost all the authors who have spoken of Louisiana have pretended that this country was full of hermaphrodites."[40] He, however, had found none. Instead, he wrote, people must have mistakenly taken for "veritable hermaphrodites"

> a certain [type of] man among the Natchez and possibly also among other savage [that is, Indigenous] nations who is called the Chief of Women. What is certain is that, although he is really a man, he has the same adornments and the same occupations as women: he has long hair and braids, he wears something like a petticoat or a little skirt (*alconand*) instead of men's shorts (*brayet*); like women, he works on the cultivation of fields, and does all other chores that women do. And, as is the case with peoples who live almost without religion and without the law, libertinage is enjoyed to the greatest excesses, so I could not confirm that these barbarians did not also abuse this pretentious Chief of Women, and did not make him satisfy their brutal passions.[41]

Such attempts to "make sense" of bodily as opposed to behavioral and sartorial difference, and to police the boundaries of "manhood" and "womanhood," were typical for this genre of writing about "the other." Thus a contemporary of Dumont de Montigny, reporting on the Choctaw, observed that the "spirit of this Nation is generally very rough and unpolished . . . . They are, besides, morally perverted, most of them being addicted to sodomy. Those degraded men wear long hair and a little petticoat like women, who despise them greatly."[42] Such eighteenth-century accounts of the sexually and gender nonconforming Louisianan Indigenous joined European explorers' earlier reports, for instance, on "sodomites" and "hermaphrodites" among the Timucua or on gender-transgressive members of the Illiniwek nations.[43] The *grands*, who ordinarily penned these high-toned observations, similarly berated the Louisianan *petits* for their perceived "depravity" and lack of propriety.

When, starting from 1720, enslaved Senegambians forcefully joined this troubled colony, they found there not only some two thousand other enslaved Africans, with whom they formed alliances regardless of socio-linguistic differences, but also the Indigenous, enslaved and free, the *petits* in all their diversity, and an ever-rising number of free people of color (*gens de couleur libres*).[44] Out of the total of 3,909 enslaved brought from Senegambian ports into French Louisiana, only 747 were (mis)gendered in the available colonial records.[45] Early censuses also refrained from gendering the enslaved, and throughout the French, Spanish, and early American periods there always remained a sizable number of enslaved whose gender could not be determined in the colonial archive.[46] Such curious archival absences, however, did not deter later historians from presenting the lifeworlds of enslaved Senegambians in Louisiana and New Orleans as strictly gender-binary. In a similar manner, their alliances with diversely racialized lower-class Louisianans were often disputed or seen as difficult to prove. The messy situation on the ground, however, suggests that enslaved Senegambians sought to connect with the others who, for a variety of reasons—including their perceived racial, gender, and class designations—found it difficult to survive or thrive under the colonial system. Work, as well as the lack thereof, turned out to be an important factor in such resistance strategies.

Because the Company insisted on charging a very high price for the enslaved, it had to provide a variety of options for an aspiring class of local planters, including "requiring slaveowners to relinquish their slaves for one month each year to work on public projects," especially in New Orleans.[47] This allowed the enslaved—most of whom, at any rate, lived on plantations within thirteen miles of the city center—to join the Company workers, enslaved or free, engaged in a variety of urban labor.[48] Many enslaved were also allowed one or two days in a week to work for themselves, sell or exchange produce at the city markets, or be hired as laborers. As Dumont de Montigny noted, "[t]here are *habitants* who give their *Nègres* Saturday and Sunday to themselves, and during that time the [planter] is not obliged to provide for them any food; they then work for other French people who have no enslaved individuals and who pay them. Those who live in the Capital or in its vicinity ordinarily turn their two hours of rest at noon to a profit [for themselves] by making bundles (*fagots*) to sell in the City; others sell ash (*cendre*), or local fruit that is in season."[49]

The adjacency of urban and rural settlements, and life, enabled mixing among the enslaved and other lower-class laborers, and for the former to access certain forms of paid work that would ordinarily be seen as contrary to their legal status. The terrain of a series of natural and human-made levees, divided by a fetid swamp, also provided for fast and, if necessary, clandestine contact: the enslaved "could reach New Orleans by paddling through the swamps almost as swiftly as [*habitants*] could by riverboat, often in five or ten minutes if coming downstream."[50] This made the capital city an epicenter of social life and the forms of labor and intimacy that were seen as "disorderly" and dangerous to the colony.

One such form was the perceived lack of work. City and state officials constantly complained to Paris, and among themselves, about the menace of the unemployed, especially if they were (former) *forçats*. In 1724, Councilor Jean-Baptiste Raguet lamented, before his fellow members of the Superior Council of Louisiana, the vice and dangers of "malcontents who stay in New Orleans," plotting "sedition and conspiracies," and who, being "idle people who have no trade, debauch and entice the French domestics, the Indigenous and enslaved Black people."[51] Years later, at the height of the Seven Years' War, Governor Kerlérec would repeat the same mantra, calling the unemployed "more dangerous to the colony than the enemy itself."[52] Another bureaucrat claimed that "the rear of the City is infested with numbers of men without profession," who "adulterate the liquors they sell [illegally] and expose the enslaved to violent maladies" in their makeshift, unlicensed taverns; "what hidden pernicious disorders have resulted!"[53] Those illegal venues—tucked away in the interior, more explicitly racially diverse and poor, parts of New Orleans—served as chief meeting places of the city's lower-class laborers, which included the ostensibly "unemployed," sex workers, and the enslaved. The city archives list by name several enslaved Senegambians who frequented such taverns; for instance, a thirty-four-year-old Alexandre, who was caught drinking with a "friend," Jupiter, "at Dusigne's tavern."[54]

Between 1725 and 1763, the Superior Council issued multiple ordinances attempting—with little success—to suppress illegal taverns and unwanted mixing of the colony's diverse underclass.[55] But such legal measures were particularly dangerous for Black people. A 1751 regulation threatened to re-enslave "all *nègres* and *négresses* who have obtained their liberty," that is, free people of color, who "led a scandalous life."[56] This was, indeed, the fate of one Jean-Baptiste, who was re-enslaved in 1757 "for licentiousness."[57] On the authority of Louisiana's infamous *Code Noir* of 1724,[58] one regulation mandated severe corporeal punishment for enslaved Black people who failed to "have enough respect and submission, [or] who, in brief, forgot that they are enslaved"—a charge that could be construed as applicable in cases involving frequenting illegal city taverns.[59] None of this, however, made such taverns disappear or, indeed, have a less diverse clientele. Starting from 1746, up to six taverns were allowed to exist legally, with licenses sold annually at auction. That first year, for example, a license was issued to one "Legros, called Latendresse" (Tenderness), for 790 livres.[60] What the city could not stop, the city intended to profit from. A long list of taverns joined the initial six during the Spanish and early American periods, and they "teemed with commercial sex," true to the city's perennial image as a "good time town."[61] But they also may have buttressed underground resistance networks, leading to conspiracies and rebellions.

Foremost of such events was the 1729 Natchez uprising, which nearly put an end to the colony and significantly altered the local dynamics of French racial capitalism. Prior to this large-scale revolt, the French had exercised an ambiguous colonial policy with the powerful, but rapidly diminishing, Natchez nation. Governor Bienville, for example, did not shy from a military "pacification" campaign against the nation in 1723, but he also, in the words of an early historian, occasionally "affected great gayety with them."[62] The new governor, Périer, saw this as overly lenient and made his intention to dispossess the Natchez of their ancestral territories—identified by the colonists as prime tobacco lands—all too obvious. When a French military commandant ordered one of their villages to swiftly vacate and "make way for tobacco cultivation," the Natchez finally decided that they had had enough of such "allyship."[63] Their attack on Fort Rosalie, a French garrison, left many dead and some 330 inhabitants captured, fifty or so described in the sources as "women and children," and as many as 280 enslaved Black people. At least one free person of color was known to have helped the Natchez four years earlier, during Bienville's "pacification" raid, "who had been instigating them against the French." And now, just before the attack on the garrison, "the Natchez assured themselves of the support" of several Black people there, who told the enslaved "that they would be free if they supported the Natchez."[64] And so, an "undisclosed but nevertheless large portion" of those 280 captured enslaved "went as allies, not hostages."[65] On the other side, fifteen enslaved Black soldiers fought against the Natchez in the ensuing military campaigns, and were, in turn, freed for their service to the colony.[66] In January 1731, Périer's forces captured some 495 Natchez, of which only forty-five were described as warriors. Those who survived the harsh conditions of their imprisonment in New Orleans were shipped off to Saint-Domingue, to be sold as enslaved laborers (only 127 of them eventually arriving on the island). According to a contemporary report, the French also captured fifty Black people out of the initial 280, "who had fought five days against the army."[67]

The French revenge was, as always, brutal. A captured Natchez woman was publicly tortured and burned to death on the square frame, starting with her sexual and reproductive organs, and "the Frenchwomen who had found themselves in the hands of the Natchez each took a pointed piece of cane and ran her through repeatedly."[68] A Company employee who left an exceedingly gruesome account of this spectacle, as well as of the earlier Natchez massacre, interrupted his narration to tell the story of an impromptu masquerade he had organized on Fat Monday in 1730, on the outskirts of New Orleans—effectively the earliest documented account of Carnival being held in Louisiana (he "dressed as a shepherdess in white," and "unless you looked at me very closely, you could not tell that I was a boy").[69] Thus the carnivalesque morbidly joined the horrendous displays of public violence, each connoted as "gender transgressions" of sorts.[70] This was hardly an exception. Many later violent acts of colonial retaliation for insurrection and insubordination continued to have a distinct gender dimension. For instance, Cecilia, a partner of Jean Saint-Malô—the legendary leader of fugitive enslaved in the Bas du Fleuve who was likely a griot and of Mande background[71]—was condemned to death along with Saint-Malô by Louisiana's Spanish colonial authorities in 1784, although she had not participated in the alleged major crimes "or even been present."[72] Cecilia's execution, temporarily stayed due to her pregnancy, must have been decided so as to make an example of her case because Saint-Malô's large community of armed, fugitive enslaved, deep in Louisiana's bayous, was another lower-class "affair" that traversed the perceived color and gender lines.[73]

Despite the brutality and gendered spectacles of colonial vengeance, the Natchez uprising had a devastating effect on the prospects of the French colonial project in Louisiana. The 1729 destruction of the French village at Fort Rosalie bankrupted the Compagnie des Indes, severely shook metropolitan investors' confidence in the colony's tobacco production capabilities and, as a result, two years later, virtually brought the trans-Atlantic influx of the enslaved into Louisiana to an end.[74] It took another empire—that of the Spanish—and some forty years before this ignominious trade could be resumed in any great numbers there. Meanwhile, New Orleans' "back o' town" remained a hub for the poor and the nonconforming, while the swamps harbored an increasing number of fugitives. Thus various forms of insurrectionary life and labor continued at pace.

COLONIAL OVERDRIVE: TEMPORAL REFUGES, INTERRUPTIVE FUTURITIES

On November 3, 1762, toward the end of the Seven Years' War, France ceded to the Spanish Empire the remnants of its Louisiana colony. By then, the French had spent millions of livres on the colony, without it ever becoming a commercial success. The new imperial rulers' corporatist concept of racial hierarchy sought to instigate separate social groupings, based on varying degrees of purported "race mixture," which led to the use of such terms of art as *cuarterón* and *octorón* (meaning "one-fourth" and "one-eighth" Black, respectively), duly translated into French and, later, English. Such groupings were intended to sow division among free Louisianans of color, who in this period emerged stronger than ever, in part due to their distinct—and gendered—survival strategies.[75] Spanish colonial law allowed the enslaved to purchase their own and their relatives' freedom, through an institution called *coartación*. Enslaved women could also achieve the same through uncompensated manumission, although it did at times involve a sexual relationship with their legal "proprietor." Those women who pursued the latter option, or those who were already free but who arranged unions with white men for the sake of their offspring and social status, did not live with these men in New Orleans. Free Black women were not expected to marry, and many more of them headed households than women of Euro-Louisianan background.[76] Besides, all free women, according to Spanish law, "exercised control over their own possessions, which for the wealthy could be considerable."[77] Still, many free Black women were poverty-stricken, facing severely restrictive choices of profession (domestic, retail, and hospitality work—the latter particularly in taverns). Across New Orleans, free Black people of all genders "bought, sold, and rented accommodations adjacent to whites," although their concentration toward the city's interior remained much higher, where taverns and other sites of resistive labor and exchange continued to trouble the city officials.[78]

The Spanish rule also brought new ways of curtailing nonconformity to its racialized, sexual, and gender mores. Had the Capuchin father Antonio de Sedella, popularly known as Père Antoine, the Spanish Inquisition's first and only commissioner in Louisiana, made any effort to use his office, there would have probably remained much more evidence of such nonconformity.[79] Luckily for New Orleanians, after an initial zeal, he gradually surrendered to such priestly duties as caring for the city's prisoners and the enslaved. Nonetheless, the incoming Governor O'Reilly, an Irishman in Spanish colonial service, saw fit to immediately enact instructions that would punish such crimes as adultery, prostitution, and sodomy. As for the latter, O'Reilly decreed, "[h]e who shall commit the detestable crime against nature shall afterwards be burned, and his property shall be confiscated to the profit of the public and royal treasuries."[80] This was despite there being only one surviving record of a trial for sodomy in the French period.[81] Another governor, Esteban Miró, imposed in 1786 a "tignon law," which targeted specifically women of color, seeking to prohibit the "extravagant luxury of their dresses" and their "wearing feathers or jewels in their hair," while, at the same time, ordering that they "cover their hair with headkerchiefs," or tignons, "as was formerly the custom."[82] The measure was intended to visually and symbolically reestablish free women of color's ties to enslavement; but it was thwarted, from the start, by them turning the kerchief into a stylish and enviable accessory. In the revolutionary 1790s, the paranoid Spanish rulers even sought to prohibit both the enslaved and free Black Louisianans from masking during Carnival—a popular way for people of color to enjoy a temporary reprieve from the stark racial and gender regime in place.[83]

Carnival was, of course, not the only occasion for the oppressed to "steal back" time. Saidiya Hartman has poignantly reflected on secret encounters that the enslaved would call "stealing the meeting"—where even short-lived "flights" from captivity would be designated as "stealing away"—just as the fugitive enslaved were described as "stealing themselves," given their legal status as property.[84] Being not only dispossessed of their freedom, the fruits of their labor, and their senses of the self beyond the dominant race, gender, and class boundaries, the enslaved sought and formed a variety of *temporal refuges* in colonial Louisiana. On plantations outside New Orleans, after a hard day's work, they would gather in nocturnal assemblages to dance, relax, and *spend time* together. And, in the city, beside the ubiquitous taverns, the Plaza de Armas (today's Jackson Square) would serve a similar purpose in the evening of a *fiesta* day. Sensing that such exercises in an alternative temporality—one that would, for a short while, escape the clutches of racial capitalist dispossession and distemporalization—Governor Miró tried to forbid all such nocturnal revelries, whether on plantations or within New Orleans.[85]

But it was both too early and too late for such colonial interventions. Too early because it was not before the advent of an Americanized Louisiana and its capital city, with the help of a new brand of racial capitalism (centered on an enormous expansion of sugar and cotton production, and the labor of, and trade in, the enslaved), that its people of color, both enslaved and free, would bear the full brunt of segregation by law. And too late because, not far northwest from the capital, in Pointe Coupée, the enslaved "of all colors and nations, free people of African descent, and poor whites: *voyageurs*, indentured servants, and soldiers," gathered to fight against enslavement and social tyranny.[86] While the Haitian Revolution (1791–1804) dramatically altered the course of the colonial, *linear* time—even if not succeeding, in the end, to derail the project of the new, American racial capitalism in Louisiana and New Orleans—events in alternative temporalities, and in insurrectionary ways of being-in-the-world, continued to interrupt the smooth progression of such violently extractive time.

In colonial New Orleans and its vital surrounding environs, work *mattered* when it was imposed as much as when it was resisted in its chief, dispossessive mode. Its simultaneous presences and absences—when one was to steal oneself from dehumanizing toil but for a brief moment, only to engage in "disorderly" forms of labor and intimacy, or when another subsisted in the guise of an "idler," working toward a "back o' town" space for self-expression and "dangerous" mingling—disrupted the terrain and timeliness of a racial capitalist system in the making. Such interruptions were momentary, oriented toward providing temporal refuges and sojourns to qualitatively specific temporal lifeworlds—such as those of eighteenth-century Greater Senegambia. Nonetheless, they happened. Because and, sometimes, in spite of the colonial archive, their presence lingers on, unsettling the presumptive linear futurity—of work, its absence, and of labors in human subjectivity.

NOTES

I would like to thank Karen Engle and Neville Hoad for their stellar stewardship of the academic encounters leading to this collection, and for the immense care and dedication they have shown throughout the editorial process. It has been a privilege and a pleasure to work (and rest from work) with you. Many thanks to Cooper Christiancy, too, for all the support and a set of incisive comments on an earlier draft of this chapter. Finally, thank you Safet Hadžimuhamedović for being my closest reader and companion, come rain or shine. I dedicate this piece to the late Gwendolyn Midlo Hall (1929–2022), Louisiana's finest, most admirable social historian. In your comforting shadow, Gwen, we all humbly walk.

1. Nine documents relative to the trial of Etienne La Rue, May 5 to May 19, 1747, Archives of the Superior Council of Louisiana (hereinafter: ASCL), at the Cabildo, New Orleans, available on microfilm at Tulane University Law Library (my translation). Unless otherwise stated, all translations in this chapter are my own.
2. In 1930, a local historian translated the trial documents into English, rendering Gaillard's swearwords "*Bonsoir, Seigneur Négritte*" into "Goodnight, Lord Little Negro," and La Rue's defiant response, "*Bonsoir, Seigneur Jean Foutre*," into "Goodnight, Lord Jack Fool." Heloise H. Cruzat, "The Documents Covering the Criminal Trial of Etienne La Rue, for Attempt to Murder and Illicit Carrying of Arms,"

Louisiana Historical Quarterly 13 (1930): 377–90. The charge of attempted murder, indicated in the title of this translation, was eventually dropped. Another local historian, who introduced the translator's work, proposed the n-word preceded by "Mr. Little" as a Jim Crow equivalent of "the ancient" *Seigneur Négritte*, adding that he hoped the reader would "be vastly entertained over the incident." Henry P. Dart, "A Criminal Trial Before the Superior Council of Louisiana, May, 1747," *Louisiana Historical Quarterly* 13 (1930): 367–76. Clearly uncomfortable with La Rue's ability to respond, in words and in kind, to racist violence, Dart concluded his remarks with the following sentence: "Doubtless he [La Rue] thereafter refrained from airing his wit in foreign ports no matter what the provocation might be." Sixty years later, in an otherwise groundbreaking book of "history from below," *Négritte* was misspelled as "Négrette" and the erstwhile English translation reaffirmed, still having paid no attention to the grammatical gender of the French word. Daniel H. Usner, Jr., *Indians, Settlers, & Slaves in a Frontier Exchange Economy: The Lower Mississippi Valley before 1783* (Chapel Hill: University of North Carolina Press, 1992), 238–39.

3. Shannon Lee Dawdy, *Building the Devil's Empire: French Colonial New Orleans* (Chicago: University of Chicago Press, 2008), 175, 291. However, her own translation of *Négritte* resorted to another racial slur, while she rendered *Seigneur Jean Foutre* into "Milord Bugger," explaining that this means "literally 'sodomite.'" See also Shannon Lee Dawdy, "Scoundrels, Whores, and Gentlemen: Defamation and Society in French Colonial Louisiana," in *Coastal Encounters: The Transformation of the Gulf South in the Eighteenth Century*, ed. Richmond F. Brown (Lincoln: University of Nebraska Press, 2007), 147.

4. My forthcoming book on gender nonconformity in eighteenth-century Senegambia and colonial Louisiana documents the rise of the French colonial gender binary, which ordinarily racialized and gendered people perceived as Black, whether enslaved or free, as *nègre* (Black man), *négresse* (Black woman), *négrillon* (Black boy), and *négrite, négritte*, or *négrillonne* (Black girl). That these terms were not devoid of social stigma in the eighteenth-century Francophone world is evident, for example, from the word used to denote trader in enslaved humans (*négrier*), although Etienne La Rue's own testimony—in which "*seigneur* La Rue, a *nègre libre*" (La Rue's father), is proudly invoked—seems to suggest that some Senegambians must have already begun to reclaim and resignify this injurious colonial vocabulary.

5. "Nine documents . . .," Doc. 1 (No. 1099), ASCL, 2; see also Doc. 2 (No. 1100), ASCL, 2. At the trial, La Rue also claimed to have said to the three assailants: "I greet you and you abuse me!"

6. Gwendolyn Midlo Hall, *Africans in Colonial Louisiana: The Development of Afro-Creole Culture in the Eighteenth Century* (Baton Rouge: Louisiana State University Press, 1992), 60.

7. "The devil's own domain" is an abiding theme of New Orleans' history, often with a reference to biblical Babylon or Sodom and Gomorrah; see, for example, Dawdy, *Building the Devil's Empire*.

8. Regarding "distemporalization," see Safet HadžiMuhamedović and Vanja Hamzić, "Distemporalities: Collisions, Insurrections and Reorientations in the Worlding of

Time" (panel, biennial conference of the Finnish Anthropological Society, Helsinki, Finland, August 29–30, 2019). Hadžimuhamedović and I have described *distemporalization* as a project of denial of time—a denial of historicity, futurity, or change, which is a significant element of various constructions of "otherness." We have also taken distemporality to signify a refusal of, and an intervention into, qualitatively specific temporal lifeworlds, such as those of eighteenth-century Senegambians forcibly brought to French Louisiana, or those of Indigenous inhabitants of that colony's unceded lands.

9. Germaine Dieterlen, *Essai sur la religion Bambara* (Paris: Presses universitaires de France, 1951), 40–56.
10. Dieterlen, *Essai sur la religion Bambara*, 87.
11. Tierno Siradiou Bah, "Fulɓe," in *Ethnic Groups of Africa and the Middle East: An Encyclopedia*, ed. John A. Shoup (Santa Barbara: ABC-CLIO, 2011), 96–100; and Alfâ Ibrâhîm Sow, *La Femme, la vache, la foi: Écrivains et poètes du Foûta-Djalon* (Paris: Julliard, 1966).
12. Helen A. Regis, *Fulbe Voices: Marriage, Islam, and Medicine in Northern Cameroon* (Boulder: Westview, 2003), 53; and Babacar M'Baye, "Afropolitan Sexual and Gender Identities in Colonial Senegal," *Humanities* 8 (2019): 166, https://doi.org/10.3390/h8040166.
13. John Barbot, *A Description of the Coasts of North and South-Guinea, and of Ethiopia Inferior, Vulgarly Angola, Being a New and Accurate Account of the Western Maritime Countries of Africa* (London: Churchill, 1732), 55.
14. Dominique Harcourt Lamiral, *L'Affrique et le people affriquain, considérés sous tous leurs rapports avec notre Commerce & nos Colonies* (Paris: Dessenne, 1789), 100.
15. René-Claude Geoffroy de Villeneuve, *L'Afrique, ou histoire, mœurs, usages et coutumes des Africains* (Paris: Nepveu, 1814), 3: 36, 3: 166. Early French texts used the word *guiriot*, which somewhat resembles the Wolof and Fulfulde terms for griot (*géwël* and *gawlo*, respectively).
16. de Villeneuve, *L'Afrique*, 4: 4, 4: 115, 4: 193–94.
17. Armand Corre, *L'Ethnographie criminelle d'après les observations et les statistiques judiciaires recueillies dans les colonies françaises* (Paris: C. Reinwald & Cie, 1894), 80n1.
18. Many West African societies connoted the artisanal caste as "foreigners." For instance, *inadan*, the collective name for the members of this status group among the Tuareg, comes from *anəd*, which means "to be apart," or "to be unlike others." See, for example, Dominique Casajus, "Crafts and Ceremonies: The Inadan in Tuareg Society," in *The Other Nomads: Peripatetic Minorities in Cross-Cultural Perspective*, ed. Aparna Rao (Köln: Böhlau Verlag, 1987), 293.
19. Michel Jajolet de la Courbe, *Premier voyage du Sieur de la Courbe fait a la coste d'Afrique en 1685* (Paris: Champion, 1913), 194.
20. de Villeneuve, *L'Afrique*, 4: 60–63.
21. "Directeurs de la Compagnie [des Indes] à St. Robert, Directeur [de la concession du] Sénégal," February 1723, COL C6 7, the Archives nationales d'outre-mer (hereinafter: ANOM), Aix-en-Provence. See also Hall, *Africans in Colonial Louisiana*, 70.
22. Hall, *Africans in Colonial Louisiana*, 77, 390–91.

23. Marc-Antoine Caillot, "Relation du voyage de la Louisianne ou Nouvelle France" (unpublished manuscript, drafted 1729–1758; the Historic New Orleans Collection, 2005.0011), 35, 46–47. See also Erin M. Greenwald, *A Company Man: The Remarkable French-Atlantic Voyage of a Clerk for the Company of the Indies* (New Orleans: Historic New Orleans Collection, 2013), 27, 35.
24. See, for example, Lawrence N. Powell, *The Accidental City: Improvising New Orleans* (Cambridge, MA: Harvard University Press, 2012), 53–56; and Jennifer M. Spear, *Race, Sex, and Social Order in Early New Orleans* (Baltimore: Johns Hopkins University Press, 2009), 56–57.
25. Jean-François-Benjamin Dumont de Montigny, *Mémoires historiques sur la Louisiane* (Paris: Bauche, 1753), 2: 240–41.
26. Powell, *Accidental City*, 54, 74–75.
27. Usner, *Indians, Settlers, & Slaves*, 55; see also Powell, *Accidental City*, 75.
28. Jean-Pierre Le Glaunec, "'Un Nègre nommé [sic] Lubin ne connaissant pas Sa Nation': The Small World of Louisiana Slavery," in *Louisiana: Crossroads of the Atlantic World*, ed. Cécile Vidal (Philadelphia: University of Pennsylvania Press, 2014), 109; Gwendolyn Midlo Hall, "African Women in French and Spanish Louisiana: Origins, Roles, Family, Work, Treatment," in *The Devil's Lane: Sex and Race in the Early South*, ed. Catherine Clinton and Michele Gillespie (New York: Oxford University Press, 1997), 257; and Kimberly S. Hanger, *Bounded Lives, Bounded Places: Free Black Society in Colonial New Orleans, 1769–1803* (Durham: Duke University Press, 1997), 59.
29. See Dumont de Montigny, *Mémoires historiques*, 2: 242, for an assertion that "[t]he *Négresses* go to work [just] like the *Nègres*."
30. Spear, *Race, Sex, and Social Order*, 57–58.
31. Sylvia Wynter, "Beyond the Categories of the Master Conception: The Counter-doctrine of the Jamesian Poiesis," in *C.L.R. James's Caribbean*, ed. Paget Henry and Paul Buhle (Durham: Duke University Press, 1992), 84.
32. Hall, "African Women," 252; and Spear, *Race, Sex, and Social Order*, 58.
33. Spear, *Race, Sex, and Social Order*, 58.
34. Paul Lachance, "The Growth of the Free and Slave Populations of French Colonial Louisiana," in *French Colonial Louisiana and the Atlantic World*, ed. Bradley G. Bond (Baton Rouge: Louisiana State University Press, 2005), 215.
35. Pierre-François-Xavier de Charlevoix, *Journal d'un voyage fait par ordre du roi dans l'Amérique septentrionnale, adressé à Madame la Duchesse de Lesdiguières* (Paris: Rollin Fils, 1744), 6: 192.
36. Spear, *Race, Sex, and Social Order*, 44–45; Powell, *Accidental City*, 69–70; Dawdy, *Building the Devil's Empire*, 150–53; and Carl A. Brasseaux, "The Moral Climate of French Colonial Louisiana, 1699–1763," in *The French Experience in Louisiana*, ed. Glenn R. Conrad (Lafayette: University of Southwestern Louisiana, 1995), 527.
37. See, for example, Sophie White, *Wild Frenchmen and Frenchified Indians: Material Culture and Race in Colonial Louisiana* (Philadelphia: University of Pennsylvania Press, 2012).
38. Antoine-Simon Le Page du Pratz, *The History of Louisiana or of the Western Parts of Virginia and Carolina* (1758; repr. London: T. Becket, 1774), 312.

39. Le Page du Pratz, *The History of Louisiana*, 326.
40. Dumont de Montigny, *Mémoires historiques*, 1: 247.
41. Dumont de Montigny, *Mémoires historiques*, 1: 248.
42. Jean-Bernard Bossu, *Nouveaux voyages aux Indes occidentales* (Amsterdam: Changuion, 1769), 1: 77.
43. Heather Martel, "Colonial Allure: Normal Homoeroticism and Sodomy in French and Timucuan Encounters in Sixteenth-Century Florida," *History of Sexuality* 22 (2013): 45; and Richard C. Trexler, *Sex and Conquest: Gendered Violence, Political Order, and the European Conquest of the Americas* (Cambridge: Polity, 1995), 66–67.
44. Apart from the ships that arrived from Senegambia and a small number of enslaved Black people who came from the French Caribbean, 1,748 enslaved Africans were brought from Wydah, in present-day Benin, between 1719 and 1728, and 295 aboard *La Néréide*, in 1721, from Cabinda, in present-day Angola. See Hall, *Africans in Colonial Louisiana*, 60.
45. This includes both embarkation and disembarkation Company records, as calculated in Hall, *Africans in Colonial Louisiana*, 60, 381–97, but excludes the privately licensed ship *Le St. Ursin* that Louisianan planter Joseph Dubreuil used in 1743 to bring 190 *captifs* from Senegambia—twelve years after the last Company voyage had done the same. The slavers' ships that attempted to gender/sex the enslaved were *L'Expédition* (1723), *Le Courrier de Bourbon* (1723), *La Mutine* (1726), and *La Flore* (1728).
46. For early censuses, see Jay K. Ditchy, trans., "Early Census Tables of Louisiana," *Louisiana Historical Quarterly* 13 (1930): 205–29. Gwendolyn Midlo Hall's excellent *Louisiana Slave Database*, freely available at http://www.ibiblio.org/laslave/index.php, which contains historical data from over 100,000 descriptions of the enslaved found in documents in Louisiana between 1718 and 1821, lists 1,897 enslaved individuals whose gender could not be identified.
47. Spear, *Race, Sex, and Social Order*, 58.
48. Powell, *Accidental City*, 72–73.
49. Dumont de Montigny, *Mémoires historiques*, 2: 242–43.
50. Powell, *Accidental City*, 72.
51. "Raguet à le Conseil Supérieur de la Louisiane," September 2, 1724, ASCL. In 1753, Raguet succeeded François Fleuriau, mentioned at the beginning of this chapter, as the *procureur general*.
52. Quoted in Brasseaux, "Moral Climate," 532–33.
53. Original unavailable in ASCL; based on the translation of a petition addressed to the Superior Council of Louisiana by *Procureur General* Nicolas Chauvin de Lafrénière, *fils*, on September 3, 1763, provided in Henry P. Dart, "Cabarets of New Orleans in the French Colonial Period," *Louisiana Historical Quarterly* 19 (1936): 580–81.
54. Dawdy, *Building the Devil's Empire*, 186.
55. Dawdy, *Building the Devil's Empire*, 185.
56. "Règlement sur la police des cabarets, des esclaves, des marchés en Louisiane," February 18 to March 1, 1751, COL C13a 35, ANOM.

57. Quoted in Spear, *Race, Sex, and Social Order*, 93.
58. *Le Code noir ou Édit du Roy, servant de règlement pour la gouvernement & l'administration de la justice, police, discipline & le commerce des Esclaves Nègres, dans la Province & Colonie de la Loüisianne*, Versailles, March 1724 (Paris: L'Imprimerie royale, 1727).
59. "Règlement sur la police," COL C13a 35, ANOM.
60. Dart, "Cabarets of New Orleans," 578–79.
61. Rashauna Johnson, *Slavery's Metropolis: Unfree Labor in New Orleans During the Age of Revolutions* (New York: Cambridge University Press, 2016), 108; and Phil Johnson, "Good Time Town," in *The Past as Prelude: New Orleans 1718–1968*, ed. Hodding Carter, William Ransom Hogan, John W. Lawrence, and Betty Werlein Carter (New Orleans: Tulane University, 1968), 233–57.
62. Grace King, *Jean Baptiste le Moyne: Sieur de Bienville* (New York: Dodd, Mead, 1893), 214.
63. Powell, *Accidental City*, 84.
64. Hall, *Africans in Colonial Louisiana*, 100.
65. Powell, *Accidental City*, 85; and Usner, *Indians, Settlers, & Slaves*, 73.
66. Gwendolyn Midlo Hall, "Epilogue: Historical Memory, Consciousness, and Conscience in the New Millennium," in *French Colonial Louisiana and the Atlantic World*, ed. Bradley G. Bond (Baton Rouge: Louisiana State University Press, 2005), 303.
67. Caillot, "Relation du voyage," 180; and Greenwald, *A Company Man*, 154.
68. Caillot, "Relation du voyage," 171.
69. Caillot, "Relation du voyage," 155, 156.
70. See generally, Sophie White, "Massacre, Mardi Gras, and Torture in Early New Orleans," *William and Mary Quarterly* 70 (2013): 497–538, https://doi.org/10.5309/willmaryquar.70.3.0497. It was relatively unusual to burn someone on the square frame who was not seen as a male Indigenous warrior. In their initial attack on Fort Rosalie, the Natchez are also thought to have spared as many "women and children" as they could.
71. There are references to Saint-Maló being "an herbal healer or a conjurer." Powell, *Accidental City*, 242. See also Hall, *Africans in Colonial Louisiana*, 212–13.
72. Gilbert C. Din, *Spaniards, Planters, and Slaves: The Spanish Regulation of Slavery in Louisiana, 1763–1803* (College Station: Texas A&M University Press, 1999), 103.
73. Hall, *Africans in Colonial Louisiana*, 212–36.
74. Spear, *Race, Sex, and Social Order*, 55. The only exception, for the remainder of the French period, was a privately licensed ship, *Le St. Ursin*, which brought, in 1743, 190 *captifs* from Senegambia.
75. Hall, "Epilogue," 305.
76. Kimberly S. Hanger, "Coping in a Complex World: Free Black Women in Colonial New Orleans," in *The Devil's Lane: Sex and Race in the Early South*, ed. Catherine Clinton and Michele Gillespie (New York: Oxford University Press, 1997), 219.
77. Hanger, "Coping in a Complex World," 220.
78. Hanger, *Bounded Lives*, 138.
79. This is true everywhere else in the Americas where the Inquisition had a chance to practice its notorious—but meticulously documented—interrogations. See, for example, Pete Sigal, ed., *Infamous Desire: Male Homosexuality in Colonial Latin America* (Chicago: Chicago University Press, 2003).

80. Alexander O'Reilly, "'Instructions,' section V: 'On Punishments,' para. 10, 25 November 1769," in *Historical Collections of Louisiana*, ed. B. F. French (New York: Lamport, Blakeman, & Law, 1853), 5:280.
81. Dawdy, "Scoundrels, Whores, and Gentlemen," 141.
82. Virginia Meacham Gould, "'A Chaos of Iniquity and Discord': Slave and Free Women of Color in the Spanish Ports of New Orleans, Mobile, and Pensacola," in *The Devil's Lane: Sex and Race in the Early South*, ed. Catherine Clinton and Michele Gillespie (New York: Oxford University Press, 1997), 237.
83. Hanger, *Bounded Lives*, 143.
84. Saidiya V. Hartman, *Scenes of Subjection: Terror, Slavery, and Self-Making in Nineteenth-Century America* (New York: Oxford University Press, 1997), 65–66.
85. Hanger, *Bounded Lives*, 145.
86. For a detailed description of the 1795 conspiracy of Pointe Coupée as a watershed event in Louisiana's antiracist history, spearheaded by "Jacobins of Louisiana of all races and nationalities," see Hall, *Africans in Colonial Louisiana*, 243–74.

CHAPTER 10

GARMENT WORK, REFUGEES, AND RESISTANCE

The Jordan Compact

JENNIFER GORDON

In this chapter, I examine an unsuccessful recent effort by the European Union, the government of Jordan, and the World Bank to take a group of "surplus" people—200,000 Syrian refugees who had previously not been permitted to work in Jordan, their host country—and turn most of them into garment workers for Jordanian export factories. I analyze why the initiative failed to materialize in ways it had been imagined from afar, emphasizing the conflict between the operating theories that animated the plan from the European perspective and the realities and responses of a range of actors on the ground in Jordan, from garment manufacturers to Syrian refugees to migrant workers.[1]

THE EU LINKS TRADE AND JOBS TO KEEP SYRIAN REFUGEES IN JORDAN

Syrian refugees emerged into European public consciousness in 2014. The flight of millions of Syrians from their homes had actually begun several years earlier, but it garnered little international attention while the refugees remained in nearby Turkey, Jordan, and Lebanon. As increasing numbers of Syrians left those countries and headed for Southern Europe, however, the media fueled a panic about a threat to Europe's borders. The European Union (EU) does not usually hesitate to assert its sovereignty, but the plight of the Syrians had garnered too much public attention and sympathy for a simple closed-door response. Facing conflicting political pressures, the EU urgently sought a way to keep the Syrians out without appearing heartless in the face of their suffering.

In late 2015, two Oxford professors proposed that the EU use trade preferences to spur the creation of employment for Syrian refugees in their host countries as a way of encouraging them to remain there.[2] Jordan would be the test case. The idea quickly gained support, and the EU-Jordan Compact was signed in early 2016.[3] Through this accord and related agreements, the European Commission and the World Bank (among other actors) promised the government of Jordan several billion dollars in aid and loans at preferential rates. In exchange, Jordan agreed to dramatically expand the right to work for the hundreds of thousands of Syrians who had taken refuge within its borders, and to increase their access to education. Once employed, the EU presumed that Syrians would stay where they were rather than leave for Europe. The model was widely hailed as a new paradigm for addressing global refugee crises.[4]

The Jordan Compact's architects highlighted the linking of trade and refugee jobs as the plan's central innovation.[5] Jordan committed to granting 200,000 work permits to Syrians, of which 150,000 were to be used for employment in free trade zones. The EU promised export factories in Jordan reductions in tariffs if at least 15 percent of their workforce was composed of Syrians. Although the compact did not specify the sectors in which the plan would be deployed, garments are Jordan's largest export, and the garment sector employs few Jordanians.[6] For these reasons, the garment sector was seen from the beginning as the primary target industry for the placement of Syrian workers. In turn, the planners emphasized the suitability of Syrian women as a labor force for garment factories. The compact initially referenced the creation of new jobs for Syrians, to be incentivized by the tariff reductions that were part of the agreement. Should those jobs fail to appear, the default assumption was that Syrian refugees would displace the industry's migrant workforce, largely consisting of women from South Asia laboring under the *kafala* visa regime.[7] The remaining work permits were for employment in other sectors of the economy selected to avoid competition with Jordanians.

The compact architects' vision of Syrians as garment workers in Jordan never came to pass. United Nations agencies, financial and development institutions, the governments of Jordan and EU nations, and scores of international humanitarian organizations poured hundreds of millions of dollars into making the compact's vision a reality. Yet six years into the plan, fewer than five hundred Syrians were employed in Jordanian garment export zones.[8] It is not that Syrians rejected the permit scheme wholesale. Outside the garment industry, less than forty thousand Syrians (95 percent of whom are men) hold active work permits granted under the compact.[9] Most of these workers used these permits to legalize existing jobs in the low-wage, largely informal sectors where Syrians were employed without authorization before the compact was signed: agriculture and construction.[10] This process formalized the workers but not the work; as a result, improvements in pay and conditions have been slow to follow.[11]

I explore why the garment plan failed, with a particular focus on the interests and dynamics in Jordan that the outside planners had failed to appreciate (or simply ignored) when they designed the intervention. The policies that the EU sought to enact through the compact are consistent with the key tenets of world-systems theory. In designing the Jordan Compact, Europe as the "core" purported to help the "periphery" (understood both as Jordan and as the Syrian refugees living there) but primarily advanced Europe's economic and political interests. The choice of export production zones as the vehicle for the compact's central intervention, and the characterization of employment in such zones as a humanitarian benefit, are consistent with neoliberal theories of export-led economic development and of the market as the solution to all problems.[12] Likewise, the compact illustrates core insights of racial capitalism regarding the uses of race and ethnicity as an economic and political sorting mechanism in ways that exemplify the manipulation of difference to reinforce the sovereignty of powerful nations and to advance the interests of global capital.

Consistent with these theories, the compact embodied a set of suppositions about the preferences and behaviors of all non-EU actors whose lives and livelihoods it would touch. Increased trade with the EU was presumed to be a gift that garment export producers in Jordan would welcome. So, too, would they be glad to hire Syrians, seeing them as essentially fungible with the South Asian migrant women currently staffing the industry. Syrian women would be eager to take jobs in Jordanian garment factories, both because in the EU imaginary they were racialized in ways that made them resemble South Asian migrants and because they would find formal jobs in export zones desirable in comparison to informal employment. The many migrants already working in Jordan could be treated as an undifferentiated group of disposable workers because there would be no politically significant consequences if their jobs were given to Syrians.

Although the assumptions behind the Jordan Compact were congruent with the interests of the EU, and with the European imperial tradition and the role the EU has historically played in core-periphery dynamics, they turned out to be weak predictors of what would actually happen on the ground. Garment export production in Jordan, although necessarily integrated into and shaped by the global market, turned out to be far less responsive to European command and incentive structures than anticipated because of the idiosyncrasies growing from its specific history in that location. Manufacturers accustomed to a labor market highly segmented by race, gender, national origin, and immigration status resisted the demand that they treat workers as fungible across these categories. Workers—Jordanian, Syrian, and migrants from a range of other countries—had their own needs and realities, and they responded to the compact plan in ways its architects had failed to imagine. As a result, things went awry.

The anthropologist Michel-Rolph Trouillot's concept of "motion in the system" captures this dynamic well.[13] Trouillot, writing against what he saw as the determinism of world-systems theory, argued that to comprehend the trajectory of history it is necessary to focus on dialectical interactions between pressures from the core and the responses from actors in the periphery.[14] Trouillot was an advocate of the specific and the contingent, calling for "a *methodology for the study of particulars as sources of change in their own right*, reacting to, but also constantly affecting, often in unexpected ways, external impulses and pressures."[15] He particularly emphasized the unit of production as a fruitful level for analysis.[16] It is in the spirit of Trouillot's work that I examine the response to the effort to employ Syrians as garment workers in Jordan. I focus on the local realities in conflict with EU assumptions at two levels: with regard to economics, especially the potential of export manufacturing and trade as tools for development of "peripheral" economies and the solution of humanitarian crises; and with regard to racialized labor, especially as to the fungibility of low-wage workers.

THE GARMENT MANUFACTURERS' PERSPECTIVE: EU ASSUMPTIONS MEET REALITY

The Jordan Compact's claim that investment in export zones would spur the Jordanian economy and create jobs for Syrians in Jordan reflects the neoliberal orthodoxy: support for export production is an effective policy tool for development of economies in the periphery.[17] Long before the Jordan Compact, that orthodoxy was under attack, in particular where the exports in question are of low-value-added products and paying low wages for tasks such as assembly.[18] Garment manufacture is a classic example of such an industry.

In Jordan, the local history of the apparel export industry amplifies these concerns. Jordan was already a major garment producer at the time the compact was signed. In 2015, seventy-five clothing factories employed fifty-five thousand workers across thirteen export zones. Yet by global supply chain standards, Jordan has few assets that would make it an obvious choice for garment production. It has no relevant raw materials, and its labor costs are high compared to other nations where the industry is concentrated. Natural resources—including the water so essential for clothing manufacture—are scarce. It entered the field only in the mid-1990s, when the United States offered Jordan low tariffs and export quota exemptions as an incentive to sign a 1994 peace deal with Israel.

With little comparative advantage in global garment production, Jordan quickly recognized that it would need to attract foreign producers and rely on imported materials and workers to make its garment industry viable. Just as Jordan was setting up its export zones in the wake of the treaty, manufacturers from the longtime garment-producing countries of India and China were seeking to relocate. Their home nations were reaching the cap on export quotas under the global Multi-Fiber Agreement. Many moved production to Jordan, where exports to the United States would not count toward their home country's quota, and where the agreement with the United States reduced tariffs significantly.[19] Reflecting this history, the Jordanian garment industry remains majority-foreign-owned today.[20]

The Jordanian garment industry has also become almost entirely dependent on foreign labor.[21] Around the world, garment manufacturers work on tight profit margins, under pressure from the brands and retailers above them in the value chain to cut costs and increase turnaround time, flexibility, and productivity. To meet these demands, they seek a workforce that will accept minimal wages, is available to labor long hours, has few distractions from work, and rarely protests the treatment they receive. From the arrival of garment export production in Jordan, Jordanian citizens had shown little interest in fitting this mold.[22]

In lieu of local workers, manufacturers in Jordan had pushed for access to migrants as a less expensive and more compliant source of labor.[23] They lobbied the Jordanian government to permit a large percentage of the garment workforce to be brought from abroad on low-wage contracts. The government responded by setting a wage for migrants in the garment industry that is only 60 percent of the minimum for Jordanians, and requiring that migrant garment workers enter through the *kafala* system on visas that tie them to a single employer for the duration of their stay and deny them the ability to bring family members.[24] Leaving the sponsoring employer—or being fired—results in deportation. Migrants in the garment export production zones are also required to live on-site in employer-controlled dorms, ensuring their availability when a rush order requires around-the-clock processing.[25] Although conditions in Jordanian garment factories are better than they once were, sexual harassment, poor housing, and issues with pay remain common.[26]

The presence of this legal regime granting employers significant control over the migrants they hire, and establishing large pay differentials between citizens and noncitizens, played a critical role in the birth and flourishing of the Jordanian garment industry. Together with the narratives based on gender, nationality, and race described in the following section, Jordanian immigration law created an ideal worker for the garment industry. Women from Bangladesh and other South Asian countries were recruited to fill this role. Their governments, reliant on the remittances sent home by migrants for a significant percentage of their GDP, assented.[27] By 2016, when the compact was signed, 75 percent of the workers in Jordanian garment factories were South and Southeast Asian women, mostly from Bangladesh, India, and Sri Lanka.[28]

Compact architects explicitly argued that Syrian refugee women would be good substitutes for these workers. They highlighted the similarities between the Syrian refugees targeted for garment employment and the existing migrant workforce: they were women, came from another country, and lived under difficult circumstances. They asserted that Syrians would be well suited for such jobs because Syria had its own garment industry, and so the refugees would bring relevant skills and experience to the field.[29] Garment employers were imagined to be eager to hire Syrians, seeing one group of foreign female workers as a good replacement for another one.[30] And Syrian refugees were imagined to reciprocate this interest. In reaching this conclusion, the compact's architects did not consult either Syrian refugees or garment employers.[31] (They also apparently did not consult an atlas. Syria had a garment industry, but it was largely located in and around Aleppo, in the north of the country near the border with Turkey, into which most refugees from that area had fled. The refugees in Jordan, in contrast, largely came from the south of Syria near the Jordanian border, where agriculture formed the basis of the economy and few women worked outside the home.[32])

The planners failed to attend to the considerable differences between the way that South Asian migrants and Syrian refugees were positioned in relation to work in Jordan. Prior to the Jordan Compact, refugees were generally barred from work in Jordan,[33] reflecting the terms of global humanitarian policy since World War II.[34] In the early stages of compact implementation, Syrians seeking permits faced requirements quite similar to those for migrant visas, including application fees, a tie to a single employer sponsor, and exemptions from the minimum wages that applied to Jordanian workers. But few Syrians applied for the permits when they were structured in this way. Faced with the need to meet the goals for permit issuance set out in the compact, the Jordanian government made a series of concessions exclusively for Syrians, waiving fees, increasing mobility between employers in agriculture and construction, and in some cases requiring higher wages for Syrians than other noncitizens.[35] The Jordanian government made clear that it would not enforce certain laws against employers as to Syrian employees with work permits for a sector other than the one in which they were employed, while continuing enforcement as to the employment of noncitizens from other countries in the same situation. It also sought to reduce visas available for migrants from other countries who ordinarily came to work in sectors now open to Syrians.

Syrian refugees were also distinct from labor migrants in that they lived outside of the zones, usually with their families, whether in camps or independently. Therefore, to be able to work, Syrian women, in particular, required transportation, child care, and shorter schedules to respond to the needs of their families.[36] To hire refugee women, firms would have had to create conditions of work that permitted the women to engage in these activities of social reproduction. In contrast, the structure of the migrant visa ensured that workers were severed from hands-on family care responsibilities, which was to firms' economic advantage.[37] Furthermore, unlike migrants, refugees could quit if they were unhappy with the pay or working conditions, turning to aid or to employment in other sectors.

To reshape the calculus of garment manufacturers in Jordan so that they would hire Syrian refugees instead of South Asian migrants would require powerful incentives. The compact sought to do this by offering increased access to the European market and lower tariffs for exports to the EU to firms that met Syrian employment targets. Again, however, the assumptions that shaped the compact did not reflect the reality of garment manufacturers in Jordan. Because of the genesis of the Jordanian garment export industry, the United States had been the primary recipient of Jordanian clothing exports since the industry's inception.[38] Expanding that focus to encompass meaningful trade with the EU was not a simple matter. Exporting to the EU would require connections to EU brands and retailers, knowledge of the quite different market there, and access to different suppliers, all of which the Jordanian firms lacked.[39] Perhaps the largest obstacle was the more stringent certification requirements for exporting to the EU, which few Jordanian firms were positioned to meet.[40] In these ways, it was a costly enterprise for manufacturers to enter the EU market. This was all the more true given that to qualify for the compact's enhanced market access, manufacturers would have to change their hiring practices so that 15 percent (and eventually 25 percent) of their workers were Syrian refugees.[41]

Once implementation began, garment manufacturers in Jordan made clear that the compact's ideas about worker fungibility and the desirability of trade on Europe's terms bore little resemblance to their preferences.[42] Citing cost pressures in the global garment industry as well as the specific history of the export sector in Jordan, manufacturers proclaimed themselves "happy with what we have" in the existing migrant workforce, configured by immigration law and in-zone dormitory housing to be a constantly available and controllable source of labor.[43] Given the path-dependent growth of the Jordanian garment industry, which had led to close ties with the United States, what the compact offered by way of incentives for trade with Europe was too little to induce manufacturers to take on the expense of contracting with Syrian workers.

THE RACIAL FUNGIBILITY OF SYRIANS AND MIGRANT WORKERS: EU ASSUMPTIONS MEET REALITY

The reluctance of garment manufacturers to hire Syrian women to replace a migrant workforce was an indication that Jordan Compact planners had misapprehended something fundamental about the fungibility of workers in Jordan. As suggested previously, part of the "something fundamental" was tied to the differing terms of work for migrants and Syrian refugees under Jordanian law. It was also deeply related to processes of racialization.

"Racialization" may strike some readers as an inapt lens to apply to the Syrian refugee crisis and the EU-Jordan Compact, where the dividing lines involve national origin, immigration status, religion, and gender, as well as skin color (including but also beyond the Black-white binary).[44] Furthermore, Jordan's history sits somewhat outside the context of colonial empire and the transatlantic slave trade—the most common settings for the racial capitalism framework.[45] I use the concept of racialization here in a broad sense, to refer to the process of assigning characteristics to groups of human beings to categorize them as suitable or unsuitable, desirable or undesirable, for particular economic, political, and social roles.[46] In Europe, those hierarchies were applied to Syrian refugees to serve the aims of sovereignty; in Jordan, a different set of racialization processes were deployed in the interests of shaping a labor force that would serve the interests of both global and local capital.

The Racialization of Syrian Refugees in Europe

In Europe, Syrians were racialized from the moment of their arrival. EU politicians and the press sought to locate Syrian refugees in a preexisting racial hierarchy of immigrants and refugees, justifying either welcome or rejection. At times, Syrians were placed at the top of the hierarchy, when Syrians (women and children, in particular) were portrayed as vulnerable, suffering, and entitled to protection in the EU under international law.[47] This claim—that Syrians were legitimate refugees—was often made by way of comparison with others who sought protection in Europe from Sub-Saharan Africa. The contrast emphasized race as a marker of merit, with the good (white) Syrian refugees opposed to the bad (Black) "illegal" immigrant from Sub-Saharan Africa whose claims to asylum were presumed to be fraudulent.[48]

In the hands of other actors, this hierarchy was inverted, with Syrians located at the bottom. Syrian men, in particular, were not infrequently characterized as the antithesis of the "European," justifying the assertion that they must be expelled to preserve the culture and sovereignty of the EU.[49] As Madeline-Sophie Abbas has argued, here skin color is only part of the story.[50] In this schema, "Europeanness functions as a 'defining logic of race' based on whiteness, Christianity, and modernity."[51] As Muslims from the Middle East, these Syrians were framed as the non-Christian, nonmodern outsider against which the inside was defined, reinforcing the urgency of closing rank against them.[52]

The Jordan Compact reflected elements of both the "deserving refugee" and the "threat to Europe" racialization processes. It recognized the merit of Syrians' claims to protection by singling them out among the world's millions of displaced people for this new type of humanitarian intervention. At the same time, it asserted that the proper place of Syrian refugees was not in Europe but in the Middle East, where the compact sought to keep them. This shored up the legitimacy of the EU's defense of its sovereignty against the threat that Syrians posed to its borders. Furthermore, by allowing the EU to claim it had a plan for the refugees who were worthy of humanitarian concern, the compact drew attention away from the rights of other refugees and migrants and provided cover for their expulsion from the EU.

Europe Looks at Jordan: The Imagined Fungibility of Syrians as Workers

When European actors turned to imagining a plan to employ Syrians in Jordan, they justified its appropriateness based on their sense of both the similarities between the refugees and their hosts (as Arabic-speaking Muslims) and the differences between them (with Syrians positioned as racially fungible with other migrants occupying the low-wage jobs that Jordanians had rejected). Here I explore the second justification.

Compact planners assumed that locating Syrians in garment factories and other "migrant jobs" would generate less opposition from Jordanians than attempting to place them in occupations where they would compete with local workers. If the trade scheme did not create substantial numbers of new jobs, Syrian workers would simply replace migrants staffing the garment industry. The fate of the migrants who would lose work as a result of this substitution was beyond the EU's realm of concern in the compact process. In reality, this plan, in which Syrian women were seen as being "like" South Asian women in their fitness for garment work, bore little resemblance to the actual divisions in the labor market in Jordan. To be clear, the point is *not* that racialization was present in the EU but absent in Jordan. Racialized distinctions between groups of workers were in fact pervasive in the Jordanian labor market. But the planners either did not perceive these distinctions or ignored them.

The Racialization of Noncitizen Workers in Jordan

Jordan's labor market is segmented by country of origin, with pervasive stereotypes about the link between gendered citizens of certain countries and their suitability for different kinds of work.[53] Egyptian men, branded as strong and tireless, do agricultural and construction labor.[54] Women from the Philippines are presented by labor recruiters as ideal domestic workers for elite families, and Sri Lankan and Indonesian women are said to be the hardest-working.[55] Women from South Asia in general are marked as compliant and diligent, essential qualities for work in garment factories, as discussed later. Palestinian men are seen as entrepreneurial. Syrian men in Jordan are also associated with entrepreneurialism, with higher-skill precision tasks in agriculture, and in the construction industry with specialty trades requiring attention to detail and with interior design.[56] Immigration status and the provisions of the compact are superimposed on, and help shape, this set of narratives based on nationality and gender.

Race is an additional axis of division between noncitizens in Jordan.[57] This is particularly evident in a comparison between the treatment of and narratives about Syrian refugees as opposed to refugees from Sub-Saharan Africa.[58] Refugees from Somalia, Sudan, and South Sudan were located at the bottom of the Jordanian hierarchy, denied the right to work (while also being criticized for an unwillingness to work), and in many cases also unable to access aid.[59] In the Jordanian context, Lewis Turner has argued that the praise offered to Syrians for their entrepreneurialism is a coded reference to whiteness, in opposition to "African refugees" looking for a handout.[60] Within Jordan, as Turner reports based on field interviews, "many humanitarians informally but explicitly position Syrian refugees as 'non-African' . . . both distinct from and superior to 'African' refugees."[61] In this way, Somali and Sudanese refugees were drafted into service as Syrians' racial opposites. This demonization of people from Africa or of African descent as "insufficiently attached to 'productive' work" is a recurring trope of racial capitalism in operation.[62]

Workers in Jordan Respond to the Compact

SYRIAN REFUGEES

Following the Jordan Compact, Syrians in Jordan were given priority over other noncitizen workers in many contexts. Syrians' privileged position came most obviously from the compact itself, the product of Europe's search for a "humane" solution to the refugee crisis that would keep Syrians in the Middle East and out of the EU. Once the compact was signed, Syrian refugees in Jordan became the focus of an enormous investment of resources by the United Nations, the World Bank, European governments, and international nongovernmental organizations.[63] The fact that large amounts of money for the Jordanian state were riding on hitting benchmarks for issuing work permits to Syrians—and only Syrians—made their access to the labor market salient to the government in a way that had not been true for migrants, much less refugees, in the past. As a result, as noted previously, the Jordanian government made work permits available to Syrians on significantly better terms than those available to other noncitizens.

Syrians used what agency they had to reject the compact's proposal that they would become garment export workers. We have already seen that garment firms were not eager to employ Syrians. The feeling, it turned out, was mutual. Once officials sought to move Syrian women into manufacturing positions in Jordanian garment factories, the women made clear that they were situated very differently in economic, social, and geographic terms than South Asian women, who traveled alone on time-limited visas and lived in dormitories within the manufacturing zones. Most Syrian women in Jordan lived with their families in cities far from export zones, with only about 20 percent residing in refugee camps. Without some provision for child care, they could not leave home at all. They could not afford—in money or in time—travel to the zones, which were often far away from where they lived. Most had little or no experience working outside of the home or family businesses, and they—and to a greater extent their male partners and relatives—had concerns about women working in factories, in particular in mixed-gender environments.[64] They feared that taking formal jobs would imperil their ability to continue to get refugee assistance or to eventually be resettled in another country. And, above all, the wages on offer in the garment export zones simply would not allow them to cover the cost of living in Jordan.[65]

Furthermore, and critically, Syrians had other options. As beneficiaries of the Jordan Compact, they had preferential access over other migrants and refugees to jobs in agriculture, construction, and other sectors. They continued to be eligible for humanitarian aid in Jordan in addition to or instead of work, giving them a small but important cushion that migrants lacked.[66] Syrians voted with their feet. Syrian women largely opted out of the work permit plan altogether, although some labored in agriculture and others worked in the service sector or ran informal home-based businesses.[67] With other more desirable occupations closed off to Syrians by order of the Jordanian government, Syrian men who applied for permits generally used them to regularize their status in existing jobs in informal sectors such as construction and agriculture.

That Syrians could and did reject garment work in Jordan is the result of deeply contextual factors. Indeed, a different set of Syrians in a different country turned toward garment work rather than away from it. Turkey is host to the largest number of Syrian refugees in the world. These refugees—unlike those in Jordan, who had little experience in apparel manufacturing—largely come from Aleppo, the heart of Syria's garment industry.[68] Without any parallel international effort to encourage the employment of Syrians in the Turkish garment industry, an estimated 650,000 Syrians in Turkey have taken work in informal garment factories whose wages and working conditions have been sharply criticized.[69] It was not garment export work per se, but garment export work in the Jordanian context, offered to Syrians with little experience in the industry, under the terms set by the compact, that Syrians turned away from.

Despite their ability to reject some elements of the work that the compact imagined for them, the circumstances of Syrians in Jordan remain terribly difficult. They are excluded from almost all "good" jobs, including those for which they have professional qualifications. In the largely informal sectors where most Syrians now labor, although their presence has generated new expressions of concern about long-standing working conditions, they continue to be treated as commodities by their employers just as other noncitizen workers are.[70] For those who continue to survive on humanitarian aid alone, the money they receive is barely enough to support the most basic existence.

SOUTH ASIAN MIGRANT WORKERS

South Asian migrant women were shielded from the impact of the Jordan Compact's replacement strategy because Syrians did not take jobs in significant numbers in the garment sector. Women from South Asia today continue to migrate to work in Jordan's industrial parks in roughly the same numbers as before the compact. Once in Jordan, the terms of their visa and the structural realities of postcolonial global inequality constrain their ability to resist the conditions of work that they face. This is not to say that they lack all agency. On an individual level, the decision to migrate itself is an exercise of autonomy, albeit within a curtailed range of options. Some Bangladeshi women in Jordan have also noted the empowering effects of migration to the zones, including a period of escape from control by family (and especially male family members), a degree of financial independence, and the chance to develop skills that may facilitate access to better job opportunities on return home.[71]

There are also some signs of collective action by—or at least on behalf of—South Asian garment workers in Jordan. The Jordanian garment workers union negotiated a contract covering migrant workers in the export zones, which went into effect in 2016.[72] Although this was initially done without the participation of migrants themselves, in 2019 twenty-six migrants were elected as union representatives.[73] Over the same period, the ILO has supported the development of a migrant workers' center in one of the largest zones, offering educational and cultural activities and support in resolving employment disputes.[74] Neither of these has yet delivered major improvements to the workers, but they suggest the potential for some degrees of resistance despite the migrants' apparent lack of bargaining power.[75]

CONCLUSION: GLOBAL THEORY, LOCAL CONTEXT

The Jordan Compact framed jobs for Syrians in Jordanian export zones as a shift away from a "purely humanitarian approach to a development approach," which would offer Syrians "far better lives" than the status quo in Jordan—while, not incidentally, keeping them from pursuing a different version of a better life in Europe.[76] But compact planners misapprehended the economic structure of garment export manufacturing in Jordan, disregarded and reinforced the racialized stratification of the local labor market, and ignored the perspectives of Syrian refugees and other migrant workers there. As a result, actors on the ground did not comply with—and ultimately stymied—the plan to put Syrians in garment factory jobs.

From a worker perspective, the primary story of resistance comes from Syrian refugees, who did not embrace the garment export work imagined for them by the World Bank, the European Commission, and the Jordanian government. In turning away from garment work, Syrian refugees undermined a much-heralded set of claims in the EU-Jordan agreement, including about the potential of trade to generate employment for refugees, the value of garment export jobs to workers, and the desirability of formal work over both informal work and humanitarian aid. Syrian refugee responses, of course, cannot be divorced from the desires of garment export firms to preserve their access to a cheap and controllable workforce. The combined effect of these two reactions scuttled the initiative. South Asian migrant workers continue to fill the majority of jobs in the Jordanian garment industry.

None of this is to say that the outcome to date of the Jordan Compact represents a victory for workers. The compact positioned Syrians as subordinate to Jordanian workers but granted them privileges other noncitizen workers lacked. This allowed them to reject garment work when it did not meet their needs; but with other occupations foreclosed, they largely continue to work in the agricultural and construction jobs they held before the compact, positions that remain largely informal despite the fact that the refugees holding them now have official work permits. Most of the work Syrians are allowed to do (and that Egyptian, Iranian, and Iraqi migrants do alongside them) is still precarious and difficult, as well as poorly paid.[77] Meanwhile, migrants from South Asia in the garment industry continue to be subjected to the *kafala* system on exploitative terms. And refugees from Somalia and Sudan bear the brunt of racism both within the humanitarian system and at the fringes of the informal economy where they seek work. Neither, however, is the compact a tale of triumph for the agenda of European sovereignty or for global capital. Realities on the ground introduced complexities that permitted resistance.

Ultimately, the fact that Syrians could and did reject garment work in Jordan was highly contingent on the specific economic structures, players, and politics surrounding the Jordan Compact. Syrians did not have to accept jobs in export manufacturing because of the bargaining position granted them by the international attention to their plight, the specific entitlements set out in the Jordan Compact, and the convergence of their interests with those of garment manufacturers. In a different context, the outcome might be entirely different. Turkey, where there is no analog to the compact and yet Syrian refugees work in the garment industry in large numbers, amply illustrates that reality.

In his book *Peasants and Capital: Dominica in the World Economy*, Trouillot asks: "Is there life beyond neocolonialism? Can we make sense of what dominated people say and do in their daily lives without keeping silent about their forced integration in the international order and yet without reducing their lives to the fact of that integration?"[78] The Jordan Compact offers one opportunity to engage in this sort of "making sense." For Syrian refugees and other actors in Jordan, as for so many other people in so many other places, options for large-scale advancement are set by the agenda of global capital and the political priorities of the Global North. At the same time, within the limited space available to them in their specific local circumstances, they have asserted their agency in ways that undermine the agenda of the core.

NOTES

1. This chapter draws on my interviews with actors engaged with various aspects of the Compact in Jordan and elsewhere in 2018 and 2019, as well as on primary documents and secondary sources. It is also informed by my interviews and observations in Ethiopia and Bangladesh in 2018 and 2019 as work on or discussion of similar approaches to refugees as export manufacturing workers was underway.
2. Alexander Betts and Paul Collier, "Help Refugees Help Themselves," *Foreign Affairs* 94, no. 6 (November/December 2015): 84–92.
3. European Commission, *Annex to the Joint Proposal for a Council Decision on the Union Position within the Association Council Set up by the Euro-Mediterranean Agreement Establishing an Association between the European Communities and their Member States, of the one part, and the Hashemite Kingdom of Jordan, of the other part, with regard to the adoption of EU-Jordan Partnership Priorities and annexed Compact*, signed by Mr. Jordi Ayet Puigarnau, JOIN(2016) 41 final ANNEX 1, Brussels, 2016, https://data.consilium.europa.eu/doc/document/ST-12384-2016-ADD-1/en/pdf, hereinafter "Jordan Compact."
4. For a more detailed discussion of the Jordan Compact alongside that of a parallel agreement in Ethiopia, see Jennifer Gordon, "Refugees and Decent Work: Lessons Learned from Recent Refugee Jobs Compacts," ILO Employment Policy Department Working Paper 256, International Labour Organization, Geneva, Switzerland, December 2019, https://www.ilo.org/employment/Whatwedo/Publications/working-papers/WCMS_732602/lang--en/index.htm.
5. The Jordan Compact embodies the trend in humanitarianism over the past decade toward "refugee self-reliance," in which "refugees are now a new experimental population who must harness the force of the market." Ali Bhagat, "Experimental Neoliberalism and Refugee Survival in Kenya," *Review of African Political Economy*, December 2019, http://roape.net/2019/12/03/experimental-neoliberalism-and-refugee-survival-in-kenya/. See also Katharina Lenner and Lewis Turner, "Making Refugees Work? The Politics of Integrating Syrian Refugees Into the Labor Market

in Jordan," *Middle East Critique* 28, no. 1 (2019): 65–95, https://doi.org/10.1080/19436149.2018.1462601; and Evan Easton-Calabria and Naohiko Omata, "Panacea for the Refugee Crisis? Rethinking the Promotion of 'Self-Reliance' for Refugees," *Third World Quarterly* 39, no. 8 (2018): 1458–74, https://doi.org/10.1080/01436597.2018.1458301.
6. At the time, textiles represented nearly half of the consumer goods exported from Jordan. "Jordan Trade Summary 2017," *World Bank*, accessed July 12, 2023, https://wits.worldbank.org/CountryProfile/en/Country/JOR/Year/2017/Summarytext.
7. Betts and Collier, "Help Refugees Help Themselves"; and Allison Spencer Hartnett, "Reflections on the Geopolitics of Refugees and Displaced Persons: The Effect of Refugee Integration on Migrant Labor in Jordan," *Review of Middle East Studies* 52, no. 2 (November 2018): 263–82, https://www.jstor.org/stable/26562582. The *kafala* (meaning "sponsorship") system refers to the migrant labor regime in Gulf countries and Jordan and Lebanon. It links the migrant's work permit and visa to a single employer sponsor, and it gives the sponsor broad control over the migrant's personal and work life while the immigrant is in the destination country. For a brief description and critique of the impact of the *kafala* system on labor standards, see "Reform of the Kafala (Sponsorship) System," Migrant Forum in Asia Policy Brief No. 2, International Labor Organization, Quezon City, Philippines, https://www.ilo.org/dyn/migpractice/docs/132/PB2.pdf. Although the *kafala* system is frequently discussed as the evolution of long-standing custom in the Middle East, Omar Hesham AlShehabi has recently argued that *Kafala* should be seen "not as an age-old practice in the Arabian Peninsula from time immemorial, but a very modern product of British colonial practices to control labour and police empire across the Gulf and the Indian Ocean." Omar Hesham AlShehabi, "Policing Labour in Empire: The Modern Origins of the Kafala Labour Sponsorship System in the Gulf Arab States," *British Journal of Middle Eastern Studies* 48, no. 2 (2021): 291–310, https://doi.org/10.1080/13530194.2019.1580183.
8. Gordon, "Refugees and Decent Work," 3.
9. Svein Erik Stave, Tewodros Aragie Kebede, and Maha Kataa, *Impact of Work Permits on Decent Work for Syrians in Jordan* (Geneva: International Labour Organization, September 2021), https://www.ilo.org/wcmsp5/groups/public/---arabstates/---ro-beirut/documents/publication/wcms_820822.pdf. In 2019, the number of Syrians holding yearly permits peaked at forty-eight thousand. Gordon, "Refugees and Decent Work," 3. It is unclear how much of the decline to under forty thousand in 2020 was due to COVID.
10. Gordon, "Refugees and Decent Work," 3, 12; and Stave, Kebede, and Kataa, *Impact of Work Permits*, 27.
11. Maha Kattaa and Meredith Byrne, "Quality of Work for Syrian Refugees in Jordan," *Forced Migration Review* 58 (June 2018): 45–46, 46. "Overall, Syrians with work permits do report an increased likelihood of having written work contracts; however, hourly wages, safety provisions and relations with employers are not necessarily any better." A more recent ILO study finds that the wages of Syrians in Jordan with work permits are now higher relative to those without. Stave, Kebede, and Kataa, *Impact of Work Permits*, 35. This study did not examine safety or relations with employers.

12. Lenner and Turner, "Making Refugees Work?," 76–77; and Katharina Lenner, "Biting Our Tongues: Policy Legacies and Memories in the Making of the Syrian Refugee Response in Jordan," *Refugee Survey Quarterly* 39, no. 3 (2020): 273–98, https://doi.org/10.1093/rsq/hdaa005.
13. Michel-Rolph Trouillot, "Motion in the System: Coffee, Color, and Slavery in Eighteenth-Century Saint-Domingue," *Review (Fernand Braudel Center)* 5, no. 3 (1982): 331–88, https://www.jstor.org/stable/40240909.
14. Trouillot, "Motion in the System," 333–34, 383.
15. Trouillot, "Motion in the System," 334 (emphasis in the original).
16. Trouillot, "Motion in the System," 374.
17. See, for example, "Global Trade Liberalization and the Developing Countries," *International Monetary Fund*, accessed January 12, 2022, https://www.imf.org/external/np/exr/ib/2001/110801.htm; and "The Role of Trade in Ending Poverty," *World Bank and World Trade Organization*, accessed January 12, 2022, https://www.worldbank.org/en/topic/trade/publication/the-role-of-trade-in-ending-poverty. Regarding the orthodoxy as applied to export processing zones in Jordan, see Lenner and Turner, "Making Refugees Work?," 76–77; and Lenner, "Biting Our Tongues," 292. The claim also reflects an assumption that increased trade and the jobs it generates would lead to a reduction in out-migration of Syrians in the short term—which I have argued is unsupported. Jennifer Gordon, "Investing in Low-Wage Jobs Is the Wrong Way to Reduce Migration," *Foreign Policy*, January 8, 2019, https://foreignpolicy.com/2019/01/28/investing-in-low-wage-jobs-is-the-wrong-way-to-reduce-migration/.
18. Xavier Cirera and Rajith Lakshman, "The Impact of Export Processing Zones on Employment, Wages and Labour Conditions in Developing Countries: Systematic Review," *Journal of Development Effectiveness* 9, no. 2 (2017): 1–17, https://doi.org/10.1080/19439342.2017.1309448.
19. Congressional Research Service, Specialist in International Trade and Finance, *Qualifying Industrial Zones (QIZs) in Jordan and Egypt: Background and Issues for Congress* (Washington, DC: Congressional Research Service, 2013), 5–6, https://www.everycrsreport.com/files/20130823_R43202_2f48bd3c6671a55402f17cf7b26cf65fb860bfcd.pdf.
20. A Jordanian garment manufacturers' association representative has asserted that 90 percent of factories in the industry are foreign-owned. Kevin Kolben, "Trade, Development, and Migrant Garment Workers in Jordan," *Middle East Law and Governance* 5, nos. 1–2 (2013): 195–226, https://doi.org/10.1163/18763375-00501006.
21. For a fuller discussion of the composition and evolution of the Jordanian garment industry, see Gordon, "Refugees and Decent Work," 14, and the sources cited therein.
22. Susan Razzaz, *A Challenging Market Becomes More Challenging: Jordanian Workers, Migrant Workers and Refugees in the Jordanian Labour Market* (Jordan: International Labour Organization Regional Office for Arab States, 2017), 97–99, https://www.ilo.org/wcmsp5/groups/public/---arabstates/---ro-beirut/documents/publication/wcms_556931.pdf.
23. Migrants were already present in Jordan in large numbers in the construction and agriculture industries, but they had not initially been conceptualized as the labor force for the garment industry. By the time the compact was signed, 1.2 million

migrants were working in Jordan, nearly as many as the 1.38 million Jordanians employed in the country. Razzaz, *A Challenging Market*, 23.

24. Alix Nasri, *Migrant Domestic and Garment Workers in Jordan: A Baseline Analysis of Trafficking in Persons and Related Laws and Policies* (Geneva: International Labour Office, Fundamental Principles and Rights at Work Branch, 2017), 3–4, https://www.ilo.org/wcmsp5/groups/public/---ed_norm/---declaration/documents/publication/wcms_554812.pdf. The government asserts that these wages are functionally the same as those paid to Jordanians, once the cost of "free" food and housing that the migrants are required to accept from employers is added in. Author's interview with ILO staff person, Amman, April 17, 2018; and Better Work Jordan, *Annual Report 2019: An Industry and Compliance Review, Jordan* (Geneva: International Labour Office and International Finance Corporation, April 16, 2019).

25. On the importance of employer-controlled dormitories to the extraction of value from workers in global supply chains, see Alessandra Mezzadri, *The Sweatshop Regime: Labouring Bodies, Exploitation, and Garments Made in India* (India: Cambridge University Press, 2017); and Pun Ngai, "Gendering the Dormitory Labor System: Production, Reproduction, and Migrant Labor in South China," *Feminist Economics* 13, nos. 3–4 (2007): 239–58, https://doi.org/10.1080/13545700701439465.

26. Charles Kernaghan, *US Jordan Free Trade Agreement Descends Into Human Trafficking and Involuntary Servitude* (New York: National Labour Committee, now the Institute for Global Labour and Human Rights, May 2006); Agulhas Applied Knowledge, *Independent Monitor's Assessment Report: Jordan Compact and Brussels Meetings* (London: Agulhas Applied Knowledge, 2019), 11–13, https://agulhas.co.uk/app/uploads/2019/11/190917-Assessment-Report-Final-1.pdf; and Business and Human Rights Resource Centre, *Jordan's Garment Sector: How Are Brands Combatting Worker Exploitation and Abuse?* (London: Business and Human Rights Resource Centre, 2018), https://media.business-humanrights.org/media/documents/Jordan_Briefing_FINAL.pdf.

27. See, for example, Elizabeth Frantz, "Of Maids and Madams: Sri Lankan Domestic Workers and Their Employers in Jordan," *Critical Asian Studies* 40, no. 4 (2008): 609–38, https://doi.org/10.1080/14672710802505323. Regarding Sri Lanka: "The Sri Lankan exodus to the Middle East was part of a deliberate labor export strategy promoted by the Sri Lankan government to generate foreign exchange." Frantz, "Of Maids and Madams," 611.

28. For 75 percent women, see Better Work Jordan, *Annual Report 2018: An Industry and Compliance Review, Jordan* (Geneva: International Labour Office and International Finance Corporation, 2018), 11. For 75 percent migrants, see Sara Elizabeth Williams, "Made in Jordan: Inside the Unexpected Powerhouse of Garment Manufacturing," *Business of Fashion*, September 15, 2015, https://www.businessoffashion.com/articles/global-currents/made-in-jordan-garment-manufacturing-industry. For statistics showing a similar percentage three years later, see Better Work Jordan, *Annual Report 2019*, 10.

29. Alexander Betts and Paul Collier, *Refuge: Rethinking Refugee Policy in a Changing World* (New York: Oxford University Press, 2017), 175; and Betts and Collier, "Help Refugees Help Themselves."

30. Lenner, "Biting Our Tongues," 294.
31. Author's interview with ILO staff person, Amman, April 17, 2018; and Veronique Barbelet, Jessica Hagen-Zanker, and Dina Mansour-Ille, "The Jordan Compact: Lessons Learnt and Implications for Future Refugee Compacts," Overseas Development Institute Policy Briefing, London, February 2018, https://cdn.odi.org/media/documents/12058.pdf.
32. "The Textile Industry in Syria: The Past and the Future," *Syrian International Business Association*, July 15, 2019, https://siba.world/textile-industry-in-syria/ (listing Aleppo as one of the major garment-producing regions in Syria); and Daniel Howden, Hannah Patchett, and Charlotte Alfred, "The Compact Experiment: Push for Refugee Jobs Confronts Reality of Jordan and Lebanon," *Refugees Deeply*, December 2017, https://s3.amazonaws.com/newsdeeply/public/quarterly3/RD+Quarterly+-+The+Compact+Experiment.pdf.
33. Jordan hosts more refugees per capita than almost anywhere else in the world. *UNHCR Jordan Factsheet* (UNHCR, October 31, 2019), https://reliefweb.int/report/jordan/unhcr-jordan-factsheet-october-2019. The more than two million Palestinian refugees and their descendants who arrived in Jordan in multiple waves, beginning in 1948 with the establishment of the State of Israel in historical Palestine, are not included this count. Geraldine Chatelard, "Jordan: A Refugee Haven," *Migration Policy Institute*, August 31, 2010, https://www.migrationpolicy.org/article/jordan-refugee-haven. The majority of Palestinians in Jordan are Jordanian citizens and thus have the right to work.
34. For an analysis of the shift that the adoption of the Refugee Convention brought about from an understanding of refugees as (potential) workers to subjects of humanitarian intervention, see Jennifer Gordon, "The International Governance of Refugee Work: Reflections on the Jordan Compact," *Global Public Policy and Governance* 1, no. 4 (2021): 239, 242–43. In this sense, one price of the unique protections granted to refugees under international law was their transformation into waste or surplus in terms of the labor market. Among the few examples of scholarship exploring the question of waste in reference to refugees, work, and racial capitalism, see Prem Kumar Rajaram, "Refugees as Surplus Population: Race, Migration and Capitalist Value Regimes," *New Political Economy* 23, no. 5 (2018): 627–39, https://doi.org/10.1080/13563467.2017.1417372; and Ali Bhaghat, "Governing Forced Migration in Racial Capitalism: Refugee Survival in Paris and Nairobi," (PhD diss., Queens University, 2019), https://qspace.library.queensu.ca/handle/1974/26667.
35. For a fuller discussion of these changes, see Gordon, "Refugees and Decent Work," 17–18. In 2021, the Jordanian government introduced a regulation to further increase permit-holders' ability to move between jobs within occupational clusters. See Stave, Kebede, and Kataa, *Impact of Work Permits*, 26–27.
36. Stave, Kebede, and Kataa, *Impact of Work Permits*, 54.
37. On distance from activities of social reproduction as a mechanism through which firms appropriate surplus value, see Alpa Shah and Jens Lerche, "Migration and the Invisible Economies of Care: Production, Social Reproduction and Seasonal Migrant Labour in India," *Transactions of the Institute of British Geographers* 45, no. 4 (2020): 719–34, https://doi.org/10.1111/tran.12401.

38. At the time the compact was signed, 81 percent of Jordanian garment production was destined for the U.S. market. See "Jordan Textiles and Clothing Exports by Country and Region 2016," *World Bank*, accessed July 12, 2023, https://wits.worldbank.org/CountryProfile/en/Country/JOR/Year/2016/TradeFlow/Export/Partner/all/Product/50-63_TextCloth. The EU's requirements for certification are also significantly more stringent than those required for trade with the United States.

39. Author's interview with Jordanian garment manufacturer, Amman, Jordan, April 17, 2018.

40. Lenner and Turner, "Making Refugees Work?", 65–79; and Agulhas Applied Knowledge, *Independent Monitor's Assessment Report*, 15. For the certification requirements themselves, see International Trade Administration, "European Union Country Commercial Guide: European Union—Standards for Trade," *Trade.Gov*, accessed January 13, 2022, https://www.trade.gov/country-commercial-guides/eu-standards-trade.

41. Although the original agreement with the EU would have increased the percentage of Syrian workers to 25 percent after two years, see "Jordan Compact," 12, it was amended in 2018 to keep the goal at 15 percent through 2030. Better Work Jordan, *Annual Report 2019*, 10.

42. Lenner and Turner, "Making Refugees Work?," 18–19.

43. Lenner and Turner, "Making Refugees Work?," 19.

44. For recent work on racialization processes beyond the Black-white binary, see, for example, Nicholas De Genova, "The 'Migrant Crisis' as Racial Crisis: Do Black Lives Matter in Europe?," *Ethnic and Racial Studies* 41, no. 10 (2018): 1765–70, https://doi.org/10.1080/01419870.2017.1361543; and Bianca Gonzalez-Sobrino and Devon R. Goss, "Exploring the Mechanisms of Racialization Beyond the Black–White Binary," in "The Mechanisms of Racialization Beyond the Black/White Binary," ed. Bianca Gonzalez-Sobrino and Devon R. Goss, special issue, *Ethnic and Racial Studies* 42, no. 4 (2019): 505–10, and other articles in this special issue of *Ethnic and Racial Studies*.

45. Joseph A. Massad, *Colonial Effects: The Making of National Identity in Jordan* (New York: Columbia University Press, 2001), 1–11. Jordan was a British protectorate from its founding in 1921 until 1946. However, its importance to the British lay more in its geographic location and political position than in natural resources—scarce then as now—or in its potential to provide labor for colonial economic projects. The enslavement of people from Africa was not central to Jordan's development, nor were Jordanians enslaved themselves. As a structural matter, then, the country has not accumulated or lost substantial wealth from slavery. At the same time, this history has by no means exempted the country from racism. Anti-Blackness is evident both on and beneath the surface in Jordanian society, accompanied by denial of its existence. Lewis Turner, "'#Refugees Can Be Entrepreneurs too!' Humanitarianism, Race, and the Marketing of Syrian Refugees," *Review of International Studies* 46, no. 1 (2020): 137–55, https://doi.org/10.1017/S0260210519000342. For one oft-cited example, it is common for Jordanians to refer to people with darker skin as "abed" or "slave." Taylor Luck, "Voicing 'Solidarity' Against US Racism, Arabs Expose Scourge at Home," *Christian Science Monitor*,

June 22, 2020, https://www.csmonitor.com/World/Middle-East/2020/0622/Voicing-solidarity-against-US-racism-Arabs-expose-scourge-at-home. For a set of personal observations on the manifestations of racism in Jordan, see Kwather Berhanu, "Constructions of Black Identities Within Jordan," *Georgetown University Junior Year Abroad Network Blog*, May 11, 2018, https://berkleycenter.georgetown.edu/posts/constructions-of-black-identities-within-jordan. The 2020 protests following the police murder of Breonna Taylor, George Floyd, and other African Americans in the United States touched off a reckoning with racism in Jordan among other Arab countries.

46. This is consistent with the foundational analysis of racial capitalism by Cedric Robinson, who in *Black Marxism: The Making of the Black Radical Tradition* (Chapel Hill: University of North Carolina Press, 2000) analyzes European feudal society and the rise of the proletariat in Europe as a racial project of capitalism before the transatlantic slave trade. See also Robin D. G. Kelley, "What Did Cedric Robinson Mean by Racial Capitalism," *The Boston Review*, January 12, 2017, http://bostonreview.net/race/robin-d-g-kelley-what-did-cedric-robinson-mean-racial-capitalism. See also Gargi Bhattacharyya, *Rethinking Racial Capitalism: Questions of Reproduction and Survival* (London: Rowman and Littlefield, 2018), 12; and Lisa Tilley and Robbie Shilliam, "Raced Markets: An Introduction," *New Political Economy* 23, no. 5 (2018): 534–43.

47. Harriet Gray and Anja Franck, "Refugees as/at Risk: The Gendered and Racialised Underpinnings of Securitisation in British Media Narratives," *Security Dialogue* 50, no. 3 (2019): 275–91, https://doi.org/10.1177/0967010619830590; and Marcello Maneri, "Breaking the Race Taboo in a Besieged Europe: How Photographs of the "Refugee Crisis" Reproduce Racialized Hierarchy," *Ethnic and Racial Studies* 44, no. 1 (2021): 4–20, https://doi.org/10.1080/01419870.2020.1723672.

48. Maneri, "Breaking the Race Taboo," 15.

49. In the second phase of UK reporting on the Syrian refugee crisis, "the image of the vulnerable feminized refugee persists. This representation, however, is overlaid with representations of the in-comers as a (racialized, masculinized) threat. The figure of the threatening terrorist that is constructed in the newspaper discourse is implicitly, and sometimes explicitly, both male and racialized." Gray and Franck, "Refugees as/at Risk," 284.

50. Madeline-Sophie Abbas, "Conflating the Muslim Refugee and the Terror Suspect: Responses to the Syrian Refugee 'Crisis' in Brexit Britain," *Ethnic and Racial Studies* 42, no. 14 (2019): 2450–69, https://doi.org/10.1080/01419870.2019.1588339; and De Genova, "The 'Migrant Crisis' as Racial Crisis," 1765.

51. Abbas, "Conflating the Muslim Refugee," 2456; see also Nicholas De Genova, "Antiterrorism, Race, and the New Frontier: American Exceptionalism, Imperial Multiculturalism, and the Global Security State," *Identities* 17, no. 6 (2010): 613, https://doi.org/10.1080/1070289X.2010.533523: "The most fundamental work accomplished through the War on Terror's global racialization of 'Muslim' identity is the production of a racial condensation that is inimical to the white (Christian, 'European') identity of 'the West,' yet one that is precisely ambiguous and inherently heterogeneous."

52. Gray and Franck, "Refugees as/at Risk."

53. For detailed explorations of current tropes about particular nationalities of workers in Jordan's economy, see generally, Razzaz, *A Challenging Market*; and Lenner and Turner, "Making Refugees Work?"
54. Razzaz, *A Challenging Market*, 50, 63. On "[t]he way in which 'difference' and 'capital' articulate," see Mezzadri, *Sweatshop Regime*, 73.
55. Frantz, "Of Maids and Madams," 613.
56. Lenner and Turner, "Making Refugees Work?," 88. The idea that Syrians are good businesspeople is oft repeated. See, for example, Norimitsu Onishi, "Scattered by War, Syrians Struggle to Start Over," *New York Times*, October 16, 2016, citing Syrians' reputation in Jordan "for being hard-working, resourceful and skilled at business"; and *Assessing the Needs of Refugees for Financial and Non-Financial Services–Jordan Final Report* (Vicenza, Italy: Microfinanza, 2018), 49, https://www.unhcr.org/5bd01f7e4.pdf, stating that Syrians generally confirm their reputation of having a strong entrepreneurial spirit and 'appetite for business.'" Tropes about the labor characteristics of particular nationalities are often inconsistent across national borders. For example, Lenner and Turner note that the jobs for which Syrians are suited are seen quite differently in Lebanon compared to Jordan. Lenner and Turner, "Making Refugees Work?," 88. Turner points out how unstable these tropes can be even within the same country. Turner, "'#Refugees Can Be Entrepreneurs too!,'" 149.
57. For explorations of immigration status as a racial sorting mechanism, see Mae Ngai, *Impossible Subjects: Illegal Aliens and the Making of Modern America* (Princeton, NJ: Princeton University Press, 2004), especially chaps. 7 and 8; Kevin Johnson, "Race, the Immigration Laws, and Domestic Race Relations: A Magic Mirror Into the Heart of Darkness," *Indiana Law Journal* 73, no. 4 (1998): 1111; E. Tendayi Achiume, "Racial Borders," *Georgetown Law Journal*, 110, no. 33 (2022): 445–507; and E. Tendayi Achiume, "Race, Refugees and International Law," in *Oxford Handbook of International Refugee Law*, ed. Cathryn Costello, Michelle Foster, and Jane McAdam (United Kingdom: Oxford University Press, 2021), 43–59.
58. Dina Baslan and Izza Leghtas, "We Need to Help Jordan's Other Refugees," *News Deeply*, October 11, 2018, https://www.newsdeeply.com/refugees/community/2018/10/11/we-need-to-help-jordans-other-refugees; Marta Vidal, "After Fleeing Conflict at Home, African Refugees Battle Racism in Jordan," *Equal Times*, March 22, 2019, https://www.equaltimes.org/after-fleeing-conflict-at-home?lang=en#.XuD0l2 pKhhE; and Zerene Haddad, "Sudanese Refugees Struggle Against Racism Every Day," *Jesuit Refugee Service*, June 18, 2012, https://reliefweb.int/report/jordan/sudanese-refugees-struggle-against-racism-everyday. Race has until recently rarely been explored in the scholarship on refugees. See Achiume, "Race, Refugees," 2; Turner, "'#Refugees Can Be Entrepreneurs too!'"; Christoper Kyriakides et al., "Introduction: The Racialized Refugee Regime," *Refuge* 35, no. 1 (2019): 3–7; and Rajaram, "Refugees as Surplus Population," 627–28.
59. A much lower percentage of Iraqi, Somali, Sudanese, and Yemeni refugees in Jordan received cash assistance through the UNHCR compared with Syrians, and none get the monthly payments for food granted to Syrians through the World Food Program. Baslan and Leghtas, "We Need to Help"; and Mennonite Central Committee, *On the Basis of Nationality: Access to Assistance for Iraqi and Other Asylum-Seekers*

and *Refugees in Jordan* (Akron, PA: Mennonite Central Committee, 2017), https://reliefweb.int/sites/reliefweb.int/files/resources/On%20the%20Basis%20of%20Nationality.pdf.
60. Turner, "'#Refugees Can Be Entrepreneurs too!,'" 138, 142, 146–47.
61. Turner, "'#Refugees Can Be Entrepreneurs too!,'" 138.
62. Bhattacharyya, *Rethinking Racial Capitalism*, 57.
63. The European Commission states that the EU has "channelled roughly €2.7 billion to Jordan through humanitarian, development and macro-financial assistance" since the Syrian crisis began in 2011. European Commission, "Jordan," *European Civil Protection and Humanitarian Aid Operation*, last modified January 9, 2021, https://ec.europa.eu/echo/where/middle-east/jordan_en. In addition, most major governmental and nongovernmental international refugee relief organizations launched programs assisting Syrian refugees in Jordan, many with multi-million-dollar annual budgets.
64. Razzaz, *A Challenging Market*, 104–6; see also Izza Leghtas, "Debunking Myths of Syrian Women's Absence from Jordan's Labor Market," *Refugees International*, July 20, 2018, https://www.refugeesinternational.org/reports/2018/7/20/debunking-myths-of-syrian-womens-absence-from-jordans-labor-market.
65. Gordon, "Refugees and Decent Work," 15–16; and Lenner and Turner, "Making Refugees Work?"
66. Indeed, as noted previously, they were entitled to aid beyond that granted to other refugees. See Baslan and Leghtas, "We Need to Help."
67. As of 2021, only 5 percent of permit holders were women. Stave, Kebede, and Kataa, *Impact of Work Permits*, 27. Taking both permitted and nonpermitted work into account, one survey indicates that only 2 percent of Syrian women are in full-time and 6 percent in part-time employment in Jordan. Salem Ajluni and Dorsey Lockhart, *The Syrian Refugee Crisis and Its Impact on the Jordanian Labour Market* (Amman: WANA Institute, 2019), https://www.mercycorps.org/sites/default/files/2019-11/3_SyrianRefugeeCrisisImpactJordanianLabourMarket.pdf. These figures appear to have held steady over time, as a 2021 ILO report estimates that between 7 and 9 percent of Syrian women in Jordan participate in the labor force. Stave, Kebede, and Kataa, *Impact of Work Permits*, 9–11. This is significantly below even the low rates of employment for Syrian and Jordanian women in their home countries (12 percent and 14 percent, respectively). ILOSTAT Database, "Labor Force Participation Rate (Female) (as % of Female Population Ages 15+)," *World Bank Data*, retrieved September 2019, https://data.worldbank.org/indicator/SL.TLF.CACT.FE.ZS.
68. Carlotta Gall, "Turkey's Radical Plan: Send a Million Syrian Refugees Back to Syria," *New York Times*, September 10, 2019, https://www.nytimes.com/2019/09/10/world/middleeast/turkey-syria-refugees-erdogan.html.
69. Business and Human Rights Resource Centre, *The Price You Pay: How Purchasing Practices Harm Turkey's Garment Workers* (London: Business and Human Rights Resource Center, 2019), https://www.business-humanrights.org/sites/default/files/Turkey%20Purchasing%20Practices%20Briefing.pdf.
70. Syrians with work permits currently are estimated to earn approximately the same amount per month as Egyptian migrants, which is substantially less than Jordanians. Stave, Kebede, and Kataa, *Impact of Work Permits*, 35.

71. Nadia Afrin, *"I Wish I Would Never Have to Wake Up Again:" Material Conditions and Psychological Well-Being of Bangladeshi Women Garment Workers in Jordan* (Geneva: Feminist Participatory Action Research Report, August 2019), 19–21, https://gaatw.org/publications/Safe_and_Fair_FPAR/FPAR_Report_Jordan.pdf.
72. "Jordan Seals Commitment to Implementing Unified Contract for Migrant Garment Workers," *ILO News*, December 10, 2015, https://www.ilo.org/beirut/media-centre/news/WCMS_435506/lang--en/index.htm.
73. "Migrant Worker Leaders Elected in Jordan Garment Factories," *IndustriALL Global Union*, April 4 2019, http://www.industriall-union.org/migrant-worker-leaders-elected-in-jordan-garment-factories.
74. "Jordan Workers' Centre Proves an Essential Lifeline for Migrants," *ILO News*, August 4, 2014, https://www.ilo.org/resource/article/jordan-workers%E2%80%99-centre-proves-essential-lifeline-migrants..
75. Suneetha Eluri, Technical Officer, International Labor Organization, "Al Hassan Migrant Worker Centre," presentation at the ILO Centenary Conference, Georgetown University, November 22, 2019.
76. Alexander Betts and Paul Collier, "Jordan's Refugee Experiment: A New Model for Helping the Displaced," *Foreign Affairs*, April 28, 2016; and Betts and Collier, "Help Refugees Help Themselves," 90.
77. Indeed there is evidence that conditions and wages in these industries for migrants to Jordan from countries other than Syria deteriorated in the wake of the compact. See Gordon, "Refugees and Decent Work," 19–21; Hartnett, "Reflections on the Geopolitics," 263–66, 268.
78. Michel-Rolph Trouillot, *Peasants and Capital: Dominica in the World Economy* (Baltimore, MD: The Johns Hopkins University Press, 1988), 181.

CHAPTER 11

DISTRIBUTIONAL ANALYSIS AND SUPPLY CHAIN INTERVENTIONS

Migrant Worker Organization in Vermont's Dairy Industry

JENNIFER BAIR

On a Friday afternoon in March 2017, Immigration and Customs Enforcement (ICE) officers in Vermont arrested José Enrique Balcazar Sanchez, twenty-four, and Zully Palacios Rodriguez, twenty-three, shortly after they left the Burlington offices of an immigrant rights group called Migrant Justice. Following their detention, fellow activists organized a series of demonstrations on their behalf, arguing that the pair was targeted because of their involvement in political organizing. Both had been active in an ongoing campaign by Migrant Justice to improve conditions for the mostly undocumented migrant workers who labor on the state's dairy farms. Specifically, Migrant Justice had been calling on Ben & Jerry's, a Burlington-based ice cream company, to sign on to a program called "Milk with Dignity," which was designed in consultation with members of Vermont's migrant worker community. Balcazar, a former dairy worker who migrated from Tabasco, Mexico at the age of seventeen, had been a particularly visible presence throughout the campaign. At the time of his arrest, he was also serving on an immigration task force convened by Vermont's attorney general in response to an uptick in immigration enforcement by ICE.[1]

Migrant rights' activists were not the only community members voicing concern about the recent expansion of immigration enforcement in Vermont. A few days after the arrest of Balcazar and Rodriguez, a local newspaper ran an article under the headline "Feds Could ICE-Out Dairy Economy." The story noted a growing sense of alarm among farmers about the expansion of immigration enforcement in the region, given the effect that mass detentions and deportations of the undocumented workforce would have on an industry that generates 70 percent of the state's agricultural sales. One dairy farmer from Addison County, Cheryl Connor, articulated a widely held view: "They keep the farms going. If we didn't have migrant workers, we wouldn't have dairy farms."[2]

The number of migrant farmworkers employed in Vermont was minimal decades ago, but their labor is now regarded as essential to "keep the farms going." The industry's collective reliance on a largely undocumented workforce coexists with insecurity on the part of individual workers, whose precarity is produced by legal regimes that make them bearers of devalued labor. Those lacking legal status are subject to immigration enforcement, and like all farmworkers—whether documented, undocumented, or "American" (as the white workers on Vermont dairies are described)—they also lack key protections provided by federal labor law, given the exclusion of agricultural labor from the National Labor Relations Act.

Yet within this seemingly inauspicious organizing context, Migrant Justice successfully orchestrated a corporate campaign targeting Ben & Jerry's, an important client of Vermont dairy farms. Activists made the company's willingness to support migrant farmworkers a litmus test for the company's progressive profile, and thus the value of its brand. The Milk with Dignity program that Migrant Justice developed, and eventually succeeded in getting Ben & Jerry's to adopt, is among a set of similar agreements negotiated in recent years between worker organizations and consumer-facing companies that sit atop supply chains.[3] The relationship between buyers like Ben & Jerry's and suppliers like Vermont dairy farmers is asymmetrical; the former, through their market power, have a disproportionate ability to govern the chain in ways that shape the distribution of risk and reward among participants.[4] Getting client firms to exercise their "buyer power" on behalf of vulnerable workers located farther down the chain typically requires "naming and shaming" campaigns that target them as the most visible, consumer-facing participants in the supply chain. Companies like Ben & Jerry's are chosen because they are more reputationally sensitive than the direct employers of workers. Moreover, when compared with their suppliers, client firms are also more likely to possess the resources necessary to effect the changes labor advocates seek.

In this chapter, I offer a distributional analysis of Migrant Justice's efforts to intervene in and disrupt the dynamics of the dairy supply chain.[5] In so doing, I draw from interviews carried out with Migrant Justice organizers, dairy farmers, and other supply chain actors.[6] I ask not only why a mostly undocumented workforce has become critical for the viability of Vermont's dairy industry, but also why efforts to improve conditions for these workers center not on federal or state government, whose laws are the most direct cause of their precarity, nor on the farmers who, as their direct employers, are the most proximate beneficiaries of their labor, but rather a premium ice cream company farther down the dairy supply chain.

The first section of the chapter documents the conditions experienced by migrant workers on Vermont dairy farms, and the ways in which they are shaped by immigration and labor law. To counter the deleterious effect of these public legal regimes, Migrant Justice turned toward private ordering, negotiating an agreement with Ben & Jerry's whereby the company agreed to redistribute some of the value it captures in the supply chain toward dairy farms and the workers they employ. The surplus that Milk with Dignity seeks to shift does not derive exclusively from the exploitation of structurally devalued migrant labor; as I explain in the second section, it is also generated by background rules that shape the industrial organization of the dairy supply chain. Prominent among such rules is competition law, and specifically the exemption of agricultural cooperatives from antitrust liability. This carve-out for cooperatives has facilitated consolidation in the dairy industry, undermining the economic security of farmers and exacerbating pressures on farmworkers. Over time, these background rules have enabled the development of marked asymmetries among supply chain participants, with small and medium-size dairy farmers particularly hard hit.

Asymmetries along the supply chain are Milk with Dignity's premise and its raison d'etre; the program aims to leverage, for the benefit of workers, the unequal bargaining relationship between buyer and supplier. Buyer power is what enables Ben & Jerry's to incentivize farmers to improve conditions for farmworkers, and to provide the support needed to make these improvements possible. Yet as cooperatives grow in size and complexity, consolidation and integration along the supply chain could alter the relative position of participants, potentially undermining the buyer power that Milk with Dignity seeks to harness on behalf of migrant workers. The distributional analysis this chapter offers explores how legal regimes and background rules contribute to the generation as well as the allocation of surplus along the dairy supply chain, and thus condition in important ways the distributive struggles that Migrant Justice is waging on behalf of farmworkers.

PRODUCING PRECARITY: MIGRANT WORKERS IN THE DAIRY INDUSTRY

Non-native-born workers account for over half of all employees in the dairy sector in the United States, and the farms on which they are employed produce more than three-quarters of the country's fluid milk supply.[7] On Vermont farms that hire nonfamily labor, some 90 percent of these employees are migrant workers, the vast majority of whom are undocumented workers, primarily from Mexico, and to a lesser extent from Central America.[8] The precise size of this labor force is unknown, but most industry observers estimate that there are around two thousand such workers on the state's dairy farms.

Some migrant workers consider milking jobs desirable because, in contrast to seasonal work such as harvesting, they entail steady year-round employment. Dairy farms provide on-site housing for migrant workers, which enables them to minimize living expenses and thus save (and repatriate as remittances) more of their earnings. This residential situation also benefits farm operators because it gives them a constant source of available labor near the milking parlor. Ensuring that cows are milked regularly is critical, both for the health of the animal and the profitability of the farm. Moreover, the imperative to increase milk production means that on most farms cows are milked three times a day instead of two, effectively making dairy farms twenty-four-hour operations. Migrant workers live in trailers that are located at variable distances from the barn; typically, their twelve-hour shifts are staggered so that those who work at night are able to rest in their shared living space during the day.

Consolidation and the industrialization of milking has driven an increase in average farm size and thus a growing demand for wage workers, particularly as children and other farm family members opt for off-farm employment. In explaining why migrant workers have become the preferred labor force for milking jobs, farmers insist that they are far more reliable than local workers. The explanation given to us by one third-generation Vermont dairy farmer we interviewed is typical: "We started hiring Hispanic workers about 2004. We started with one or two, and then we grew to the whole staff. They fit our needs much better. . . . They are a more stable workforce than American workers. It's really hard to get guys to do the milking. It's twelve-hour shifts, six days a week, and it wears on you." Another Vermont farmer attributed the decision to hire migrant workers to a superior work ethic that "far exceeds [that of] American workers." This emphasis on the reliability and dependability of migrant workers is echoed in research from other dairying regions, such as Wisconsin and upstate New York.[9]

Agricultural industry representatives have long advocated for expanded access to immigrant workers on the grounds that native-born workers are unable or unwilling to meet the demand for farm labor. Yet many dairy farms that hire migrant workers also have one or more local employees who perform tasks other than milking. Milking jobs are among the least desirable in the industry, given the repetitive, difficult, and dangerous nature of the work and the punishing schedule. In most cases, even migrant workers with years of experience in the dairy industry will not experience mobility beyond these jobs, perhaps because employers perceive that such workers lack interest in diversifying their skill set.[10]

Describing migrant workers as hard-working but unambitious serves to justify both employers' preference for hiring them over "American" workers and delimiting their opportunities to the jobs that are most onerous and difficult to fill. Such discursive constructions, which draw distinctions between laboring bodies and then use these distinctions to naturalize the kinds of work bodies are assigned to do and the conditions under which they do it, are hallmarks of racial capitalism as it has operated across space and time. Racial capitalism, as Ruth Wilson Gilmore has observed, is a historical formation "developed in agriculture, improved by enclosure in the Old World, and captive land and labor in the Americas, perfected in slavery's time motion field-factory choreography."[11] It is also a framework for analyzing how this enduring but dynamic formation has evolved over the longue durée, enabling us to recognize that contemporary capitalism "exploits through culturally and socially constructed differences such as race, gender, region, and nationality, and is lived through these."[12]

The importation of racialized labor runs like a red thread through the agrarian history of the United States. In 1867, Southern planters looking to replace or supplement a recently emancipated Black labor force seized on the idea of importing Chinese workers from the Caribbean, where they had been laboring as indentured servants on sugar plantations.[13] In the nineteenth and early twentieth centuries, laborers from Europe and Asia worked alongside African Americans on farms and plantations, although employers were continuously frustrated in their quixotic quest to find and retain an industrious but compliant workforce that would neither agitate for higher wages nor leave for better opportunities.[14] By the middle of the twentieth century, the dependence of U.S. farmers on Mexican and Mexican American workers was well-established. Some workers came to the United States as guestworkers under the auspices of temporary migrant labor programs, but then, as now, many more lacked legal authorization to work.[15]

Agricultural workers are exposed to considerable risks, including but not limited to health and safety hazards. In 2019 the occupational fatality rate for farmworkers was five times higher than the average for workers in all other industries.[16] The dangers posed by unsafe conditions in the U.S. dairy industry, including injuries from animals and exposure to harmful chemicals, have been well documented.[17] These risks are exacerbated by the fact that most employees receive little in the way of training when arriving on a farm, and language barriers often impede communication between farm owners or managers and migrant workers. Exhaustion is an additional factor, given the prevalence of excessive work hours, with some laborers on Vermont farms noting that sixty- and even eighty-hour workweeks are not uncommon. Crowded and substandard housing is another frequent problem migrant workers encounter.

Undocumented farmworkers navigate the labor market and the workplace in the looming shadow of immigration law. In the case of Vermont's dairy sector, where workers both live and labor on farms in rural communities, concerns about legal status exacerbate feelings of isolation. Many workers find it difficult to access services or move in spaces beyond the farm, even when they have access to transportation.[18] In a state that is 93 percent white, migrant workers are aware of the risks implicit in going into town to buy groceries, remit earnings to their families back home, or see a doctor, especially because their presence in public space may be sufficient reason for a passerby to alert immigration authorities to "suspicious activity."[19] Immigration enforcement is conducted not only by ICE but by the U.S. Customs and Border Patrol, whose agents are given wide latitude to stop, question, and search individuals within one hundred miles of the U.S.-Canada border—a distance that encompasses two-thirds of the state and most of its dairy farms.

At the time of our first research trip to Vermont in 2019, anxiety about the ratcheting up of immigration enforcement was shared by farmers as well as their employees. Agricultural producers in other sectors have responded to the absence of immigration reform by increasing their reliance on the H-2A temporary visa program; the number of guestworker visas granted under this program increased fivefold between 2005 and 2019. Dairy farmers, however, are not eligible to use the H-2A program, which is intended for seasonal labor, not the year-round employment that dairy farms offer. The industry association representing dairy farmers, the National Milk Producers Federation (NMPF), has lobbied legislators and government officials vigorously and repeatedly to open the H-2A program to its members. Proponents of such a change argue that the industry's exclusion creates undue hardship for dairy farmers because it denies them a "sufficient labor force, and by virtue of the lack of willing domestic workers, does nothing to protect U.S. jobs" and ultimately "contributes to the trend of illegal employment of agricultural workers."[20]

In comparison to the arm of the state that enforces the immigration regime, government labor inspectors are a less visible presence in Vermont's dairy sector. Federal law prohibits Vermont's Occupational Safety and Health Administration (OSHA) from using federal funds to investigate accidents resulting in injury on farms that employ fewer than ten nonfamily laborers.[21] The vast majority of dairy farms in Vermont fall below this threshold, meaning that officials will not come to the farm or investigate potential health violations, even in the event of a reported fatality. In contrast to their blanket exclusion from the National

Labor Relations Act, agricultural workers are covered by some provisions of the Fair Labor Standards Act, although farmers are exempted from its overtime pay provisions. In short, the combined influence of immigration law and labor law condition the bargaining power of migrant workers and leave them vulnerable to hardships ranging from inadequate housing and health risks to detention and deportation.

Given the obstacles posed by these legal regimes, when organizers in Vermont began looking for ways to address the problems confronting migrant workers, they reached out to the Coalition of Immokalee Workers (CIW), the Florida-based farmworker organization that designed the Fair Food Program. Under this program, fast food restaurants and food retailers commit to purchasing tomatoes only from growers that are certified to meet minimum standards laid out in a Fair Food Code of Conduct, which was developed with extensive input from migrant workers.[22] A delegation from CIW traveled to Vermont and facilitated a series of meetings or *encuentros* in which farmworkers and organizers from Florida and Vermont shared their experiences and concerns. Inspired by CIW's Fair Food Program, Migrant Justice decided to emulate its approach and create a supply chain agreement for the dairy industry. The goal would be to get the clients of dairy farms—analogous to the fast food and grocery chains that participate in the Fair Food Program—to secure commitments from dairy farmers to improve conditions for workers and, critically, to provide those suppliers with the resources to do so.

Migrant Justice launched this strategy by targeting Ben & Jerry's, a highly visible Burlington-based company with a reputation for being socially and environmentally responsible. In 2015, following a relatively brief campaign, Ben & Jerry's and its parent company Unilever signed a memorandum of understanding (MoU) with Migrant Justice, committing it to accept a program involving five elements: (1) a worker-authored Milk with Dignity Code of Conduct; (2) worker education regarding the code; (3) third-party monitoring of its implementation by a body called the Milk with Dignity Standards Council; (4) payment of a premium to farms that comply with the code, a portion of which is passed on to farmworkers; and (5) a legally binding agreement affirming commitment to these principles. Working out the details of the MoU proved to be a complicated and protracted affair. Negotiations regarding implementation took another two years to complete, during which time Migrant Justice maintained public pressure on the company, organizing demonstrations and holding rallies in Burlington and throughout the state. A final agreement between Migrant Justice and Milk with Dignity was concluded on October 3, 2017, and the Milk with Dignity program got underway in early 2018.

During its first three years in operation, Milk with Dignity grew to cover migrant workers on more than five dozen farms that are part of Ben & Jerry's supply chain for cream; these farms generate approximately 20 percent of Vermont's total dairy production. Over $1 million has been redistributed to workers though wage increases, monthly bonuses, and improved housing. Among the most notable changes has been improved working conditions regarding health and safety, such as expanded access to personal protective equipment and the ability to take sick days when needed. At the time of writing, Ben & Jerry's is the only company that has signed on to the Milk with Dignity program, although in 2019 Migrant Justice launched a campaign targeting the grocery store chain Hannaford, which is discussed in greater detail later.

The supply chain design of the Milk with Dignity program recognized that many of the dairy farms employing migrant workers lack the resources to provide the improved conditions that Migrant Justice sought. Meaningful change for migrant workers would therefore require two distributions: a transfer of resources from Ben & Jerry's to the dairy farms that supply the company, and second, a transfer of resources from those dairy farms to the migrant workers they employ. The premium that Ben & Jerry's pays to participating farmers that comply with the Milk with Dignity Code of Conduct functions as this distributive mechanism. It is intended not only to reward farms for compliance but also to defray the costs that compliance entails, such as upgrades to the trailers that house farmworkers or the provision of health and safety equipment. These costs also include giving each qualifying worker a monthly Milk with Dignity premium of $50, which is included as a line item in their paycheck.[23] Additionally, farmers must agree to pay their workers an hourly wage equivalent to the state minimum, even though a Vermont statute exempts agricultural employers from the minimum wage requirement.[24] Even if most farmers spend the bulk of the premium on the costs of code compliance, they may use some portion of it to supplement generally low milk prices, thereby padding what are, for many, exceedingly thin margins.

The scale of the program remains modest to date, but Migrant Justice has succeeded in giving greater visibility to the value being generated by migrant workers. Although this population buttresses Vermont's agrarian economy, migrant workers are absent from the bucolic pictures of dairy farms that figure prominently in the "marketing of the state's agricultural products and the celebration of its rural livelihoods."[25] Via a corporate campaign that targeted a well-known, national company and its customers, organizers were able to achieve a degree of recognition for a labor force made precarious by the absence of legal protections. Alongside recognition, Migrant Justice also sought a redistribution of economic gains along the supply chain so that this workforce could capture a greater share of the value generated by its labor. But the future viability of the program may depend, in part, on a set of background rules that shape the industrial organization of the contemporary agricultural sector. Among these rules antitrust law figures prominently.

COMPETITION LAW, COOPERATIVE CONSOLIDATION, AND SUPPLY CHAIN ASYMMETRIES

So far, my distributional analysis has focused on legal regimes that (even through their exclusions) govern the availability and treatment of migrant labor by dairy farmers, and on the development of Milk with Dignity as an intervention that enlists Ben & Jerry's buyer power to push improved conditions up the supply chain. But if Ben & Jerry's is the lynchpin of the Milk with Dignity program, and dairy farmers are the direct implementers of the program's standards, there is one other supply chain actor whose participation is required: the dairy cooperative that connects the two. Ben & Jerry's does not buy directly from dairy farms; instead, it procures its cream from a dairy cooperative located near one of the company's ice cream manufacturing facilities outside of Burlington.

The cooperative, St. Alban's, receives and processes milk from more than three hundred farms. Ben & Jerry's is among St. Alban's largest clients, but the cooperative has multiple customers from Vermont and surrounding states. Because Ben & Jerry's is not the sole destination for St. Alban's output, Milk with Dignity uses "mass balancing" as a kind of proxy supply chain; the volume of milk produced by farms participating in Milk with Dignity is equivalent to the volume of milk that the company sources for its North American ice cream production. St. Alban's tracks the amount of premium each participating farm is supposed to receive and administers these premium payments.

To appreciate the role of St. Alban's in the distributional struggle playing out along Ben & Jerry's supply chain requires understanding the position of the agricultural cooperative in the broader political economy of milk. The American dairy industry has experienced wrenching change over the last half century. In just the three decades, between 1970 and 2000, the number of dairy farms declined from 648,000 to 105,000.[26] By 2019, fewer than 35,000 farms remained. The environment has been particularly challenging for producers in the Midwest and Northeast who face daunting domestic competition from industrial dairies in the West and Southwest, where confined feeding operations provide economies of scale unavailable in traditional dairy states.

In Vermont, the number of dairy farms fell by more than a third in less than a decade, plummeting from 1,015 farms in 2010 to 636 in 2020. This decline has been driven primarily by the closure of many small (less than 200 cows) and medium-size (200 to 699 cows) operations. Even as the number of dairies in the state has declined, the number of large farms (more than 700 cows) almost doubled, from eighteen in 2011 to thirty-three in 2019. At 192 cows, the mean size of Vermont's dairy farms continues to be lower than the national average (234), but this number has been increasing steadily, as smaller operations exiting the business sell their herds to larger ones.[27] The farms that remain require more wage labor, fueling the dependence on migrant workers who, as the Vermont dairy farmer quoted earlier noted, "keep the farms going."

Among the challenges dairy farmers face is a steady decline in fluid milk consumption, which has fallen about 6 percent per year since 2015 as dairy substitutes such as soy and oat milk gain in popularity. Although domestic consumption is decreasing, the milk supply continues to grow (albeit modestly) year on year because of herd consolidation and increasing productivity per animal. In this context, trade policy has become central to the fortunes of U.S. dairy farmers. Exports accounted for just under 16 percent of the industry's output in 2018, as compared with 5 percent twenty years earlier.

Much of the export growth has been fueled by increased shipments to Mexico, which dismantled its price-setting system for domestic milk producers in 1998. U.S. dairy exports to Mexico increased from $193 million in 1994, the year that NAFTA went into effect, to $1.5 billion in 2019.[28] Mexico is now the largest destination market for the U.S. dairy industry, absorbing about a quarter of all exports. After the 2016 presidential election, the uncertainty generated by the Trump administration's trade policies, and fears that Mexico might impose retaliatory tariffs against U.S. dairy in the event of further disputes, caused anxiety for dairy farmers, who also confront heightened global competition from the expansion of dairy production in China and India.

Milk prices, like those of other agricultural commodities, fluctuate, and although farmers are accustomed to such fluctuations, price volatility has been unusually pronounced in the dairy industry over the past decade. After reaching a record high price of $23.63 per hundredweight of milk in 2014, prices plummeted to $16.59 the following year. In 2017, the year that Milk with Dignity began enrolling dairy farms in the program, the average price was $15.44. In 2019, milk prices were below the cost of production for modest-sized farms in the northeast for the fifth consecutive year.

When Ben & Jerry's signed the Milk with Dignity agreement, St. Alban's was the twenty-first largest cooperative nationwide.[29] Processing around 1,200 million pounds of milk annually, St. Alban's was among a shrinking set of regional cooperatives. Many of these regional cooperatives were themselves products of mergers that had occurred during the 1960s and 1970s, when a wave of consolidation swept smaller cooperatives sourcing from and supplying local markets.[30] In July 2019, St. Alban's member farms voted to join Dairy Farmers of America (DFA), which promised to invest $30 million in the cooperative's processing plant.[31] Based in Kansas City, DFA is the largest dairy cooperative in the nation; it controls about 30 percent of the country's milk supply nationally, although the percentage is markedly higher in some areas. Created in 1998 through a merger of four regional cooperatives, DFA claims to represent more than twelve thousand farmers in forty-eight states. In 2020, DFA's member farmers sold fifty-six billion pounds of milk, some of which was bottled in the thirty-one processing plants that DFA owns.[32]

As a result of DFA's purchase of St. Alban's, DFA's member farms now include the dozens of Ben & Jerry's suppliers participating in Milk with Dignity. At the time of sale, DFA committed to maintaining St. Alban's role in administering the agreement, but the implications of the acquisition for the future of the program remain unclear. On the one hand, the Milk with Dignity premium may become even more attractive to participating dairies if, as some farmers fear, DFA lowers the base price it pays farms for their milk. However, the design of Milk with Dignity was premised on St. Alban's willingness to facilitate the program, at a time when Ben & Jerry's was among the cooperative's most important customers. The purchase of St. Alban's by DFA may erode this privileged status, shifting the balance of power between the client firm and its supplier, as cooperatives consolidate and expand their reach along the supply chain.

Agricultural cooperatives were initially created to permit farmers to pool output and thereby increase the bargaining power of many small producers vis-à-vis a more concentrated set of buyers. As a body of antitrust law developed in the United States in the late nineteenth and early twentieth centuries, farmers repeatedly pushed for clarification of its applicability to cooperatives. Section 6 of the 1914 Clayton Act created an antitrust exemption for associations of farmers pursuing the "legitimate objects" of cooperation. Yet concerns about the antitrust liability of cooperatives—and what was meant by "legitimate objects"—continued. Efforts to achieve greater clarity culminated in the 1922 passage of the Capper-Volstead Act, which granted antitrust immunity to associations of farmers that engage in the cooperative marketing of agricultural products. Cooperatives qualifying for this exemption must meet several conditions, including that they are "operated for the mutual benefit of the members" and "deal primarily in the products" of those members. Over the years, the exemption has been generally granted, even as the scale and form of cooperatives have changed.

The antitrust exemption for cooperatives was intended to provide a degree of protection to the individual producers comprising the cooperatives, who would otherwise be disadvantaged in their negotiations with the processors and middlemen that they relied on to get their milk to market. The power imbalance between the corporate buyer and the individual producer was exacerbated by the nature of the commodity; the perishability of raw milk means that farmers have little ability to withhold supply from the market in the hopes of finding better terms. In this sense, the law encouraged "the formation of agricultural cooperatives intended to countervail the monopsony power then held by the corporate purchasers." Yet "with the help of regulation and permissive application of antitrust principles to cooperative activities, the balance of power has shifted. In some markets, [large] cooperatives . . . *supervail* buyer power."[33]

Concerns about this shifting balance of power tend to focus on the implications of cooperatives' market power for milk prices, and thus consumer welfare, but farmers are also affected by the growth in corporate cooperatives. Critics suggest that the antitrust exemption today primarily advantages large cooperatives like DFA, arguably at the expense of the farmers they were supposed to help.[34] Today, cooperatives are often involved in joint ventures with other supply chain actors, and some have vertically integrated from production to retail. Yet these complex businesses can be opaque to their farmer members, who lack the kind of rights granted to the shareholders of publicly traded corporations. There is little federal regulation regarding the governance of cooperatives, beyond a limited oversight role for the Department of Agriculture.[35] Cooperatives are not required, for example, to disclose executive compensation.[36]

Dairy industry observers have long expressed worry about concentration among milk processors, and recent developments have intensified these concerns. In November 2019, five months after DFA's acquisition of St. Alban's, Dean Foods, the owner of brands such as Garelick Farms, Dean's, and Dairy Pure, filed for bankruptcy. Among the reasons for its declining fortunes the company cited the drop in milk consumption and competition from retailers' own milk bottling operations.[37] When, shortly thereafter in January 2020, it was announced that Dean Foods and DFA were in talks about a merger, the Department of Justice reported that it was looking into the possible deal. At the time, Dean Foods was the country's largest processor of milk and the largest customer of DFA, itself the largest dairy cooperative in the United States. The resulting joint company would control 60 percent of the fluid milk market in the upper Midwest.[38]

In April 2020, DFA announced its intention to purchase Dean Foods' forty-four processing milk facilities for $433 million. Independent farmers, cooperatives, and grocery stores filed more than one hundred objections, claiming irregularities in the bidding process.

However, Justice Department officials approved the merger the following month, allowing DFA to acquire the processing facilities. The only condition imposed was divestiture of three of DFA's own processing plants—a requirement that was added in response to a civil antitrust lawsuit filed by attorneys general in three states worried about the implications of DFA acquiring Dean Foods' processing plants in northeastern Illinois, Wisconsin, and New England. The lack of alternative buyers for Dean Foods' assets and the destabilizing effects of the COVID-19 pandemic on an already beleaguered industry appeared to motivate the decision. The Justice Department statement announcing the approval noted that "its investigation was conducted against the backdrop of unprecedented challenges in the dairy industry, with the two largest fluid milk processors in the US, Dean and Borden Dairy Company, in bankruptcy, and Dean faced with imminent liquidation."[39]

The acquisition of Dean Foods by DFA was not the first time the two companies had caught the attention of regulators. In 2004, Justice Department officials opened an inquiry into their relationship, and although they recommended that enforcement action be taken against both, the investigation was dropped in 2006 with no charges filed.[40] Scrutiny of the DFA-Dean Foods relationship continued, however, in the form of two class action lawsuits filed by dairy farmers. In 2007, a group of dairy farmers from the Southeast filed an antitrust lawsuit against the two companies, accusing them of making a sweetheart deal designed to suppress milk prices and eliminate competition in the region. Specifically, the suit alleged that Dean Foods agreed to make DFA its sole supplier in the region in exchange for DFA offering lower prices, thereby excluding from the market independent milk producers and competing cooperatives in fourteen states.

A similar lawsuit, alleging a mixed vertical and horizontal conspiracy among DFA, Dean Foods, and another large processor, Hood, was filed in Vermont district court in 2009. The class action complaint, brought on behalf of dairy farmers located within the region covered by Federal Milk Marketing Order One, claimed that DFA colluded with Dean Foods and Hood to create a monopsony that would keep milk prices low. Settlements were reached in both cases, squelching the hopes of some dairy industry observers that the cases would go to trial and that the subsequent litigation "would set guidelines and provide limitations on DFA's seemingly overpowering reach."[41]

Critics point out that DFA has expanded "to the point that it owns or controls entities up and down the entire dairy industry supply chain, from milk truckers to food processors to marketers." Diversification of this sort creates "an obvious conflict of interest: the less these entities have to pay DFA farmers for their milk, the more money they—and DFA—make."[42] Importantly, member farms do not see any proceeds from the majority of DFA's net income (about 75 percent of the profit earned on nearly $18 billion in revenue in 2020) that derives from "non-member business earnings."

These developments pose questions, yet unanswered, about the scope of the antitrust exemption provided in the Clayton and Capper-Volstead acts, and what counts as "legitimate objects" of cooperation for today's cooperatives, many of which are far more complex and diversified than the regional marketing associations and processing plants traditionally associated with the term "cooperative." Although membership is voluntary for farmers, the mergers occurring among previously independent cooperatives means that small and medium-sized farmers looking to secure a guaranteed outlet for their milk have few alternatives to membership, particularly when chronic oversupply is causing some cooperatives to refuse new members.

A conflict of interest between DFA and farmers could have several possible implications for Milk with Dignity. It may further exacerbate cost pressures on dairy farmers attempting to manage a period of low milk prices. This pressure could, in turn, manifest in deteriorating conditions for the migrant workers they employ, but it could also make the Milk with Dignity premium even more highly valued by the Vermont farmers eligible to participate in the program. On the other hand, as cooperatives increase their bargaining power vis-à-vis their farmer members, so too might they be gaining clout in negotiations with buyers. The expansion of cooperatives' market power both upstream and downstream could affect the size and distribution of the surplus in ways that affect the feasibility of a supply chain intervention such as Milk with Dignity, which is premised on the ability and willingness of a reputationally sensitive client to redistribute along the supply chain some of the value that it captures.

DISTRIBUTIONAL ANALYSIS, BACKGROUND RULES, AND STRUGGLES FOR SURPLUS

Through an analysis of the Milk with Dignity program, I have sought to illuminate the rules that structure the dairy supply chain and allocate a particular distribution of risk and reward among its participants. Given the long devaluation of racialized labor in U.S. agriculture, it is perhaps not surprising that immigration and labor law loom large as legal regimes that help explain why migrant workers are deemed necessary to secure the future of Vermont's dairy industry. Perhaps less obvious are the background rules that structure the market within which dairy farms operate.

Over time, these rules have enabled the development of marked asymmetries among supply chain participants. Of course, supply chain interventions such as Milk with Dignity are premised on power imbalances; Migrant Justice's efforts to improve working and living conditions on Vermont dairy farms center on Ben & Jerry's not because the company employs farmworkers, but because, as a significant buyer of local cream, it has influence over the dairy farms that do. Like all strategic supply chain interventions, Migrant Justice's campaign starts from an assumption about where the surplus in the dairy supply chain is and how it can be put into play. As consolidation and integration along the supply chain play out, the industry could evolve in ways that undermine the buyer power on which Milk with Dignity is based.

As a distributive intervention in the dairy supply chain, the question to be asked of Milk with Dignity is the same one that Janet Halley has asked about the value of distributional analysis for feminist inquiry: "what distributions does it leave in place, and what distributions does it shift?"[43] Migrant Justice's attempts to improve conditions for migrant workers implicate multiple distributions: of voice, of profit, of cost, of risk. I have argued that Migrant Justice's efforts gained an important measure of recognition for the migrant worker community and redistributed, modestly but meaningfully, some of the power between employers and workers—for example, by subjecting farms to audits by the Milk with Dignity Standards Council and by creating a hotline employees can use to report when a participating farm fails to comply with the standards laid out in the Milk with Dignity Code. Particularly in an industry context where workplaces can be hazardous and state enforcement is weak, a worker's ability to report health and safety concerns, and to credibly believe that such concerns will be acted upon, constitutes a significant redistribution of risk. The program also achieves a shift in the distribution of material resources; the financial support that Ben & Jerry's provides to participating farms in the form of the Milk with Dignity premium redistributes some of the profit generated along the supply chain from the ice cream brand and its parent corporation to dairy farmers and their workers.

Yet there are also distributions of risk and reward that Milk with Dignity is unable to shift. These include the substantial costs created by immigration enforcement—most acutely, of course, for workers, but also for their employers, whose cows' milking schedules cannot be altered to accommodate a worker's detention by Border Patrol. The dairy industry association, the National Milk Producers Federation, continues to present authorized guestworkers as a solution to this problem. In an April 2020 letter addressed jointly to the U.S. secretaries of Labor and Agriculture, the group implored the Labor Department's Office of Foreign Labor Certification to "accept and approve H-2A applications from dairy farmers offering temporary employment up to 364 days in a 12-month period." In justifying the request, the NMPF cited the dislocations caused by COVID-19, which, it claimed, were dramatically exacerbating the dairy industry's chronic labor shortage.[44] The letter failed to generate the response its signatories hoped for, but efforts to expand the H-2A program to include dairy workers will almost surely continue. The effects of such a change in the rules governing labor's incorporation into the dairy supply chain, and its implications for Milk with Dignity, are unclear.

Also falling outside of the distributive intervention Milk with Dignity effects are dairy workers on nonparticipating farms. Increasing the scope of the program would require identifying other lead firms that might join Ben & Jerry's in signing on to the Milk with Dignity program. In October 2019, Migrant Justice launched a public campaign targeting Hannaford, a Maine-based supermarket chain that procures milk from Vermont farms for its store brand line of dairy products. Although Hannaford is based in New England, it lacks the close association with the region that Ben & Jerry's cultivated for decades after opening its first "scoop shop" in a converted Burlington gas station in 1978.[45] It also lacks a brand asset whose value relies on the consumer's perception of it as a company committed to progressive causes. In short, Ben & Jerry's unique profile may have made it a particularly tractable target.

Although Migrant Justice has orchestrated a corporate campaign against Hannaford similar to the one it deployed against Ben & Jerry's, including a seven-state tour around the northeast aimed at putting pressure on the company to join Milk with Dignity, the supermarket chain has resisted requests to engage with the organization. Some dairy farmers are even worried that Migrant Justice's public efforts may damage an already embattled industry fighting for shelf space. One official in Vermont's agriculture department we spoke with observed that Hannaford has an extensive supply chain that gives it room to maneuver in relation to Migrant Justice's demands. If the company is concerned that the group's efforts will increase costs, "then [its] milk will just come from out of state," where Milk with Dignity is not active.

This sentiment aptly captures the challenge for advocates of any supply chain intervention: how to shift the distribution of surplus toward workers without disrupting the supply chain in such a way that the surplus is placed out of reach. This question is made all the more fraught by the fact that the surpluses activists seek to capture frequently rely on and reproduce the very dynamics of exploitation and appropriation that they seek to mitigate. There are no easy answers, only a set of strategic choices about who bears the costs of distributions left in place.

NOTES

1. In 2020, the Trump administration settled a lawsuit brought by Migrant Justice, alleging that the U.S. Department of Homeland Security unlawfully targeted the group's members in an effort to "intimidate and chill" immigrant rights advocates. Eli Rosenberg, "Trump Administration Settles with Latino Farm Activists Who Said They Were Targeted Over Political Work," *Washington Post*, April 17, 2017, https://www.washingtonpost.com/business/2020/10/28/dhs-farmworkers-lawsuit-immigration/.
2. Gaen Muphree, "Feds Could ICE-Out Dairy Economy: Deporting Workers Would 'Devastate' Farms," *Addison County Independent*, March 22, 2017, https://www.addisonindependent.com/2017/03/22/feds-could-ice-out-dairy-economy-deporting-workers-would-devastate-farms/.
3. Sean Sellers, "Assessing Feasibility for Worker-Driven Social Responsibility Programs," in *Power, Participation, and Private Regulatory Initiatives: Human Rights Under Supply Chain Capitalism*, ed. Daniel Brinks, Julia Dehm, Karen Engle, and Kate Taylor (Philadelphia: University of Pennsylvania Press, 2021), 139–52.
4. For other examples in a range of industries, see Jeremy Blasi and Jennifer Bair, *An Analysis of Multiparty Bargaining Models for Global Supply Chains* (Geneva: International Labour Office, 2019).
5. Among the three critical methods that orient this book's collective project, my chapter is inspired most directly by the mode of distributional analysis associated with American Critical Legal Studies (CLS) and elaborated here by Duncan Kennedy in chapter 4. However, racial capitalism and world-systems theory also critically inform this work because these frameworks underscore the historical dynamics of exploitation and inequality that structure the more proximate "conflict[s] . . . between strong and weak parties" at the heart of distributional analysis. For discussion of the influence of world-systems theory on the type of analysis I engage in here, see Jennifer Bair, "Global Capitalism and Commodity Chains: Looking Back, Going Forward," *Competition and Change* 9, no. 2 (2005): 153–80.
6. Between June 2019 and July 2021, Kathryn Babineau and I carried out interviews with the participants in the Milk with Dignity program as well as with other industry actors and public sector officials. We also had the opportunity to shadow Milk with Dignity audits, which include conversations with migrant workers and, separately, the farmers employing them.
7. Flynn Adcock, David Anderson, and Parr Rosson, *The Economic Impacts of Immigrant Labor on U.S. Dairy Farms* (College Station, TX: Texas A&M University Center for North American Studies, 2015).

8. Claudia Radel, Birgit Schmook, and Susannah McCandless, "Environment, Transnational Labor Migration, and Gender: Case Studies from Southern Yucatán, Mexico and Vermont, USA," *Population and Environment* 32, nos. 2–3 (2010): 177–97, https://doi.org/10.1007/s11111-010-0124-y.
9. For Wisconsin, see Jill Lindsey Harrison and Sarah E. Lloyd, "Illegality at Work: Deportability and the Productive New Era of Immigration Enforcement," *Antipode* 44, no. 2 (2011): 365–85, https://doi.org/10.1111/j.1467-8330.2010.00841.x; and for New York, see Kathleen Sexsmith, "Decoding Worker 'Reliability': Modern Agrarian Values and Immigrant Labor on New York Dairy Farms," *Rural Sociology* 84, no. 4 (2019): 706–35, https://doi.org/10.1111/ruso.12267.
10. Jill Lindsey Harrison and Sarah E. Lloyd, "New Jobs, New Workers, and New Inequalities: Explaining Employers' Roles in Occupational Segregation by Nativity and Race," *Social Problems* 60, no. 3 (2013): 281–301, https://doi.org/10.1525/sp.2013.60.3.281.
11. Ruth Wilson Gilmore, "Abolition Geography and the Problem of Innocence," in *Futures of Black Radicalism*, ed. Gaye Theresa Johnson and Alex Lubin (London: Verso, 2017), 225–40; see also Kris Manjapra, "Plantation Dispossessions: The Global Travel of Agricultural Racial Capitalism," in *American Capitalism: New Histories*, ed. Sven Beckert and Christine Desan (New York: Columbia University Press, 2018), 361–88.
12. Lisa Lowe, *The Intimacies of Four Continents* (Durham, NC: Duke University Press, 1995), 149.
13. Moon-Ho Jung, *Coolies and Cane: Race, Labor, and Sugar in the Age of Emancipation* (Baltimore, MD: Johns Hopkins University Press, 2006), 83.
14. Lowe, *Intimacies of Four Continents*.
15. Cindy Hahamovitch, *No Man's Land: Jamaican Guestworkers in America and the Global History of Deportable Labor* (Princeton, NJ: Princeton University Press, 2011), 88.
16. Teresa Mares, *Life on the Other Border: Farmworkers and Food Justice in Vermont* (Berkeley: University of California Press, 2019), 18. Migrant Justice was formed in the aftermath of a workplace fatality on a Vermont dairy farm. In December 2009, José Obeth Santiz Cruz, a young migrant worker from Chiapas, was strangled when his clothing became tangled in a manure scraper. Community members originally came together to raise the funds necessary to repatriate his body, with a small delegation traveling to Mexico for Santiz Cruz's funeral. This group evolved into the organization now known as Migrant Justice. Thatcher Moats, "After Migrant Worker's Farm Death, Advocates Hope to Bring Changes," *Barre Montpelier Times Argus*, January 9, 2010, https://www.timesargus.com/news/after-migrant-worker-s-farm-death-advocates-hope-to-bring/article_2ca40b29-3bb8-5b5a-82d7-2d264acf89e4.html.
17. Julie C. Keller, Margaret Gray, and Jill Lindsey Harrison, "Milking Workers, Breaking Bodies: Health Inequality in the Dairy Industry," *New Labor Forum* 26, no. 1 (January 2017): 36–44.
18. Mares, *Life on the Other Border*, 44.
19. Arvind Dilawar, "Undocumented Workers Are Especially Vulnerable to Border Patrol in Vermont," *Pacific Standard*, July 19, 2019, https://psmag.com/social-justice/undocumented-workers-are-especially-vulnerable-to-border-patrol-in-vermont.

20. Merrill Bent, "A Land of Milk and Honey: Dairy Farms, H-2A Workers, and Change on the Horizon," *Vermont Law Review* 35, no. 3 (2011): 746–47.
21. Timothy Kelsey, "The Agrarian Myth and Policy Responses to Farm Safety," *American Journal of Public Health* 84, no. 7 (July 1994): 1171–77, https://doi.org/10.2105/ajph.84.7.1171; see also Eli Wolfe, "Death on a Small Farm," *The Atlantic*, November 28, 2018.
22. James J. Brudney, "Decent Labour Standards in Corporate Supply Chains," in *Temporary Labour Migration in the Global Era: The Regulatory Challenges*, ed. Joanna Howe and Rosemary Owens (Oxford: Hart, 2016), 351–76.
23. Nonmigrant workers that meet the program's definition for "qualifying workers" also receive the $50 monthly bonus and enjoy all the same protections (access to health and safety equipment, etc.) that migrant workers receive under the program. However, because they typically live in the surrounding community, they are less likely to experience the housing upgrades that are a significant benefit for the migrant workers living on the farm.
24. Vermont's minimum wage was raised to $10 an hour in 2017 by a state law that also mandates for an automatic inflation-related adjustment to the wage on January 1 of each year. On January 1, 2021, the minimum wage increased from $10.96 to $11.75. The following year it increased to $12.55. However, the Vermont statute excludes "any individual employed in agriculture," along with a few other groups, from these minimum wage protections. 21 V.S.A. § 383 (2021).
25. Mares, *Life on the Other Border*, 12.
26. James MacDonald et al., *Profits, Costs, and the Changing Structure of Dairy Farming*, United States Department of Agriculture Economic Research Service Report Number 47 (2007), https://www.ers.usda.gov/publications/pub-details?pubid=45870.
27. Vermont Department of Financial Regulation, Act No. 129 (2020), *Report: Vermont Dairy Industry Price Regulation: Assessment and Recommendations*, January 15, 2021.
28. Congressional Research Service, *Dairy Provisions in USMC*, IF11149, ver. 3, https://fas.org/sgp/crs/row/IF11149.pdf.
29. Government Accountability Office, *Dairy Cooperatives: Potential Implications of Consolidation and Investments in Dairy Processing for Farmers*, GAO-19-695R Dairy Cooperative, https://www.gao.gov/assets/710/701795.pdf.
30. David L. Baumer, Robert T. Masson, and Robin A. Masson, "Curdling the Competition: An Economic and Legal Analysis of the Antitrust Exemption for Agriculture," *Villanova Law Review* 31, no. 1 (1986): 183–252.
31. With 108 of the 307 voting members of St. Alban's participating, the vote was 99 to 9 in favor of the merger.
32. Dan Kaufman, "Is It Time to Break Up Big Ag?" *New Yorker*, August 17, 2021.
33. Baumer, Masson, and Masson, "Curdling the Competition," 185.
34. Sarah Phillips, "The Future of Dairy Cooperatives in the Modern Marketplace: Redeveloping the Capper-Volstead Act," *Dickinson Law Review* 124, no. 1 (2019): 175–202.
35. Peter C. Carstensen, "Agricultural Cooperatives and the Law: Obsolete Statutes in a Dynamic Economy," *South Dakota Law Review* 58, no. 3 (2013): 462–98.

36. Kaufman, "Is It Time to Break Up Big Ag?"
37. Dean Foods was particularly affected by Walmart's decision to forward integrate into bottling. The retailer built a large bottling plant in Indiana to bottle its store brand of milk, which had previously been done by Dean Foods. The loss of Walmart's private label business led Dean Foods to terminate supply relationships with more than a hundred independent dairy farmers. Other grocery chains, including Kroger and Food Lion, preceded Walmart in making the move into milk bottling.
38. Jacob Bunge, "Regulators Probe Potential Dean Foods Merger," *Wall Street Journal*, January 27, 2020, https://www.wsj.com/articles/regulators-probe-potential-dean-foods-merger-11580147236.
39. Department of Justice, Office of Public Affairs, "Justice Department Requires Divestitures as Dean Foods Sells Fluid Milk Processing Plants to DFA Out of Bankruptcy," May 1, 2020, https://www.justice.gov/opa/pr/justice-department-requires-divestitures-dean-foods-sells-fluid-milk-processing-plants-dfa.
40. Andrew Martin, "In Dairy Industry Consolidation, Lush Paydays," *New York Times*, October 27, 2012.
41. Phillips, "The Future of Dairy Cooperatives," 196. In July 2011, Dean Foods and the plaintiffs in the southeast case, *Sweetwater Valley Farm, Inc. v. Dean Foods Co.*, No. 2:07–CV 208 (E.D. Tenn. Jun. 15, 2012) reached a settlement of $140 million. In January 2013, the same month that the price-fixing trial was set to open in Greenville, Tennessee, a settlement between DFA and the farmers, also in the amount of $140 million, was entered. In the northeast case, *Allen v. Dairy Farmers of America, Inc.*, No. 5:09-cv-00230 (D. Vt. Aug. 15, 2011), Dean Foods settled the case in 2010 for $30 million. Seven more years passed before a $50 million settlement between DFA and two subclasses of farmers was finalized in April 2017. Allen v. Dairy Farmers of Am., Inc., No. 5:09-CV-230 (D. Vt. June 7, 2016), *aff'd sub nom*. Haar v. Allen, 687 F. App'x 93 (2d Cir. 2017). Subsequent years saw additional legal action against DFA, including a case brought by farmers that opted out of the 2016 settlement, which was settled in September 2020. In 2022, two lawsuits were brought against DFA by farmers alleging the cooperative engaged in anti-competitive practices in different regions of the United States. One class action lawsuit, filed in U.S. District Court in Vermont on behalf of dairies in the northeast, was dismissed in 2023, but at the time of writing a second case involving dairy farmers in the southwest was proceeding in U.S. District Court in New Mexico. See Mike Scarella, "Dairy Collectives Must Face Farmers' Milk Price-Fixing Lawsuit, US Judge Rules," *Reuters*, March 12, 2024, https://www.reuters.com/legal/litigation/dairy-collectives-must-face-farmers-milk-price-fixing-lawsuit-us-judge-rules-2024-03-12/.
42. Leah Douglas, "How Rural America Got Milked," *Washington Monthly*, January 7, 2018, 28, https://washingtonmonthly.com/2018/01/07/how-rural-america-got-milked/
43. Janet Halley, "Distribution and Decision: Assessing Governance Feminism," in *Governance Feminism: An Introduction*, ed. Janet Halley, Prabha Kotiswaran, Rachel Rebouché, and Hila Shamir (Minneapolis: University of Minnesota Press: 2018), 253 (italics removed).
44. The letter explained that COVID-19 had transformed the lack of dairy workers from a persistent problem into an acute crisis because "as more and more Americans have

to remain home to care for children who are out of school or care for other loved ones, there are even fewer workers available to work on our nation's farms." National Milk Producers Federation to Eugene Scalia and Sonny Purdue, April 9, 2020, https://www.nmpf.org/wp-content/uploads/2020/04/Letter-NMPF-on-H2A-Enrollment-DOL-USDA-4.09.2020.pdf. It is perhaps telling that a *global* pandemic, which affects workers and their families worldwide, is enlisted to explain why *foreign* workers are needed to fill the dairy industry's workforce needs, as if H-2A visa holders are uniquely invulnerable to the disruptions caused by COVID.

45. Hannaford's parent company is the Dutch multinational Ahold Delhaize, which acquired it in 2000.

CHAPTER 12

BEYOND ESSENTIAL

Growth, a Pandemic, and the Future of Expendable Workers in a "Progressive" Texas Boomtown

KAREN ENGLE AND SAMUEL TABORY

In this chapter, we take seriously the possibility of an urban-regional political economy not centered around growth—whether economic, physical, or population growth. Specifically, we consider what projects that aim to distribute along visions of diminished or limited growth, sometimes termed "degrowth," might mean for the future of work and workers in a particular urban-regional political economy for which growth itself, as well as the workers who enable it, have been deemed essential. At the same time, we contemplate the challenges of even questioning growth-oriented orthodoxy.

Using the situation of low-wage Latino construction workers in the rapidly growing Austin, Texas, region (Austin region)—many of whom are undocumented—we revisit and engage with two related moments during the COVID-19 pandemic. We use the juxtaposition of these moments as a window into an interrogation of the past, present, and future of Austin's specific brand of growth politics, which has long represented and promoted Austin as a "progressive" boomtown economy.[1] What work does that economy deem essential? Which workers does it render expendable, and how? Who bears the cost of social reproduction in the boomtown? What livelihoods might be pursued in a differently oriented economy?

In the first moment, early in the pandemic, the state of Texas declared workers in the already dangerous and under regulated Texas construction industry "essential." As a result, low-income workers in the industry bore outsized health risks, in part because of long-standing cumulative economic insecurity that made it difficult, if not impossible, for many not to work during the early stages of the pandemic. In the second moment, only a few months later, local officials decided to provide tens of millions of dollars of tax incentives to attract a major corporate manufacturing project to the region. It did so even as local resources for pandemic emergency response efforts aimed at low-income undocumented workers were proving inadequate.

Growth is at the center of both stories. Between 2010 and 2019, the Austin region was the fastest growing major metropolitan area in the United States in terms of population.[2] From 2016 to 2021, it ranked as the third fastest growing metropolitan economy by real GDP.[3] The transformation of the built environment via a robust construction sector constitutes one of the most significant physical effects of this growth. From 2010 to 2020, employment in the construction sector in the Austin region grew by some 28,000 jobs, or nearly 70 percent, with more than 69,000 construction workers employed in the region by the first quarter of 2020.[4] Latino workers, many undocumented, perform a large number of the low-income jobs in that sector. Austin's high rate of growth has received a great deal of national attention. Yet growth—with its attendant narratives, imaginaries, aspirations, and fears—has been for decades at the center of heated local-regional debates about issues ranging from gentrification to environmental harm.

In what follows, mobilizing the methodologies and critical traditions of distributional analysis, world-systems theory, and racial capitalism, we trace some of the background(ed) rules conditioning each of these stories, ultimately charting connections between Austin's specific brand of growth politics—reinforced by a legal and policy apparatus spanning multiple levels of government—and the conditions of precarity that define the low-income construction workforce. Although their work was deemed essential, these workers have long been made expendable due to highly racialized laws and politics involving labor, immigration, and growth. We then consider what insights we might glean from this combination of stories, occurring during (even if not unique to) the pandemic, for attempts to distribute differently. Specifically, how might we confront or curtail certain manifestations of growth politics while also attending to the precarity of workers who seem to depend upon growth?

THE AUSTIN REGION IN AN AGE OF PANDEMIC

On March 24, 2020, in response to COVID-19, the City of Austin and Travis County, of which Austin is the seat, issued stay-at-home orders for all but those engaged in "essential work," a term defined in reference to activities that support "critical infrastructure." That order designated only some limited construction, such as of public works and affordable housing, as essential.[5]

A week later, the Texas governor Greg Abbott provided a different understanding of critical infrastructure, and therefore of essential work. On March 31, he issued an executive order to supersede local orders, effectively defining "essential" services in Texas to include *all* construction.[6] The governor based his order on then recent changes in the U.S. Department of Homeland Security's (DHS) Guidance on the Essential Critical Infrastructure Workforce, which, though only advisory and not followed by all states, had been promoted by the construction industry.[7] A core assumption baked into the governor's order, and the updated DHS guidance it was based on, was that infrastructure services (including construction) to support physical—and attendant economic and population—growth are essential.

In the months that followed, clinical and public health data, media reporting, and, ultimately, epidemiological modeling, pointed toward the construction sector as an early COVID-19 hotspot in Austin. Low-income Latino construction workers, many undocumented, were hit hard. The University of Texas at Austin's Dell Seton Medical Center, a hospital that primarily serves low-income and uninsured individuals—85 percent of whom are Latino—began noticing alarming trends in occupational data from the COVID-19 patients it was treating. Between late March 2020 and late May 2020, some 37 percent of patients reported working in construction, far surpassing other large occupational categories including cleaning and hotel workers (10 percent), health care workers (10 percent), and food service workers (14 percent).[8] Epidemiological analysis of COVID-19 hospitalization risk for workers in the Austin region released in late October 2020 associates the decision to allow "unrestricted construction work" with construction workers being five times more likely than workers in other occupational categories to have been hospitalized for COVID-19.[9]

If in principle protected by most labor and employment law, undocumented immigrants are not entitled to federal emergency relief or social services, some of which might have eased economic pressures that compelled many to continue working during the early stages of the pandemic. In response to this gap in relief services, a number of states (although not Texas) and local governments (including the City of Austin and Travis County) made available funds for those who did not qualify for federal relief. Travis County residents could apply for City of Austin RISE (Relief in a State of Emergency) funds, which provided up to $2,000 to eligible households. At least initially, with the hope of reaching those who might be wary of applying for relief directly from the government, local government enlisted nonprofit community-based and advocacy organizations to distribute the funds.[10]

The RISE funds are in line with many attempts by the City of Austin and Travis County to push back on, or at least mitigate, state and federal policies on a number of issues concerned with the well-being of workers, often undocumented workers. These efforts range from improved working conditions and secure housing to so-called sanctuary city policies around immigration enforcement. As explained later, conservatives have aggressively and often successfully sought to block the ability of local jurisdictions in Texas to enact these policies, thereby contributing to the production of very particular forms of social vulnerability for Latino construction workers.

At the same time that the city and county have attempted to provide at least some worker protections, they have also participated in—both independently and via complex interactions with the state—the perpetuation of a racialized labor market and larger urban-regional political economy that depends upon the exploitation and dispossession of the very people who literally build the region. The average annual wage for construction workers in Austin ($32,960) is lower than both the statewide average for such workers ($34,980) and the national average ($43,000).[11] This disparity is indicative of the challenges that low-wage workers face, even and especially in the "progressive" Austin region.

In July 2020, amid a surge of coronavirus cases in the Austin region, both Travis County and the Del Valle Independent School District (DVISD) were separately finalizing negotiations with Tesla to locate a billion-dollar electric vehicle manufacturing plant for its future Cybertruck in Del Valle, an edge community some fifteen minutes southeast of downtown Austin. DVISD, which is 85 percent Latino, is one of the lowest-income communities in the Austin region, not having benefited from the same level of investment and economic growth that has been so central to the experience of the larger Austin region in the last several decades. In these negotiations, Tesla sought—and ultimately received—significant tax incentives from both the school district and the county. In negotiations that took shape rapidly (over the course of two months in June and July 2020), DVISD offered $46 million in property tax breaks, and Travis County agreed to provide an additional $14 million in tax incentives.

DVISD's offered tax relief mobilized a specific incentive program that was then in effect, known as Chapter 313 (named after its place in the Texas Tax Code), which provided tax incentives for corporations that claimed the relevant tax incentives would be a "determining factor" in their decision to invest.[12] Using a formula in the code, the Tesla plant's property value for tax purposes was capped for ten years at $80 million, resulting in $776,000 per year in taxes for that period. In fact, the facility was estimated to have a value of $1.1 billion, which would have resulted in $5 million per year in taxes. Chapter 313 also allowed qualifying companies to make "supplemental payments" to school districts for their unrestricted use, with a cap based on the number of students in average daily attendance. Tesla agreed to pay the maximum supplemental amount allowed to DVISD, which will yield nearly $1 million per year for the school district through 2034.[13]

Travis County used its own policies and procedures for "competitively sited projects" to offer Tesla tax incentives.[14] As a condition for that tax relief, the county required that the project create as least 5,001 new full-time jobs by 2023 with a minimum wage of $15 per hour, provided that the average annual salary for employees at the plant totals at least $47,147 before benefits (to be annually adjusted based on the Consumer Price Index). As a result of the work of labor advocates, the agreement also required that not only Tesla employees, but all contracted construction, janitorial, and food service workers at the plant, be paid at least $15 per hour.

With the negotiation and public comment processes for both the school board and county commissioners court happening parallel to one another (each clearly influencing the other), the terms of debate emerging from each process were largely similar. Public comments—from speakers representing community development organizations, labor advocacy organizations, industry groups, interfaith community representatives, individual workers, and residents, among others—generally acknowledged the importance of a project that could bring relatively high-paying jobs to both the region, generally, and to Del Valle, specifically, particularly for workers without a college degree.[15] To the extent that concerns were expressed, they were largely related to the rushed nature of the deliberation process or to the lack of sufficient enforcement and accountability mechanisms to hold Tesla to its commitments. The somewhat staid pushback to the project seemed to indicate a general belief in, or at least strategic acquiescence to, a stance that sees growth as necessary for the region even, if not especially, in the uncertain age of a pandemic.

Even progressive labor advocates generally did not explicitly oppose the use of subsidies, at least publicly (despite having expressed general opposition to them in the past).[16] Instead, they used their public comments to leverage the subsides as a tool for shaping specific protections and monitoring mechanisms to make any agreement as robust as possible for workers. Given the history of the state's undermining of local governmental efforts to achieve fair wages and working conditions, perhaps leveraging the incentive agreement seemed the most promising avenue to secure protections for workers.

Proponents of the project touted the middle-class manufacturing jobs and the economic investment the project promised to bring to a largely under-invested-in part of the Austin region. For example, Travis County Commissioner Jeff Travillion characterized the project as "transformational" because it would "address poverty and opportunity in [Del Valle] for generations."[17] The DVISD superintendent Annette Tielle separately said, "we want our students to have opportunities, and this is something we know will take them to high heights."[18] The DVISD trustee Susana Woody, who was more ambivalent about the project (ultimately voting against the agreement, citing the rushed deliberations), underscored the generally neglected position of Del Valle in larger conversations about regional prosperity, remarking that she had "never seen so much attention given to the Del Valle area and the Del Valle community since [Tesla's] announcement of possibly relocating here. To all of those who have ignored us for decades, welcome to Del Valle."[19]

Relevant to the school district's negotiating and decision-making posture were two interacting state laws regarding school finance. The first is a 1993 law referred to as the "Robin Hood" law.[20] It redistributes the portion of local property tax that "property rich" districts collect above the state-determined per-pupil funding levels to "property poor" districts without a sufficient tax base to meet those levels. The second relevant law concerns the already mentioned Chapter 313 program, the state's largest corporate tax incentive program. Combined, these two laws created an incentive structure in which school districts, whether "property-rich" or "property-poor," have no financial reason *not* to agree to lower tax valuations for large corporate investments. Per-pupil funding levels are determined by the state and do not depend upon property taxes collected in any given district. Raising additional tax revenues would therefore not increase per-pupil funding levels.

This arrangement makes Chapter 313's provision for supplemental payments particularly attractive. In the Tesla case, DVISD is set to receive close to $15 million over fifteen years, none of which, because it is not tax revenue, could be subject to recapture under the so-called Robin Hood law. That DVISD would not have benefited from taxing Tesla at its full property value, of course, does not mean that the State of Texas did not take a hit in terms of lost public revenue potential. That the cumulative effect of Chapter 313 agreements statewide has yielded significantly lower property tax revenues, even beyond the terms of the agreements, led to the program's failure to attract enough support for renewal. Governor Abbott, however, has called for the program's reinstatement, and several other incentive arrangements are under consideration.[21] Regardless of whether Chapter 313 is reinitiated, the effects of the program will continue to be felt for years to come.

Lack of significant opposition to the specific deployment of corporate subsidies for Tesla, during a time of open debate about the adequacy of public relief expenditure amid the pandemic, is striking. For example, just two months earlier, when Travis County had announced an allocation of $10 million in emergency funds specifically for rental and mortgage assistance, community advocates and county economic development staff alike acknowledged that allocated funds would represent only "a drop in the bucket" of overall community need across the county, with Commissioner Brigid Shea acknowledging a "tsunami of need" even prepandemic.[22] And when the city made available $40 million in various forms of relief (including but not limited to the above-mentioned RISE funds), community advocates argued that addressing the real level of pandemic-related need at the time would have required allocations of funds closer to $70 million. Furthermore, as one union representative for state employees pointed out during the public comments on Tesla, the county had recently denied cost-of-living raises to even its own employees on the ground that the "funds weren't there."[23]

Of course, the pandemic did not create, but rather exacerbated and exposed, long-standing racialized legal, political, geographic, and economic drivers of precarity and risk experienced by low-income construction workers in the region.[24] But the background(ed) laws and policies that we chart in the next two sections played out in particularly stark and dramatic ways during the pandemic.

THE MAKING OF ESSENTIAL WORK BUT EXPENDABLE WORKERS: AN ARRAY OF BACKGROUND RULES

When construction workers started showing up in Austin hospitals with severe COVID-19 in disproportionate numbers, many advocates, quite rightly, began to focus on drafting and enforcing public and occupational health regulations designed to address immediate worker risk. The City of Austin, for example, issued updated guidance from its original regulations at the very outset of the pandemic, outlining additional safety requirements for construction sites with more than ten workers.[25] These policies, however useful in directly addressing acute concerns of immediate risk, had limited impact on the long-term, structurally produced precarity that these workers and other members of their communities face.

As others have identified for some time, several aspects of the construction industry play a significant role in the production of Latino worker precarity in this industry in Austin (and elsewhere). These factors, although often stated neutrally, in fact both depend upon and produce differentiations based on ethnicity, language, and documentation status. They include (1) wide reliance on subcontractors and the challenge of regulating safety across dispersed, small-scale work sites;[26] (2) the specific prevalence of a U.S. model of low investment in worker skills and safety training, resulting in high turnover due to lack of sustainable career paths, injury, and burnout;[27] (3) a general industry posture of deferring safety-net costs onto society at large;[28] and (4) an industry standard of cutting labor costs in order to enhance profit margins.[29]

An array of legal rules permits, if not produces, these factors and their distributive effects, which are of course neither necessary nor unique to the construction industry. In this section, we foreground some of the broad overlapping and intersecting legal and policy regimes that play a significant role in producing the precarity of low-income Latino construction workers, including as manifested during the COVID-19 pandemic, with a focus on immigration and state preemption of local regulations. These legal and policy regimes build on and interact with the legal and policy postures undergirding Austin's model of boomtown growth, discussed in the next section.

Immigration Law and Policy

An anti-immigrant climate looms over much of the United States, even in those cities and regions that claim to be safe zones for undocumented immigrants. At the same time, the U.S. economy has long depended on undocumented migration, particularly from Latin America, to fill low-paying jobs, with push-pull processes that are difficult to disentangle from the history of U.S. imperialism and the U.S. role in the global capitalist world-system. U.S. immigration law, particularly through strategic enforcement uncertainty, facilitates employer exploitation of workers' irregular immigration status to produce long-standing patterns of labor force racialization. These patterns manifest themselves in the construction sector at the global, national, and local levels.[30] In Texas, as many as 70 percent of construction workers are Latino, mostly from Mexico and Central America, and half of those Latino workers are estimated to be undocumented.[31]

It is well-established that undocumented workers are reluctant to express concerns about unsafe working conditions or wage theft, both of which are rife in the construction industry.[32] Dramatic and high-profile escalations of federal immigration enforcement actions under the first Trump administration heightened that reluctance in the early stages of the pandemic, with particularly significant health consequences for the many undocumented workers—and their household members—whose work was deemed essential in the early days of the pandemic.

The fear of immigration surveillance and enforcement also complicated undocumented immigrants' decisions about seeking medical testing and care.[33]

Even documented immigrants have not been immune to the effects of immigration law on access to relief and medical care. The Trump administration's "public charge rule," through which accessing public benefits could lead to ineligibility for citizenship, in effect from February 2020 until March 2021, significantly complicated decisions to seek relief.[34] Even before COVID-19, for example, the rule was leading some immigrants, including those in mixed-status households, to forgo access to benefits to which they or their family members were otherwise entitled out of fear of inadvertently attracting scrutiny.[35] Moreover, although COVID-19 testing and care in emergency rooms or free clinics formally had no bearing on public charge evaluations, there was substantial confusion on this point, in part because of statements issued by the U.S. Citizenship and Immigration Services suggesting that applicants would need to submit "evidence of any benefits used for such testing or treatment."[36]

Both generally and under pandemic conditions, immigration law and its enforcement dictate a large number of decisions that migrant workers face daily, including whether to seek medical, financial, or legal assistance, whether to organize as workers, or even whether to talk to researchers. As discussed in the next section, although immigration law is federal, states and municipalities often affect how and when it is enforced. Even when undocumented workers have jobs that are deemed essential, their potential deportability—and expendability—always looms in the background.

State Preemption: Thwarted Local Policy Agendas

As exemplified by the first moment discussed earlier, the State of Texas has often preempted decisions of local government, with significant impact on the ability of local governments to protect workers.[37] Specifically, it has thwarted local efforts to provide various types of protections for immigrants, mandate minimum wage and sick leave, and make available affordable housing policy tools. In doing so, the state has asserted its authority over immigration enforcement and reinforced the background legal rules of property and contract that construct and maintain the balance of power in favor of employers over employees. In the Austin region, this preemption has yielded cumulative social and economic effects that compound low-income Latino worker precarity in ways that are emblematic of a state-level policy commitment to a pro-business and pro-growth environment that is both dependent upon and at the expense of certain workers.

LOCAL SANCTUARY POLICIES

The City of Austin and Travis County have long attempted to push back against anti-immigrant sentiments. By 2016, many people called Austin a sanctuary city, based on some immigrant friendly, if unenforceable, measures adopted by the City Council.[38] In 2017, Travis County elected a sheriff who campaigned on a promise to protect immigrant communities from federal immigration enforcement.[39] Once in office, she put in place a policy against complying with U.S. Immigration and Customs Enforcement (ICE) detainers placed on individuals who were not charged with serious offenses.[40]

Shortly thereafter, the Texas legislature passed Senate Bill 4 (SB 4), which prohibits city and county officials from passing laws or policies that prevent local cooperation with ICE and other federal immigration enforcement agencies.[41] A number of local jurisdictions, including Austin and Travis County, brought legal challenges against SB 4.[42] In 2018, a federal court of appeals rejected those challenges, largely leaving the law in place.[43] In 2019, the number of ICE detainers honored by Travis County grew by 82 percent. Cooperation between the Austin Police Department and ICE also increased, notwithstanding two additional ordinances passed by the Austin City Council to attempt to reduce SB 4's impact.[44]

The controversy around SB 4 in Austin (and in other large cities in Texas) has been one of the highest profile examples to date of state preemption. SB 4 both contributes to the anti-immigrant policy and legal climate and highlights the limits of local leadership's ability to respond to harms generated by state and federal policies.

MINIMUM WAGE AND SICK LEAVE REQUIREMENTS

The City of Austin has attempted to improve worker benefits but has been undermined by state legislative action and judicial interpretation. As the Tesla example shows, there would likely be political will for the city to increase the minimum wage, but the 2003 Texas Minimum Wage Act (TMWA) bars local governments from establishing a mandatory minimum wage higher than the federal minimum wage.[45]

The TMWA has been interpreted broadly, in one instance in response to a 2018 City of Austin ordinance requiring all private employers to provide paid sick leave.[46] A number of private businesses and business associations brought suit to enjoin the ordinance, claiming that it was preempted by the TMWA. The state intervened on behalf of the plaintiffs. A Texas appeals court ruled against the city, reasoning that sick leave constituted a "wage" under the TMWA.[47] Courts enjoined similar ordinances in Dallas and San Antonio. While awaiting judicial rulings, worker advocates successfully blocked state legislation that would have explicitly prohibited municipalities from requiring private employers to pay sick leave. Even without the legislation, however, judicial interpretation ultimately achieved the same result.

By taking away this power from cities, the state effectively offers a subsidy to employers who might otherwise be compelled to pay living wages more appropriate for their urban-regional context. In the Austin region, that wage has generally been identified as at least $15 per hour, with many community advocates contending that it would need to be much higher.

AFFORDABLE HOUSING POLICY TOOLS

In 2014, the City of Austin passed an ordinance prohibiting housing discrimination based on source of rental income, aimed at ensuring that individuals would not be denied housing if they were to pay rent with federal housing vouchers or other forms of listed assistance.[48] Shortly thereafter, Governor Abbott signed Senate Bill 267, which preempted a portion of the ordinance by prohibiting municipalities from adopting or enforcing laws that prohibit discrimination against individuals who would pay rent with federal housing assistance.[49]

Low-income workers in general have a difficult time finding housing when source of income discrimination is permitted. Although undocumented immigrants are excluded from receiving federal housing assistance, they too might be affected by such discrimination. Undocumented immigrants may live, either in moments of acute need or on a semipermanent basis, in mixed status households that also include citizens or lawful residents.

Additional affordable housing tools that are banned by Texas law but regularly used by local governments in other states include so-called linkage fees, which charge developers—as part of the development approval process—fees to be used in the creation of local affordable housing supply; inclusionary zoning for owner-occupied units requiring that a certain percentage of units of a given project be priced below market rate; and laws limiting the conversion of rental units to condominiums.[50] The broad preemption of these policy instruments directly affects housing affordability for low-income workers, including Latino construction workers.

"ESSENTIAL" GROWTH IN A "PROGRESSIVE" BOOMTOWN

The previous section highlighted several attempts by the City of Austin to enact and defend laws and policies that explicitly aim to provide greater protection for the work and livelihood of some of the most vulnerable members of the regional community. That it pushes actively against the state on so many issues is one reason the city has built and claimed a reputation as progressive, even as a boomtown.

Yet many have long questioned Austin's self-understood progressive identity, pointing to the ways that the city's "growth machine" is implicated in explicit histories of racialized dispossession, wealthy (largely white) property owners' hostility to affordable housing and accessible density, racialized environmental harm, and the city's pursuit of superficial and commodified postures of sustainable urbanism in service of neoliberal place branding.[51] Building on these critiques, we aim to show how Austin uses its progressive identity, particularly as a blue city within a red state, to sustain a model of growth that has decidedly nonprogressive effects. Furthermore, we demonstrate how important city and county actors use that progressive identity to disguise many of the ways in which local government provides numerous subsidies to corporate interests in the interest of growth. Law and policy decisions undergird and fundamentally shape the deeply racialized social and political landscape of the Austin region's "boomtown" economy.

Over the past two decades, the increasingly high cost of living in the Austin area and the demolition of older (often more affordable) housing stock for new (often luxury) residential or commercial development have driven communities of color from the City of Austin, particularly from the long-standing Black and Latino neighborhoods of central east Austin.[52] This gentrification has pushed many Latino residents to the larger "eastern crescent" of Travis County, which includes Del Valle. Some of DVISD has been annexed by the City of Austin, and other parts remain unincorporated. Even parts of the "eastern crescent" are now experiencing displacement pressures.[53] In recent years, the size of the Latino population has declined in the City of Austin, while increasing dramatically in neighboring counties.[54]

The effects of displacement can be exacerbated by jurisdictional fragmentation across a wider metropolitan region. For example, when low-income Latino construction workers are pushed by economic factors to relocate outside of the City of Austin or Travis County, they may be moving to jurisdictions with a substantially different capacity or ethos in terms of providing services and support for low-income and undocumented workers, or with a more permissive approach to collaboration and cooperation with federal immigration authorities.

The precarity experienced by communities of color facing displacement in the region has a long trajectory, a not insignificant part of which can be traced to a 1928 Austin city plan that formally racially divided east and west Austin. Among other effects, that plan facilitated racial "redlining" of mortgage underwriting well into the 1940s.[55]

Current displacement pressures interact not only with histories of explicit racial segregation but also with more recent histories of competing environmental movements in Austin dating to the 1980s and 1990s. Specifically, concern for sensitive ecological zones on Austin's wealthier and whiter west side, and the related activism that eventually led to an ordinance (Save Our Springs, or SOS) that protected the west side's Barton Creek Watershed from development, is directly entangled with gentrification in Austin's previously majority-minority east side. As a result of the so-called smart growth policy paradigm emerging out of SOS activism, and what many see as a compromise with private development interests, the city designated much of the central east side as a "targeted development zone," intended to allow, but still spatially contain, new development that might otherwise have spread west.[56]

Capitalizing on depressed ground rents that were a function of a long history of racist segregation and disinvestment, that move exacerbated decades of racist zoning policies that had already pushed undesirable and polluting industrial land uses to the east side. While activists on the west side rallied around blocking development in the name of protecting a watershed, activists and community advocates on the east side made powerful and damning, although to some degree less successful, arguments about the long-standing lack of environmental justice considerations for east side residents. They pushed for the preservation of green space and won the closure of at least some polluted industrial sites; at the same time, they were fighting against displacement to ensure that residents would have the opportunity to stay and benefit from hard-won environmental justice gains.[57]

Hidden Subsidies of Growth

Notwithstanding these policies, both past and present, Austin has managed for decades to sell itself as "progressive," including to potential corporate investors. The Austin Chamber of Commerce, for instance, answers the question it poses on its website, "Why the Austin region?," with the following: "Austin is a one-of-a-kind place that defies stereotypes. It is progressive and fiercely entrepreneurial; pro-business and pro-environment; easy going and hardworking."[58] This message interacts with related narratives around Austin being a "creative city" home to a "high-skilled knowledge economy."[59] Austin is not alone in this strategy. Detailed academic literature charts mutually reinforcing relationships across such narratives and how they are used to establish urban-regional competitive economic advantage.[60]

The Austin Chamber of Commerce also boasts that the region has an "affordable cost of living" that is "significantly lower than many major markets," even as the cost of living relative to local benchmarks is rising dramatically.[61] Businesses might benefit, but who is paying the costs associated with the social and economic arrangements that make any so-called regional low-cost of living possible? This question is fundamentally about the distribution of the costs of growth. Many of those costs are borne by low-income workers, including those who put their labor toward the physical construction involved in growth, when—due to lack of individual or social safety nets—they have an economic imperative to work for low wages even amid dangerous conditions. At the same time, multiple subsidy mechanisms ensure that large corporate actors actively benefit from, but are only minimally saddled with responsibility for supporting, broader conditions of urban-regional social reproduction. In addition to a low minimum wage and the absence of required sick leave prohibited by preemption, a variety of legal and policy rules that promote boomtown growth conditions create subsidies that distribute often unacknowledged value to large corporate actors, while pushing the costs of growth increasingly onto individual workers and residents.

LOW TAX BURDEN

The individual tax burden in the Austin region is roughly 15 to 18 percent less than the national average. The Austin Chamber of Commerce touts Texas's lack of a state personal income tax as an enticing proposition for corporations wanting to court employees.[62] With no personal income tax, state and local sales tax makes up a combined 44 percent of all tax collected in the state. Local property tax provides nearly 35 percent, making Texas fifth in the country in its reliance on property tax and eleventh on sales tax.[63] Sales tax is a particularly regressive form of taxation, with the poor paying a higher share of their income than the wealthy on the tax. Although in principle progressive, on-the-ground assessment and collection of property taxes in Texas raise concerns for those who might wish to ensure that wealthy corporations (and wealthy homeowners) shoulder a greater burden of supplying public revenue.

Specifically, corporations are particularly well positioned to reduce their property tax liability because Texas law favors those who challenge the assessed value of their property by not requiring sales disclosure information to establish objective market value and by making local governments liable for the attorney costs of challengers who succeed. The law thus creates strong incentives for local governments to settle such proceedings, resulting in corporations being able to achieve assessed values of corporate land and property holdings well below their market value in an otherwise high-priced regional property market.[64] Although property tax assessment challenge processes are common nationwide and are seen by some as a key relief valve for individual homeowners overwhelmed by potentially dramatic increases in property taxes associated with fast-rising home values, they offer an easy mechanism for large corporations (and often, wealthy homeowners) to reduce their contributions to the tax base that supports the public infrastructures on which the thriving urban-regional economy from which they benefit is based. Such a scenario is doubly perverse because low-income homeowners who are most at risk of facing displacement pressures due to rising property tax liability (often pegged to rapidly rising property values in gentrifying markets) are generally less able to avail themselves of such safety valve reassessment measures, given the expense and bureaucratic wherewithal involved.

SUSTAINED PUBLIC INVESTMENT IN A HIGH-SKILLED KNOWLEDGE ECONOMY

The region's "knowledge economy" credentials, from which corporate actors benefit substantially, rest on a foundation of decades of public investment in and by the University of Texas at Austin's major research facilities as well as state and federal subsidies for the region's high-technology research and development industries.[65] In 1983, for example, amid the Austin region's nascent technology industry, the city successfully—and surprisingly—attracted the high-profile Microelectronics and Computer Consortium, which was conducting a national search for a suitable location. As a part of its bid, the university committed to funding thirty-two one-million-dollar endowed research chairs in engineering and computer science.[66]

Public investment in universities and other research institutions, independent of whether it is a direct means to lure corporations to the region, obviously generates broader social benefits. Although corporations widely recognize the importance of access to a highly educated workforce, the sustained public funds that make the university and research environments contributing to such a workforce possible in the first place are rarely acknowledged as a type of corporate subsidy. In the Austin region, private companies benefit substantially from decades of public participation in the planning of and investment in the locational economic agglomeration advantages of the region's particular style of high-skilled, high-technology economy.[67]

INCENTIVES FOR CORPORATE INVESTMENT/RELOCATION

Especially given the state's reliance on property taxes, tax abatements offered to Tesla and other large corporations significantly affect state revenue. This tax relief is a principal subsidy offered by local governments and taxing entities throughout the region to encourage businesses to relocate to the area.[68] To be sure, incentives offered by Travis County are generally contingent on a corporation meeting certain minimum wage and other conditions, with implications for first-order worker protections, such as those that cover workers directly involved in constructing a company's new site.[69] Or, as Travis County ultimately negotiated with Tesla, they might even set conditions involving employees who will eventually hold jobs either with the company or its subcontractors.

As noted previously, Chapter 313 agreements with school districts in Texas are aimed at projects for which the incentives are a "determining factor" in the company's decision to move to the state. Similar requirements are used around the country, notwithstanding a great deal of academic and policy analysis that has cast doubt on their necessity.[70] These criteria are of course premised on a counterfactual that is subject to a range of often unspecified qualitative and quantitative interpretive factors. In the Texas case, measures for verifying "determining factor" validity under the Chapter 313 program were woefully inadequate, according to Dick Lavine, Senior Fiscal Analyst for Every Texan. As he argued in testimony to the Texas House Ways and Means Committee, companies should have to do more than write "boiler plate letters saying, 'Well, you know, we do business in other states. We might not come to Texas.'" Instead, "[w]hat you really need is the CEO or the CFO to sign a sworn statement about the competing locations, why Texas is better. . . . They're asking for a special benefit, and they should be willing to open their books, at least to the extent that we can judge whether or not they really need this to come to Texas."[71]

The relative vagueness of Chapter 313's "determining factor" and the county's similarly constructed "competitively sited" project standards fail to require deeper reflection about the broader locational advantages sought by companies.[72]

That reflection should consider not only narrow approaches to tax relief but the entire set of regulatory, economic, and cultural dynamics that affect the attractiveness of a region.

Tesla Comes to Austin

The combined interaction of these various subsidies is captured well by the second moment with which we began this chapter: the saga of Tesla's recruitment to the region and ultimate decision to locate a billion-dollar electric vehicle manufacturing plant in Del Valle. It later announced its decision to relocate its company headquarters to the Austin region as well. As one of the richest people in the world, and as the founder of both Tesla and SpaceX, Elon Musk has made no secret of his interest in being less subject to the public regulatory and taxation regime he encountered in California. That he moved the Tesla headquarters, his personal foundation offices, and his own permanent residence to Texas further confirms this point.[73] Musk's move is part of a trend of high-technology companies decamping from California to establish or expand their presence in and around Austin, which they have found possesses a particularly attractive combination of ostensibly liberal cultural capital, an advanced research and development ecosystem, and a highly trained workforce, absent high public taxation and regulatory burdens. The software company Oracle, which already had a major campus in Austin, made public its decision to move its headquarters from California to Austin within days of Musk's announcement.[74]

Although Tesla made much of its intention to hire workers from the Del Valle and Austin areas, including many without a college degree, it has done little to acknowledge the roles that both historical disinvestment in east Austin and public investment in Austin's broader high-skilled, high-technology economy have played in its business interests. Tesla relies on the latter for the recruitment and retention of its own high-skilled employees, as well as for its larger sense of fit in a regional high-technology ecosystem.

Returning to the entanglements between the "Robin Hood" recapture plan regarding school financing (requiring the redistribution of local property tax revenue collected beyond what is required to meet state-determined per-pupil funding levels) and the Chapter 313 program, DVISD had no reason to take a risk that it might lose out on the broader opportunities that it believed a Tesla relocation could offer, even beyond the supplemental payments. Tesla might be making a direct investment in the physical jurisdiction of the Del Valle school district, but many of the thousands of future workers at the plant will have been educated by public school systems across the Austin region and the state of Texas (if not beyond), the very systems Tesla is substantially relieved of contributing to due to the tax abatement it received under Chapter 313. Policy makers who designed the recapture law created a mechanism for ensuring a general degree of formal equity in school financing, but that is not the same as prioritizing ongoing investments in public education.[75] An aggressively pro-business state legislature that works diligently to encourage local level tax abatements for corporate relocations by removing nearly all local downside cost via policy design is a constituent component of that lack of investment.

Musk has entered the growth politics fray directly, using his substantial public discourse influence via social media to make "urgent" calls for new housing construction in the Austin region, as well as to extend a call to workers from across the country to move to the region to work for Tesla and SpaceX.[76] At issue here is not only how Tesla, or any other major technology company moving to Austin, might treat their direct employees or those who are contracted to work on their sites. It is about the ways in which they shape and exacerbate the unequal distribution of burdens and benefits in a large, urban-regional political and economic unit. What would it mean for them to account more fully for their impact on the livelihoods of *all* workers in the region, including those who will be building the housing that Musk has called for? And what might it mean not to begin from the presumption that all growth is good for the region?

DISTRIBUTING DIFFERENTLY

Did someone die while building your office space or condo? Was the person who built your home actually paid for their work?
—Workers Defense Project 2019 Annual Report

For all the local critique of state preemption of broad areas of law and policy that might otherwise have favorable distributive effects for workers, that same preemption—alongside conservative state policies—also allows the Austin region to promote its low regulatory burdens and low taxes, as well as to underemphasize the extent to which it produces public subsidies for particular kinds of industry and workers. Consideration of low-income Latino construction workers offers both a stark example of, and a particularly fruitful inquiry into, the Austin region's growth economy, specifically into the degree to which growth is understood as essential, as well as into who reaps the benefits and bears the burdens of growth. In the region's current political economy, construction workers literally depend upon growth for their jobs and economic security, even as they live and work in conditions of precarity to facilitate that growth. But does it need to be this way? Could value be distributed differently, particularly within or through a degrowth posture, or simply in an economy less oriented toward growth?

Bringing together critical approaches to law and planning, we suggest four analytical pathways that might aid both academic and political projects seeking to engage with the retooling of value distributions that are embedded in the current background rules and dominant logics described in the legal and policy drivers already mentioned. First, any attempt to distribute differently needs to foreground the ways that private corporate viability and surplus accumulation depend upon public subsidies that go well beyond those explicitly made by local governmental entities to recruit specific businesses to the region. And it needs to highlight the role of law, including private law, in supporting them. Low tax burden, low wages, poor working conditions, and even the legal preemption that secures them, all function as subsidies, often grounded in underlying doctrinal understandings of property and contract. Furthermore, much of the economic value that new businesses bring to the region is heavily premised on, and made possible by, decades of public investment—and select disinvestment—that has directly benefited them. Foregrounding these subsidies is a necessary part of calling for local and state governments to require that large corporate players, specifically those that overtly benefit from Austin's urban-regional economic configuration and identity, carry a greater share of the costs of urban-regional social reproduction.[77]

Second, and related, a different distribution requires thinking differently about the responsibilities associated with a given company's role in inducing increments of growth in the larger urban-regional economy. Specifically, it requires making visible and valuing the work of *all* labor undergirding that urban-regional growth. Even incentive-based agreements with corporations that mandate living wage and benefits requirements for workers directly employed or contracted by corporations only account for first-order vulnerability. They also do not always work. Two years into the Tesla agreement, for instance, safety and wage theft concerns emerged, with workers hired by project subcontractors alleging physically unsafe working conditions, falsified safety training certificates, and unpaid wages.[78] Even were those protections effective, the focus on these directly employed or subcontracted workers is insufficient, given the role that corporations' locational decisions play in bolstering and inducing increments of growth that extend well beyond their direct employment base. What protections exist for those workers who, for example, will build the apartments and houses that a given corporation's employees will inevitably live in, as well as for the low-wage service workers who will provide labor more generally in the larger regional economy in which a corporation's employees will be enjoying a "lower cost of living" relative to national averages?

Third, place-specific dynamics and dependencies can be identified and mobilized to challenge "progressive" boomtown narratives. With its particular position in national imaginaries of culture, politics, technology, and urban prosperity, Austin embodies and is in many ways dependent on a set of place-based dynamics that could potentially be deployed in service of projects that seek to distribute differently, including through visions of prosperity and well-being in which growth plays a less central role. Those concerned with the level of inequality on which Austin's growth patterns seem to depend might continue to criticize, but also exploit, Austin's equally important dependence on its self-identification as a "progressive" region. In its 2019 annual report, the Workers Defense Project, a statewide membership-based worker organization provocatively asks: "Did someone die while building your office space or condo? Was the person who built your home actually paid for their work?" These are the types of questions that might be able to spur larger reflection across an urban-regional polity about the nature of what it means to be a "progressive" region. Such a strategy might be used to support and further the worker protections and social provisioning gains that activist communities have successfully lobbied and fought for, not least the protections and relief that were so critical for workers (particularly undocumented workers) during the early stages of the pandemic.[79] Scholarship on policy advocacy around "degraded work" suggests that an intersection between place-based dynamics and "local-serving industries," such as construction, which by definition must occur in the place where the service is offered, may offer key leverage points for the political struggles being waged by labor advocates.[80]

Public attitudes can change; norms of what is acceptable can shift. High profile, strategic, and place-based discourse challenges, highlighting and contesting the legal and political background rules that lead to radically unequal distribution, are part of such change. Local activists and their allies, for instance, might make tactical use of the colocation of major dialogues among ostensibly culturally, if not economically, progressive industries that are at the center of the high-profile "South by Southwest" (SXSW) festivals and conferences in Austin. Those dialogues—about technology, entertainment, and media—not coincidentally involve industries that are broadly implicated in Austin's particular model of growth, both past and present. Activists might work toward creating a larger climate in which certain corporate leaders in these industries find an increasingly critical local reception, both inside the festival and out. They might, for example, organize protests or counterprogramming that leverage the now-expansive SXSW universe of events as a focal point for bringing regional and national attention to the unaccounted-for costs and externalities of the growth models in which SXSW sectors are implicated, in the Austin region and beyond.

Finally, we need to take seriously arguments for pursuing an urban-regional policy posture of degrowth, which would mean, at a minimum, decentering and deemphasizing growth as it is currently configured in contemporary urban-regional political economies. Serge Latouche and others maintain that the concept of degrowth is a flexible, nonunitary, and malleable "keyword" or interpretive frame.[81] In that vein, and with an eye toward low-income Latino construction workers, we argue that ideas of degrowth should be actively held open to being molded, contested, and defined in ways that will work for real people in real places.

Entertaining any version of degrowth requires taking seriously the complex question of what logics or limiting principles could or ought to govern constraints on urban-regional growth. At the same time, it also calls for grappling with the complicated terrain of individual emotional and material investments in the project of growth, even and especially of those who are most exposed to its costs. Specifically, it means heeding Stefania Barca's insistence that "the degrowth movement desperately needs to reach out to and mobilize waged workers and their organizations." That is, it needs to "take seriously workers' conditions and needs, as well as labour movements' concerns and dilemmas vis-à-vis ecology and the climate," even while pushing forward both theoretical and practical considerations of possible degrowth futures.[82]

For all of degrowth's conceptual malleability, delinking the presumed relationship between growth and worker well-being is incredibly difficult, encountering deep seated political, if not economic, truths that predominate even in "progressive" urban-regional contexts.[83] The degrowth literature to date has generally not foregrounded the conditions of specific, situated workers or their potential material and symbolic investment in projects of growth. The literature is also scant in terms of detailed engagement with what degrowth futures, in concrete terms, might mean for undocumented workers and transnational migration dynamics. Construction work offers a complicated field in which to consider such questions, as much of the work would not exist in the absence of at least physical growth. Yet some limited interviews we conducted with low-income Latino construction workers in Austin about their experiences early in the pandemic suggest both challenges to and promises for the project of delinking the relationship between worker well-being and growth.[84]

Although many workers and worker advocacy organizations expressed concern about the governor's designation of all construction work as essential, at least some workers early in the pandemic were understandably more afraid of losing work than they were of contracting the virus. When asked about their general perceptions of growth and the economy in the Austin region, and whether they see themselves as having benefited from the region's growth, worker assessments of their own economic security and prosperity revealed a complicated picture. Nearly all associated growth in the region with a strong employment market for construction workers. They spoke of plentiful work, and in more limited instances, of rising wages, but often while acknowledging challenges around dramatically rising costs of living. Multiple workers noted feeling, both pre- and mid-pandemic, as though they were working paycheck to paycheck, unable to get ahead or build foundations of economic security.

When asked whether they saw a future for themselves (and their families) in the region, as well as whether they had considered moving, none of the workers indicated that they were thinking of imminently leaving the region. Many had long-standing ties to and were actively building lives for themselves and their immediate families in the region. Yet some of the workers living in the City of Austin noted a desire to move outside the city proper to less congested areas where property is more affordable.

These interview responses suggest that whatever level of economic security workers might hope to cultivate or hold onto is directly tied to regional economic and physical growth. Yet, our questions only probed the current landscape. We did not ask workers about other types of livelihoods they might imagine for themselves or about alternative political economies or growth policies that might privilege greater security of income and well-being. These are questions we need to explicitly ask workers across sectors to identify the contours of new systems configurations around which political mobilization might be both possible *and* desirable.

CONCLUSION

Workers and worker advocacy groups may take for granted the necessity of economic and physical growth to the future of work, even when they are grappling with growth's downsides. But they do so in ways that are inseparable from an on-the-ground interpretation of the constraints and opportunities afforded them by the larger context in which they are operating. The limited livelihood possibilities and overall economic vulnerability of low-income Latino construction workers in Austin are shaped and produced in part by the multiple, often backgrounded, legal and policy regimes we have highlighted in this chapter. Surfacing those regimes helps illuminate the grossly unequal distribution of the surplus yielded by Austin's growth, as well as the broader landscape against which Latino construction workers are responding and within which they are formulating complex understandings of risk, well-being, and opportunity. If for some powerful actors in Texas the project of growth was deemed essential during the pandemic, some workers, even those who were empirically subjected to greater risk of COVID hospitalization, also seemed to see growth as an essential part of their own understanding of economic opportunity and prosperity.

Building on long-fought struggles in the Austin region, we have begun in this chapter to identify additional pathways for imagining and promoting alternative urban-regional political economies, ones not centered around growth. Continuing this work will require not only more structural historical excavation but also creativity, trying to imagine something for which we do not necessarily have exemplary models. Perhaps we might even take a page from growth boosters in Austin who have no trouble entertaining elaborate and speculative ideas about the region's role in the future of electric mobility, the logistics of private space navigation, or the colonization of Mars. Although those boosters might be at a loss when it comes to imagining significant (re)configurations of distribution and growth that would support the future well-being and aspirations of *all* workers, we do not need to be so stymied.

NOTES

This chapter builds on a report that we coauthored in the summer of 2020 in consultation with Neville Hoad, Snehal Patel, Dan Danielsen, and Lucie White, and with the research support of Adaylin Alvarez, Jacob Blas, and Michael Bass. That report would not have been possible without collaboration with the Workers Defense Project and the Equal Justice Center in Austin; we are grateful to both organizations and especially to the construction workers who agreed to be interviewed for the project. The chapter has benefited from generous engagement during a number of presentations at the University of Texas School of Law as well as from comments on various parts of the draft by Dick Lavine, Liz Mueller, Sara McTarnaghan, and Heather Way.

1. For discussion of the roles that Austin's identity as "progressive," "a creative city," and "a knowledge economy" play in constructing an understanding of the region's urban competitive advantage, see Andrew Busch, "Building 'A City of Upper-Middle Class Citizens': Labor Markets, Segregation, and Growth in Austin, Texas, 1950–1973," *Journal of Urban History* 39, no. 5 (September 2013): 975–96;

and Eugene J. McCann, "Livable City/Unequal City: The Politics of Policy-Making in a 'Creative' Boomtown," *Political Economy* 37 (February 2008), https://doi.org/10.4000/interventionseconomiques.489.

2. U.S. Census Bureau, "Most of the Counties with the Largest Population Gains Since 2010 Are in Texas," news release no. CB20-53, March 26, 2020, https://www.census.gov/newsroom/press-releases/2020/pop-estimates-county-metro.html.

3. Beverly Kerr, "Gross Domestic Product by Metro & County," Austin Chamber of Commerce, February 27, 2023, https://www.austinchamber.com/blog/02-28-2023-gross-domestic-product.

4. Texas Workforce Commission, "Quarterly Census of Employment and Wages (QCEW)," last accessed June 14, 2023, https://texaslmi.com/LMIbyCategory/QCEW. Compare first quarter 2020 average employment for "Construction" NAICS Code 23 in the Austin-Round Rock Metro against first quarter 2010 average employment.

5. The order made exceptions specifically for "public works construction, and construction of affordable housing or housing for individuals experiencing homelessness, social services construction and other construction that supports essential uses, including essential businesses, government functions, or critical infrastructure." Travis County, Texas County Judge Order No. 2020-5 at 13, March 24, 2020, https://www.traviscountytx.gov/images/docs/covid-19-order-5.pdf.

6. Texas Executive Order No. GA-14, "Relating to Statewide Continuity of Essential Services and Activities During the COVID-19 Disaster," March 31, 2020, https://gov.texas.gov/uploads/files/press/EO-GA-14_Statewide_Essential_Service_and_Activity_COVID-19_IMAGE_03-31-2020.pdf.

7. U.S. Department of Homeland Security, Cybersecurity and Infrastructure Security Agency, "Guidance on the Essential Critical Infrastructure Workforce: Ensuring Community and National Resilience in COVID-19 Response (Version 2.0)," March 28, 2020, https://www.cisa.gov/sites/default/files/publications/CISA_Guidance_on_the_Essential_Critical_Infrastructure_Workforce_Version_2.0_1.pdf.

8. COVID-19 patient data by occupation type from March 29, 2020 to May 17, 2020 for patients seen at Dell-Seton Medical Center in Austin, TX. Provided by Snehal Patel, MD of the University of Texas at Austin Dell Medical School. These findings were consistent with others reported in the media. See, for example, Mark Wilson, "Many Construction Workers Testing Positive for Coronavirus, Austin Health Officials Say," *Austin American-Statesman*, May 5, 2020.

9. Remy F. Pasco et al., "Estimated Association of Construction Work with Risks of COVID-19 Infection and Hospitalization in Texas," *JAMA Network Open* 3, no. 10 (2020): e2026373, https://doi.org/10.1001/jamanetworkopen.2020.26373.

10. City of Austin, Texas, Resolution No. 20200409-081, "COVID-19 Relief in a State of Emergency (RISE)," April 9, 2020, https://www.austintexas.gov/edims/document.cfm?id=339008.

11. Ruth Ellen Wasem et al., *Advancing Immigrant Incorporation in Austin, TX* (Austin: Lyndon B. Johnson School of Public Affairs, The University of Texas at Austin, 2021), 21.

12. Tex. Tax Code Ann. § 313.026(c)(2) (West 2008 & Supp. 2012). The provision gives the state comptroller the ability to override that requirement if the comptroller makes

a "qualitative determination that other considerations . . . result in a net positive benefit to the state." Tex. Tax Code Ann. § 313.026(f).

13. Texas State Comptroller, "Agreement for the Limitation of Appraised Value of Property for School District Maintenance and Operations Taxes by and Between Del Valle Independent School District and Colorado River Project, LLC," July 9, 2020, arts. II and VI, https://assets.comptroller.texas.gov/ch313/1496/1496-del-colorado-agmt.pdf.

14. Travis County Commissioners Court, "Economic Development Performance Agreement Colorado River Project, LLC," July 14, 2020, https://financialtransparency.traviscountytx.gov/Reports/EcoDev/TeslaAgreement.pdf.

15. Travis County Commissioners Court, "Voting Session June 16, 2020, XII Executive Session, Agenda Item 24413," June 16, 2020, TravisCountyTX.gov; Travis County Commissioners Court, "Voting Session 6/23/2020, X Planning and Budget, Agenda Item 24461," June 23, 2020, TravisCountyTX.gov; and Del Valle Independent School District, "Public Hearing on Application of Colorado River Project, LLC for Appraised Value Limitation on Qualified Property," June 25, 2020, https://delvalleisdtx.new.swagit.com/videos/235612.

16. Heath Prince and Bethany Boggess, *The Failed Promise of the Texas Miracle* (Austin, TX: Workers Defense Project, 2016).

17. Bob Sechler, "Travis County Gives Thumbs-Up," *Austin American-Statesman*, July 14, 2020.

18. Del Valle Independent School District, "Public Hearing on Application."

19. Del Valle Independent School District, "Public Hearing on Application."

20. Tex. Educ. Code Ann. §§ 41.001–42.411 (Vernon 2012).

21. For the first time since its passage, the Texas legislature responded to significant pushback against the law and allowed it to expire in December 2022, although Governor Greg Abbott and others are encouraging its reinstatement. Some of the criticism of the law centered on the practice of many companies to challenge the valuation of their taxable assets just as their incentive agreements are coming to an end, thereby substantially reducing their tax liability and the revenues that local school districts can expect upon expiration of the incentives. Patrick Svitek, "Gov. Greg Abbott Says Texas Will Revamp Economic Development Program After Property Tax Incentive Expires," *Texas Tribune*, February 22, 2023, https://www.texastribune.org/2023/02/22/greg-abbott-chapter-313/ (with the governor claiming that Texas had lost out to New York on a bid to recruit a large computer chip factory to the region); and Justin Miller, "Texas' Largest Corporate Welfare Program Is Leaving Companies Flush and School Districts Broke," *Texas Observer*, May 12, 2021, https://www.texasobserver.org/texas-largest-corporate-welfare-program-is-leaving-companies-flush-and-school-districts-broke/.

22. Jessi Devenyns, "Travis County Approves $10M for Direct Rental and Mortgage Assistance," *Austin Monitor*, May 13, 2020, https://www.austinmonitor.com/stories/2020/05/travis-county-approves-10m-for-direct-rental-and-mortgage-assistance/.

23. Travis County Commissioners Court, "Voting Session June 16, 2020."

24. For discussion of some of these factors prepandemic, see Rebecca Torres et al., "Building Austin, Building Justice: Immigrant Construction Workers, Precarious Labor Regimes

and Social Citizenship," *Geoforum* 45 (2013): 145–55; Workers Defense Project, *Build a Better Nation: A Case for Comprehensive Immigration Reform* (Austin, TX: Workers Defense Project, 2013); and Workers Defense Project, *Build a Better Texas: Construction Working Conditions in the Lone Star State* (Austin, TX: Workers Defense Project, 2013).

25. April 2020 guidelines required prework health screenings, worker sign-in documentation, handwashing station requirements, a ban on community water coolers, cleaning requirements for tools and "collective touchpoints" between use, and physical distancing requirements. City of Austin, Texas, Order 20200324-007, "Supplemental Guidance Based on Executive Order No. GA-14," April 2, 2020, http://austintexas.gov/sites/default/files/files/GUIDANCE%20-%20Response%20to%20GA-14%20%20FINAL.pdf. In July 2020, the Austin-Travis County Public Health Authority called for additional measures including masking for all work sites (in response to capitulation by Governor Abbott allowing local leaders to establish their own mask mandates based on the advice of health experts) and for larger sites, specifically, staggered shifts, additional provision and placement of restrooms and hand washing facilities, and the designation of a site safety monitor. City of Austin, Texas, "Notice of Emergency Rules Adoption," July 14, 2020, http://www.austintexas.gov/edims/document.cfm?id=343206.

26. Gerhard Bosch and Peter Philips, eds., *Building Chaos: An International Comparison of Deregulation in the Construction Industry* (New York: Routledge, 2003); and Workers Defense Project, *Build a Better Texas*.

27. Bosch and Phillips, *Building Chaos*.

28. Bosch and Phillips, *Building Chaos*; and Workers Defense Project, *Build a Better Texas*.

29. Workers Defense Project, *Build a Better Texas*.

30. Workers Defense Project, *Build a Better Texas*; Torres et al., "Building Austin, Building Justice"; and Michelle Buckley, "On the Work of Urbanization: Migration, Construction Labor, and the Commodity Moment," *Annals of the Association of American Geographers* 104, no. 2 (February 2014): 338–47.

31. Workers Defense Project, *Build a Better Texas*.

32. Workers Defense Project, *Build a Better Texas*.

33. Miriam Jordan, "'We're Petrified': Immigrants Afraid to Seek Medical Care for Coronavirus," *New York Times*, March 18, 2020, https://www.nytimes.com/2020/03/18/us/coronavirus-immigrants.html.

34. See, generally, Jose F. Figueroa, Fabiola Molina, and Benjamin D. Sommers, "The Trump Administration's 'Public Charge' Rule and Covid-19: Bad Policy at the Worst Time," *Stat*, August 21, 2020, https://www.statnews.com/2020/08/21/the-trump-administrations-public-charge-rule-and-covid-19-bad-policy-at-the-worst-time/; and Hamutal Bernstein et al., *Amid Confusion Over the Public Charge Rule, Immigrant Families Continued Avoiding Public Benefits in 2019* (Washington, DC: Urban Institute, May 2020).

35. See Olga Khazan, "Some Immigrants Choose Between Food Stamps and a Green Card," *The Atlantic*, April 25, 2019, https://www.theatlantic.com/health/archive/2019/04/trumps-immigration-proposal-hurting-immigrant-health/587908/;

see also Helen Branswell, "Federal Rules Threaten to Discourage Undocumented Immigrants from Vaccinating Children," *Stat*, August 26, 2019, https://www.statnews.com/2019/08/26/federal-rules-threaten-to-discourage-undocumented-immigrants-from-vaccinating-children/.

36. Muzaffar Chishti and Sarah Pierce, "Crisis Within a Crisis: Immigration in the United States in a Time of COVID-19," *Migration Policy Institute*, March 26, 2020, https://www.migrationpolicy.org/article/crisis-within-crisis-immigration-time-covid-19.

37. For the identification and discussion of a national trend of state preemption of local government progressive legislation, see Richard Briffault, "The Challenge of the New Preemption," *Stanford Law Review* 70 (2018): 1995–2027.

38. Audrey McGlinchy, "Is Austin a Sanctuary City? Good Question," *KUT News*, November 16, 2016, https://www.kut.org/austin/2016-11-16/is-austin-a-sanctuary-city-good-question.

39. Julián Aguilar, "Travis County Sheriff Announces New 'Sanctuary' Policy," *Texas Tribune*, January 20, 2017, https://www.texastribune.org/2017/01/20/travis-county-sheriff-announces-new-sanctuary-poli/.

40. Specifically, the sheriff stated that she would not honor ICE detainers unless the person was charged or convicted of capital murder, murder, aggravated sexual assault, or human trafficking. Audrey McGlinchy, "Here's What We Learned About Requests from ICE to Pick Up Travis County Inmates," *Austin Monitor*, June 1, 2017, https://www.austinmonitor.com/stories/2017/06/heres-learned-requests-ice-pick-travis-county-inmates/.

41. Tex. Gov't Code Ann. § 752.053. The law was passed after President Trump and Governor Abbott had both threatened to withdraw funds from local entities that had sanctuary policies. See Martin Kaste, "Trump Threatens 'Sanctuary' Cities with Loss of Federal Funds," *NPR*, January 26, 2017, https://www.npr.org/sections/thetwo-way/2017/01/26/511899896/trumps-threatens-sanctuary-cities-with-loss-of-federal-funds; and Sedria Renee, "Texas Gov. Abbot [sic] Halts Travis County Funding Over Sanctuary Policy," *NBC News*, February 2, 2017, https://www.nbcnews.com/news/us-news/texas-gov-abbot-halts-travis-county-funding-over-sanctuary-policy-n716201.

42. City of El Cenizo v. Texas, 890 F.3d 164, 176 (5th Cir. 2018) (explaining that "field preemption occurs when States are precluded from regulating conduct in a field Congress, acting within its proper authority, has determined must be regulated by its exclusive governance" (quotations and citations omitted)).

43. *City of El Cenizo*, 890 F.3d at 185. An additional provision of SB 4 prohibiting local officials from "endorsing" sanctuary policies in their private lives was struck down.

44. Mary Tuma, "Austin Struggles to Adjust as SB 4 Takes Its Toll on Immigrants," *Austin Chronicle*, April 5, 2019, https://www.austinchronicle.com/news/2019-04-05/austin-struggles-to-adjust-as-sb-4-takes-its-toll-on-immigrants/.

45. Tex. Labor Code § 62.051 (West 2003); Tex. Labor Code Ann. § 62.0515 (West 2003).

46. City of Austin, Tex., Ordinance No. 20180215-049 (2018) (codified at Austin, Tex., Code of Ordinance § 4-19 (2021)).

47. Texas Ass'n of Bus. v. Austin, 565 S.W.3d 425 (Tex. App—Austin 2018, pet. denied.).

48. City of Austin, Tex., Ordinance No. 20141211-050 (2014) (codified at Austin, Tex., Code of Ordinance § 5-1-13 (2021)) (defining source of income as "lawful, regular,

and verifiable income including, but not limited to, housing vouchers and other subsidies provided by government or non-governmental entities, child support, or spousal maintenance, but does not include future gifts").

49. Tex. Loc. Gov't Code § 250.007.
50. Heather Way, Elizabeth Mueller, and Jake Wegmann, *Uprooted: Displacement in Austin's Gentrifying Neighborhoods and What Can Be Done About It* (Austin, TX: Center for Sustainable Development, University of Texas at Austin School of Architecture and the Entrepreneurship and Community Development Clinic, University of Texas at Austin School of Law, 2018).
51. "Growth Machine" is a term introduced in the 1970s to describe competitive elite-based urban growth coalitions. See Harvey Molotch, "The City as a Growth Machine: Toward a Political Economy of Place," *American Journal of Sociology* 82, no. 2 (1976): 309–32. For just some of the literature critiquing inequalities in Austin's growth policies and practices, see Joseph Straubhaar et al., eds., *Inequity in the Technopolis: Race, Class, Gender, and the Digital Divide in Austin* (Austin: University of Texas Press, 2012); see also Busch, "Building 'A City of Upper-Middle Class Citizens'"; Eliot Tretter, "Contesting Sustainability: 'SMART Growth' and the Redevelopment of Austin's Eastside," *International Journal of Urban and Regional Research* 37, no. 1 (2013): 297–310; and Joshua Long, "Constructing the Narrative of the Sustainability Fix: Sustainability, Social Justice and Representation in Austin, TX," *Urban Studies* 53, no. 1 (2016): 149–72.
52. For an analysis of demolition on Austin's east side, see Sara McTarnaghan, "Development and Displacement: Single Family Home Demolitions in Central East Austin, 2007 to 2014," *Planning Forum*, 16 (2015), 47–66.
53. Way, Mueller, and Wegmann, *Uprooted*.
54. Luz Moreno-Lozano, "Hispanic Flight from Austin Tied to Affordability, Gentrification, Experts Say," *Austin American-Statesman*, November 20, 2020, https://www.statesman.com/story/news/2020/11/21/hispanic-flight-from-austin-tied-to-affordability-gentrification-experts-say/115016122/.
55. For detailed discussions of historical anti-Black and anti-Latinx redlining and segregation in Austin, see Eliot M. Tretter and Moulay A. Sounny-Slitine, *Austin Restricted: Progressivism, Zoning, Private Racial Covenants, and the Making of a Segregated City* (Austin: Institute for Urban Policy Research and Analysis, University of Texas at Austin, 2012). For detailed treatment of gentrification and displacement pressure in contemporary Austin, see Eric Tang and Bisola Falola, *Those Who Left: Austin's Declining African American Population* (Austin: Institute for Urban Policy Research and Analysis, University of Texas at Austin, 2016); Eric Tang and Bisola Falola, *Those Who Stayed: The Impact of Gentrification on Longstanding Residents of East Austin* (Austin: Institute for Urban Policy Research and Analysis, University of Texas at Austin, 2018); and Way, Mueller, and Wegmann, *Uprooted*.
56. See Elizabeth Walsh and Bjørn Sletto, *East Austin Environmental Justice History* (Austin, TX: East Austin Environmental Justice Project, 2007).
57. For accounts of prominent environmental justice activism on Austin's east side, see the website of People Organized in Defense of Earth and Her Resources (PODER), which was formed in 1991 by a group of Chicana and Chicano activists "to increase

East Austin residents' participation in corporate and government decisions related to economic development, environmental hazards and the impact on our East Austin neighborhoods." "About Us," PODER, accessed June 20, 2023, https://www.poderaustin.org/about.

58. Austin Chamber of Commerce, "Why the Austin Region?," archived June 9, 2023, http://web.archive.org/web/20230609082608/https://www.austinchamber.com/economic-development/why-austin.

59. See Busch, "Building 'A City of Upper-Middle Class Citizens'"; and McCann, "Livable City/Unequal City."

60. See, generally, Richard Florida, *Cities and the Creative Class* (New York: Routledge, 2005); Allen J. Scott, "Creative Cities: Conceptual Issue and Policy Questions," *Journal of Urban Affairs* 28, no. 1 (2006): 1–17; and Andy C. Pratt, "The Cultural Contradictions of the Creative City," *City, Culture and Society* 2, no. 3 (2011): 123–30.

61. Austin Chamber of Commerce, "Why the Austin Region?"; and Raven Ambers, "Cost of 'Living Comfortably' in Austin Nearly $20k More Expensive Than Previous Year," *CBS Austin*, December 10, 2018, https://cbsaustin.com/news/local/cost-of-living-comfortably-in-austin-nearly-20k-more-expensive-than-previous-year.

62. Austin Chamber of Commerce, "State & Local Taxes & Incentives," archived June 9, 2023, http://web.archive.org/web/20230609080048/https://www.austinchamber.com/economic-development/taxes-incentives.

63. Janelle Cammenga, "To What Extent Does Your State Rely on Property Taxes?," *Tax Foundation*, January 19, 2021, https://taxfoundation.org/state-property-taxes-reliance-2021/ (based on 2018 data); and Janelle Cammenga, "To What Extent Does Your State Rely on Sales Taxes?," *Tax Foundation*, January 27, 2021, https://taxfoundation.org/state-sales-tax-reliance-2021/ (based on 2018 data).

64. Shannon Najmabadi, "When Big Businesses Want to Fight Their Property Tax Bills, Texas Law Hands Them an Easy Way, Critics Say," *Texas Tribune*, March 26, 2019, https://www.texastribune.org/2019/03/26/equity-appeals-help-texas-big-businesses-fight-their-property-tax-bill/.

65. The Austin Chamber of Commerce boasts that Austin has the "5th highest concentration of college-educated adults," is the "6th best educated major metro area," and has a concentration of STEM occupations that makes it the "6th most concentrated among large U.S. metros." Austin Chamber of Commerce, "Why the Austin Region?" For academic discussion of Austin's high technology economy and related conversations of growth and equity, see, generally, Kent S. Butler and Dowell Meyers, "Boomtime in Austin, Texas: Negotiated Growth Management," *Journal of the American Planning Association* 50, no. 4 (1984): 447–58; Lisa Hartenberger, Zeynep Tufekci, and Stuart Davis, "A History of High Tech and the Technopolis in Austin," in Straubhaar et al., *Inequity in the Technopolis*, 63–83; and Busch, "Building 'A City of Upper-Middle Class Citizens.'"

66. Lawrence Wright, "The Astonishing Transformation of Austin," *New Yorker*, February 6, 2023, https://www.newyorker.com/magazine/2023/02/13/the-astonishing-transformation-of-austin.

67. For discussion of agglomeration economics, generally, see Diego Puga, "The Magnitude and Causes of Agglomeration Economies," *Journal of Regional Science* 50,

no. 1 (2010): 203–19; and Richard Florida, "Why US Tech Inventors Are So Highly Clustered," *CityLab, Bloomberg*, October 1, 2019, https://www.bloomberg.com/news/articles/2019-10-01/why-u-s-tech-inventors-are-so-highly-clustered.

68. Austin Chamber of Commerce, "Local Incentives Summary," archived August 10, 2023, https://web.archive.org/web/20230810124408mp_/https://www.austinchamber.com/economic-development/taxes-incentives/local-incentives; and City of Austin, Texas, "Business Expansion Incentive Program," archived May 30, 2023, http://web.archive.org/web/20230530083221/https://www.austintexas.gov/department/business-expansion-incentive-program.

69. Travis County, Texas, "Economic Development," accessed June 21, 2023, https://www.traviscountytx.gov/planning-budget/economic-development.

70. See, for example, Timothy J. Bartik, " 'But For' Percentages for Economic Development Incentives: What Percentage Estimates Are Plausible Based on the Research Literature?," Upjohn Institute Working Paper 18–289, Kalamazoo, MI: W. E. Upjohn Institute for Employment Research, June 2018; Nathan M. Jensen, "Bargaining and the Effectiveness of Economic Development Incentives: An Evaluation of the Texas Chapter 313 Program," *Public Choice* 177, nos. 1–2 (2018): 29–51; Prince and Boggess, *The Failed Promise of the Texas Miracle*; and Stephan Goetz et al., "Sharing the Gains of Local Economic Growth: Race-to-the-Top Versus Race-to-the-Bottom Economic Development," *Environment and Planning C: Politics and Space* 29, no. 3 (2011): 428–56.

71. Texas House of Representatives, "House Ways and Means Committee Hearing, Interim Charge 4—Non-Renewal of Chapter 313, Tax Code," September 8, 2022, https://tlchouse.granicus.com/MediaPlayer.php?view_id=46&clip_id=23501.

72. This tax relief requires companies to attest that they are actively seeking tax relief incentives in another jurisdiction, and thereby considering locating their investment elsewhere. See 28.002 of Travis County Commissioner's Court, "Chapter 28-Travis County Economic Development Program Policy Guidelines and Criteria," January 14, 2014, https://www.traviscountytx.gov/images/planning_budget/Docs/final_policy.pdf.

73. Heather Somerville, "Elon Musk Moves to Texas, Takes Jab at Silicon Valley," *Wall Street Journal*, December 8, 2020, https://www.wsj.com/articles/elon-musk-to-discuss-teslas-banner-year-despite-pandemic-silicon-valleys-future-11607449988.

74. Somerville, "Elon Musk Moves to Texas"; see also Aaron Tilley, "Oracle Moves Corporate Headquarters to Austin, Texas," *Wall Street Journal*, December 11, 2020, https://www.wsj.com/articles/oracle-moves-corporate-headquarters-to-austin-texas-11607724881.

75. Chandra Kring Villanueva, *Recapture: The Most Misunderstood Aspect of the Texas School Finance System* (Austin: Every Texan, 2022).

76. Grace Kay, "Elon Musk Issues 'Urgent' Plea for More Housing in Austin, Texas, as Tesla and SpaceX Look to Fill Hundreds of Jobs," *Business Insider*, April 5, 2021, https://www.businessinsider.com/elon-musk-austin-texas-housing-tesla-spacex-boring-job-postings-2021-4.

77. For academic treatment of debates around social reproduction in urban-regional or city-regional contexts, see Andrew E. G. Jonas and Kevin Ward, "Introduction to a Debate on City-Regions: New Geographies of Governance, Democracy and

Social Reproduction," *International Journal of Urban and Regional Research* 31, no. 1 (2007): 169–78; and Alan Harding, "Taking City Regions Seriously? Response to Debate on 'City-Regions: New Geographies of Governance, Democracy and Social Reproduction,'" *International Journal of Urban and Regional Research* 31, no. 2 (2007): 443–58. For discussion of such dynamics in Austin specifically, see Eugene J. McCann, "Inequality and Politics in the Creative City-Region: Questions of Livability and State Strategy," *International Journal of Urban and Regional Research* 31, no. 1 (2007): 188–96.

78. Alexandra Villareal, "Tesla's Construction Workers at Texas Gigafactory Allege Labor Violations," *The Guardian*, November 15, 2022, https://www.theguardian.com/technology/2022/nov/14/tesla-texas-construction-workers-gigafactory-lawsuit-labor-violations.

79. See Ryan Autullo, "Group to Austin Leaders: Give $40 Million Cut from Coronavirus Funds to Renters," *Austin American-Statesman*, May 13, 2020, https://www.statesman.com/story/news/coronavirus/2020/05/14/group-to-austin-leaders-give-40-million-cut-from-coronavirus-funds-to-renters/1205619007/; see "Austin City Council Votes in Favor of Replenishing Direct Cash Assistance Fund for Most Directly Impacted Austinites, But Is It Enough?," *Grassroots Leadership*, June 4, 2020, http://web.archive.org/web/20230617234807/https://www.grassrootsleadership.org/in-the-news.

80. Marc Doussard, *Degraded Work* (Minneapolis: University of Minnesota Press, 2013).

81. Serge Latouche, "Degrowth Economics," *Le Monde Diplomatique*, November 2004. See also Federico Demaria et al., "What Is Degrowth? From an Activist Slogan to a Social Movement," *Environmental Values* 22, no. 2 (2013): 191–215; and Giorgos Kallis et al., *The Case for Degrowth* (Cambridge: Polity, 2020).

82. Stefania Barca, "An Alternative Worth Fighting For: Degrowth and the Liberation of Work," in *Towards a Political Economy of Degrowth*, ed. Ekaterina Chertovskaya et al. (New York: Rowman and Littlefield, 2019), 175–91, quotes at 181 and 184.

83. Richard Schragger, "Is a Progressive City Possible? Reviving Urban Liberalism for the Twenty-First Century," *Harvard Law and Policy Review* 7 (2013), 231–52.

84. Interviews were conducted between July 2020 and March 2021 with fifteen respondents who are Latino and who work broadly in the construction industry in the Austin region. The interviews, conducted in Spanish over the phone or via video call, were part of a larger project on which this chapter draws. For more detailed discussion of interviews, see Samuel Tabory and Karen Engle, with others, *COVID-19, Structural Inequality, and the Past and Future of Low-Income Latinx Construction Workers in Austin, Texas* (Austin: Rapoport Center for Human Rights and Justice, University of Texas at Austin, 2020).

CHAPTER 13

LAND AND LABOR IN THE COLOMBIAN PALM OIL INDUSTRY

HELENA ALVIAR GARCÍA AND JORGE GONZÁLEZ JÁCOME

On November 5, 2019, one of Colombia's main palm oil producers, Indupalma, announced it would be closing down. The company defended its decision by pointing to the rising costs of worker pensions, labor unrest, environmental pressure from the European Union, and difficulties in marketing the product.[1] This announcement came only a year after the association of Colombian palm producers (La Federación Nacional de Cultivadores de Palma de Aceite, or Fedepalma) announced it expected a 20 percent increase in palm output as the result of conservative president Iván Duque coming into office in 2018.[2] Workers alleged that Indupalma was shutting down as a result of poor managerial decisions that union representatives had highlighted during several meetings. The company, however, was not bankrupt and announced that they would be liquidating the corporation and thus paying outstanding debts and offering compensation for workers. A majority of the workers accepted the settlements offered, but others did not. A year after announcing that the company was closing down, union workers noticed that other companies were still harvesting palm crops and producing palm oil. In their view, closing down Indupalma was merely a strategy to terminate the agreements previously established in collective bargaining. For workers, Indupalma's strategy was in line with other decisions in the past where capital won and workers lost.[3]

The debate around the motivations or strategies involved in Indupalma's decision to close down raises questions about the history of palm oil production and the relationship between capital and labor in Colombia during the second half of the twentieth century. If workers are right, and Indupalma's decision is a façade for evading prior obligations, why does Indupalma have so much power to determine its future without significant participation of workers? Part of the answer might lie with the history of palm oil production in the country. As Angela Serrano's research points out, Indupalma's dissolution process is a new—probably final—step in the company's historical strategies to elude workers' pressures and create more favorable scenarios for palm oil production.[4] History confirms that closing shop and looking for new places to invest capital is one of the alternatives powerful business elites have used in the past to protect their investment.

The perplexing nature of Indupalma's decision to dissolve—apparently shutting down while the business is still profitable—helps us frame the goal of this chapter: to propose that distributional analysis provides important and useful insights about the legal framework behind the Colombian palm oil industry that allows capital to prevail over work. We argue that the transformation of development policies and property regulations are in the background of the Colombian palm oil industry and have crucially aided the unequal distribution of resources. Our analysis shows that palm oil entrepreneurs have used the legal system, especially background rules, to avoid transformations that could eventually give more power to workers. Hence, as an alternative to neoliberal explanations of production problems caused by rising costs—which were at the center of Indupalma's public justifications for its dissolution—we explain the dynamic of palm oil production in Colombia as elites' successful capturing state rents as an illustration of the intricate relationship between property and work and as an example of racial dispossession. We hope this analysis will inform contemporary debates about work and its futures.

Colombia is the largest palm oil producer in Latin America and the fourth largest in the world. Palm oil is the second most important agricultural export in the country after coffee.[5] It is harvested in twenty-one of the thirty-two departments of the country.[6] Palm oil production needs to take place near the crops because the seed has to be processed within twelve hours after being picked. Processing therefore requires substantial financial investments, which in turn has promoted a considerable degree of property concentration. In fact, 41 percent of palm oil is produced on plots of land larger than two thousand hectares, and at the other end of the spectrum, 80 percent of the plots that harvest oil palm are fifty hectares or less and represent 8.6 percent of Colombian agricultural production.[7] Small producers need to create cooperative associations and sell the palm seed to big players for processing.[8] The interaction between these two styles of production has triggered extensive labor and land conflicts. Palm has been at the core of the Colombian armed conflict during the twentieth and twenty-first centuries.

One of the dominant narratives about the centrality of palm oil production for the Colombian economy portrays it as the successful implementation of neoliberal policies. In this story, the emphasis lies on the privileged climate conditions that make palm oil production desirable in the country, sound public policy that supports export led growth, and technical advice from the World Bank.[9] The classical theory of comparative advantage lies beneath this explanation. Colombia is located, the story goes, in a tropical zone that makes the country more suitable to produce palm oil than other products. Domestic policy makers and international organizations thus believe that cultivation of palm and production of palm oil is obvious for countries that have a specific climate and a sufficient amount of land to hold this crop. The common sense of mainstream literature thus argues that the main determinant for palm oil production is the comparative advantage that it has vis-à-vis other products that could be cultivated in a country.[10]

In this chapter, we depart from this dominant framing by arguing that the expansion of oil palm production was not simply a consequence of objective and enlightened decisions by entrepreneurs and policy makers that potentialized palm cultivation in light of a natural comparative advantage. Rather, the conditions that led to the expansion of this production were the outcome of a struggle between business, the state, and workers. This struggle produced a particular set of laws and legal institutions that *distributed* public and private resources in a very specific way. In short, powerful economic actors created comparative advantage with the help of legal regimes. Both economic development models we examine, import substitution industrialization (ISI) and export led growth, contributed to cementing the dominance of capital over labor in the palm oil industry. Development strategies affected agrarian reform policies, which in turn led to property regulations that contributed to strengthening the power of capital vis-à-vis labor.

Along with exploring the success of rent-seeking initiatives of palm producers and their violent practices against unions, our analysis here aims for a further critique. Even when governments were embracing neoliberalism as a discourse, we illustrate how they continued to center their practice on prizing certain entrepreneurs at the expense not only of workers but of consumers as well. Finally, in relation to labor, our goal is to provide more depth to the conditions of exploitation that are framed in relation to property and determined by race. For palm oil business owners to capture rents and exploit workers, collective titling for Afro-descendants and the dispossession of their land must coexist as well. We detail how the forces of capitalist expansion and racial capitalism frame palm production and are crystallized through law. We propose a legal narrative aligned with Nancy Fraser's revisiting of the Marxist analysis of capitalism, one that makes relevant the inextricable relationship between exploitation and expropriation. According to Fraser, "Marx leads us from *accumulation through exploitation*, which is a legally sanctioned form of rip-off that works through—and mystified by—the labor contract, to *accumulation by expropriation*, which is an overtly brutal process, with no pretense of equal exchange. The latter process, which David Harvey calls 'dispossession,' lies behind contractualized exploitation and renders it possible."[11]

To explore these ideas, the text is divided into two sections. First, we lay out the legal frame that allowed capitalist expansion through worker exploitation, property accumulation, and the interaction between labor and property. The second part homes in on a specific region, Chocó, to illustrate the legal tools that made expropriation possible and are telling illustrations of racial capitalism.[12] Subsequently, we juxtapose the neoliberal narrative against a corporatist one. Here our aim is to underscore how oil palm production is explained through a lens that hides the struggle between relevant actors with and within the state via the neoliberal story told by palm oil entrepreneurs. We stress how their narrative about the emergence, consolidation, and strengthening of the palm oil economy demonstrates that these entrepreneurs were acutely determined to translate their private interests into state policy. Then we delve into the blind spots in the neoliberal story by proposing a detailed analysis of the legal rules that palm oil entrepreneurs have successfully lobbied for since the 1970s. This account illustrates the number of public resources that were transferred to the private sector, which in turn undermines the idea that the state was a neutral umpire distributing economic, social, and political entitlements.

CAPITALIST EXPANSION: THE LEGAL STRUCTURE OF EXPLOITATION AND EXPROPRIATION

In this section, we foreground the laws and policies in Colombia that were designed to promote capitalist expansion, exploit workers, and expropriate the labor and land of the Afro-descendant population through the protection and privileging of palm oil production. These numerous regulations show not only why palm producers are so powerful in the country and why they have fought so hard to maintain their rents, but also how these sets of privileges have made the sector an important site for money laundering, which in turn crystallizes in capitalist expansion.[13] In addition, protectionism and privilege explain the value of land, which led to its dispossession from and the economic displacement of peasants and Afro-descendants.

Paving the Ground for Exploitation:
The Interaction Between Labor and Land

Colombian palm producers have long argued that the high costs of labor in the country make their product uncompetitive on the international market. As a consequence, the last thirty years have seen a shift in the production model from direct to indirect employment schemes. Scarcity of workers during the 1970s gave employees an upper hand in negotiating their labor conditions, allowing some workers to unionize and improve their bargaining position after violent strikes. This strength was short lived. Companies shifted their strategy, and instead of hiring workers they offered to buy the harvested palm from associations of small and medium-sized producers. Labor unions have argued that they were sidelined by property owners and the government beginning in the early 1980s and up to 2017, when the Ministry of Labor (of a not particularly progressive government) fined Indupalma for engaging in practices that hindered workers' bargaining position.[14]

The labor side of the equation is encapsulated in what has been termed indirect employment. Indirect employment entails the establishment of associations of workers or cooperatives of small property owners, who in turn sell their production to companies that transform palm into palm oil. The associations affiliate individuals are not called workers but "associates." Because of the type of contract they sign, "associates" are not owed overtime or welfare benefits such as health, pension, or unemployment insurance.[15] Workers raised complaints regarding this contracting style in the late 1990s.[16] It took the Colombian government almost twenty years to punish companies that had contracts with workers' associations, under the justification that such contracts were set forth to avoid labor rights protections.[17]

The property side of the equation is equally problematic. Cooperative structures illustrate an initiative by large agribusiness owners to promote the acquisition of small and medium-sized plots by peasant families. To acquire the land, peasants were offered twelve-year lines of credit, and for the first four years no payment was due (to facilitate setting up production).[18] Despite being described as a generous initiative to empower small landholders and increase productivity, the reality was far grimmer. In fact, cooperatives have shifted many costs and responsibilities to the small producer: price fluctuations in international markets; shifts in environmental conditions; and harms induced by pesticides and additional labor costs, among others. However, once the cooperatives were set in place, big companies could concentrate on the most profitable part of the equation: the industrial process of producing oil and its sale in local and international markets.

Against the backdrop of these struggles, unionized workers, associates, and small peasants of the palm oil industry have drifted toward new legal and political language with the hope of affecting land and labor regulations. Memory and human rights are part of the language these actors use to retell their decades old struggle to new generations for the purposes of generating class consciousness and revamping unionization, which were negatively affected by the previously mentioned strategies. Within the framework of the explosion of memory and transitional justice in the last couple of decades in Colombia, in 2018 workers' unions from the northern part of the country published a report coauthored with the government run Centro Nacional de Memoria Histórica (National Center for Historical Memory).[19] In this report, business associations protested because their voice was not included.[20] Workers stressed that memory entailed the remembrance of past struggles that led to victories through proper labor organization. In workers' recollections of events, the unionization of the 1970s challenged traditional economic powers that then reacted violently against them.[21] In their narrative, workers argue that the rise of violence is a consequence of their mobilization, their success in raising class consciousness, and the strengthening of their bargaining power, which threatened to affect distributional outcomes traditionally favoring capitalists, and thus provoked an elite backlash.[22] Hence workers see in labor organization the main tool that will enable them to counter the lobbying and legal reforms that have favored business during the twentieth century. This state of affairs echoes one of the aspects that Hale highlighted in his writings about law and coercion, which ultimately became relevant for distributional analysis: through organization and unionization, workers can take advantage of the background rules of property if they can withhold their personal activities—the labor that they own—from the capitalist and can thus create situations where capitalists do not have suitable alternatives to evade workers' demands.[23]

EXPROPRIATION: THE CASE OF CHOCÓ

Entrepreneurs, workers, peasants, and other actors have framed their legal struggle in different vocabularies around the country. The social and ethnic diversity of the different regions where palm oil is cultivated explains these differences. In the northeast Pacific region of Colombia lies the *departamento* of Chocó. It covers 46,530 square kilometers and is one of the rainiest places on Earth, which also makes it one of the most biodiverse. The region has great tracts of forest, which has made it important for logging industries, along with rich mineral sources such as gold and platinum. Close to 80 percent of its population is Afro-Colombian. Historically, Chocó has been a region neglected by Colombian centralist elites based in Bogotá. The only style of economic development it experienced was a model based on the outright extraction of resources through mining and logging. During the early twenty-first century, the appeal of the area has increased, not only because of the resources previously mentioned but also due to pharmaceutical uses of its biodiversity and its possibilities as a more direct transportation route to Asian countries.

Palm oil has been present in the region since the 1960s, when the Colombian state made it easy for big companies to invest in its production. In return, businesses would receive property rights in protected forest areas and publicly owned land (lands that were only to be used for agrarian reform purposes). Since the 1960s, the government has granted concessions on land that Afro-Colombians argued they had ancestrally occupied.[24] The conflict regarding who were the rightful landowners was transformed in 1993 when Afro-descendants were allowed to demand collective property. Law 70 of 1993 specifically states: "The purpose of this law is to recognize the right to collective property of the black communities that have been occupying *tierras baldías* [empty or unused land] in the river-side rural zones of the rivers of the Pacific Basin in accordance with their traditional practices of production."[25]

Granting collective titling could be understood as a triumph for Afro-Colombians, but it has many dark sides. As Karen Engle argues in her in-depth of analysis of the law and the regulations (*decretos*) implementing it, there were restrictions on what could be produced on titled land and what methods could be employed. This, in turn, excluded this population from the benefits of economic development programs on their titled land, including large-scale palm production. Along these same lines, the law assumes that all Afro-Colombians are environmental protectors: "Law 70 and the decretos implementing it not only assume, *but require*, that black communities use the land in ecologically sustainable ways."[26] In fact, as Engle argues, the Afro-Colombian community is deeply divided on these issues, with some of them arguing that rural Afro-Colombians should have a chance to reap the benefits of their land. Engle quotes a human rights report that states this point brilliantly: "Some assert that the crop is 'good business,' but that the current practices of the industry exclude the local communities from its benefits, leaving them only to fill positions as low-paid, manual laborers. Indeed, if palm oil cultivation were to follow the guidelines of [prior consultation], ecological sustainability, and community participation outlined in [Law 70], perhaps it would have the potential to be a much-needed development tool for these communities."[27]

The case of Chocó illustrates how the background rules of property, which in the region largely revolve around Law 70, are essential for grassroots mobilization and identity formation. Communities' participation in economic development is framed by their capacity to mobilize background rules to change the distribution of existing resources. Therefore, as we show later, the legalization of land dispossession has been one of the key factors in the development of the palm sector and the consolidation of big businesses in this sector.

Very early on white Colombian business owners opposed Law 70. They were worried that this law would not only affect the four thousand hectares of palm crops but also the more than six million hectares of the Pacific "conquered without firing a bullet but imposed by subversive forces."[28] To counteract the territorial redefinition that collective titling would entail, current and future entrepreneurs used a combination of violence that led to displacement and migration by means of intimidation to secure lower land prices and forgery of property deeds.[29] This strategy was confessed by a paramilitary leader in the following terms: "I was given the name of 10 to 12 people—I don't remember their names—who were part of a corporation owned by politicians from Medellín. This group had high level connections who would help us acquire legal land deeds that would be used for palm production."[30]

By 2004, this capitalist expansion (through legal and illegal means) significantly transformed collective property into an agro-industrial compound. In 2004, according to the Colombian Institute for Rural Development (INCODER), 4,993 hectares that had been granted to Afro-Colombians had been illegally expropriated and were used for oil palm production. In addition, documents indicated an aimed expansion of 21,142 hectares more.[31] In this situation, it is impossible to think about the future of work and workers without assessing the background rules and actions that shape the distribution of large tracts of land that are relevant for palm oil cultivation and exploitation.

Capitalist Expansion Through Property Accumulation:
The Effects of Economic Development Policies Over Property

As described in the introduction and developed further in the second section of this chapter, palm oil was considered strategically important for economic development, and as a consequence, considerable amounts of public resources have been made available for its production (directly in the form of subsidies or subsidized credits; as well as indirectly in the form of tax exemptions), which in turn have stimulated land concentration and the appropriation of barren land. Barren land is the unused, publicly owned frontier land. Mainstream accounts describe its distribution as historically following three objectives: economic development purposes; improving the livelihood of poor landless peasants; and solving pressing social issues.[32] If we consider the myriad incentives surrounding palm oil production, the account seems more biased toward privileging elites with a specific view of growth and distribution and clear ideas regarding how to extract surplus. In fact, promoting palm oil production meant that many occupants of barren land were expelled to make space for wealthy, well connected businesspeople who had access to public resources. They used both legal and illegal instruments to accumulate land.[33] In fact, from 2000 to 2017, the amount of land dedicated to palm production increased 200 percent, going from 157,000 to 516,000 hectares.

In addition, big land plots where palm is produced are the result of Civil Code provisions (in place since the late nineteenth century) that distributed barren land to expand the agricultural frontier. After several agrarian reforms, accumulating big land extensions through the adjudication of publicly owned plots was greatly limited because this land could only be given to landless peasants.[34] This didn't prevent property concentration through buying out small and medium-sized landowners. In areas where work was hard to find, land was bought from small landowners who were heavily indebted (as palm oil production can be expensive), and part of the exchange was a job in their previously owned plots. Along with legal ways of acquiring property, there have been accusations of paramilitary groups displacing people from plots that were later used by industrialists to plant palm. However, violent displacement was not the general rule; economic and environmental displacement were most common. Research has demonstrated that once a region started to produce palm oil, subsistence farming almost disappeared because of new plagues, water pollution, changes in the quality of the soil, and decreased access to water resources.[35] In addition, in some regions there are conflicts regarding titling in collective property zones such as in the departments of Chocó, Cauca, and Bolívar.[36] Racial capitalism thus enables the emergence of background rules of land regulation, which are also shaped by a narrative of economic development that has constructed an idea of comparative advantage of palm cultivation in Colombia. As the next section shows, the narrative of comparative advantage has been useful for appropriating the rents of the business during paradigmatic changes in the idea of development—namely, the fall of the ISI model and the rise of the market economy.

NEOLIBERALISM AND CORPORATIVISM: OPPOSING NARRATIVES

In this section, we describe the power of the palm oil elite, how they tell the narrative of their success, and how they were able to successfully achieve robust protections for their sector despite the commitment of successive governments to the neoliberal agenda. In a way, this story shows that far from being a cohesive, comprehensive economic development program, neoliberal ideas were more a superficial discourse (probably aimed at multilateral institutions). The superficiality of the neoliberal discourse also illustrates that, far from allowing market forces to distribute resources, the state effectively privileged a particular sector and selected economic winners.

The Neoliberal Story: The Growing Importance of Palm Oil and the Strengthening of Comparative Advantage

Palm oil became an important commodity in world trade after the final decade of the twentieth century. It has become important because of changes in attitudes toward the preparation of food and its relationship to health, ethical debates regarding the welfare of animals, and pressing concerns about climate change. As a matter of fact, the food, cosmetic, and biodiesel industries are largely responsible for this boom that led to the quadruplication of palm oil production worldwide between 1995 and 2015.

In the food industry, palm oil increased in importance when people discovered that it was healthier than other fats and was relatively cheap for daily cooking. Discovery of the lower fat content of palm oil emerged after giants in the global food industry (like Unilever) invested in scientific research to replace products high in trans fat. Likewise, in the cosmetics industry, the animal-friendly drive led to replacing tallow as a prime ingredient in soaps. Palm oil was a versatile substitute for the animal fat found in these cosmetic products, and its uptake was supported by the argument that people should be more conscientious of animal rights. Finally, ecological concerns in the late twentieth century about carbon monoxide emissions led to research investigating the possibility of using biofuels. Although oil from other products is also useful for biofuels, palm oil is cheaper and has become the most important substitute for fossil fuels. The desirable goal of fostering diverse sustainable sources of energy had the unintended consequence of increasing the demand for palm oil, which is produced in conditions that exploit workers, promote land dispossession, and importantly, also negatively affect soil conditions and water sources.[37] In sum, one of the main characteristics of the palm oil industry is that a primary product found its way up the supply chain to a very diverse array of industries.[38]

STRENGTHENING COLOMBIA'S COMPARATIVE ADVANTAGE

Colombia's great advantage is that it has almost forty-four million hectares of land that is adequate for agriculture. At the moment, the country is only cultivating 8.5 million hectares, which means that palm oil plantations can increase drastically without deforestation.[39]

The palm tree mainly grows in the tropics—West Africa, South Asia, and South America. This fact frames the classical comparative advantage argument in favor of its production. Indonesia, Malaysia, Thailand, and Colombia are the main growers and producers of palm oil. In Colombia, palm oil crops were originally promoted during ISI in the 1950s to diminish the amount of imported vegetable oil.[40] Protectionist policies included controlling imports of other vegetable oils, thereby keeping national prices higher than international prices. With the change of the development model and a rise in the demand for palm oil for food, cosmetics, and biofuel production, in the early 1990s the area of palm cultivation began to increase exponentially. Domestic capital investment has been central to this increase in production.[41] Producers in Colombia are organized around a specific association, Fedepalma, that seeks to protect their interests and cooperates in publishing scientific studies about palm cultivation and its benefits.[42]

In the era of the rise of market economies, the World Bank has pushed forward the comparative advantage argument by recommending palm oil cultivation as a recipe to alleviate poverty in countries close to the Equator because there can be year-round production of the tree and it requires relatively little preparation of the land vis-à-vis other crops.[43] Hence domestic capital investment decisions also are related to ideas about best practices and definitions of economic development designed by multilateral institutions that have identified economic growth as the main instrument to attack poverty. This approach contrasts with other definitions of economic development, such as those that make the protection of national production the main goal; combine growth with redistribution; define growth in terms of sustainability; or more recently, center well-being, the environment, care, and a good living, *buen vivir*, for all.[44]

The Other Story: Corporativism and Rent-Seeking in the Palm Oil Industry

One of the striking features about the history of palm oil production in Colombia is that it demonstrates that there was more continuity than rupture between ISI policies and neoliberal ones. In fact, the rise of the neoliberal state in Colombia did not produce what technocrats had envisioned: a government that would not intervene in markets to avoid rent-seeking behavior. Neoliberal economists had called out rent-seeking practices when criticizing ISI models, arguing that industrialization projects directed by states encouraged firms to obtain financial gains out of the manipulation of their privileged position. Instead of creating wealth through activities that would benefit the economy as a whole, rent-seekers merely wanted to increase their own profits by, for example, investing in political lobbying, which in turn provided them with access to subsidies.[45]

THE RISE OF THE PALM INDUSTRY IN THE VOICE OF BUSINESSPEOPLE

Fedepalma (the association of palm producers) and the government developed important links beyond the fall of ISI and the rise of neoliberalism. The strength of these links demonstrates how corporatist ideas have been central to the management of the Colombian economy. For the purpose of this chapter, we understand corporatism as a social ideology that took hold of the imagination of important members of the Colombian legal and political elite during most of the twentieth century. Where Catholicism was preponderant, corporatism was read through papal encyclicals to assert that society was not merely a group of individuals regulated by the state; rather, individuals were part of associations (or institutions) such as the family, the municipality, and unions, among others. One of the main goals of corporatism was to resist the Marxist explanation of social conflict, which highlighted social class as the key unit of social organization and struggle. Corporatists believed that they had to resist class conflict and the threat of a socialist revolution by advancing a vision of organic integration of society that could harmonize class conflict. Individuals did not advance their interests exclusively, but mainly promoted the interests of the organizations or associations to which they belonged. Society would advance its political, social, and economic goals by harmonizing the interests of these different organizations—many of them multiclass—and thus avoid class conflict.[46]

As a result of these ideas, Colombian economic elites created organizations that allegedly represented interests that went beyond social classes. In the

1940s, for example, merchants created FENALCO and industrialists organized around ANDI to bargain with and press the government for the adoption of economic policies that favored their sectors.[47] As a country implementing ISI after the 1940s, Colombia saw important clashes between the interests of these elitist organizations. For example, discussion about tariffs on manufactured goods frequently led to debates between merchants and industrialists insofar as the former pressed for low tariffs to sell more commodities at low prices and the latter pressed for higher tariffs and protection of their industries to sell their goods at high prices in domestic markets. Their struggle showed that a corporatist organization, far from deactivating social conflict, actually produced other battle sites. At the same time, it illustrated the possibilities of achieving specific economic policies.

Fedepalma was a latecomer to this trend of creating organizations, but nonetheless shared the purposes and inhabited the same milieu from which prior associations emerged. To the extent that palm plantations and palm oil production were not particularly relevant for the Colombian economy during the first half of the twentieth century, this association would only emerge in the 1960s when the country was still under an ISI model and cultivation expanded to several regions of the nation.

Fedepalma's official documents narrate how it became a relevant association in the middle of the financial crisis in the late 1960s and in opposition to the very low tariffs on imported oils from Perú. In fact, the price of palm oil had decreased after 1967, and the association followed a path well-known by entrepreneurs, merchants, and industrialists in the past: reach out to the government and convince public officials of the need for adopting favorable credit policies that accommodated their interests. In the words of Fedepalma, the organization "sought to solve these delicate financial problems through an intensive campaign to convince the Minister of Agriculture and Development, the Board of Directors of the Central Bank and all public officials working in credit policies to cooperate in designing new credits and restructure the current loans to palm oil industries."[48]

During the 1970s, the palm oil industry started its path toward consolidation. According to Fedepalma, a deep monetary crisis and the oil crisis of the early 1970s led to high prices of imported goods. The country turned to domestic products, such as palm oil, to satisfy the demand of domestic markets. In the words of the entrepreneurs, palm oil became the cherished girl, *"niña bonita,"* of industrialists that needed their product. The expansion of palm cultivation during the decade evidenced the rising importance of the crop, as well as the decision of one of the biggest financial groups of the moment, *Grupo Grancolombiano*, to buy shares of several companies involved in this business.

Despite the privileges granted by the Colombian government (which are summarized later), Fedepalma's official documents narrate how they had to fight to convince officials of the problems of liberalizing trade in competing oils. In the late 1970s, the government adopted low tariffs for vegetable oils (1 percent), which alarmed the organization of palm oil businessmen. According to a former chairman of Fedepalma:

> One of the most important tasks that I had between 1979 and 1981 was to *have some conversations* with the Vice minister of Agriculture . . . in which we agreed on several strategies to dynamize and save the African palm sector, seriously affected with the policies of free imports and 1 percent tariffs. In April 1981, the floor prices for vegetable oils *were settled* and the prices of palm recovered. On December 2 a new tariff of 40 percent for vegetable oil was established. I couldn't believe it! Was it a dream? No, it wasn't, and the 1980s started, the so-called golden era of palm in Colombia.[49]

It is worth noticing several aspects of the relationship between the association of palm businesspeople and the government, which emerge from how they tell the story of their struggle to include palm oil production as one of the sectors worth shielding during ISI and how successful they were in extending their privileged position after free market policies were embraced. As Fedepalma's documents illustrate, liberalization was dreaded by a nascent industry that was seeking to capture the rents of a protectionist state on the verge of moving toward free markets. Palm industrialists resisted, in their words, by talking (*conversando*) with the government. They did not describe their activities as a negotiation but merely as a gentlemen's conversation. Hence the passive verbs: floor prices and high tariffs "were settled," and the subject of the action is erased, producing the idea that perhaps these decisions were natural and obvious solutions to the problem. The previous quote conveys an image of low bargaining power for Fedepalma. However, the organization was aware of the need to strengthen their status: by the late 1970s the main financial group of the country, Grupo Grancolombiano, became a major stockholder in several palm oil businesses, thereby leading to their "consolidation" (*consolidación gremial*), an essential feature in the increase of their lobbying power.[50] This consolidation of power was demonstrated by their success in obtaining favorable policies for their industry.

What happened after 1990 demonstrates how a corporatist economy can survive (neo)liberalization. The government appointed businesspeople related to the palm industry to high government positions. The connection between the private and public realms emerges in a story told by a former president of

Fedepalma in the 1980s, Alfredo Guerra, when he inadvertently stated that he headed the organization after having lunch with Carlos Murgas, then one of the main palm oil entrepreneurs and in the late 1990s the Minister of Agriculture, who convinced him to turn down an offer from the president to head the Colombian Consulate in Houston and instead lead the association.[51] The profile that entrepreneurs were looking for to lead the association included not only technical expertise but also political acumen for the purposes of bargaining and pressing the state on policy decisions. Murgas himself would later be appointed the Minister of Agriculture in 1998, after consolidating his position as an important palm oil entrepreneur since the second half of the 1970s. Aside from telling a story that defended protectionist policies of the Colombian government during these decades and the higher influence of Fedepalma in broader associations that represent the agricultural sector in general, Guerra finishes his account by confirming how the palm business consolidated a close relationship with the government when in 1989 he was appointed Vice-Minister of Agriculture.[52]

According to Fedepalma, the transformation from an ISI development paradigm to neoliberalism in the early 1990s was detrimental to the palm oil business. Not only did special credits and subsidies for the palm industry disappear, but also the rise of public expenditures led to a burdensome fiscal situation for many sectors that was compensated by high international prices of palm oil.[53] Likewise, Fedepalma complained about the 1991 Constitution, which "created extremely expensive and extravagant institutions for our milieu."[54] Law 70 of 1993, which enshrined collective land titles in the Pacific region as *acción de tutela*, allowing Colombians to seek judicial remedies for violations of social and economic rights, were part of the institutions that the business sector consistently criticized during the 1990s and the 2000s.

The 1991 Constitution, however, was not friendly only to rights activists. In fact, it embodied a tension between neoliberalism and the expansion of social rights, which allowed businesspeople to advance their project in the former realm. With the rise of neoliberalism, Fedepalma actually found a way to continue securing friendly policies. Businesspeople sought to expand crops and maintain prices to stay competitive in international markets and to improve marketing and selling conditions within the country. Most of these privileges are described in the next section. But for the purposes of this section, it is interesting to notice how broad shifts in the economic development strategy were counterbalanced by powerful actors seeking rents. For example, one of the main mechanisms designed to achieve these goals in the heyday of free markets was, ironically, the *Fondo de Estabilización de Precios*, a special account of the government administered by Fedepalma. In 1993, when market economics allegedly took over Colombian officials' ideas about economic policies, Congress enacted a statute that allowed the government to create special accounts administered by business organizations (*gremios*) that sought to protect producers from changing prices in domestic and international markets. The statute (Law 101 of 1993) protected the production of agricultural products and thus established that producers had to pay a special contribution to a government account (*parafiscales*) run by Fedepalma. The special account uses these resources and others to compensate producers when prices drop below a reference price calculated according to several factors.[55]

Business associations, and in this case Fedepalma, strongly lobbied for the creation of these types of accounts. These accounts might challenge the ideal of free markets and free competition that took hold of the global economy after the 1980s, and they have been at the eye of a storm of economic debates in the country. For some, neoliberal principles should yield to incentives that seek to stabilize basic economic sectors that contribute to the "general conditions of the country's economy."[56] Others believe that these accounts are not necessarily the best way to compensate producers when international prices are too low and thus criticize this mechanism.[57] The tension between ideas of free markets ("let the market get the prices right") and these accounts is evidence that corporatism in palm oil production still has an important influence in Colombia to the extent that Fedepalma had the muscle to press for this *Fondo*. To justify this approach, Fedepalma argued that running the economy is a task in which both the government and private parties should cooperate. Private parties should develop schemes to increase productivity, especially through expanding crop cultivation, and the government should engender the appropriate "economic milieu," generating incentives for palm oil producers. Expansion and favorable government policies were the targets of Fedepalma in the early 2000s.[58]

The expansion of crop cultivation was evident between the 1980s and the early 2000s. In 2002, the president of Fedepalma argued that between 1980 and the early 2000s production of palm oil increased at a rate of nearly 8 percent each year. Producers starting to export nearly 20 percent of total production, and when projecting their business to 2020, Fedepalma stressed the need to further expand the agricultural frontier.[59] In 2018, Fedepalma showed that in less than two decades cultivation of oil palms grew 200 percent, from 157,000 to 516,000 hectares between 2000 and 2017.[60] Government cooperation in these years crystallized not only in the Fondo de Estabilización de Precios but also in more aggressive support from the Colombian president, Álvaro Uribe. In a public address in 2004, for example, he stressed that "it is necessary to grow [palm] oil. Not one day should go by without planting this crop."[61] The government was largely responsible for the success story of palm oil in Colombia as a key sector for the country's economic development. Behind this spectacular development, however, lies a decades old strategy by Fedepalma regarding the interaction between their interests and the government's. The fluid frontier between working for the government and for business associations, which we saw earlier in the 1980s, became more evident during Uribe's government. Palm producers partially funded his presidential campaign, and he appointed several individuals who were related—sometimes evidently and sometimes tenuously—to palm oil interests.[62] Aside from other strategies, the expansion of palm oil production was related to an idea of a mixed economy in which businesspeople of this sector reached government positions.

In 2009, Jens Mesa Dishington, president of Fedepalma and spouse of then-Minister of Communications, awarded the Order of the Palm Merit—*Orden al Mérito Palmero*—to Álvaro Uribe for his accomplishments during his eight years as president of Colombia.[63] The main achievement of Uribe, according to Fedepalma, was ensuring appropriate security conditions for the expansion of the agricultural frontier. Security had been a concern for Fedepalma since the 1970s. The formation of guerrilla movements appeared, although marginally, in their reconstruction of the story. However, during the first decade of the current century, the security problem became a central concept that the government and businesspeople took into account while considering expansion of the cultivation of palm crops. Public debates about the convenience of palm oil cultivation interpreted decades old worker struggles connected to the lack of "security" in large parts of Colombia, which led to the association of guerrillas and workers. Distributive debates were replaced by the overwhelming goal of security that President Álvaro Uribe placed as the most important policy of his term in office (2002 to 2010). The security debate thus contributed to the expansion of palm cultivation without addressing old demands about inequality in the realms of work and land ownership in the production chain.

In sum, Fedepalma tells a story about the palm oil industry in which the private sector and the state cooperate in achieving common interests. The association thus tells an evolutionary history in which entrepreneurs and the government overcome hurdles for this collaboration. From a more critical perspective, we can read this history differently: old corporatist tactics developed during the ISI period have survived during market liberalization as businesspeople of the palm sector take over key positions in the state. The lack of concern for economic inequality or even the social function of industry is swept under the rug in their narrative, or perhaps swept under the label of "security conditions." Businesspeople repeatedly complained about security conditions—violent tactics of trade unions, guerrilla warfare—without even mentioning the background of economic inequality that led to this problem in the first place. Security is the discursive place where inequalities lie hidden. In Fedepalma's narrative, there is not a particular concern about the causes for "insecurity" but mainly a "labeling" of a problem that the state has to solve. Hence the insistence in 2002 that in a mixed state or economy—which the palm industry praised—the state's role was chiefly to provide security. But under security discourse, there are histories of dispossession that businesspeople block from emerging in their public reconstructions of palm oil history. Land and work are out of the picture. This is what palm oil workers' organizations showed in a report on memory that retells their struggles since the 1960s. The permanent emphasis on security led to an official narrative that associated workers with guerrillas, thereby underestimating their legal and political claims against inequality between capitalists and workers. Insofar as the latter were associated with armed conflict, businesspeople and government argued that their demands were contaminated and could not be taken seriously. Workers not only lost in their bargaining for improving work conditions, but also suffered from ruthless violence of paramilitary groups that identified union leaders as guerrilla members. Several lost their lives.[64]

Fedepalma's narrative shows how businesspeople operated as rent-seekers both in the ISI moment and after the rise of the market economy and export-led growth. Therefore, the palm oil industry has been privileged by ISI policies, neoliberal policies, and policies that mix both frameworks. These economic development policies have had an impact on agricultural production patterns, the migration of peasants from rural areas to cities or between rural areas, the configuration of property, the adjudication of publicly owned plots, and the price of land.

For example, during the implementation of the ISI model in the 1970s, Colombia's demand for oil reached 160 tons, yet it produced only 10 tons. Partly justified by ideas regarding import substitution industrialization and partly to limit some areas of the country's dependence on cotton, the government designed a set of policies that effectively generated a bias in favor of big land parcels. Executive Decree 290 of 1957 contained the blueprint to promote palm oil against this new arrangement to the extent that it included financial aid for plantations that surpassed five hundred hectares, provided seeds and technical assistance for small-scale producers, imposed tariffs on vegetable oil imports, and allowed the government to buy all production.[65]

Later on this policy was transformed into Law 26 of 1959, which set forth a range of incentives for the agricultural sector requiring all banks (private and public) to dedicate at least 15 percent of their available credit lines to the promotion of agriculture, including livestock production and fishing. These ten-year loans should be granted at a preferential rate, with an initial five-year period where no interests would be demanded.[66] The state also partnered with private companies to support the initial capital needs of setting up plantations (including the time it takes for a plant to produce fruits) and sites for oil production. Once the initial investment period passed, the government would sell its stake back to the private company.[67] Incentives proved useful: by the mid-1970s palm was being cultivated in 23,000 hectares, and by the late 1980s it had reached close to 100,000 hectares.[68]

Benefits during export-led growth in the late 1980s were also evident and even more beneficial to the expansion of palm oil capital than in the ISI model. Although the government dismantled explicit subsidies for agriculture, Law 101 of 1993 (briefly described earlier) created a series of tools to promote the production of agricultural goods, among them palm oil. The bundle of incentives included the creation of a fund of public resources (*Fondo de Estabilización de Precios*) designed to protect producers from internal price fluctuations and guarantee a stable income for cultivators and to promote exports; financial subsidies designed to increase technological advances in agricultural and agro-industrial production (*Incentivo a la Capitalización Rural*); and a government funded guarantee account (*Fondo Agropecuario de Garantías*) that would back agricultural loans.[69]

From the year 2000, the number of laws and policies geared toward privileging and strengthening palm oil were multiplied.[70] The trend started with Law 812 of 2003 and its regulatory framework, which stated that the government would subsidize land purchases, provided that they were used in developing agribusinesses. Later on, in 2004, another law was passed to stimulate the production and sale of biofuels. The stimulus included prioritizing biofuel production and increasing the amount of tax incentives available for it.[71] As a consequence, six production sites were built.[72] The government of Uribe Vélez was particularly interested in boosting the local market for palm oil to sell domestically whatever wasn't exported. This was done by demanding that the gasoline sold in most regions of Colombia (with the exception of those bordering Venezuela) had to have between 5 and 10 percent palm oil content.[73]

During negotiations of the free trade agreement with the United States (TLC, for its initials in Spanish), Congress approved a law (*Ley de Agro Ingreso Seguro*) geared toward directly aiding the agricultural and agribusiness sector to prepare it for trade with the United States. This support included direct aid that didn't have to be paid back; preferential access to credit; strengthening the fund dedicated to support capital formation; and an increase in technical assistance.[74] Implementation of these incentives in the palm sector were highly controversial because it was proved that the resources had only benefited large landowners.[75] Among these business owners were those who had links with paramilitary groups or were paramilitary members themselves.[76] Colombian unions opposed signing the treaty, arguing that jobs would be lost, that the country would continue to export primary products, and that the country would gain little in terms of technological transfer or the establishment of U.S. companies. According to a study developed by major unions ten years after signing the treaty, the situation is exactly as was predicted.[77]

Generous tax incentives were also part of the deal. Law 788 of 2002 cut in half the value added tax for the sale of palm oil; Law 939 of 2004 eliminated income taxes for palm producers until 2014 and included tax exemptions for the selling of biodiesel; and Law 1111 of 2006 allowed tax deductions for those who invested in assets dedicated to palm oil production.

Despite the fact that palm producers weren't so central to President Uribe's successor, Juan Manuel Santos, his economic development program (focused on five growth engines—agriculture, mining, infrastructure, housing, and innovation) also benefited the sector, including through the elimination of limits on the amount of rural property that could be owned by a single individual or company to further enhance agribusiness.[78] In addition to Colombian public funds, U.S. cooperation resources (aimed at helping peasants shift from coca production to other agricultural goods) ended up funding palm oil producers, some of them with links to the paramilitary.[79]

The reluctance to eliminate direct and indirect subsidies during the export led growth phase shows not only that law and policy decisions create comparative advantage but also reveals that in the case of palm oil the alleged liberalization did not deliver the promise of "let the market get the prices right." A collusion of public and private interests created a regime that gave the upper hand to producers, allowing them to capture rent and preserve the capital-work hierarchy despite shifts of development paradigms.

CONCLUSIONS

The goal of this chapter was to propose a different way of analyzing the importance of palm oil for the Colombian economy. Contrary to the neoliberal and corporate story of success, we explored the legal structure that allowed the capture of rents, the exploitation of workers, and the expropriation of land. The expansion of this crop was not simply a consequence of objective and enlightened decisions by entrepreneurs and policy makers that potentialized palm cultivation in light of comparative advantage. In contrast, we highlighted how the conditions that led to the expansion of its production were the outcome of a struggle between businesspeople, the state, and workers. This struggle produced a particular set of laws and legal institutions that *distributed* public and private resources in a very specific way. In short, comparative advantage is a situation that powerful economic actors can create with the help of legal regimes. In this analysis of the creation of comparative advantage, our aim was to unveil two interrelated tools through which capital is accumulated: exploitation and dispossession.

We offered a perspective on how distributional analysis tools can be used to understand the emergence of background rules in a specific industry, and how they operate. Racial capitalism and the economic development models explain how these rules come into being in a specific setting. The Colombian palm industry shows that entrepreneurs' decisions—like Indupalma's dissolution—have to be analyzed bearing in mind the struggles between capital and labor, the implementation of economic models, and the background regulations that open or close the possibilities for different actors involved in a specific industry.

NOTES

1. Redacción Economía y Negocios, "Por Temas Laborales y Comerciales Liquidan Indupalma," *El Tiempo*, November 5, 2019, https://www.eltiempo.com/economia/empresas/indupalma-junta-directiva-decide-liquidar-la-empresa-429740.
2. "Producción de Aceite de Palma en Colombia podría aumentar un 20 percent," *El Espectador*, July 11, 2018, https://www.elespectador.com/economia/produccion-de-aceite-de-palma-en-colombia-podria-aumentar-un-20-articulo-799653.
3. Agencia de Información Laboral—Escuela Nacional Sindical, "Colombia: Tras la liquidación de Indupalma, trabajadores luchan por sus derechos colectivos," *Centro de Información sobre Empresas y Derechos Humanos*, November 19, 2020, https://www.business-humanrights.org/es/%C3%BAltimas-noticias/colombia-tras-la-liquidaci%C3%B3n-de-indupalma-trabajadores-luchan-por-sus-derechos-colectivos/.
4. Angela Serrano, "Oil Palm Workers Confront a Fatal Blow Against Unions in Colombia," *Collective of Agrarian Scholar-Activists from the South-Casas*, April 13, 2021, https://casasouth.org/oil-palm-workers-confront-a-fatal-blow-against-unions-in-colombia/.
5. "Las Metas del Gremio de la Palma Colombiana Tras 55 años," *Revista Dinero*, February 1, 2018, https://www.semana.com/edicion-impresa/negocios/articulo/metas-de-la-agroindustria-de-la-palma-colombiana-en-2018/254802/.
6. "En 2017, Colombia exportó mas de 800,000 Toneladas de Aceite de Palma," *Portafolio*, June 7, 2018, https://www.portafolio.co/economia/exportacion-en-colombia-de-aceite-de-palma-durante-el-2018-517865.

7. Juan Diego Murcia, "Fedepalma proyecta una producción de aceite de palma de 1.8 toneladas," *Agronegocios*, February 15, 2023, https://www.agronegocios.co/agricultura/produccion-de-aceite-de-palma-para-2023-3546342.
8. Centro Nacional de Memoria Histórica, *Tierras y Conflictos Rurales: Historia, Conflictos Rurales y Protagonistas* (Bogotá: Central Nacional de Memoria Histórica, 2016), 460.
9. "Among the success factors for the National Plan for Colombian Biofuels, Mesa mentioned political will, the soundness of technical standards, the quality of the product, the strength of the producers' associations, the building of trust between actors in the [supply] chain, and the environmental sustainability of the biofuel industry." "Colombia, Cuarto Productor de Aceite de Palma en el Mundo," *Portafolio*, September 18, 2014, https://www.portafolio.co/economia/finanzas/colombia-cuarto-productor-aceite-palma-mundo-59140 (authors' translation).
10. Hansen Tandra, Arif Imam Suroso, Yusman Syaukat, and Mukhamad Najib, "The Determinants of Competitiveness in Global Palm Oil Trade," *Economies* 10 (2022): 132, https://doi.org/10.3390/economies10060132.
11. Nancy Fraser and Rahel Jaeggi, *Capitalism: A Conversation in Critical Theory* (Cambridge: Polity, 2018), 30.
12. It is relevant to stress that several regions of Colombia host palm oil production. Ethnic, racial, social, and gender dynamics are different in each of these regions. As we consider the case of Chocó, we do not want to delve too deeply into the specifics of this region, but we use it to illustrate how transformation or preservation of background rules about land have an impact on the distribution of economic resources.
13. Several NGOs have suggested the connection between forced displacement, government incentives for palm cultivation, and money laundering. In 2009, for example, "The Nation" reported that part of the money the USAID donated to the Colombian government meant for investing in new crops—i.e., oil palm—that would replace coca plantations were sent to corporations owned by drug lords and paramilitary leaders. Even Fedepalma acknowledged that some entrepreneurs were using the palm oil business for money laundering, but stressed that this was not a main feature of the businesses affiliated with the association. See Sandra Seeboldt and Yamile Salinas Aldana, *Responsabilidad y sostenibilidad de la Industria de la Palma* (Bogóta: Oxfam-Indepaz, 2010), http://www.indepaz.org.co/wp-content/uploads/2018/08/Responsabilidad-y-sostenibilidad-de-la-industria-de-la-palma.pdf.
14. Redacción Economía y Negocios, "Por temas laborales y comerciales liquidan a Indupalma," *El Tiempo*, November 5, 2019, https://www.eltiempo.com/economia/empresas/indupalma-junta-directiva-decide-liquidar-la-empresa-429740.
15. Grupo Semillas, "El Agronegocio de la Palma Aceitera en Colombia ¿Desarrollo Para Las Poblaciones Locales o Una Crónica Para el Desastre?," *Revista Semillas* 34/35, February 4, 2008, https://www.semillas.org.co/es/revista/el-agronegocio-de-la-palma-aceitera-en-colombia-desarrollo-para-las-poblaciones-locales-o-una-crnica-para-el-desastre.
16. Agencia de Información Laboral, "Colombia: Trabajadores Tercerizados en Indupalma Alegan Abusos Laborales e Intimidación," *Centro de Información Sobre Empresas y Derechos Humanos*, January 26, 2018, https://www.business-humanrights.org/es/últimas-noticias/colombia-trabajadores-tercerizados-en-indupalma-alegan-abusos-laborales-e-intimidación/.

17. Sebastián Forero Rueda, "La Lucha de los Trabajadores de Indupalma, un Conflicto de Vieja Data," *El Espectador*, October 14, 2018, https://www.elespectador.com/colombia/mas-regiones/la-lucha-de-los-trabajadores-de-indupalma-un-conflicto-de-vieja-data-article-817928/.
18. María M. Aguilera Díaz, "Palma Africana en la Costa Caribe: Un Semillero de Empresas Solidarias," Documentos de Trabajo sobre Economía Regional, No. 30, Banco de la República—Sucursal Cartagena, Cartagena de Indias, Colombia, July 2002, 35.
19. See Centro Nacional de Memoria Histórica et al., *Y a la vida por fin daremos todo: memorias de las y los trabajadores y extrabajadores de la agroindustria de la palma de aceite en el Cesar 1950–2018* (Bogotá: Centro Nacional de Memoria Histórica, 2018).
20. Edinson Arley Bolaños and Sebastián Forero, "El Informe que el Centro de Memoria se niega a lanzar," *El Espectador*, April 10, 2019, https://www.elespectador.com/colombia-20/paz-y-memoria/el-informe-que-el-centro-de-memoria-se-niega-a-lanzar-article/.
21. Centro Nacional de Memoria Histórica, *Y a la vida*, 25.
22. Centro Nacional de Memoria Histórica, *Y a la vida*, 22.
23. Robert Hale, "Coercion and Distribution in a Supposedly Non-Coercive State," *Political Science Quarterly* 38, no. 3 (1923): 471–74, https://doi.org/10.2307/2142367.
24. Natalia Arenas, "Colombia: La Palma de Aceite en Medio de Los Conflictos por la Tierra en Tumaco," *Mongabay*, December 3, 2018, https://es.mongabay.com/2018/12/restitucion-de-tierras-palma-de-aceite-colombia/.
25. Law 70 of 1993, L. 70/1993, August 27, 1993, Diario Oficial [D.O.], translated in Karen Engle, *The Elusive Promise of Indigenous Development: Rights, Culture, History* (Durham, NC: Duke University Press, 2010), 223.
26. Engle, *The Elusive Promise*, 241 (emphasis added).
27. Engle, *The Elusive Promise*, 251, quoting Bernard and Audre Rapoport Center for Human Rights and Justice, Robert S. Strauss Center for International Law and Security, and Lozano-Long Institute for Latin American Studies, *Unfulfilled Promises and Persistent Obstacles to the Realization of the Rights of Afro-Colombians: A Report on the Development of Ley 70 of 1993* (Austin, TX: Rapoport Center, Strauss Center, and Lozano-Long Institute, 2007).
28. Letter sent by businessman Gabriel Jaramillo Sierra to the Minister of Agriculture on September 27, 2007, quoted in Vilma Liliana Franco R. and Juan Diego Restrepo E., "Empresarios Palmeros, Poderes de Facto y Despojo de Tierras en el Bajo Atrato," in *La Economía de los Paramilitares: Redes de Corrupción, Negocios y Política*, ed. Mauricio Romero Vidal (Bogotá: Debate, 2011), 308 (authors' translation).
29. "The initial stages of the expropriation-appropriation story were the forced displacement produced by the military-paramilitary alliance in early 1997 . . . this generated a separation between the community and its livelihood after the destruction of their goods." Franco R. and Restrepo E., "Empresarios Palmeros," 310 (authors' translation).
30. Account by paramilitary leader Fredy Rendón Herrera quoted in Franco R. and Restrepo E., "Empresarios Palmeros," 311 (authors' translation).
31. Franco R. and Restrepo E., "Empresarios Palmeros," 311.
32. Juanita Villaveces Niño and Fabio Sánchez, "Tendencias Históricas y Regionales de la Adjudicación de Baldíos en Colombia," Documentos de Trabajo 179, Universidad del Rosario, Facultad de Economía, February 2015, Rosario, Colombia, 10.

33. "In San Alberto Cesar, in 1958, several methods were used. These included displacing peasants who occupied the land as well as small property owners w produced rice or had cattle. The company would come and offer to buy at a very low price." Centro Nacional de Memoria Histórica, *Y a La Vida*, 34.
34. Helena Alviar García, "The Unending Quest for Land: The Tale of Broken Constitutional Promises," *Texas Law Review* 89 (2015): 1895–1914.
35. Centro Nacional de Memoria Histórica, *Tierras y Conflictos*, 462; "El Cultivo de Palma Aceitera seca a los Montes de María," *Semana-Sostenible*, June 6, 2017, https://www.semana.com/medio-ambiente/articulo/palma-aceitera-y-su-cultivo-seca-a-los-montes-de-maria-en-bolivar/37966/.
36. "Lo que hay detrás del negocio de palma de aceite," *Agronegocios e Industria de Alimentos-AneIA, Universidad de Los Andes*, March 21, 2016, https://aneia.uniandes.edu.co/lo-que-hay-detras-del-negocio-de-la-palma-de-aceite/.
37. Centro Nacional de Memoria Histórica, *Y a la vida*, 37.
38. See Paul Tullis, "How the World Got Hooked on Palm Oil," *The Guardian*, February 19, 2019, https://www.theguardian.com/news/2019/feb/19/palm-oil-ingredient-biscuits-shampoo-environmental.
39. "Producción de aceite de palma en Colombia podría aumentar un 20 percent," *El Espectador*, July 11, 2018, https://www.elespectador.com/economia/produccion-de-aceite-de-palma-en-colombia-podria-aumentar-un-20-article-799653/.
40. Centro Nacional de Memoria Histórica, *Tierras y Conflictos*, 457.
41. There is some foreign investment—famously, Poligrow (the Italian/Spanish agribusiness) was involved in a land accumulation scandal in Mapiripan, Meta. For more on this, see "Lupa a la Multinacional Poligrow que opera en Mapiripán, Meta," *Verdad Abierta*, November 5, 2015, https://verdadabierta.com/lupa-a-la-multinacional-poligrow-que-opera-en-mapiripan-meta/.
42. Ian Henson, Rodrigo Ruiz, and Hernán Mauricio Romero, "The Growth of the Oil Palm Industry in Colombia," *Journal of Oil Palm Research* 23 (2011): 1121–28.
43. See Tullis, "How the World Got Hooked on Palm Oil."
44. For more on diverse definitions of development, see Helena Alviar García, *Legal Experiments for Development in Latin America: Modernization, Revolution and Social Justice* (London: Routledge, 2021).
45. On the transformation of development ideas in Latin America, see Luis Bértola and José Antonio Ocampo, *The Economic Development of Latin America Since Independence* (Oxford: Oxford University Press, 2012).
46. For a description of twentieth-century corporatism, see Stanley G. Payne, *A History of Fascism 1914–1945* (Madison: University of Wisconsin Press, 1995), 38–40.
47. On the rise of these associations in Colombia, see Eduardo Sáenz Rovner, *La ofensiva empresarial: Industriales, políticos y violencia en los años 40 en Colombia* (Bogotá: Universidad Nacional de Colombia, 2007).
48. Ernesto Vargas Tovar, "Décadas de 1960 y 1970: La Palma de aceite: de fincas a empresas," *Palmas* 23, no. 3 (2002): 87 (authors' translation).
49. Tovar, "Décadas de 1960 y 1970," 92 (authors' translation).
50. Tovar, "Décadas de 1960 y 1970," 92.

51. "Carlos Roberto Murgas Guerrero: Más de 40 años dominando la Palma de Aceite," *Rutas del Conflicto*, accessed September 16, 2022, https://rutasdelconflicto.com/especiales/acuatenientes/murgas.html; and Antonio Guerra de la Espriella, "Década de 1980: la época dorada de la palma," *Palmas* 23, no. 3 (2002): 93.
52. Guerra de la Espriella, "Década de 1980," 93–96.
53. Eliseo Restrepo Londoño, "Decada 1990: consolidación institucional," *Palmas* 23, no. 3 (2002): 97–100.
54. Restrepo Londoño, "Decada 1990," 97 (authors' translation).
55. For a detailed description of this special account, see Law 101 of 1993, L. 101/93, December 23, 1993, Diario Oficial [D.O.], https://www.funcionpublica.gov.co/eva/gestornormativo/norma.php?i=66787.
56. "Fondos de estabilización de precios, desde las normas de la competencia," *Portafolio*, accessed September 16, 2022, https://www.portafolio.co/economia/finanzas/fondos-estabilizacion-precios-normas-competencia-350310 (authors' translation).
57. Guillermo Trujillo Estrada, "Fondo de estabilización de precios," *La República*, June 26, 2018, https://larepublica.co/analisis/guillermo-trujillo-estrada-505837/fondo-de-estabilizacion-de-precios-2742576.
58. Amy C. Offner, *Sorting Out the Mixed Economy. The Rise and Fall of Welfare and Developmental States in the Americas* (Princeton, NJ: Princeton University Press, 2019).
59. Jens Mesa Dishington, "La Palmicultura colombiana de cara al 2020," *Palmas* 21, special issue (2000): 9–17.
60. Taran Volckhausen, "How Colombia Became Latin America's Palm Oil Powerhouse," *Mongabay*, May 31, 2018, https://news.mongabay.com/2018/05/how-colombia-became-latin-americas-palm-oil-powerhouse/.
61. lmarin, "Genealogía de la palma en el gobierno de Álvaro Uribe," *La Silla Vacía*, March 30, 2009, https://www.lasillavacia.com/silla-nacional/genealogia-de-la-palma-en-el-gobierno-de-alvaro-uribe/ (authors' translation).
62. lmarin, "Genealogía"; "Quién es quién. Las conexiones del poder," *La Silla Vacía*, September 16, 2022, https://www.lasillavacia.com/quien-es-quien/jens-mesa-dishington.
63. See pictures of this award on Uribe's personal webpage at Agosto 11, Alvaro Uribe Velez, accessed September 16, 2022, https://alvarouribevelez.com.co/2009-08-11-foto10/.
64. See, generally, Centro Nacional de Memoria Histórica, *Y a la vida*.
65. Alejandra Rueda Zárate and Pablo Pacheco, *Políticas, Mercados y Modelos de Producción: Un Análisis de la Situación y Desafíos del Sector Palmero Colombiano, Documentos Ocasionales* (Bogor, Indonesia: Centro Para la Investigación Forestal Internacional, 2015), 7, https://www.cifor.org/publications/pdf_files/OccPapers/OP-128.pdf.
66. See Law 26 of 1959, L. 26/1959, May 25, 1959, Diario Oficial [D.O.], https://www.funcionpublica.gov.co/eva/gestornormativo/norma.php?i=72953.
67. Many private companies benefited from this scheme, including Caribe Oleaginosas Hipinto (1960) in San Alberto, Cesar; Palmas Oleaginosas de Ariguaní Palmariguaní (1961) in Bosconia, Cesar; and Palmas Oleaginosas de Cascará, Palmacará (1963) in Codazzi, Cesar. See Rueda-Zárate and Pacheco, *Políticas*, 8.
68. Rueda-Zárate and Pacheco, *Políticas*, 9.

69. In fact, in 1998, Fedepalma, achieved a specific fund for palm oil. See Rueda-Zárate and Pacheco, *Políticas*, 9. For government funding, see Law 101 of 1993.
70. As mentioned in the first section, President Álvaro Uribe Vélez was responsible for this golden era of palm oil.
71. See Law 939 of 2004, L. 939/2004, December 31, 2004, Diario Oficial [D.O.], https://www.funcionpublica.gov.co/eva/gestornormativo/norma.php?i=15594; and Documento Conpes DNP 3510 of 2008, March 31, 2008, https://gestornormativo.creg.gov.co/gestor/entorno/docs/CONPES_DNP_3510_2008.htm.
72. Alejandra Rueda Zárate and Marlyn Ahumada, *Biodiesel de palma colombiano: De la Ficción energética a la Realidad de un Negocio* (Bogotá: Fedepalma, 2013).
73. Documento Conpes DNP 3510 of 2008.
74. Law 1133 of 2007, L. 1133/2007, April 9, 2007, Diario Oficial [D.O.], https://www.funcionpublica.gov.co/eva/gestornormativo/norma.php?i=68093.
75. Of the fifty-one businesses that were granted aid, 20 percent were palm producers. In fact, palm producers received more than 14 billion pesos in subsidies and more than 7 billion pesos in preferential lines of credit. For more on this, see Juan Esteban Lewin, "Estos son los 51 beneficiarios de Agro Ingreso Seguro que Aportaron a Campañas de Uribe," *La Silla Vacía*, October 29, 2009, https://www.lasillavacia.com/historias/silla-nacional/estos-son-los-51-beneficiarios-de-agro-ingreso-seguro-que-aportaron-a-campanas-de-uribe.
76. Nazih Richani describes the fact that paramilitaries were also successful businesspeople in the following terms: "In Colombia an individual can alternate roles: that is, one can start as drug trafficker and end up as an agro-industrialist farming African palm and owning another parcel for cattle ranching used for speculation and to shelter capital gains. For example, Salvatore Mancuso, a leading paramilitary figure, is a cattle rancher and owns a rice business; Pedro Oliviero "Cuchillo" Guerrero commanded a paramilitary force of 1,100 fighters until his death in December 2010 and other drug traffickers became owners of several African palm businesses." Nazih Richani, "The Agrarian Rentier Political Economy: Land Concentration and Food Insecurity in Colombia," *Latin American Research Review* 47, no. 2 (2012): 68, https://www.jstor.org/stable/23321732.
77. "Centrales Obreras no ven con Buenos Ojos los 10 años del TLC con Estados Unidos," *El Espectador*, May 18, 2022, https://www.elespectador.com/economia/centrales-obreras-no-ven-con-buenos-ojos-los-10-anos-del-tlc-con-estados-unidos/.
78. Law 1776 of 2016, L. 1776/2016, January 26, 2016, Diario Oficial [D.O], https://www.funcionpublica.gov.co/eva/gestornormativo/norma.php?i=74057.
79. Teo Ballvé, "The Dark Side of Plan Colombia: Is Plan Colombia Subsidizing Narco-Traffickers to Cultivate Biofuels on Stolen Lands?," *The Nation*, May 27, 2009, https://www.thenation.com/article/archive/dark-side-plan-colombia/.

CHAPTER 14

DEAD ENDS AND BLIND ALLEYS IN THE FUTURE OF WORK

Notes from Italy

JORGE L. ESQUIROL

Italy is a democratic Republic founded on labor.
—Italian Constitution (1947), Article 1, Sentence 1.

What we are confronted with is the prospect of a society of laborers without labor, that is, without the only activity available to them. Surely, nothing could be worse.
—Hannah Arendt, *The Human Condition* (1958)

In an age of highly mobile capital, national governments are struggling to promote quality jobs and suitable job substitutes. Fiscal incentives, import tariffs, subsidies for industries, universal basic income, lower (or higher) retirement age, and partial state ownership of private enterprises are some of the common proposals. But no single policy prescription, realistically considered, appears especially promising. Most national governments lack the coercive instruments to constrain powerful multinationals. Large enterprises refuse to absorb the environmental and social externalities demanded by democratic politics. And international institutions fail to equitably reconcile the divergent objectives of heterogeneous global constituencies. This absence of traction, at every level, is a characteristic aspect of the contemporary debate over decent employment.

Of course, material realities such as resource scarcity and innovation challenges are certainly part of the difficulty. However, quite common beliefs about government capacity, private sector constraints, and international institutional limits equally truncate both action and thought on issues concerning workers. These disconnects undermine the ability of policy makers to think more effectively about the future of work and work substitutes and to propose reforms with any anticipated success. Instead, they engender mostly rearguard action in which governments are simply reacting to popular discontent with few apparent tools at their disposal.

Certainly, work and its substitutes are only one way of organizing societies. Productive employment is not the singular frame for human experience. An altogether different framing could well begin with personal satisfaction, cooperation in society, and collective well-being as the background paradigm. Yet, even universal basic income programs operate mostly as a temporary substitute for work, and retirement benefits equally track the model of productive work when individual labor is no longer possible or expected. In any case, even retaining the limited approach of productive work as the starting point, additional policy alternatives may come into focus—if we note the current dead ends and blind alleys of prevailing debates.

The focus here is specifically on Italy. That country is by all measures a developed nation in the Global North, part of the European Union. It has extensive labor legislation and social protections, a mixed legacy of workers' union activism, and nationalist syndicalism. Indeed, it is one of the Western countries with the highest levels of worker protections. Moreover, the country's leaders are not preemptively hamstrung by geopolitical unimportance, a peripheral economy, and global racial disadvantage. Its people do not suffer the same obstacles, whether material or ideational, of developing countries in the Global South. At the same time, it does face its own challenges of structural inequities between the north and the south of the country, continuing presence of organized crime and corruption, one of the highest governmental debts in the EU, and the generalized perception of rampant inefficiency, extensive bureaucracy, and less than uniformly liberal legal culture. As such, Italy provides a useful example of mixed advantages and constraints characteristically associated with both developed and developing countries.

Not unlike some other places, the prospects of quality employment in Italy have increasingly eroded. Firms and factories are frequently enticed to relocate to lower wage countries. Worker unions and labor authorities are incapable of stopping them. The realities of mobile capital and disparate labor conditions across the world combine to limit any effective counterpressure. Even the national government is at a loss to coerce private firms, or even to convince them to stay. At the same time, there is demographic pressure from continuing immigration from the Global South, for which Italy is a main entry point. Local administrations struggle to process new arrivals while national politics are buffeted by deepening waves of xenophobia and anti-immigrant populism. It seems that national authorities are only capable of standing by and compensating the losers of globalization, in piecemeal and partial ways, for lower quality or no employment. At the same time, the only effective expression of national sovereignty consists of keeping immigrants off Italian shores and in perpetual states of precarity once they have arrived.

My objective here is to examine this perceived lack of effective legal instruments to make meaningful change in the arena of employment. The institutions presumably advancing worker interests are patently lacking, and labor legislation in Italy (and elsewhere) appears to be unequal to the complexities of the current moment. Instead, worker demands for satisfactory employment and income stability routinely abut in dead ends. Some obstacles are the product of the legal system itself. Background legal rules, government bureaucracies, international legal commitments, and informal allocations of power produce a situation in which democratic demands—such as worker interests—cannot permeate the protected encasement of neoliberal policies. Certain arrangements have been effectively placed beyond democratic control. But that is not the only way blockages are created. They are equally erected by limitations of legal consciousness. Traditional legal concepts—despite their widely recognized contingency—continue to reign and to restrict options. Common yet misleading distinctions, such as public versus private law, state intervention versus free market, and intentional discrimination versus disparate impact, all remain pervasive. They resurface more or less explicitly when debating employment policies and their alternatives and are part of the explanation for muddled public debate and policy prescriptions.

The discussion here addresses some of these troubling impasses. The paper is divided into three parts. The first describes two relatively recent events in Italy. One is a high-profile case arising from the steady influx of migrants to Italy from Africa, the Middle East, and South Asia. It highlights the negligible legal protections afforded to migrant workers. The second event retraces the vicissitudes of the ILVA steel plant in southern Italy. The plant has been the object of continuing controversy over employment, health, and the environment. Even with the full array of labor protections afforded by a functioning welfare state, workers at ILVA are confronted with a dilemma between keeping their jobs and threats to their health, environment, and conditions of employment.

The second part of the paper examines the way labor demands and policies are commonly framed. Specifically, appeals to "the social" predominate—in Italy, harkening back to its fascist origins but progressing well beyond. Relying principally on this strategy for labor empowerment, and the types of remedies it suggests, may be part of the problem.

The concluding part of the paper begins to sketch out some alternative thinking.

TWO TAKES ON THE FUTURE OF WORKERS IN ITALY

The discussion in this part focuses on the ILVA steel plant saga in southern Italy as well as the plight of migrants aboard the Italian Coast Guard ship, the *U. Diciotti CP 941*. By examining them together, I explore the positions of government officials, private individuals, and international institutions in contemporary debates about work and work substitutes. Their unfolding in Italy certainly gives a particular shape to these issues, embedded as they are in that country's specific history and political economy. The events described here garnered widespread international attention, affected many individuals, and became the topic of heated public debate about various issues, including work. Adopting the focus of employment as a way of understanding them, admittedly, limits the discussion in advance. It perpetuates the notion of productive activity as the main goal of human life in society. However, it does offer some new perspectives on that paradigm.[1]

Caso Diciotti

Starting with the *Diciotti* case, in August 2018, the Italian Minister of the Interior ordered the detention of 177 migrants on board an Italian Coast Guard ship for ten days. Its unfolding cannot be understood without the background politics that preceded it. Earlier in 2018, Italy held regular parliamentary elections. These elicited the most energetic opposition to mainstream parties from populists of the right and the left. The *Movimento Cinque Stelle* (Five-Star Movement), hard to pin down in terms of its ideological commitments, and the *Lega* (the League), a clearly right-wing party—some would say radical right—both did exceedingly well.[2] Without an outright majority for either party, however, they formed a coalition government. They were unable to agree on the prime ministership, so they decided on a nonpolitician professor of civil law, Giuseppe Conte, to lead them. The heads of the main coalition parties, Luigi di Maio of Five-Star and Matteo Salvini of *Lega*, would both become vice prime ministers. Additionally, di Maio took over the ministry of work and economic development, and Salvini took over the ministry of the interior. The rest of the ministries were distributed more or less proportionally among them. The Yellow-Green government was born, corresponding to the colors of each party.

It was a tumultuous government while it lasted.[3] Practically enemies divided by vast political differences, they repeatedly disputed their political agenda and its relation to a coalitional pact. Salvini was a particularly controversial figure. His approach to government was unmistakably authoritarian. He may best be remembered in those days for requesting from the Italian people "full powers" to rule: "I ask Italians, if they so will, to give me full powers to do that that we have promised to do to the fullest without delays and without chains [balls] on our feet.... We are in democracy, who chooses Salvini knows what he chooses."[4] It is difficult to know what he was truly thinking. At the time, it came across as a call for state power freed from counterbalancing constraints of unelected officials, such as national judges and international institutions. It chillingly recalled Italy's fascist past and the figure of "il duce."[5]

During Salvini's tenure as minister of the interior, he took many controversial actions, including two security decrees that informally bear his name. They imposed strict restrictions on immigration, prohibition of immigrant rescue ships docking in Italy, vast diminution of humanitarian permits, and evictions of refugees from government facilities. No doubt, Italy's immediate immigration problem stems *in part* from the vacuum of effective government in Libya. In practice, the decrees were focused on limiting the large numbers of African and South Asian immigrants who were attempting to enter Italy from North Africa. In July 2018, the Salvini decrees closed Italian ports to nongovernment organization (NGO) ships bringing immigrants attempting to cross and those rescued at sea. The rescue ships that forced their way in were subject to arrest and detention. The decrees even prevented the Italian Coast Guard (which routinely conducts rescue operations) from picking up migrants whose vessels had stalled or broken apart or who were flung overboard by fleeing smugglers.

On August 16, 2018, patrol boats rescued and transferred to a Coast Guard ship, the *U. Diciotti*, 190 immigrants adrift in the Mediterranean. Most were from Eritrea, a former Italian colony. Following authorization from the minister of transportation on August 20, the ship headed to the port of Catania in Sicily. However, Salvini countermanded that no one except thirteen individuals with grave medical conditions be allowed to disembark, effectively detaining 177 people on board a cramped and ill-equipped ship. He made clear that he would refuse entry until other European Union member states agreed to take some of the migrants. In the subsequent days, the EU Commission repeatedly failed to obtain the consent of member states to take any significant number. EU treaties herald solidarity and shared burdens among member states in handling immigration flows, but there is no legally binding obligation.[6]

Although not the only incident of its kind during Salvini's ministry, it gained him international scorn because the sequester produced much human hardship.[7] Some individuals on board badly needed medical attention. State officials allowed to board were hardly sufficient to tend to the extensive human suffering. The news traveled internationally, and the government ultimately relented. Nonetheless, the incident seared the image of an Italy closed to immigrants, whether refugees or not, if they came from Africa or the Middle East. Notably, despite the opposition's rallying cry to repeal the Salvini decrees, the successor government took more than two years to overturn them.[8] Recently, some of the special protections afforded by previous law—like humanitarian status—have been reinstated.

ILVA Taranto

The second story involves the potential shutting down of Europe's biggest single-site steel mill, located in Taranto at the heel of the Italian peninsula.[9] Taranto is deep in the heart of southern Italy in the Puglia region, in the lesser industrialized parts of the country, where quality jobs are at a steep premium. The steel mill, which accounts for 75 percent of the gross domestic product of the province of Taranto, is an icon of Italian industrialization established in 1905 in Genoa. It was rebuilt by the state in Taranto and consolidated with other holdings as *ILVA di Taranto*. When it was reinaugurated in 1965, it was the largest iron and steel plant in Europe. It was publicly owned and privatized only following the economic crisis of the 1980s.[10]

The ILVA plant's modern history dates to the 1995 sale to the Riva family. Years of environmental pollution ensued, leading to the prosecution of owners, managers, and certain public officials for environmental crimes.[11] In 2012, a court ordered seizure of the plant for serious environmental violations. Since then, the Italian state has sought to save the company from closure, to avoid the loss of thousands of jobs and because of its fundamental importance to the Italian economy. In 2015, it placed the plant under "extraordinary administration" to restore the plant both environmentally and economically and then sell it.[12] In June 2017, it awarded the plant through a public tender offer to a multinational, the world's largest steel company, ArcelorMittal.[13] The express condition of the sale was that its new buyers maintain ten thousand jobs until 2023, with a 150,000 euro penalty for each worker dismissed under that number.

After a year of running the plant, the new foreign owners threatened to reduce the work force by 4,700 or shut down the business altogether.[14] Ostensibly, they took advantage of the zeal of the then recently elected to government Five-Star Movement, which proposed removing the plant's legal immunity for past environmental harms.[15] In the past, ILVA had continued operations on the authority of government decrees, despite adjudicated environmental harms and attempts to close the plant down.[16] The cost of clean-up was estimated at 8 billion euros.[17] However, based on strategic national security interests, the government decrees immunized officers and managers—including future acquirers—from criminal and administrative liability. Those government orders were challenged in the Italian Constitutional Court and the European Court of Human Rights on the basis of rights to health and to life, nondiscrimination, and safety at work.[18] The Italian high court upheld them.[19] The European court faulted the Italian court's reasoning.[20] But the plant remained open.

In any case, lifting the environmental shield was prominently heralded by the new populist government. The investors reacted immediately. The new owners cried foul and additionally demanded to renegotiate the deal over job guarantees. The purchase contract between the multinational and the state contains a rescission provision in case of later changes in laws and regulations in effect at the time of purchase.[21] A later decree-law reestablished the liability shield but only for *past* environmental violations; new deviations from the plant-specific environmental plan would henceforth be actionable. Still, ArcelorMittal threatened to pull out, and as a result legislation was introduced to reinstate the full shield to even new violations, although the immunity would progressively fade out over time. However, that proposal did not pass, and the government's remaining reassurances to ArcelorMittal consisted simply in emphasizing that abiding by the law—including the plant's environmental plan—would protect the company from any criminal liability.[22] The steel multinational ultimately sued for rescission of the concession contract.

The whole event caused deep national consternation and exposed the government's limited power. The latter engaged in intense negotiations with the steel giant and affected parties throughout. In an attempt to placate striking steel workers, Italy's prime minister went personally to meet with them. The workers feared for their jobs, despite ArcelorMittal's contractual obligations, in the face-off between the multinational and the government over the liability shield. In an unprecedented move, the sitting prime minister, Giuseppe Conte, threw himself into the melee of agitated workers to speak with them face to face. His resounding message, despite transmitting much personal empathy, was that he "does not have a solution in his pocket" to keep their jobs.[23] "The solution to the ex-ILVA crisis I don't have it in my pocket, I am not a smoke-and-mirrors salesman . . . I am not a superman, nor a [superhuman] phenomenon. If there would have been a solution in hand, it would have already been undertaken."[24]

In April 2021 the new government of Mario Draghi proceeded to take a 38 percent equity stake in the company while obtaining 50 percent of the voting rights. The government would keep the liability shield intact for environmental harm and presumably seek a waiver of European Union rules on government budget deficits. Italy every year is at the edge or just above the 3 percent of GDP budget deficit maximum imposed by the European Union.[25] Any additional government expenditures—for universal basic income, social policy, or significant environmental clean-up like at ArcelorMittal—must be coordinated with Brussels.[26] Influencing corporate policies, even by the state, was not possible simply through public law mechanisms. It required a significant ownership stake.

Takeaways from the Two Cases

The combination of policies and institutions, highlighted by these accounts, reveal an evolving paradigm for workers within society. The national and international institutions, legislative and regulatory jurisdictions, and legal rules and distinctions are increasingly contributing to the construction of a particular identity of "workers." These developments function on more than one register—both political and cultural. The crisscross of rules and jurisdictions marginalize worker interests from fuller democratic expression, restricting their participation to weakened national institutions at the cost of jeopardizing their physical integrity and environment. It also projects the paradigm of identity onto industrial and low-level workers—both in the sense of marginalizing them socioeconomically as well as provoking a reactionary identitarian backlash from this subject position. It would not be the first time powerful economic interests make use of racialization to their benefit. Even workers in the Global North—especially those underemployed or unemployed workers—are both vulnerable and susceptible to it.

Subordinating entire groups, such as manual workers or the immigrants arriving on Italian shores, increasingly becomes possible when presumed to be the result of their own particular traits. Patterns of hegemony and domination appear to be the natural workings of inherent, or near-inherent, attributes of groups. This makes the problem seem cultural or specific to certain demographics and not the product of policy and institutional decisions, of which culture and race are only back-formations. Indeed, it makes diminishing opportunities and marginalization of workers increasingly tolerable by society as a whole. It is not altogether surprising that one common reaction has been nationalist populism by those affected. That reaction to contemporary developments, in many ways misguided, is commonly expressed in the language of antidiscrimination movements against globalists and elites—the world's nonworkers.

Furthermore, continual reliance on notions of the "social" as a form of worker protection is rather ineffective. Legal protections for social groups may indeed be a natural paradigm in which to promote worker interests. It typically stands for needed changes in the rules of private, commercial, and corporate law to empower workers as well as the incapacitated and "weaker parties." Its doctrines are long-standing monuments to "politics from below." However, the particular versions of the social inherited from Italian fascism as well as the 1970s welfare state are too limited. They do not consider the changed political economy in which foreign investors, multinational corporations, and international economic institutions—armed with their own legal powers and protections—are a central part of the mix. In a nutshell, going forward, the interests of workers should be integrated in the background rules of the market, not merely segregated to offer protections from it. Below is the argument why.

BLIND ALLEYS AND DEAD ENDS

Calls for "protection" from interest groups may be heard in all legal systems, if in varying degrees and forms.[27] Advocates for consumers, the environment, and workers appear most prominently in this connection. And, indeed, consumer protection laws, environmental law, and labor law are direct responses to these calls—but so are trade barriers, foreign investment treaties, international financial organizations, and independent central banks, responding to quite different interests. The Italian political context—no less than others—is heavily punctuated by claims to such legal protection from various sectors.[28] Broadly referred to as "*tutela*," which is discussed later, the concept is the common currency of national legal politics, quite evident from even minimal exposure to Italian public debate.

Indeed, framing legal alternatives as questions of autonomy versus protection, individualism versus altruism, or formalism versus the social does significant political work.[29] Societies and individuals that fiercely defend "individualism" are generally loath to accept the language of altruism or protection. Those tending the other way more readily embrace the rhetoric of protectionism. The discourse in the end mostly muddies the practical effects and real distributional consequences.[30] Outcomes post hoc are more a question of *whose* interests are protected rather than whether there is protection. Still, the conceptual dichotomy orients the cardinal directions along which "labor" has traditionally sought to obtain relative advantages in solidly capitalist countries.[31]

The demands of ILVA workers described here echo this strategy.[32] They draw on the long history of *tutela*, the specific Italian version of "the social" inflected by its particular past. For the survivors of the *Diciotti*, this same kind of *tutela* is completely inaccessible. The concept's historical and jurisdictional limitations render it unavailable to migrants and most foreign workers. Instead, legal protection must be sought elsewhere, such as in international norms, political morality, or even criminal law. Still, the history of *tutela* for collective interests is relevant to these stories. It frames the development of "the social" in a society that in the past turned to fascism for protection. It is part of the institutional legacy of a certain form of legal protectionism, in some ways still relevant today.[33] Moreover, it provides a historical lesson of the challenges for workers and worker empowerment from another era of labor crisis and its own anticipated future of work.

My main point is that the conception of labor protection, as inherited from Italian (and world) legal history and projected onto current policy debates, is excessively limited. To the point, *tutela* as currently understood is incapable of protecting workers from multinationals, and it is incapable of protecting migrant, prospective workers from the state. A more robust conception of the social is needed. Below are some of the problems with relying solely on state *tutela* of workers.

The Indeterminacy of Tutela

The legal concept of *tutela* appears in nineteenth-century civil codes modeled on the *Code Napoléon*, such as Italy's, as a form of protection for vulnerable individuals—then defined as the incompetent, married women, and minors. The doctrine served to restrict an individual's legal capacity and provide for the appointment of a legal guardian. Workers were not included in this category. They were not understood to be in need of protection. Classical private law perceives individual workers as willing sellers of their hours of work, or piecemeal production, in mutually agreed contracts with purchasers—or, as may be alternatively conceptualized, in lease agreements with lessors for their bodies or energy.

However, faced with the extensive commodification of labor created by factory work in the industrial era, it soon became evident that "no society could stand the effects of such a system of crude fictions even for the shortest stretch of time unless its human and natural substance as well as its business organization was protected against the ravages of this satanic mill."[34] The unequal bargaining conditions between employers and employees, and the affront to the dignity and professional identity of workers, required protection. The historic turn in the early twentieth century to "the social" experienced in many countries was the common response.[35] According to Karl Polanyi, from whom the quote is taken, the clashing forces of the "satanic mill" and the social ultimately led around the world to dictatorial socialism in the Soviet Union, fascism as in Italy, and the New Deal in the United States.[36]

Post–World War I Italy witnessed a period of escalating labor struggles, strikes, and unrest provoking violent reaction by the bourgeoisie and ruling classes. It culminated in the *biennio rosso* (the red biennial), the two years (1919 to 1920) in which worker strikes paralyzed significant sectors of the economy.[37] These years paved the way for basic labor protections in Italy: mandatory unemployment insurance, an eight-hour work day, minimum wage, and a rise in real wages near 50 percent.[38] Social programs provided assistance to needy families, credits for the poor, disability insurance, and old-age pensions.

These developments helped provoke fascism, at root inimical to labor empowerment.[39] Worker gains were perceived as contrary to virtues of austerity and economy and as illegitimately extracted from a weak liberal government.[40] It thus required repressive force to overturn them. Polanyi himself sharply observed that "in Italy alone were the conservatives unable to restore work-discipline in industry without providing the fascists with a chance of gaining power."[41] By stopping labor unrest and bringing all sectors of the economy to heel within the corporatist state, fascism redefined the legal subject. As Maria Rosaria Marella has argued, the legal subject became the "worker," in a redefined way that included entrepreneurs.[42] Indeed, fascism took up the "social" in a quite particular form.[43] It embraced class solidarity not conflict, corporativism not liberalism, and productivism not social welfare as conventionally understood.[44] Work became a social *duty*.[45] And the definition of "worker" included all productive agents in society, most importantly capitalists in pride of place.[46]

The entrepreneur was the linchpin of the economy and of national administration, deserving protection in the form of rights to profits and hierarchical power.[47] To implement this vision, the fascist government gained "full powers," by vote of the Chamber of Deputies, to make all necessary bureaucratic and financial reforms.[48] The program consisted of fiscal budget cuts, regressive taxation (increased burdens on households with lower incomes), layoffs in the public sector, privatizations of public entities, liberalization of financial markets, and colonial expansion in Africa.[49] These policies were reinforced after the Great Depression in 1929, imposing a generalized reduction of production costs, lower interest rates, reduced tariffs, and timely repayment of government debts.[50] An inherent part of this program was a new idea about law.

SOCIAL LAW

Prior to the rise of fascism, Italian syndicalism was a political program based on an idealized model of industrial worker relations. Some of the main ideas of the social emerged in this environment. In the interwar period, however, the general movement came to identify worker protection with nationalism and imperialism. The historical commitment to international socialism was abandoned as a disappointing delusion, belied by the lack of solidarity among workers of different nations. The ill treatment and discrimination faced by Italian workers abroad, especially in the United States and Argentina, were not insignificant to these developments.[51] Indeed, more prosperous countries at the time generally limited the entry of Italian immigrants and tolerated discriminatory pay and harsh working conditions against them. Italian workers would thus have to create socialism within their own borders. Additionally, imperialism was not altogether unattractive. It offered the promise of raw materials in short supply in Italy, additional markets, and other opportunities for excess Italian labor.[52] The thought was, if Italian workers did not support it, workers in other countries would. Providing jobs was especially crucial in this period of massive Italian emigration—before the fascist regime restricted departures.

During the fascist regime, many of the earlier syndicalist ideas reemerged but changed in authoritarian-type ways. All productive agents of society were to be organized in associations—manual workers, industrialists, artisans, and others. In turn, all associations were to be operated under sectoral "corporations" directed by the state.[53] For example, only approved labor unions, under the supervision of designated corporations, could negotiate enforceable collective contracts. Even worker-owned cooperatives, which Italy leads in numbers and have existed since the early twentieth century, were remade in the fascist era.[54] They were controlled by the single-party state under their respective national organizations.[55] Fascism transformed what was a class-based "labor unionism" to a sort of "mixed unionism" with all sides working in collaboration, at least in theory.[56] Directives emanating from the corporations set baseline conditions for workers such as vacation time, overtime pay, sick days, and the like; prohibitions on strikes and lockouts; and mandatory adjudication of industrial disputes in specialized labor courts.[57] Salaries were still formally to be decided by collective bargaining, within reasonable limits.[58] Workers benefited from insurance for accidents and occupational hazards, maternity leave, and involuntary unemployment.[59] If the national interest warranted, the state reserved the right to intervene, encourage, and directly manage the enterprise.[60]

Concomitantly, theorists of the social made significant inroads into classical legal thought and the liberal order.[61] They introduced the concept of social interests within both public and private law and openly engaged in what we would call "the politics of private law."[62] New legal doctrines were fashioned to place limits on the purely consensual and absolute nature of private law rights.[63] Social function replaced individualism as the key organizing concept.[64] Both property and contracts were no longer thought of as merely voluntaristic and absolute within their respective spheres. Rather, legal entitlements were contingent on fulfilling their social mission. The particular function involved depended on the area and activity to be defined in legislation and other pronouncements.

With respect to property, it was no longer one unified abstract idea but rather multiple contextual definitions.[65] In rural areas, it could mean a duty to cultivate the land; in factories, to maintain production; in urban settings, it may require making housing available.[66] The same for contracts. Their objective and terms may be equally restricted to their respective social functions. For example, the doctrine of "abuse of rights" sought to check the unbridled exercise of absolute individual rights. Collective contracts such as labor agreements were theorized as capable of binding those not formally expressing consent, thus acknowledging their quasi-public character. And the firm or economic enterprise became the focus of legal regulation and state protection.[67]

These revamped doctrines and concepts were not platforms for judges and legislators to equalize unfair bargains between private parties or to protect the individual interests of weaker parties.[68] Rather, they offered a legal and technical way to interject the state's overriding policy objectives within private law transactions—with whatever proposals the state decided constituted the "social function" or "social interests" at the time.

THE "PRODUCTIVIST" SOCIAL

Indeed, labor law in Italy was born in this environment. Its quintessential creations are the 1926 fascist labor laws and the 1927 Labor Charter. The latter proclaims: "the consequences of crises in production and in monetary phenomena must be divided equally among all factors of production."[69] This was the formal bargain enshrined in the 1942 civil code.[70] According to the noted Italian labor scholar Mario Casanova, what it produced in effect was: "An intransigently statist ideology reflexively [that] inspired the entire legal system even labor law. That ideology was met, in the political arena, with the gradual eclipse of all personal liberties of individual citizens before the power of the State."[71]

But it was not limited to fascism or to Italy alone. Corporativism, social protection, and the Labor Charter were influential the world over.[72] They provided the main sources of ideas and policies constituting the globalized "social," which remains a significant part of Western legal thought today.[73] Yet the labor protections of the "productivist social" were not primarily designed to benefit workers.[74] They were intended to promote industrial peace, productivity, and Italy's place in the world. The 1942 Civil Code embodies this structure. It separates labor contracts from regular contracts under the heading of *tutela* for workers—while simultaneously mandating the hierarchical superiority of entrepreneurs, as essentially *pater familias* of their enterprises.[75]

Moreover, these socially "protective" ideas were implemented by a totalitarian regime.[76] What should have been institutions of the social, the intermediate associations in between the state and the individual, were highly centralized within the state itself—ultimately disempowering workers and illegitimately discriminating against certain groups.[77] The micro-requirements of social function on the shop floor were exacting and hierarchical.[78] The fascist social was "a model rendering law apt to the dispensation of *tutelas* and super-*tutelas*, maybe even favors, but incapable of redistributing power," in the words of noted Italian labor scholar Umberto Romagnoli.[79] This explanation is the standard reconstruction for those seeking to salvage "the social" from the wreckage of fascism. In this reading, the social introduced many positive ideas, but they were instrumentalized and distorted.

The 1942 Italian Civil Code still in effect constitutes only a small aspect relevant to workers today. And the fascist labor legislation has since been repealed, of course. Other more recent laws and regulation, discussed later, take a more important role. Still, that era's code reveals the multiple meanings of the social and the productivist form of *tutela*.[80] Since then, commentators have noted the splintering of the legal subject in contemporary times.[81] Instead of a unified historical subject such as labor or the enterprise, multiple identities or interests figure as differential bearers of legal personality. Consumers, people of color, gender identities, the environment, foreign investors, undocumented aliens, and heteronomous workers all have their own differential status in law. And, indeed, one way to conceptualize this—and the main mode in which it is publicly articulated, especially in Italy—is by types and degrees of *tutela*.

In this connection, the high point of worker interests *specifically* was the 1970 Workers' Statute.[82] This piece of legislation drew on the same conceptual basis for legal protection. However, it was significantly severed from productivism. It set the ground rules for more adversarial relations between unions and capitalist associations, workers, and employers. By then, labor strikes were no longer a crime and instead were given constitutional protection. The legislation includes both substantive rights and safeguards for union representation. Labor unions gained greater autonomy to set their own goals. This period of Italian legal history cannot be separated from the mass mobilization of the left, including armed insurgency. The Italian economic miracle of the 1960s was accompanied by a heightened consciousness of class warfare, both figurative and literal. The Workers' Statute, if anything, reflects a return—or progression—to a more partisan notion of worker interests, transcending its 1942 civil code tutelage of private enterprises generally.

Still, the productivist social reappears in some unexpected ways. It is manifest, for example, in the Italian Constitutional Court decisions upholding the decrees overturning the judicial closure of the ILVA plant in 2012 because of environmental crimes.[83] These latter cases preceded the sale to ArcelorMittal but occurred after the plant's privatization in 1995. National prosecutors convinced the local courts to shut down the plants based on continuing environmental damage. The plants emit an extraordinary amount of iron-ore dust and other gases and vapors into the air that harm the health of workers and residents of Taranto. The closures were subsequently countermanded by government orders.[84] Executive decrees, later converted to law, authorized the reopening of the plants and criminal and administrative liability shields, citing strategic national interests in employment and production. These executive orders were reviewed by the Italian Constitutional Court for their compatibility with fundamental rights and separation of powers.[85] The Court engaged in a balancing of the interests of employment and production against the right to health and derivative environmental interests.[86] It sided with employment and production, delegating the management of environmental concerns to the administrative board established by law to mandate precautions at the plant.[87]

As commentators have noted, the Court unjustifiably juxtaposed employment— employment no matter how unsafe—with health.[88] The decisions were also read as a throwback to the "entrepreneurial state."[89] Not unlike the Civil Code, that approach fuses the interests of workers to private enterprise under the mantle of strategic national interests. And, in the process, worker interests are reduced to productivity. The mayor of Taranto again attempted to shut down the plant using his emergency powers based on ongoing environmental harm.[90] That order was rescinded by the Council of State, Italy's highest administrative tribunal, due to insufficient evidence of an emergency thus precluding the mayor from exercising his powers.[91]

Narrowed Legal Protections

Another drawback of the productivist social is receding actual protections. Indeed, in the protests of ILVA workers, one can hear echoes of the type of *tutela* that had traction in an earlier era of labor mobilization—whether of the type integral to national enterprise as in fascism or competing with capitalist accumulation as in the Workers' Statute. Faced with only bad options, they can at best hope the government will succeed in imposing the national productivist social over private enterprises—to keep their jobs despite health and environmental costs and foreign investor prerogatives.

Under either paradigm, whether productivist or social welfare, heteronomous workers are unpropertied claimants in the process of national production,[92] with contractual claims for hours worked or items produced as negotiated by unions,[93] limited say in comparison to other claimants and creditors,[94] and protected mostly by legislated floors on employment terms and conditions. Even these minimums have been eroded in recent laws on "for cause only" dismissals,[95] pension reform,[96] increased leverage of multinational firms, as well as the limited ability for democratic change due to the EU rules, international treaties, and contractual guarantees for foreign investors. Indeed, international institutions like the WTO Dispute Resolution Bodies, the European Commission, and the European Court of Justice have the power to invalidate national legislation contrary to their preferred model of political economy. Especially in Italy's case, EU fiscal spending caps and limits on state aid greatly affect social policy alternatives.[97] And this is just a partial listing of the background legal architecture painting worker interests into a corner.[98] It does not even begin to address the reduction of job supply generally through artificial intelligence and worldwide trends toward monopoly production.

Moreover, whatever *tutela* obtains for subordinate workers is assigned to national public law institutions that are underfunded, less than effective, and culturally expected to fail.[99] The Italian Constitution of 1948 recognizes the right of workers to take part in management.[100] This constitutional right however has had minimal practical effect.[101] No implementing law has ever specified its scope.[102] And no firm has ever been required to reorganize its corporate structure as a result of this constitutional provision.[103] Worker participation through "management councils" in business decisions, distribution of profits, and ownership participation has never succeeded nor been seriously pursued by most labor unions. Its prototype during the interwar years, in the form of internal workers' commissions in Torino factories, was stifled by fascism. And the 1970s Workers' Statute limited itself to strengthening union representation by imposing requirements of information and consultation on management,[104] shifting some of the power from entrepreneurs to labor.[105] More recently, the government of Matteo Renzi of the Democratic Party introduced a neoliberal labor flexibility law in 2014 to reduce costs, eliminating even some of the protections of the Workers' Statute.[106] Certainly, the few cases of limited profit-participation and stock option plans for workers may be a sign of a certain type of participation, yet one translating simply to increased remuneration and a vote on exceptional types of decisions placed collectively before shareholders.[107]

Finally, enforcement of public law regulations on businesses—perceived as added costs to be borne by private employers—is perennially less effective. There are never enough agents and controls, and incentives for corruption are high. Indeed, all of these labor protections operate strictly within a national frame of interests and pressure points.[108] The globalization of capital and international economic institutions, however, adds different parties to the table. National labor is confronted by mobile foreign investors armed with special rights—a modern version of Italian national syndicalism's *tutela* for entrepreneurs, this time for foreign investors and their enterprises.

Indeed, investor protections in the form of international treaties, European Union causes of action, and negotiated concession agreements skew the traditional negotiating table. Faced with this imbalance, collective bargaining is not principally a matter involving national labor and capital. It is national governments, in the best of cases, negotiating on behalf of labor. The most relevant collective bargaining regulations in this case are, in effect, bilateral investment treaties and foreign investor special rights. Yet no careful balance between government/labor interests and foreign investors exists. No national labor law is capable of establishing that. The scales tilt heavily in favor of foreign industrialists and like-minded governments. The only leverage at ministry tables is the prospect of loss of future business in the country, the threat of national legal processes over remaining corporate assets and executives, and general international reputation.

However, not all the routes to be taken by labor need line up neatly with altruism or protection, and not all market capitalism lines up with individualism or autonomy.[109] It is not as determinate as that.[110] The grammars may be scrambled.[111] Indeed, that is the point here: an overemphasis on labor laws as solely national government "protection" may skew the possible legal alternatives into an overly narrow range of options. Moreover, viewing "free" market actors, foreign investors, and multinational corporations as operating in the realm of individualistic rights also obscures the many ways in which *they* are the beneficiaries of legal protection, state welfare, and other special rights.

Racialized Levels of Protection

Finally, the social has been historically intertwined with race. Turning more squarely to the *Diciotti* case as a prime example, it is not as if Italy had no use for migrants. For those migrants hoping to remain in Italy, rather than the majority heading elsewhere in Europe, they predominantly engage in manual work. Indeed, a large part of agricultural and other forms of "usurious" work are performed precisely by people like those disembarking from the *Diciotti*, accepting jobs that native Italians will not take. Their lack of effective *tutela* is a result of the racial limits of social protection. These are effectively withheld from migrants from the Global South and increasingly diminished for newly racialized Italian workers.

It is interesting to note that among the survivors of the *Diciotti* were many citizens of Italy's former colony, Eritrea. That area was colonized in the late nineteenth century, but Mussolini made it a central part of his imperial productivist regime.[112] In fact, the fascist government was not content with its long-standing colony in Eritrea alone in East Africa, and it invaded neighboring Ethiopia in 1935. The few Italian colonies that already existed including Libya and Somalia were there to expand productivist opportunities for Italian colonists.[113] Colonized natives were increasingly racialized and marginalized under fascism.[114] Education levels were kept minimal so that natives would not be able to compete with Italian workers.[115] Targeted by imperialism and racism, the colonized were geographically segregated, limited to three years of schooling, and politically disenfranchised by a combination of direct colonial rule and complicit chieftains handpicked by Italy.[116] Eritrean men, for example, were mostly recruited as fighters for the Italian colonial forces. For the most part, it was dictatorial apartheid military rule.

The colonies served *rhetorically* as "social protection" for excess labor within Italy.[117] To the extent they emigrated, working class Italian colonists were assured stable employment and worker housing. However, the anticipated emigration shift to the colonies—away from third countries—fell short of expectations.[118]

Practically, the colonies served as opportunities for Italian businesses and imperial power. And businesses were the beneficiaries. They were incentivized with subsidies and state contracts for ports, roads, railroads, and infrastructure.

Indeed, the characteristics of productivist *tutela* become even more evident when considered in light of colonialism. In the interwar period, the paradigm of "the social" did not prioritize better working conditions or social and racial justice.[119] Rather, its main imperative was productivism.[120] Where it did provide "social protection," it operated in very insidious ways. For example, racial laws in 1938 and 1939, mimicking Nazi Germany, instituted the state policy of anti-Semitism, and the domination of so-believed inferior races.[121] Such laws quite literally sent those populations to their deaths. The experience in the African colonies was a precursor.[122] Italian citizenship was denied to colonized peoples of color, although it was initially granted to mixed-race children of Italian-Eritrean unions. By 1936 even they were excluded from citizenship, and mixed-race unions were criminalized.[123] A virtual system of apartheid was instituted.[124]

In those later years, fascist colonial policy turned away from any semblance of either assimilation of native populations or indirect rule. Rather, it aimed at segregating and dominating colonized peoples and ultimately replacing them with peninsular Italians and presumably their progeny. The concept of *tutela* was made applicable to the colonized in a perverse way.[125] It was the kind of "protection" afforded to individuals permanently lacking legal capacity, those incapable of ever reaching any level of autonomy.[126] Thus, in the colonies, *tutela* meant promoting Italian enterprises and securing markets for increased production and oversupply in Italy. For Eritreans, Ethiopians, and colonized others, it meant keeping them out of the way, under a regime of oppressive tutelage.

Italy lost its colonies after World War II, and the racial laws were dismantled. However, neocolonial paradigms still structure much current thinking. Contemporary policies toward Global South migrants reveal two perverse epistemic legacies. It visits the need for the policies to repel them, and the exacerbation of their negative effects in society, on this class of workers. And two, it reinforces the systemic marginalization of worker interests by polarizing types of workers: a parallel labor market of others whose lack of *tutela* is invisibilized through racial prejudice and the construction of immigration illegality, contrary to principles of equality and a real demand for labor. As such, the limited scope of guarantees reinforces the marginality of a class of workers through race and law.

Notably, the immigration policies during the Salvini regime entailed a reduction of intermediate legal statuses, such as humanitarian permits to remain in the country legally. And Italian citizens and officials formally and informally assisting irregular immigrants were criminalized.[127] These irregular workers were thus left in the hands of informal employers, often those who already operate organized crime structures. In the Italian context, these workers fall prey to already highly developed and entrenched mafias. The institution of gang-mastering is thriving in the country, particularly in the southern agricultural areas.[128] The gang-masters round up illegal immigrants and recruit them for day labor. Laborers are paid a fraction of the amount the gang-master negotiates with the farm owner or other employer. It is a criminal practice, but one that is nonetheless widely tolerated.

CONCLUSION

Advancing worker interests principally as claims for *tutela* granted by the state is a strategy of the "social." Its invocation today erroneously assumes the same historical pressure points among labor, capital, and governments of another era. In the current moment, these are no longer configured the same way. Instead, the political economy has changed, and claims of *tutela*—when articulated by the unemployed and laid-off factory workers—appear merely anachronistic or wishful thinking. Representatives of the state, who know better, have not been sufficiently forthcoming to dispel this myth—declarations of Giuseppe Conte to ILVA workers notwithstanding. That is, in fact, why his comments were so jarring. They cut through the collective suspended disbelief. To whatever degree Conte was correct, he expressed an increasingly common perception: the state does not have ready solutions for worker demands.

In contrast, populist pretensions to "full powers" episodically emerge as the alternative: a sovereigntist, antidemocratic, authoritarian regime. Pulling out of the European Union, the end of the Euro monetary union, and xenophobic racist action become part of the new form of *tutela* envisaged. And in the current political economy of dead ends and blind alleys for workers, these may very well seem acceptable. However, the ultimate untenability of holding African migrants hostage indefinitely equally demonstrates the impossibility of the state lending "protection" to nativists opposed to migration. International migration flows, Italy's demand for manual labor, the porousness of borders, freedom of movement within the EU, and current migration accords within the Union all make it quite unlikely. That makes the task of thinking about options all the more crucial.

One possible route, suggested here, is to extend beyond a restricted notion of *tutela* as state protection—whether left- or right-wing versions. Instead, it may require more thoroughly exploring the mechanisms identified with individualism, autonomy, and formalism: reconfiguring the terrain of baseline private law rules, corporate regulation, international norms, and constraints. The full map of those critical nodal points must remain for another day. However, the references in this chapter to some of the main laws and institutions provide an initial sketch of the key points for intervention.

NOTES

1. "Workers" here refers to individuals performing functionally "heteronomous" work, i.e. not autonomous—whether they are nominally labeled employees or independent contractors.
2. Originally a secessionist movement of regions of the North, "Lega" was formerly known as "Lega Nord."
3. The coalition government lasted no more than a year as a result of Salvini's withdrawal—in the hopes of an off-year parliamentary election that would propel him to unrivaled victory. That did not happen. Instead, another odd-bedfellows coalition, the Five-Star and PD parties, unexpectedly allied to keep the country from going to untimely elections.
4. Oreste Pollicino and Giulio Enea Vigevani, "Perché Salvini non può chiedere «pieni poteri»," *24 ORE*, August 9, 2019, https://perma.cc/JA4J-Z82S.
5. Salvini later walked back the purported intent of these comments. But at the time, commentators noted the eerie resemblance to a Mussolini speech in the 1920s. Pollicino and Vigevani, "Perché Salvini."
6. Contrast the 2020 European Court of Justice decision condemning certain Member States for not complying with emergency measures (Emergency Relocation Scheme) passed in 2015 by the EU Council to redistribute immigrants arriving in Italy and Greece. Joined Cases C-715/17, C-718/17 and C-719/17, Commission v Poland, Hungary and the Czech Republic, ECLI:EU:C:2020:257. The EU Dublin Treaty requires the country of entry to process refugee applications. Italy has been attempting to extend "burden sharing" to include initial processing of refugees, relocated after they arrive on Italian shores. France and Germany, however, view burden sharing as simply a financial obligation, not any requirement to apportion asylum seekers among them. The *Diciotti* stand-off was not resolved until August 26, 2018, when the Episcopal Conference of the Catholic Church (on Italian soil), Ireland, and Albania (a non-EU state) agreed to take charge of the remaining immigrants on board, and all were allowed to disembark. About twenty-seven minors had been previously released.
7. For his actions while minister, Salvini was personally indicted for kidnapping, abuse of power, and other charges corresponding to his detaining the *Diciotti* survivors. However, under Italian procedures, the legislature must lift his official immunity for criminal charges to proceed. With respect to the *Diciotti* case, the legislature gave him cover and did not lift immunity. Salvini's defense is that this was a governmentwide action of which all cabinet members were aware.

8. Decreto Legge n. 130, October 21, 2020, converted to Law n. 173, December 18, 2020; and Judith Sunderland, "Finally, Good News for Asylum Seekers in Italy: New Decree Rolls Back Some of the Worst Aspects of Immigration Policy," *Human Rights Watch*, October 7, 2020, https://perma.cc/378H-WNVK.
9. "ArcelorMittal Gets Its Fingers Burned in Italy's Ilva Steel Mill," *Economist*, December 7, 2019, https://www.economist.com/business/2019/12/07/arcelormittal-gets-its-fingers-burned-in-italys-ilva-steel-mill.
10. Barbara Massaro, "Ilva di Taranto, la storia infinita di un pasticcio all'italiana," *Panorama*, November 6, 2019, https://www.panorama.it/news/economia/ilva-taranto-storia-tappe-fallimento-italia-tumore-ambiente.
11. After twenty years of litigation, the Riva couple were condemned to twenty-two years and twenty years in prison, respectively, and the former governor of the Puglia region to three years for pressuring authorities to keep the plant open. Domenico Palmiotti, "Sentenza ex Ilva: 22 e 20 anni per Fabio e Nicola Riva, 3 anni e mezzo a Vendola," *Il Sole 24 Ore*, May 31, 2021, https://perma.cc/8VDZ-Z3KA.
12. See Fabio Di Cristina, "Gli stabilimenti di interesse strategico nazionale e i poteri del Governo," *Giornale di Diritto Amministrativo* 4 (2013): 369–78.
13. "ArcelorMittal Completes Transaction to Acquire Ilva S.p.A. and Launches Arcelor Mittal Italia," *ArcelorMittal*, November 1, 2018, https://corporate.arcelormittal.com/media/press-releases/arcelormittal-completes-transaction-to-acquire-ilva.
14. See F.Q., "Ex Ilva, ArcelorMittal rischia di pagare 700 milioni di penale per i 4700 esuberi. 'Clausola nel contratto da 150 mila euro a lavoratore,'" *Il Fatto Quotidiano*, December 5, 2019, https://www.ilfattoquotidiano.it/2019/12/05/ex-ilva-arcelormittal-rischia-di-pagare-700-milioni-di-penale-per-i-4700-esuberi-clausola-nel-contratto-da-150mila-euro-a-lavoratore/5596531/.
15. Decreto Legge n. 1/2015, art. 2, para. 6 (the so-called criminal shield: conduct under the remediation plan cannot give rise to the criminal or administrative liability of the extraordinary commissioner and of the subjects functionally delegated by him. The Lega-M5S government, by Decreto Legge n. 34/2019, eliminated the legal immunity granted to ArcelorMittal for violations of health and safety at work (even under cover of remediation plan)).
16. Law decrees no. 136/2013 of December 10, 2013; no. 1/2015 of January 5, 2015; no. 92/2015 of July 4, 2015; and no. 98/2016 of June 9, 2016.
17. Court of Taranto, Examining Judge Office, Preventive Seizure Decree, May 22, 2013, following appeal R.G.N.R. 938/2010; and M. Sanna, R. Monguzzi, N. Santili, and R. Felici, *Conclusioni della perizia chimica sull'Ilva di Taranto* (2012), 514–54, https://download.repubblica.it/pdf/repubblica-bari/2012/ilva_Relazione_conclusioni.pdf.
18. Maddalena Neglia, "Striking the Right(s) Balance: Conflicts Between Human Rights and Freedom to Conduct a Business in the ILVA Case in Italy," *Business and Human Rights Journal* 5, no. 1 (June 20, 2019): 143, https://doi.org/10.1017/bhj.2019.3; Italian Constitutional Court, No. 58/2018 (*decreto legge* challenged did not take into account fundamental rights to life; but plant remains open on basis of other decrees); Cordella et al v Italy, Eur. Ct. H.R. 54414/13, 54264/15 (2019) (Italian government violated article 8 of the European Convention on Human Rights); and Franco Giampietro,

"Sull'inquinamento dell'ILVA la CEDU dichiara la responsabilità dello stato italiano per violazione dei diritti dell'uomo," *Ambiente e Sviluppo*, no. 4 (2019): 263.
19. Italian Constitutional Court, April 9, 2013, no. 85.
20. *Cordella et al. v Italy* (condemning Italy and its courts for not conducting a fair balancing between the applicants' interest in not being harmed by serious damage to the environment and the interest of society as a whole in the continuation of production activity).
21. Despite ArcelorMittal's threat to withdraw from the contract, in the conversion of this last decree into law (as Law November 2, 2019, n. 128), Parliament deleted art. 14 with the consequence of leaving in force the text of the standard as modified by the previous Law Decree April 30, 2019, n. 34 (converted with amendments by Law June 18, 2019, n. 58), which limited the effectiveness of the "scudo penale" through September 6, 2019.
22. "ArcelorMittal lascia ex Ilva: cos'è lo scudo penale, tra le cause del recesso di contratto," *Sky TG24*, November 4, 2019, https://perma.cc/94KL-SH8Q.
23. See F.Q., "Ex Ilva, Conte a Taranto: 'Stato ci metterà la faccia, vogliamo migliorare il piano. Saremo intransigenti, ad Morselli mia antagonista,'" *Il Fatto Quotidiano*, December 24, 2019, https://www.ilfattoquotidiano.it/2019/12/24/ex-ilva-conte-a -taranto-stato-ci-mettera-la-faccia-vogliamo-migliorare-il-piano-saremo-intransigenti -ad-morselli-mia-antagonista/5637587/.
24. "Ex Ilva. Conte a Taranto: "Non sono un superuomo e non ho soluzioni in tasca," *la Repubblica* video, 2:39, November 8, 2019, https://perma.cc/9X9R-224J.
25. Alberto Magnani, "Che cos'è il deficit al 3 percent del Pil e perché non solo Salvini vuole rivederlo," *Il Sole 24 Ore*, May 15, 2019, https://www.ilsole24ore.com/art/che-cos -e-deficit-3percento-pil-e-perche-non-solo-salvini-vuole-rivederlo-AC5CyzC.
26. See Giampietro, "Sull'inquinamento," 263.
27. Karl Polanyi, *The Great Transformation: The Political and Economic Origins of Our Time* (Boston: Beacon, 2001), 76–77.
28. Duncan Kennedy, "Three Globalizations of Law and Legal Thought," in *The New Law and Economic Development*, ed. David Trubek and Alvaro Santos (Cambridge: Cambridge University Press, 2006), 19–73.
29. For a depiction of this market-versus-protection distinction, see Polanyi, *The Great Transformation*.
30. Duncan Kennedy, "Form and Substance in Private Law Adjudication," *Harvard Law Review* 89, no. 8 (June 1976): 1685, https://doi.org/10.1515/9780691186429-018.
31. Many workers in the Global North (although not so much so in Italy) do not depend solely on salaries. They are often invested in the stock market, participate in company stock option plans, and have significant pension holdings in mutual funds and other investments. Such individuals may personally identify more with owners than with workers. This is in part structural, as reflected by their financial investments, but also ideological. It further contributes to the marginalization of labor organizations—and workers themselves. See Silvio Sonnati, "Low-Income Workers' Financial Participation in Italy: A Proposal de Iure Condendo," *Italian Law Journal* 5, no. 5 (2019): 197–206.
32. Karl Renner, *The Institutions of Private Law and Their Social Function* (New York: Routledge, 2010), 92, describing the advent of classical civil code and industrial

revolution: "An institution of private law . . . takes the place of the regulation of labour by public law."

33. James Q. Whitman, "Consumerism Versus Producerism: A Study in Comparative Law," *Yale Law Journal* 117, no. 3 (2007): 340–406, https://doi.org/10.2307/20455797; James Q. Whitman, "Consumerism Versus Producerism: On the Global Menace of 'Consumerism' and the Mission of Comparative Law," manuscript (2006), https://openyls.law.yale.edu/handle/20.500.13051/4983. "Nobody thinks that European countries are still fascist, but thoughtful observers continue to see lines of filiation between the economics of the '30s and the economics of today." Whitman, "Consumerism Versus Producerism," 26.

34. Polanyi, *The Great Transformation*, 76–77.

35. Kennedy, "Three Globalizations," 50: "Enemies of the social never tired of pointing out that it was a 'regression' from contract to status, and that it was 'demeaning' to the beneficiaries to be treated as though, like the member of the Roman or feudal household, they lacked legal capacity."

36. Polanyi, *The Great Transformation*, 245–56, 252.

37. David D. Roberts, *The Syndicalist Tradition and Italian Fascism* (Manchester: Manchester University Press, 1979), 137–38.

38. Clara Elisabetta Mattei, "Austerity and Repressive Politics: Italian Economists in the Early Years of the Fascist Government," *European Journal of the History of Economic Thought* 24, no. 5 (April 2017): 998, 1001–2, https://doi.org/10.1080/09672567.2017.1301510.

39. Mattei, "Austerity and Repressive Politics," describing the agreement of prominent liberal and fascist economists on austerity measures; see also Roberts, *The Syndicalist Tradition*, describing the syndicalist intellectual influence on Italian fascism. Although syndicalism is based on the centrality of worker unions, it came to reject class conflict in favor of class solidarity and corporatism.

40. Mattei, "Austerity and Repressive Politics," 1011, citing one of Fascism's early economists, Maffeo Pantaleoni: "In my judgment, as a consequence of the laws and actions of Government, their [workers'] wages are much higher than the marginal return of their labour. This is the outcome, first, of the pressure of the war, and, then, of the pressure of socialism and Bolshevism."

41. Polanyi, *The Great Transformation*, 249; and Antonio Gramsci, *La questione meridionale* (Raleigh, NC: Lulu, 2019).

42. See Maria Rosaria Marella, "Antropologia del soggetto di diritto. Note sulle trasformazioni di una categoria giuridica," in *Il Soggetto di Diritto: Storia ed Evoluzione di un Concetto nel Diritto Privato*, ed. Francesco Bilotta and Fabio Raimondi (Napoli: Jovene Editore, 2020), 57.

43. See Roberts, *The Syndicalist Tradition*, 70, commenting on Italian fascism's syndicalists roots: early syndicalists believed that "the workers could be counted upon to lead only because, through a difficult process of psychological maturation, they were coming to embody values diametrically opposed to those underlying the liberal capitalist system. The workers were learning to live according to the principle of solidarity on a day-to-day basis. . . . The foundation of the new solidarity would be common productive labor."

44. Kennedy, "Three Globalizations," 41–42. Also see Polanyi, *The Great Transformation*, 247: "People often did not feel sure whether a political speech or a play, a sermon or a public parade, a metaphysics or an artistic fashion, a poem or a party program was fascist or not. There were no accepted criteria of fascism, nor did it possess conventional tenets." Compare with Marco Sabbioneti, "Raymond Saleilles," in *Great Christian Jurists in French History*, ed. Olivier Descamps and Rafael Domingo (Cambridge: Cambridge University Press, 2019), 328–33, examining the "social citizen" version of the welfare state espoused by Raymond Saleilles in France.
45. See *Carta del Lavoro* [Charter of Labour of 1927], Paragraph II, adopted 1927 by Gran Consiglio del Fascismo, entered into "force" as interpretive guidelines in 1941 and preface to 1942 Italian Civil Code (abrogated 1944) (in the collective bargaining agreement all opposing interests are subordinate to the superior interests of production, para. IV).
46. Umberto Romagnoli, *Storia del Diritto del Lavoro*, Il Digesto, 1989. "A *tutela* that for him implies a recognition of the right to profit as well as a remuneration of his work as an organizer of the factors of production." See also Galgano, *L'imprenditore* (Bologna: Zanichelli, 1980), 25.
47. Galgano, *L'imprenditore*, 25.
48. "Near Dictatorship Given to Mussolini," *New York Times*, November 26, 1922; and Legal Decree for the Delegation of full powers to Sir Majesty's government for the rearrangement of the taxation system and of public administration. Law 1601/1922 (Official Gazette, December 15, 1922, number 293).
49. Mattei, "Austerity and Repressive Politics," 998, 1005.
50. Benito Mussolini, "Per il Consiglio Nazionale delle Corporazioni," in *Scritti e discorsi dal 1929 al 1931* (Milano: Hoepli, 1934), 194–98; see also Gian Paolo Calchi Novati, *L'Africa d'Italia: Una Storia Coloniale e Postcoloniale* (Roma: Carocci, 2011), 103, discussing the connection between the Great Depression and the 1934 Italian colonial invasion of Ethiopia to provide greater opportunities for émigré Italian farmers and workers.
51. Roberts, *The Syndicalist Tradition*, 108.
52. Roberts, *The Syndicalist Tradition*, 109. "As imperialism followed protection, workers in favored countries found that they too had a stake in the imperialistic successes of their ruling classes."
53. Ultimately, Mussolini's plan was to eliminate the Chamber of Deputies and replace it with an Assembly of Corporations as the representatives of the people. Julian Stone, "Theories of Law and Justice of Fascist Italy," *Modern Law Review* 1, no. 3 (December 1937): 177–202, https://www.jstor.org/stable/1089318. ("From the ... internal viewpoint, the groups represent the absolute antithesis of the Marxian notion of the class struggle. From the latter, the external viewpoint, they indicate a close connection between political organisation and economic organisation which is thoroughly Marxian."); and Carta del Lavoro, Article VII. ("corporations" are organs of state with power to issue binding rules; all private enterprises are grouped under such corporations).
54. For a history of Italian cooperatives, see "Labor Conditions in Fascist Italy," *Monthly Labor Review* 57, no. 5 (November 1943): 911, 931, https://www.jstor.org/stable

/41817276. "[Under Mussolini] the cooperatives did not represent a free movement controlled by the membership. Italy lost its membership in the International Cooperative Alliance for that reason, shortly after the Fascist Government took over control of the cooperative associations."
55. Regio Decreto n. 1130, July 1, 1926, Art. 8. Three main organizations of this type continue to exist to this day. Although not centrally controlled by the state, they are still heavily reliant on government support and subsidies.
56. Rocco D'Alfonso, "Oltre lo Stato Liberale: Il Progetto di Alfredo Rocco," *Il Politico* 64, no. 3 (1999): 341, 345–46, referred to in Italy by their historical preliberalism analogues, i.e., "corporations" and thus "corporatism."
57. Legge, April 3, 1926, n. 563 (GU n. 087 del 14/04/1926) (Italy) Disciplina Giuridica dei Rapporti Collettivi del Lavoro (published in La Gazzetta Ufficiale N.87, April 14, 1926).
58. "Labor Conditions in Fascist Italy," 921–22. "Actually . . . there was little freedom in such matters." From 1929–38 real wages remained stationary but direct comparisons are difficult because of changing family allowances, social insurances, and benefits as well as union dues and salary deductions for social programs.
59. Stone, "Theories of Law," 183.
60. *Carta del Lavoro*, Paragraph IX; see also Paolo Grossi, *Scienza Giuridica Italiana: Un Profilo Storico 1860–1950* (Milano: Giuffrè, 2000), on the origins in this period of the term "impresa" or "enterprise" as distinctively "social" and opposed to the individualism of productive agents.
61. Grossi, *Scienza Giuridica Italiana*, 174–77, defending the valuable juristic debates and theorizations of corporativism in this period that Italian fascism ultimately instrumentalized and deformed. According to Grossi, corporativism stressed collectivities within society [not just the individual and the State as did liberalism], the wide plurality of collective interests needing accommodation within the superior national interest, and legal pluralism proper to the internal norms of the collectives.
62. See generally, Jorge L. Esquirol, "Making the Critical Moves: A Top Ten of Progressive Legal Scholarship," *Colorado Law Review* 92, no. 4 (July 2021): 1079–128.
63. Contrast with Giovanni Cazzetta, "Legge e Stato sociale. Dalla legislazione operaia ai dilemmi del welfare 'senza legge,' " in *XLVI Quaderni Fiorentini* (Milano: Giuffrè, 2017), 103, 127–30, 132–37, arguing that the social paradigm of "*tutela*," applied to multiple constituencies has not sufficiently transformed the structure of private law.
64. See Stone, "Theories of Law," 186–88, discussing the likely connections between fascism and the social solidarity of Emile Durkheim and Leon Duguit, in which social function replaces the will theory and rights as the quintessence of law. Under these new theories, the social function of enterprises is efficiency.
65. Jorge L. Esquirol, "Formalizing Property in Latin America," in *Comparative Property Law*, ed. Michele Graziadei and Collegio Carlo Alberto (Cheltenham: Edward Elgar, 2017), discussing the Colombian implementation of "social function" of property in the countryside, requiring land cultivation by owners at the risk of losing their property without compensation.
66. Grossi, *Scienza Giuridica Italiana*, 232–34. Property was not principally the rights of an identifiable owner but the duties owed by the holder.

67. Grossi, *Scienza Giuridica Italiana*, 207–14.
68. Alessandro Somma, "Il diritto fascista dei contratti: un confronto col modello nazionalsocialista," in *Diritto Economia e Istituzioni nell'Italia Fascista*, ed. Aldo Mazzacane (Baden-Baden: Nomos, 2002), 205–10.
69. *La Carta del Lavoro*, Article 13.
70. Alessandro Somma, "Fascismo e diritto, una ricerca sul nulla," in *Rivista Trimestrale di diritto e Procedura Civile* (Milano: Giuffrè, 2001), discussing the studied neglect and denial by Italian legal scholars of the fascist, or productivist social, elements of the 1942 Italian Civil Code.
71. Mario Casanova, "Il Diritto del Lavoro nei Primi Decenni del Secolo: Rievocazioni e Considerazioni," in *Rivista Italiana di Diritto del Lavoro* (Milano: Giuffrè, 1986), 231, 253.
72. Matteo Pasetti, "The Fascist Labour Charter and Its Transnational Spread," in *Corporatism and Fascism*, ed. Antonio Costa Pinto (Oxfordshire: Taylor & Francis, 2017), 61. "While Fascism had a 'temporary' effect, corporatism had an epochal dimension." See also Alvaro Santos, "The Trouble with Identity and Progressive Origins in Defending Labour Law," in *Global Governance: Critical Legal Perspectives* (Oxford: Hart, 2014), on the social's influence on legendary Mexican labor laws and their originality.
73. See, generally, Kennedy, "Three Globalizations," describing the hodge-podge of current globalization that included classical legal thought and the social.
74. Natascia Ridolfi and Ada Di Nucci, "Il Corporativismo: un Paradosso della Politica Economica dello Stato Fascista," *Pecvnia* 19, no. 1 (July–December 2014): 61, 64, describing fascist labor legislation as excluding internal union committees on the shop floor, thereby reinforcing the power of owners over which there was no effective control in the enforcement of labor contracts.
75. See discussion of fascist era framing of corporate law privileging the entrepreneur as hierarchical leader in Francesco Ferrara and Francesco Corsi, *Gli Imprenditori e le Società* (Milano: Giuffrè, 1994).
76. Guglielmo Negri, "The Rise and Fall of the Fascist Constitution," *Il Politico* 47, no. 3 (1982): 449, 465–67, https://www.jstor.org/stable/43096918.
77. Irene Stolzi, "Politica sociale e regime fascista: un'ipotesi di lettura," in *XLVI Quaderni Fiorentini* (Milano: Giuffrè, 2017), 241, 262–64, describing the shift between unionist and corporativist phases of Italian fascism and the latter's only instrumental reliance on "social policy" and bottom-up steering of society and its total disregard for "social rights." According to the author, syndicalism (unionism) was only a phase to more effectively access the protected sphere of private or individual rights and protections.
78. D'Alfonso, "Oltre lo Stato Liberale: Il Progetto di Alfredo Rocco," 341, 345, referring to the legal architect of Mussolini's industrial policy, "Rocco's corporativist conception has its model in the ideal structure of a modern and efficient monopolistic enterprise, characterized by a rigid hierarchical organization of professional roles and capable"; and Umberto Romagnoli, *Storia del Diritto del Lavoro*, Il Digesto, 1989. "Labor law (in the law of 3 April 1926, n. 563) encountered certain death by overdose of state protectionism. Even if all was attempted, after the end of its historical cycle, to hide its demise and make it appear in good health, many subsequent generations of legal operators are forced to deal with it."

79. Umberto Romagnoli, "Il diritto del lavoro durante il fascismo: Uno sguardo d'insieme," *Lavoro e diritto* 1 (2003):77, 87.
80. See Stone, "Theories of Law," 186–88.
81. Ernesto Laclau and Chantal Mouffe, *Hegemony and Socialist Strategy: Towards a Radical Democratic Politics* (New York: Verso, 2001).
82. Statuto dei Lavoratori, Legge May 20, 1970 n. 300, a "Norme sulla *tutela* della libertà e dignità dei lavoratori, della libertà sindacale e dell'attività sindacale nei luoghi di lavoro e norme sul collocamento."
83. Corte costituzionale, April 9, 2013, n. 85.
84. Decreto Legge n. 207 del 2012, converted to law L. n. 231/2012. "Disposizioni urgenti a *tutela* della salute, dell'ambiente e dei livelli di occupazione, in caso di crisi di stabilimenti industriali di interesse strategico nazionale."
85. Corte costituzionale, April 9, 2013, n. 85.
86. See Camilla Crea and Luca Ettore Perriello, "Health, Environment and Economic Interests: From Balancing to Ensuring Effective Remedies," *Journal of European Tort Law* 11, no. 3 (2020): 247–85.
87. A third case by the Constitutional Court found the authorization unconstitutional due to a lack of administrative oversight, which in this case was not included in the law.
88. Tatiana Guarnier, "Della Ponderazione di un 'Valore primario.' Il caso ILVA sotto la lente della Corte Costituzionale," *Diritto e Società* 2 (2018): 173, 183.
89. Cristina Fabio, Il Decreto "SALVA ILVA" D.L. 03-12-2012, n. 207 L. 24-12-2012, n. 231, 4 Giornale Dir. Amm. 369 (2013).
90. Comune di Taranto, Direzione Ambiente, Salute e Qualità di Vita, Ordinanza no. 15, 27 October 2020.
91. Giuliano Foschin, "Ex Ilva, no allo stop degli impianti dell'area a caldo: il Consiglio di Stato tiene aperto il siderúrgico," *la Repubblica*, June 23, 2021, https://perma.cc/J7NS-NGYP.
92. Regio Decreto March 16, 1942, n. 262 Approvazione del testo del Codice civile. (042U0262) (GU Serie Generale n.79 del 04-04-1942), Article 832 (owners enjoy absolute legal rights over production machines and work product "full and exclusive.")
93. Regio Decreto March 16, 1942, n. 262 Approvazione del testo del Codice civile, Article 2060. (Adopts a "protective" or social model of industrial relations.)
94. The situation in Italy—where workers are recognized a legal privilege for past wages—means they are far better off than in the United States, for example, where no such priority obtains.
95. Legge no. 183/2014 (the "Jobs Act"); and Alberto Pizzoferrato, "Economic Crisis and Labour Law Reform in Italy," *International Journal of Comparative Labour Law and Industrial Relations* 3, no. 2 (2015): 187, 205, offering an extensive overview of the history and characteristics of the Jobs Act.
96. Decreto Legge 201/2011, converted with amendments, by Law 214/2011 (so-called Fornero Law) (set the requirements for old-age pensions until 2050); Law Decree January 28, 2019 n. 4—converted with amendments by Law 28 March 2019, n. 26—provides for new provisions to access early retirement, in force from January 1, 2019; and Francesca Barbieri, "Pensioni, con quota 100 salgono a 12 le possibilità di uscita dal lavoro," *24 ORE*, September 12, 2019, https://perma.cc/427X-BMYE.

97. Achim Seifert, "European Economic Governance and the Labor Laws of the E.U. Member States," *Comparative Labor Law and Policy Journal* 35, no. 3 (2014): 312. The EU's overall effect is described as: "a progressive deterioration in working conditions as a way of ensuring the stability of financial markets. In Italy, the impact has been greater than in other European countries." See generally, for example, Law March 28, 2019, n. 26, of conversion of Law Decree January 28, 2019, n. 4, Citizenship Income are established; compare with Giuliano Cazzola, "Il reddito di cittadinanza," *Il lavoro nella giurisprudenza* 5 (2019): 446–60.
98. See Official Journal of the European Communities, STATE AID C 29/97—C 30/97—C 31 /97 (ex NN 125/96) Italy; see, generally, Marcelo Vieta, "The Italian Road to Creating Worker Cooperatives from Worker Buyouts: Italy's Worker-Recuperated Enterprises and the Legge Marcora Framework," Euricse Working Papers no. 78 (2015).
99. See, for example, Stefano Rodotà, *Il diritto di avere diritti* (Roma-Bari: Laterza, 2012), 232; and Maria Rosaria Marella, "Il diritto all'esistenza," *Rivista critica del diritto privato* 4 (Napoli: Jovene, 2012), 673–78 (critiques of conditional basic income schemes, like the *reddito di cittadinanza*).
100. Italian Constitution of 1947, Article 46.
101. Giampaolo De Ferra, "La partecipazione dei lavoratori alla gestione delle aziende (rectius delle imprese)," *Rivista delle Società* 6 (Milano: Giuffrè, 2015), 1298. Italian S.p.A.s [stock companies] are even prohibited from having workers on their "supervision boards"—one of the two corporate boards required for certain statutory corporations—unless they are publicly traded.
102. Federico Caporale and Emiliano Frediani, "La Costituzione «Dimenticata» dai Consigli di Gestione alla Partecipazione di Rischio delle Imprese," *Rivista Trimestrale di Diritto Pubblico* 1 (Milano: Giuffrè, 2021), 279, 293, 297–98.
103. Caporale and Frediani, "La Costituzione," 299, describing how the few worker-participation schemes in effect today are voluntary on the part of management and mostly intended to strengthen employee loyalty but not involving them in investment decisions or production methods.
104. Giampiero Proia, "La partecipazione dei lavoratori tra realtà e prospettive: Analisi della normativa interna," *Diritto delle Relazioni Industriali* 20, no. 1 (2010): 60.
105. See, generally, Lorenzo Stanghellini, "Corporate Governance in Italy: Strong Owners, Faithful Managers. An Assessment," *Indiana International & Comparative Law Review* 6, no. 1 (January 1995): 91–159, https://doi.org/10.18060/17591; and Lorenzo Segato, "A Comparative Analysis of Shareholder Protections in Italy and the United States," *Northwestern Journal of International law and Business* 26, no. 2 (Winter 2006): 373–79.
106. Law no. 183/2014 (so-called Jobs Act) provides for numerous and wide-ranging delegations to the government for reforming the labor market. Eight legislative decrees (and a corrective decree) have followed; and see Maurizio del Conte, "Re-structuring the Standard Employment Relationship: Italy and the Increasing Protection Contract," in *Core and Contingent Work in the European Union A Comparative Analysis*, ed. Edoardo Ales, Olaf Deinert, and Jeff Kenner (London: Bloomsbury, 2017), 111–28.

107. Proia, "La partecipazione dei lavoratori," 60.
108. See Kerry Rittich, "The Future of Law and Development: Second Generation Reforms and Incorporation of the Social," in *The New Law and Economic Development: A Critical Appraisal*, ed. David Trubek and Alvaro Santos (Cambridge: Cambridge University Press, 2006), 203–52, arguing that a weak version of the "social" incorporated within the remit of international financial institutions works to give the appearance of addressing social protection without making any significant changes in policy.
109. See, for example, the long history of worker-owned cooperatives in Italy, which predated fascism and survive through today. Essentially, these are private entities whose scope is mutual support and salaries rather than profit maximization.
110. For example, Evgeny Pashukanis, *The General Theory of Law and Marxism* (1924; repr., London: Taylor and Francis, 2017), provides a critique of bourgeois legal form (and Soviet-state legal form) as determined by the underlying characteristics of commodity exchange, presuming individuals are equally entitled to an equivalent exchange.
111. On *relative* indeterminacy, see Ferdinand de Saussure, *Course in General Linguistics* (New York: Philosophical Library, 1959), in which linguistic structuralism reveals seemingly transcendental meanings as human-developed conventions, fitting nonetheless within a finite pattern of permutations; and Claude Levi-Strauss, *Structural Anthropology* (New York: Basic Books, 1963), maintaining the existence of common relational archetypes across groups that are differentially expressed as distinct cultures.
112. Angelo Del Boca, "Le leggi razziali nell'Impero di Mussolini," in *Il Regime Fascista: Storia e Storiografia* (Roma: Laterza, 1995), 339.
113. Valeria Deplano, "Dalla colonia all'impero: l'Africa e il progetto nazionale fascista," in *Il Fascismo Italiano*, ed. Giulia Albanese (Roma: Carocci, 2021), describing the self-proclaimed fascist identification with an "empire of labor" as based on increasing racialization and racial hierarchy compared to the previous Italian colonial period.
114. Chiara Giorgi, "Borders and Boundaries in Italy's Colonial Administration," in *Mussolini's National Empire* (Cambridge: Cambridge University Press, 2017), describing extreme segregation of the Indigenous population—residential, occupational, and political under Italian colonialism and the lack of intervening associations between the colonizing state and Indigenous Africans.
115. Calchi Novati, *L'Africa d'Italia*, 226.
116. Calchi Novati, *L'Africa d'Italia*, 183–228.
117. Compare "Labor Conditions in Fascist Italy," 921, citing relatively low numbers of Italians in East Africa: "the total number going to Italian East Africa in 1938 was 5,795, making a total of 199,382."
118. Calchi Novati, *L'Africa d'Italia*, 110. Emigration fell short of expectations despite doubling of the Italian population in Libya from 1936 to 1940.
119. Calchi Novati, *L'Africa d'Italia*, 110.
120. See, for example, Elisabetta Fiocchi Malaspina, "Techniques of Empire by Land Law: The Case of the Italian Colonies (Nineteenth and Twentieth Centuries)," *Comparative Legal History* 6, no. 2 (July 2018): 233, 241, 249–50, https://doi.org/10.1080/2049677X.2018.1534780, arguing that Italian law in the colonies shifted from

providing for registrable property to promote settlement to one of continuing state control over land in the form of concessions to promote productivist goals.

121. Decree Law no. 1728, November 17, 1938, and Decree Law no. 1004, June 29, 1939; and Mathias Siems, "Malicious Legal Transplants," *Legal Study* 38, no. 1 (March 2018): 103, 105–6, https://doi.org/10.1017/lst.2017.4, arguing conflicting theories behind racial laws: political expediency vis-à-vis German allies; anti-Semitism as a strategy for dictatorial consolidation; Italian "spiritual" racism as opposed to German "biological" racism. See Olindo De Napoli, "The Origin of the Racist Laws Under Fascism. A Problem of Historiography," *Journal of Modern Italian Studies* 17, no.1 (January 2012): 106–22, https://doi.org/10.1080/1354571X.2012.628112.

122. Mussolini himself denied imitating Germany. He associated racism with a necessary element of imperialism that he vigorously championed. Benito Mussolini, *Scritti e discorsi, vol. XII* (Milano: Hoepli, 1939), 46.

123. Law no. 822, May 13, 1940.

124. Del Boca, "Le leggi razziali nell'Impero di Mussolini," 336.

125. Mussolini's regime defended the invasion of Ethiopia on humanitarian grounds as *protecting* against ongoing slavery, while forced labor was accepted in European colonies and League mandates elsewhere in Africa. See also Adom Getachew, *Worldmaking After Empire: The Rise and Fall of Self-Determination* (Princeton, NJ: Princeton University Press, 2019), 64–66.

126. See Lidio Cipriani (one of the theoreticians of Italian racism), cited in Del Boca, "Le leggi razziali nell'Impero di Mussolini," 334–35.

127. Alessia Candito, "Riace, il sindaco Lucano arrestato per favoreggiamento dell'immigrazione clandestina," *la Repubblica*, October 2, 2018, https://www.repubblica.it/cronaca/2018/10/02/news/immigrazione_arrestato_il_sindaco_di_riace-207913366/.

128. Tomaso Ferrando, "Gangmastering Passata: Multi-Territoriality of the Food System and the Legal Construction of Cheap Labor Behind the Globalized Italian Tomato," *FIU Law Review* 14, no. 3 (February 2021): 521–44.

CONTRIBUTORS

Helena Alviar García is professor at the Sciences Po Law School and former dean of the law school at the Universidad de Los Andes in Bogotá, Colombia. An expert in law and development, property law, social and economic rights, feminism, and transitional justice, she is the author of notable publications including *Legal Experiments for Development in Latin America: Modernization, Revolution and Social Justice Law* (2021) and coeditor of *Social and Economic Rights in Theory and Practice Critical Inquiries* (2015). She is also the cofounder of Dejusticia, one of the leading human rights NGOs in the Global South.

Jennifer Bair is professor of sociology and senior associate dean for academic affairs in the College and Graduate School of Arts and Sciences at the University of Virginia. Her research interests are at the intersection of global political economy, work, and development, and she has written extensively about global value chains and world-systems theory. She is editor of *Frontiers of Commodity Chain Research* (2008) and coeditor of *Putting Labour in Its Place: Labour Process Analysis and Global Value Chains* (2015) and several special issues, including "Power and Inequality in Global Value Chains" (*Global Networks*, 2023) and "The Arrighian Approach to Agrarian Political Economy" (*Journal of Agrarian Change*, 2019). Prof. Bair is currently studying efforts to ensure human rights protections for migrant workers in U.S.-based agricultural supply chains.

Nicole Burrowes is a historian of the African Diaspora and an assistant professor in the Department of History at Rutgers University, New Brunswick. Her scholarly interests include social justice movements, relational histories of racialization and colonialism, Black internationalism, and the politics of solidarity.

Her current book project, *Seeds of Solidarity: African-Indian Relations and the 1935 Labor Rebellions in British Guiana*, explores the historical possibility of a movement forged by those at the edges of empire in the middle of economic, environmental, and political crises, and is forthcoming from Cambridge University Press. Beyond academia, she draws on an extensive portfolio of experience working with communities for transformative justice.

Dennis Davis is a professor at the University of Cape Town Faculty of Law and a recently retired judge who served in the High Court of Cape Town, appointed by former South African president Nelson Mandela. His scholarly interests include constitutional law, labor law, socioeconomic rights, and human rights and litigation. He has published extensively in academic journals on poverty and supply chain governance and has cowritten eight books, including *Rights and Constitutionalism* (1994) and *Beyond Apartheid: Labour and Liberation in South Africa* (1991). He is the former chair of the Davis Tax Committee, tasked with assessing South Africa's tax policy framework and its role in supporting the objectives of inclusive growth, employment, development, and fiscal sustainability.

Karen Engle is Minerva House Drysdale Regents chair in law and codirector of the Bernard and Audre Rapoport Center for Human Rights and Justice. She teaches and writes on international human rights law, labor and employment law, global inequality, law and social movements, and critical legal theory. She is the author of numerous scholarly articles and *The Grip of Sexual Violence in Conflict: Feminist Interventions in International Law* (2020) and *The Elusive Promise of Indigenous Development: Rights, Culture, Strategy* (2010), the latter of which received the Best Book Award from the American Political Science Association Section on Human Rights. She is also coeditor of *Power, Participation, and Private Regulatory Initiatives: Human Rights Under Supply Chain Capitalism* (2021), *Anti-Impunity and the Human Rights Agenda* (2016), and *After Identity: A Reader in Law and Culture* (1995). She has received a Bellagio Residency Fellowship from the Rockefeller Foundation, a Fulbright Senior Specialist assignment in Bogotá, and the Deborah Lunder and Alan Ezekowitz Founders' Circle Membership at the Institute for Advanced Study in Princeton.

Jorge L. Esquirol is a founding faculty member and the founding international programs director of the Florida International University College of Law. He previously taught at Northeastern University School of Law and before that was academic affairs director for the Graduate Program at Harvard Law School. He was the Fulbright Distinguished Chair in Law for 2015–2016 at the University of Trento; visiting research professor at the Watson Institute Brown University Spring 2008; and currently affiliate professor at SciencesPo—Paris. He is the author of numerous publications, including *Ruling the Law: Legitimacy and Failure in Latin American Legal Systems* (2020). He researches and teaches in the fields of comparative law, law and development, international trade law, property, and commercial law. He is fluent in Spanish, French, Portuguese, and Italian.

Jorge González Jácome is associate professor of law at Universidad de los Andes in Bogotá, Colombia. He teaches and writes in the areas of Latin American legal and political history, law and literature, critical legal theory, and human rights. His most recent publications include *Law's Will to Truth in 'The Sound of Things Falling'* (2024) and *Revolución, Democracia y Paz: Trayectorias de los Derechos Humanos en Colombia (1973–1985)* (2019). In his ongoing research, Prof. González is exploring the distributive effects of legal narratives of memory in Latin America.

Jennifer Gordon is the John D. Feerick Chair and professor of law at Fordham University School of Law in New York City, where she teaches immigration law and labor and employment law, as well as an introductory course on legislation and regulation. She is the author of *Suburban Sweatshops: The Fight for Immigrant Rights* (2005), and of multiple scholarly pieces on migration, trade, and labor standards in the context of globalization. She has also written on these topics for the *New York Times*, *Foreign Policy*, and numerous other media outlets. The recipient of a MacArthur Prize Fellowship and an Open Society Fellowship, she has been named one of the "Outstanding Woman Lawyers in the United States" by the National Law Journal. Earlier in her career, Prof. Gordon founded and directed the Workplace Project, a pioneering immigrant workers' center in the United States.

Vanja Hamzić is reader in law, history, and anthropology at SOAS University of London. His work considers colonial, postcolonial, and decolonial subjectivity making—with a particular focus on gender nonconformity—in South and Southeast Asia, West Africa, and Louisiana. His published books include *Sexual and Gender Diversity in the Muslim World: History, Law and Vernacular Knowledge* (2016, 2019), and *Control and Sexuality: The Revival of Zina Laws in Muslim Contexts* (with Ziba Mir-Hosseini) (2010). His current book project explores gender diversity and cosmological pluralism in eighteenth-century Senegambia, the ways enslaved gender nonconforming West Africans survived the Middle Passage, and the gender regime of colonial Louisiana. Dr. Hamzić was a 2016/17 member of the School of Social Science in the Institute for Advanced Study at Princeton.

Neville Hoad is associate professor of English and codirector of the Audre and Bernard Rapoport Center for Human Rights and Justice at the University of Texas at Austin, and works at the intersection of legal, literary, and gender/sexuality studies, mostly in contemporary southern Africa. He is the author of *Pandemic Genres: Imagining Politics in a Time of AIDS* (2025) and *African Intimacies: Race, Homosexuality and Globalization* (2007) and the coeditor of *Sex & Politics in South Africa: Equality/Gay & Lesbian Movement/the Anti-Apartheid Struggle* (2005), as well as several journal special issues, including "Queer Valences in African Literatures and Film," *Research in African Literature* 47, no. 2 (2016); "Solidarity Here and Everywhere: The Lifework of Barbara Harlow," *Race & Class*, Vol.60, no. 3 (2019); and "Time Out of Joint: The Queer and the Customary in Africa," *GLQ: A Journal of Lesbian and Gay Studies* 26, no, 3 (2020).

David Kennedy is Manley O. Hudson professor of law and faculty director of the Institute for Global Law and Policy at Harvard Law School, where he teaches international law, international economic policy, legal theory, law and development, and European law. His research uses interdisciplinary materials from sociology and social theory, economics, and history to explore issues of global governance, development policy, and the nature of professional expertise. He is the author of numerous articles, book chapters, and monographs. His recent books include *A World of Struggle: How Power, Law and Expertise Shape Global Political Economy* (2016) and *Of Law and the World: Critical Conversations on Power, History and Political Economy* (with Martti Koskenniemi) (2023). He is a member of the U.S. Council on Foreign Relations and past chair and member of the World Economic Forum's Global Advisory Council on Global Governance.

Duncan Kennedy is the Carter Professor of General Jurisprudence Emeritus at Harvard Law School. He was a founding member of the Critical Legal Studies movement. He is the author of dozens of articles and five books, including *Legal Reasoning: Collected Essays* (2008), and *The Rise and Fall of Classical Legal Thought* (1998 [1975]). His publications have contributed significantly to legal and social theory, the history of legal thought, law and economics, contract law, and legal education.

CONTRIBUTORS

Vasuki Nesiah is professor of practice in human rights and international law at the Gallatin School, New York University. She is also currently a Yip fellow at Magdalene College, Cambridge University. She has published extensively on the history and politics of international law, human rights, transnational feminisms, reparations, and decolonization. She recently completed *International Conflict Feminism* (2024). A founding member of Third World approaches to international law (TWAIL), she is coediting the *Handbook on Third World Approaches to International Law (TWAIL)*. Her previous coedited work also speaks to this tradition, *A Global History of Bandung and Critical Traditions in International Law* (2017). Her current focus is on her book project on reparations, tentatively titled *Reading the Ruins: Slavery, Colonialism and International Law*.

Kerry Rittich is professor at the Faculty of Law and the Women and Gender Studies Institute at the University of Toronto. She writes in the areas of labor law, global governance, law and development, human rights, and gender and critical theory. Her recent works include, "Informal Labour Through the lens of TWAIL," in the *TWAIL Handbook* (forthcoming); "In the Middle of Things: The Political Economy of Labour Beyond the Market," *European Law Open* (2023); "Labour and Labour Law in the Project of International Development" (with Diamond Ashiagbor), in *Oxford Handbook of International Law and Development*, and "Historicizing Labour and Development: Labour Market Formalization Through the Lens of British Colonial Administration," in *Re-Imagining Labour Law for Development* (2019). She has been a Jean Monnet fellow at the EUI and a visiting professor at Harvard, Brown, Sciences Po Law School, and the Center for Transnational Legal Studies, London.

Samuel Tabory is a PhD candidate in urban and regional planning at the Harvard University Graduate School of Design. His research examines the governance and negotiation of urban-regional systems transitions, paying particular attention to how such transitions interact with evolving spatial and temporal understandings of crisis under conditions of global environmental change. His work considers how conventions of both growth and polity are implicated by ideas of crisis. Trained as a planner and a Latin Americanist, comparative and global perspectives inform his work. His research interests are interdisciplinary and multiscalar across planning, law, and territorial transformation.

INDEX

Page locators in italics indicate figures

Abbas, Madeline-Sophie, 244
Abbott, Greg, 283, 286, 291, 305n21
Abnet, Dustin, 150–51
abolition movements, 130–31
abstractions, used to defend ideological formations, 106
academics and activism, integration of, 49
Acer, 197
Achiume, Tendayi, 135
Ackerman, Bruce, 114–16, 121n66
Africa: automation as potential block against access to global economy, 197; as net exporter of capital, 151; Pan-Africanism, 6, 46, 49, 52–53; Senegambia region, 216; Sub-Saharan Africa, refugees from, 244, 245–46, 249. *See also* Senegambia; South Africa; Syrian refugees
Africana Studies and Research Center (Cornell University), 55
African National Congress (ANC), 33, 39, 40–41
After London; Or, Wild England (Jefferies), 146
agriculture: demand for food, 87–88, *88*; direct aid in Colombia, 330–31, 337n75; excluded from National Labor Relations Act, 184, 261, 265–66; exemption of antitrust law, 262; farmer's offers to landlord, 90–91; fertility of soil, 87, 89–90; Florida workers, 266; H-2A temporary visa program, 265, 275; importation of racialized labor in history of, 264; laborers as destitute agricultural population, 89; landlords and farmers, 88–89; market price for product, 90–91; monocultures, 128; population and unproductive land linked, 82, 118n25; racial capitalism developed in, 264; rental market for land, 89–90; rent-seeking process, *87*, 87–94, *88*, *91*, *92*. *See also* dairy industry; dairy industry (Vermont); landlords; palm oil industry (Colombia); Ricardo, David
Alabama, 184
Alagraa, Bedour, 5
Alexander, Neville, 4, 5, 8, 31–44, 46, 57; 2010 speech, 41; background, 33–34; language policy advocacy, 33–34; nonracial society, concept of, 39; and racial capitalism, 34–38; toward liberation from racial capitalism in thought of, 38–39

alienated labor, 13, 82, 103, 148; distemporalization, 216, 230–31n8
alternative imaginaries, 21–24
Alviar García, Helena, 16, 19–20, 23, 129, 132
Amazon, Black warehouse worker struggles against, 184
The American Dilemma (Myrdal), 9
Anghie, Antony, 129–30
Anner, Mark, 202–3, *203*
anticapitalism, 25n12, 38, 57
anti-imperialism, 57, 123, 128
antitrust law, 17, 174, 175; exemption of agricultural cooperatives from, 18–19, 262, 268–73
apartheid, 8; "Bantustan policy," 36–37; capitalism as twin of, 33; economic aims of, 34–35; education policy, 37; formal end of, 39; native reserves, 32, 35–36; racial capitalism as response to, 31. *See also* South Africa
ArcelorMittal, 343–44, 352, 360n21; and legal immunity laws, 344, 359n15
Arendt, Hannah, 338
Arrighi, Giovanni, 150
artificial intelligence, 12, 173, 196; algorithms, expanded wage discrimination through, 174; in developing economies, 196, 200
artisan class, Greater Senegambia, 16, 215, 217–18, 220, 231n18
assembly line: dehumanization of, 103–4, 118n46; global, 197–98, 205–6; mechanization of, 101, 103
Austin, Texas region, 19, 23; Black and Latino population displaced from, 292–93; Chamber of Commerce, 294; "competitively sited" project standards, 296; COVID-19 health measures, 306n25; Del Valle area, 284–86, 292, 297–98; as early COVID-19 hotspot, 283; environmental justice advocacy, 293, 308–9n47; as fastest growing major metropolitan area, 282; gentrification, 292, 293; "growth machine" as counter to progressive claims, 292; hidden subsidies of growth, 293–
economy, public investment in, 295–96; local governmental efforts thwarted by state, 285, 289–90; as "progressive" boomtown, 281, 284, 292–98; racist zoning policies, 293; RISE (Relief in a State of Emergency) funds, 283–84, 287; sanctuary policy, 290; Save Our Springs (SOS) ordinance, 293; "South by Southwest" (SXSW) festivals and conferences, 300–301; stay-at-home orders, 282–83; Texas "Robin Hood" law, 286, 297. *See also* construction workers (Austin, Texas)
automation, 1, 12–14, 173, 196–97, 200, 205
Azania, 31, 32
Azmanova, Albena, 3

background legal rules, 7, 86, 100; during COVID-19, 19; and dispossession, 132–33; and growth policies, 282; Italy, 340, 341, 346, 353; layers of, 126; and palm oil industry, 313, 317–20, 327, 329–32; and Vermont dairy industry, 262, 268, 273–76; worker countering of, 317
Bair, Jennifer, 13–14, 16, 18, 27–28n31
Balcazar Sanchez, José Enrique, 260
Bandung Conference (1955), 128
bankruptcy, 20, 99, 226, 271, 272, 312
Barca, Stefania, 23–24, 301
bargaining power, 7, 10, 28n34; affected by legal arrangements, 83; in Colombia, 317; as determinant of the distribution of surplus, 107–8; harms that can be inflicted in course of, 109; Italy, 350; private law's influence on, 112–13; threats, overt and implied, 107, 109–10; zero, picture of, 107
Barsoom series (Burroughs), 154
Baud, Céline, 204–5
Baxi, Upendra, 136
Beckles, Hilary, 52
Bellamy, Edward, 146

INDEX

Ben & Jerry's, 18–19, 260–62, 266–67, 273, 275; buyer power, 262, 268; redistribution of value, 262, 267. *See also* Milk with Dignity
Berle, Augustus, 96–97
Bessemer, Alabama, 184
Bhatia, Amar, 136
Bienville, Governor, 225
"black heretical tradition," 58
The Black Jacobins (James), 47
Black Marxism: The Making of the Black Radical Tradition (Robinson), 4–5, 32, 58, 256n46
Black nationalism, 53
Blackness, class-based definition of, 48–49
Black Power, 48
Black Power Revolution (Trinidad), 49
Black radical tradition, 46, 58–59, 123, 182–83. *See also* Robinson, Cedric; Rodney, Walter
Black workers, excluded from National Labor Relations Act, 184
Bleak House (Dickens), 151
Bogues, Anthony, 46, 48, 49
boom-and-bust cycles, 70–72, 103
bourgeoisie, capitalist, 89, 93
British Empire, 53, 56, 59, 127, 160
Bromwich, David, 176
buen vivir (good living), 23, 322
Bulwer-Lytton, Edward, 22, 145–47, 154, 159–62; as British Colonial Secretary, 159
Bureau of Labor Statistics, 206
Burma (now Myanmar), 177
Burnham, Forbes, 54–55, 57
Burroughs, Edgar Rice, 154
Burrowes, Nicole, 5, 8–9
Butler, Samuel, 146, 147
buyer power, 262, 268, 271, 274

California, tech decamping from, 296
cannibalism, 155–59
capital, whiteness as form of, 130, 184
capital accumulation: boom-and-bust cycles, 70–72, 103; "civilization capital," 127; endless, 69, 76, 82; enslaved women as source of, 183; expansion through, 319–20; in human rights, 127–28, 134; labor's contribution to, 124–25; legitimated by individual rights doctrine, 36; logic of, 100–101; in manufacturing, 10; mechanics of ("how" question), 129–30, 131–33, 141n47; monopoly power, 66, 69–71, 80; nested, 126; "sovereignty capital," 129; tracking, 124–28. *See also* capitalism; exploitation; expropriation; surplus value
Capital in the 21st Century (Piketty), 3
capitalism: apartheid as twin of, 33; capitalist world-economy, 68; continuous growth required for, 23, 101, 167; culture of, 6; "disaster capitalism," 159; division between wage and surplus labor created by, 37–38; dominant structural mechanism in, 69; evolutionary theory as ideology of, 153; expansion, 315–20; foundational role played by race and racial categories in, 15; illusion of optimum conditions, 36; imbricated in histories of genocide, imperialism, and enslavement, 57; indenture as central to, 57; labor, relationship with, 182–83; nonracial, 39; philanthrocapitalism, 152; racial capitalism as central to, 8, 31–32, 38, 46, 58; shift from mercantile to industrial, 131; socialism in the womb of, 100–105; socialization of production, 101–2; socially beneficial option versus dark option, 103; Wilde's interpretation of, 147–53; as a world-system, 5. *See also* farmers (capitalist); global capitalism; racial capitalism; world-systems
Capitalism and Slavery (Williams), 11, 131
Capitalism as Civilisation (Tzouvala), 126
capitalists: as appendix to giant bureaucracy, 102; average rate of profit for, 90–91; explanation of gross over-reward of, 110–11; miserly behavior of, 101, 102; as owners, 89, 94; social role of, 102–3; as tenants, 89. *See also* landlords

capital markets, 98, 205
Capper-Volstead Act (192), 270–71, 273
captifs (captives), 218–20
care work, 184, 185, 187. *See also* social reproduction; unpaid work
Caribbean, 8, 46; "Caribbean/black radical tradition," 58; intellectual tradition, 49; South Asians in, 48, 53–56, 264
Casanova, Mario, 351
Central Intelligence Agency (CIA), 53
Centro Nacional de Memoria Histórica (National Center for Historical Memory), Colombia, 317, 329
Césaire, Aimé, 48
The Challenge of Blackness: The Institute of the Black World and Political Activism in the 1970s (White), 53
Chapter 313 tax relief (Texas), 284, 286, 296, 298, 305n21
Cherry, Miriam, 13
Chimni, Bhupinder, 133, 135
China, 206, 240, 264
Choctaw people, 222–23
circular causation, 9, 74–81
civilization: imperative of work/labor for, 161; racial-capitalist and imperial logics of, 127; Victorian views of, 148–50, 153, 157, 161–62
"civilizing mission," 152–53, 159–60, 184
Civil Rights Acts, 113
classical economics, 85, 86, 188n32
class struggle, 52–53, 119n48; corporativism as response to, 323–24; Italy, 352. *See also* capitalism
Clayton Act (1914), 270, 273
climate change and ecological crises, 14, 23–24, 146, 167; and palm oil industry, 301–21
Coalition of Immokalee Workers (CIW), 266
coartación, 227
Code Napoléon, 347
Code Noir (Louisiana), 225
coercion, 7, 36, 83, 176, 178, 182, 317
cognitive injustice, 128

Cole, Teju, 151–52
collective titling, 314, 318–20, 326
Collins, Jane, 15
Colombia, 16, 19–20, 23, 321–37; Afro-descendant population in, 314, 315, 318–20; armed conflict over palm oil, 313; background legal rules, 313, 317–20, 327, 329–32; Catholicism, 323; Chocó region, 314, 317–19, 333n12; Civil Code, 320; "consolidation" (*consolidación gremial*), 325; Constitution (1991), 326; corporativism in, 323–31; direct aid to agricultural and agribusiness sector, 330–31, 337n75; displacement of workers, 315, 319–20, 333n12, 334n29, 335n33; economic development policies, 319–20; environmental harms, 312, 316, 318, 320, 321, 333n9; Executive Decree 290 of 1957, 329; Fondo de Estabilización de Precios, 326–27, 330; free trade agreement with United States, 330–31; guerrilla movements, 328; inequality in, 129, 328–29; legislation, 318–19, 327, 329–31; Order of the Palm Merit—Orden al Mérito Palmero, 328; paramilitary groups, 320, 329, 331, 333n13, 334n49, 337n76; protectionism, 315, 322, 325–26; regional diversity, 317, 333n12; security concerns, 328–29; *tierras baldías*, 318, 320
Colombian Institute for Rural Development (INCODER), 319
colonialism: afterlives of, 10–11, 123, 136; colonial ordinary, 214; colonial power/knowledge nexus, 124–25; colonial racial capitalism, 56, 59; colonizer decivilized by, 48; divide and rule strategies, 53, 57, 59; Dutch, 32; and future of work, 150–51; gender binary of, 215, 219, 223; Italy, 349, 355–56, 362n50, 367–68n120, 367n113, 368n125; metaphors of, 148; pillage as necessary for, 150; and racialization of work, 184; spatial difference of colonized peoples, 157; and surplus appropriation,

132; Utopia/futurity linked with, 159; violent and unjust law, 215

The Coming Race (Bulwer-Lytton), 22, 145–46, 154, 159–62; as intraracial allegory, 160; inversion of gender in, 160–61

commodities: chains, 27–28n31; decommodification, 114; fetish, 125, 159; production and sale of, 94–95

commodity form, 105–6, 111–12

commons, 156

Compagnie des Indes, 219–21

comparative advantage theory, 100, 197, 240; and palm oil production, 20, 314, 320, 321–22, 331–32

competition: among suppliers, 202; among workers, 81–82; among workers in globalized markets, 171–72; average rate of profit equalized by, 90–91; competitive advantages, 95; and desperate conditions of work, 176; between developing countries, 197; and monopoly power, 71–72, 80; reinvestment needed to stave off, 101

competition law. *See* antitrust law

Congress of Berlin (1885), 149

Connor, Cheryl, 261

Conrad, Joseph, 152, 154

construction industry: DHS guidelines promoted by, 283; minimum wage, 285, 290–91; production of hierarchies, 287–88; state preemption of local policy, 285, 289–91; subcontractors, 287; wage theft in, 288, 299

construction workers (Austin, Texas region), 16, 18, 19, 23; average annual wage, 284; increased COVID-19 hospitalization risk for, 283, 303; medical care avoided due to fears of immigration policy, 288–89; precarity of, 282–83, 289, 294; sick leave requirements, 290–91; strategies for distributing differently, 298–302. *See also* Austin, Texas region

Consumer Protection Bureau, 115

Conte, Giuseppe, 341, 344–45, 357

convict labor, 184

cooperatives, 18–19, 262, 268–73; Colombia, 316–17; consolidation of, 270–73; exemption from antitrust law, 262, 268–73; Italy, 349, 362–63n54; premium payments made by, 268

core competencies, 200–201

"core (center)" and "periphery," 5, 9, 17, 50, 51, 68, 70–72, 80–81, 83, 238, 239, 250. *See also* periphery; world-systems analysis

Cornell University, 55

"corn laws," 82, 99–100, 104, 111

corporativism: Colombia, 323–31; Italy, 348, 350–51, 363n61, 364nn77, 78; private and public realms connected, 325–26

COVID-19, 16, 281–311; Austin construction industry as early hotspot, 283; background legal rules during, 19; construction workers declared "essential" in Texas, 281, 282–87; and dairy industry, 272, 275, 279–80n44; and unpaid work, 186

Cox, Oliver Cromwell, 52

"creative destruction," 159, 171

criminal law, 7, 109–10, 127, 130, 346, 347, 356

critical legal studies (CLS), 6–7, 85, 100, 110, 122–23, 276n5; appropriation of Ricardo/Marx model, 112–17; distributive agenda, 112–13. *See also* legal distributional analysis

critical race theory, 123, 130, 183

critical system analysis, 9, 65–84; and legal analysis, 79–83; Marx and Ricardo as theorists of, 81–82; search for systematic patterns, 66–67; society and governance system, default images of, 66; "spread effects" and "backwash effects," 76–77, 81–83; structure as concept, 65–69, 73, 75, 76; "system" as term, 66

Customs and Border Patrol, 265, 275

Dairy Farmers of America (DFA), 270–73, 279n41
dairy industry: China and India, 269; and COVID-19, 272, 275, 279–80n44; decline in consumption, 269; distributional analysis of, 273–76; exports, 269; legal regime of, 270–73; national political economy of, 268–69; occupational hazards, 263, 264–65, 267, 274, 276n16
dairy industry (Vermont), 16, 18, 260–80; "American" workers not preferred, 263–64, 265; and competition law, 262, 268–73; conditions experienced by workers, 262; detentions and deportations, effect on, 260–61, 274–75; excluded from government labor inspection, 265–66; "Feds Could ICE-Out Dairy Economy" article, 260; H-2A visas not available for, 265, 275; housing, 263, 265, 267; industrial organization of supply chain, 262; migrant workers in, 260–68, 274–75; "naming and shaming" campaigns, 261; nonmigrant workers in, 278n23; precarity in, 262–68; racial capitalism applied to, 264; redistribution in, 262, 267; twenty-four-hour operation, 263; undocumented workforce necessary to, 261, 262–63. *See also* Migrant Justice (Vermont); Milk with Dignity
Dalla Costa, Mariarosa, 186
Dar es Salaam, 49–50
Darwin, Charles, 160
Darwinian theories of evolution, 146, 147, 153, 155, 160–62
Davies, Carol Boyce, 58, 61n16
Davis, Angela, 6
Davis, Dennis, 8
Dean Foods, 271–72, 279nn37, 41
debt, 178–79; credit schemes for enslaved people, 221; "odious debt," legal principle of, 135; and sovereignty, 11, 135; Third World debt crisis, 205

decolonization, 11, 12, 50, 126; migration as form of, 11, 135
Decolonising International Law (Pahuja), 126
decommodification, 114
degeneration, 155–58, 162
"degraded work" policy advocacy, 300
degrowth, 23–24, 281, 299, 301–3
Dehm, Julia, 132, 134
De Lara, Juan, 13
Del Valle Independent School District (DVISD), 284–86, 292; and Tesla relocation, 297–98
demand, 87–88, *88*; demand curve, 88, *88, 91*, 91–92, 96; and population growth, 91, 98–99
Department of Homeland Security (DHS), 283
dependency theory, 5, 6, 9, 51, 68, 123
De Profundis (Wilde), 149
The Descent of Man (Darwin), 160
de Soto, Hernando, 132
de Sousa Santos, Boaventura, 128
development, 19–20; comparative advantage argument, 322; dispossession through, 132; disruption of through advanced automation, 196–97, 205; international economics of, 73; "ruling rationality" of, 126. *See also* degrowth; growth; underdevelopment
Diciotti (*U. Diciotti CP 941*) (Italian Coast Guard ship), 16–17, 341–43, 347, 355, 358n6
Dick, Philip K., 154
Dickens, Charles, 151
di Maio, Luigi, 341–42
"disaster capitalism," 159
Dishington, Jens Mesa, 328
displacement of workers, 169, 176; and anti-immigration sentiment, 292–93; by artificial intelligence, 196; Colombia, 315, 319–20, 333n12, 334n29, 335n33; and technology, 12, 173, 196–97
dispossession, 19, 23, 125–27, 214–15; by legal frameworks for property, 132–33; built

into slave and colonial economies, 125; and collective titling, 314, 318–20, 326; of Global South, 126; as ordinary, 214; racialized, 132, 225, 228–29, 292, 313–15. *See also* exploitation; expropriation
distemporalization, 216, 230–31n8
distraint, 110, 114
distribution: agricultural land examples, *87*, 87–94, *88, 91, 92*; alternative distributive outcomes, 136, 346–48; bargaining power as determinant of, 107–8; CLS agenda, 112–13; cost curve, *87*, 96; critique and reconstruction of the role of law in Ricardo and Marx, 105–12; demand curve, 88, *88, 91*, 91–92, 96; ethical argument, 94, 97, 116; and factory legislation, 104–5; law's role in, 2, 4, 10; Marx's theory of profit, 94; modeling on basis of actual rules and practices, 108–10; more important than redistribution, 7; neo-Ricardian account of Marxian profit, 95–96; neo-Ricardian neoclassical case against capitalist appropriation of surplus, 96–97; radically different approach needed, 3–4; Ricardo on rent, *87*, 87–94, *88, 91, 92*; social roles of landlord and capitalist, 102–3; system threatens to destroy itself, 103–4; through changing legal rules, 85–86; and welfare economics, 21, 74, 94, 106, 112; in world-systems, 68. *See also* legal distributional analysis; ownership; production; redistribution; surplus value
distributional analysis. *See* legal distributional analysis
divide and rule strategies, 53, 57, 59
division of labor, 37–38; "axial," 72; in production process, 101; in world-systems, 68–70, 72
domination, conditions of, 2, 46, 60, 111, 131, 220
Draghi, Mario, 345
Dumont de Montigny, Jean-François-Benjamin, 222–24

Duque, Iván, 312
Durand, Cédric, 202, 204–5
Dutch colonialism, 32

Economic and Philosophical Manuscripts (Marx), 148
efficiency, 86, 168, 173; and factory legislation, 104–5; and socialization of production, 101–2; and taxation of landlords, 93–94
Emergency, Empire and International Law (Reynolds), 127
employment relationship: off-loading, 200–203; standard employment relationship (SER), 13–14, 21, 147, 169, 201, 207. *See also* financialization; fissuring; informal work; outsourcing
Engels, Friedrich, 153
Engle, Karen, 16, 18, 19, 23–24, 318
entitlements, 71, 80, 82–83; as marking the "fault lines" between winners and losers, 83; of firms, 174–75
entrepreneurialism, 96, 257n56; in post–World War I Italy, 348–49, 351
environmental harms, 130–32, 266, 282; in Austin, Texas region, 292–93, 308–9n47; in Colombia, 312, 316, 318, 320, 321, 333n9; international environmental law, 132; in Italy, 20, 338, 343–46, 352–53; multinational circumvention of responsibility for, 343–45, 352–53; sustainable development policies, 134; in Victorian era writing, 146–47
Erakat, Noura, 136
Erewhon (Butler), 146, 147
Eritrea, 342; migrants from, 16–17, 355
Eslava, Luis, 133
Esquirol, Jorge, 16, 21
"essential work," 148; construction work considered as, 281, 282–87, 302; expendable workers created by background rules, 287–91; limited effect of safeguards, 287; in "progressive" boomtown, 281, 284, 292–98

ethical and epistemic capital, 11
ethics, and landlords, 97, 103, 116
Ethiopia, 355, 362n50
EU-Jordan Compact (2015). *See* Jordan Compact
Europe: imperial tradition of, 238; power struggles within, 216–17; racialism as rooted in feudal society, 58; "threat to Europe" racialization processes, 244
European Court of Human Rights, 344
European Union, 207; attempt to keep Syrian refugees in Jordan, 236–39; as "core," 238; and detention of migrants, 16–17; GDP budget deficit maximum, 345; imaginary of fungibility, 244–45; investment of resources in Jordan, 246, 258n63; media panic about refugees, 237; and palm oil industry, 312; racialization of Syrian refugees in, 243–44; trade preferences used by, 237; and *U. Diciotti* refugees, 342–43, 358n6. *See also* Italy
evolutionary theory, 146, 147, 153, 155, 160–62
expansion, 315–20; security concerns, 328–29; through accumulation, 319–20
exploitation, 10, 15, 17–18, 112–13, 126, 332; accumulation through, 314–15; in South Africa, 32, 35, 37–38, 41–42; interaction between labor and land, 316–19; Rodney's explanation of, 49–51, 53, 57–59; structure of, 315–20; "super-exploitation" of Black women, 184. *See also* dispossession; expropriation
export zones, 17, 28n34, 238, 241–42
expropriation: accumulation by, 314–15; and collective titling, 314, 318–20, 326; of expropriators, 111; illegal, 319; structure of, 315–20. *See also* dispossession; exploitation

Fair Food Code of Conduct, 266
Fair Food Program, 266
Fair Labor Standards Act, 266

farmers (capitalist), 88–89, 118n25; offers to landlord, 90–91
fascism, 21, 342, 346–48, 364n74, 367n113; legal subject redefined by, 348
Fedepalma, 312, 322, 323–29
Federal Milk Marketing Order One, 272
Federici, Silvia, 14–15
feminist theory, 183, 274; governance feminism, 7, 124; international conflict feminism (ICF), 130; and social reproduction, 126, 185, 189
Fernand Braudel Center (State University of New York), 55
feudal society, 58, 256n46
"financial inclusion," 178
financialization, 2, 13, 209–10n20; "offshoring-financialization" linkage, 204–5; and palm oil industry, 20; valorization of intangible assets, 203–5
fissuring, 2, 196, 207–8; "fissured workplace," 13–14, 200; and global value chains, 13–14, 169; global value chains as product of, 202; "human supply chains," 16; internal subcontracting, 200; and off-loading of employment relationship, 200–203; outsourcing, 13–14; and palm oil industry, 20; shareholder value as central to, 200–201; trouser import example, 202–3, *203*, 208n10; wage share, decline in, 202–3
Five-Star Movement (*Movimento Cinque Stelle*), Italy, 341, 344
Fleuriau, François, 213
forced labor, 147, 176, 180, 184
formalization, 14, 172–73, 177; of workers but not work, 17–18, 238
Francis, Pope, 3
Fraser, Nancy, 314–15
free market, 6–7, 110; as fantasy, 69–70, 102; prone to crises, 103
free people of color (*gens de couleur libres*), 213–14, 223, 224–25; *coartación*, 227
French recordkeeping, 214
Freud, Sigmund, 158

fungibility of workers: in colonial New Orleans, 220; EU assumptions versus reality, 243–48; imagined by EU, 244–45; racial, of Syrians and migrant workers, 17, 238–39, 241–48
Furnivall, John Sydenham, 177
future of work, 1–4; challenging dominant framings, 12; as colonial, 150–51; current challenges, 167–68; and debt, 178–79; and degeneration, 155–58, 162; dominant discourses of, 15; global, 196–210; imagined alternatives, 21–24; inevitability of constant upheaval and change at, 171; Italian cases, 341–46; late-twentieth- and early twenty-first-century framings of, 147; overlapping and converging institutional visions, 170–73; and past speculations, 148; prospects for research, 187–89; racialization at work, 182–84; research agenda as work of, 181; revisiting, 187–89; as speculative, 147; as story of the present and the past of work, 168; unpaid work, 185–87. *See also* financialization; fissuring; informal work; past of work; Victorian past, future of work seen from; work (labor)

Gaillard, Jean, 213–14
Gariep River metaphor, 40
garment industry, 236–59; manufacturers' perspective, 239–43; path-dependent growth of, 243; trouser import example, 202–3, *203*, 208n10; Turkey, 247, 249; worker responses to Jordan Compact, 246–48. *See also* Jordan; Jordan Compact
Garvey, Marcus, 55
Gathii, James, 126, 131
gender: divisions of work, 14–15, 147–48, 156; future of in Wells's novella, 156–57, 161; hierarchies, 1, 14–15, 172, 238, 245–46; inversion of in *The Coming Race*, 160–61. *See also* feminist theory; women

Gender, Alterity, and Human Rights (Kapur), 127–28
gender nonconformity, 16, 213–35; among Indigenous peoples, 222–23; and artisanal status group, 16, 215, 217–18, 220, 231n18; circum-Atlantic Black and Indigenous, 214–15; "hermaphrodites," 217, 222–23; and insurrectionary potential, 214, 215, 216, 221–26; *jeliw* (griots), 218–29; racialized and genderized insults, 213–14; resistance to colonial binary, 215; in Senegambia, 215, 217–18; "sodomites," 222–23
gentrification, 19, 113, 292, 293
George, Henry, 94
gig work, 13, 169, 178
Gilman, Charlotte Perkins, 163n6
Gilmore, Ruth Wilson, 264
"global black tradition," 58
global capitalism: coexistence of free and unfree labor, 176; organization of, 1–2; racial, gender, and geographic differentiation tied to, 11. *See also* capitalism; financialization; fissuring; global value chains; racial capitalism; world-systems; world-systems analysis;
global competition for work, 171–72
global financial crisis of 2008, 2, 65
"global governance," 79, 81
globalization: division of labor, 68–70, 72; inequality "between" nations as focus, 79; soft goods production, 197; of soft goods production, 197; territorial diversity as guardrail against global policy, 70; Wallerstein as critic of, 67; "world market" as virtual, 69–70
Global North, 11, 14, 23, 207; "informal" types of work, 169–70; NGOs, 151; nostalgia for "full" and "standard" employment, 21; surplus appropriation from Global South, 77, 125–26; White Savior Industrial Complex, 151–52. *See also* Italy; United States
global supply chains. *See* supply chains

Global South, 8, 14, 19, 23, 123, 141n7; capital dispossession of, 126; expressions of dissent in, 134–35; informal sector, 28n34, 169, 173, 177, 207; migration to from Italy, 339–40, 355–56; present organization of work as referent, 179–80; surplus appropriation from, 77, 125–27, 138n13; Third World debt crisis, 205
global value chains (GVCs), 13–14, 169, 171, 202; garment industry, 202–3, *203*, 208n10, 240; "intangible" activities, 198; lead firms, 202–5, 208–9n12; as product of fissuring, 202; proliferation of in 1990s and 2000s, 204; reverse smile curve, *199*; smile curve, 197–99, *198*, 202–5; under strain, 205–6. *See also* Third World approaches to international law (TWAIL)
Goldsmith, Oliver, 176
González, Jorge, 16, 19–20, 23
Gopal, Priyamvada, 134
Gordon, Jennifer, 16, 17–18
governance feminism, 7, 124
Gramsci, Antonio, 39
Great Depression, 349, 362n50
grounding, concept of, 49
The Groundings with My Brothers (Rodney), 48–49, 61n16
growth policies: degrowth, 23–24, 281, 299, 301–3; hidden subsidies of, 293–97, 299; local-regional debates about, 282; Texas, 281–82
Grupo Grancolombiano, 324–25
Guerra, Alfredo, 325–26
Guidance on the Essential Critical Infrastructure Workforce (DHS), 83
Guyana, 49, 52–55

H-2A visas, 265, 275
Haitian Revolution, 47, 55–56, 229
Hale, Robert, 7, 108, 317
Halley, Janet, 7, 11, 124, 128, 274
Hamzić, Vanja, 16, 22
Hannaford (grocery chain), 267, 275

Harding, Vincent, 45, 46, 55, 60
Harney, Stefano, 136
Harris, Cheryl, 130
Hartman, Saidiya, 228
Harvey, David, 315
Heart of Darkness (Conrad), 152, 154
Hegel's philosophy, 102–5, 118n47
Herland (Gilman), 163n6
hierarchies, 238; gendered and racialized, 1, 14–15, 172, 238, 245–46; global, 15–21; inequality seen as métier of, 80; Italy, 345–46, 351–52; law as device of categorical ordering, 215, 238; by nationality, 245, 257n56; racialization of low-level workers, 345–46; and universal standard, 129–30; vulnerable feminized refugee, 243–44, 256n49
Hill, Robert, 45, 55, 60
History of Guyanese Working People, 1885–1905 (Rodney), 55–56, 58
Hoad, Neville, 12–13, 15, 22
Hobbes, Thomas, 153
homosexual panic defense, 158, 165–66n53
housing, low-income, 10, 114–15; affordable housing policy tools, 291; linkage fees, 291; pro-tenant rules, 86; "redlining" of mortgage underwriting, 293; source of income discrimination, 291
How Britain Underdeveloped the Caribbean (Beckles), 52
How Europe Underdeveloped Africa (Rodney), 5, 6, 45, 46, 50–52
human capital, 170, 171, 175, 178, 197
humanitarian capital, 127–28, 134
humanitarian policy, 125, 130–32; and ICF projects, 130; Italy, 341–43; and Jordan Compact, 237–38, 241, 244, 246–49; refugees barred from work, 241; trend toward "refugee self-reliance," 250n5
human rights, 127, 132, 170, 317–18; capital accumulation in, 127–28, 134

"idleness," 215
ILVA steel plant (southern Italy), 340, 341, 343–45, 352–53, 357; environmental

harms caused by, 343–44; sale to ArcelorMittal, 343–44; sale to Riva family, 343, 359n11; *tutela* demands of, 347

immigration law, 18, 288–89; and dairy industry, 265; effect on Vermont dairy workers, 260, 262; Jordanian, 241–42; *kafala* visa regime, 237, 240, 249, 251n7imperialism: cannibalism as allegory for, 159; "civilizing mission," 152–53, 159–60, 184; extractive economies, 152–53; "imperial labor reallocation" strategy, 56; Italian views of, 349, 362n52; rivalries of, 37; travel fiction in era of, 154; "white man's burden," 151, 160

Imperialism, Sovereignty and the Making of International Law (Anghie), 129–30

Imperialism: The Highest Stage of Capitalism (Lenin), 150

import substitution industrialization (ISI), 20, 35, 314, 320, 322–26, 328–30

indentured labor, 48, 55–57, 127, 176, 264

independence movements, 47

independent contractors, 13, 175, 200, 206, 358n1

India, 56, 240

Indigenous communities: dispossessed by legal frameworks for property, 132–33; extreme segregation of under Italian colonialism, 367n114; in Louisiana, 15, 16, 215, 221–22, 231n8

indirect employment, 316

individualism, 153, 346; private property as condition for, 156; replaced by social function in Italy, 350

Indo-Caribbean peoples, 48–49, 53

Indupalma, 20, 312–13, 316, 332

industrial capitalism, 12, 131, 137n4, 138n13, 155, 348

industrial revolution, 176, 360n32; fourth, 147, 154; started by plundering of New World silver, 150

inequality, economic, 1–4; billionaire wealth, 3, 24n7; circular causation of, 9,

74–81; as distributional point of larger structures, 3–4; due to gendered and racialized distinctions, 14–15; income and wealth inequality, 1–2, 3, 11, 43n25, 65, 66, 68, 70, 82, 122, 177, 210n26; intra-country, 206; legacy inheritance of, 79–80; nonrecognition of unpaid care work as central to, 185; and predictable patterns, 66–67, 75; South Africa, 40, 43n25. *See also* fissuring; gender; hierarchies; racialization

informal work, 17, 21, 28n34, 168–72, 177–81, 188, 207; gig work, 178; as global norm, 14; Jordan, 237–38; and organized crime structures, 356–57. *See also* garment industry

Institute of the Black World (IBW), 45, 53, 55

institutionalist analysis, 66, 73–78, 112, 126–27. *See also* Myrdal, Gunnar

intangible activities and assets, 14, 203–5

intellectual property, 171, 204

international conflict feminism (ICF), 130

international criminal law (ICL), 130

International Financial Institutions (IFIs), 141n47

international institutions, 21, 126–27, 141n47, 204; future-of-work projects, 168, 170–73

International Labor Organization (ILO), 13, 170–71, 207; migrant workers' center in Jordan, 248

international law, 10–11, 122, 142n51, 254n34; background laws, 126, 132, 133; as complement to demands of global capital, 127; environmental, 132; hierarchies within, 243–44; public/private dichotomy naturalized in, 133. *See also* Third World approaches to international law (TWAIL)

International Law from Below (Rajagopal), 126–27

investment: reinvestment, 100–101, 103; strangled by higher and higher rent, 98

Italian Coast Guard, 17, 341–42

Italian Constitutional Court, 344, 352
Italy, 16, 338–68; "abuse of rights" doctrine, 350; appeals to "the social" in, 339–40; austerity measures, 348, 361n39; background legal rules, 340, 341, 346, 353; *biennio rosso* (red biennial), 348; Civil Code (1942), 350–52; coalition (Yellow-Green) government, 341–42, 358n3; colonialism, 349, 355–56, 362n50, 367–68n120, 367n113, 368n125; Constitution (1948), 338, 353–54; cooperatives, 349, 362–63n54; Council of State, 353; emigration from, 349; entrepreneurialism, 348–49, 351; environmental harms in, 20, 338, 343–46, 352–53; Eritrean migrants in, 355–56; fascism, 21, 342, 346–48, 364n74; fascist labor laws (1926), 350; foreign investors, 254; "full powers," 342, 348–49, 357, 362n48; future of workers, two cases on, 341–46; hierarchies, 345–46, 351–52; ILVA steel plant, 340, 341, 343–45, 347, 352–53, 357; immigration to from Global South, 339–40, 355–56; intermediate legal statuses reduced, 356–57; Labor Charter (1927), 350–51; left mobilization, 352; legal immunity laws, 344, 359n15; migrants kept at bay, 16–17, 21; organized crime, 339, 357; racialized levels of protection, 355–57; relocation of private firms, 339; "social," concept of, 21, 340–41, 346, 349–51, 367n108; social law, 349–50; state policy of anti-Semitism, 356; syndicalism, 339, 349, 354, 361nn39, 43, 364n77; *tutela*, 21; "*tutela*," 346–48; work as social duty in, 348; Workers' Statute (1970), 352–54

Jamaica, 48–49, 61n16
James, C. L. R., 47, 49, 52
James, Selma, 47, 49, 186
Jefferies, Richard, 146, 147
jeliw (griots), 218–19, 226

Jones, Claudia, 52, 61n16, 184
Jordan, 17–18, 236–59; actual divisions in labor market, 245; Aleppo as base for garment industry, 241, 247; Bangladeshi women in, 248; export zones, 17, 28n34, 238, 241–42; garment industry as majority-foreign-owned, 240; garment manufacturers' perspective, 239–43; garment work due to peace deal with Israel, 240; geographical location, 255n45; *kafala* visa regime, 237, 240, 249, 251n7; number of refugees hosted by, 254n33; as "periphery," 238; racialization of noncitizen workers in, 245–46; refugees barred from work in, 241; scarcity of natural resources, 239–40, 255n45; South Asian migrants in, 238, 241–42, 245; Syrian women's employment in, 247, 258n67; tariff reduction, 17, 237, 240, 242; work permits granted to Syrians, 17, 237–38, 246, 247, 251n11. *See also* garment industry
Jordan Compact, 17, 237–41; enhanced market access, 242; global theory versus local context, 248–50; neoliberal orthodoxy of, 239; racialization through, 244; worker responses to, 246–48; work permits granted under, 17, 237–38, 246, 247, 251n11
Justice Department, 271–72
Justice for Some (Erakat), 136
just-in-time manufacturing, 13

kafala visa regime (Jordan), 237, 240, 249, 251n7
Kale, Madhavi, 56
Kang'ara, Sylvia, 132
Kapur, Ratna, 127–28, 131, 134, 136
Kelley, Robin D. G., 60
Kempf, Edward J., 165–66n53
Kennedy, David, 3, 7, 9–10, 17, 23, 28n31
Kennedy, Duncan, 6, 7, 8, 10, 11, 18, 81, 122–23, 136
Kerlérec, Governor, 224

Khan, Adil, 136
Kipling, Rudyard, 160
knowledge: colonial power/knowledge nexus, 124–25; dominant patterns interrupted in New Orleans, 216; ecologies of, 128; politics of, 122–23; public investment in knowledge economy, 295–96; subjugated, 128
Koskenniemi, Martii, 133
Krippner, 209–10n20
Kundnani, Arun, 38

labor. *See* work (labor)
Labor Department's Office of Foreign Labor Certification, 275
labor-intensive manufacturing, disruption of, 196–97, 205
labor law, 17–19, 169, 176, 180, 182; National Labor Relations Act, 183, 261, 265–66
labor markets, formalization of, 14, 171–72
labor theory of value, 10, 86, 95–97, 105, 107, 111
Lamming, George, 58–59
landlords, 10; appropriation of all the surplus, 91–93, 97–100, 106–7; enforcement by, 106–7; explanation of gross over-reward of, 110–11; and farmers as tenants, 88–89; impoverishment as strategy against, 82; improving, 89, 96, 113, 118n25; no efficiency cost through taxation of, 93–94; no ethical claim to respect, 97, 103, 116; non-improving, 89, 93–94, 96; social role of, 102–3. *See also* agriculture; capitalists; ownership
Lansdowne Commission on Mine Wages (South Africa), 35
La Paperson, 132
La Rue, Etienne, 213–14, 219, 230n2
Latouche, Serge, 301
Lavine, Dick, 296
law: constitutive of political and economic disparities, 66; as device of categorical ordering, 215; facilitation of racialized and geographic hierarchies by, 1; formalization through, 14, 171–73; internal critique of, 132; mainstream, 6–7, 105–6; positive, 106, 108, 111; role in unequal distribution of wealth and resources, 2; seen as nonproblematic and neutral, 7, 41, 112, 183–84, 287, 315; shadow of, 7, 110, 141n47, 265. *See also* legal distributional analysis; legal rules
"Law and the Global Dynamics of Distribution" (Kennedy), 7
"lead" industries, 70–72, 81
League of Nations mandate system, 129
Le Courrier de Bourbon (slavers' ship), 219
Lee, Cynthia, 165–66n53
left and multiracial coalitions, 54–55
Lega (the League), 341, 358n2
legacy inheritance, 79–80
legal distributional analysis, 2, 10, 100; applied to TWAIL scholarship, 11, 122, 124; arguments favoring the poor, 114; beyond labor and capital, 182–84; of dairy industry, 273–76; distributional analysis invented by Marx and Ricardo, 85–86; invented by Marx and Ricardo, 85–86; neo-Ricardian, 113–14; normative blinders addressed by, 128–31; normative orientation of subordinated groups, 86; overview, 6–7; post-realist legal lens, 86, 97; of pro-tenant rules, 86; and reparative interventions, 22, 133–36; revisited, 180–82; strong and weak parties, 85–86, 115–16, 138n12, 276n5; of supply chain interventions, 260–80; three steps of, 124. *See also* distribution; Marx, Karl; Ricardo, David
legal formalism, 85, 105–6
legalism, liberal political, 117, 123, 129
legal realism, 7, 10, 132, 182
legal rules: backgrounded and naturalized, 7, 18–19, 86; bargaining power affected by, 108; contingency of, 105, 108, 111; distribution through changing, 85–86; "law of work," 168, 180, 186. *See also* law

Lenin, Vladimir Il'ich, 150
liberation movements, 53
Libya, 342, 355
London Labour and the London Poor (Mayhew), 147
Looking Backward (Bellamy), 146
"lost decade" of the 1980s, 205
Louisiana: Canadian traders in, 221–22; chartered to Compagnie des Indes, 221; *Code Noir*, 225; free people of color (*gens de couleur libres*), 213–14, 223, 224–25; insurrectionary potential in, 214, 215, 216, 221–26, 228–29; Natchez uprising, 225; Pointe Coupée conspiracy, 228–29, 235n86; Spanish, 215, 227; Spanish racial hierarchies created, 227; "tignon law," 228. *See also* New Orleans

management function, 97, 101–2
Mandela, Nelson, 32, 34, 39, 40
manufacturing: labor as "fertile," 94–95; neo-Ricardian account of Marxian profit, 95–96; reinvestment required, 100–101; technological innovation required, 101
Marella, Maria Rosaria, 348
market: owner-entrepreneur in, 97; price for product, 90–91; reserve labor, 33; state as all organized interferences with, 78; "virtual," 69; "world market" as virtual, 69–70. *See also* free market
market engagement, 168, 176, 178, 185
market value, 94, 115, 295
maroon settlements, 33
Marx, Karl, 8, 10, 11, 81–82, 85–86, 122–23, 138n13; alienation of labor, concept of, 103, 148; on assembly line as dehumanizing, 103–4, 118n46; dynamic analysis, 94; on labor's contribution to capital accumulation, 124–25; legal formalism of, 105–6; legal rules in theory of, 105; "mere ownership" and appropriation of all the surplus, 97; neo-Ricardian neoclassical case against, 96–97; theory of profit, 94–97; Works: *Economic and Philosophical Manuscripts*, 148
Marxism, 4–5, 9, 31–33, 46–47, 60–61n7, 122–23, 314–15, 323. *See also* Black Marxism: The Making of the Black Radical Tradition (Robinson); capitalism; racial capitalism; socialism
Mayhew, Henry, 147
McKinsey Global Institute, 206
Means, Gardiner Coit, 96–97
mechanization, 101, 103
"media," 77–78, 80–82
medievalism, literary, 146, 147, 148
Mémoires historiques sur la Louisiane (Dumont de Montigny), 222–24
Mexico, dairy exports to, 269
Mickelson, Karin, 132
Microelectronics and Computer Consortium, 295
Migrant Justice (Vermont), 18, 260–62, 266–68, 277n16
migrants, 28n34; aboard *U. Diciotti CP 941*, 16–17, 341, 342–43, 347, 358n6; activism in agricultural industries, 18, 260–62, 266; "human supply chains," 16; Italian, 349; *kafala* visa regime (Jordan), 237, 240, 249, 251n7; remittances sent by, 241, 263; structurally devalued labor of, 262; undocumented not entitled to relief, 283, 287; in Vermont dairy industry, 260–68. *See also* construction workers (Austin, Texas); dairy industry (Vermont); immigration law; refugees; Syrian refugees
migration, 177; as decolonization, 11, 135; as "imperial labor reallocation" strategy, 56; internal, Colombia, 19; to Italy from Global South, 339–40, 355–56
Milberg, Will, 202, 205
Milk with Dignity, 18, 266–67; attempts to shift surplus, 262; Code of Conduct, 266, 267, 274; hotline, 274; "mass balancing," 268; Standards Council,

266, 274; supply chain design, 267. *See also* Ben & Jerry's
minimum wage, 278n24, 285, 290–91
Miró, Esteban, 228
The Modern World-System (Wallerstein), 5
money laundering, 315, 333n13
monopoly power, 66, 69–72, 80; quasi-monopolies, 71–72
Morris, William, 146, 147, 148, 154
Moten, Fred, 136
"motion in the system," 17, 239
Movement for Black Lives, 60
Multi-Fiber Agreement, 240
multinational corporations: and global value chains, 202; governments lack of tools to constrain, 338–39, 344–45, 352–53; *tutela* as incapable of protecting workers from, 347. *See also* ILVA steel plant (southern Italy)
Murgas, Carlos, 326
Musk, Elon, 154, 297–98
Muslims, 244, 256n51
Mussolini, Benito, 355, 362n53, 368n122
Myanmar. *See* Burma (now Myanmar)
Myrdal, Gunnar, 8, 9–10, 17, 23; "circular causation" theory, 9, 74–78, 80–81; complexity in theory of, 73, 76, 78; economic institutionalism, 73–78; generality of analytic, 75, 76, 78; "social system," analysis of unequal development within, 9, 66, 67; "spread effects" and "backwash effects," 76–77, 81–83; "structure" lacking in system of, 78

NAFTA, 269
Napoleonic wars, 99
Natarajan, Usha, 130, 131
Natchez nation, 222, 225–26
National Labor Relations Act, 183, 261, 265–66
National Liberation Front (South Africa), 34
National Milk Producers Federation (NMPF), 265, 275

National Party (South Africa), 36
"Nation and Ethnicity in South Africa" (Alexander), 31
Native Labour Code, 183
Nazi Germany, 355
nègre, as designation for captives, 219–20, 230nn2, 4
neoclassical economics, 10, 15, 94, 106, 112
neocolonialism, 10–11, 47–48, 53, 122–23, 250
neoliberalism, 113–14, 321–22; export-led economic development theories, 238, 239; humanitarian rhetoric of, 238; in Italy, 354; and palm oil production, 313–14; postures of sustainable urbanism, 292; and rent-seeking practices, 323. *See also* comparative advantage theory
"neo-*terra nullius*" discourse, 132
Nesiah, Vasuki, 8, 10–11, 22
New Orleans, 16, 22, 213–35; "back o' town," 226, 229; blacksmiths from Senegambia in, 220; Carnival, 228; classed and racialized "justice" in, 213–14; as devil's own domain, 215–16.221; French recordkeeping, 214; as gendered name, 221; knowledge dominant patterns interrupted in, 216; number of enslaved people in, 220, 223, 233n44; perceived lack of work in, 224; Senegambians in, 16, 213–24; socio-temporal contexts of, 214–15; Superior Council of Louisiana, 213; taverns, 215, 224–25, 227. *See also* Louisiana
News from Nowhere (Morris), 146, 147, 154
Nixon, Richard, 113
"normal" work, 21, 169–70; informality as, 179–80
normative assessment, 7; "double move" of, 129–31
Nyerere, Julius, 49

Obama, Barack, 2
Obregón, Liliana, 135
Occupational Safety and Health Administration (OSHA), 265–66

OECD countries, 206
offshoring-financialization linkage, 205
"On the Principles of Political Economy and Taxation" (Ricardo), 94
Oracle, 296
O'Reilly, Governor, 227–28
organizational change, 200, 205
"outside" of labor, 168, 179–80
outsourcing, 13, 14, 20, 178, 200–205
ownership, 14, 20–21; control separated from, 96–97; costless transfer of, 94; estate owners and smallholders, 93; laborer divested of means of survival, 59; legal regime of, 82; of the means of production, 94, 96; "mere," 96, 97–100; owner-entrepreneur, 97; priority over citizenship, 70; social and legal concepts of, 97. See also distribution; landlords
Oxfam, 3, 24n7

Pahuja, Sundhya, 126
Palestinian refugees, 254n33
palm oil industry (Colombia), 16, 19–20, 312–37; amount of land dedicated dedicated to, 320; background legal rules, 313, 317–20, 327, 329–32; and climate change, 301–21; collective titling and expropriation, 314, 318–20, 326; comparative advantage theory, 20, 314, 320, 321–22, 331–32; at core of armed conflict, 313; dissolution of businesses, 312–13; Fedepalma, 312, 322, 323–29; government account (*parafiscales*), 327; government incentives for, 329–30; history of, 312–13; and import substitution industrialization (ISI), 20, 314, 320, 322–26, 328–30; indirect employment schemes, 316; memory of workers, 317, 329; and money laundering, 315, 333n13; production increases, 327, 329; protectionist policies, 315, 322, 325–26; struggle between business, the state, and workers, 314; unintended consequences of, 321–22

Pan-Africanism, 6, 46, 49, 52–53
Parmar, Pooja, 136
past of work, 167–95; distributional analysis beyond labor and capital, 182–84; distributional analysis revisited, 180–82; efforts to improve work, 168, 175; landscape of work, 169–70; "outside" of labor, 168, 179–80; in the present, 175–79, 187. *See also* future of work; legal distributional analysis; Victorian past, future of work seen from
Pater, Walter, 150, 161
Peasants and Capital: Dominica in the World Economy (Trouillot), 250
Périer, Governor, 225
periphery, 5, 9, 14, 17, 28n31, 68, 70–72; Colombia in, 20; in dependency theory, 51. *See also* "core (center)" and "periphery"
Perry, Keisha-Khan, 48, 58, 61n16
philanthrocapitalism, 152
Philippe (Duc d'Orléans), 221
Pickett, Kate, 3
The Picture of Dorian Gray (Wilde), 152
pièce d'Inde, as unit of value, 220
Piketty, Thomas, 3
plantation economies, 56, 58–59
platform work, 170, 206
play, forms of, 136
Polanyi, Karl, 176, 177, 348
political economy: current use of term, 65–66; Marxist critique of, 124–26; racialized, 53; urban-regional, 19, 23, 281, 284, 291, 294–95, 298–301; Victorian-era imaginings, 145, 146
population: growth and demand, 91, 98–99; Malthusian theory, 99, 153; and unproductive land linked, 82
post-realist legal lens, 86, 97
poverty, decline in, 206, 210n26
precarity, 14, 17–19, 79; of alternative forms of work, 169; of construction workforce, 282; in dairy industry, 262–68; growth policies as source

of, 23; of immigrants to Italy, 340; informal labor as complex response to, 180; profitability of, 10, 18; for white collar professionals, 196. *See also* financialization; fissuring

private law, 6–7, 360n32; and bargaining power, 112–13; ignored by reforms, 111–12; Italy, 349–50; mid-nineteenth-century Western Europe, 105; pro-poor rules, 86, 112–13; and public/private dichotomy, 133; structuring work of, 78; supposedly neutral, 7; workers as willing sellers in, 347–48. *See also* property law

production: capitalist socialization of, 101–2; and competition among workers, 81–82; "core-like products and peripheral products," 72; and costless transfer of ownership, 94; costs of, *87*, 87–93, 97–99, 101, 105, 110, 269; labor and nonlabor elements, 95; management function, 97, 101–2; mechanization of assembly line, 101, 103; nonlabor means of, 105; organizational dimension, 101; ownership of the means of, 94, 96; rationalization of, 101–2; and specialization, 70; transnationalized world of, 167

"productivism," 351–53, 355–56

profit: Marx's theory, 94–97; rent distinguished from, 90, 96

progressive legal scholarship, 182

Project for the Study of Alternative Education in South Africa, 34

"The Promise of International Law," 135

property: as condition for individualism, 156; international legal frameworks for, 132; ownership prohibited to Blacks in South Africa, 32; public, 112; racial privilege as, 130; and social function in Italy, 350; "social function" of, 363n65; technologies for making land into, 132; and unpaid work, 186. *See also* dispossession; expropriation

property law, 7, 83, 125, 182

pro-poor private law rules, 86, 112–13; rent-seeking on behalf of the poor, 10, 86, 115–17

protectionism, 141n47, 315, 322, 325–26, 346–47, 364n78

Protestant work ethic, 145

"public charge rule," 289

public interest, not prioritized by state, 65, 78

Putin, Vladimir, 2–3

racial capitalism, 2, 15–16, 147, 153, 182–83, 256n46, 276n5; agriculture as source of, 264; American, 228–29; as central to capitalism, 8, 31–32, 38, 46, 58; challenges to, 31; concept developed in South Africa, 31–32, 60n4; critiques of, 1–2; in dairy industry, 264; early articulations of, 57; gender binary of, 16, 214–15, 219; overview, 4–5; and palm oil industry, 332; socioeconomic alienation of gender and bodily labor, 215–16; South African, 8, 31–44; temporality of work and selfhood in, 214; toward liberation from, 38–39; as world-system, 22; world-systems analysis linked with, 5–6. *See also* Alexander, Neville; capitalism; Robinson, Cedric; Rodney, Walter

racialization: as central to structure of work, 183; and dispossession, 132, 225, 228–29, 292, 313–15; and Jordan Compact, 243–48; Italy, and levels of protection, 355–57; of labor, 149; of low-level workers, 345–46; of noncitizen workers in Jordan, 245–46; of primitive accumulation, 147; of refugees from Sub-Saharan Africa, 244, 245–46, 249; as stealth material distribution, 130; of Syrian refugees in Europe, 17, 243–44; at work, 182–84

Rajagopal, Balakrishnan, 126–27

Rastafarians, 48–49, 61n16

redemption, 149

redistribution, 3; distribution more important than, 7; and efficiency cost, 94; and factory legislation, 104–5; harms to people being helped, 86; and regulation, 104–5, 111–16; in Vermont dairy industry, 262, 267. *See also* distribution

reform, 3, 6, 65–66; agrarian, 314, 318, 320; Colombia, 129; expropriate the expropriators, 111; focus on, 80; four modes of, 111–12; proposal to repeal "corn laws," 82, 99–100, 104, 111; rent-seeking on behalf of the poor, 10, 86, 115–17; Ricardo's, 82, 111; Wilde's views, 151

refugees: assistance for, 242, 247, 249, 257n59; hierarchies of, 243–44; from Sub-Saharan Africa, 244, 245–46, 249; vulnerable feminized refugee image, 243–44, 256n49. *See also* migrants

"Regulating Slum Housing Markets on Behalf of the Poor: Of Housing Codes, Housing Subsidies and Income Redistribution Policy" (Ackerman), 114–16

regulation, 78, 172; calls for increase in, 3, 12, 86; of gender binary, 214–15; of "idleness," 215; and redistribution, 104–5, 111–16; social democratic regulatory regimes, 111; statutory, 6–7

remittances, 77, 241, 263

rents, 83; compared with Marx's theory of profit, 94; leasehold rights, 90; and perpetuation of racial thinking, 41; profit distinguished from rent, 90; reconstruction legal presuppositions of, 106–7; reinvested in politics, 99; Ricardo's model, *87*, 87–94, *88, 91, 92*; South African inequalities, 41

rent-seeking: "on behalf of the poor," 10, 86, 115–17; in palm oil industry, 314, 323–31

Renzi, Matteo, 354

reparative interventions, 22, 133–36

retirement benefits, 239

Reynolds, John, 127

Rhodes, Cecil, 35, 150

Ricardo, David, 8, 10, 11, 81–82, 85–86, 122–23; demand for food, 87–88, *88*; improving landlord, concept of, 89, 93–94, 96, 113, 118n25; landlords and farmers, 88–89; legal context neglected by, 105; "mere ownership" and appropriation of all the surplus, 97; neo-Ricardian account of Marxian profit, 95–96; neo-Ricardian neoclassical case against capitalist appropriation of surplus, 96–97; population growth and demand, 91, 98; on rent, *87*, 87–94, *88, 91, 92*; on repeal of "corn laws," 82, 99–100, 104, 111; stagnation argument, 98–100; Works: "On the Principles of Political Economy and Taxation," 94. *See also* agriculture

Richani, Nazih, 337n76

"right to work" laws, 184

RISE (Relief in a State of Emergency) funds, 283–84, 287

Rittich, Kerry, 13–15

Robinson, Cedric, 4–6, 8, 17, 25n12, 46, 57, 153, 256n46; European feudal society, view of, 58; racial capitalism in thought of, 32–33, 37–38; on racism in capitalism, 32–33; Works: *Black Marxism: The Making of the Black Radical Tradition*, 4–5, 32, 58, 256n46

Rodney, Patricia, 49, 52, 54

Rodney, Walter, 5, 6, 8–9, 45–64, 138n14; assassination of, 45, 56–57; banned from Jamaica, 48; children of, 49, 52; class-based definition of Blackness, 48–49; global, but locally grounded, interventions, 46; influence on Wallerstein, 9, 46, 55; key tenets of project, 46–47; in left and multiracial coalitions, 54–55; Works: *The Groundings with My Brothers*, 48–49, 61n16; *A History of Guyanese Working People, 1881–1905*, 46, 55, 58;

How Europe Underdeveloped Africa, 5, 6, 45, 46, 50–52; "Towards the Sixth Pan-African Congress: Aspects of the International Class Struggle in Africa, the Caribbean and America," 52–53
Rodriguez, Zully Palacios, 260
Romagnoli, Umberto, 351
rule of law, 14, 126, 172–73, 175, 177
Ruskin, John, 148, 150, 152–53

Saint-Maló, Jean, 226
Salvini, Matteo, 341–43, 356, 358nn3, 5, 7
Samour, Nahed, 135
sanctuary policies, 290
Santiz Cruz, José Obeth, 277n16
Santos, Juan Manuel, 331
School of Oriental and African Studies (SOAS), 47
Seabrooke, Leonard, 204
"security capital," 127
Sedella, Antonio de, 227
Sedgwick, Eve, 134
selfhood, temporality of, 213–14, 216
Senegambia: artisan class, 16, 215, 217–18, 220, 231n18; gender nonconformity in, 215, 217–18; Senegambians in New Orleans, 16, 22, 213–24
Sepoy Rebellion (1857), 149
Serrano, Angela, 313
Seven Years' War, 224, 227
shareholder value, doctrine of, 200–201
Shea, Brigid, 287
Shearer, Hugh, 48
Shih, Stan, 197–98
Sixth Pan-African Congress, 52–53
slave-machines, 148–50
slavery: afterlives of, 11, 123, 136; and agriculture, 264; alliances between enslaved people and others, 215; capitalist view of as necessity, 33; *captifs* (captives), 218–20; compensation for "lost property," 56; economics as reason for development of, 57–58; griots as captives, 218–19; indentured labor schemes to replace, 48, 55–56, 176; misgendering of Africans, 215; *pièce d'Inde* as unit of value, 220; plantation, 16; reenslavement of free people of color, 224–25; slave trade in Senegambia region, 216–17; and TWAIL analysis, 125
slave trade, 32, 127, 138n14; rebellion on ships, 215, 219
smile curve, 197–99, *198*, 202–5
Smith, Adam, 182
Smith, Gregory, 57
"social," concept of, 21, 340–41, 346, 349–57, 361n35, 367n108; "productivist," 351–53, 355–56; racialized, 355–57
Social Darwinism, 153, 157
social democracy, 104
socialism, 100–105; abandonment of, 347; class split within, 154; Wilde's view, 148–53. *See also* Marx, Karl; Marxism
social reproduction: and backgrounded legal rules, 16; and boomtown economy, 281; and care work, 184–85; design for social living, 58–60; disruption of, 17; feminist theory and, 189; mystification of, 185; new imaginaries of work, 16; unpaid work, 14, 185–87; of women garment workers, 242
social responsibility model, 16, 18
"social system": circular causation in, 9, 74–81; as relationship among regions, 77–78; state as part of, 78. *See also* Myrdal, Gunnar; systems; world-systems analysis
Somalia, 355
"The Soul of Man Under Socialism" (Wilde), 12–13, 145–46, 147, 148–53, 162
South Africa, 31–44; agriculture and secondary industries, 34–35; "Bantustan policy," 36–37; class perspective, 38–39; Constitution (1996), 41; continued inequality, 40, 43n25; democracy, movement for, 33, 34, 38–40; dividing of people in, 38, 40; education, 37, 41; Gariep River metaphor, 40; genealogy

South Africa (*continued*)
of racial capitalism, 8; language policy advocacy, 33–34; leadership of the Black working class, 8; Marxist theories applied to, 32–33; material conditions, 40; mining sector, 32, 33, 35; national bourgeoisie, 32; National Liberation Front, 34; need for cohesive conception of nation, 38; precious gems and metals, 35; property ownership prohibited to Blacks, 32; racial capitalism as system in, 31–32, 60n4; racial capitalism now, 40–42; rainbow nation concept, 40; reserve labor market, 33; Robben Island prison, 32, 34, 39, 40; service delivery protests, 41; state-owned and parastatal corporations, 35; subsidization of labor, 35–36; workers' movement needed, 40–42. *See also* Africa; African National Congress (ANC); apartheid

South Asians: in Caribbean, 48, 53–56, 264; collective action by, 248; in Jordan, 17, 238, 241–42, 245; responses to Jordan Compact, 247–48; women in gendered hierarchies by country, 245

"South by Southwest" (SXSW) festivals and conferences (Austin), 300–301

sovereignty: of European Union, 244; hierarchy within, 129–30; imbrication of with debt, 11; Italy, 340; "sovereignty capital," 129; territory equated with, 70, 82

Spanish Empire, 215, 227

specialization, 66, 68, 70, 217; and technological innovation, 100–101

The Spirit Level: Why More Equal Societies Almost Always Do Better (Wilkinson and Pickett), 3

Spivak, Gayatri Chakravorty, 128

St. Alban's (dairy cooperative), 268–69, 270

standard employment relationship (SER), 13–14, 21, 147, 169, 201, 207

Star Trek (television series), 154

State University of New York at Binghamton, 55

statutory regulation, 6–7

Strickland, William, 45, 53, 55, 60

strong and weak parties, 85–86, 115–16, 138n12, 276n5

subcontracting, 20, 287, 296, 299; internal, 200

Sub-Saharan Africa, refugees from, 244, 245–46, 249

subsistence labor, 180, 185, 187, 320

subsistence wages, 89, 90, 95–96, 103, 118n25

sugar industry, 56

supply chains, 14, 18, 170, 171, 172, 203, 206; asymmetries along, 262; buyer power, 262, 268, 271, 274; coercive forms of labor in, 176; "human," 16; industrial organization of in diary industry, 262, 263; Vermont dairy industry, 260–80. *See also* Migrant Justice (Vermont). *See also* global value chains (GVCs)

surplus value, 10–11, 38, 111, 131, 132–34, 254n37; all appropriated by landlord, 91–93, 97–100, 106–7; bargaining power as determinant of the distribution of, 107–8; and civilizational discourse, 127; and cost of production, *87*, 87–93, 97–99, 101, 105, 110, 269; defended against neoliberal attack, 114; and demand, 87–88, *88*, 91; derived from exclusion of cooperatives, 18–19, 262, 268–73; epistemic, 128; flow of in world-systems, 72; identifying, 124–28; landlord's strategy for accumulating, 91–93, *92*; "mere" ownership permits appropriation of all, 97–100; neo-Ricardian neoclassical case against capitalist appropriation of, 96–97; Ricardo and Marx on distribution of, 86–94; shifted toward intangible activities, 14; sources of, 95; "surplus sovereignty," 130; tracking capital accumulation, 124–28; TWAIL analyses of, 123–25, 132–34. *See also* capital accumulation; legal distributional analysis

Sweeney, Shauna, 58
syndicalism, 339, 349, 354, 361nn39, 43, 364n77; authoritarian changes to, 349–50
Syrian refugees, 16–17, 236–59; ability to opt out of garment work, 242, 247, 249; EU attempt to keep in Jordan, 236–39; framed as non-African, 245–46; framed as non-Christian, nonmodern outsider, 244; imagined as fungible, 17, 238–39, 241–48; low wages paid to, 240, 253n24; as "periphery," 238; racialization of in Europe, 17, 243–44; rejection of export zone work, 28n34, 246–47; responses to Jordan Compact, 246–47
systems: conventional understandings of, 72–73, 79; institutionalist theories of, 66, 73–78; mechanical or logical determinism about, 67, 72; patterns of subordination and inequality in, 66–67; reframing understandings of, 80–81; routine legal arrangements in, 67, 80; structural accounts of, 67–68. See also "social system"; world-systems analysis

Tabory, Samuel, 16, 18, 19, 23–24
Tanzania, 49–50
tariffs, 35, 82; "corn laws," 82, 99–100, 104, 111; Jordan, 17; as legal device, 100; and palm oil industry, 324–25
taxation: Chapter 313 tax relief (Texas), 284, 286, 296, 298, 305n21; efficiency cost, 94; and growth policies, 294–95; and intangible assets, 204; on non-improving landlord, 93–94, 113; and palm oil industry, 331; private law operational prior to, 112; regressive sales taxes, 294–95
technology, 21; centrality of to organization and reorganization of work, 171; controlled by firms, 174–75; governed by legal rules, 174; as hybrid actor, 13, 174; imagined evolutionary advantage of, 148–49, 154–55, 162; and job displacement, 12, 173, 196–97; just-in-time manufacturing, 13; for making land into property, 132; new modes of exercising control over workers, 173–74; prevailing preoccupation with, 1–2; reducing cost of production as main driver of, 101; Victorian views of, 146–51, 154–55, 161–62, 163n10; at work, 168, 170, 173–82; and workers' rights, 174
techno-optimism, 12, 22, 146, 147, 154, 162, 163n10
techno-pessimism, 22, 147, 162
temporality: colonial as linear, 229; of selfhood, 213–14, 216; "stealing away," 228; temporal refuges, 216, 227–29; of work, 214. See also distemporalization
tenants, 88–89
terra nullius, Indigenous land framed as, 132–33
Tesla, 284–86, 290, 297–99
Texas: lack of state personal income tax, 294; property tax assessment challenge processes, 295; Senate Bill 4 (SB 4), 290; Senate Bill 267, 291; state-level preemption of local policy, 285, 289–91. See also Austin, Texas region
Texas Minimum Wage Act (TMWA), 290–91
Texas "Robin Hood" law, 286, 297
Third World approaches to international law (TWAIL), 8, 10–11, 122–42; anti-imperialist project of, 128; bracketing of the normative, 129–31; distributional analysis applied to, 11, 122, 124; double move on normative questions, 128–31; four strategies of, 122, 124; interventions, history of, 134–35; material distribution, focus on, 125, 130; reparative interventions, 22, 133–36; risks of, 136; surplus value, analyses of, 123–25, 132–34; three foci of, 122–23; TWAIL I thinkers, 123
Thirteenth Amendment, 184
Thompson, E. P., 123

Thornton, John, 62n24
Tielle, Annette, 286
The Time Machine (Wells), 12, 145–46, 153–59, 161; collapse of private property in, 155–56; future of gender in, 156–57; touch in, 157–58
Total Recall (film), 154
Totem and Taboo (Freud), 158
Trade-Related Aspects of Intellectual Property Rights (TRIPS), 204
trade unions, 104; development of, 56; exclusions in National Labor Relations Act, 184, 261; Italy, 349–50, 352; and palm oil industry, 314, 316, 331; and transitional justice, 317; undermining of, 169
transitional justice, 317
travel literature, 154, 218
Travillion, Jeff, 285
Travis County. *See* Austin, Texas region
Trinidad, 49, 55
Trouillot, Michel-Rolph, 17, 250
Trump administration: escalation of immigration enforcement, 288–89; "public charge rule," 289; trade policies, 269, 276n1
Turkey, garment industry in, 247, 249
Turner, James, 55
Turner, Lewis, 245–46
tutela ("the social" in Italy), 21, 346–58, 363n63; extension of restrictions, 357–58; indeterminacy of, 347–49; narrowed legal protections, 353–55; racialization of, 355–57
Tutu, Desmond, 40
TWAIL. *See* Third World approaches to international law (TWAIL)
Tzouvala, Ntina, 126

"Ujamaa," 49
underdevelopment, 6; in Myrdal's work, 9, 23, 74, 76; in Rodney's work, 6, 50–51. *See also* development
undocumented workers. *See* construction workers (Austin, Texas); dairy industry (Vermont); migrants

Unilever, 266, 321
United Nations trusteeship system, 129
United States: anti-immigrant climate, 288, 290, 292–93; Colombia, free trade agreement with, 330–31; federal funding, 115; idea of equality as constraint on analysis, 66, 79; labor's share of national income, 206; liberal approaches in, 86; migrant labor in, 16; "neo-Ricardian" approach in, 86; New Deal, 348; patterns of subordination in, 66; police murders of Black people, 256n45; political/economic crisis of late 1960s and early 1970s, 113; racial oppression in, 9; as recipient of Jordanian garment industry, 242, 255n38; regional economy, 18, 19; urbanization of, 113. *See also* construction workers (Austin, Texas); dairy industry (Vermont)
universal basic income (UBI), 146, 338–39, 345
universities, public investment in, 295–96
University of Guyana, 54
University of Texas at Austin, 295, 309n66; Dell Seton Medical Center, 283
unpaid work, 14, 185–87. *See also* care work; social reproduction
Uribe, Álvaro, 327–28
U.S. Citizenship and Immigration Services, 289
U.S. Immigration and Customs Enforcement (ICE), 260, 265, 290
"usurious" work, 355
utopia, 12–13, 102; colonizing metaphors for, 149–50, 159; Victorian-era imagining of, 148–53

value, 86; market value, 94, 115, 295; and reallocation of resources, 181. *See also* global value chains (GVCs); surplus value
Vélez, Uribe, 330
Vermont. *See* dairy industry (Vermont)
Verwoerd, Hendrik, 37

Victorian past, future of work seen from, 145–66; civilization, views of, 148–50, 153, 157, 161–62; degeneration theories, 155–58, 162; homosexual panic, 158; imbrication of sexuality, gender, race, and labor, 154–62; political economy, imaginings of, 145–46; progressivism, 154; science fiction writing, 22, 154; technology, views of, 146–51, 154–55, 161–62, 163n10; utopian empire imagined in, 148–53; working class, stereotypes of, 157. *See also* Bulwer-Lytton, Edward; Wells, H. G.; Wilde, Oscar

wage share, decline in, 202–3, 206–7; due to enslaved artisan class, 220
Wallerstein, Immanuel, 5, 8, 14, 66, 178; Rodney's influence on, 9, 46, 55; world-systems analysis of, 67–73
war: Hobbes' theory of, 153; modern law of, 116–17
Weber, Max, 14, 102, 145, 178
Weil, David, 13, 200, 201, 205, 206
welfare economics, 21, 74, 94, 106, 112
Wells, H. G., 12, 145–46, 154–59
White, Derrick, 53
white collar professionals, 196
"white man's burden," 151n60
whiteness, 184, 245
"Whiteness as Property" (Harris), 130
"White Savior Industrial Complex," 151–52
Wigan, Duncan, 204
Wilde, Oscar, 22, 145–53; aristocracy for everyone, 149; Eurocentrism of, 153; as techno-optimist, 147, 163n10; *Works: De Profundis*, 149; *The Picture of Dorian Gray*, 152; "The Soul of Man Under Socialism," 12–13, 145–53, 162
Wilkinson, Richard, 3
Williams, Eric, 8, 11, 58, 131
Winkler, Deborah, 205
women: enslaved, as source of capital accumulation, 183; social reproduction of garment workers, 242; South Asian, 245; "super-exploitation" of Black women, 184; unpaid work as "tax" on, 185. *See also* feminist theory; gender; gender nonconformity
Woody, Susana, 286
work (labor): ahistorical and racialized nostalgia for "full" and "standard" employment, 21; alternative forms, 169; antonyms and cognates for, 147; aspirations for democracy and justice as questions of, 167; becoming "good," 179; capitalism, relationship with, 182–83; at center of political issues, 167; at center of social and political issues, 167; "decent" or "better," 168, 185; "disorderly" forms of, 229; distributive justice at, 168, 180; fundamental purpose of negated by hostile forms of ownership, 59; gendered and racialized distinctions and hierarchies, 14–15, 147–48, 172; imperative of for civilization, 161; increased precarity, 167; labor as "fertile," 94–95; labor equivalents, 86, 95; lack of, 338, 340; legal infrastructure of, 168; "normal," 21, 169–70, 179–80; racialization as central to structure of, 183; racialization at, 182–84; social and political challenges central to conditions of, 167; social organization through, 339; standard employment relationship, 13–14, 21, 147, 169; subsistence wages for, 89, 90, 95–96, 103, 118n25; technology at, 168, 170, 173–82; unpaid, 185–87. *See also* future of work; informal work; past of work
worker advocacy groups, 298, 300, 302
workers: alternative visions of, 45, 60; as "associates," 316; circumscribed lives of dues to capitalism, 59; competition among, 81–82; differences among in need of analysis, 188; displacement of, 12, 169, 173, 176, 196–97; encumbered, 186–87; fungibility of, 17, 220, 238–39, 241–48; identity of constructed by

workers (*continued*)
  policies and institutions, 345; and income inequality, 1–2, 43n25, 177, 210n26; indentured labor, 48, 55–56, 57; left and multiracial coalitions, 54–55; limited feasibility for concerted action, 57–58, 96; in Marx's theory, 94–97, 119nn48, 49; racialization of low-level, 345–46; racism used to divide, 57–58; stock option plans and worker participation, 354, 360n31, 366n103; "unencumbered," 186; as unpropertied claimants, 353; wage share, decline in, 202–3, 206–7, 220
Workers Defense Project, 298, 300
Workers' Statute (Italy, 1970), 352–54
working class, 39–42, 51, 55, 104, 119n48; Black, 8, 31; creation of through backlash, 176; nineteenth-century stereotypes of, 157
Working People's Alliance (WPA), 54, 56–57
work permits, 17, 237–38, 246, 247, 251n11
World Bank, 170–71, 185; on average global markup, 202–3; comparative advantage argument, 322; and palm oil production, 314
World Development Report, 205
World of Struggle (Kennedy), 7
world-systems, 2, 5; animating driver within, 69, 70; as capitalist, 69–70; division of labor in, 68–70, 72; limited exposure to competition for core firms, 71–72; patterns of subordination and inequality in, 66–67, 75; political units within, 68, 70; racial capitalism as, 22; specialization in, 68, 70; TWAIL analysis of, 125
world-systems analysis, 66, 67–73, 276n5; "core (center)" and "periphery," 5, 68, 70–71, 83; inequalities identified by, 72–73; racial capitalism linked with, 5–6; of Rodney, 8–9; of Wallerstein, 67–73; Rodney's influence on, 59. *See also* Myrdal, Gunnar; Rodney, Walter; systems; Wallerstein, Immanuel
World Trade Organization (WTO), 126, 131, 135, 141n47; Trade-Related Aspects of Intellectual Property Rights (TRIPS), 204Wynter, Sylvia, 220

GPSR Authorized Representative: Easy Access System Europe, Mustamäe tee 50, 10621 Tallinn, Estonia, gpsr.requests@easproject.com